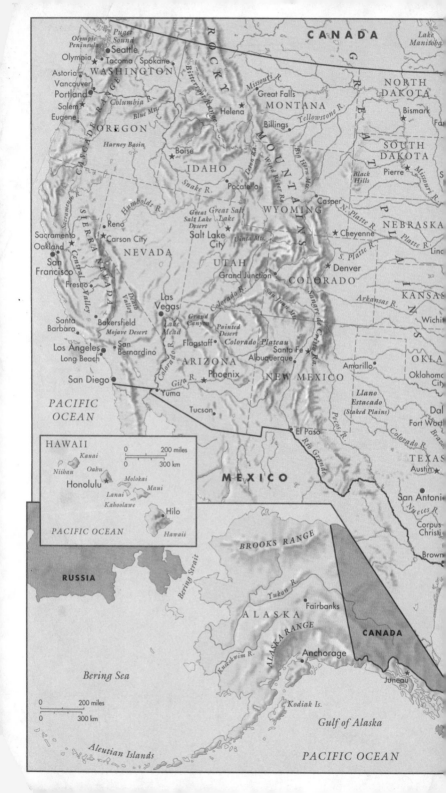

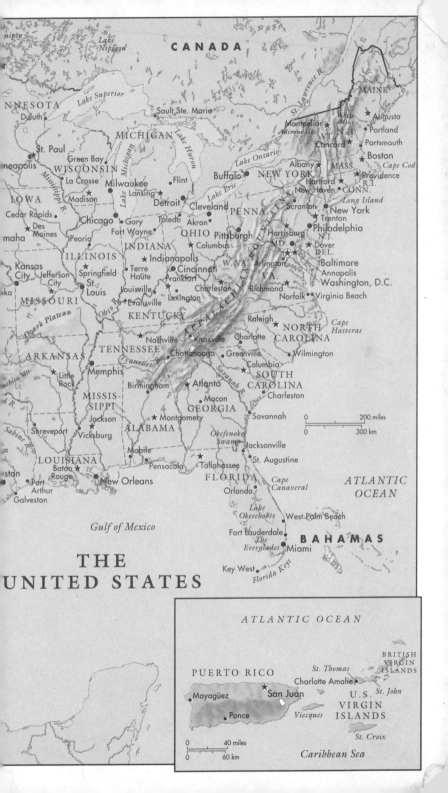

AMERICA

AMERICA

A NARRATIVE HISTORY

FOURTH EDITION

VOLUME I

GEORGE BROWN TINDALL
DAVID E. SHI

W • W • NORTON & COMPANY • NEW YORK • LONDON

The text of this book is composed in Caledonia,
with the display set in Torino Roman.
Composition by ComCom, Inc.
Manufacturing by R.R. Donnelley.
Book design by Antonina Krass.
Cover illustration: Pavel Petrovich Svinin (1737–1839), *Deck Life on the
Paragon*, The Metropolitan Museum of Art, Rogers Fund, 1942. (42.95.7)

The Library of Congress has cataloged the one-volume edition as follows:

Tindall, George Brown.
America : a narrative history/ George Brown Tindall and David E. Shi.—4th ed.
p.   cm.
Includes bibliographical references and index.
ISBN 0-393-96873-1
1. United States—History.   I. Shi, David E.   II. Title.
E.178.1.T55   1996
973—dc20   95–42495

ISBN 0-393-96874-X (pbk.)

W. W. Norton & Company, Inc., 500 Fifth Avenue, New York, N.Y. 10110
http://web.wwnorton.com
W. W. Norton & Company Ltd., 10 Coptic Street, London WC1A 1PU

2 3 4 5 6 7 8 9 0

FOR BRUCE AND SUSAN
AND FOR BLAIR

_____

FOR JASON AND
JESSICA

CONTENTS

PART THREE | AN EXPANSIVE NATION

MAPS

PREFACE

Just as history is never complete, neither is a historical textbook. We have learned much from the responses of readers and instructors to the first three editions of *America*. Perhaps the most important and reassuring lesson is that our original intention has proved valid: to provide a compelling narrative history of the American experience, a narrative animated by human characters, informed by analysis and social texture, and guided by the unfolding of events. Readers have also endorsed the book's unique format. *America* is designed to be read and to carry a moderate price. For this reason, we have refused to clutter the text with distracting inserts and expensive color illustrations. In an attempt to help students grasp the major themes and developments in particular periods more easily, we have added a new element to the Fourth Edition. *America* is now divided into seven Parts, each with a brief opening essay that provides an overview of the chapters ahead.

The revisions that set off the Fourth Edition of *America: A Narrative History* highlight frontiers: the experiences of men and women on America's frontiers and the significance of frontiers in shaping the nation's history. Frontiers can be understood in many ways. In announcing that the American frontier had closed in 1893, the historian Frederick Jackson Turner described the frontier as the source of American democratic values and institutions. For Turner the frontier was the place where Americans reinvented themselves, made better lives, tamed the wilderness, and set it on the path to civilized development. The frontier experience forged the distinctive American character and the independence, acquisitiveness, and boldness often attributed to it. Turner's frontier incorporated images already being conjured in American popular culture: savage Indians, virtuous settlers, gritty desperadoes, and gallant mothers and wives.

Turner's "frontier thesis" dominated the teaching of American history for almost half a century. Yet his uncritical celebration of the dramatic process of westward expansion overlooked many tragedies and failures along the way. It also was highly selective. His cast of characters was made up almost exclusively of white males. He left out many other important actors: Indians, women, Hispanics, Asians, and African Americans, among others.

Despite the flaws in Turner's version of the frontier, the concept itself remains viable. Many historians still find the frontier a useful frame for understanding important aspects of the American experience (not to mention other societies as well). In tracing the significance of the frontier experience in the development of American society and culture, we adopt an expansive definition and an inclusive treatment of its participants.

America has had many frontiers. They were places of fast-paced change. The unsettled conditions in many areas helped alter social relations, including those between women and men. Frontiers also served as crossroads where ethnic and racial groups formed new configurations, often with violent overtones. And the frontier exists in the minds of Americans as a powerful metaphor for change, for the chance to start anew.

There is much that is new in the Fourth Edition of *America*. The frontier theme surfaces in fresh treatments of the Spanish Southwest in the colonial period and the ways Native Americans and Spanish settlers reacted and adapted to each other (Chapters 1 and 4). In Chapter 2 there are new discussions of Indian cultures and societies in the colonial Atlantic region. The French empire in America and its interactions with the Native Americans receive fresh attention in Chapter 4. There are new sections detailing Anglo-Indian relations (Chapters 1, 2, 4, and 5), and expanded treatments of the old Southwest (Chapters 14 and 15), the mining frontier (Chapters 16 and 19), the Civil War in the West (Chapter 17), and the development of the West in the late nineteenth century (Chapter 19). This edition of *America* also provides more extensive coverage of the West in the twentieth century, with new discussions of the West during the Great Depression of the 1930s and World War II, and the particular experiences of Hispanics.

This Fourth Edition, like its predecessor, integrates more social history into the narrative of American experience, detailing the folkways and contributions of those groups often underrepresented in historical treatments—women, blacks, and ethnic Americans. New sections have been added dealing with the Salem witch trials, Andrew Jackson, Clara Barton, Woodrow Wilson, Eleanor Roosevelt, the D-Day invasion, the social impact of the GI Bill, the "black power" movement, cultural conservatism, and the Clinton administration. This edition also features new material about religious life in general and revivalism in particular.

In preparing this Fourth Edition of *America* we have benefitted from the insights and suggestions of many people. The following scholars provided close readings of the manuscript at various stages: Holly Mayer (Duquesne University), Jean B. Lee (University of Wisconsin, Madison), Elizabeth Leonard (Colby College), Bruce Field (Northern Illinois University), Virginia DeJohn Anderson (University of Colorado), Fred Anderson (University of Colorado), Charles Eagles (University of Mississippi), and David Parker (Kennseaw College). Once again we thank our friends at W. W. Norton, especially Margaret Farley, Kate Brewster, Tim Holahan, and Steve Forman, for their care and attention along the way.

—George B. Tindall
—David E. Shi

AMERICA

PART ONE

A NEW WORLD

Long before Christopher Columbus accidentally discovered the New World in his effort to find a passage to Asia, the tribal peoples he mislabeled "Indians" had occupied and shaped the lands of the Western Hemisphere. The first people to settle the New World were nomadic hunters and gatherers who migrated from northeastern Asia during the last glacial advance of the ice age, nearly twenty thousand years ago. By the end of the fifteenth century, when Columbus began his voyage west, there were millions of Native Americans living in the Western Hemisphere. Over the centuries, they had developed stable, diverse, and often highly sophisticated societies, some rooted in agriculture, others in trade or imperial conquest.

The native American cultures were, of course, profoundly affected by the arrival of peoples from Europe and Africa. They were exploited, enslaved, displaced, and exterminated. Yet this conventional tale of conquest oversimplifies the complex process by which Indians, Europeans, and Africans interacted. The Indians were more than passive victims; they were also trading partners and rivals of the transatlantic newcomers. They became enemies and allies, neighbors and advisors, converts and spouses. As such they fully participated in the creation of the new society known as America.

The Europeans who risked their lives to settle in the New World were themselves quite diverse. Young and old, men and women, they came from Spain, Portugal, France, Great Britain, the Netherlands, Italy, and the various German states. A variety of motives inspired them to undertake the transatlantic voyage. Some were adventurers and fortune seekers, eager to find gold and spices. Others were fervent Christians determined to create kingdoms of God in the New World. Still others were convicts, debtors, indentured servants, or political or religious exiles. Many were simply seeking higher wages and greater economic opportunity. A settler in Pennsylvania noted that "poor people (both men and women) of all kinds, can here get three times the wages for their labour than they can in England or Wales."

Yet such enticements were not sufficient to attract enough workers to keep up with the rapidly expanding colonial economies. So the Europeans began to force Indians to work for them. But there were never enough of them to meet the unceasing demand. Moreover, they often escaped or were so obstreperous that several colonies banned their use. The Massachusetts legislature did so because Indians were of such "a malicious, surly and revengeful spirit; rude and insolent in their behavior, and very ungovernable."

Beginning early in the seventeenth century, more and more colonists turned to the African slave trade for their labor needs. In 1619 white traders began transporting captured Africans to the English colonies. This development would transform American society in ways that no one at the time envisioned. Few Europeans during the colonial era saw the contradiction between the New World's promise of individual freedom and the expanding institution of race slavery. Nor did they reckon with the problems associated with introducing into the new society peoples they considered alien and unassimilable.

The intermingling of peoples, cultures, and ecosystems from the three continents of Africa, Europe, and North America gave colonial American society its distinctive vitality and variety. In turn, the diversity of the environment and climate led to the creation of quite different economies and patterns of living in the various regions of North America. As the original settlements grew into prosperous and populous colonies, the transplanted Europeans had to fashion social institutions and political systems to manage growth and control tensions.

At the same time, imperial rivalries among the Spanish, French, English, and Dutch produced numerous intrigues and costly wars. The monarchs of Europe had a difficult time trying to manage and exploit this fluid and often volatile colonial society. Many of the colonists, they discovered, brought with them to the New World a feisty independence that led them to resent government interference in their affairs. A British official in North Carolina reported that the residents of the Piedmont region were "without any Law or Order. Impudence is so very high [among them], as to be past bearing." As long as the reins of imperial control were loosely applied, the two parties maintained an uneasy partnership. But as the British authorities tightened their control during the mid-eighteenth century, they met resistance, which became revolt, and culminated in revolution.

1

THE COLLISION OF CULTURES

The first Americans were immigrants whose origins are lost in the mists of time, where legends abound. Over the centuries Native Americans have passed down various creation myths explaining the origins of their society. Some claim that the first people descended from the sky; still others speak of miraculous events, such as the union of the Sky Father and Earth Mother. In the Southwest the Pueblo people had a place of worship called the kiva, a stone pit in which a deeper opening symbolized Sipapu, a place of mystery in the north where people entered the world from underground.

The likelihood—now almost a certainty—is that Indian peoples entered the New World, not from underground but from Siberia to Alaska, either by island-hopping across the Bering Strait or by crossing a broad land bridge (Beringia) from which the waters receded during the Ice Ages. They came in pursuit of deer and elephants (the extinct American mammoth). Given the advance and retreat of the ice sheets over North America, a crossing might have been possible 50,000–40,000 years ago, but the most likely time for the latest crossings would have been just after the last heavy ice coverage, 18,000–16,000 years ago, when people could still walk across and then filter southward toward warmth through passes in the melting ice.

Once the ice sheets melted and the sea rose again, these migrants to the New World were cut off from the rest of humanity (except for the short-lived Viking settlements on Greenland and Newfoundland) until Columbus arrived in 1492. Their story remains in the realm of prehistory, the domain of archeologists and anthropologists who must salvage a record from the rubble of the past: stone tools and weapons, bones, pottery, figurines, ancient dwellings, burial places, scraps of textiles and basketry, and finally bits of oral tradition and the reports of early explorers, all pieced together with the adhesive of informed guesswork.

PRE-COLUMBIAN INDIAN CIVILIZATIONS

Archeological digs add yearly to the fragments of knowledge about the varied and complex societies of pre-Columbian America. The richest finds have been made on either side of the Isthmus of Panama, where Indian civilization peaked in the high altitudes of Mexico and Peru. Indeed, researchers have reconstructed a remarkable sequence of events in Middle America, a story of peoples who built great empires and a monumental architecture, supported by large-scale agriculture and a far-flung commerce: the Olmecs, Mayas, Toltecs, Aztecs, Incas, and others.

EARLY CULTURAL STAGES   By 1492 some 40 million people lived in the Western Hemisphere, about 2 million (or 5 percent) in what is now the United States. Their cultures ranged from those of Stone Age nomads to the life of settled communities which practiced agriculture, although none of them ever achieved the sophistication of the cultures to the south.

Remnants of stone choppers and scrapers suggest the presence of people in the Americas long before the development, by about 9500 B.C., of projectile points for use on spears and, later, on arrows. As hunting and gathering became a way of life at around 5000 B.C., diet became more varied. It included a number of small creatures such as raccoons and opossums, along with fish and shellfish (hooks, nets,

Out of the mists of time, a carved jade head of the Olmec culture, found in Chiapas, Mexico.

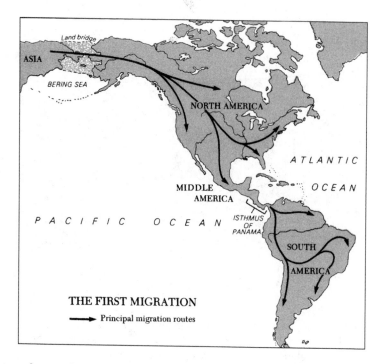

THE FIRST MIGRATION

→ Principal migration routes

and weirs from this period have been found) and wild plants: nuts, greens, berries, and fruits. The Indians then began to settle in permanent or semipermanent villages. They invented fiber snares, basketry, and mills for grinding nuts; they domesticated the dog and the turkey. In southern California tribes lived off sea animals, shellfish, and acorns.

A new cultural stage arrived with the introduction of farming and pottery. In these developments Middle Americans outpaced the tribes farther north and became the center of innovation and cultural diffusion. By about 5000 B.C., Indians of the Mexican highlands were cultivating or gathering plant foods that became the staples of the New World: chiefly maize (Indian corn), beans, and squash, but also such plants as chili peppers, avocados, pumpkins, and many more. These evolved into the forms now familiar by cross-breeding, accidental in part, but believed to have been also the product of experiments by Indian horticulturists.

THE MAYAS, AZTECS, AND INCAS   By about 2000–1500 B.C., permanent towns dependent on farming had appeared in Mexico. The more settled life in turn provided leisure for more complex cultures, for the cultivation of religion, crafts, art, science, administration—and warfare. A

A fresco depicting the social divisions of Mayan society. The king, on the top step, is surrounded by nobles; below, prisoners are guarded by warriors.

stratified social structure began to emerge. From about A.D. 300–900, Middle America reached the flowering of its classic cultures, with great centers of religion, gigantic pyramids, temple complexes, and courts for ceremonial games, all supported by the surrounding peasant villages. The Mayas had developed enough mathematics (including a symbol for zero) and astronomy to devise a calendar more accurate than that the Europeans were using at the time of Columbus. Then, about A.D. 900, the classic cultures collapsed and the religious centers were abandoned. The disappearance of Mayan culture has baffled scholars. Numerous civil wars helped weaken the social fabric, but other factors also played a role. Pollen recovered from underground debris suggests that the Mayas overexploited the rain forest upon whose fragile ecosystem they depended for survival. Overpopulation also placed added strain on Mayan society. Skeletal remains reveal evidence of widespread malnutrition. Whatever the reasons, the Mayans succumbed to the Toltecs, a warlike people who conquered most of the region in the tenth century. But around A.D. 1200, they too mysteriously withdrew.

During the time of troubles that followed, the Aztecs arrived from somewhere to the northwest, founded the city of Tenochtitlán (now Mexico City) in 1325, and gradually expanded their control over central Mexico. When the Spaniards arrived in 1519, the Aztec Empire under Montezuma II ruled over perhaps 5 million people—estimates range as high as 20 million. They were held in fairly loose subjugation

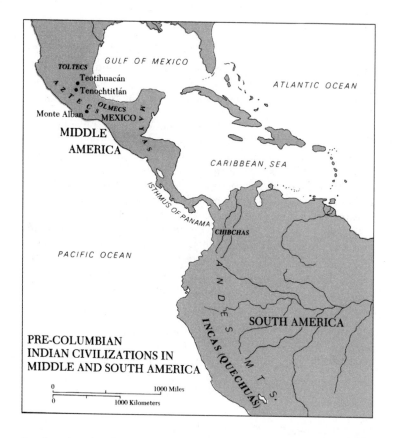

PRE-COLUMBIAN
INDIAN CIVILIZATIONS IN
MIDDLE AND SOUTH AMERICA

for the sake of trade and tribute. They also furnished captives to sacrifice on the altars of their bloodthirsty sun god, Huitzilopochtli (symbolized by the hummingbird), to feed and strengthen him for his daily journey across the sky.

Farther south, in what is now Colombia, the Chibchas built a similar empire on a smaller scale. Still farther south the Quechua peoples (better known by the name of their ruler, the Inca) by the fifteenth century controlled an empire that stretched a thousand miles along the Andes Mountains from Ecuador to Chile. It was connected by an elaborate system of roads and organized under an autocratic government that dominated life.

INDIAN CULTURES OF NORTH AMERICA   The Indians of the present-day United States reached the stage of agricultural settlements only in the last thousand years before Christ. There were three identifiable cultural peaks: the Adena-Hopewell culture of the Northeast (800 B.C.–A.D.

600); the Mississippian of the Southeast (A.D. 600–1500); and the Pueblo-Hohokam culture of the Southwest (400 B.C.–present). None of these developed as fully as the classic cultures of Middle America, although they showed strong influences from the Mayas, Aztecs, and Incas.

The Adena culture, centered in the Ohio Valley, was older but overlapped the similar Hopewell in the same area. The Adena-Hopewell peoples left behind enormous earthworks and burial mounds—sometimes elaborately shaped like great snakes, birds, or other animals. Evidence from the mounds suggests a developed social structure and a specialized division of labor. There were signs too of an elaborate trade network that spanned the continent. The Hopewellians made ceremonial blades from Rocky Mountain obsidian, bowls from seashells of the Gulf and Atlantic, ornamental silhouettes of hands, claws, and animals from Appalachian mica, and breastplates and ornaments from copper found near Lake Superior. The Northeastern Indians at the time of colonization were distant heirs to the Hopewellian culture after its decline.

The Mississippian culture of the Southeast, centered in the central Mississippi Valley, probably derived its impulse from the Hopewellians, but reached its height later and under greater influence from Middle America—in its intensive agriculture, its pottery, its tem-

A wooden carving of a mother carrying a child, found in a Hopewell burial mound in southern Ohio.

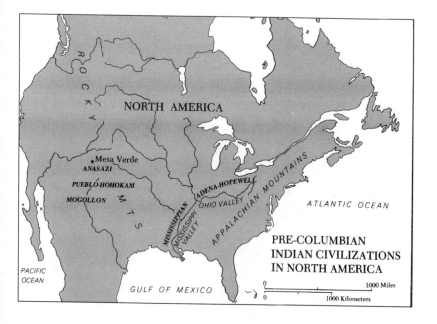

NORTH AMERICA

Mesa Verde
ANASAZI

PUEBLO-HOHOKAM

MOGOLLON

ADENA-HOPEWELL
OHIO VALLEY
MISSISSIPPI VALLEY
APPALACHIAN MOUNTAINS

ROCKY MTS

ATLANTIC OCEAN

PACIFIC OCEAN

GULF OF MEXICO

PRE-COLUMBIAN
INDIAN CIVILIZATIONS
IN NORTH AMERICA

1000 Miles
1000 Kilometers

ple mounds (vaguely resembling pyramids), and its death cults, which involved human torture and sacrifice. The Mississippian culture peaked in the fourteenth and fifteenth centuries, and collapsed finally because of diseases transmitted from European contacts.

The Mississippian culture touched all the peoples of the Southeast and also those far into the Midwest. As late as the eighteenth century, tribes of the Southeast still practiced their annual busk, or green corn ceremony, a ritual of renewal in which pottery was smashed, dwellings were cleaned out, all fires were quenched, and a new fire was kindled in the temple.

The greatest capacity for survival in their homeland was displayed by the irrigation-based cultures of the arid Southwest, elements of which persist today and heirs of which (the Hopis, Zunis, and others) still live in the adobe pueblos of their ancestors. The most widespread and best-known of the cultures, the Anasazi ("the ancient ones," in the Navajo language), developed in the "four corners" where the states of Arizona, New Mexico, Colorado, and Utah now meet.

The Anasazis never gave up their traditional patterns of hunting and gathering, eating small mammals, rodents, reptiles, birds, and insects, along with seeds, mesquite beans, yucca fruits, and berries. With the coming of agriculture they perfected techniques of "dry farming," using the traces of ground water and catching the runoff in garden terraces or, in some cases, extensive irrigation works. They lived in baked-mud

Ruins of Anasazi cliff dwellings at Mesa Verde, Colorado. The circular chamber to the left is a ceremonial kiva.

adobe structures that were built four and five stories high and were often located, as at Mesa Verde, Colorado, in canyons underneath protective cliffs.

In contrast to the Middle American and Mississippian cultures, Anasazi society lacked a rigid class structure. The religious leaders and warriors labored much as the rest of the people. In fact, they engaged in warfare only as a means of self-defense (Hopi means "the peaceful people"), and there was little evidence of human sacrifice or human trophies. Toward the end of the thirteenth century a lengthy drought and the pressure of new arrivals from the north began to restrict the territory of the Anasazis. Into their peaceful world came the aggressive Navajos and Apaches, followed two centuries later by Spaniards marching up from the south.

Even the most developed Indian societies of the sixteenth century were ill-equipped to resist the dynamic European cultures invading their world. There were large and fatal gaps in Indian knowledge and technology. Southwestern Indians had invented etching, but the wheel was found in the New World only on a few toys. The Indians of Mexico had copper and bronze but no iron except a few specimens of meteorites. Messages were conveyed by patterns in beads in the Northeast and by knotted cords among the Incas, but there was no true writing except for the hieroglyphs of Middle America. The Indians had domesticated dogs, turkeys, and llamas, but horses were unknown until the Spaniards came astride their enormous "dogs."

Disunity everywhere—civil disorders and rebellions plagued the Aztecs, Mayas, and Incas—left the peoples of the New World open to division and conquest. As it turned out, however, the centralized societies in the south were as vulnerable as the scattered tribes farther north. The capture or death of their rulers left them in disarray and subjection. The loosely organized tribes of North America (over one thousand in all) made the Europeans pay more dearly for their conquest, but when open conflict erupted, arrows and tomahawks were seldom a match for guns.

Despite such disadvantages, the Indians resisted European invaders for centuries. They displayed an amazing capacity for adapting to changing circumstances, incorporating European technology and weaponry, forging new alliances, changing their own community structures, and, in numerous instances, converting the Europeans to their way of life. For centuries scholars glossed over the awkward fact that many Spanish, English, and French settlers had voluntarily joined Indian society or had chosen to stay after being captured. As a French colonist in America noted, "thousands of Europeans are Indians," yet "we have no examples of even one of those aborigines having from choice become Europeans."

EUROPEAN VISIONS OF AMERICA

Long before Columbus, America lived in the fantasies of Europeans. The vast unknown beyond the sea held a prominent place in the mythology of ancient Greece. In the west, toward the sunset which marked the end of day and symbolically the end of life, was supposedly an earthly paradise. The vision of America as a place of rebirth, a New Eden freed from the historic sins of the Old World, still colors the self-image of the American people.

Norse discoveries of the tenth and eleventh centuries are the earliest that can be verified, and even they have dissolved into legend. Like Eskimos crossing the Bering Strait to the east, the Norsemen went island-hopping across the North Atlantic to the west. Before about A.D. 870 they conquered Iceland from Irish settlers while other Vikings terrorized the coasts of Europe. Around 985 an Icelander

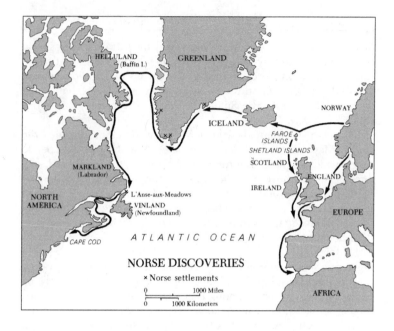

NORSE DISCOVERIES

× Norse settlements

0 _____ 1000 Miles

0 _____ 1000 Kilometers

named Erik the Red colonized the west coast of an icebound island he deceptively called Greenland—Erik was the New World's first real-estate booster—and about a year later a trader missed Greenland and sighted land beyond. Knowing of this, Thorvald Eriksson, son of Erik the Red, sailed out from Greenland about A.D. 1001 and sighted the coasts of Helluland (Baffin Island), Markland (Labrador), and Vinland (Newfoundland), where he settled for the winter. After Thorvald's death the Norse sagas began to tell of places such as Vinland and Krossanes.

"This is a beautiful place," Thorvald declared in one such account. "I should like to build myself a home here." That night, however, Indians attacked the Norse camp with bows and arrows. A mortally wounded Eriksson told his men: "You must carry me to the headland where I thought it would be good to live." He said to bury him there and "put a cross at my head and another one at my feet, and from then on you must call the place Krossanes [Cross Head]."

Three attempts to colonize Vinland followed over the next fifteen years, but they were all abandoned after fierce attacks by natives. The sagas then told no more of Vinland. Speculation had long placed Vinland as far south as Rhode Island or Chesapeake Bay, but in 1963 a Norwegian investigator uncovered the ruins of a number of Norse houses at L'Anse-aux-Meadows, on the northern coast of Newfoundland. This almost surely was the Vinland of the sagas.

The Norse discoveries of the New World are fascinating, but they have no connection to later American history unless Columbus heard of them, which is doubtful. The Norsemen withdrew from North America in the face of hostile natives, and the Greenland colonies vanished mysteriously in the fifteenth century. Nowhere in Europe had the forces yet developed that would impel adventurers and subdue the New World.

THE EMERGENCE OF EUROPE

During the five centuries from Eriksson to Columbus, Europe emerged slowly from the invasions and disorders that had plagued it since the fall of Rome. In the twelfth century, a time often called the High Middle Ages, western Europe achieved comparative stability. The age of discovery, in turn, coincided with the opening of the modern period in European history. Indeed, the burst of energy with which Europe spread its power and culture around the world was the epoch-making force of modern times. The expansion of Europe derived from, and in turn affected, the peculiar patterns and institutions that distinguished modern times from the medieval. These included the revival of learning and the rise of the inquiring spirit; the rise of trade, towns, and modern corporations; the decline of feudalism and the rise of national states; the Protestant Reformation and the Catholic Counter-Reformation; and, on the darker side, some old sins—greed, conquest, exploitation, oppression, racism, and slavery—that quickly defiled the fancied innocence of the New Eden.

RENAISSANCE GEOGRAPHY   For more than two centuries before Columbus, the mind of Europe quickened with the fledgling Renaissance: the rediscovery of ancient classics, the rebirth of secular learning, the spirit of inquiry, all of which spread the more rapidly after Johan Gutenberg's invention of movable type around 1440. Learned Europeans of the fifteenth century held in almost reverential awe the authority of ancient learning. The most direct though by no means the only contribution of antiquity to the age of discovery was in geography. As early as the sixth century B.C. the Pythagoreans had taught the sphericity of the earth, and in the third century B.C., the earth's size was computed very nearly correctly. All this had been accepted in Renaissance universities on the word of Aristotle, and the story that Columbus was trying to prove this theory is one of those durable falsehoods that will not disappear in the face of the evidence. No informed person at that time thought the earth was flat.

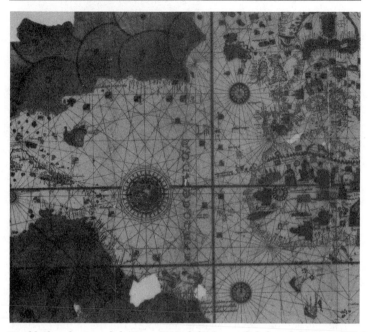

World Chart by Juan de la Cosa, 1500; de la Cosa sailed aboard the Nina on Columbus's second voyage.

Progress in the art of navigation accompanied the revival of learning. The precise origin of the magnetic compass is unknown, but the principle was known by the twelfth century, and in the fifteenth century mariners employed the astrolabe and cross-staff long used by land-locked astronomers to sight stars and find the latitude. Steering across the open sea, however, remained a matter of dead reckoning. A ship's master set his course along a given latitude and calculated it from the angle of the North Star, or with less certainty the sun, estimating speed by the eye. Longitude remained a matter of guesswork, since accurate timepieces were needed to obtain it. Ship's clocks were too inaccurate until more precise chronometers were developed in the eighteenth century.

THE GROWTH OF TRADE, TOWNS, AND NATION-STATES   The forces that would invade and reshape the New World found their focus in the rising towns, the centers of a growing trade which slowly broadened the narrow horizons of feudal Europe. In its farthest reaches, this trade moved either overland or through the eastern Mediterranean all the way to East Asia, whence Europeans imported medicine, silks, precious stones, dye-woods, perfumes, and rugs. There they also purchased the spices—pepper, nutmeg, clove—so essential to the preserving of food, especially in the countries of southern Europe, where the warm, humid climate accelerated spoilage. The trade gave rise to a merchant class, and they in turn developed the idea of corporations through which stockholders would share the risks and profits.

The trade was both chancy and costly. Goods commonly passed from hand to hand, from ships to pack trains and back to ships along the way, subject to levies by all sorts of princes and potentates, with each middleman pocketing whatever he could. The Muslim world, from Spain across North Africa into Central Asia, lay athwart all the more important routes and this added to the hazards. Little wonder, then, that Europeans should dream of an all-water route to the riches of East Asia and the Indies. Travelers' stories also stirred interest in the Orient. The Venetian Marco Polo provided the most famous account in 1298–1299. Christopher Columbus had a Latin version, with margins heavily annotated in his own hand.

Another spur to exploration was the rise of national states, with

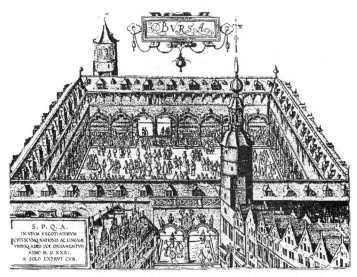

The Antwerp Bourse, or Exchange, was erected in this Netherlands trade center for the use of merchants of every nation and language.

kings and queens who had the power and the means to sponsor the search. The growth of the merchant class went hand in hand with the growth of centralized power. Traders wanted uniform currencies, trade laws, and the elimination of trade barriers. They thus became natural allies of the sovereigns who could meet their needs. In turn, merchants and university-trained professionals supplied the monarchs with money, lawyers, and officials. The Crusades to capture the Holy Land (1095–1270) had also advanced the process of international trade and exploration. They had brought the West into contact with Eastern autocracy and had decimated the ranks of the feudal lords. And new means of warfare—the use of gunpowder and standing armies—further weakened the independence of the nobility. By 1492 the map of western Europe showed several united kingdoms: France, where in 1453 Louis XI had emerged from the Hundred Years' War as head of a unified state; England, where in 1485 Henry VII emerged victorious after thirty years of civil strife, the Wars of the Roses; Spain, where in 1469 Ferdinand of Aragon and Isabella of Castile united two great kingdoms in marriage; and Portugal, where even earlier, in 1384, John I had fought off the Castilians and assured national independence.

THE VOYAGES OF COLUMBUS

It was in Portugal, with the guidance of John's son, Prince Henry the Navigator, that exploration and discovery began in earnest. About 1418 Prince Henry set up an information service to collect charts and data on winds and currents. In 1422 he sent out his first expedition to map the coast of Africa. Driven partly by the hope of outflanking the Islamic world, partly by the hope of trade, the Portuguese by 1446 reached Cape Verde, then the equator, and by 1482 the Congo River. In 1488 Bartholomew Diaz rounded the Cape of Good Hope at Africa's southern tip, and in 1498 Vasco da Gama went on to India.

Christopher Columbus meanwhile was learning his trade in the school of Portuguese seamanship. Born in 1451, the son of an Italian weaver, Columbus took to the sea at an early age, making up for his lack of formal education by teaching himself geography, navigation, and Latin. By the 1480s Columbus—a tall, red-haired, long-faced man with a ruddy complexion, oval eyes, and a prominent nose—was an experienced seaman. Dazzled by the prospect of Asian riches, he hatched a scheme to reach the Indies (India, China, the East Indies, or Japan) by sailing west. After the courts of Portugal, England, and France showed little interest in his plan, Columbus turned to Spain for backing. He won the support of Ferdinand and Isabella, the Spanish monarchs, and himself raised much of the money needed to finance the voyage. The legend that the queen had to hock the crown jewels is as spurious as the fable that Columbus set out to prove the earth was round.

Columbus chartered one seventy-five-foot ship, the *Santa María,* and the Spanish city of Palos supplied two smaller caravels, the *Pinta* and *Niña.* From Palos this little squadron, with eighty-seven officers and men, set sail westward for what Columbus thought was Asia. The first leg of the journey went well, thanks to a strong trade wind. But then the breeze lagged, the days passed, and the crew began to grumble about their captain's farfetched plan. To rally flagging morale, he reminded the crew of the dazzling riches awaiting them. Yet skepticism remained rife, and he finally promised that the expedition would turn back if land were not sighted in three days.

Early on October 12, 1492, after thirty-three days at sea, a lookout on the *Santa María* yelled *"Tierra! Tierra!* [Land! Land!]" It was an island in the Bahamas that Columbus named San Salvador (Blessed Savior). According to Columbus's own reckoning he was near the Indies, so he called the island people *los Indios.* He described the Indians as naked people, "very well made, of very handsome bodies and very good faces." The Arawak Indians paddled out in dugout logs, which they called canoes, and offered gifts to the strangers. Their warm generosity and docile temperament led Columbus to write in his journal that "they invite you to share anything that they possess, and show as much love as if their hearts went with it." Yet he added that "with fifty men they could all be subjugated and compelled to do anything one wishes."

A 1493 woodcut depicting Columbus's discovery of America. At left is Spain's King Ferdinand, who with Queen Isabella authorized the expedition.

At the moment, however, Columbus was not interested in enslaving noble savages; he was seeking the Indies. He therefore continued to search through the Bahamian Cays down to Cuba, a place name which suggested Cipangu (Japan), and then eastward to the island he named Española (or Hispaniola, now the site of Haiti and the Dominican Republic), where he first found significant amounts of gold jewelry. Columbus learned of, but did not encounter until his second voyage, the fierce Caribs of the Lesser Antilles. The Caribbean Sea was named after them, and, because of their alleged bad habits, the word "cannibal" was derived from a Spanish version of their name (Caníbal).

On the night before Christmas the *Santa María* ran aground off Hispaniola, and Columbus, still believing he had reached Asia, decided to return home. He left about forty men behind in camp and seized a dozen natives to present as gifts to Spain's royal couple. When Columbus finally reached Palos, the news of his discovery spread rapidly throughout Europe, and Ferdinand and Isabella instructed him to prepare for a second voyage. They also set about shoring up their legal claim against Portugal's pretensions to the newly discovered lands. When the pope, who was Spanish, interceded on Spain's behalf, Spain and Portugal reached a compromise agreement called the Treaty of Tordesillas (1494), which drew an imaginary line 370 leagues (roughly a thousand miles) west of the Cape Verde Islands and stipulated that the area west of the line would be a Spanish sphere of exploration and settlement.

Columbus returned across the Atlantic in 1493 with seventeen ships and some 1,200 men, as well as royal instructions to "treat the Indians very well and affectionately without causing them any annoyance whatever." Once back in the New World, Admiral Columbus discovered the camp he had left behind in chaos. The unsupervised soldiers had run amok, raping native women, robbing Indian villages, and, as Columbus's son later added, "committing a thousand excesses for which they were mortally hated by the Indians." The Indians finally struck back and killed ten Spaniards. A furious Columbus immediately launched a wholesale attack on the Indian villages. The Spaniards, armed with crossbows, guns, and ferocious dogs, decimated the native defenders and loaded 500 of them onto ships bound for the slave market in Spain.

Columbus thereafter ventured out across the Caribbean Sea. He found the Lesser Antilles, explored the coast of Cuba, discovered Jamaica, and finally returned to Spain in 1496. On a third voyage in 1498 Columbus found Trinidad and explored the northern coast of South America. Back in Hispaniola he displayed a disastrous vacillation

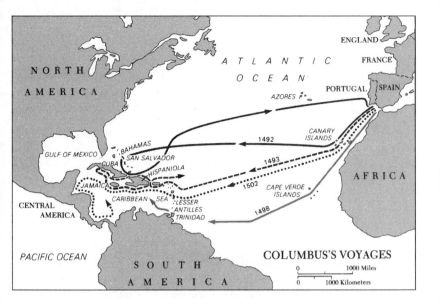

NORTH AMERICA

A T L A N T I C   O C E A N

ENGLAND

FRANCE

PORTUGAL | SPAIN

AZORES

CANARY ISLANDS

GULF OF MEXICO

BAHAMAS

SAN SALVADOR

CUBA

HISPANIOLA

1492

1493

JAMAICA

1502

CAPE VERDE ISLANDS

AFRICA

CENTRAL AMERICA

CARIBBEAN SEA

LESSER ANTILLES

TRINIDAD

1498

PACIFIC OCEAN

SOUTH AMERICA

COLUMBUS'S VOYAGES

0   1000 Miles

0   1000 Kilometers

in dealing with a rebellion, and was arrested by Spanish troops and sent back to Spain in chains. But he regained enough favor to lead a fourth voyage in 1502, during which he sailed along the coast of Central America, still looking in vain for Asia. Marooned on Jamaica more than a year, he finally returned to Spain in 1504. He died two years later.

To the end Columbus refused to believe that he had discovered anything other than outlying parts of Asia. Full awareness that a great land mass lay between Europe and Asia dawned on Europeans very slowly. By one of history's greatest ironies, this led the New World to be named not for its discoverer but, in what one writer has called a comedy of errors, for another Italian, Amerigo Vespucci.

Vespucci was a Florentine merchant and navigator sent to Spain as an agent of the ruling de Medici family. He knew Columbus and may have been among those who welcomed him back from the first voyage. He certainly helped outfit his ships for the second and third. Later, Vespucci himself made several voyages to the New World. Both he and Columbus used the expression "New World," but an Italian printer pulled it out of a Vespucci letter to his patron, Lorenzo de Medici, and used it as the title of a Latin translation, *Mundus Novus*. Then, in 1507, the young geographer Martin Waldseemüller published a new Latin edition of Ptolemy's *Cosmography*. Out to make a name for himself, Waldseemüller appended another Vespucci letter which, either by design or by a printer's error, credited Vespucci with having reached

South America in 1497, one year before Columbus did. For that reason Waldseemüller suggested that the new continent, "the fourth part of the world"—along with Europe, Asia, and Africa—be named "America" in his honor.

Actually, Amerigo Vespucci's first voyage began in 1499, and there is no firm evidence that he, any more than Columbus, ever believed he had touched anything more than a part of East Asia—or perhaps a continent to its southeast. So many writers and mapmakers followed Waldseemüller's idea, however, that the name was entrenched before Vespucci's right to the honor was questioned.

The Great Biological Exchange

Immigration has been the most salient characteristic of the American experience. Since the end of the fifteenth century, nearly seven out of ten immigrants to what is now the United States came from Europe. During that time, some 60 million Europeans have migrated overseas, most of them to the United States. They brought with them distinctive customs, languages, and aspirations—as well as unexpected ecological and biological effects.

The first European contacts with this New World began a diffusion of cultures, an exchange of such magnitude and pace as humanity had never known before. It was in fact more than a diffusion of cultures: it was a diffusion of distinctive biological systems. If anything, the plants and animals of the two worlds were more different than the people and their ways of life. Europeans, for instance, had never seen such creatures as the fearsome (if harmless) iguana, flying squirrels, fish with whiskers like cats, snakes that rattled "castanets," or anything quite like several other species: bison, cougars, armadillos, opossums, sloths, tapirs, anacondas, electric eels, vampire bats, toucans, Andean condors, and hummingbirds. Among the few domesticated animals, they could recognize the dog and the duck, but turkeys, guinea pigs, llamas, and alpacas were all new. Nor did the Indians know of horses, cattle, pigs, sheep, goats, and (maybe) chickens, which soon arrived from Europe in abundance. Within a half century, for instance, whole islands of the Caribbean were overrun by pigs, whose ancestors were bred in Spain.

The exchange of plant life worked an even greater change, a revolution in the diets of both hemispheres. Before the Great Discovery three main staples of the modern diet were unknown in the Old World: maize, potatoes (sweet and white), and many kinds of beans (snap, kidney, lima, and others). The white potato, although commonly called "Irish," actually migrated from South America to Europe and only reached North America with the Scotch-Irish immigrants of the 1700s.

A tortoise, drawn by John White, one of the earliest English settlers in America.

Other New World food plants were manioc (soon a staple in tropical Africa, and consumed in the United States chiefly as tapioca), peanuts, squash, peppers, tomatoes, pumpkins, pineapples, sassafras, papayas, guavas, avocados, cacao (the source of chocolate), and chicle (for chewing gum). Europeans soon introduced rice, wheat, barley, oats, wine grapes, melons, coffee, olives, bananas, "Kentucky" bluegrass, daisies, and dandelions.

The beauty of the exchange was that the food plants were more complementary than competitive. They grew in different soils and climates, or on different schedules. Indian corn, it turned out, could flourish almost anywhere—high or low, hot or cold, wet or dry. It spread quickly throughout the world. Before the end of the 1500s, American maize and sweet potatoes were staple crops in China. The green revolution exported from the Americas thus helped nourish a worldwide population explosion probably greater than any since the invention of agriculture. Plants domesticated by American Indians now make up about a third of the world's food plants.

Europeans, moreover, adopted many Indian devices: canoes, snowshoes, moccasins, hammocks, kayaks, ponchos, dogsleds, toboggans, and parkas. The rubber ball and the game of lacrosse had Indian origins. New words entered the languages of Europeans in profusion: wigwam, teepee, papoose, succotash, hominy, tobacco, moose, skunk, opossum, woodchuck, chipmunk, tomahawk, mackinaw, hickory, pecan, raccoon, and hundreds of others—and new terms in translation: warpath, warpaint, paleface, medicine man, firewater. And the natives left the map dotted with place names of Indian origin long after they were gone, from Miami to Yakima, from Penobscot to Yuma.

There were still other New World contributions: tobacco and a number of other drugs, including coca (for cocaine and novocaine), curare (a muscle relaxant), and cinchona bark (for quinine), and one common medical device, the enema tube. But Europeans also exposed the New World inhabitants to exotic new illnesses they could not handle. Even minor European diseases such as measles turned killer in the bodies of Indians who had never encountered them and thus had built up no immunity. Major diseases like smallpox and typhus killed all the more speedily. According to an account from the first English colony, sent by Sir Walter Raleigh to Roanoke Island, within a few days after Englishmen visited the Indian villages of the neighborhood "people began to die very fast, and many in short space. . . . The disease also was so strange that they neither knew what it was, nor how to cure it; the like by report of the oldest man in the country never happened before, time

Native Americans fishing, in an engraving by Theodor de Bry based on a watercolor by John White.

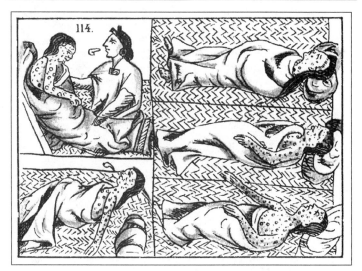

A devastating smallpox epidemic depicted in an Aztec manuscript.

out of mind." Now it happened time and time again. Epidemics ravaged the native population. In central Mexico alone, some 8 million people, perhaps a third of the entire population, died of disease within a decade after the Spaniards arrived. In what is now Texas, one Spanish explorer noted, "half the natives died from a disease of the bowels and blamed us."

PROFESSIONAL EXPLORERS

Undeterred by new diseases and encouraged by Columbus's discoveries, professional explorers, mostly Italians, hired themselves out to the highest bidder to look for that open sesame to riches, a western passage to the Asia. One after another these men probed the shorelines of America during the early sixteenth century in the vain search for an opening, and thus increased by leaps and bounds European knowledge of the New World. The first to sight the North American continent was John Cabot, a Venetian whom Henry VII of England sponsored. Acting on the theory that China was opposite England, Cabot sailed across the North Atlantic in 1497. His landfall at what the king called "the new founde lande" gave England the basis for a later claim to all of North America. During the early sixteenth century, however, the English grew so preoccupied with internal divisions and conflicts with France that

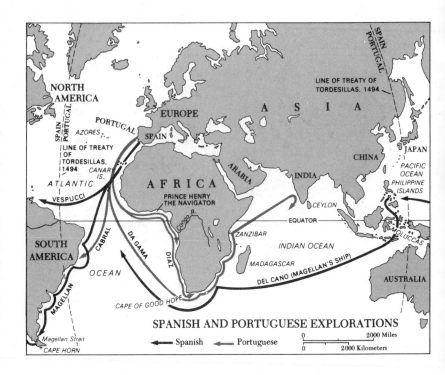

SPANISH AND PORTUGUESE EXPLORATIONS

⬅ Spanish ⬅ Portuguese

| 0 | | 2000 Miles |
| 0 | | 2000 Kilometers |

they failed to capitalize on Cabot's discoveries. Only fishermen exploited the teeming waters of the Grand Banks. In 1513 the Spaniard Vasco Núñez de Balboa became the first European to sight the Pacific Ocean, but only after he had crossed the Isthmus of Panama on foot.

The Portuguese, meanwhile, went the other way. In 1498, while Columbus prowled the Caribbean, Vasco da Gama sailed around Africa and soon afterward set up the trading posts of a commercial empire stretching from India to the Moluccas (or Spice Islands) of Indonesia. The Spaniards, however, reasoned that the line of demarcation established by the Treaty of Tordesillas ran around the other side of the earth as well. Hoping to show that the Moluccas lay near South America within the Spanish sphere, Ferdinand Magellan, a Portuguese seaman in the employ of Spain, set out to find a passage through or around South America. Departing Spain in 1519, he found his way through the dangerous strait which now bears his name, then moved far to the north. On a journey far longer than he had anticipated, he touched upon Guam and eventually made a landfall in the Philippines, where he lost his life in a fight with the natives.

Magellan's remaining crew members made their way to the Moluccas, picked up a cargo of spices, and returned to Spain in 1522. This first voyage around the globe quickened Spanish ambitions for empire in the East, but after some abortive attempts at establishing themselves there, the Spaniards, beset by war with France, sold Portugal their claims to the Moluccas. From 1565, however, Spaniards would begin to penetrate the Philippines, discovered by Magellan and named for the Spanish prince who became Philip II. In the seventeenth century, the English and the Dutch would oust Portugal from most of its empire, but for a century the East Indies were Portuguese.

The Spanish Empire

During the sixteenth century, the New World was a Spanish preserve, except for the Portuguese colony of Brazil. The Caribbean Sea served as the funnel through which Spanish power entered the New World. After establishing colonies on Hispaniola and at Santo Domingo, which became the capital of the West Indies, the Spanish proceeded eastward to Puerto Rico (1508) and westward to Cuba (1511–1514). Their motives were explicit. Said one soldier: "We came here to serve God and the king, and also to get rich."

A CLASH OF CULTURES   The encounter between Spaniards and Indians in North America involved more than a clash between different peoples. It also involved quite different forms of technological development. Where Indians used dugout canoes for transport, Europeans sailed on sophisticated, heavily armed, ocean-going vessels. The Spanish ships not only carried human cargo; they also brought with them steel swords, firearms, explosives, and armor. These advanced military tools were so shocking and lethal that they struck fear into many Indians. A Spanish priest in Florida observed that gunpowder "frightens the most valiant and courageous Indian and renders him slave to the white man's command." Such weaponry helps explain why the Europeans were able to defeat far superior numbers of Indians.

The Europeans also enjoyed other cultural advantages. The only domestic four-legged animal in North America, for example, was the dog. The Spaniards, on the other hand, brought with them horses, pigs, and cattle, all of which offered sources of food and leather. Horses provided greater speed in battle and also introduced a decided psychological advantage. "The most essential thing in new lands is horses," reported one of Coronado's soldiers. "They instill the greatest fear in the enemy and make the Indians respect the leaders of the army." Even more feared among the Indians were the greyhound dogs that the Spanish used to guard their camps. Incredibly fast, they were trained to attack Indians, tearing their limbs away and scaring them into surrender.

CORTÉS'S CONQUEST   In the islands Spaniards found only primitive cultures of hunters and gatherers. On the mainland, however, it was different, for there they discovered civilizations in some ways equal to their own, but almost as vulnerable to their power and to the infectious diseases carried by the Europeans. The great adventure of mainland conquest began in 1519, when Hernando Cortés and 600 men landed on the site of Vera Cruz, which he founded. Then, far exceeding his orders, Cortés's men set about a daring conquest of the Aztec Empire. The 200-mile march from Vera Cruz through difficult mountain passes to the magnificent Aztec capital of Tenochtitlán (Mexico City), and the subjugation of the Aztecs, was one of the most remarkable—and tragic—feats in human history.

Cortés made the most of his few assets. An acute judge of character and a gifted diplomat as well as military leader, he landed in a region where the local Indians were still fighting off the spread of Aztec power

In this 1599 woodcut, Cortés holds out his hand in friendship to the Aztec ruler Montezuma; Cortés's wiles would soon destroy Montezuma and enslave the Aztec nation.

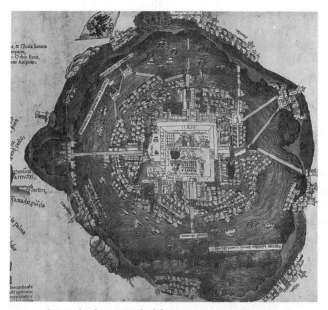

A *map of Tenochtitlán, capital of the Aztec empire, drawn by Cortés,
1524.*

and were ready to embrace new allies, especially those possessing
strange animals (horses) and powerful weapons. By a combination of
threats and deceptions, Cortés entered Tenochtitlán peacefully and
made the emperor, Montezuma, his puppet. Cortés explained to Montezuma why the invasion was necessary: "We Spaniards have a disease of
the heart that only gold can cure."

After taking all the gold the Aztecs had already gathered, the Spanish
forced Montezuma to provide Indian laborers to mine more. This state
of affairs lasted until the spring of 1520, when disgruntled Aztecs,
regarding Montezuma as a traitor, rebelled, stoned him to death, and
attacked Cortés's forces. The Spaniards lost about a third of their men as
they fought their way out of the city. Their Indian allies remained loyal,
however, and Cortés gradually regrouped. In 1521 he took the city again.
After that the resistance collapsed, and Cortés and his officers simply
replaced the former Aztec overlords as rulers over the Indian empire.

In doing so they set the style for other conquistadores to follow, who
within twenty years had established a Spanish empire far larger than

Rome's had ever been. Between 1522 and 1528 various lieutenants of Cortés conquered the remnants of Indian culture in Yucatán and Guatemala. In 1531 Francisco Pizarro led a band of soldiers down the Pacific coast from Panama toward Peru, where they attacked and subdued the Inca Empire. From Peru conquistadores extended Spanish authority through Chile by about 1553 and to the north, in present-day Colombia, in 1536–1538.

The Spanish were great believers in form. Before entering upon each new conquest, Spanish generals read a *Requerimiento* (Requirement) to the native people. This curious document recited Christian history from the creation to the time of the current pope and called upon the Indians to accept the authority of the crown, as granted by the pope. Failure to do so would result in subjugation and loss of property, and even more dire consequences. "The resultant deaths and damages shall be your fault," the paper added, not that of the Spaniards. The *Requerimiento* was repeatedly pronounced before battle, and while it may have helped to salve consciences, it required a strange naïveté. "It is not Christianity that leads them on," the great Spanish dramatist Lope de Vega had the devil say in his play *The New World,* "but rather gold and greed."

SPANISH AMERICA   The course of empire was nevertheless marked by Spain's centuries-long crusade to expel the Islamic Moors from their foothold in the Iberian peninsula. By coincidence it was in 1492, the very year of discovery, that the Catholic monarchs captured the last Moorish stronghold, Granada, and there ordered the expulsion of all Jews (previously tolerated by the Moors) unless they converted to Christianity.

The conquest of America seemed almost like an extension of this crusade into a new world—first conquest, then conversion, by force if need be. Spanish culture and Catholicism would displace the "pagan" civilizations throughout the Americas. Believing that God was on their side in this cultural exchange, the Spaniards carried with them an intoxicating sense of mission that bred both intolerance and zeal. The conquistadores transferred to America a system known as the *encomienda,* whereby favored officers took over Indian villages or groups of villages. As *encomenderos* they were called upon to protect and care for the villages and support missionary priests. In turn they could levy tribute in goods and labor. Spanish America therefore developed from the start a society of extremes: conquistadores and encomenderos who sometimes found wealth beyond the dreams of avarice, if more often just a crude affluence, and subject peoples who were held in poverty.

What were left of them, that is. By the mid-1500s Indians were nearly extinct in the West Indies, reduced more by European diseases than by

Spanish brutalities. To take their place, the colonizers as early as 1503 began to transport slaves from Africa, the first in a wretched traffic that eventually would carry over 9 million people across the Atlantic in bondage. In all of Spain's New World empire, by one informed estimate, the Indian population dropped from about 50 million at the outset to 4 million in the seventeenth century, and slowly rose again to 7.5 million. Whites, who totaled no more than 100,000 in the mid-sixteenth century, numbered over 3 million by the end of the colonial period.

The Indians, however, did not always lack advocates. In many cases Catholic missionaries offered a sharp contrast to the conquistadores. Setting examples of self-denial, they ventured into remote areas, usually without weapons or protection, to spread the gospel—and often suffered martyrdom for their efforts. Among them rose defenders of the Indians, the most noted of whom was Bartolomé de las Casas, a priest in Hispaniola and later bishop of Chiapas, Guatemala, author of *A Brief Relation of the Destruction of the Indies* (1552). Las Casas won some limited reforms from the Spanish government, but ironically had a more lasting influence in giving rise to the so-called Black Legend of Spanish cruelty which the enemies of Spain gleefully spread abroad, often as a cover for their own abuses.

From such violently contrasting forces Spanish America gradually developed into a settled society. The independent conquistadores were replaced quickly by a second generation of bureaucrats and the *encomienda* was replaced by the *hacienda* (a great farm or ranch) as the claim to land became a more important source of wealth than the claim to labor. The empire was organized first into two great regions, the Viceroyalties of New Spain and Peru; eventually the Viceroyalties of New Granada and La Plata were split off from the latter. From the outset these were separate realms, united with Spain and with each other only in the person of the monarch. From the outset, in sharp contrast to the later English experience, the crown regulated every detail of colonial administration. After 1524 the Council of the Indies, directly under the crown, issued laws for America, served as the appellate court for civil cases arising in the colonies, and administered the bureaucracy.

The culture of Spanish America would be fundamentally unlike the English-speaking world that would arise to the north. In fact a difference already existed in pre-Columbian America, with largely nomadic tribes to the north and the more complex civilizations in Mesoamerica. On the latter world the Spaniards imposed an overlay of their own peculiar ways, but without uprooting the deeply planted cultures they found. Just as Spain itself harbored reminders of the one-time Arab rule, so its colonies preserved reminders of the Aztec and Incan cultures. Catholicism, which for long centuries had absorbed pagan gods and transformed pagan feasts into such holy days as Christmas and Easter, in turn adapted

Indian beliefs and rituals to its own purposes. The Mexican Virgin of Guadalupe, for instance, evoked memories of feminine divinities in native cults. Thus Spanish America, in the words of Mexican writer Octavio Paz, became a land of superimposed pasts. "Mexico City was built on the ruins of Tenochtitlán, the Aztec city that was built in the likeness of Tula, the Toltec city that was built in the likeness of Teotihuacán, the first great city on the American continent. Every Mexican bears within him this continuity, which goes back two thousand years."

SPANISH EXPLORATIONS   For more than a century after Columbus no European power other than Spain had more than a brief foothold in the New World. Spain had the advantage not only of having sponsored the discovery, but of having stumbled onto those parts of America that would bring the quickest profits. While France and England struggled with domestic quarrels and religious conflict, Spain had forged an intense national unity. Under Charles V, heir to the throne of Austria and the Netherlands, and Holy Roman Emperor to boot, Spain dominated Europe as well as the New World. The treasures of the Aztecs and the Incas added to Spain's power, but they would prove to be a mixed blessing. The easy reliance on American gold and silver undermined the basic economy of Spain and tempted the government to live beyond its means, while American bullion contributed to price inflation throughout Europe.

For most of the colonial period, much of what is now the United States belonged to Spain, and Spanish culture has left a lasting imprint upon American ways of life. Spain's colonial presence lasted more than three centuries, much longer than either England's or France's, and its possessions were much more far-reaching. The Viceroyalty of New Spain was centered in Mexico, but its frontiers extended from the Florida Keys to Alaska and included areas not currently thought of as formerly Spanish, such as the Deep South (Memphis was founded as San Fernando, Vicksburg as Nogales) and the lower Midwest. Hispanic place names—San Francisco, Santa Barbara, Los Angeles, San Diego, Tucson, Santa Fe, San Antonio, Pensacola, and St. Augustine—survive to this day, as do Hispanic influences in art, architecture, literature, music, law, and cuisine.

The Spanish encounter with native Indian populations and their diverse cultures produced a two-way exchange by which the two societies blended, coexisted, and interacted. To be sure, each side was more concerned with preserving its own integrity and dealing with its own internal squabbles than with understanding the other. But even when locked in mortal conflict and riven with hostility and mutual suspicion, the two cultures necessarily affected each other. The imperative of sur-

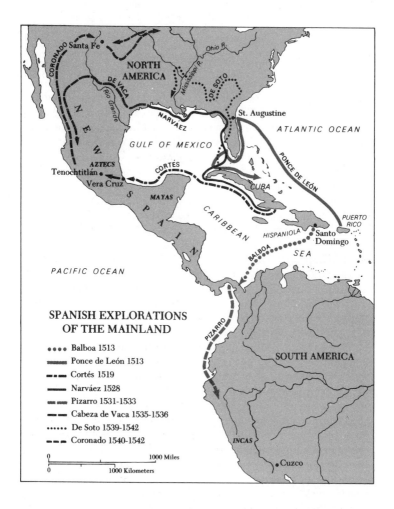

SPANISH EXPLORATIONS
OF THE MAINLAND

•••• Balboa 1513
▬▬▬ Ponce de León 1513
▬ ▬ Cortés 1519
▬▬▬ Narváez 1528
▬▬ Pizarro 1531-1533
▬ ▬ Cabeza de Vaca 1535-1536
••••• De Soto 1539-1542
▬ ▬ Coronado 1540-1542

0 ————————— 1000 Miles
0 ————————— 1000 Kilometers

vival forced both natives and conquerors to devise creative adaptations. In other words this frontier world, while permeated with violence, coercion, and intolerance, also produced mutual accommodation that enabled two living traditions to persist side by side. For example, the Pueblo Indians of the Southwest practiced two religious traditions simultaneously, adopting Spanish Catholicism while at the same time retaining the essence of their own inherited faith.

The "Spanish borderlands" of the southern United States preserve many reminders of the Spanish presence. The earliest known exploration (of Florida) was made in 1513 by Juan Ponce de León, then governor of Puerto Rico. Meanwhile, Spanish explorers skirted the Gulf coast from Florida to Vera Cruz, scouted the Atlantic coast from Cuba to Newfoundland, and established a short-lived colony on the Carolina coast.

Sixteenth-century knowledge of the interior came mostly from would-be conquistadores who sought but found little to plunder in the hinterlands. The first, Pánfilo de Narváez, landed in 1528 at Tampa Bay, marched northward to Appalachee, an Indian village in present-day Alabama, then back to the coast near St. Marks, where his party contrived crude vessels in hope of reaching Mexico. Wrecked on the coast of Texas, a few survivors under Núñez Cabeza de Vaca worked their way painfully overland and after eight years stumbled into a Spanish outpost in western Mexico. Hernando de Soto followed their example. With 600 men he landed on the Florida west coast in 1539, hiked up as far as western North Carolina, then westward beyond the Mississippi, and up the Arkansas River. In the spring of 1542 de Soto died near the site of Memphis; the next year the survivors floated down the Mississippi and 311 of the original band found their way to Mexico. In 1540 Francisco Vásquez de Coronado, inspired by rumors of gold, traveled northward into New Mexico and eastward across Texas and Oklahoma as far as Kansas. He returned in 1542 without gold but with a more realistic view of what lay in those arid lands.

The Spanish established provinces in North America not so much as commercial enterprises but as defensive buffers protecting their more lucrative trading empire in Mexico and South America. They were concerned about French traders infiltrating from Louisiana, English settlers crossing into Florida, and Russian seal hunters wandering down the California coast. Yet the Spanish settlements in what is today the United States never flourished. The Spaniards failed to realize that a prosperous and enduring colonial empire depended on self-sustaining economic development. Preoccupied with exploitive and extractive economic objectives, they never understood the central significance of developing a viable market economy. The primary reason why England and France surpassed Spain in the development of an American presence was that Spain mistakenly assumed that developing a thriving Indian trade in goods was more important than the conversion of "heathens" and the vain search for gold and silver. Capitalism, rather than mercantilism, became the fulcrum of successful colonial development.

The first Spanish base in the present United States emerged in response to French encroachments on Spanish claims. In the 1560s French Huguenots (Protestants) established short-lived colonies in South Carolina and Florida. In 1565 a Spanish outpost, St. Augustine, became the first European town in the present-day United States, and is now its oldest urban center except for the pueblos of New Mexico. While other outposts failed, St. Augustine survived as a defensive base perched on the edge of a continent.

THE SPANISH SOUTHWEST   The Spanish eventually established other permanent settlements in what is now New Mexico, Texas, and California. Eager to pacify rather than fight the far more numerous Indians of the region, the Spanish used religion as an effective instrument of colonial control. Missionaries representing the various monastic orders, particularly the Franciscans and Jesuits, ventured into the frontier to establish isolated Catholic missions where they taught Christianity to the Indians. After about ten years, a mission was secularized; its lands were divided among the converted Indians, the mission chapel became a parish church, and the inhabitants were given full Spanish citizenship—including the privilege of paying taxes. The soldiers who were sent to protect the missions were housed in *presidios,* or forts, while their families and the merchants accompanying the soldiers lived in adjacent villages.

The Franciscans were an order of celibate males founded in 1209. To be eligible for the order, applicants had to surrender all their personal property and live only on charitable contributions. The friars donned simple robes, wore sandals rather than shoes, and walked rather than rode. To demonstrate the intensity of their piety, some wore hairshirts, walked barefoot, or flagellated themselves. In 1526 the Spanish monarchy ordered that at least two Franciscan friars accompany each colonial expedition to ensure that the "conquest be a Christian apostolic one and not a butchery," as Mexico's first bishop explained.

The Franciscans not only wanted to save the souls of "heathen" Indians; they also sought to transform their cultures. They smashed, burned, or confiscated the objects deemed sacred by the Indians and suppressed spiritual rituals and ceremonial dances. Even recreational sports native to the region were banned. The Franciscans regarded the Indians as childlike innocents who could form the basis for ideal Christian communities in which property was owned in common and worked together, not unlike the original Puritan utopia envisioned by John Winthrop and the settlers of Massachusetts Bay.

The land that would later be called New Mexico was the first center of mission activity in the American Southwest. In 1598 Juan de Oñate, the wealthy son of a prominent family in Mexico, received a patent for the territory north of Mexico above the Rio Grande. With an expeditionary military force, he took possession of New Mexico, established a capital at San Gabriel, and sent out search parties looking for evidence of gold and silver deposits. He promised the Pueblo Indian leaders that Spanish dominion would bring them peace, justice, prosperity, and protection. Conversion to Catholicism offered even greater benefits: "an eternal life of great bliss" instead of "cruel and everlasting torment."

*A Dominican friar forcing the native women to weave,
in a print by Felipe Guamán Puma de Ayala, an
Andean who depicted the conquest of America, late
sixteenth century.*

One of Oñate's aides recorded that the Indians thereupon "spontaneously" agreed to become Spanish vassals and Christians.

Some Indians welcomed the missionaries as "powerful witches" capable of easing their burdens. Others tried to use the Spanish as allies against rival Indian tribes. Still others saw no alternative but to submit. The Indians living in Spanish New Mexico were required to pay tribute to their *encomenderos*—privileged landowners given control over a specified number of natives. The annual tribute usually entailed a bushel of maize and a blanket or deer hide. But often Indians were required to perform personal tasks for the *encomenderos,* including sexual favors. Disobedient Indians were flogged, by both soldiers and priests. In one instance, a friar whipped a Hopi Indian suspected of idolatry and then smeared burning turpentine over the open wounds. The Indian died. In the struggle with Satan all means were considered appropriate.

Before the end of the province's first year, the Indians discovered that the Spanish were not keeping their promises of just treatment. They revolted, killing several soldiers and incurring Oñate's wrath. During three days of relentless fighting, the Spanish killed 500 Pueblo men and 300 women and children. Surviving women were enslaved. Indian males over the age of twenty-five had one foot severed in a public ritual intended to strike fear in the hearts of the Indians. Children were taken from their parents and placed under the care of a Franciscan mission where, Oñate remarked, "they may attain the knowledge of God and the salvation of their souls."

During the first three-quarters of the seventeenth century, Spanish New Mexico expanded very slowly. The hoped-for deposits of gold and silver failed to materialize, and a sparse food supply also helped dull interest among potential colonists. In 1608 the Spanish government decided to turn New Mexico into a royal province. The following year they dispatched a royal governor, and in 1610, at the same time that the English settlers were struggling to survive at Jamestown, the Spanish moved the capital of New Mexico to Santa Fe, the first seat of government in the present-day United States. By 1630 there were fifty Catholic churches and friaries in New Mexico and some 3,000 Spaniards. The leader of the Franciscan missionaries claimed that 86,000 Pueblo Indians had been converted to Christianity. In fact, however, resentment among the Indians increased with time. In 1680 a charismatic Indian leader named Popé organized a massive rebellion that involved some 17,000 Indians living in separate villages spread across hundreds of miles. To coordinate the timing of the attacks, Popé sent ropes with knots in them to the outlying pueblos, each knot indicating how many days until the assault was to begin. When the Spanish intercepted two Indian messengers and discovered the ropes, Popé ordered the fighting to commence. Within a few weeks, the Spaniards had been driven from New Mexico. Almost 400 of the 2,500 Europeans were killed in the uprising. The outraged Indians burned churches, tortured and executed priests, and destroyed all relics of Christianity. "The heathen," wrote one Spanish officer, "have concealed a mortal hatred for our holy faith and enmity for the Spanish nation." It took fourteen years and four military assaults for the Spaniards to reestablish their control over New Mexico. Thereafter, except for sporadic raids by Apaches and Navajos, the Spanish exercised stable control over New Mexico. Spanish outposts on the Florida and Texas Gulf coasts and in California did not appear until the eighteenth century.

THE PROTESTANT REFORMATION

While Spain built her empire, a new movement was growing elsewhere in Europe, the Protestant Reformation. It would embitter

Martin Luther.

national rivalries, and, by encouraging serious challenges to Catholic Spain's power, profoundly affect the course of early American history. When Columbus sailed in 1492, all of western Europe acknowledged the Catholic church and its pope in Rome. The unity of Christendom began to crack in 1517, however, when Martin Luther, a German monk and theologian, posted his "Ninety-five Theses" in protest against abuses in the church and especially against the sale of indulgences, whereby priests would forgive sins in exchange for money or goods. Sinners, Luther argued, could win salvation neither by good works nor through the mediation of the church, but only by faith in the redemptive power of Christ and through a direct relationship to God—the "priesthood of all believers." The only true guide to the will of God, he insisted, was the Bible.

Fired with these beliefs, Luther set out to reform the church and ended by splitting it. Lutheranism spread rapidly among the people and their rulers—some of them with an eye to seizing church properties. When the pope expelled Luther from the church in 1520, reconciliation became impossible. The German states fell into conflict over religious differences until 1555, when they finally patched up a peace whereby each prince determined the religion of his subjects. Generally, northern Germany, along with Scandinavia, became Lutheran. The principle of close association between church and state thus carried over into Protestant lands, but Luther had unleashed volatile ideas that ran beyond his personal control.

Other Protestants pursued Luther's doctrine to its logical end and preached religious liberty for all. Further divisions on doctrinal matters led to the appearance of various sects such as Anabaptists, who rejected infant baptism and favored the separation of church and state. Other offshoots including the Mennonites, Amish, Dunkers, Familists, and Schwenkfelders appeared later in America, but the more numerous like-minded groups would be Baptists and Quakers, who derived from English origins.

CALVINISM   Soon after Luther began his revolt, a number of Swiss cantons began to throw off the authority of Rome. In Geneva the reform movement looked to John Calvin, a French scholar who had fled to Switzerland and who brought his adopted city under the sway of his beliefs. In his great theological work, *The Institutes of the Christian Religion* (1536), Calvin set forth a stern doctrine. All people, he taught, were damned by the original sin of Adam, but the sacrifice of Christ made possible their redemption. The experience of faith, however, was open only to those whom God had elected and thus predestined to salvation from the beginning of time. It was a hard doctrine, but the infinite wisdom of God was beyond human understanding.

Calvinism required a stern moral code, for the outward sign of true faith was correct behavior. If this did not of itself prove that one was of the elect, an immoral life clearly proved the opposite. Calvin therefore insisted upon strict morality and hard work, a teaching which especially suited the rising middle class. Moreover, he taught that people serve God through any legitimate calling, and permitted lay members a share in the governance of the church through a body of elders and ministers called the consistory or presbytery. The doctrines of Calvin became the basis for the beliefs of the German Reformed and Dutch Reformed churches, the Presbyterians in Scotland, some of the Puritans in England, and the Huguenots in France. Through these and other groups, Calvin later exerted more effect upon religious belief and practice in the English colonies than any other single leader of the Reformation.

THE REFORMATION IN ENGLAND   In England the Reformation, like so many other things, followed a unique course. The Church of England, or Anglican church, took form through a gradual process of Calvinizing

John Calvin.

"Look here the Queen, whom no mishap can move." A 1563 woodcut portrait of Queen Elizabeth I.

English Catholicism. Purely political reasons initially led to the rejection of papal authority. Henry VIII (1509–1547), the second of the Tudor dynasty, had in fact won from the pope the title of Defender of the Faith, for refuting Luther's ideas. But Henry's marriage to Catherine of Aragon had produced no male heir, and for that reason he required an annulment. In the past popes had found ways to accommodate such requests, but Catherine was the aunt of Charles V, king of Spain and emperor of the Holy Roman Empire, whose support was vital to the church's cause on the continent. So the pope refused to grant an annulment. Unwilling to accept the rebuff, Henry severed the connection with Rome, named a new archbishop of Canterbury who granted the annulment, and married the lively Anne Boleyn. In one of history's great ironies, she presented him not with the male heir he sought, but with a daughter, who as Elizabeth I would reign from 1558 to 1603 over one of England's greatest eras.

Elizabeth could not be a Catholic, for in the Catholic view she was illegitimate. During her reign, therefore, the Church of England became Protestant, but in its own way. The structure of organization, the bishops and archbishops, remained much the same, but the doctrine and practice changed: the Latin liturgy became, with some changes, the English *Book of Common Prayer,* the cult of saints was dropped, and the clergy were permitted to marry. For the sake of unity the "Elizabethan Settlement" allowed some latitude in theology and other matters, but this did not satisfy all. Some tried to enforce the letter of the law, stressing traditional Catholic practices. Many others, however, especially those under Calvinist influence from the continent, wished to "purify" the church of all its Catholic remnants so that it more nearly fit their views of biblical authority. Some of these Puritans would leave England to build their own churches in America. Those who broke altogether with the Church of England were called Separatists. The religious controversies associated with the English Reformation so dominated the political life of the nation that interest in colonizing the New World was forced to the periphery of concern.

CHALLENGES TO SPANISH EMPIRE

The Spanish monopoly of New World colonies remained intact throughout the sixteenth century, but not without challenge from national rivals spurred now by the emotion unleashed by the Protestant Reformation. The French were the first to pose a serious threat as Huguenot seamen promised to build France into a major sea power. Spanish treasure ships from the New World were tempting targets for French privateers. In 1524 the French king sent an Italian named Giovanni da Verrazano in search of a passage to Asia. Sighting land (probably at Cape Fear, North Carolina), Verrazano ranged along the coast as far north as Maine. On the way he viewed Pamlico Sound across the North Carolina Outer Banks and, beguiled by hope, mistook it for the Pacific Ocean. On a second voyage in 1538, his career met an abrupt end in the West Indies at the hands of the fierce Caribs.

Unlike the Verrazano voyages, those of Jacques Cartier about a decade later led to the first French effort at colonization. On three voyages Cartier explored the Gulf of St. Lawrence and ventured up the St. Lawrence River looking for another fantasy kingdom compounded of European greed and Indian tall tales. Twice he got as far as present-day Montréal, and twice wintered at or near the site of Québec, near which a short-lived French colony appeared in 1542–1543. From that time forward, however, French kings lost interest in Canada. France after mid-century plunged into religious civil wars, and the colonization of Canada had to await the coming of Samuel de Champlain, the "Father of New France," after 1600.

From the mid-1500s forward, greater threats to Spanish power arose from the growing strength of the Dutch and English. The provinces of the Netherlands, which had passed by inheritance to the Spanish king, and which had become largely Protestant, rebelled against Spanish rule in 1567. A protracted and bloody struggle for independence ensued. Spain did not accept the independence of the Dutch Republic until 1648.

Almost from the beginning of the revolt, the Dutch "Sea Beggars," privateers working out of both English and Dutch ports, plundered Spanish ships in the Atlantic and carried on illegal trade with the Span-

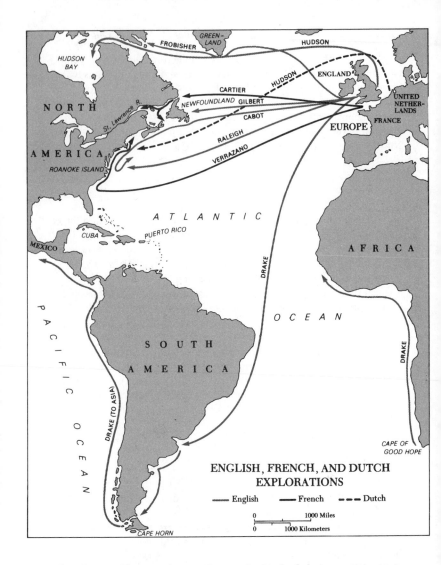

ENGLISH, FRENCH, AND DUTCH EXPLORATIONS

— English   — French   - - - Dutch

0   1000 Miles

0   1000 Kilometers

ish colonies. The Dutch "Sea Beggars" soon had their counterpart in the Elizabethan "Sea Dogges": John Hawkins, Francis Drake, and others. While Elizabeth steered a tortuous course to avoid open war with Catholic Spain, she encouraged both Dutch and English captains to engage in smuggling and piracy. In 1577 Drake embarked on his famous adventure around South America to raid Spanish towns along the Pacific and surprise a treasure ship from Peru. Continuing in a vain search for a passage back to the Atlantic, he spent seven weeks at

Drake's Bay in "New Albion," as he called California. Eventually he found his way westward around the world and back home in 1580. Elizabeth, who had secretly backed the voyage, shared a profit of 4,600 percent, and knighted Drake as "Sir Francis" upon his return.

THE ARMADA'S DEFEAT Such plundering of Spanish shipping by English privateers continued for some twenty years before circumstances provoked open war. In 1568 Elizabeth's cousin Mary, "Queen of Scots," ousted by Scottish Presbyterians in favor of her infant son, fled to refuge in England. Mary, who was Catholic, had a claim to the English throne by descent from Henry VII, and soon became the focus for Spanish-Catholic intrigues to overthrow Elizabeth. Finally, after an abortive plot to kill Elizabeth and elevate Mary to the throne, Elizabeth yielded to the demands of her ministers and had Mary beheaded in 1587.

In revenge Spain's king, Philip II, decided to crush once and for all the Protestant power of the north and began to gather his ill-fated Armada, whereupon Francis Drake destroyed part of the fleet before it was ready. His "singeing of the King of Spain's beard" postponed for a year the departure of the "Invincible Armada," which set out in 1588.

The defeat of the Spanish Armada, depicted in a contemporary English oil painting.

From the beginning it was a case of incompetence and mismanagement compounded by bad luck. The heavy Spanish galleons, however, could not cope with the smaller, faster English vessels. Drake and the English harried the Spanish ships through the English Channel on their way to the Netherlands, where the Armada was to pick up an invasion force. But caught up in a powerful "Protestant Wind" from the south, the storm-tossed fleet was swept into the North Sea instead. What was left of it finally found its way home around the British Isles, leaving wreckage scattered on the shores of Scotland and Ireland.

Defeat of the Armada marked the beginning of English naval supremacy and cleared the way for English colonization of America. It was the climactic event of Elizabeth's reign, and it brought to a crescendo the surging patriotism that had been born of the epic conflict with Spain. The great literature of the Elizabethan age reflected a spirit of confidence and pride. The historical plays of William Shakespeare, especially, celebrated the glories of the House of Tudor and linked them to the spirit of the nation: "This blessed plot, this earth, this realm, this England." England at the end of the sixteenth century was in the springtime of its power, filled with a youthful zest for new worlds and new wonders that were opening up before the nation.

ENGLISH EXPLORATIONS   A significant figure in channeling this energy was Richard Hakluyt, an Oxford clergyman, who became an active promoter of colonization. In 1584, at the request of Sir Walter Raleigh, he prepared for the queen *A Discourse of Western Planting* (first published three centuries later) in which he pleaded for colonies to accomplish diverse objects: to extend the reformed religion, to expand trade, to supply England's needs from her own dominions, to provide bases in case of war with Spain, to enlarge the queen's revenues and navy, to discover a Northwest Passage to the Orient, and to employ the growing number of people made idle by the surge of population growth. He lamented that England was "swarminge at this day with valiant youths rusting and hurtfull by lacke of employment."

The history of English colonization begins with Sir Humphrey Gilbert and his half-brother, Sir Walter Raleigh. In 1578 Gilbert, who had long been a confidant of the queen, secured a royal patent to possess and hold "heathen and barbarous landes countries and territories not actually possessed of any Christian prince or people." Significantly, the patent guaranteed to settlers and their descendants in such a colony the rights and privileges of Englishmen "in suche like ample manner and fourme as if they were borne and personally residaunte within our sed Realme of England." And laws had to be "agreable to the forme of the lawes and pollicies of England."

Gilbert, after two false starts, finally set out with a colonial expedition in 1583, intending to settle near Narragansett Bay (in present-day Rhode Island). He landed in Newfoundland, and took possession of the land for Elizabeth by right of John Cabot's discovery in 1497. With the season far advanced and his largest vessels lost, Gilbert resolved to return home. On the last day of his life he was seen with a book in his hand—probably Sir Thomas More's *Utopia,* which inspired his last recorded words. From the deck of his pinnace, the *Squirrel,* Gilbert shouted across to his other ship the haunting words: "We are as near to heaven by sea as by land." The following night his ship vanished and was never seen again.

RALEIGH'S LOST COLONY   The next year, 1584, Raleigh persuaded the queen to renew Gilbert's colonizing mission in his own name, and sent out a ship to reconnoiter a site. Sailing by way of the West Indies, they came to the Outer Banks of North Carolina and discovered Roanoke Island, where the soil seemed fruitful and the natives friendly. After several false starts, Raleigh in 1587 sponsored an expedition of 117 men, women, and children, under Governor John White. After a month in Roanoke, Governor White returned to England to get supplies, leaving behind his daughter Elinor and his granddaughter Virginia Dare, the

The English arrival at the Outer Banks, with Roanoke Island at left.

first English child born in the New World. White, however, could not get back because of the war with Spain. He finally returned in 1590 to find the city of "Ralegh" abandoned and pillaged.

No trace of the "Lost Colonists" was ever found. Hostile Indians may have destroyed the colony, or hostile Spaniards—who certainly planned to attack—may have done the job. The only clue was one word carved on a doorpost, "Croatoan," the name of a friendly tribe of Indians and also of their island, the present Ocracoke. A romantic legend later developed that the colonists joined the Croatan Indians. There is no solid evidence for this, and while some may have gone south, the main body of colonists appears to have gone north to the southern shores of the Chesapeake Bay, as they had talked of doing, and lived there for some years until killed by local Indians. Such stories were picked up from the Indians by English settlers at Jamestown some two decades later. Unless some remnant of the Lost Colony did survive in the woods, there was still not a single English colonist in North America when Queen Elizabeth died in 1603.

FURTHER READING

A fascinating study of pre-Columbian migration is Brian M. Fagan's *The Great Journey* (1987). On the Aztecs, see Inga Clendennin, *Aztecs: An Interpretation* (1991). A comprehensive anthropological account of American Indian life is Harold E. Driver's *Indians of North America* (2nd ed., 1969). Recent historical treatments include Alvin M. Josephy's *The Indian Heritage of America* (1968), *America in 1492* (1992), and Wilcomb E. Washburn's *The Indian in America* (1975).°
For a revisionist view of the Inca Empire's history, see Thomas C. Patterson's *The Inca Empire*.

On the theme of cultural conflict, see James Axtell's *The Invasion Within* (1986) and *Beyond 1492: Encounters in Colonial North America* (1992). Karen O. Kupperman's *Settling with the Indians: The Meeting of English and Indian Cultures in America, 1580–1640* (1980) stresses the racist nature of the conflict. R. C. Padden's *The Hummingbird and the Hawk* (1967) describes Cortés's conquest of the Aztecs; also useful is Charles Gibson's *The Aztecs under Spanish Rule* (1964).

Alfred W. Crosby, Jr.'s *The Columbian Exchange* (1972) discusses the biological aspects of the cultural collision. Crosby's *Ecological Imperialism: The Biological Expansion of Europe, 900–1900* (1986) is a full exploration of the ecological side of European expansion.

For evidence that Viking explorers came to North America before

°These books are available in paperback editions.

Columbus, see Paul H. Chapman's *The Norse Discovery of America* (1981).°

The most comprehensive overviews of European exploration are two volumes by Samuel E. Morison, *The European Discovery of America: The Northern Voyages,* A.D. *500–1600* (1971), and *The Southern Voyages,* A.D. *1492–1616* (1974). David B. Quinn's *North America from Earliest Discovery to First Settlements* (1977) is also useful. A good outline of the forces of exploration is John H. Parry's *The Age of Reconnaissance* (1963).

Scholarship on Columbus is best handled by Samuel E. Morison's *Admiral of the Ocean Sea* (2 vols., 1942), which was condensed into *Christopher Columbus, Mariner* (1955).° See also Michael Paiewonsky's *Conquest of Eden, 1493–1515: The Other Voyages of Columbus* (1990), Foster Provost's *Columbus: An Annotated Guide to the Scholarship on His Life and Writings* (1990), and Vincent Sinovcic's *Columbus—Debunking of a Legend* (1990). On the recent controversy regarding the site of the first landfall, see the articles on Columbus and the New World in *National Geographic,* November 1986, pp. 566–605.

David J. Weber offers a comprehensive survey of Spanish colonization in *The Spanish Frontier in North America* (1993). James Lang's *Conquest and Commerce: Spain and England in the Americas* (1975) compares the Spanish and English processes of colonization. See also Charles Gibson's *Spain in America* (1966), and for the French experience, William J. Eccles's *France in America* (1972). The most comprehensive view of how European mercantile practices led to the "modernization" of the rest of the world is presented in Louis Hartz's *The Founding of New Societies: Studies in the History of the United States, Latin America, South Africa, Canada, and Australia* (1964).

The English efforts that led to the Roanoke Island colony are documented in David B. Quinn's *England and the Discovery of America, 1481–1620* (1974). The most readable account of the colony itself is Karen O. Kupperman's *Roanoke* (1984); Quinn's *Set Fair for Roanoke* (1985) is more comprehensive. For background on the motives for English exploration and settlement, see Alfred L. Rouse's *The Expansion of Elizabethan England* (1955) and Carl Bridenbaugh's *Vexed and Troubled Englishmen, 1590–1642* (1968). The link between English settlements and the Irish experience is explored in David B. Quinn's *The Elizabethans and the Irish* (1966).

°These books are available in paperback editions.

2

ENGLAND AND ITS COLONIES

The England that Elizabeth bequeathed to James I, like the colonies it would plant, was a unique blend of elements. The language and the people themselves mixed Germanic and Latin ingredients. The Anglican church mixed Protestant theology and Catholic forms in a way unknown on the continent. And the growth of royal power paradoxically had been linked with the rise of English liberties, in which even Tudor monarchs took pride. In the course of their history, the English people have displayed a genius for "muddling through," a gift for the pragmatic compromise that defied logic but in the light of experience somehow worked.

THE ENGLISH BACKGROUND

Set off from continental Europe by the English Channel, England had safe frontiers after the union of the English and Scottish crowns in 1603. Such comparative isolation enabled England to develop institutions unlike those on the continent. By 1600 the decline of feudal practices was far advanced. The great nobles, decimated by the Wars of the Roses, had been brought to heel by Tudor monarchs and their ranks filled with men loyal to the crown. In fact the only nobles left, strictly speaking, were those who sat in the House of Lords. All others were commoners, and among their ranks the aristocratic pecking order ran through a great class of landholding squires, distinguished mainly by their wealth, and bearing the simple titles of "esquire" and "gentleman," as did many well-to-do townsmen. They in turn mingled freely and often intermarried with the classes of yeomen (small freehold farmers) and merchants.

ENGLISH LIBERTIES   It was to these middle classes that the Tudors looked for support and, for want of bureaucrats or a standing army, for

The House of Commons in 1640.

local government. Chief reliance in the English counties was on the country gentlemen, who usually served as officials without pay. Government, therefore, allowed a large measure of local initiative. Self-rule in the counties and towns became a habit—one that, along with the offices of justice of the peace and sheriff, English colonists took along to the New World as part of their cultural baggage.

In the making of laws, the monarch's subjects consented through representatives in the House of Commons. Subjects could be taxed only with the consent of Parliament. By its control of the purse strings, Parliament drew other strands of power into its hands. This structure of powers formed a constitution that was not only not written in one place, but, for that matter, not fully written down at all. The Magna Carta (Great Charter) of 1215, for instance, had been a statement of privileges wrested by certain nobles from the king, but it became part of a broader assumption that the people as a whole had rights that even the monarch could not violate.

A further buttress to English liberty was the great body of common law, which had developed since the twelfth century in royal courts established to check the arbitrary power of local nobles. Without laws to cover every detail, judges had to exercise their own ideas of fairness in settling disputes. Decisions once made became precedents for later decisions, and over the years a body of judge-made law developed, the outgrowth more of experience than of abstract logic. The courts evolved the principle that people could be arrested or their goods seized only upon a warrant issued by a court, and that individuals were entitled to a trial by a jury of their peers (their equals) in accordance with established rules of evidence.

ENGLISH ENTERPRISE   English liberties inspired a certain initiative and vigor of which prosperity and empire were born. The ranks of entrepreneurs and adventurers were constantly replenished by the young sons of the squirearchy, cut off from the estate that the oldest son inherited by the law of primogeniture (or first born). The formation of joint-stock companies spurred commercial expansion. These companies were the ancestors of the modern corporation, in which stockholders shared the risks and profits, sometimes for a single venture but more and more on a permanent basis. In the late 1500s some of the larger companies managed to get royal charters that entitled them to monopolies in certain areas and even governmental powers in their outposts. Such companies would become the first instruments of colonization.

For all the vaunted glories of English liberty and enterprise, it was not the best of times for the common people of the realm. For more than two centuries, serfdom had been on the way to extinction, as the feudal duties of serfs were transformed into rents. But while tenancy gave a degree of independence, it also allowed landlords to increase demands, and, as the trade in woolen products grew, to enclose farmlands and evict the tenants in favor of sheep. The enclosure movement of the sixteenth century gave rise to the great numbers of sturdy beggars and rogues who peopled the literature of Elizabethan times and gained immortality in Mother Goose: "Hark, hark, the dogs do bark. The beggars have come to town." The needs of this displaced population became another argument for colonial expansion.

PARLIAMENT AND THE STUARTS   With the death of Elizabeth, the Tudor line ran out and the throne fell to the first of the Stuarts, whose dynasty spanned most of the seventeenth century, a turbulent time during which the English planted an overseas empire. In 1603 James VI of Scotland, son of the ill-fated Mary, Queen of Scots, and great-great-grandson of Henry VII, became James I of England—as Elizabeth had planned. A man of ponderous erudition, James fully earned his reputation as the "wisest fool in all Christendom." He lectured the people on every topic but remained blind to English traditions and sensibilities. Where the Tudors had wielded absolute power through constitutional forms, the learned James demanded a more consistent logic and advanced at every chance the theory of divine right, by which monarchs answered only to God for their actions. Where the Puritans hoped to

James I, the successor to Queen Elizabeth and the first of England's Stuart kings.

find a Presbyterian ally in their opposition to Anglican trappings, they found instead a testy autocrat who promised to "harry them out of the land." He even offended Anglicans by deciding to end Elizabeth's war with Catholic Spain.

Charles I, who succeeded his father in 1625, proved even more stubborn about royal prerogative. He ruled without Parliament from 1628 to 1640 and levied taxes by royal decree. The archbishop of Canterbury, William Laud, directed a systematic persecution of Puritans but finally overreached himself when he tried to impose Anglican worship on Presbyterian Scots. In 1638 Scotland rose in revolt and in 1640 Charles called Parliament to rally support and raise money for the defense of his kingdom. The "Long Parliament" impeached Laud instead, condemned to death the king's chief minister, and abolished the king's "prerogative courts." In 1642, when the king tried to arrest five members of Parliament, civil war erupted between the "Roundheads," who backed Parliament, and the "Cavaliers," who supported the king.

In 1646 royalist resistance collapsed, and parliamentary forces captured the king. Parliament, however, could not agree on a permanent settlement. A dispute arose between Presbyterians and Independents (who preferred a congregational church government), and in 1648 the Independents purged the Presbyterians, leaving a "Rump Parliament" that then instigated the trial and execution of Charles I on charges of treason.

Oliver Cromwell, commander of the army, operated like a military dictator, ruling first through a council chosen by Parliament (the Commonwealth), and, after forcible dissolution of Parliament, as Lord Protector (the Protectorate). Cromwell extended religious toleration to all except Catholics and Anglicans, but his arbitrary governance and his moralistic codes made the regime increasingly unpopular. When, after his death in 1658, his son proved too weak to carry on, the army once again took control, permitted new elections for Parliament, and supported the restoration of the monarchy under Charles II, son of the martyred king, in 1660.

Charles accepted as terms of the Restoration settlement the principle that he must rule jointly with Parliament. By tact or shrewd maneuvering, he managed to hold his throne. His younger brother, the duke of York (who became James II upon succeeding to the throne in 1685) was less flexible. He openly avowed Catholicism and assumed the same unyielding stance as the first two Stuarts. The people could bear it so long as they expected one of his Protestant daughters, Mary or Anne, to succeed him. In 1688, however, the birth of a son who would be reared a Catholic finally brought matters to a crisis. Leaders of Parliament invited Mary and her husband, William of Orange, a Dutch prince, to assume the throne jointly, and James fled the country.

By this "Glorious Revolution," Parliament finally established its freedom from royal control. Under the Bill of Rights, in 1689, William and Mary gave up the prerogatives of suspending laws, erecting special courts, keeping a standing army, or levying taxes except by Parliament's consent. They further agreed to hold frequent legislative sessions and allow freedom of speech in Parliament, freedom of petition to the

Charles I, in a portrait by Van Dyck that vividly captures the ill-fated monarch's arrogance.

crown, and restrictions against excessive bail and cruel and unusual punishments. The Toleration Act of 1689 extended a degree of freedom of worship to all Christians except Catholics and Unitarians, although dissenters from the established church still had few political rights. In 1701 the Act of Settlement ensured a Protestant succession through Queen Anne (1702–1714). And by the Act of Union in 1707, England and Scotland became the United Kingdom of Great Britain.

SETTLING THE CHESAPEAKE

During these eventful years all but one of the thirteen North American colonies and several more in the islands of the Caribbean had their start. After the ill-fated efforts of Gilbert and Raleigh, the joint-stock company of merchants and gentlemen became the chief vehicle of colonization. In 1606 James I chartered a Virginia Company with two divisions, the First 'Colony of London and the Second Colony of Plymouth. The London group could plant a settlement between the 34th and 38th parallels, the Plymouth group between the 41st and 45th parallels, and either between the 38th and 41st parallels, provided they kept a hundred miles apart. The stockholders expected a potential return from gold and other minerals; products, such as wine, citrus fruits, and olive oil, to free England from dependence on Spain; trade with the Indians; pitch, tar, potash, and other forest products needed for naval use; and perhaps a passage to East Asia. Some investors dreamed of finding another Aztec or Inca Empire. Few if any investors foresaw what the first English colony would actually become: a place to grow tobacco.

From the outset the pattern of English colonization diverged significantly from the Spanish. For one thing the English had a different model in their experience. The Spanish had retaken their homeland from the Moors and in the process worked out patterns of colonization later used in America. The English, after four centuries of sporadic intervention in Ireland, proceeded under Elizabeth to conquer the Irish by military force. While the interest in America was growing, the English were already involved in planting settlements, or "plantations," in Ireland. Within their own pale (or limit) of settlement the English set about reconstructing their familiar way of life insofar as possible. The term "wild Irish," which today seems more comic than serious, was then taken in dead earnest. The English considered Ireland a barbaric country. To them, Irish Catholicism was mere paganism. What the English saw as a "savage nation" that lived "like beastes" could therefore be subjected without compunction. The same pattern would apply to the Indians of North America. In America the English settled along the Atlantic

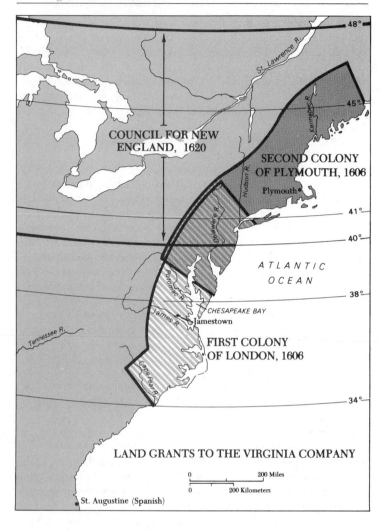

COUNCIL FOR NEW
ENGLAND, 1620

SECOND COLONY
OF PLYMOUTH, 1606

Plymouth

St. Lawrence R.

Kennebec R.

Hudson R.

Delaware R.

*ATLANTIC
OCEAN*

Potomac R.

James R.

CHESAPEAKE BAY

Jamestown

Tennessee R.

FIRST COLONY
OF LONDON, 1606

Cape Fear R.

48°

45°

41°

40°

38°

34°

LAND GRANTS TO THE VIRGINIA COMPANY

| 0 | | 200 Miles |

| 0 | | 200 Kilometers |

St. Augustine (Spanish)

seaboard, where the native populations were relatively sparse. There was no Aztec or Inca Empire to conquer and rule. The colonists thus had to establish their own communities within a largely wilderness setting.

VIRGINIA   The London Company planted the first permanent colony in Virginia, named after Elizabeth I, the "Virgin Queen." On May 6, 1607, three ships carrying about 100 men reached Chesapeake Bay after four storm-tossed weeks at sea. They chose a river with a northwest bend—in hope of a passage to Asia—and settled about 40 miles from the sea to hide from marauding Spaniards. One of the settlers noted that they found "fair meadows and goodly, tall trees, with such fresh waters running through the woods as I was almost ravished with the first sight thereof."

The river they called the James, and the colony, Jamestown. The sea-weary colonists began building a fort, thatched huts, a storehouse, and a church. They then set to planting, but most were either townsmen unfamiliar with farming or "gentleman" adventurers who scorned manual labor. They had come to find gold, not to establish a farm settlement. Ignorant of woodlore, they did not know how to exploit the area's abundant game and fish. Supplies from England were undependable, and only some effective leadership and their trade with the Indians, who taught the colonists to grow maize, enabled them to survive.

The Indians of the region were loosely organized. Powhatan, chief of the Pamunkey tribe, had gained shaky control over some thirty Algonquian-speaking tribes (14,000 people) in the coastal area. Largely an agricultural people, they focused on the raising of several varieties of corn. They lived along rivers in fortified towns and resided in framed houses sheathed with bark. Despite occasional clashes with the colonists, the Indians of Virginia initially adopted a stance of nervous assistance and watchful waiting. Powhatan developed a lucrative trade with the colonists, exchanging corn for hatchets, swords, and muskets; he realized too late that the newcomers intended to expropriate his lands and subjugate his people. As one Indian said in 1608, "We hear you are come from under the World to take our World from us."

The colonists, as it happened, had more than a match for Powhatan in Captain John Smith, a swashbuckling soldier of fortune with rare powers of leadership and self-promotion. The story goes that earlier in his career, while fighting with the Austrians against the Turks in Hungary, he had beheaded three Turks in hand-to-hand challenges staged in front of a Turkish fortress. The grateful Austrians supposedly awarded him the title of captain, a horse, a scimitar, and a coat of arms. Thereafter Smith was wounded, captured, and enslaved in Turkey, but he freed himself by killing his overseer. After fleeing across Russia and sailing in a pirate ship off the coast of Africa, the twenty-four-year-old Smith was "befriended by a gentlewoman" who facilitated his return to England in 1604.

The Virginia Company, understandably impressed by Smith's exploits, appointed him a member of the resident council to manage the new colony in America. It was a wise decision. With the colonists on the verge of starvation, Smith imposed strict discipline and forced all to labor, noting that "he that will not work shall not eat." Smith also

Captain Smith taketh the King of Pamaunkee prisoner, *1608*,
from John Smith's map of "Ould Virginia," 1624.

bargained with the Indians and explored and mapped the Chesapeake
region. Through his efforts, Jamestown survived, but Smith's dictatorial
acts did not endear him to many of the colonists. One called him "ambitious, unworthy, and vainglorious."

In 1609 the Virginia Company moved to reinforce the Jamestown
colony. A new charter redefined the colony's boundaries and replaced
the largely ineffective council with an all-powerful governor whose
council was only advisory. The company then lured new subscribers
from all ranks of society and attracted new settlers with the promise of
free land after seven years of labor. The company in effect had given
up hope of prospering except through the sale of lands which would rise
in value as the colony grew. The governor, the noble Lord De La Warr
(Delaware), sent as interim governor Sir Thomas Gates. In May 1609
Gates set out with a fleet of nine vessels and about 500 passengers and
crew. On the way Gates was shipwrecked on Bermuda, where he and
the other survivors wintered in comparative ease, subsisting on fish,
fowl, and wild pigs. (Their story was transformed by William Shakespeare into his play *The Tempest.*)

Most of the fleet, however, did reach Jamestown. Some 400 settlers overwhelmed the remnant of about 80. These leaderless settlers, said one observer, included "many unruly gallants packed thether by their friends to escape il destinies." But their destinies were "il" indeed. All chance that John Smith might control things was lost when he suffered a gunpowder burn and sailed back to England in October 1609. The consequence was anarchy and the "starving time" of the winter of 1609–1610, during which most of the colonists, weakened by hunger, fell prey to pestilence. By May, when Gates and his companions made their way to Jamestown on two small ships built in Bermuda, only about 60 remained alive. All poultry and livestock (including horses) had been eaten, and one man was even said to have dined on his wife. Jamestown was falling into ruins and was abandoned.

In June 1610, as the colonists made their way down the river, the new governor, Lord Delaware, providentially arrived with three ships and 150 men, whereupon instead of leaving Virginia, the colonists returned to Jamestown and created the first new settlements upstream at Henrico (Richmond) and two more downstream near the mouth of the river. It was a critical turning point for the colony, whose survival required a

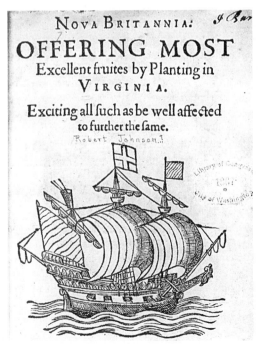

A 1609 handbill of the Virginia Company attempts to lure settlers to Jamestown.

combination of stern measures and not a little luck. In 1611 Thomas Gates took charge of the Virginia colony and established a strict system of *Lawes Divine, Moral, and Martiall,* inaccurately called "Dale's Code," after Thomas Dale who enforced them as marshal. Severe even by the standards of a ruthless age, the code enforced a militaristic discipline needed for survival. The new colonial regime also assaulted the local Indians. Deputy Governor Gates had arrived with orders to exact tribute from the Indians in the form of labor, corn, and furs. English soldiers thereafter attacked Indian villages and destroyed their crops. One commander reported that they marched a captured Indian queen and her children to the river where they "put the Children to death . . . by throwing them overboard and shooting out their brains in the water."

Over the next seven years the colony limped along until it gradually found a reason for being: tobacco. In 1612 John Rolfe had begun to experiment with the harsh, biting Virginia tobacco. Eventually he got hold of some seed for the more savory Spanish varieties, and by 1616 the weed had become an export staple.

Meanwhile Rolfe had made another contribution to stability by marrying Pocahontas, the daughter of Powhatan. Pocahontas (a nickname usually translated as "frisky"—her given name was Matowaka) had been a familiar figure in Jamestown almost from the beginning. In 1607, then only eleven, she figured in perhaps the best-known story of the settlement, her plea for the life of John Smith, who credited to his own charm what was perhaps the climax to a ritual threat of execution—that is, a bit of playacting to impress Smith with Powhatan's authority. In 1613, however, on a foray to extort corn from the Indians, settlers captured Pocahontas and held her for ransom. To fend off the crisis, Rolfe proposed marriage to Pocahontas, Powhatan agreed, and a wary peace ensued. By now Pocahontas had been baptized in the Anglican church, and she was given a new name, "Lady Rebecca." In 1616 Rolfe took Rebecca and their infant son Thomas to London, where the young princess drew excited attention from the royal family and curious Londoners. But only a few months after arriving, Rebecca grew gravely ill from pneumonia or smallpox and died at the age of twenty. Distinguished Virginians still boast of their descent from the Indian "princess."

In 1618 Sir Edwin Sandys, a prominent member of Parliament, became head of the company and set about a series of reforms. First of all he inaugurated a new "headright" policy: anyone who bought a share in the company and who could transport himself to Virginia could have fifty acres, and fifty more for any servants he might send or bring. The following year, 1619, was memorable in several ways. The company now relaxed the tight regimen of the *Lawes* and promised that the settlers should have the "rights of Englishmen," including a representative assembly.

Engraving of Pocahontas, from John Smith's Generall Historie.

A new governor arrived with instructions to put the new order into effect, and on July 30, 1619, the first General Assembly of Virginia, including the governor, six councilors, and twenty-two burgesses, met in the church at Jamestown and deliberated for five days, "sweating & stewing, and battling flies and mosquitoes." It was an eventful year in two other respects. The promoters also saw a need to send out wives for the men who, Sandys noted, "By defect thereof (as is credibly reported) stay there but to get something and then return for England." During 1619 a ship arrived with ninety young women, to be sold to likely husbands of their own choice for the cost of transportation (about 125 pounds of tobacco). And a Dutch man-of-war, according to an ominous note in John Rolfe's diary, stopped by and dropped off "20 Negars," the first blacks known to have reached English America. It would be another year before the fabled *Mayflower* came.

Despite its successes, however, the company again fell upon evil days. The profitable tobacco trade intensified the settlers' lust for land. The colonists especially coveted Indian fields because they had already been cleared and were ready to be planted. In 1622 the Indians, led by Opechancanough, Powhatan's brother and successor, tried to repel the land-grabbing English. They killed some 350 colonists, including John Rolfe, only to provoke a vengeful counterattack. John Smith denounced the Indian assault as a "massacre" and dismissed the "savages" as "cruel beasts" whose "brutishness" exceeded that of wild animals. Others declared that the dead colonists certified the English claim to the lands of the New World: "We who hitherto have had no more ground than their [Indian] waste, and our purchase . . . may now by right of War, and law of Nations, invade the Country, and destroy them who sought to destroy us." Whatever moral doubts had earlier plagued English settlers were now swept away. "We shall enjoy their cultivated places. . . . Now their cleared grounds in all their villages (which are situated in the fruitfulest places of the land) shall be inhabited by us."

The English thereafter sought to wipe out the Indian presence along their frontier. In 1623 Captain William Tucker led a band of soldiers into a Powhatan village, ostensibly to negotiate a settlement. After signing a treaty, Tucker invited the Indians to drink a toast to celebrate their truce. Unwittingly, the Indians drank the proffered wine, only to realize too late that it had been poisoned. Two hundred Indians died from the doctored brew. The soldiers then killed another fifty and "brought home part of their heads." This process of "continual incursions" into Indian territory continued throughout the decade.

Yet the English foothold in Virginia remained tenuous. Some 14,000

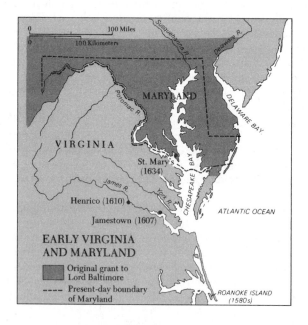

EARLY VIRGINIA
AND MARYLAND

The Virginia Company recommended that prospective settlers bring to America these "provisions necessary to sustain themselves." At bottom is the company's new headright policy.

men, women, and children had migrated to the colony since 1607, but the population in 1624 stood at a precarious 1,132. Despite the broad initial achievements of the company, after about 1617 a handful of insiders had appropriated large estates and began to monopolize the indentured workers. In a tobacco boom of those years some made fortunes, but most of the thousands sent out died before they could prove themselves. At the behest of Sandy's opponents, the king appointed a commission to investigate, and on its recommendation a court dissolved the company. In 1624 Virginia became a royal colony.

The king did not renew instructions for an assembly, but his governors found it impossible to rule the troublesome Virginians without one. Annual assemblies met after 1629, although not recognized by the crown for another ten years. After 1622, relations with the Powhatan confederates continued in a state of what the governor's council called "perpetual enmity" until the aging Opechancanough staged another concerted attack in 1644. The English suffered as many casualties as they had twenty-two years before, but put down the uprising with such ferocity that nothing quite like it happened again.

Sir William Berkeley, who arrived as governor in 1642, presided over the colony's growth for most of the next thirty-four years. The brawling populace of men on the make over which he held sway was a far cry from the cultivated gentry of the next century. But among them were the Byrds, Carters, Masons, and Randolphs who made the fortunes that nurtured the celebrated aristocrats of later generations.

During the 1630s and 1640s the instability and turmoil of Virginia's early days gave way to a more settled and stable period. Tobacco prices peaked, and the large planters began to consolidate their economic gains through political action. They assumed key civic roles as justices of the peace and sheriffs, helped initiate internal improvements such as roads and bridges, supervised elections, and collected taxes. They also formed the able-bodied males into local militias. Despite the presence of a royal governor, the elected assembly continued to assert its sovereignty, making laws for the colony and resisting the governor's encroachments.

Virginia at midcentury continued to serve as a magnet for new settlers. Indentured servants streamed into the colony. As the sharp rise in tobacco profits leveled off, planters began to grow corn and raise cattle. The increase in the food supply helped lower mortality rates and fuel the rapid rise in population. By 1650 there were 15,000 residents of Virginia. As servants fulfilled their indentures, they gained access to land. Many former servants became planters in their own right. Women typically improved their status through marriage. If they outlived their husbands—and many did—they inherited the property and often leveraged their growing wealth through second and even third marriages.

As was the case throughout North America, the relentless stream of new white settlers exerted constant pressure on Indian lands and produced unwanted economic effects. The increase in the number of planters resulted in a dramatic rise in production. This in turn caused the cost of land to soar and the price of tobacco to plummet. To sustain their competitive advantage, the largest planters bought up the most fertile lands along the coast, thereby forcing freed servants to become tenants or to claim less fertile lands along the frontier. In either case they found themselves at a disadvantage. Tenants grew dependent on planters for land and credit, while small farmers along the frontier became more vulnerable to Indian attacks.

The plight of common folk worsened after 1660, when a restored monarchy under Charles II instituted new trade regulations for the colonies. By 1676 a fourth of the free white men in Virginia were landless. Vagabonds roamed the roads, squatting on private property, working at odd jobs, or poaching game or engaging in other petty crimes in order to survive. Alarmed by the growing social unrest, the large planters controlling the assembly lengthened the indentures, passed more stringent vagrancy laws, stiffened punishments, and stripped the landless of their political rights. Such repressive efforts only increased social unrest and spawned a wave of uprisings.

BACON'S REBELLION   A variety of simmering tensions—caused by depressed tobacco prices, rising taxes, and crowds of freed servants greedily eyeing Indian lands—contributed to the tangled events that have come to be labeled Bacon's Rebellion. Just before the outbreak,

Governor William Berkeley had remarked in a letter: "How miserable that man is that Governes a People where six parts of seaven at least are Poore, Endebted, Discontented and Armed."

The discontent turned to violence in July 1675 when a petty squabble between a frontier planter and the Doeg Indians on the Potomac led to the murder of the planter's herdsman, and in turn to retaliation by frontier militiamen who killed ten or more Doegs and, by mistake, fourteen Susquehannocks. Soon a force of Virginia and Maryland militiamen laid siege to the Susquehannocks, murdered in cold blood five chieftains who came out to negotiate, and then let the enraged survivors escape to take their revenge on frontier settlements. Scattered attacks continued on down to the James River, where Nathaniel Bacon's overseer was killed.

By then, their revenge accomplished, the Susquehannocks pulled back. What followed had less to do with a state of war than with a state of hysteria. Berkeley proposed that the assembly support a series of forts along the frontier. But that would not slake the thirst for revenge—nor would it open new lands to settlement. Besides, it would be expensive. Some thought Berkeley was out to preserve a profitable fur trade, although there is no evidence that he was deeply involved personally.

In May 1676 Nathaniel Bacon defied Governor Berkeley's authority by assuming command of a group of frontier vigilantes. The tall, slender, black-haired, twenty-nine-year-old Bacon, a graduate of Cambridge University, had been in Virginia only two years, but he had been well set up by an English father relieved to get his vain, ambitious, hot-tempered son out of the country. Later historians would praise Bacon as the "Torchbearer of the Revolution" and leader of the first struggle of common man versus aristocrat, of frontier versus tidewater. In part this was true. The rebellion he led was largely a battle of servants, small farmers, and even slaves against Virginia's wealthy planters and political leaders. But Bacon was also the spoiled son of a rich squire who had a talent for trouble. It was his ruthless assaults against peaceful Indians rather than any commitment to democratic principles that brought him into conflict with the governing authorities.

Bacon was early in the line of one lamentable American tradition. Indians, he said, were "all alike," in that they were "wolves, tigers, and bears" who preyed upon "our harmless and innocent lambs," and therefore were fair game. After threatening to kill the governor and members of the assembly if they tried to intervene, Bacon began preparing for a total war against all the local Indians. To prevent any governmental interference, he ordered the governor arrested. Berkeley's forces resisted—but only feebly—and Bacon's men burned Jamestown in September. Bacon, however, could not savor the victory long; he fell ill and died of swamp fever a month later.

Governor Berkeley quickly regained control and subdued the leaderless rebels. In the process he hanged twenty-three and confiscated several estates. When his men captured one of Bacon's closest lieutenants, Berkeley gleefully exclaimed: "I am more glad to see you than any man in Virginia. Mr. Drummond, you shall be hanged in half an hour." For such severity the king recalled Berkeley to England, and a royal commission made treaties of pacification with the remaining Indians, some of whose descendants still live in Virginia on tiny reservations guaranteed them in 1677. The fighting opened new lands to the colonists and confirmed the power of an inner group of established landholders who sat in the council.

MARYLAND   In 1634, ten years after Virginia became a royal colony, a neighboring settlement appeared on the northern shores of Chesapeake Bay. Named Maryland in honor of Queen Henrietta Maria, it was granted to Lord Baltimore by King Charles I and became the first proprietary colony—that is, it was owned by an individual, not a joint-stock company. Sir George Calvert, the first Lord Baltimore, had announced in 1625 his conversion to Catholicism and sought the colony as a refuge for English Catholics who were subjected to discriminations at home. His son, Cecilius Calvert, the second Lord Baltimore, actually founded the colony. The charter, which set a precedent for later proprietary grants, gave the proprietor powers similar to those of an independent monarch, though the charter specified that the laws must be in accordance with those of England. References to religion were vague except for a mention that chapels should be established according to the ecclesiastical law of England.

In 1634 Calvert planted the first settlement in Maryland at St. Mary's on a small stream near the mouth of the Potomac. St. Mary's in fact was already there, a native settlement purchased from friendly Indians along with the cleared fields around it. Calvert brought Catholic gentlemen as landholders, but a majority of the servants were Protestants. The charter gave Calvert power to make laws with the consent of the freemen (all property holders). The first legislative assembly met in 1635, and divided into two houses in 1650, with governor and council sitting separately. This was instigated by the predominantly Protestant freemen—largely servants who had become landholders, or immigrants from Virginia. The charter also empowered the proprietor to grant manorial estates, and Maryland had some sixty before 1676, but the Lords Baltimore soon found that to draw settlers they had to offer farms. The colony was meant to rely on mixed farming, but its fortunes, like those of Virginia, soon came to depend on tobacco.

EARLY NEW ENGLAND SETTLEMENTS

0   100 Miles

0   100 Kilometers

MAINE

Piscataqua R.
Merrimack R.

York
Portsmouth
NEW HAMPSHIRE

CAPE ANN

Salem **MASSACHUSETTS**
Boston **BAY**

Connecticut R.

Springfield

Provincetown

Windsor
Hartford   Providence
Wethersfield **CONN.**
New Haven

Plymouth

CAPE COD

PLYMOUTH

Hudson R.

NEW HAVEN
LONG ISLAND SOUND

Newport
NARRAGANSETT BAY
RHODE ISLAND

ATLANTIC OCEAN

LONG I.

New Amsterdam

SETTLING NEW ENGLAND

PLYMOUTH   Far to the north of the Chesapeake Bay colonies, quite different settlements were taking shape. In 1607 the Virginia Company of Plymouth founded a colony along the Sagadahoc River in what is now Maine. The settlement, however, survived only one winter, after which interest in the northern region of America waned. Reports of rich cod fisheries off the New England coast helped revive interest, and in 1620 the Virginia Company reorganized itself into the Council for New England. But before the Council could mount its own colonizing expedition, a band of settlers initially headed for Virginia strayed off course and made landfall at Cape Cod. There they decided to establish a colony, naming it Plymouth after the English port from which they embarked.

The Pilgrims who established Plymouth colony belonged to the most extreme and uncompromising sect of Puritans, the Separatists, who had severed all ties with the Church of England. They stemmed from a congregation established at Scrooby in eastern England, members of which had slipped away to Holland in 1607 to escape persecution. The Calvin-istic Dutch granted them asylum and toleration, but restricted them mainly to unskilled labor. After ten years in the Dutch city of Leyden, they had wearied of the struggle. Watching their children take up Dutch habits and customs, drifting away to become sailors, soldiers, or worse, so that "their posterity would be in danger to degenerate and be cor-rupted," they longed for English ways and the English flag. If they could not have them at home, perhaps they might transplant them to the New World. King James would not promise outright toleration if they set up a colony, but did agree to leave them alone, or, as he put it, to "connive at them."

The Leyden group secured a land patent from the Virginia Company and set up a joint-stock company. In September 1620, 101 men, women, and children, led by William Bradford, crammed aboard the *Mayflower*. Their ranks included both "saints" (people recognized as having been elected by God for salvation) and "strangers" (those yet to receive the gift of grace). The latter group included John Alden, a cooper, and Miles Standish, a soldier hired to organize their defenses. A stormy voyage led them in November to Cape Cod, far north of Vir-ginia. Heading south, they encountered rough waters and turned back to seek safety at Provincetown. "Being thus arrived at safe harbor, and brought safe to land," William Bradford wrote, "they fell upon their knees and blessed the God of Heaven who had brought them over the vast and furious ocean." Since they were outside the jurisdiction of any organized government, forty-one of the Pilgrim leaders entered into a formal agreement to abide by laws made by leaders of their own choos-ing—the Mayflower Compact of November 21, 1620.

On December 26 the *Mayflower* reached Plymouth harbor and stayed there until April to give shelter and support while the Pilgrims built and occupied their dwellings amid the winter snows. Nearly half the colonists died of exposure and disease, but friendly relations with the neighboring Wampanoag Indians proved their salvation. In the spring of 1621 the colonists met Squanto, an Indian who spoke English and showed the colonists how to grow maize. By autumn the Pilgrims had a bumper crop of corn, a flourishing fur trade, and a supply of lum-ber for shipment. To celebrate, they held a harvest feast in company with Chief Massasoit and the Wampanoags. But after the ship *Fortune* arrived with thirty-five new colonists, the enlarged group again faced hunger before a food supply arrived in the spring. To make matters worse, on the way home the *Fortune* lost its cargo of furs and lumber to a French privateer.

But the colony soon stabilized. In 1621 it received a land patent from the Council for New England. Two years later it gave up its original communal economy to the extent that each settler was to provide for his family from his own land. A group of settlers bought out the sponsoring merchants in 1626. In 1630 Governor Bradford secured a new title, the "Bradford Patent," from the Council for New England, which confirmed possession and defined the boundaries more clearly.

Throughout its separate existence, until absorbed into Massachusetts in 1691, the Plymouth colony remained in the anomalous position of holding a land grant but no charter of government from any English authority. The government grew instead out of the Mayflower Compact, which was neither exactly a constitution nor a precedent for later constitutions. Rather it was the obvious recourse of a group who had made a covenant (or agreement) to form a church and who believed that God had made a covenant with them to provide a way to salvation. Thus the civil government grew naturally out of the church government, and the members of each were identical at the start. The signers of the compact at first met as the General Court, which chose the governor and his assistants (or council). Later others were admitted as members, or "freemen," but only church members were eligible. Eventually, as

A sixteenth-century ocean-going vessel, sketched by Holbein, 1532.

The Plymouth Meetinghouse, built in 1683 with funds from the sale of confiscated Indian lands.

the colony grew, the General Court became in 1639 a body of representatives from the various towns.

Plymouth's area, Cape Cod and the neighboring mainland, had relatively poor land, lacked ready access to furs from the interior, and was not in the best location for fisheries. But its imprint on the national mind would be greater than its size would warrant—William Bradford's unpretentious history, *Of Plymouth Plantation* (completed in 1651), brought the colony vividly to life. And Plymouth invented Thanksgiving—at least later generations persuaded themselves that its 1621 harvest feast was the first Thanksgiving.

JOHN WINTHROP AND THE BEGINNINGS OF MASSACHUSETTS BAY The Plymouth colony's population never rose above 7,000, and after ten years it was overshadowed by its larger neighbor, Massachusetts Bay colony. It, too, was originally intended to be a holy commonwealth made up of religious folk bound together in the harmonious worship of God and the pursuit of their "callings." Like the Pilgrims, the Puritans who colonized Massachusetts Bay were primarily Congregationalists who sought to form self-governing churches with membership limited to "visible saints"—those who could demonstrate receipt of the gift of God's grace. But unlike the Plymouth Separatists, the Puritans who settled Massachusetts Bay were still hopeful that they could help to reform the Church of England and therefore they were called Non-Separating Congregationalists.

In 1628 a group of Puritans and merchants formed the New England

Company, and got a land patent from the Council for New England. To confirm its legality, the company turned to Charles I, who issued a charter in 1629 under the new name of Massachusetts Bay Company. Leaders of the company at first looked upon it mainly as a business venture, but a majority faction led by John Winthrop, a well-to-do lawyer from East Anglia recently discharged from a government job, resolved to use the colony as a refuge for persecuted Puritans and as an instrument for building a "wilderness Zion" in America.

Winthrop was a courageous, committed leader who reflected the strengths and weaknesses of the Puritan movement. In 1606 he had experienced an intense religious conversion and soon joined the Puritan movement, determined to rid the Church of England of its Catholic trappings and to lead a life of intense piety. By 1629 Winthrop was forty years of age, had a large family, and found himself in control of a floundering estate that could not support his seven sons. Even more unsettling to him was the heightened persecution of Puritans and other dis-

Governor John Winthrop, in whose vision the Massachusetts Bay colony would be as "a city upon a hill."

senters by the Stuart monarchy. Hence he eagerly supported the idea of establishing a spiritual plantation in the New World, and he agreed to head up the enterprise.

Winthrop shrewdly took advantage of a fateful omission in the charter for the Massachusetts Bay Company: the usual proviso that the company maintain its home office in England. Winthrop's group thus decided to take the charter with them, thereby transferring the entire government of the colony to Massachusetts Bay, where they hoped to ensure Puritan control. By the Cambridge Agreement of 1629 twelve leaders resolved to migrate on these conditions, and the company's governing body agreed.

In 1630 the *Arbella,* with Governor John Winthrop and the charter aboard, embarked with six other ships for Massachusetts. In a sermon, "A Model of Christian Charity," delivered on board, Winthrop told his fellow Puritans "we must consider that we shall be a city upon a hill"— an exemplary beacon to all people of what a godly community could be. By the end of the year seventeen ships bearing 1,000 more colonists arrived. As settlers—both Puritan and non-Puritan—poured into the region, Boston became the new colony's chief city and capital.

The *Arbella* migrants proved to be the vanguard of a massive movement, the Great Migration, that carried some 80,000 men, women, and children away from their homeland to new settlements around the world over the next decade. Fleeing persecution and economic depression at home, they gravitated to Ireland, the Netherlands, and the Rhineland. But the majority traveled to the New World. They went not only to New England and the Chesapeake, but now also to new English settlements in the Lesser Antilles: St. Christopher (first settled in 1624), Barbados (1625), Nevis (1632), Montserrat (1632), and Antigua (1632). The West Indian islands started out to grow tobacco but ended up in the more profitable business of producing cane sugar.

The transfer of the Massachusetts charter, whereby an English trading company evolved into a provincial government, was a unique venture in colonization. Under this royal charter, power in the company rested with the General Court, which elected the governor and assistants. The General Court consisted of shareholders, called freemen (those who had the "freedom of the company"), but only a few besides Winthrop and his assistants had such status. This suited Winthrop and his friends, but then over 100 settlers asked to be admitted as freemen. Rather than risk trouble, the inner group invited applications and finally admitted 118 in 1631. They also stipulated that only church members, a limited category, could become freemen.

At first the freemen had no power except to choose assistants, who in turn chose the governor and deputy governor. The procedure violated provisions of the charter, but Winthrop kept the document hidden and few knew of the exact provisions. In the Watertown Protest of

THE WEST INDIES, 1600 – 1800

0   300 Miles

0   300 Kilometers

GULF OF MEXICO

ATLANTIC OCEAN

FLORIDA

VIRGIN ISLANDS (BR. 1672)

ST. CHRISTOPHER (BR. 1624)

NEVIS (BR. 1632)

ANTIGUA (BR. 1632)

MONTSERRAT (BR. 1632)

GUADELOUPE (FR. 1635)

DOMINICA (FR. 1632, BR. 1763)

MARTINIQUE (FR. 1635)

ST. VINCENT (BR. 1763)

BARBADOS (BR. 1625)

GRENADA (BR. 1763)

BAHAMA ISLANDS (BR. 1612, 1670)

Havana

CUBA (SPAIN)

GREATER

TURKS ISLANDS (BR. 1672)

CAYMAN ISLANDS (BR. 1655)

SANTO DOMINGO (SPAIN)

AREA OF INSET MAP

BELIZE (BR. 1648) BRITISH HONDURAS (BR. 1786)

JAMAICA (BR. 1655)

Port Royal (Kingston)

HAITI (FR. 1640, 1697)

ANTILLES

PUERTO RICO (SPAIN)

GUADELOUPE

MARTINIQUE

HONDURAS (SPAIN)

MOSQUITO COAST (BR. 1665)

NICARAGUA

CARIBBEAN SEA

LESSER ANTILLES

BARBADOS

TOBAGO (FR. 1677, BR. 1763, FR. 1783)

TRINIDAD (BR. 1802)

PACIFIC OCEAN

NEW GRANADA (SPAIN)

1632, the people of one town objected to paying taxes levied by the governor and assistants "for fear of bringing themselves and posterity into bondage." Winthrop rebuked them, but that year restored to the body of freemen election of the governor and his deputy. Controversy simmered for two more years until 1634, when each town sent two delegates to Boston to confer on matters coming before the General Court. There they demanded to see the charter, which Winthrop reluctantly produced, and they read that the power to pass laws and levy taxes rested in the General Court. Winthrop argued that the body of freemen had grown too large, but when it met, the General Court responded by turning itself into a representative body with two or three deputies to represent each town. They also chose a new governor, and Winthrop did not resume the office until three years later.

A final stage in the evolution of the government, a two-house legislature, came in 1644 when, according to Winthrop, "there fell out a great business upon a very small occasion." The "small occasion" involved a classic melodrama which pitted a poor widow against a well-to-do merchant over ownership of a stray sow. The General Court, being the supreme judicial as well as legislative body, was the final authority in the case. Popular sympathy and the deputies favored the widow, but

THE

OATH
OF A
FREE-MAN

I A.B. being by Gods Providence an Inhabitant and FREEMAN within the Iurifdiction of this Commonwealth; doe freely acknowledge myfelfe to be fubject to the Government thereof.

AND therefore doe here fweare by the Great and Dreadful NAME of the Everliving GOD, that I will be true and faithfull to the fame, and will accordingly yield affiftance & fupport thereunto with my perfon and eftate as in equity I am bound; and will alfo truly endeavour to maintaine& preferve all the liberties & priviledges thereof, fubmitting myfelfe to the wholefome Lawes & Orders made and eftablifhed by the fame. +++ AND further that I will not Plot or practife any evill againft it, or confent to any that fhall fo doe: but will timely difcover and reveal the fame to lawfull authority now here eftablifhed, for the fpeedy preventing thereof.

MOREOVER I doe folemnly bind myfelfe in the fight of GOD, that when I fhall be called to give my voyce touching any fuch matter of this State in which FREEMEN are to deale +++ I will give my vote and fuffrage as I fhall judge in mine own confcience may beft conduce and tend to the publicke weale of the body without refpect of perfon or favour of any man.

So help me GOD in the LORD IESVS CHRIST.

Printed at Cambridge in New England:
by Order of the Generall Courte:
Moneth the Firft – 1639

The Oath of a Free-Man: "I will give my vote and suffrage as I shall judge in mine own conscience . . ." (1639).

the assistants disagreed. The case was finally settled out of court, but the assistants feared being outvoted on some greater occasion. They therefore secured a separation into two houses, and Massachusetts thenceforth had a bicameral assembly, the deputies and assistants sitting apart, with all decisions requiring a majority in each house.

Thus over a period of fourteen years the Massachusetts Bay Company, a trading corporation, was transformed into the governing body of a commonwealth. Membership in a Puritan church replaced the purchase of stock as the means of becoming a freeman, which was to say, a voter. The General Court, like Parliament, became a representative body of two houses: the House of Assistants corresponding roughly to the House of Lords, and the House of Deputies to the House of Commons. The charter remained unchanged, but practice under the charter was quite different from the original expectation.

ROGER WILLIAMS AND ANNE HUTCHINSON   More by accident than design Massachusetts became the staging area for the rest of New England as new colonies grew out of religious quarrels within the fold. Puritanism created a volatile mixture: on the one hand the search for God's will could lead to a rigid orthodoxy; on the other hand it could lead troubled consciences to diverse, radical, even bizarre convictions.

Young Roger Williams, who arrived in 1631, was among the first to cause problems, precisely because he was the purest of Puritans, troubled by the failure of Massachusetts Nonconformists to repudiate the Church of England entirely. He held a brief pastorate in Salem, then tried Separatist Plymouth. Governor Bradford found Williams to be gentle and kind in his personal relations as well as a charismatic speaker. But he charged that Williams "began to fall into strange opinions," specifically questioning the king's right to grant Indian lands "under a sin of usurpation of others' possession"; Williams then returned to Salem. Williams's belief that a true church must have no truck with the unregenerate led him eventually to the conclusion that no true church was possible, unless perhaps consisting of his wife and himself—and he may have had doubts about her.

But eccentric as some of Williams's beliefs may have been, they led him to principles that later generations would honor for other reasons. The purity of the church required complete separation of church and state and freedom from coercion in matters of faith. Williams therefore questioned the authority of government to impose an oath of allegiance and rejected laws imposing religious conformity. Such views were too advanced even for the radical church of Salem, which finally removed him, whereupon Williams retorted so hotly against churches that were "ulcered and gangrened" that the General Court in 1635 banished him to England. Governor Winthrop, however, out of personal sympathy, permitted him to slip away with a few followers among the Narragansett Indians, whom he had befriended. In the spring of 1636 Williams established the town of Providence at the head of Narragansett Bay, the first permanent settlement in Rhode Island, and the first in America to legislate freedom of religion.

Anne Hutchinson quarreled with the Puritan leaders for different reasons. The articulate, strong-willed, and intelligent wife of a promi-

Religious quarrels within the Puritan fold led to the founding of new colonies. Here a seventeenth-century cartoon shows wrangling sects tossing a Bible in a blanket.

nent merchant, she raised thirteen children, served as a healer and mid-wife, and hosted meetings in her Boston home to discuss sermons. Soon, however, the discussions turned into forums for Hutchinson to provide her own commentaries on religious matters. She disclosed that she had experienced direct revelations from the Holy Spirit which convinced her that only two or three Puritan ministers actually preached the appropriate "covenant of grace." The others, she claimed, were deluded and incompetent; the "covenant of works" they promoted led people to believe that good conduct would ensure salvation.

Hutchinson's beliefs were provocative for several reasons. Puritan theology was indeed grounded in the Calvinist doctrine that people could be saved only by God's grace rather than through their own willful actions. But Puritanism in practice also insisted that ministers were necessary to interpret God's will for the people so as to "prepare" them for the possibility of salvation. In challenging the very legitimacy of the ministerial community as well as the hard-earned assurances of salvation enjoyed by current church members, Hutchinson was undermining the stability of an already fragile social system. Moreover, her critics likened her claim of direct revelations from the Holy Spirit to the antinomian heresy, technically a belief that one is freed from obeying the moral law by one's own faith and by God's grace. And what made the situation worse in the male-dominated society of seventeenth-century New England was that a *woman* had made such charges and assertions. Mrs. Hutchinson had both offended authority and sanctioned a disruptive individualism.

Hutchinson, now pregnant again, was hauled before the General Court in 1637, and for two days she verbally sparred on equal terms with the presiding magistrates and testifying ministers. Her skillful deflections of the charges and her ability to cite chapter-and-verse defenses of her actions led an exasperated Governor Winthrop at one point to explode: "We do not mean to discourse with those of your sex." He found Hutchinson to be "a woman of haughty and fierce carriage, of a nimble wit and active spirit, and a very voluble tongue." As the trial continued, an overwrought Hutchinson was eventually lured into convicting herself by claiming direct divine inspiration—blasphemy in the eyes of orthodox Puritans.

Banished in 1638 as "a woman not fit for our society," Hutchinson walked through the wilderness to Providence and then settled with her family and a few followers on an island near what is now Portsmouth. But the arduous journey had taken its toll. Hutchinson grew sick and her baby was stillborn, leading her critics back in Massachusetts to assert that the "monstrous birth" was God's way of punishing her for her sins. Hutchinson's spirits never recovered. After her husband's death in 1642 she moved to Long Island, then under Dutch jurisdiction, and the following year she and five of her children were massacred during an Indian attack. Her fate, wrote an unusually vindictive Winthrop, was "a special manifestation of divine justice."

Thus the colony of Rhode Island and Providence Plantations, the smallest in America, grew up in Narragansett Bay, as a refuge for dissenters who agreed that the state had no right to coerce belief. In 1640 they formed a confederation and in 1644 secured their first charter—from the Puritan Parliament. Williams lived until 1683, an active and beloved citizen of the commonwealth he founded in a society which, during his lifetime at least, lived up to his principles of religious freedom and a government based on the consent of the people.

CONNECTICUT   Connecticut had a more orthodox beginning. In 1633, a group from Plymouth settled Windsor, ten miles farther up the Connecticut River. Three years later Thomas Hooker led three entire church congregations from Massachusetts Bay to the Connecticut River towns of Wethersfield, Windsor, and Hartford, which earlier arrivals had laid out the previous year.

For a year the settlers in the river towns were governed under a commission from the Massachusetts General Court, but the inhabitants organized the self-governing colony of Connecticut in 1637. The impulse to organize came when representatives of the towns met to consider ways of meeting the danger of attack from the Pequot Indians, who lived east of the river. Before the end of the year the Pequots had attacked Wethersfield, and the settlers, with help from Massachusetts, responded with ferocity, surprising and burning the chief Pequot town on the Mystic River and slaughtering some 400 men, women, and children; stragglers were sold into slavery. All but a remnant of the Pequots perished in the holocaust.

In 1639 the Connecticut General Court adopted the "Fundamental Orders of Connecticut," a series of laws which provided for a government like that of Massachusetts, except that voting was not limited to church members. New Haven had by then appeared within the later limits of Connecticut. A group of English Puritans, led by their minister and a wealthy merchant, had migrated first to Massachusetts and then, seeking a place to establish themselves in commerce, to New Haven on Long Island Sound in 1638. Mostly city dwellers, they found themselves reduced to hardscrabble farming, despite their intentions. The New Haven colony became the most rigorously Puritan of all. Like all the other offshoots of Massachusetts, it too lacked a charter and maintained a self-governing independence until 1662, when it was absorbed into Connecticut under the terms of that colony's first royal charter.

NEW HAMPSHIRE AND MAINE   To the north of Massachusetts, most of what are now New Hampshire and Maine was granted in 1622 by the Council for New England to Sir Ferdinando Gorges and Captain John Mason and their associates. In 1629 Mason and Gorges divided their territory at the Piscataqua River, Mason taking the southern part which he named New Hampshire. In the 1630s Puritan immigrants began filtering in, and in 1638 the Reverend John Wheelwright, one of Anne Hutchinson's group, founded Exeter. Maine consisted of a few scattered and small settlements, mostly fishing stations, the chief of them being York.

An ambiguity in the Massachusetts charter brought the proprietorships into doubt, however. The charter set the boundary three miles north of the Merrimack River and the Bay colony took that to mean north of the river's northernmost reach, which gave it a claim on nearly the entire Gorges-Mason grant. During the English time of troubles in the early 1640s Massachusetts took over New Hampshire, and in the 1650s extended its authority to the scattered settlements in Maine. This led to lawsuits with the heirs of the proprietors, and in 1677 English judges and the Privy Council decided against Massachusetts in both cases. Two years later New Hampshire became a royal colony, but Massachusetts bought out the Gorges heirs and continued to control Maine as its proprietor. A new Massachusetts charter in 1691 finally incorporated Maine into Massachusetts.

INDIANS IN NEW ENGLAND

The English settlers who poured into New England found not a "virgin land" of uninhabited wilderness but a developed region populated by over 100,000 Indians. To the white colonists the Native Americans represented both an alien race and an impediment to their economic and spiritual goals. To the Indians the newcomers seemed like magical monsters. As one Indian leader explained, the white adventurers "strike awe and terror to our hearts." But the interactions of the two cultures were more complex than the conventional story of conquest and subjugation. Indians coped with the newcomers and changing circumstances in a variety of different ways. Some resisted, others sought accommodation, and still others grew dependent on white culture. In some areas Indians survived and even flourished in concert with European settlements over long periods of time and with varying degrees of advantage. In other areas land-hungry newcomers quickly displaced or decimated the native populations. The interactions of the two cultures thus involved misunderstandings, the mutual need for trade and adaptation, and sporadic outbreaks of epidemics and warfare.

In general, the English colonists adopted a quite different strategy for dealing with the Native Americans than that of the French and the Dutch. Merchants from France and the Netherlands were preoccupied with exploiting the fur trade. To do so they established permanent trading outposts among the Indians. This led them to establish stable and even amicable relations with the far more numerous Indians in the region. In contrast, the English colonists were more interested in fish and farms. They were quite willing to manipulate and exploit Indians rather than deal with them on an equal footing. Their goal was subordination rather than reciprocity.

THE NEW ENGLAND INDIANS   In Maine the Abenakis were mainly hunters and gatherers dependent upon the natural offerings of the land and waters. The men did the hunting and fishing while the women retrieved the dead game and prepared it for eating. Women were also responsible for setting up and breaking camp, gathering fruits and berries, and raising the children. The Algonquian tribes of southern New England—the Massachusetts, Nausets, Narragansetts, Pequots, and Wampanoags—were more horticultural. Their highly developed agricultural system centered on three primary crops: corn, beans, and pumpkins. While the men still hunted, fished, or traded surplus grain, women planted crops in regularly spaced mounds or "hills" so as to allow the roots of the plants to intertwine and thereby protect the young tendrils from wind and birds. A Rhode Island colonist reported that the Indian "woman of the family will commonly raise two or three heaps of twelve, fifteen, or twenty bushels, a heap, which they dry in round broadheaps; and if she have help of her children or friends, much more."

For centuries the Indians had used the "slash-and-burn" technique to transform densely wooded forests into fields or parklike hunting preserves. They set fires to burn the underbrush and to nourish the soil.

This not only facilitated planting but also allowed for the emergence of succulent new plants that enticed deer. Burning the thick underbrush under the forest canopy also made it easier for Indians to track game and to gather nuts and berries.

The Indians' dependence on nature for their survival shaped their religious beliefs. They believed in a Creator who provided them with the land and its bountiful resources. Many rituals, ceremonies, and taboos acknowledged their dependence on the gods. Rain dances, harvest festivals, and sacrificial offerings bespoke a culture whose fate was dependent on supernatural powers.

Initially, the coastal Indians helped the white settlers develop a subsistence economy. They taught the Europeans how to plant corn and to use fish for fertilizer. They also developed a flourishing trade with the newcomers, exchanging furs for manufactured goods and "trinkets." Although often portrayed as a monolithic group, the various Indian tribes of New England often fought among themselves, usually over disputed land. Had they been able to forge a solid alliance, they would have been better able to resist the encroachments of white settlers. As it was, they not only were fragmented but also vulnerable to the infectious diseases carried on board the ships transporting European settlers to the New World. Epidemics of smallpox soon devastated the Indian population, leaving the coastal areas "a widowed land." Between 1610 and 1675 the Abenakis declined from 12,000 to 3,000, and the southern New England tribes from 65,000 to 10,000. Governor William Bradford of Plymouth reported that the Indians "fell sick of the smallpox, and died most miserably." Their bodies were covered with "the pox breaking and mattering and running one into another, their skin cleaving" to their sleeping mats. By the hundreds, they died "like rotten sheep."

Many of the Puritan leaders interpreted these epidemics as divine harvests intended to clear the region of Indians and thereby facilitate white settlement. After all, they reasoned, the Indians were heathens doing the devil's work. They must be rooted out. Those Indians who survived the epidemics and refused to yield their lands were often dislodged by force. In 1636 white settlers in Massachusetts accused a Pequot of murdering a colonist. Joined by Connecticut colonists, they exacted their revenge by setting fire to a Pequot village on the Mystic River. As the Indians fled their burning huts, the Puritans shot and killed them—men, women, and children. In less than an hour, all but seven escapees were dead.

Sassacus, the Pequot chief, then organized the survivors among his followers and attacked the whites. During the Pequot War of 1637, the colonists and their Narraganset allies indiscriminately killed 700 Pequots in their village near West Mystic, in the Connecticut River valley. A white participant described the horrible scene: "Many were burnt

*The Puritans and their Indian allies, the Narragansetts, mount a
ferocious attack on the Pequots at Mystic, Connecticut (1637).*

in the fort, both men, women, and children. . . . There were about four
hundred souls in this fort, and not above five of them escaped out of
our hands. Great and doleful was the bloody sight." The magisterial
Puritan minister Cotton Mather described the slaughter as a "sweet sacrifice" and "gave the praise thereof to God." Only a few colonists regretted the massacre. Roger Williams warned that the lust for land would
become "as great a God with us English as God Gold was with the
Spanish." With poignant clarity, Pequot survivors recognized the
motives of the English settlers: "We see plainly that their chiefest desire
is to deprive us of the privilege of our land, and drive us to our utter
ruin." Indeed, the white colonists captured most of the surviving
Pequots and sold them into slavery in Bermuda. Under the terms of the
Treaty of Hartford (1638), the Pequot nation was declared dissolved.

After the Pequot War the prosperous fur trade contributed to peace-

The official seal of the Massachusetts Bay colony after 1675. The Indian is depicted as saying "Come over and help us."

ful relations between whites and the remaining Indians, but the relentless growth of the colony and the decline of the animal population began to reduce the eastern tribes to relative poverty. The colonial government repeatedly encroached upon the Indian settlements, forcing them to acknowledge English laws and customs. Colonial leaders used a variety of arguments to rationalize their action. Several argued that the Indians should be deprived of their land because they were not using it as efficiently as the English would. "The Indians," declared a Bostonian, "are not able to make use of the one-fourth part of the land, neither have they any settled places, as towns to dwell in, nor any ground as they challenge for their own possession but change their habitation from place to place." Another Englishman explained that the Indians "are not industrious, neither have they art, science, skill, or faculty to use either the land or the commodities of it, but all spoils, rots, and is marred for want of manuring, gathering, ordering, etc." At the same time that colonial leaders expropriated Indian lands, Puritan missionaries sought to convert the tribes. One missionary, John Eliot, translated the Bible into the Algonquian language. By 1675 hundreds of converts had settled in special "praying Indian" towns.

The era of fairly peaceful coexistence that began with the Treaty of Hartford came to an end during the last quarter of the seventeenth century. In 1675 Philip (Metacomet), chief of the Wampanoags, forged an alliance among the remaining tribes of southern New England—the Narragansetts, Mohegans, and Wampanoags. The spark that set New England ablaze resulted from the murder of Sassamon, a "praying Indian" who had attended Harvard, later strayed from the faith while serving Metacomet, and then returned to the Christian fold. The officials of Plymouth colony tried and executed three Wampanoags for the murder of Sassamon. In retaliation the Indians attacked and burned colonial settlements throughout Massachusetts and Plymouth colony.

Both sides suffered incredible losses. It is estimated that some 20,000 people were killed in what came to be called either King Philip's War or Metacomet's War. Within a year the Indians were threatening Boston itself. Finally, however, depleted supplies and the casualty toll wore down Indian resistance. Philip's wife and son were captured and sold into slavery. Some of the tribes surrendered, a few succumbed to disease, while others fled to the west. Those who remained behind were forced to resettle in villages supervised by white settlers. Philip initially escaped, only to be hunted down and killed in 1676. Sporadic fighting continued in Maine and New Hampshire until 1678.

This pattern of relentless white encroachment upon Indian lands continued over the years. The survivors of the wars had to submit to colonial authority and accept confinement to ever-dwindling plots of land. In 1735 twenty-seven Pequots submitted a petition to Connecticut's royal governor, complaining that the white settlers had planted wheat and were grazing cattle on their lands. Yet their plea fell on deaf ears. In a similar petition to the Connecticut legislature in 1789, the Mahicans plaintively recognized that "the times" had been "exceedingly alter'd."

THE ENGLISH CIVIL WAR IN AMERICA

Before 1640 English settlers in New England and around Chesapeake Bay had established two great beachheads on the Atlantic coast, separated by the Dutch colony of New Netherland in between. After 1640, however, the struggle between king and Parliament distracted attention from colonization, and migration dwindled to a trickle of emigrants for more than twenty years. During the time of civil war and Oliver Cromwell's Puritan dictatorship, the struggling colonies were left pretty much to their own devices, especially in New England where English Puritans saw little need to intervene.

In 1643 four of the New England colonies—Massachusetts Bay, Plymouth, Connecticut, and New Haven—formed the New England Confederation. The purpose was mainly joint defense against the Dutch, French, and Indians, but the colonies agreed also to support the Christian faith, to render up fugitives, and to settle disputes through the machinery of the Confederation. Two commissioners from each colony met annually to transact business. In some ways the Confederation behaved like a sovereign power. It made treaties with New Netherland and French Acadia, and in 1653 voted a war against the Dutch who were supposedly stirring the Indians against Connecticut. Massachusetts, far from the scene of trouble, failed to cooperate, however, and this greatly weakened the Confederation. The commissioners nevertheless continued to meet annually until 1684, when Massachusetts lost its charter.

Virginia and Maryland remained almost as independent as New England. At the behest of Governor William Berkeley, the Virginia burgesses in 1649 denounced the execution of Charles and recognized his son, Charles II, as the lawful king. In 1652, however, the assembly yielded to parliamentary commissioners and overruled the belligerent governor. In return for the surrender, the commissioners let the assembly choose its own council and governor, and the colony grew rapidly

Oliver Cromwell, England's Lord Protector from 1653 until his death in 1658.

in population during its years of independent government—some of the growth came from the arrival of royalists who found a friendly haven in the Old Dominion, despite its capitulation to the English Puritans.

The parliamentary commissioners who won the submission of Virginia proceeded to Maryland, where the proprietary governor faced particular difficulties with his Protestant majority, largely Puritan but including some earlier refugees from Anglican Virginia. At the governor's suggestion, the assembly had passed, and the proprietor had accepted, the Maryland Toleration Act of 1649, an assurance that Puritans would not be molested in their religion. In 1652 the commissioners revoked the Toleration Act and deprived Lord Baltimore of his governmental rights, though not of his lands and revenues. Still, the more extreme Puritan elements were dissatisfied and a brief clash in 1654 brought civil war to Maryland, deposing the governor. But the Calverts had a remarkable skill at retaining favor. Oliver Cromwell took the side of Lord Baltimore and restored him to full rights in 1657, whereupon the Toleration Act was reinstated. The act deservedly stands as a landmark to human liberty, albeit enacted more out of expediency than conviction, and although it limited toleration to those who professed belief in the Holy Trinity.

Although Cromwell let the colonies go their own way, he was not indifferent to the nascent empire. He fought trade wars with the Dutch and harassed England's traditional enemy, Catholic Spain, in the Caribbean. In 1655 he sent out an expedition that wrested Jamaica from the Spaniards, thereby improving the odds for English privateers and pirates who pillaged Spanish ships—and often any others that chanced by.

The Restoration of King Charles II in England led to an equally painless restoration of previous governments in the colonies. The process involved scarcely any change, since little had occurred under Cromwell. Emigration rapidly expanded the populations in Virginia and Maryland. Fears of reprisals against Puritan New England proved unfounded, at least for the time being. Agents hastily dispatched by the colonies won reconfirmation of the Massachusetts charter in 1662 and the very first royal charters for Connecticut and Rhode Island in 1662 and 1663. All three retained their status as self-governing corporations. Plymouth still had no charter, but went unmolested. New Haven, however, disappeared as a separate entity, absorbed into the colony of Connecticut.

SETTLING THE CAROLINAS

The Restoration of Charles II opened a new season of enthusiasm for colonial expansion, directed mainly by royal favorites. Within twelve years the English had conquered New Netherland, had settled

Carolina, and very nearly filled out the shape of the colonies. In the middle region formerly claimed by the Dutch, four new colonies sprang into being: New York, New Jersey, Pennsylvania, and Delaware. Without exception the new colonies were proprietary, awarded by the king to men who had remained loyal, or had brought about his restoration, or in one case to whom he was indebted. In 1663 he granted Carolina to eight prominent allies who became Lord Proprietors of the region.

NORTH CAROLINA   Carolina was from the start made up of two widely separated areas of settlement, which finally became separate colonies. The northernmost part, long called Albemarle, had been entered as early as the 1650s by stragglers who drifted southward from Virginia. For half a century Albemarle remained a remote scattering of settlers along the shores of Albemarle Sound, isolated from Virginia by the Dismal Swamp and lacking easy access for ocean going vessels. Its reputation had long suffered from the belief that it served as a rogue's harbor for the outcasts of Virginia. Later the aristocratic William Byrd, who helped survey the dividing line between Virginia and North Carolina, dubbed the neighboring colony Lubberland: "Surely there is no place in the world where the inhabitants lived with less labor than in North Car-

EARLY SETTLEMENTS IN THE SOUTH

olina. . . . When the weather is mild, they stand leaning with both their arms upon the cornfield fence and gravely consider whether they had best go and take a small beat at the hoe but generally find reasons to put it off. . . ." Albemarle had no governor until 1664, no assembly until 1665, and not even a town until a group of French Huguenots founded the village of Bath in 1704.

SOUTH CAROLINA   The eight Lords Proprietors to whom the king gave Carolina neglected Albemarle from the outset, and focused on more promising sites to the south. They sought settlers who had already been seasoned in the colonies, and from the outset Barbadians showed a lively interest, for the rise of large-scale sugar production in Barbados had persuaded small planters to try their luck elsewhere. In 1669 three ships left London with about 100 settlers recruited in England. The expedition sailed first to Barbados, to pick up more settlers, then north to Bermuda. They settled in South Carolina at a place several miles up the Ashley River, where Charles Town (later known as Charleston) remained from 1670 to 1680, when it was moved across and downstream to Oyster Point, overlooking Charleston Harbor. There, as proud Charlestonians later claimed, the Ashley and Cooper rivers "join to form the Atlantic Ocean."

The government of this colony rested on one of the most curious documents of colonial history, the "Fundamental Constitutions of Carolina," drawn up by one of the proprietors, Lord Ashley-Cooper, with the help of his secretary, the philosopher John Locke. Its cumbersome frame of government and its provisions for an elaborate nobility had little effect in the colony except to encourage a practice of large land grants, but from the beginning smaller "headrights" were given to every immigrant who paid for the cost of transit. The provision that had greatest effect was a grant of religious toleration, designed to encourage immigration, which gave South Carolina a greater degree of indulgence (extending even to Jews and heathens) than either England or any other colony except Rhode Island and, once it was established, Pennsylvania.

For two decades the South Carolina proprietors struggled to find a staple crop. Indeed, the colonists at first had trouble providing their own subsistence. The first profitable enterprise was a flourishing trade in deerskins and Indian slaves. Ambitious Barbadians, case-hardened by African slavery in the tropics, dominated the colony and did not scruple at organizing a major trade in Indian slaves, whom the Westo Indians obligingly drove to the coast for shipment to the Caribbean. The first major export other than furs and slaves was cattle, and a staple crop was not developed until the introduction of rice in the 1690s. South

An Indian village in North Carolina, in an engraving by
Theodor de Bry based on a sketch by John White.

Carolina became a separate royal colony in 1719. North Carolina remained under the proprietors' rule for ten more years, when the proprietors surrendered their governing rights to the crown.

THE SOUTHERN INDIAN TRADE   The major Indian tribes in Florida, the Carolinas, Georgia, and what is today Alabama and Mississippi—the Apalachee, Timucua, Catawba, Cherokee, Chickasaw, Choctaw, Creek, and Tuscarora—combined farming with hunting and fishing to produce a thriving culture. They clustered in matrilineal clans (in which authority and property descended through the maternal line). The women raised beans, potatoes, and especially corn. The men hunted, traded, and made war. Beginning in the late seventeenth century, the Creeks developed a flourishing trade with the British settlers, exchanging deerskins for manufactured goods—hoes, copper kettles, knives, beads, blankets, and clothing.

In the late seventeenth century English merchants—mostly illiterate adventurers—began traveling southward from Virginia down the Occaneechi trading path into the piedmont region of Carolina, where they developed a prosperous exchange with the Catawbas. By 1690 traders from Charleston, South Carolina, made their way up the Savannah River to arrange deals with the Cherokees, Creeks, and Chickasaws. Between 1699 and 1715 Carolina exported an average of 54,000 deer-skins per year. The voracious demand for the soft skins almost exterminated the deer population.

The growing trade with the English exposed the Indians to contagious diseases that decimated their population. Commercial activity also entwined the Indians in a dependent relationship that would prove disastrous to their traditional way of life. Eager to receive more finished goods, weapons, and ammunition, the Indians became pliable trading partners, easily manipulated by wily English entrepreneurs and government officials. The English traders began providing the Indians with firearms and rum as incentives to convince them to capture rival tribesmen to be sold as slaves.

During the early eighteenth century Indians equipped with British weapons and led by English soldiers crossed into Spanish territory in south Georgia and north Florida. They were intent upon destroying Spanish missions and capturing Indian slaves from the Timucua and Apalachee tribes. One large campaign destroyed thirteen missions, killed several hundred Indians and Spaniards, and enslaved over three hundred Indian men, women, and children. By 1710 the Florida tribes were on the verge on extinction.

One white Carolinian rationalized enslaving Indians by arguing that "it both serves to lessen their numbers before the French can arm them, and it is a more Effectuall way of Civilizing and Instructing [them] than all of the efforts used by the French missionaries." In 1708, when the total population of South Carolina was 9,580, including 2,900 blacks, there were 1,400 Indian slaves. Because the captive Indians frequently escaped or revolted, many were relocated to New England or the West Indies.

The continuing Indian trade led to repeated troubles. In 1711 the Tuscaroras in North Carolina grew alarmed at the unrelenting pace of white settlement. They also were goaded by the Iroquois to abandon their accommodating ways and oust the Europeans. The catalyst for their uprising was the severe punishment of a Tuscarora accused of a petty offense. In a vengeful outburst the Tuscaroras captured and killed a white colonist, then assaulted several plantations using weapons bartered from Virginia traders. When South Carolina dispatched a relief expedition of whites and Indian allies, the Tuscaroras held out in forts of their own. But in 1713 they succumbed to a massive assault. Hundreds of Tuscaroras were killed and over four hundred enslaved. Most of the survivors of this Tuscarora War retreated north, where they joined the League of the Iroquois.

A contemporary print depicting seven "Chiefs of the Cherokee Indians" who had been taken from Carolina to England in 1730.

Two years later, in 1715, Creeks, Choctaws, and members of smaller tribes organized a more massive revolt against English control. This, the Yamasee War, began when Indians killed several English traders, including the Indian agent for South Carolina. When a war party arrived at John Hearn's outpost, he gave them food "according to our Usual friendly manner"—and then they killed him. A similar incident resulted in twenty-two whites being killed. Word of the uprising provoked similar attacks on traders throughout South Carolina. The English attributed the attacks to French and Spanish intrigues, but it now seems likely that the Indians acted on their own. The English colonists won out by playing the Indians against one another, convincing the Cherokees to join their side. When the Creek leaders visited the Cherokees in an effort to gain their support, the Cherokees killed them, an incident that engendered hatred between the two tribes for years thereafter.

The Yamasee War ended in 1717, when the Creeks signed a peace treaty. But infighting among the Indians continued. For the next ten years or so, the Creeks and Cherokees engaged in a costly blood feud, much to the delight of the English. One Carolinian explained that their challenge was to figure "how to hold both as our friends, for some time, and assist them in cutting one another's throats without offending either. This is the game we intend to play if possible." The French played the same brutal game, doing their best to excite hatred between the Choctaws and the Chickasaws.

New Amsterdam in 1667.

SETTLING THE MIDDLE COLONIES AND GEORGIA

NEW NETHERLAND BECOMES NEW YORK   Charles II resolved early to pluck out that old thorn in the side of the English colonies—New Netherland. The Dutch colony was older than New England, and had been planted when the two Protestant powers enjoyed friendly relations in opposition to Catholic Spain. The Dutch East India Company (organized in 1620) had hired an English captain, Henry Hudson, to seek the elusive passage to China. Sailing along the upper coast of North America in 1609, Hudson had discovered Delaware Bay and explored the river named for him, to a point probably beyond Albany where he and a group of Mohawks made merry with brandy. From the contact stemmed a lasting trade relation between the Dutch and the Iroquois nations. In 1614 the Dutch established fur-trading posts on Manhattan Island and upriver at Fort Orange (later Albany). In 1626 Governor Peter Minuit purchased Manhattan from the resident Indians and a Dutch fort appeared at the lower end of the island. The village of New Amsterdam, which grew up around the fort, became the capital of New Netherland.

Dutch settlements gradually dispersed in every direction where furs might be found. In 1638 a Swedish trading company established Fort Christina at the site of the present Wilmington and scattered a few hundred settlers up and down the Delaware River. The Dutch, at the time allied to the Swedes in the Thirty Years' War, made no move to challenge the claim until 1655, when a force outnumbering the entire Swedish colony subjected them without bloodshed to the rule of New Netherland. The chief contribution of the short-lived New Sweden to American culture was the idea of the log cabin, which the Swedes and a few Finnish settlers with them had brought from the woods of Scandinavia.

Like the French, the Dutch were interested mainly in the fur trade and were less interested in agricultural settlements. In 1629, however, the Dutch West India Company provided that any stockholder might obtain a large estate (a patroonship) if he peopled it with fifty adults within four years. The patroon was obligated to supply cattle, tools, and buildings. His tenants, in turn, paid him rent, used his gristmill, gave him first option on surplus crops, and submitted to a court he established. It amounted to transplanting the feudal manor into the New World, and met with as little luck as similar efforts in Maryland and South Carolina. Volunteers for serfdom were hard to find when there was land to be had elsewhere; most settlers took advantage of the company's provision that one could have as farms (*bouweries*) all the lands one could improve.

The colony's government was under the almost absolute control of a governor sent out by the Dutch West India company, subject to little check from his council or from the directors back in Holland. The governors were mostly stubborn autocrats, either corrupt or inept, especially at Indian relations. They depended on a small professional garrison for defense, and the inhabitants (including a number of English on Long Island) betrayed almost total indifference in 1664 when Governor Peter Stuyvesant called them to arms against a threatening British fleet. Almost defenseless, old soldier Stuyvesant blustered and stomped about on his wooden leg, but finally surrendered without a shot and stayed on quietly at his farm in what had become the colony of New York.

The plan of conquest had been hatched by the king's brother, the duke of York and Albany, later King James II. As lord high admiral and an investor in the African trade, York had already harassed Dutch shipping and forts in Africa. When he and his advisers counseled that New Netherland could easily be conquered, Charles II simply granted the region to his brother as proprietor, permitted the hasty gathering of an invasion force, and the English transformed New Amsterdam into New York and Fort Orange into Albany. The Dutch, however, left a permanent imprint on the land and the language: the Dutch vernacular faded away but place names such as Block Island, Wall Street (the original wall was for protection against Indians), and Broadway (*Breede Wegh*) remained, along with family names like Rensselaer, Roosevelt, and Van Buren. The Dutch presence lingered in the Dutch Reformed church; in words like boss, cookie, crib, snoop, stoop, spook, and kill (for creek); and in the legendary Santa Claus, Rip Van Winkle, and the picturesque Dutch governors, preserved in the satirical caricatures of Washington Irving's *Knickerbocker History.*

THE IROQUOIS LEAGUE   One of the most significant effects of European settlement in North America during the seventeenth century was the intensification of warfare between Indian peoples. The same combination of forces that decimated the Indian population of New England and the Carolinas befell the tribes around New York City and the lower Hudson valley. Dissension among the Indians and susceptibility to infectious disease left them vulnerable to exploitation by whites and by other Indians.

In the interior of New York, however, a different situation arose. There the Iroquois (an Algonquian term signifying "snake" or "terrifying man") nation would eventually forge a strong alliance, a league so strong

Iroquois wampum belts.

and numerous that the outnumbered Dutch and, later, English traders were forced to work with the Indians in exploiting the lucrative fur trade. Initially, the Mahicans (an offshoot of the Pequots) supplied the Dutch with pelts. By 1625, however, the game animals in the Mahican territory had been hunted almost to extinction, so the Dutch turned to the Iroquois, a federation of five tribes who spoke related languages— the Mohawk, Oneida, Onondaga, Cayuga, and Seneca (a sixth tribe, the Tuscaroras, joined them in 1712). Legend has it that a Mohawk sachem (chief) named Hiawatha unified the "Five Nations" in the early fifteenth century.

By the early 1600s some fifty chiefs governed the 12,000 members of the Iroquois League. The sachems made decisions for all the villages and served to minimize tribal rivalries and dissension within the confederacy. The well-organized, firmly knit Iroquois tribes lived in rectangular "long houses" sheathed in bark. These multifamily dwellings could house fifty or sixty members of an extended family. Iroquois men hunted deer, bear, and beaver; women grew corn, beans, and squash. They used belts of colored beads, known as wampum, to symbolize words intended to certify treaties or record transactions with other Indians and whites. The rejection or return of a wampum belt meant that its message or proposal was unacceptable. Although a patriarchal society, the Iroquois granted considerable powers to women; they controlled the nominations for the tribal councils and could remove ineffective or corrupt leaders.

When the Iroquois began to deplete the local game during the 1640s, they used firearms supplied by their Dutch trading partners to seize the Canadian hunting grounds of the neighboring Hurons and Eries. During the so-called Beaver Wars, the Iroquois defeated the western tribes and thereafter hunted the region to extinction. Other Indian nations such as the Fox, Sac, and Kickapoo fled in terror at the approach of the Iroquois. The lucrative trade in pelts led the Iroquois to emphasize hunting at the expense of farming. This in turn accentuated the warrior-hunter ideal as the masculine archetype.

Iroquois men were proud, ruthless warriors. Indeed, warfare was an essential part of aboriginal culture. Participation in a war party served as the crucial rite of passage for young men. They fought opponents to gain status and revenge and to ease the grief caused by the death of friends and relatives. Their skill and courage in battle determined their social status. A warrior's success was not only measured by his fighting prowess but also by his ability to capture prisoners and bring them back alive for adoption or ritual execution. This helps explain the Indian preference for surprise attacks and ambushes rather than conventional frontal assaults.

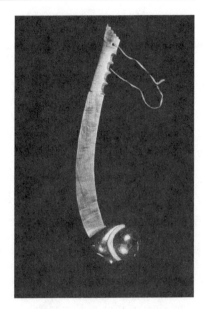

An Onondaga (Iroquois) war club.

If captured themselves, the Iroquois expected to be tortured. They, in turn, tortured, roasted, and occasionally ate their foes. A captive slated for execution was daubed with red and black paint, given a death feast, and invited to recite his own feats in war. On the appointed day he was tied to a stake, and villagers of all ages then took turns burning him with red-hot objects. A courageous victim was expected to endure such torments stoically, but few could do so for long. Eventually the prisoner was scalped, hot sand was thrown onto the exposed skull, and a hatchet blow to the neck ended his suffering.

While providing profitable new hunting grounds, wars against other Indian tribes depleted the Iroquois population. This led them to replace lost relatives by allowing elder women to "adopt" able-bodied captives after they had been tortured so as to break their allegiance to their native group or culture. In 1657 a French missionary noted that "more Foreigners than natives of the country" resided in Iroquoia. By the 1660s more than two-thirds of the residents of some Iroquois villages were adoptees.

During the second half of the seventeenth century, the relentless search for furs and captives led Iroquois war parties to range far and wide across what is today eastern North America. They gained control over a huge area from the St. Lawrence River to Tennessee and from

Maine to Michigan. These wars helped reorient the political relationships in the whole eastern half of the continent, especially in the area from the Ohio Valley northward across the Great Lakes basin. Besieged by the Iroquois Confederacy, the western tribes forged defensive alliances with the French.

For over twenty years warfare raged across the Great Lakes region. In 1689 Iroquois warriors attacked the French village of Lachine, near Montreal. A Jesuit priest reported that the Iroquois attacked while the people were asleep. They began "by massacring the men; then they set fire to the houses. . . . [The Iroquois] opened the bodies of pregnant women, to tear out the fruit that they bore; they put children alive on the spit, and forced the children to turn and roast them. They invented a number of other unheard-of tortures; and thus, in less than an hour, 200 persons of every age and both sexes, perished in the most frightful tortures."

In the 1690s the French and their Indian allies gained the advantage over the Iroquois. They destroyed their crops and villages, infected them with smallpox, and reduced the male population by more than a third. Facing extermination, the Iroquois made peace with the French in 1701. They claimed to be tired of serving the English as a "Pack of Hounds" to harass the French. During the first half of the eighteenth century, they maintained a shrewd neutrality between the two rival European powers that enabled them to play the British off against the French, all the while creating a thriving fur trade for themselves. Iroquois warriors intermarried and intermingled with women of the western tribes and occasionally went to war against reluctant trading partners such as the Catawbas to the south.

NEW JERSEY   Shortly after the conquest of New Netherland, still in 1664, the duke of York granted his lands between the Hudson and the Delaware rivers to Sir George Carteret and Lord John Berkeley (brother of Virginia's governor), and named the territory for Carteret's native island of Jersey. The New Jersey proprietorship then passed through a sequence of incredible complications. In 1674 Berkeley sold his share to a Quaker leader, whose affairs were so encumbered that their management fell to three trustees, one of whom was William Penn, another prominent Quaker. In 1676, by mutual agreement, the colony was divided by a diagonal line into East and West New Jersey, with Carteret taking the east. Finally in 1682 Carteret sold out to a group of twelve, including Penn, who in turn brought into partnership twelve more proprietors, for a total of twenty-four! In East New Jersey, peopled at first by perhaps 200 Dutch who had crossed the Hudson, new settlements gradually arose: some disaffected Puritans from New

Haven founded Newark, Carteret's brother brought a group to found Elizabethtown (Elizabeth), and a group of Scots founded Perth Amboy. In the west, which faces the Delaware River, a scattering of Swedes, Finns, and Dutch remained, soon to be overwhelmed by swarms of English Quakers. In 1702 East and West New Jersey were united as a royal colony.

PENNSYLVANIA AND DELAWARE   The Quaker sect, as the Society of Friends was called in ridicule, was the most influential of many radical groups that sprang from the turbulence of the English Civil War. Founded by George Fox in about 1647, the Quakers carried further than any other group the doctrine of individual inspiration and interpretation—the "inner light," they called it. Discarding all formal sacraments and formal ministry—all spoke only as the spirit moved them— they refused deference to persons of rank, used the familiar "thee" and "thou" in addressing everyone, refused to take oaths because that was contrary to Scripture, and embraced pacifism. Quakers were subjected to intense persecution— often in their zeal they seemed to invite it—but never inflicted it on others. Their toleration extended to complete religious freedom for all, of whatever belief or disbelief, and to the equality of sexes and the full participation of women in religious affairs.

In 1673 George Fox had returned from an American visit with the vision of a Quaker commonwealth in the New World and had enticed others with his idea. The entrance of Quakers into the New Jersey proprietorships had encouraged Quakers to migrate, especially to the Delaware River side. And soon, across the river, arose Fox's "Holy Experiment," William Penn's Quaker commonwealth, the colony of Pennsylvania. Penn was the son of Admiral Sir William Penn, who had supported Parliament in the Civil War and had led Cromwell's conquest of Jamaica but later helped in the Restoration. Young William was reared as a proper gentleman, but as a student at Oxford he had turned to Quakerism. His father disowned him, then after a reconciliation sent him off to France to get his mind on other things. It worked for a while, but Penn later came back to the Quaker faith.

Upon his father's death Penn inherited the friendship of the Stuarts and a substantial estate, including a claim of £16,000 his father had lent the crown. Whether in settlement of the claim or out of imple friendship he got from Charles II in 1681 proprietary rights to a tract extending westward from the Delaware River for 5 degrees of longitude and from the "beginning" of the 43rd degree on the north to the "beginning" of the 40th degree on the south. The land was named, at the king's insistence, for Penn's father: Pennsylvania (liter-

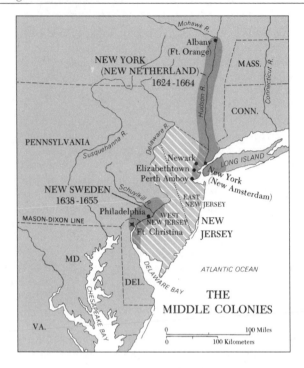

ally Penn Woods). The boundary overlapped lands granted to both
New York and Maryland. The New York boundary was settled on
the basis of the duke of York's charter at 42° North, but the Maryland boundary remained in question until 1767 when a compromise
line (nineteen miles south of the 40th parallel) was surveyed by
Charles Mason and Jeremiah Dixon—the celebrated Mason-Dixon
line.

When Penn assumed control of the area there was already a scattering of Dutch, Swedish, and English settlers on the west bank of the
Delaware, but Penn was soon making vigorous efforts to bring in more
settlers. He published glowing descriptions of the colony, which were
translated into German, Dutch, and French. They were favorably
received, especially by members of Pietist sects whose beliefs paralleled
those of the Quakers. By the end of 1681 Penn had about 1,000 settlers
in his province, and in October of the next year arrived himself with 100
more. By that time a town was growing up at the junction of the

Schuylkill and Delaware Rivers. Penn called it Philadelphia (the City of Brotherly Love). Because of the generous terms on which Penn offered land, because indeed he offered aid to emigrants, the colony grew rapidly.

The relations between the Indians and the Quakers were cordial from the beginning, because of the Quakers' friendliness and because of Penn's careful policy of purchasing land titles from the Indians. Penn even took the trouble to learn the language of the Delawares, something few colonists even tried. For some fifty years the settlers and the natives lived side by side in peace, in relationships of such trust that Quaker farmers sometimes left their children in the care of Indians when they were away from home.

The government, which rested on three Frames of Government promulgated by Penn, resembled that of other proprietary colonies, except that the freemen (taxpayers and property owners) elected the councilors as well as the assembly. The governor had no veto—although Penn, as proprietor, did. "Any government is free . . . where the laws rule and the people are a party to the laws," Penn wrote in the 1682 Frame of Government. He hoped to show that a government could run in accordance with Quaker principles, that it could maintain peace and order without oaths or wars, and that religion could flourish without an established church and with absolute freedom of conscience. Because of its tolerance, Pennsylvania became a refuge not only for Quakers but for a variety of dissenters—as well as Anglicans—and early reflected the ethnic mixture of Scotch-Irish and Germans that became common to the middle colonies and the southern backcountry. Penn himself stayed only two years in the colony. Although he returned in 1699 for two more years, he continued at home the life of an English gentleman—and Quaker.

In 1682 the duke of York also granted Penn the area of Delaware, another part of the Dutch territory. At first Delaware became part of

William Penn, the Quaker who founded the Pennsylvania colony in 1681.

*A Quaker meeting. The presence of women is evidence
of Quaker views on the equality of the sexes.*

Pennsylvania, but after 1701 it was granted the right to choose its own assembly. From then until the American Revolution it had a separate assembly, but had the same governor as Pennsylvania.

GEORGIA Georgia was the last of the British continental colonies to be established, half a century after Pennsylvania. During the seventeenth century English settlers pushed southward into the borderlands between the Carolinas and Florida. They brought with them their African slaves and a desire to win over the Indian trade from the Spanish. Each side used guns, goods, and alcohol to influence the Indians, and the Indians, in turn, effectively played off the English against the Spanish in order to gain the most favorable terms.

In 1663, despite Spanish claims, Charles II had granted the area from the 31st to 36th parallels to the Carolina proprietors, but in 1732 George II gave the land between the Savannah and Altamaha rivers to the twenty-one trustees of Georgia. In two respects Georgia was unique among the colonies: it was set up as both a philanthropic experiment and a military buffer against Spanish Florida. General James E. Oglethorpe, who accompanied the first colonists as resident trustee, represented both concerns: as a soldier who organized the defenses, and as a philanthropist who championed prison reform and sought a colonial refuge for the poor and persecuted.

In 1733 a band of 120 colonists founded Savannah near the mouth of the Savannah River. Carefully laid out by Oglethorpe, the old town with its geometrical pattern and its numerous little parks remains a monument to the city planning of a bygone day. A group of Protestant refugees from Salzburg began to arrive in 1734, followed by a number of Germans and German-speaking Moravians and Swiss, who made the colony for a time more German than English. The addition of Highland Scots, Portuguese Jews, Welsh, and others gave the early colony a cosmopolitan character much like that of Chareleston.

As a buffer against Florida the colony succeeded, but as a philanthropic experiment it failed. Efforts to develop silk and wine production had little success. Land holdings were limited to 500 acres, rum was prohibited, and the importation of slaves was forbidden, partly to leave room for servants brought on charity, partly to ensure security. But the utopian rules soon collapsed. The regulations against rum and slavery were widely disregarded, and finally abandoned. By 1759 all restrictions on landholding were removed.

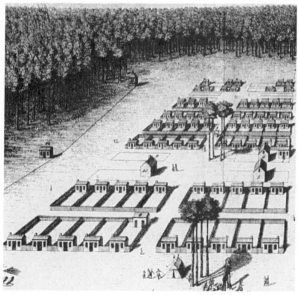

A view of Savannah in 1734. The town's layout was carefully planned.

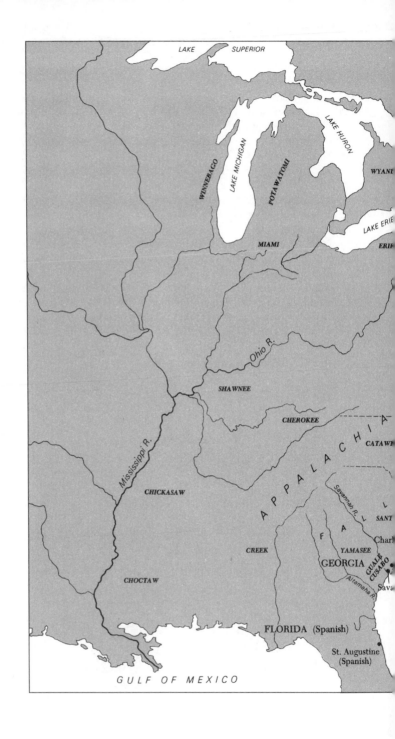

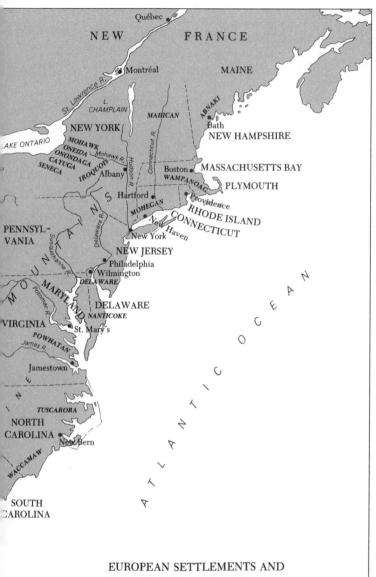

NEW FRANCE

Québec

Montréal

MAINE

St. Lawrence R.

L. CHAMPLAIN

MAHICAN

ABNAKI

Bath

NEW HAMPSHIRE

LAKE ONTARIO

NEW YORK

MOHAWK
ONEIDA
ONONDAGA
CAYUGA
SENECA

IROQUOIS

Mohawk R.

Hudson R.

Connecticut R.

Albany

Boston

MASSACHUSETTS BAY

WAMPANOAG

PLYMOUTH

Hartford

MOHEGAN

Providence

RHODE ISLAND

CONNECTICUT

New Haven

PENNSYL-VANIA

Delaware R.

Susquehanna R.

A P P A L A C H I A N   M O U N T A I N S

New York

NEW JERSEY

Philadelphia

Wilmington

DELAWARE

MARYLAND

Potomac R.

DELAWARE

NANTICOKE

St. Mary's

VIRGINIA

POWHATAN

James R.

Jamestown

F A L L   L I N E

TUSCARORA

NORTH CAROLINA

New Bern

WACCAMAW

SOUTH CAROLINA

ATLANTIC OCEAN

EUROPEAN SETTLEMENTS AND
INDIAN TRIBES IN EARLY AMERICA

0   200 Miles

0   200 Kilometers

In 1753 the trustees' charter expired and the province reverted to the crown. As a royal colony Georgia acquired for the first time an effective government. The province developed slowly over the next decade, but grew rapidly in population and wealth after 1763. Instead of wine and silk, Georgians exported rice, indigo, lumber, naval stores, beef, and pork, and carried on a lively trade with the West Indies. Georgia's products fitted well into the British economic system, and Georgians prospered. The colony, which got off to such a late start, had become a commercial success.

THRIVING COLONIES

A British historian once wrote that England acquired an empire "in a fit of absence of mind." In the abstract it seems an unlikely way to build an empire, but after a late start the English outstripped both the French and the Spanish in the New World. The lack of plan was the genius of English colonization, for it gave free rein to a variety of human impulses. The centralized control imposed by the monarchs of Spain and France got them off the mark more quickly but eventually brought about their downfall because it hobbled innovation and responsiveness to new circumstances. The British acted by private investment and with a minimum of royal control. Not a single colony was begun at the direct initiative of the crown. In the English colonies, poor immigrants had a much greater chance of getting at least a small parcel of land. The English, unlike their rivals, welcomed people from a variety of nationalities and dissenting sects who came in search of a new life or a safe harbor. And a degree of self-government made the English colonies more responsive to new circumstances—if sometimes stalled by controversy.

The compact pattern of English settlement contrasted sharply with the pattern of Spain's far-flung conquests or France's far-reaching trade routes to the interior by way of the St. Lawrence and Mississippi rivers (discussed in Chapter 4). Geography reinforced England's bent for concentrated occupation and settlement of its colonies. The rivers and bays that indented the coasts served as veins of communication along which colonies first sprang up, but no great river offered a highway to the far interior. About a hundred miles back in Georgia and the Carolinas, and nearer the coast to the north, the "fall line" of the rivers presented rocky rapids that marked the head of navigation and the end of the coastal plain. About a hundred miles beyond that, and farther back in Pennsylvania, stretched the rolling expanse of the Piedmont, literally the foothills. And the final backdrop of English America was the Appalachian Mountain range, some 200 miles from the coast in the south, reaching down to the coast at points in New England, with only one significant break—up the Hudson-Mohawk Valley of New York. For 150 years the farthest outreach of settlement stopped at the slopes of the mountains. To the east lay the wide expanse of ocean, which served as a highway for the transit of civilization from Europe to America, but also as a barrier beyond which civilization took to new paths in a new environment.

FURTHER READING

Several general interpretations handle the sweep of English settlement during the early colonial period. The first volume of Charles M. Andrews's *The Colonial Period of American History* (4 vols., 1934–1938) is detailed and comprehensive. Bernard Bailyn's multivolume work *The Peopling of British North America,* the first two volumes of which have appeared (*The Peopling of British North America: An Introduction,* 1986, and *Voyagers to the West: A Passage in the Peopling of America on the Eve of the Revolution,* 1986), will provide a comprehensive view of European migration. Shorter and more interpretive is John E. Pomfret and Floyd M. Shumway's *Founding the American Colonies, 1583–1600* (1970). A valuable summary of recent scholarship is *Colonial British America* (1984),° edited by Jack P. Greene and J. R. Pole. For the effect of English settlement on Native Americans see D. W. Meining's *Atlantic America* (1986) and Alfred W. Crosby's *Ecological Imperialism: The Biological Expansion of Europe, 900–1900* (1986).

Carl Bridenbaugh's *Vexed and Troubled Englishmen, 1590–1642* (1968) helps explain why so many sought a new home in a strange land. A pathbreaking book on the social conditions of pre-industrial England is Peter Laslett's *The World We Have Lost* (3rd ed., 1984). A study of the political institutions of the time is Wallace Notestein's *The English People on the Eve of Colonization, 1603–1630* (1954). English constitutional traditions and their effect on the colonists are examined in Edmund S. Morgan's *Inventing the People: The Rise of Popular Sovereignty in England and America* (1988), Julian H. Franklin's *John Locke and the Theory of Sovereignty* (1978), and David S. Lovejoy's *The Glorious Revolution in America* (1972).° John Phillips Kenyon documents the internal dynamics of English politics in *Stuart England* (2nd ed., 1985).°

Carl Bridenbaugh's *Jamestown, 1544–1699* (1980) traces the English experience on the Chesapeake. See also *The Chesapeake in the 17th*

°These books are available in paperback editions.

Century: Essays on Anglo-American Society and Politics (1980),° edited by Thad Tate and David Ammerman. On the role of Captain John Smith, see Alden T. Vaughan's *American Genesis: Captain John Smith and the Founding of Virginia* (1975).°

Still a good starting point for the northern colonies is James T. Adam's *The Founding of New England* (1921). A more recent treatment is Francis J. Bremer's *The Puritan Government* (1976).° A useful and enlightening primary source is William Bradford's narrative of the Pilgrim experience, *Of Plymouth Plantation, 1620–1647* (1952),° edited by Samuel E. Morison. See Daniel K. Richter's *The Ordeal of the Longhouse: The Peoples of the Iroquois League in the Era of European Colonization* (1992) for a history of the northeastern Iroquois Nation.

Scholarship abounds on Puritanism. To learn about the English roots of the movement, see Charles H. George and Katherine George's *The Protestant Mind of the English Reformation, 1570–1640* (1961). David G. Allen's *In English Ways* (1981)° traces the migration of English societies to Massachusetts. The classic works of Perry Miller demonstrate how Puritan ideology evolved once transplanted to the New World; see especially *The New England Mind* (2 vols., 1939–1953)° and *Errand into the Wilderness* (1956).° The problem of translating idea into governance is treated elegantly in Edmund S. Morgan's *The Puritan Dilemma: The Story of John Winthrop* (1958).° Andrew Delbanco's *The Puritan Ordeal* (1989)° is a powerful study of the tensions inherent in the Puritan outlook.

Useful works on the problem of dissent in a theocracy include Edmund S. Morgan's *Roger Williams, the Church, and the State* (1967)° and Emery Battis's *Saints and Sectaries: Anne Hutchinson and the Antinomian Controversy in Massachusetts Bay Colony* (1962). The religious theme in the settlement of Connecticut is handled in Mary J. A. Jones's *Congregational Commonwealth: Connecticut, 1636–1662* (1968). See also Sydney V. James's *Colonial Rhode Island* (1975).

No comprehensive work explores the overall pattern of settlement in the middle colonies, yet good scholarship exists for each colony. Thomas J. Condon's *New York Beginnings: The Commercial Origins of New Netherland* (1968) examines the Dutch connection, and Randall Balmer's *A Perfect Babel of Confusion: Dutch Religion and English Culture in the Middle Colonies* (1989) describes how the English conquest of New Netherland intensified the cultural complexity of the middle colonies.

°These books are available in paperback editions.

A good account of Bacon's Rebellion is found in Wilcomb E. Washburn's *The Governor and the Rebel* (1957).

The influence of Quakers can be studied through Gary B. Nash's *Quakers and Politics: Pennsylvania, 1681–1726* (1968). Other useful studies on the colony level include Michael G. Kammen's *Colonial New York* (1975), Joseph E. Illick's *Colonial Pennsylvania* (1976), John E. Pomfret's *Colonial New Jersey* (1973), and John A. Munroe's *History of Delaware* (1979).

Settlement of the areas along the south Atlantic is traced in Wesley F. Craven's *The Southern Colonies in the Seventeenth Century, 1607–1689* (1949) and Clarence L. Ver Steeg's *Origins of a Southern Mosaic* (1975). The early chapters of Hugh T. Lefler and Albert R. Newsome's *North Carolina* (3rd ed., 1973) and Robert M. Weir's *Colonial South Carolina* (1983) cover the activities of the Lords Proprietors. For an imaginative study of race and the settlement of South Carolina, see Peter Wood's *Black Majority: Negroes in Colonial South Carolina from 1670 through the Stono Rebellion* (1975).° To study Oglethorpe's aspirations, consult Paul S. Taylor's *Georgia Plan: 1732–1752* (1971) and *Oglethorpe in Perspective: Georgia's Founder after Two Hundred Years* (1989), edited by Phinizy Spalding and Harvey H. Jackson. A brilliant book on relations between the Catawba Indians and their black and white neighbors is James H. Merrell's *The Indians' New World: Catawbas and Their Neighbors from European Contact Through the Era of Removal* (1989).°

°These books are available in paperback editions.

3

COLONIAL WAYS OF LIFE

The colonial period witnessed the emergence of prominent leaders and colorful figures—John Smith, Pocahontas, William Bradford, John Winthrop, Roger Williams, Anne Hutchinson, and others. Yet students of American history too often forget that the process of carving a new civilization out of an abundant yet menacing and violent frontier was largely the story of thousands of diverse folk engaged in the everyday tasks of building homes, planting crops, raising families, enforcing laws, and worshipping their God.

Those who colonized America during the seventeenth and eighteenth centuries were part of a massive pattern of social migration occurring throughout Europe and Africa. Everywhere, it seemed, people were on the move. They were moving from farms to villages, from villages to cities, and from homelands to colonies. They came from varied locales—the streets of London and other cities in southern and central England, the farms of Yorkshire and the Scottish Highlands, the villages of Germany, Switzerland, and Protestant Ireland, and the savannas and jungles of west Africa. They moved for different reasons. Most were responding to powerful social and economic forces, as rapid population growth and the rise of commercial agriculture squeezed people off the land. Many traveled in search of political security or religious freedom. Africans were moved to new lands against their will.

America's settlers were mostly young (over half were under twenty-five), and mostly male. Almost half were indentured servants or slaves, and during the eighteenth century England would transport some 50,000 convicted felons to the North American colonies. About a third of the settlers came with their families; most arrived alone. A very few were wealthy; more were impoverished. Most were of the "middling sort," neither very rich nor very poor. Whatever their status or ambition, however, this extraordinary mosaic of ordinary yet adventurous people was primarily responsible for creating the American institutions and values we have all inherited.

BRITISH FOLKWAYS   The vast majority of early settlers came from the British Isles. They clustered in four mass migrations from distinct regions of Britain over the seventeenth and eighteenth centuries. The first involved some 20,000 Puritans who settled Massachusetts between 1629 and 1641, most of whom hailed from the East Anglian counties east of London. A generation later a smaller group of wealthy Royalist cavaliers and their indentured servants migrated from southern England to Virginia. These English aristocrats, mostly Anglicans, were already accustomed to severe social inequalities and so had few qualms about the introduction of African slavery. The third migratory wave brought some 23,000 Quakers from the North Midlands of England to the Delaware Valley colonies of West Jersey, Pennsylvania, and Delaware. They imported with them a social system distinctive for its sense of spiritual equality, suspicion of social hierarchy and powerful elites, and a commitment to plain living and high thinking. The fourth and largest surge of colonization occurred between 1717 and 1775 and included hundreds of thousands of Celtic Britons and Scotch-Irish from northern Ireland, the Scottish lowlands, and the northern counties of England; these were mostly coarse, feisty, clannish folk who settled in the rugged backcountry along the Appalachian Mountains.

It was long assumed that the strenuous demands of the American frontier environment served as a great "melting pot" that stripped such immigrants of their native identities and melded them into homogeneous Americans. In the late eighteenth century, J. Hector St. John de Crèvecoeur, an articulate Frenchman who took up farming in Orange County, New York, sounded this theme when he wrote that the American was a European who, "leaving behind him all his ancient prejudices and manners, receives new ones from the new mode of life he has embraced. . . . Here individuals of all nations are melted into a new race of men, whose labors and posterity will one day cause great changes in the world." But it was not that simple. For all of the transforming effects of the New World, the persistence of disparate British ways of life was remarkable. Although most British settlers spoke a common language and shared the Protestant faith, they carried with them—and retained—sharply different cultural attitudes and customs from their home regions. They spoke distinct dialects, cooked different foods, named and raised their children differently, adopted different educational philosophies and attitudes toward time, built their houses in quite different architectural styles, engaged in disparate games and forms of recreation, and organized their societies differently.

Echoes of these divergent regionally based folkways still resonate through American culture. Houses in New England still favor two styles brought from East Anglia: the "saltbox"—featuring two stories in front and one in back—and the one-and-a-half-story Cape Cod. People in the South prefer fried foods in part because their ancestors from southern and western England did so. And people in the hollows of Appalachia who manufacture "moonshine" are simply continuing a pattern of home distilling begun in the borderlands of northern Britain. Other examples of cultural continuity abound. The distinctive high-pitched nasal twine associated with the New England dialect, for instance, is a product not of the American environment but of a transplantation of the "Norfolk whine" still evident in England's East Anglia region. Likewise, the slow drawl associated with Virginia cavaliers replicates a dialect common in southern and western England, and the speech pattern common in Appalachia that pronounces *where* as *whar* and *there* as *thar* is a product of the Scottish and Irish borderlands. Terms common to the Appalachian backcountry such as "hoosier," "redneck," and "cracker" were also imported from England rather than homegrown.

The British cultural legacy extends well beyond linguistics. In gender relations, religious practices, criminal propensities, and dozens of other ways, many Americans in the 1990s still reflect age-old British customs. Of course, such cultural continuity is not unique to British-Americans. Enduring folkways are also evident among the descendants of settlers from Africa, Europe, Latin America, the Middle East, and Asia. Americans thus constitute a mosaic rather than a homogeneous mass, and they share a quite varied social and cultural heritage.

SEABOARD ECOLOGY   One of the cherished legends of American history has it that those settling British America arrived to find a pristine environment, an unspoiled wilderness little touched by human activity. But that was not the case. For thousands of years, the pre-Columbian inhabitants of the eastern seaboard had modified their environment. Indian hunting practices had over the centuries produced what one scholar has called the "greatest known loss of wild species" in the continent's history. The Indians had burned forests and dense undergrowth in order to provide cropland, to ease travel through hardwood forests, and to make way for grasses, berries, and other forage for the animals they hunted. Farming Indians worked cleared lands for six to eight years until the nutrients in the soil were depleted, and then they moved on to new areas. This migratory "slash-and-burn" agriculture increased the rate at which plant nutrients were recycled and also allowed more sunlight to reach the forest floor. These conditions in turn created rich soil and ideal grazing grounds for elk, deer, turkey, bear, moose, and beaver. Nutrients from the topsoil also fertilized the streams and helped pro-

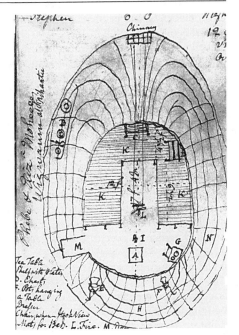

A sketch of Niantic wigwams in 1761, by Ezra Stiles.

duce teeming schools of sturgeon, smelt, and small herrings called alewives. Indian farming practices also halted the normal forest succession and, especially in the Southeast, created large stands of longleaf pines, still the most common source of timber in the region.

Equally important in shaping the ecosystem of America was the European attitude toward the environment. Where the native Americans tended to be migratory, considering land and animals as communal resources to be shared and consumed only as necessary, many European colonizers viewed natural resources as privately owned commodities. Settlers thus looked with disdain upon the subsistence level of Indian agriculture and quickly set about evicting Indians, clearing, fencing, improving, and selling land, growing surpluses, and trapping game for commercial use. These practices transformed the seaboard environment. In many places—Plymouth, for instance, or St. Mary's, Maryland—settlers occupied the sites of former Indian towns, and maize, corn, beans, and squash quickly became colonial staples, along with new crops brought from Europe.

In time a more dense population of humans and their domestic animals created a new landscape of fields, meadows, fences, barns, and houses. Such innovations further altered the ecology of the New World environment. Colonists brought with them new domesticated animals—pigs, sheep, cattle, and horses—as well as new weeds and pests such as dandelions, black flies, and cockroaches. Animal crowding forced further deforestation. So, too, did the ravenous demand for timber to construct ships and houses, a demand that devoured many of the white oak, white pine, cedar, and hickory trees in the East.

There followed consequences no one had anticipated. Because cleared and grazed land is warmer, drier, and more compacted, it is more easily subject to flooding and erosion. Foraging cattle, sheep, horses, and pigs gradually changed the distribution of trees, shrubs, and grasses. The transformed landscape made regions such as New England sunnier, windier, and colder than they had been before colonization. And many Indians, far from being passive observers in this frenzy of environmental change, contributed to the process by trading furs for metal or glass trinkets. This ravaged the populations of large mammals that had earlier been central to Indian culture. By 1800 the physical environment of the eastern seaboard had changed markedly from what it had been in 1600.

POPULATION GROWTH   England's first footholds in America were bought at a fearful price. The beachhead in Virginia, one historian pointed out, "cost far more casualties, in proportion to numbers engaged, than did the conquest of any of the Japanese-held islands in World War II." But once the brutal seasoning time was past and the colony was on its feet, Virginia and all its successors grew rapidly. After the last major Indian uprising in 1644, Virginia's population quadrupled from about 8,000 to 32,000 over the next thirty years, then more than doubled, to 75,000, by 1704. Throughout the mainland colonies the yearly growth rate during the eighteenth century ran about 3 percent. In 1625 the English colonists numbered little more than 2,000 in Virginia and Plymouth together; by 1700 the population in the colonies was perhaps 250,000, and during the eighteenth century it doubled at least every twenty-five years. By 1750 the number of colonists had passed 1 million; by 1775 it stood at about 2.5 million. In 1700 the English at home outnumbered the colonists by about 20 to 1; by 1775, on the eve of the American Revolution, the ratio was about 3 to 1.

The prodigious increase of colonial population did not go unnoticed. Benjamin Franklin of Pennsylvania, a keen observer of many things, published in 1751 his *Observations Concerning the Increase of Mankind* in which he pointed out two facts of life which distinguished the colonies from Europe: land was plentiful and cheap; labor was scarce and dear. Just the opposite conditions prevailed in the Old World. From this reversal of conditions flowed many if not most of the changes which European culture underwent in the New World—not the least being that good fortune beckoned the immigrant and induced the settlers to replenish the earth with large families. Where labor was scarce, children could lend a hand, and once they were grown could find new land for themselves if need be. Colonists tended, as a result, to marry and start new families at an earlier age.

BIRTH AND DEATH RATES The initial scarcity of women in the colonies had significant social effects. Where in England the average age at marriage for women was twenty-five or twenty-six, in America it dropped to twenty or twenty-one. Men also married younger in the colonies than in the Old World. The birth rate rose accordingly, since those who married earlier had time for about two additional pregnancies during the childbearing years. Later a gradual reversion to a more even gender ratio brought the average age at marriage back toward the European norm. Even so, given the better economic prospects in the colonies, a greater proportion of American women married and the birth rate remained much higher than in Europe. In eighteenth-century Virginia, William Byrd II of Westover asserted, matrimony thrived "so excellently" that "an Old Maid or an Old Bachelor are as scarce among us and reckoned as ominous as a Blazing Star." And early marriage remained common. The most "antique Virgin" Byrd knew was his twenty-year-old daughter.

Equally responsible for the burgeoning population in the colonies was a much lower death rate in the New World. After the difficult first years of settlement, infants generally had a better chance to reach maturity, and adults had a better chance to reach old age. In seventeenth-century New England, apart from childhood mortality, men could expect to reach seventy and women nearly that age. This longevity resulted from several factors. Since the land was more bountiful, famine seldom occurred after the first year, and while the winters were more severe than in England, firewood was plentiful. Being younger on the whole—the average age in the new nation in 1790 was sixteen!—Americans were less susceptible to disease than were Europeans. More widely scattered, they were also less exposed to disease. This began to change, of course, as population centers grew and trade and travel increased. By the mid-eighteenth century the colonies were beginning to have levels of contagion much like those in Europe. In 1735–1737, for instance, a diphtheria epidemic swept the northern colonies, taking the lives of thousands. In this case the lack of previous exposure now left the young especially vulnerable for want of a chance to develop immunity.

The greatest variations on these patterns occurred in the earliest testing times of the southern colonies. During the first century after the Jamestown settlement, until about 1700, a high rate of mortality and a chronic shortage of women meant that the population increase there

Mr. John Freake, and Mrs. Elizabeth Freake and Baby Mary. Elizabeth married John at age nineteen; Mary, born when Elizabeth was thirty-two, was the Freakes' eighth and last child.

could be sustained only by immigration. In the southern climate, English settlers proved vulnerable to malaria, dysentery, and a host of other diseases. The mosquito-infested rice paddies of the Carolina tidewater were notoriously unhealthy. And ships that docked at the Chesapeake tobacco plantations brought in with their payloads unseen cargoes of smallpox, diphtheria, and other infections. Given the higher mortality, families were often broken by the early death of parents. One consequence was to throw children on their own at an earlier age. Another was probably to make the extended family support network, if not the extended household, more important in the South.

SEX RATIOS AND THE FAMILY   Whole communities of religious or ethnic groups migrated more often to the northern colonies than to the southern, bringing more women in their company. There was no mention of any women at all among the first arrivals at Jamestown. Virginia's seventeenth-century sex ratio of two or three white males to each female meant that many men never married, although nearly every adult woman did. Counting only the unmarried, the ratio went to about eight men for every woman. In South Carolina around 1680 the sex ratio stood at about three to one, but since about three-quarters of the women were married, it was something like seven to one for singles.

A population made up largely of bachelors without strong ties to family and to the larger community made for instability of a high order in the first years. And the high mortality rates of the early years further loosened family ties. While the first generations in New England proved to be long-lived, and many more children there knew their grandparents than in the motherland, young people in the seventeenth-century South were apt never to see their grandparents, and in fact to lose one or both of their parents before reaching maturity. But after a time of seasoning, immunities built up. Eventually the southern colonies reverted to a more even sex ratio and family sizes approached those of New England.

Survival was the first necessity, and for the 90–95 percent of colonists who farmed, a subsistence or semi-subsistence economy remained the foundation of being. Not only food, but shelter, implements, utensils, furnishings, and clothing had to be made at home from the materials at hand. As the primary social and economic unit, the family became a "little commonwealth" which took on functions performed by the community in other times and places. Production, religion, learning, health care, and other activities centered on the home. Fathers taught sons how to farm, hunt, and fish. Mothers taught daughters how to tend to the chickens, the gardens, and the countless household chores that fell to the women of that time. Extended kinship ties added meaning to life and stability to communities.

Though colonists began in the early years to manifest such traditional American traits as practicality, acquisitiveness, restlessness, and a

"A little commonwealth." This eighteenth-century American family shows the "stairstep" pattern of childbearing, in which children were born at approximately two-year intervals.

propensity for violence, it would be far too easy to read back into colonial times exaggerated notions of American individualism. Whatever the changes to be wrought by environment, the earliest settlers were transplanted Europeans whose ideas and practices adjusted to new circumstances only by degrees. Clusters of ethnic and religious groups that sprang up, such as the Puritans in New England, or the German settlements in Pennsylvania, suggest that European values persisted in the New World for some time. Conditions in America did cause changes in family life, the implications of which social historians have only begun to explore, but this much seems clear. The conjugal unit, or nuclear family of parents and children, was not a new development in the colonies but the familiar arrangement in both England and America. The household that included an extended family of three or more generations was rare, although given the greater life span, large networks of kinship ties did develop. These networks included servants attached to households, who were often young kinspeople apprenticed to learn a trade.

THE SOCIAL HIERARCHY   The earliest settlers also brought in their cultural baggage certain fixed ideas of social hierarchy and rank. People of the lower orders deferred to their "betters" almost without question. Devereux Jarratt, son of a carpenter and later an Episcopal evangelist, recalled that in the Virginia of his youth: "We were accustomed to look upon, what were called *gentle folks,* as beings of a superior order. . . . Such ideas of the differences between *gentle* and *simple,* were, I believe, universal among all of my rank and age." John Winthrop, looking out from a higher station in life, asserted it to be God's will that "some must be rich, some poore, some high and eminent in power and dignitie, others meane and in subjection."

But the breadth of opportunity impelled settlers to shake off the sense of limitations that haunted the more crowded lands of Europe. The new experience of social mobility took some getting used to. The fear lingered that it threatened the equilibrium of society, and efforts persisted to keep the "meaner sort" in their place. But attempts to regulate dress as the outward sign of social class ran up against a human weakness for finery. Even in Puritan New England, which got an undeserved reputation for pinched austerity, the scorn of fancy dress was reserved mainly for those who affected to rise above their station. In 1651 the Massachusetts General Court declared its "utter detestation and dislike" that persons of mean condition "should take upon them the garb of gentlemen" and prescribed fines for those with estates of less than £200 who wore gold or silver lace and other such finery.

WOMEN IN THE COLONIES   Most colonists brought to America deeply rooted convictions concerning the inferiority of women. God and nature, it was widely assumed, had made these "weaker vessels" smaller in stature, feebler in mind, and more prone to both heightened emotions and psychological dependency. As one preacher stressed, "the woman is a weak creature not endowed with like strength and constancy of mind." Their prescribed role in life was clear: to obey and serve their husbands, nurture their children, and endure the taxing labor required to maintain their households. As John Winthrop insisted, "A true wife accounts her subjection [as] her honor and freedom" and would find true contentment only "in subjection to her husband's authority." His sister, Lucy Winthrop Downing, accepted such a subordinate position. In a letter to her brother, she confessed: "I am but a wife and therefore it is sufficient for me to follow my husband."

Even high-spirited women such as Virginia's Lucy Parke Byrd submitted to their husbands' absolute authority. The imperious patrician William Byrd II managed his wife's estate without consulting her, kept a tenacious grip on his property— even to the point of forbidding her to borrow a book from his library without explicit permission—and saw fit to interfere in her own field of domestic management. In his secret diary he recorded their stormy relationship:

> [April 7] I reproached my wife with ordering the old beef to be kept and the fresh beef to be used first, contrary to good management, on which she was pleased to be very angry . . . then my wife came and begged my pardon and we were friends again. . . .
> [April 8] My wife and I had another foolish quarrel about my saying she listened at the top of the stairs . . . she came soon after and begged my pardon.
> [April 9] My wife and I had another scold about mending my shoes, but it was soon over by her submission.

Both social custom and legal codes ensured that most women, like Lucy Byrd, remained deferential. In most colonies they could not vote, preach, hold office, attend public schools or colleges, bring suits, make contracts, or own property.

WOMEN'S WORK   In the eighteenth century, "women's work" typically involved activities in the house, garden, and yard. Farm women usually rose at four in the morning and prepared breakfast by five-thirty. They then fed and watered the livestock, awakened the children, churned butter, tended the garden, prepared lunch, played with the children, worked the garden again, cooked dinner, milked the cows, got the children ready for bed, and cleaned the kitchen before retiring about nine. Women also combed, spun, spooled, wove, and bleached wool for clothing, knitted linen and cotton, hemmed sheets, pieced quilts, made can-

Prudence Punderson's needlework, "The First, Second, and Last Scene of Mortality" (c. 1776), shows the domestic path, from cradle to coffin, followed by most colonial women.

dles and soap, chopped wood, hauled water, mopped floors, and washed clothes. Martha Ballard, a farm woman in Maine, reported in her diary that when a sheep returned from the pasture with a gash in its neck, she "drest it with Tarr," and when a lamb was born with its "entrails hanging out," she sewed it up.

Despite the conventional mission of women to serve in the domestic sphere, the scarcity of labor opened new lines of action. Quite a few women by necessity or choice went into gainful occupations. In her role as a paid midwife, for example, Martha Ballard delivered almost 800 babies. In the towns women commonly served as tavern hostesses and shopkeepers, but occasionally women also worked as doctors, printers, upholsterers, glaziers, painters, silversmiths, tanners, and shipwrights— often, but not always, widows carrying on their husbands' trades. Some managed plantations, again usually carrying on in the absence of husbands. One exceptional early case was "Mistress Margaret Brent, Spinster," of Maryland, who arrived in 1638 with two brothers and a sister. All four came on their own ventures, with servants and patents for large tracts of land. Margaret Brent ran her plantation so well that her brothers entrusted their affairs to her in their absence. As executrix of Governor Leonard Calvert's estate, she settled his complex affairs and arranged to pay the local militia and avert a mutiny. As "his Lordship's Attorney," she boldly demanded a vote in the assembly so as to see after his affairs. The governor, in response, acknowledged her gifts, but denied her request. When she became perhaps the first American suffragist, she had overstepped the bounds of acceptance.

Yet the New World environment did generate slight improvements in the status of women. The acute shortage of women in the early years made them more highly valued than in Europe, and the Puritan emphasis on well-ordered family life led to laws protecting wives from physical abuse and allowing for divorces. In addition, colonial laws allowed wives greater control over property that they had contributed to a marriage or that was left after a husband's death. But the central notion of female subordination and domesticity remained firmly entrenched in the New World. As a Massachusetts boy maintained in 1662, the superior aspect of life was "masculine and eternal; the feminine inferior and mortal."

SOCIETY AND ECONOMY IN THE SOUTHERN COLONIES

CROPS   The southern colonies had one unique advantage —the climate. They could grow exotic staples (market crops) prized by the mother country. Virginia, as Charles I put it, was "founded upon smoke." By 1619 tobacco production had reached 20,000 pounds, and in the year of the Glorious Revolution, 1688, it was up to 18 million pounds. "In Virginia and Maryland," wrote Governor Leonard Calvert in 1729, "Tobacco as our Staple is our All, and indeed leaves no room for anything else."

After 1690 rice was as much the staple in South Carolina as tobacco in Virginia or sugar in Barbados. The rise and fall of tidewater rivers made the region ideally suited to a crop that required alternate flooding and draining of the fields. In 1699 the young colony exported at least 366 tons of rice.

Much later, in the 1740s, another exotic staple appeared—indigo, the blue dyestuff which found an eager market in the British woolens industry. An enterprising young woman named Eliza Lucas, daughter of the governor of Antigua, produced the first crop on her father's Carolina plantation, left in her care when she was only seventeen. She thereby founded a major industry, and as the wife of Charles Pinckney, later brought forth a major dynasty which flourished in the golden age of Charleston.

The southern woods provided harvests of lumber and naval stores (tar, pitch, and turpentine) as well. From their early leadership in the latter trade, North Carolinians would later earn the nickname of Tar Heels. In the interior a fur trade flourished, and in the Carolinas, a cattle industry that presaged the later industry on the Great Plains—with cowboys, roundups, brandings, and long drives to market.

English customs records showed that for the years 1698–1717 South

Working the tobacco crop (late eighteenth century).

Carolina and the Chesapeake colonies enjoyed a favorable balance of trade with England. But the surplus revenues were more than offset by "invisible" charges: freight payments to shippers, profits, commissions, storage charges, and interest payments to English merchants, insurance premiums, inspection and customs duties, and outlays to purchase indentured servants and slaves. Thus began a pattern that would plague the southern staple-crop system into the twentieth century. Planter investments went into land and slaves while the profitable enterprises of shipping, trade, investment, and manufacture fell under the sway of outsiders.

LAND   Land could be had almost for the asking throughout the colonial period, although many a frontier squatter who succumbed to the lure ignored the formalities of getting a deed. In colonial law, land titles rested ultimately upon grants from the crown, and in colonial practice, the evolution of land policy in the first colony set patterns that were followed everywhere save in New England. In 1614 every colonist could claim a plot of land. In 1618 the Virginia Company, lacking any assets other than land, sold each investor a fifty-acre "share-right" and gave each settler a "headright" for paying his own way or for bringing in others. When Virginia became a royal colony in 1624, the headright system continued to apply, administered by the governor and his council. Lord Baltimore adopted the same practice in Maryland, and successive proprietors in the other southern and middle colonies adopted variations on the plan.

As time passed certain tracts were put up for sale and throughout the colonies special grants (often sizable) went to persons of rank or persons who had performed some meritorious service, such as fighting the Indians. Since land was plentiful and population desired, the rules tended to be generously interpreted and carelessly applied. With the right connections, persons or companies might amass handsome estates and vast speculative tracts in the interior, looking toward future growth and rising land values. From the beginning of colonization—and even before that—the real-estate boomer was a stock figure in American history, and access to power was often access to wealth. But by the early 1700s acquisition of land was commonly by purchase under more or less regular conditions of survey and sale by the provincial government.

Some promoters of colonization, including Lord Baltimore and the Lords Proprietors of Carolina, had dreams of reviving the feudal manor in the New World. Their plans went awry, it is commonly said, because of the New World environment. With land aplenty, there was little call to volunteer for serfdom. Yet in unexpected ways the southern colonies gave rise to something analogous, a new institution with a new name: the plantation. The word originally carried the meaning of colony. The plantations in the New World were the colonies and planters were the

An idyllic view of a tidewater plantation. Note the easy access to oceangoing vessels.

settlers who had "planted" them. Gradually the name attached itself to large individual estates.

If one distinctive feature of the South's staple economy was a good market in England, another was a trend toward large-scale production. Those who planted tobacco soon discovered that it quickly exhausted the soil, thereby giving an advantage to the planter who had extra fields to rotate in beans and corn or to leave fallow. With the increase of the tobacco crop, moreover, a fall in prices meant that economies of scale might come into play—the large planter with lower cost per unit might still make a profit. Gradually he would extend his holdings along the riverfronts, and thereby secure the advantage of direct access to the oceangoing vessels that moved freely up and down the waterways of the Chesapeake, discharging goods from London and taking on hogsheads of tobacco. So easy was the access, in fact, that the Chesapeake colonies never required a city of any size as a center of commerce, and the larger planters functioned as merchants and harbormasters for their neighbors.

LABOR   If the planter found no volunteers for serfdom, and if wage labor was scarce and expensive, he could still purchase the labor of an indentured servant for £6 to £30 (a substantial sum, which in much of the seventeenth and eighteenth centuries would equal perhaps 900 to 5,000 pounds of tobacco). Voluntary indentured servitude accounted for probably half the arrivals of white settlers (mostly from England, Ireland, or Germany) in all the colonies outside New England. The name derived from the indenture, or contract, by which a person promised to labor for a fixed number of years in return for transportation to the New World. Usually one made the contract with a shipmaster who would then sell it to a new master upon arrival. Not all went voluntarily. The London underworld developed a flourishing trade in "kids" and "spirits," who were "kidnapped" or "spirited" into servitude. One servant recalled how he and others were "stolen in Ireland" by English soldiers. Taken from their beds during the night "against their Consents," they were whisked away to a waiting ship, "weeping and crying." After 1717, by act of Parliament, convicts guilty of certain crimes could escape the hangman by "transportation" to the colonies. Most of these, like Moll Flanders, the lusty heroine of Daniel Defoe's novel, seem to have gone to the Chesapeake Bay region.

In due course, however, usually after four to seven years, the indenture ended and the servant claimed the freedom dues set by custom and law—money, tools, clothing, food, and occasionally small tracts of land. Some did very well for themselves. In 1629 seven members of the Virginia legislature were former indentured servants. Others, including Benjamin Franklin's maternal grandmother, married the men who bought their services. Many servants died before completing their indenture, and recent evidence suggests that most of those who served their term remained relatively poor thereafter. With the increase of the colonies, servants had a wider choice of destination. Pennsylvania became more often the chosen land, "one of the best poor man's countries in the world," in the verdict of a judge at the time.

SLAVERY   But most captive Africans, although they might cost a bit more than indentured servants, had no choice over their fate and served for life. Slavery, long a dying institution in Europe, had undergone a revival in Spanish America a full century before the Jamestown colony. It evolved in the Chesapeake after 1619, when a Dutch vessel dropped off twenty Africans in Jamestown. Some of the first were treated as indentured servants, with a limited term. Court records indicate that black and white servants occasionally escaped together. A Virginia court, for instance, declared that six white servants and a "negro Servant" who had run away from their masters be given "thirty-nine lashes well layed on." Those African servants who worked out their term of indenture gained freedom and a fifty-acre parcel of land. They themselves sometimes acquired slaves and white indentured servants. Gradually, however, with rationalizations based on color difference or heathenism, the practice of perpetual slavery became the custom of the land. Evidence that in 1640 some blacks were being held in hereditary life service appears in Virginia court records. By the 1660s colonial assemblies recognized slavery by laws that later expanded into elaborate and restrictive slave codes.

RUN away from the fubfcriber, a negro fellow named BOW, about five feet fix inches high, well made, about forty years of age, late the property of capt. Francis Lander, deceafed, and is well known about At'ley-Ferry; alfo his fon, named SANDY, a boy about twelve years old. Whoever delivers them to me in Charles-Town, or to the warden of the work-houfe, fhall receive ten pounds reward for each and all reafonable charges.   tbctf.   JOHN EDWARDS.

N. B. If the above negroes will return to their mafter they fhall be forgiven.

A notice for a runaway slave in the South Carolina Gazette, *1762.*

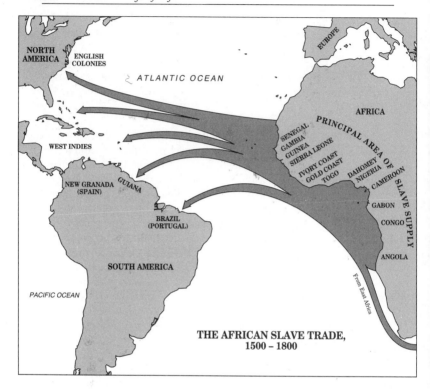

**THE AFRICAN SLAVE TRADE,
1500 – 1800**

The sugar islands of the French and British Antilles and the cane fields of Portuguese Brazil had the most voracious appetite for human cargoes, using them up in the tropical heat on the average within seven years. By 1675 the English West Indies had over 100,000 slaves while the colonies in North America had only about 5,000. But as the staple crops became established on the American continent, the demand for slaves grew. As readily available lands diminished, Virginians were less eager to bring in indentured servants who would lay claim to them at the end of their service. Though British North America took less than 5 percent of the total slave imports to the Western Hemisphere during the more than three centuries of that squalid traffic—400,000 out of some 9,500,000—it offered better chances for survival if few for human fulfillment. The natural increase of black immigrants in America approximated that of whites by the end of the colonial period. By that time, every fifth American was either an African or a descendant of one.

Slavery was recognized in the laws of all the colonies, but flourished in the tidewater South—one colony, South Carolina, had a black majority through most of the eighteenth century. By one estimate, about 40 percent of the slaves imported into North America came in through Sullivan's Island in Charleston Harbor, which was to African Americans what New York's Castle Garden and Ellis Island were later to millions of European immigrants or what San Francisco's Angel Island was to Asians.

AFRICAN ROOTS   Slaves are so often lumped together as a social group that their great ethnic diversity is overlooked. They came from lands as remote from each other as Angola and Senegal, on the west coast of Africa, and they spoke Mandingo, Ibo, Kongo, and countless other tongues. Still, the many peoples of Africa did share similar kinship and political systems. Not unlike native American cultures, African societies were often matrilineal. Property and political status descended through the mother rather than the father. When a couple married, the wife did not leave her family; the husband left his family to join that of his bride.

West African tribes were organized hierarchically. Priests and the nobility lorded over the masses of farmers and craftspeople. Below the masses were the slaves, typically war captives, criminals, or debtors. African slaves, however, did have certain rights. They could marry, be educated, and have children. Their servitude was not permanent, nor

Bronze relief of a Portuguese soldier cast in sixteenth-century Benin, now coastal Nigeria.

were children automatically slaves by virtue of their parentage, as would be the case in North America.

West Africans were predominantly agricultural people. Their economy centered on hunting, fishing, planting, and animal husbandry. Men and women typically worked alongside one another in the fields. Religious belief served as the spine of West African life. All tribal groups believed in a supreme Creator and an array of lesser gods tied to specific natural forces such as rain, fertility, and animal life. These gods directly intervened in daily life. West Africans were pantheistic in that they believed that spirits resided in trees, rocks, and streams. Those who died were also subjects of reverence because they served as mediators between the living and the gods.

Herded up by traders and frequently branded with a company mark, Africans were packed tightly together in slave ships and subjected to a four- to six-week Atlantic passage so brutal that one in seven captives died en route. Once in America they were thrown indiscriminately together and treated like work animals. More than a few arriving "saltwater" slaves rebelled against their new masters, resisting work orders, sabotaging crops and tools, or running away to the frontier. In a few cases they organized rebellions that were ruthlessly suppressed. "You would be surprised at their perseverance," noted one white planter.

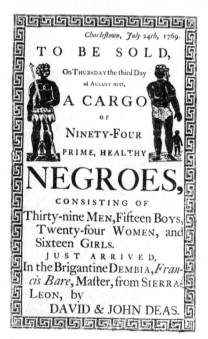

Advertisement for the sale of slaves—men, boys, women, and girls.

Neck and wrist irons used to subdue slaves during the passage from Africa.

"They often die before they can be conquered." Those still alive when captured frequently faced ghastly retribution. After rounding up slaves who participated in the Stono uprising in South Carolina in 1739, enraged planters "Cutt off their heads and set them up at every Mile Post."

SLAVE CULTURE   With the odds so heavily stacked against resistance, most slaves resigned themselves to the overwhelming authority of the "peculiar institution." Yet in the process of being forced into lives of bondage, diverse blacks from diverse homelands forged a new identity as African Americans, while at the same time leaving entwined in the fabric of American culture more strands of African heritage than historians and anthropologists can ever disentangle. Among them were new words that entered the language, such as *tabby, tote, cooter, goober, yam,* and *banana,* and the names of the Coosaw, Peedee, and Wando rivers.

More important were African influences in music, folklore, and religious practices. On one level slaves used such cultural activities to distract them from their servitude; on another level they used songs, stories, and sermons as coded messages expressing their distaste for masters or overseers. Slave religion, a unique blend of African and Christian beliefs, was frequently practiced in secret. Its fundamental theme was deliverance: God would eventually free them from slavery and open up the gates to Heaven's promised land. As one popular slave spiritual said:

> And it won't be long. And it won't be long,
> And it won't be long, Poor sinner suffer here.
> We'll soon be free.
> The Lord will call us home.

The survival of African culture among American slaves is evident in this late-eighteenth-century painting of a South Carolina plantation. The musical instruments, pottery, and clothing are of African origin, probably Yoruba.

The planters, however, sought to strip slave religion of its liberationist hopes. They insisted that being "born again" had no effect upon their workers' status as slaves. In 1667 the Virginia legislature declared that "the conferring of baptism does not alter the condition of the person as to his bondage or freedom."

Africans also brought with them to America powerful kinship ties. Even though most colonies outlawed slave marriages, many masters soon realized that slaves would work harder and be more stable if allowed to form families. Though many families were broken up when one or more members were sold, slave culture retained its powerful domestic ties. It also developed gender roles distinct from white society. Most slave women were by necessity field workers as well as wives and mothers responsible for household affairs. Since they worked in close proximity to black men, they were treated more equally than most of their white counterparts.

Most of the slaves were fated to become fieldhands, but not all did. Many of those from the lowlands of Africa used their talents as boat-men in the coastal waterways. Some had linguistic skills that made them useful interpreters. Others tended cattle and swine in the wilderness, or hacked away at the forests and operated sawmills. In a society forced to construct itself, they became skilled artisans: blacksmiths, carpenters, coopers, bricklayers, and the like. Some of the more fortunate entered domestic service.

Slavery and the growth of a biracial South had economic, political, and cultural effects far into the future, and set America on the way to tragic conflicts. Questions about the beginnings of slavery still have a bearing on the present. Did a deep-rooted color prejudice lead to slavery, for instance, or did the existence of slavery produce the prejudice? Clearly, slavery evolved because of the desire for a supply of controlled labor, and the English adopted a trade established by the Portuguese and Spanish more than a century before —the very word "Negro" is Spanish for "black." But while English settlers often enslaved Indian captives, they did not bring their white captives into slavery. Color was the crucial difference, or at least the crucial rationalization.

One historian has marshaled evidence that the seeds of slavery were already planted in Elizabethan attitudes. The English associated the color black with darkness and evil; they stamped the different appearance, behavior, and customs of Africans as "savagery." At the very least such perceptions could soothe the consciences of people who traded in

An English tobacco label depicting black labor (eighteenth century).

human flesh. On the other hand, most of the qualities that colonial Virginians imputed to blacks to justify slavery were the same qualities that the English assigned to their own poor to explain *their* status: their alleged bent for laziness, improvidence, treachery, and stupidity, among other shortcomings. Similar traits, moreover, were imputed by ancient Jews to the Canaanites and by the Mediterranean peoples of a later date to the Slavic captives sold among them. The names Canaanite and Slav both became synonymous with slavery—the latter lingers in our very word for it. Such expressions would seem to be the product of power relationships and not the other way around. Dominant peoples repeatedly assign ugly traits to those they bring into subjection.

THE GENTRY   By the early eighteenth century Virginia and South Carolina were moving into the golden age of the tidewater gentry, leaving the more isolated and rustic colony of North Carolina as "a valley of humiliation between two mountains of conceit." The first rude huts of Jamestown had given way to frame and brick houses, but it was only as the seventeenth century yielded to the eighteenth that the stately country seats in the Georgian, or "colonial," style began to emerge along the banks of the great rivers. In South Carolina the mansions along the Ashley, Cooper, and Wando, or along the tidal creeks that set the Sea Islands imperceptibly off from the mainland, boasted spacious gardens and avenues of moss-draped live oaks.

The new aristocracy patterned its provincial life-style after that of the English country gentlemen. The great houses became centers of sumptuous living and legendary hospitality to neighbors and passing strangers. In their zest for the good life, the planters kept in touch with the latest refinements of London style and fashion, living on credit extended for the next year's crop and the years' crops beyond that, to such a degree that in the late colonial period Thomas Jefferson called the Chesapeake gentry "a species of property annexed to certain English mercantile houses." Dependence on outside capital remained a chronic southern problem far beyond the colonial period.

In season the carriages of the Chesapeake elite rolled to the villages of Annapolis and Williamsburg, and the city of Charleston became the center of political life and high fashion where the new-issue aristocrats could reel and roister for days on end and patronize the taverns, silversmiths, cabinetmakers, milliners, and tailors. Through much of the year the outdoors beckoned planters to the pleasures of hunting, fishing, and riding. Gambling on horse races, cards, and dice became consuming passions for men and women alike. But a cultivated few courted high culture with a diligence that violated genteel indulgence. William Byrd II of Westover pursued learning with a passion. He built a library of some 3,600 volumes and often rose early to keep up his Latin, Greek,

South Carolina planters at leisure (1754).

and Hebrew. The Pinckneys of the Carolina low country, when they were at home, practiced their musical instruments and read from such authors as Vergil, Milton, Locke, Addison, Pope, and Richardson. These families commonly sent their sons—and often their daughters—abroad for an education, usually to England, sometimes to France.

RELIGION   It has often been said that Americans during the seventeenth century took religion more seriously than at any time since. That may have been true, but it is important to remember how many early Americans were not active communicants. One estimate holds that fewer than one in fifteen residents of the southern colonies were church members. There the tone of religious belief and practice was different from that in Puritan New England or Quaker Pennsylvania. As in England, colonial Anglicans tended to be more conservative, rational, and formal in their forms of worship than their Puritan, Quaker, or Baptist counterparts. Anglicans tended to stress collective rituals over personal religious experience.

After 1642 Virginia governor William Berkeley decided that the colony was to be Anglican, and he passed laws requiring "all nonconformists . . . to depart the colony with all conveniency." Puritans and Quakers were hounded out of the colony. By the end of the seventeenth

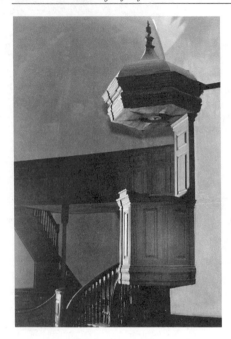

The elegant pulpit at Christ's Church, an eighteenth-century Anglican church in Virginia.

century Anglicanism predominated in the region, and it proved especially popular among the large landholders. In the early eighteenth century it became the established church in all the South—and some counties of New York and New Jersey, despite the presence of many dissenters. In the new environment, however, the Anglican church evolved into something quite unlike the state church of England. The scattered population and the absence of bishops made centralized control difficult. After 1632 the bishop of London held theoretical jurisdiction over the colonial churches, but regulation was generally entrusted to governors more concerned with political matters.

In practice therefore, if not in theory, the Anglican churches became as independent of any hierarchy as the Puritans of New England. Governance fell to lay boards of vestrymen, who chose the ministers, and usually held them on a tight rein by granting short-term contracts. In Virginia ministerial salaries depended on the taxes paid in the parish, and in 1662 they were set uniformly at the value of 13,333 pounds of leaf; the salary therefore fluctuated with the price of tobacco. Often the parishes were too large for an effective ministry. Isolated chapels might have lay readers and get only infrequent visits by clergymen. Standards were often lax, and the Anglican clergy around the Chesapeake became notorious for its "sporting parsons," addicted to fox-hunting, gambling, drunkenness, and worse. Few among the conscientious and upright Anglican ministers preached fire-and-brimstone sermons. Their congregations showed little toleration for being chastised from the pulpit. One minister lamented that the powerful planters removed any preacher who "had the courage and resolution to preach against any Vices taken into favor by the leading Men of his Parish."

SOCIETY AND ECONOMY IN NEW ENGLAND

TOWNSHIPS   In contrast to the seaboard planters who transformed the English manor into the southern plantation, the Puritans transformed the English village into the New England town, although there were several varieties. Land policy in New England had a stronger social and religious purpose than elsewhere. Towns shaped by English precedent and Puritan policy also fitted the environment of a rockbound land, confined by sea and mountains and unfit for large-scale cultivation.

Neither headrights nor quitrents ever took root in New England. There were cases of large individual land grants, but the standard system was one of township grants to organized groups. A group of settlers, often gathered already into a church, would petition the General Court for a town (what elsewhere was commonly called a "township") and then divide it according to a rough principle of equity—those who invested more, or had larger families or greater status, might receive more land—retaining some pasture and woodland in common and holding some for later arrivals. In some early cases the towns arranged each settler's land in separate strips after the medieval practice, but with time land was commonly divided into separate farms to which landholders would move, away from the close-knit village. Still later, by the early eighteenth century, the colonies used their remaining land as a source of revenue by selling townships to proprietors whose purpose, more often than not, was speculation and resale.

ENTERPRISE   The life of New England farmers was a hardscrabble subsistence. Simply clearing the glacier-scoured soil of rocks might require sixty days of hard labor per acre. The growing season was short, and no exotic staples grew in that harsh climate. If the town resembled the English village, the crops and livestock too were those familiar to the English countryside: wheat, barley, oats, some cattle, swine, and sheep. By the end of the seventeenth century New England farmers were developing some surpluses for export but never any staples that met the demands of the English market.

With virgin forests ready for conversion into masts, lumber, and ships, and rich fishing grounds that stretched northward to Newfound-

A sketch of Deerfield, Massachusetts, in 1728 by Dudley Woodbridge, a student at Harvard.

land, it is little wonder that New Englanders turned to the sea for their livelihood—the fisheries in fact antedated settlement by more than a century. The Chesapeake region afforded a rich harvest of oysters, but New England, by its proximity to waters frequented by cod, mackerel, halibut, and other varieties, became the more important maritime center. Whales, too, abounded in New England waters and supplied oil for lighting and lubrication, as well as ambergris, a secretion used in perfumes. New England ships eventually were chasing whales from Baffin Bay to Antarctica and out across the Pacific on voyages that lasted years.

The fisheries, unlike the farms, supplied a staple of export to Europe, while lesser grades of fish went to the West Indies as food for slaves. Fisheries encouraged the development of shipbuilding, and experience at seafaring spurred commerce. This in turn encouraged wider contacts in the Atlantic world and a degree of materialism and cosmopolitanism which clashed with the Puritan credo of plain living and high thinking. In 1714 an anxious Puritan deplored the "great extravagance that people are fallen into, far beyond their circumstances, in their purchases, buildings, families, expenses, apparel, generally in the whole way of living."

By the mid-seventeenth century shipyards had developed at Boston, Salem, Dorchester, Gloucester, Portsmouth, and other towns. New England remained the center of shipbuilding throughout the colonial period. Lumber provided not only raw material for ships but a prime cargo. As early as 1635 what may have been the first sawmill appeared at Portsmouth, New Hampshire. Sawmills soon abounded throughout the colonies, often together with gristmills using the same source of waterpower.

TRADE   Commercially the colonies by the end of the seventeenth century had become part of a great North Atlantic connection, trading not only with the British Isles and the British West Indies, but also —and often illegally—with Spain, France, Portugal, Holland, and their colonies from America to the shores of Africa. Out of necessity the colonists had to import manufactured goods from Britain and Europe: hardware, machinery, paint, instruments of navigation, various household items. The function of the colonies as a market for English goods was important to the mother country. The central problem for the colonies was to find the means of paying for the imports—the eternal problem of the balance of trade.

The mechanism of trade in New England and the middle colonies differed from that of the South in two respects: their lack of staples to exchange for English goods was a relative disadvantage, but the abundance of their own shipping and mercantile enterprise worked in their

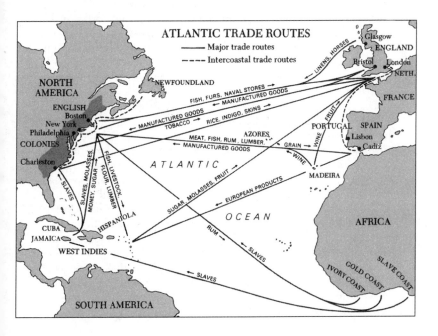

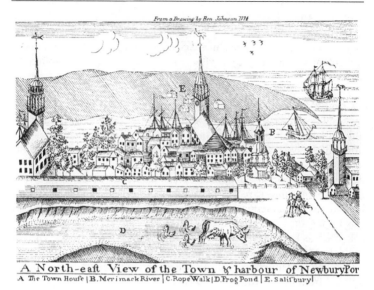

From a Drawing by Ben Johnson 1774

A North-east View of the Town & harbour of NewburyPor

A The Town Houfe | B. Merimack River | C. RopeWalk | D. Frog Pond | E. Salifbury

Newburyport, Massachusetts, in 1774.

favor. After 1660, in order to protect English agriculture and fisheries, the English government raised prohibitive duties against certain major exports of these colonies: fish, flour, wheat, and meat, while leaving the door open to timber, furs, and whale oil, products in great demand in the home country. As a consequence, New York and New England in the years 1698–1717 bought more from England than they sold there, incurring an unfavorable trade balance.

The northern colonies met the problem partly by using their own ships and merchants, thus avoiding the "invisible" charges for trade and transport, and by finding other markets for the staples excluded from England, thus acquiring goods or bullion to pay for imports from the mother country. American lumber and fish therefore went to southern Europe, Madeira, and the Azores for money or in exchange for wine; lumber, rum, and provisions went to Newfoundland; and all of these and more went to the West Indies, which became the most important outlet of all. American merchants could sell fish, bread, flour, corn, pork, bacon, beef, and horses to West Indian planters who specialized in sugarcane. In return they got money, sugar, molasses, rum, indigo, dye-woods, and other products, much of which went eventually to England.

This gave rise to the famous "triangular trade" (more a descriptive convenience than a rigid pattern) in which New Englanders shipped rum to the west coast of Africa and bartered for slaves, took the slaves on the "Middle Passage" to the West Indies, and returned home with various commodities including molasses, from which they manufactured rum. In another version they shipped provisions to the West Indies, carried sugar and molasses to England, and returned with manufactured goods from Europe.

The colonies suffered from a chronic shortage of hard money, which drifted away to pay for imports and invisible charges. Various expedients met the shortage of currency: the use of wampum or commodities, the monetary value of which colonial governments tried vainly to set by law. For a time Massachusetts coined silver "pine-tree" shillings, but lost the right after the loss of its charter in 1684. Promissory notes of individuals or colonial treasurers often passed as a crude sort of paper money. Most of the colonies at one time or another issued bills of credit, on promise of payment later (hence the dollar "bill"), and most set up land banks which issued paper money for loans to farmers on the security of their lands, which were mortgaged to the banks. Colonial farmers began to recognize that an inflation of paper money led to an inflation of crop prices, and therefore asked for more and more paper. Thus began in colonial politics what was to become a recurrent issue in later times, the question of currency inflation. Whenever the issue arose, debtors commonly favored growth in the money supply, which would make it easier for them to settle accounts, whereas creditors favored a limited money supply, which would increase the value of their capital. In 1751 Parliament outlawed legal-tender paper money in New England, and in 1764 throughout the colonies.

RELIGION The Puritans for many years had a bad press. By the standards of later ages they were judged bigots, but they had come to America to escape error, not to tolerate it in their New Zion. The picture of the dour Puritan, hostile to anything that gave pleasure, is false. Puritans, especially those of the upper class, wore colorful clothing, enjoyed secular music, and imbibed prodigious quantities of rum. "Drink is in itself a good creature of God," said the Reverend Increase Mather, "but the abuse of drink is from Satan." If found incapacitated by reason of strong drink, a person was subject to arrest. A Salem man, for example, was tried for staggering into a house where he "eased his stomak in the Chimney." Repeated offenders were forced to wear the letter "D" in public.

Moderation in all things except piety was the Puritan guideline, and it applied to sexual activity as well. Contrary to prevailing images of Puritan prudery, they quite openly acknowledged natural human desires. One minister emphasized that "the Use of the Marriage Bed" is "founded in man's Nature." He also stressed that intimacy between marriage partners was a necessary component of a successful marriage.

Any unwillingness to engage in sexual intercourse on the part of husband or wife "Denies all reliefe in Wedlock unto Human necessity: and sends it for supply unto Beastiality." Churches occasionally expelled male and female members for failing to satisfy their partner's sexual needs. Sexual activity outside the bounds of marriage was strictly forbidden, but like most social prohibitions it may have provoked transgression. New England court records are filled with cases of adultery and fornication. A man found guilty of coitus with an unwed woman could be jailed, whipped, fined, disenfranchised, and forced to marry the woman. Women offenders were also jailed, whipped, and in some cases adulterers were forced to wear the letter "A" in public. In part the abundance of sex offenses is explained by the disproportionate number of men in the colonies. Many were unable to find a wife and were therefore tempted to satisfy their sexual desires outside of marriage.

The Puritans who settled Massachusetts, unlike the Separatists of Plymouth, proposed only to form a purified version of the Anglican church. They believed that they could remain loyal to the Church of England, the unity of church and state, and the principle of compulsory uniformity. But their remoteness from England led them very quickly to a congregational form of church government identical with that of the Pilgrim Separatists, and for that matter little different from the practice of southern Anglicans.

Certain aspects of the Puritan faith were pregnant with meaning for the future. In the Puritan's version of Calvin's theology God had voluntarily entered into a covenant, or contract, with people through which they could secure salvation. By analogy, therefore, an assembly of true Christians could enter into a church covenant, a voluntary union for the common worship of God. From this it was a fairly short step to the idea of a voluntary union for purposes of government. The history of New England affords examples of several such limited steps toward constitutional government: the Mayflower Compact, the Cambridge Agreement of John Winthrop and his followers, the Fundamental Orders of Connecticut, and the informal arrangements whereby the Rhode Island settlers governed themselves until they secured a charter in 1663.

The covenant theory contained certain kernels of democracy in both church and state, but democracy was no part of Puritan political thought, which like so much else in Puritan belief began with original sin. Humanity's innate depravity made government necessary. "If people be governors," asked the Reverend John Cotton, "who shall be governed?" The Puritan was dedicated to seeking not the will of the people but the will of God, and the ultimate source of authority was the Bible. But the Bible had to be known by right reason, which was best applied by those trained to the purpose. Hence most Puritans deferred to an intellectual elite for a true knowledge of God's will. Church and state were but two aspects of the same unity, the purpose of which was to carry out God's will on earth. The New England way might thus be summarized in the historian Perry Miller's phrase as a kind of "dictatorship of the regenerate."

The church exercised a pervasive influence over the life of the town, but unlike the Church of England it technically had no temporal power. Thus while Puritan New England has often been called a theocracy, the church was entirely separated from the state—except that the residents were taxed for its support. And if not all inhabitants were church members, they were required to attend church services. So complete was the consensus of church member and nonmember alike that the closely knit communities of New England have been called peaceable kingdoms.

It was a peace, however, under which bubbled a volcano of soul-searching. Puritans were assailed by doubts, by a fear of falling away from godly living, by the haunting fear that despite their best outward efforts they might not be among God's elect. Add such concerns to the long winters that kept the family cooped up during the dark, cold months, and one has a formula for seething resentments and recriminations that, for the sake of peace in the family, had to be projected outward toward neighbors. The New Englanders of those peaceable kingdoms therefore built a reputation as the most litigious people on the face of God's earth, continually quarreling over fancied slights, business dealings, and other issues, and building in the process a flourishing legal profession.

DIVERSITY AND SOCIAL STRAINS   Increasing diversity and social discord combined to challenge the idyllic consensual society envisioned by the founding settlers. Despite long-enduring myths, New England towns were not always pious, harmonious, static, and self-sufficient peasant utopias populated by praying Puritans. Many communities were founded not as religious farming utopias but as secular centers of fishing, trade, or commercial agriculture, and the animating concerns of residents in such towns tended to be more entrepreneurial than spiritual. After a Puritan minister delivered his first sermon to a congregation in the fishing port of Marblehead, a crusty fisherman admonished him: "You think you are preaching to the people of the Bay. Our main end was to catch fish." Similar priorities appeared in highly commercialized inland towns such as Springfield, Massachusetts. There, too, material opportunity rather than religious communalism governed individual behavior. Yet such acquisitive individualism, while generating marked social inequalities, was accompanied by growing social stability as an economic elite came to exercise paternalistic control over town affairs.

In many of the godly backwoods communities, however, social strains

School Street, Salem, around 1765. The mansion of a wealthy merchant dominates this street scene in Salem, a prosperous port town.

increased as time passed, a consequence primarily of population pressure on the land and rising disparities of wealth. "Love your neighbor," said Benjamin Franklin's Poor Richard, "but don't pull down your fence." Initially, among the first settlers, fathers exercised strong authority over sons through their control of the land. They kept the sons and their families in the town, not letting them set up their own households or get title to their farmland until they reached middle age. In New England as elsewhere, fathers tended to subdivide their land among all the male children. But by the eighteenth century, with land scarcer, the younger sons were either getting control of property early or moving on. Often they were forced out, with family help and blessings, to seek land elsewhere or new kinds of work in the commercial cities along the coast or inland rivers. With the growing pressure on land in the settled regions, poverty and social tension increased in what had once seemed a country of unlimited opportunity.

Interestingly enough, however, in seaport towns such as Salem, Marblehead, and Gloucester, settled by contentious English immigrants eager to succeed, community and family life grew more cohesive, stable, and visibly religious with the passage of time, the growth of population, and the advance of prosperity. Increasing concentrations of wealth enabled a social and economic elite to coalesce and dominate the political process. Aspects of the original Puritan vision—civic consciousness, deference to leaders and institutions, church membership, and family authority—remained strong well into the eighteenth century. Rather than witnessing a decline from communitarian standards, these maritime communities attained greater equilibrium as time passed.

Yet sectarian disputes and religious indifference were on the rise in many communities. The emphasis on a direct accountability to God, which lay at the base of all Protestant theology, itself caused a persistent tension and led believers to challenge authority in the name of private conscience. Massachusetts repressed such heresy in the 1630s, but it resurfaced during the 1650s among Quakers and Baptists, and in 1659–1660 the colony hanged four Quakers who persisted in returning after they were expelled. These acts caused such revulsion—and an investigation by the crown—that they were not repeated, although heretics continued to face harassment and persecution.

More damaging to the Puritan utopia was the increasing worldliness of New England, which placed growing strains on church discipline. More and more children of the "visible saints" found themselves unable to give the required testimony of regeneration. In 1662 an assembly of ministers at Boston accepted the "Half-Way Covenant," whereby baptized children of church members could be admitted to a "halfway" membership and secure baptism for their own children in turn. Such members, however, could neither vote in church nor take communion. A further blow to Puritan control came with the Massachusetts royal charter of 1691, which required toleration of dissenters and based the right to vote in public elections on property rather than on church membership.

THE DEVIL IN NEW ENGLAND   The strains accompanying Massachusetts's transition from Puritan utopia to royal colony reached an unhappy climax in the witchcraft hysteria at Salem Village (now the town of Danvers) in 1692. Belief in witchcraft was widespread throughout Europe and New England in the seventeenth century. Prior to the dramatic episode in Salem, almost three hundred New Englanders (mostly middle-aged women) had been accused as witches and more than thirty hanged. New England was, in the words of Cotton Mather, "a country . . . extraordinarily alarum'd by the wrath of the Devil."

Still, the outbreak in Salem was distinctive in its scope and intensity. Salem Village was about eight miles from the larger Salem Town, a thriving port. A contentious community made up of independent farm families and people who depended on the commercial activity of the port, Salem Village struggled to free itself from the influence and taxes of Salem proper. These different loyalties provoked tensions that apparently made the residents especially susceptible to the idea that the devil was at work in the village.

During the winter of 1691–92, several adolescent girls began meeting in the kitchen of the town minister, the Reverend Samuel Parris. There they gave rapt attention to the voodoo stories told by Tituba, Parris's West Indian slave. They also tried to envision their future husbands

*Four women being hanged as witches in seventeenth-century
England. At Salem, nineteen people were hanged for witchcraft.*

through a fortune-telling ritual that involved dropping an egg white into
a glass and watching what shape it took.

As the days passed, the entranced girls began to behave oddly—
shouting, barking, groveling, and twitching for no apparent reason. A
doctor concluded that the girls were bewitched. Their parents and other
adults questioned the girls: "Who torments you?" They replied that
three women—Tituba, Sarah Good, and Sarah Osborne—were Satan's
servants.

Authorities thereupon arrested the three women. At a special hearing
before the magistrates, the "afflicted" girls rolled on the floor in convulsive fits as the accused women were questioned. In the midst of the
hearing, Tituba shocked listeners by not only confessing to the charge
but also divulging the names of many others in the community who she
claimed were also performing the devil's work. Soon thereafter, dozens
more girls and young women began to experience the same violent con-
tortions. The accusations of witchcraft now spread throughout the community. Within a few months, the Salem Village jail was filled with
townspeople—men, women, and children—accused of practicing
witchcraft. The villagers panicked as word spread that the devil was in
their midst.

At the end of May the authorities arrested Martha Carrier. A farmer
had testified that several of his cattle suffered "strange deaths" soon
after he and Carrier had an argument. Little Phoebe Chandler added
that she had been stricken with terrible stomach pains soon after she
heard Carrier's voice telling her she was going to be poisoned. Even

Carrier's own children testified against her: they reported that their mother had recruited them as witches. But the most damning testimony was provided by several young girls. When they were brought into the hearing room, they began writhing in agony at the sight of Carrier. They claimed that they could see the devil whispering in her ear. The magistrate found this evidence compelling: "You see, you look upon them and they fall down," he told Carrier. She answered that it was "a shameful thing that you should mind these folks that are out of their wits. I am wronged." A few days later she was hanged. Rebecca Nurse, a pious seventy-one-year-old matriarch of a large family went to the gallows in July. George Jacobs, an old man whose servant girl accused him of witchcraft, dismissed the whole chorus of accusers as "bitch witches." He was hanged in August.

But as the net of accusation spread wider, extending far beyond the confines of Salem, leaders of the Massachusetts Bay colony began to worry that the witch-hunts were out of control. When the afflicted girls charged Samuel Willard, the distinguished pastor of Boston's First Church and president of Harvard College, the stunned magistrates had seen enough. Shortly thereafter, the governor intervened when his own wife was accused of serving the devil. He disbanded the special court in Salem and ordered the remaining suspects released. A year after it had begun, the fratricidal event was finally over. Nineteen people (including some men married to women who had been convicted) had been hanged; one man—the stubborn Giles Corey—was pressed to death by heavy stones, and more than one hundred others were jailed. Nearly everybody responsible for the Salem executions later recanted, and nothing quite like it happened in the colonies again.

What explains the witchcraft hysteria at Salem? Some have argued that it may have represented nothing more than a contagious exercise in adolescent imagination intended to enliven the dreary routine of everyday life. Yet it was adults who pressed the formal charges against the accused and provided most of the testimony. This has led some scholars to speculate that long-festering local feuds and property disputes may have triggered the prosecutions. One of the leaders of the young girls, for instance, was twelve-year-old Ann Putnam, whose older male kinfolk pressed many of the complaints. The Putnam clan were landowners whose power was declining, and their frenetic pursuit of witches might have served as a psychic weapon to restore their prestige.

More recently, historians have focused on the most salient fact about the accused witches. Almost all of them were women. Many of the accused women, it turns out, had in some way defied the traditional roles assigned to females. Some had engaged in business transactions outside the home; others did not attend church; some were sour curmudgeons. Most of them were middle-aged or older and without sons or brothers. They thus stood to inherit property and live as independent women. The notion of autonomous spinsters flew in the face of prevailing social conventions.

Whatever the precise cause, there is little doubt that the witchcraft hysteria reflected the peculiar social dynamics of the Salem community. Late in 1692, as the hysteria in Salem subsided, several of the afflicted girls were traveling through nearby Ipswich when they encountered an old woman resting on a bridge. "A witch!" they shouted and began writhing as if possessed. But the people of Ipswich were unimpressed. Passersby showed no interest in the theatrical girls. Unable to generate either sympathy or curiosity, the girls picked themselves up and continued on their way.

SOCIETY AND ECONOMY IN THE MIDDLE COLONIES

AN ECONOMIC MIX   Both geographically and culturally the middle colonies stood between New England and the South, blending their own influences with elements derived from the older regions on either side. In so doing they more completely reflected the diversity of colonial life and more fully foreshadowed the pluralism of the later American nation than the regions on either side. Their crops were those of New England but more bountiful, owing to better land and a longer growing season, and they developed surpluses of foodstuffs for export to the plantations of the South and the West Indies: wheat, barley, oats, and other cereals, flour, and livestock. Three great rivers—the Hudson, Delaware, and Susquehanna—and their tributaries gave the middle colonies a unique access to their backcountry and to the fur trade of the interior, where New York and Pennsylvania long enjoyed friendly relations with the Iroquois, Delaware, and other tribes. As a consequence the region's commerce rivaled that of New England, and indeed Philadelphia in time supplanted Boston as the largest city of the colonies.

Land policies followed the headright system of the South. In New York the early royal governors carried forward, in practice if not in name, the Dutch device of the patroonship, granting to influential favorites vast estates on Long Island and up the Hudson and Mohawk valleys. These realms most nearly approached the Old World manor, self-contained domains farmed by tenants who paid fees to use the landlords' mills, warehouses, smokehouses, and wharfs. But with free land available elsewhere, New York's population languished, and the new waves of immigrants sought the promised land of Pennsylvania.

AN ETHNIC MIX   In the makeup of their population the middle colonies stood apart from both the mostly English Puritan settlements and the

A member of a Pennsylvania German sect, the "Spiritual Virgins," in the habit of the order (1745).

biracial plantation colonies to the South. In New York and New Jersey, for instance, Dutch culture and language lingered for some time, along with the Dutch Reformed church. Along the Delaware River the few Swedes and Finns, the first settlers, were overwhelmed by the influx of English and Welsh Quakers, followed in turn by the Germans and Scotch-Irish.

The Germans came mainly from the Rhineland, a region devastated by war. (Keep in mind that until German unification in 1871, ethnic Germans—those Europeans speaking German as their native language—lived in a variety of areas and principalities in central Europe.) Penn's brochures on the bounties of Pennsylvania circulated in German translation, and his promise of religious freedom brought a response from persecuted sects, especially the Mennonites, German Baptists whose beliefs resembled those of the Quakers. In 1683 a group of Mennonites founded Germantown near Philadelphia. They were but the vanguard of a swelling migration in the eighteenth century which included Lutherans, Reformed Calvinists, Moravians, Dunkers, and others, a large proportion of whom paid their way as indentured servants, or "redemptioners," as they were commonly called. West of Philadelphia they created a belt of settlement in which the "Pennsylvania Dutch" (a corruption of *Deutsch,* meaning German) predominated,

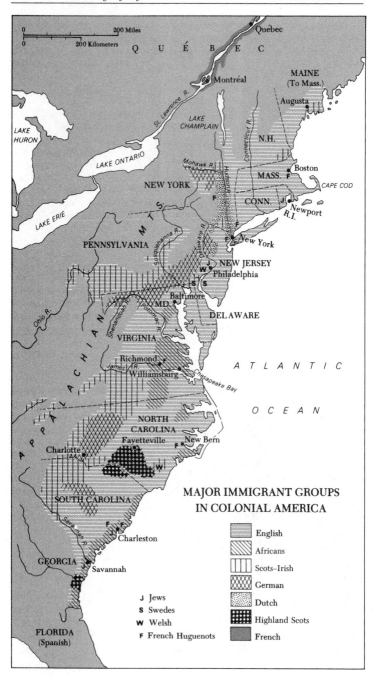

MAJOR IMMIGRANT GROUPS
IN COLONIAL AMERICA

- English
- Africans
- Scots–Irish
- German
- Dutch
- Highland Scots
- French

J Jews
S Swedes
W Welsh
F French Huguenots

as well as a channel for the dispersion of German populations throughout the colonies.

The more aggressive and grasping Scotch-Irish began to arrive later and moved still farther out in the backcountry. "Scotch-Irish" is an enduring misnomer for Ulster Scots, Presbyterians transplanted from Scotland to confiscated lands in northern Ireland to give that country a more Protestant tone. The Ulster plantation dated from 1607 to 1609, the years when Jamestown was fighting for survival. A century later the Ulster Scots, mostly Presbyterians, were on the move again, in flight both from Anglican persecution and from economic disaster caused by English tariffs. These and other "border Britons" constituted a truly mass migration. Between 1717 and 1775 over a quarter million of them left northern England, southern Scotland, and northern Ireland for America. This time they looked mainly to Pennsylvania and the fertile valleys stretching southwestward into Virginia and Carolina.

The Germans and Scotch-Irish became the largest non-English elements in the colonies, but other groups enriched the population in New York and the Quaker colonies: French Huguenots (Calvinists whose privilege of toleration was revoked in 1685), Irish, Welsh, Swiss, Jews, and others. New York had inherited from the Dutch a tradition of toleration which had given the colony a motley population before the English conquest: French-speaking Walloons and French, Germans, Danes, Portuguese, Spaniards, Italians, Bohemians, Poles, and others, including some New England Puritans. The Protestant Netherlands had given haven to the Sephardic Jews expelled from Spain and Portugal, and enough of them found their way into New Netherland to found a synagogue there.

What could be said of Pennsylvania as a refuge for the persecuted

PERCENTAGE OF AFRICAN AMERICANS IN THE TOTAL POPULATION OF THE BRITISH COLONIES, 1660–1780

Year	New England	Middle Colonies	Upper South	Lower South	West Indies
1660	1.7	11.5	3.6	2.0	42.0
1700	1.8	6.8	13.1	17.6	77.7
1740	2.9	7.5	28.3	46.5	88.0
1780	2.0	5.9	38.6	41.2	91.1

SOURCE: U.S. Bureau of the Census, *Historical Statistics of the United States, Colonial Times to 1970* (Washington, D.C.: U.S. Government Printing Office, 1975), 2:1168 (Ser.Z1-19).

might be said as well of Rhode Island and South Carolina, which practiced a similar religious toleration. Newport and Charleston, like New York and Philadelphia, became centers of minuscule Jewish populations. French Huguenots made their greatest mark on South Carolina, more by their enterprise than by their numbers, and left implanted in the life of the colony such family names as Huger, Porcher, DeSaussure, Legare, Lanneau, and Lesesne. A number of Highland Scots came directly from their homeland rather than by way of Ulster, especially after suppression of a rebellion in 1745 on behalf of the Stuart pretender to the throne, "Bonnie Prince Charlie." A large group of them went to Fayetteville, North Carolina, where Gaelic-speaking Scots settled beside Lumbee Indians who had spoken English for nearly a century.

The eighteenth century was the great period of expansion and population growth in British North America, and during those years a large increase of the non-English stock took place. A rough estimate of the national origins of the white population as of 1790 found it to be 60.9 percent English, 14.3 percent Scots and Scotch-Irish, 8.7 percent German, 5.4 percent Dutch, French, and Swedish, 3.7 percent Irish, and 7 percent miscellaneous or unassigned. If one adds to the 3,172,444 whites in the 1790 census the 756,770 nonwhites, not even considering uncounted Indians, it seems likely that only about half the populace, and perhaps fewer, could trace their origins to England. Of the blacks about 75 percent had been transported from the bend of the African coastline between the Senegal and Niger rivers; most of the rest came from Congo-Angola.

THE BACKCOUNTRY   Pennsylvania in the eighteenth century became the great distribution point for the diverse ethnic groups of European origin, just as the Chesapeake Bay region and Charleston became the distribution points for African peoples. Before the mid-eighteenth century, population in the Pennsylvania backcountry was coming up against the Appalachian barrier and, following the line of least resistance, the Scotch-Irish and Germans filtered southward along what came to be called the Great Philadelphia Road, the primary internal migration route during the colonial period. It headed west from the port city, traversing Chester and Lancaster counties, and turned southwest at Harris' Ferry (now Harrisburg), where it crossed the Susquehanna. Continuing south across western Maryland, it headed down the Shenandoah Valley of Virginia, and on into the Carolina and Georgia backcountry. Germans were first in the upper Shenandoah Valley, and to the south of them Scotch-Irish filled the lower valley. Migrants of both stocks continued to move into the Carolina and Georgia backcountry, while others found their way up from Charleston.

Along the fringes of the frontier were commonly found the Scotch-Irish, who had acquired in their homeland and in Ulster a stubborn fighting spirit that brooked no nonsense from the "savages" of the woods. And out on the cutting edge life might be in that "state of nature" described by Thomas Hobbes: "poor, nasty, brutish, and short." It was a lonely life of scattered settlements, isolated log cabins set on plots of land which the pioneer owned or at least occupied, furnished with crude furniture hacked out with axe and adze and pieced together with pegs.

The frontier regions bred a rough democracy, because most people were on a nearly equal status, and instilled a stubborn individualism in people who got accustomed to deciding things for themselves. With time, of course, neighborhoods grew up within visiting distance, animal and Indian trails broadened into wagon roads, and crossroads stores grew up into community gathering places where social intercourse could be lubricated with the whiskey that was omnipresent on the Scotch-Irish frontier.

The backcountry of the Piedmont, and something much like it on up to northern New England (Maine, New Hampshire, and what would become Vermont), became a fourth major region that stretched the length of the colonies across the abstract imaginary boundaries separating the political units. Government was slow to reach these remote settlements, and the system of "every man for himself" sometimes led frontier communities into conditions of extreme disorder.

Colonial Cities

During the seventeenth century the colonies remained in comparative isolation, evolving subtly distinctive ways and unfolding separate histories. Boston and New York, Philadelphia and Charleston were more likely to keep in closer touch with London than with each other. The Carolina upcountry had more in common with the Pennsylvania backcountry than either had with Charleston or Philadelphia. Colonial cities faced outward to the Atlantic. Since commerce was their chief reason for being, they hugged the coastline or, like Philadelphia, sprang up on rivers where oceangoing vessels could reach them. Never holding more than 10 percent of the colonial population, they exerted an influence in commerce, politics, and civilization generally out of proportion to their size.

Five major port cities outdistanced the rest. By the end of the colonial period Philadelphia, with some 30,000 people (counting adjacent suburbs), was the largest city in the colonies and second only to London in the British Empire. New York, with about 25,000, ranked second; Boston numbered 16,000; Charleston, 12,000; and Newport, 11,000. Falling in a range of about 8,000 down to 4,000 were secondary ports and inland towns such as New Haven and Norwich, Connecticut; Norfolk; Baltimore; Lancaster, Pennsylvania; Salem; New London; Providence; and Albany.

THE SOCIAL AND POLITICAL ORDER   The upper crust of urban society were the merchants who bartered the products of American farms and forests for the molasses and rum of the West Indies, the wines of Madeira, the manufactured goods of Europe, and the slaves of Africa. Their trade in turn stimulated the activities of rum distilling, ropewalks, sail lofts, instrument makers, and ship chandlers who supplied vessels leaving port. After the merchants, who constituted the chief urban aristocracy, came a middle class of craftspeople, retailers, innkeepers, and small jobbers who met a variety of needs. And at the bottom of the pecking order were sailors, unskilled workers, and some artisans.

Class stratification in the cities became more pronounced as time passed. One study of Boston found that in 1687 the richest 15 percent of the population owned 52 percent of the taxable wealth; by 1771 the top 15 percent owned about two-thirds and the top 5 percent owned some 44 percent of the wealth. In Philadelphia the concentration of wealth was even more pronounced.

Problems created by urban growth are nothing new. Colonial cities had traffic requiring not only paved streets and lighting but regulations to protect children and animals in the streets from reckless riders. Regulations restrained citizens from creating public nuisances by tossing their garbage into the streets. Fires that on occasion swept through closely packed buildings led to preventive standards in building codes, restrictions on burning rubbish, and the organization of volunteer and finally professional fire companies. Crime and violence made necessary more police protection than could be provided by the constable and by the watch duty that at first was required of ordinary citizens. And in cities the poor became more visible than in the countryside. Colonists brought with them the English principle of public responsibility. The number of Boston's poor receiving public assistance rose from 500 in 1700 to 4,000 in 1736, New York's from 250 in 1698 to 5,000 in the 1770s. Most of it went to "outdoor" relief in the form of money, food, clothing, and fuel, but almshouses also appeared in colonial cities.

Town governments were not always equal to their multiple tasks. Of the major cities, Boston and Newport had the common New England system of town meetings and selectmen, while New York after 1791 had an elected council responsive to the citizens, although its mayor and other officials were still appointed by the governor. Philadelphia, however, fell under a self-perpetuating closed corporation in which the common run of citizens had no voice, and colonial Charleston never achieved status as a municipal corporation at all, but remained under the thumb of the South Carolina assembly.

THE URBAN WEB   Transit within and between cities was difficult at first. Little of the colonial population lived far from the navigable streams, except in the interior. The first roads were likely to be Indian trails, which themselves often followed the tracks of bison and perhaps the ancient mastodon through the forests. The trails widened with travel, then were made roads by order of provincial and local authorities. Land travel at first had to go by horse or by foot. The first stagecoach line for the public, opened in 1732, linked Burlington and Perth Amboy, New Jersey, connecting by water to Philadelphia and New York, respectively. That same year a guidebook published in Boston gave roads connecting from Boston through Providence, New York, Philadelphia, and eventually on to Williamsburg and Charleston, with connecting branches. From the main ports good roads might reach thirty or forty miles inland, but all were dirt roads subject to washouts and mudholes. There was not a single hard-surfaced road during the entire colonial period, aside from city streets.

Taverns were an important adjunct of colonial travel, since movement by night was too risky, and they became social and political centers to which the local people repaired to learn news from travelers, to discuss the current issues, to socialize, drink, and gamble. Postal service through the seventeenth century was almost nonexistent—people entrusted letters to travelers or sea captains. Massachusetts set up a provincial postal system in 1677, and Pennsylvania in 1683. Under a parliamentary law of 1710, the postmaster of London named a deputy in charge of the colonies and a system eventually extended the length of the Atlantic seaboard. Benjamin Franklin, who served as deputy postmaster from 1753 to 1774, speeded up the service with shorter routes and night-traveling post riders, and increased the volume by inaugurating lower rates.

More reliable deliveries gave rise to newspapers in the eighteenth century. Before 1745 twenty-two newspapers had been started, seven in New England, ten in the middle colonies, and five in the South. An important landmark in the progress of freedom of the press was John Peter Zenger's trial for seditious libel for publishing criticisms of New York's governor in his newspaper, the New York *Weekly Journal.* Imprisoned for ten months and brought to trial in 1735, he was defended by the aged Andrew Hamilton of Philadelphia. The established rule in English common law held that one might be punished for criticism which fostered "an ill opinion of the government." The jury's function was only to determine whether the defendant had published

Fighting a fire in colonial New York, 1762.

the opinion. Hamilton startled the court with his claim that Zenger had published the truth—which the judge ruled an unacceptable defense. The jury, however, agreed with the assertion and held the editor not guilty. The libel law remained standing as before, but editors thereafter were emboldened to criticize officials more freely.

THE ENLIGHTENMENT

DISCOVERING THE LAWS OF NATURE   It was the cities that, through their commercial contacts, through their newspapers, and through other activities, became the centers for the dissemination of fashion and ideas. In the world of ideas a new fashion was abroad: the Enlightenment. During the first century of English colonization the settlers' contemporaries in Europe went through a scientific revolution in which the old Ptolemaic view of an earth-centered universe was overthrown by the new heliocentric (sun-centered) system of Polish astronomer Nicolaus Copernicus. A climax to the revolution came with Sir Isaac Newton's *Principia* (*Mathematical Principles of Natural Philosophy*, 1687), which set forth his theory of gravitation. Newton had, in short, hit upon the design of a mechanistic universe moving in accordance with natural laws which could be grasped by human reason and explained by mathematics.

By analogy from Newton's world machine, one could reason that natural laws governed all things—the orbits of the planets and also the orbits of human relations: politics, economics, and society. Reason could make people aware, for instance, that the natural law of supply and demand governed economics or that natural rights to life, liberty, and property determined the limits and functions of government.

Much of enlightened thought could be reconciled with established beliefs—the idea of natural law existed in Christian theology, and religious people could reason that the worldview of Copernicus and Newton simply showed forth the glory of God. Puritan leaders accepted Newtonian science from the start. Yet when carried to its ultimate logic, as the Deists did, the idea of natural law left God eliminated or at best reduced to the position of a remote Creator—as the French *philosophe* Voltaire put it, the master clockmaker who planned the universe and set it in motion. Evil in the world, in this view, resulted not from original sin and innate depravity so much as it did from an imperfect understanding of the laws of nature. Man, the English philosopher John Locke argued in his *Essay on Human Understanding* (1690), is largely the product of his environment, the human mind a blank tablet on which experience is written. The evils of a corrupt society therefore might corrupt the mind. The way to improve both society and human nature was by the application and improvement of Reason—which was the highest Virtue (enlightened thinkers often capitalized both words).

THE ENLIGHTENMENT IN AMERICA   However interpreted, such ideas profoundly affected the climate of thought in the eighteenth century. The premises of Newtonian science and the Enlightenment, moreover, fitted the American experience. In the New World people no longer moved solely in the worn grooves of tradition that defined the roles of priest or peasant or noble. Much of their experience had already been with observation, experiment, and the need to think anew. America was therefore receptive to the new science. Anybody who pretended to a degree of learning revealed a curiosity about natural philosophy, and some carried it to considerable depth.

John Winthrop, Jr. (1606–1676), three times governor of Connecticut, wanted to establish industries and mining in America. These interests led to his work in chemistry and membership in the Royal Society of London. He owned probably the first telescope brought to the colonies. His cousin, John Winthrop IV (1714–1779), was a professional scientist, Hollis Professor of Mathematics and Natural Philosophy at Harvard, who introduced to the colonies the study of calculus and ranged over the fields of astronomy, geology, chemistry, and electricity. David Rittenhouse of Philadelphia, a clockmaker, became a self-

Benjamin Franklin (1767).

taught scientist who built probably the first telescope made in America. John Bartram of Philadelphia spent a lifetime traveling and studying American plant life, and gathered in Philadelphia a botanical garden now part of the city's park system.

FRANKLIN'S INFLUENCE   Benjamin Franklin stood apart from all these men as the person who epitomized the Enlightenment, in the eyes of both Americans and Europeans. It was fitting that Franklin came from Pennsylvania, which in the eyes of Voltaire had fulfilled the Quaker virtues of toleration and simplicity. William Penn, Voltaire wrote, had "brought to the world that golden age of which men talk so much and which probably has never existed anywhere except in Pennsylvania." Franklin came from the ranks of the common folk and never lost the common touch, a gift that accounted for his success as a publisher. Born in Boston in 1706, he was the son of a candle and soap maker. Apprenticed to his older brother, a printer, Franklin left home at the age of seventeen, bound for Philadelphia. There, before he was twenty-four, he owned a print shop where he edited and published the *Pennsylvania Gazette,* and when he was twenty-seven he brought out *Poor Richard's Almanac,* filled with homely maxims on success and happiness. Before he retired from business at the age of forty-two, Franklin, among other achievements, had founded a library, set up a fire company, helped start the academy which became the University of Pennsylvania, and started a debating club which grew into the American Philosophical Society. After his early retirement he intended to devote himself to public affairs and the sciences.

The course of events allowed him less and less time for science, but that was his passion. Franklin's *Experiments and Observations on*

Electricity (1751) went through many editions in several languages and established his reputation as a leading thinker and experimenter. His speculations extended widely to the fields of medicine, meteorology, geology, astronomy, physics, and other aspects of science. He invented the Franklin stove, the lightning rod, and a glass harmonica for which Mozart and Beethoven composed. In his travels as colonial agent to London and later American ambassador to France, his insatiable curiosity led to suggestions (some of them later adopted) for improvements in ship design. The triumph of this untutored genius further confirmed the Enlightenment trust in the powers of Nature.

EDUCATION IN THE COLONIES   The heights of abstract reasoning, of course, were remote from the everyday concerns of most colonists. For the colonists at large, education in the traditional ideas and manners of society—even literacy itself—remained primarily the responsibility of family and church, and one not always accepted. The modern conception of universal free education as a responsibility of the state was slow in coming and failed to win universal acceptance until the twentieth century. Yet there is evidence of a widespread concern almost from the beginning that steps needed to be taken lest the children of settlers grow up untutored in the wilderness.

Conditions in New England proved most favorable for the establishment of schools. The Puritan emphasis on Scripture reading, which all Protestants shared in some degree, implied an obligation to ensure literacy. The great proportion of highly educated people in Puritan New England (Massachusetts probably had a greater proportion of college

From the "Rhymed Alphabet" of The New England Primer, first published in America in the 1680s.

G   As runs the Glafs,
Man's Life doth pafs.

H   My Book and Heart
Shall never part.

I   Job feels the rod,
Yet bleffes God.

K   King George the good,
No Man of Blood.

graduates in the early seventeenth century than in the twentieth) ensured a common respect for education. And the compact towns of that region made schools more feasible than among the scattered people of the southern colonies. In 1635 the inhabitants of Boston established the Boston Latin Grammar School, which had a distinguished career to the twentieth century, and the same year the General Court voted to establish a college that, begun in 1636, grew into Harvard University. In 1647 the colony enacted the famous "ye olde deluder Satan" Act (designed to thwart the Evil One), which required every town of fifty or more families to set up a grammar school (a Latin school which could prepare a student for college). Although the act was widely evaded, it did signify a serious purpose to promote education. Massachusetts Bay set an example which the rest of New England emulated.

The Dutch in New Netherland were nearly if not equally as active as the New England Puritans, and more active than the English who succeeded them after 1664. In Pennsylvania the Quakers never heeded William Penn's instructions to establish public schools, but did respect the usefulness of education and financed a number of private schools teaching practical as well as academic subjects. In the southern colonies efforts to establish schools were hampered by the more scattered populations, and in parts of the backcountry by indifference and neglect. Some of the wealthiest planters and merchants of the tidewater sent their children to England or hired tutors, who in some cases would also serve the children of neighbors. In some places wealthy patrons or the people collectively managed to raise some kind of support for "old field" schools and academies at the secondary level.

THE GREAT AWAKENING

STIRRINGS   Amid the new currents of learning and the Enlightenment, many people seemed to be drifting away from the old moorings of piety. If the Lord had allowed great Puritan and Quaker merchants of Boston and Philadelphia to prosper, the haunting fear arose that the devil had lured them into the vain pursuit of worldly gain. Intellectually the educated classes were falling into deism and skepticism. And out along the fringes of settlement there grew up a great backwater of the unchurched, people who had no minister to preach or administer sacraments or perform marriages, who fell, according to some, into a primitive and sinful life, little different from the heathens who lurked in the woods. One Anglican divine called the backcountry preachers in the Carolinas "ignorant wretches, who cannot write," and he compared a Baptist communion service to "A Gang of frantic Lunatics broke out of Bedlam." By the 1730s the sense of falling-away provoked a revival of faith, the Great Awakening, a wave of evangelism that within a few years swept the colonies from one end to the other.

In 1734–1735 a remarkable spiritual refreshing occurred in the congregation of Jonathan Edwards, a Congregationalist minister in Northampton, Massachusetts. One of America's most brilliant philosophers and theologians, Edwards was the only son among eleven children. He entered Yale in 1716 at age thirteen and was graduated valedictorian four years later. While a college student, he developed a mystical religious strain. Following his conversion, he wrote: "God's excellency, his wisdom, his purity and love, seemed to appear in everything; in the sun, moon and stars; in the clouds, and blue sky; in the grass, flowers, trees; in the water, and all nature; which used greatly to fix my mind."

The intense, studious Edwards met and courted Sarah Pierrepont, the charming, witty, and fervently pious daughter of New Haven's most prominent minister. They married in 1727 and by all accounts enjoyed a remarkably joyous union. A friend recalled how striking was "the perfect harmony and mutual love and esteem that subsisted between them." Sarah Edwards eventually bore eleven children, all of whom survived infancy during a period of high infant mortality, and most of whom became distinguished figures in their own right.

In 1726 Edwards was called to serve the Congregational church in Northampton. There he found the congregation's spirituality at low ebb. "Licentiousness for some years greatly prevailed among the youth of the town: there were many of them much addicted to night walking and frequenting the tavern, and lewd practices wherein some by their example exceedingly corrupted others." He was convinced that Christians had become too preoccupied with making and spending money, and that religion had become too intellectual, thereby losing its animating force. "Our people," he said, "do not so much need to have their heads stored as to have their hearts touched." He added that he considered it a "reasonable thing to endeavor to fright persons away from hell." His own vivid descriptions of the torments of hell and the delights of heaven helped rekindle spiritual fervor among his congregants. By 1735 he could report that "the town seemed to be full of the presence of God; it never was so full of love, nor of joy."

About the same time, William Tennent, the Irish-born Presbyterian revivalist, set up a "Log College" in Neshaminy, Pennsylvania, for the education of ministers to serve the Scotch-Irish Presbyterians around Philadelphia. The Log College specialized in turning out zealots who disdained complacency and proclaimed the need for revival. Among the most successful of these was Tennent's son, Gilbert. He became the leader of the so-called New Light faction and eventually helped raise funds for the College of New Jersey (now Princeton University), of which he was a trustee. Critics scorned Tennent and his fellow back-woods evangelists, branding them "half educated enthusiasts," but two of these rustic preachers later became presidents of Princeton.

The true catalyst of the Great Awakening, however, was a twenty-seven-year-old English minister, George Whitefield, whose reputation as a spellbinding evangelist in the Wesleyan revivals then under way in England preceded him to the colonies. Congregations were lifeless, he claimed, "because dead men preach to them." Too many ministers were "slothful shepherds and dumb dogs." His objective was to restore the fires of religious fervor to American congregations. In the autumn of 1739 he arrived in Philadelphia, and late in that year preached to crowds in the area of as many as 6,000. After visiting Georgia, he made a triumphal procession northward to New England, drawing great crowds and releasing "Gales of Heavenly Wind" that blew gusts throughout the colonies.

Young and magnetic, possessed of a golden voice, Whitefield in the pulpit was a dramatic actor who impersonated the agonies of the damned and the joys of the regenerate. He enthralled audiences with his unparalleled eloquence. Even the skeptical Ben Franklin, who went to see the show in Philadelphia, found himself so carried away that the frugal Franklin emptied his pockets into the collection plate—perhaps the ultimate tribute to Whitefield's persuasiveness. The English revival-ist urged his listeners to experience a "new birth"—a sudden, emotional moment of conversion and salvation—and warned of the dangers of a ministry that had not experienced such rebirth. By the end of his ser-mon, one listener reported, the entire congregation was "in utmost Con-fusion, some crying out, some laughing, and Bliss still roaring to them to come to Christ, they answering, *I will, I will, I'm coming, I'm coming.*"

Jonathan Edwards heard Whitefield preach and found the experience so moving that he wept through most of the sermon. Thereafter he took advantage of the commotion stirred up by Whitefield to spread his own revival gospel. In his view, a religion of the heart was central to true faith. The Christian, Edwards explained, "does not merely rationally believe that God is glorious, but he had a sense of the gloriousness of God in his heart." But Edwards, an intellectual himself, was never given to the excesses or to the histrionics of Whitefield. His magnum opus was an elaborate theological reconciliation of Calvinism and the Enlightenment: *Of Freedom of Will* (1754). In that book as well as other writings Edwards acknowledged that religion should not be reduced to sheer emotionalism, nor should it shift its focus from the grace of God to the intensity of an individual's conversion experience. Instead he sought to use his remarkable powers as a theologian and preacher to remind people of the sovereignty of God and the irresistible attraction of his glory, beauty, and love.

The Reverend Jonathan Edwards awoke many congregants to their plight in sermons such as "Sinners in the Hands of an Angry God."

The Awakening in New England reached its peak in 1741, when Edwards delivered his most famous sermon at Enfield, Massachusetts. Entitled "Sinners in the Hands of an Angry God," it represented a devout appeal to repentance. Edwards reminded the congregation that hell was real and that God's vision was omnipotent, his judgment certain. "The bow of God's wrath is bent," he declared, "and the arrow made ready on the string, and justice bends the arrow at your heart, and strains the bow, and it is nothing but the mere pleasure of God, and that of an angry God, without any promise or obligation at all, that keeps the arrow one moment from being made drunk with your blood." In an even more compelling metaphor, Edwards noted that God "holds you over the pit of hell, much as one holds a spider, or some loathsome insect, over the fire, abhors you, and is dreadfully provoked . . . he looks upon you as worthy of nothing else, but to be cast into the fire." But for all the terror of his theme, Edwards did not rant or engage in theatrics. Instead he delivered the carefully reasoned sermon in a soft, solemn voice and a calm manner. When he finished, he had to wait several minutes for the congregation to quiet down before leading them in a closing hymn.

Edwards and Whitefield inspired many imitators, some of whom carried the fiery language to extremes. Once unleashed, spiritual enthusiasm is hard to control. In many ways the Awakening backfired on those who had intended it to bolster church discipline and social order. Some of the revivalists began to court those at the bottom of the social scale—laborers, seamen, servants, and farm folk. The Reverend James Davenport, for instance, a fiery itinerant New England Congregationalist, set about shouting, raging, and stomping on the devil, beseeching his listeners to renounce the established clergy and become the agents of their own salvation. The churched and unchurched flocked to hear his mesmerizing sermons. Seized by the terror and ecstasy, they groveled on the floor or lay unconscious on the benches, to the chagrin of more decorous churchgoers. One never knew, the more traditional clergymen warned, whence came these enthusiasms—perhaps they were devilish delusions intended to discredit the true faith.

PIETY AND REASON   Everywhere the Awakening brought splits, especially in the more Calvinistic churches. Presbyterians divided into the "Old Side" and "New Side"; Congregationalists into "Old Lights" and "New Lights." New England would never be the same. The more traditional clergy found its position being undermined as church members chose sides and either dismissed their ministers or deserted them. Many of the "New Lights" went over to the Baptists, and others flocked to Presbyterian or, later, Methodist groups, which in turn divided and subdivided into new sects.

New England Puritanism was now finally divided. The precarious tension in which the founders had held the elements of piety and reason was now sundered. In consequence New England attracted more and more Baptists, Presbyterians, Anglicans, and other denominations, while the revival tradition scored its most lasting victories along the chaotic frontiers of the middle and southern colonies. In the more sedate churches of Boston, moreover, the principle of reason gained the upper hand in a reaction against the excesses of revival emotion. Boston ministers such as Charles Chauncey and Jonathan Mayhew assumed the lead in preaching a doctrine of rationality. They reexamined Calvinist theology and found it too forbidding and irrational that people could be forever damned by predestination. The rationality of Newton and Locke, the idea of natural law, crept more and more into their sermons. They were already on the road to Unitarianism and Universalism.

In reaction to taunts that the "born-again" ministers lacked learning, the Awakening gave rise to the denominational colleges that became so characteristic of American higher education. The three colleges already in existence had grown earlier from religious motives: Harvard, founded in 1636, because the Puritans dreaded "to leave an illiterate ministry to the church when our present ministers shall lie in the dust"; the College of William and Mary, in 1693, to serve James Blair's purpose of strengthening the Anglican ministry; and Yale College, in 1701, set up to educate the Puritans of Connecticut, who felt that Harvard was drifting from the strictest orthodoxy. The Presbyterian College of New Jersey, later Princeton University, was founded in 1746 as successor to William Tennent's Log College. In close succession came King's College (1754) in New York, later Columbia University, an Anglican institution; the College of Rhode Island (1764), later Brown University, Baptist; Queen's College (1766), later Rutgers, Dutch Reformed; and Congregationalist Dartmouth (1769), the outgrowth of an earlier school for Indians. Among the colonial colleges only the University of Pennsylvania, founded as the Philadelphia Academy in 1754, arose from a secular impulse.

The Great Awakening, like the Enlightenment, set in motion currents that still flow in American life. It implanted in American culture the evangelical principle and the endemic style of revivalism. The movement weakened the status of the old-fashioned clergy and encouraged believers to exercise their own judgment, and thereby weakened habits of deference generally. By encouraging the proliferation of denominations it heightened the need for toleration of dissent. But in some respects the counterpoint between the Awakening and the Enlightenment, between the principles of piety and reason, led by different roads to similar ends. Both emphasized the power and right of individual decision-making, and both aroused millennial hopes that America would become the promised land in which people might attain the perfection of piety or reason, if not of both.

FURTHER READING

The diversity of colonial societies may be seen in Jack P. Greene's *Pursuits of Happiness: The Social Development of the Early Modern British Colonies and the Formation of American Culture* (1988)° and in David Hackett Fischer's *Albion's Seed: Four British Folkways in America* (1989).° Other useful works include Richard F. Hofstadter's *America at 1750: A Social Portrait* (1971),° and James A. Henretta's *The Evolution of American Society, 1700–1815* (1973). Timothy H. Breen's *Puritans and Adventurers: Change and Persistence in Early America* (1980)° concentrates on Virginia and Massachusetts. Gary B. Nash examines early race relations in *Red, White, and Black* (2nd ed., 1982).° Also see Jack P. Greene's *Imperatives, Behaviors, and Identities: Essays in Early American Cultural History* (1992) and Mitchell Robert Breitwieser's *Cotton Mather and Benjamin Franklin: The Price of Representative Personality* (1993).

Until recently Puritan communities received the bulk of scholarly attention. Studies of the New England town include Darrett B. Rutman's *Winthrop's Boston: Portrait of a Puritan Town, 1630–1649* (1965)°; Sumner C. Powell's *Puritan Village* (1963),° on the origins and

°These books are available in paperback editions.

social structure of Sudbury, Massachusetts; Kenneth A. Lockridge's *A New England Town: The First One Hundred Years* (2nd ed., 1985),° which looks at the relationship of family and authority in Dedham, Massachusetts; John Frederick Martin's *Profits in the Wilderness: Entrepreneurship and the Founding of New England Towns in the Seventeenth Century* (1991) indicates that economic concerns rather than spiritual motives were driving forces in many New England towns; Richard Johnson's *John Nelson, Merchant Adventurer* (1991) provides perspective on New England businessmen. Philip J. Greven, Jr.'s *Four Generations: Population, Land, and Family in Colonial Andover, Massachusetts* (1970),° a similar study; and Paul S. Boyer and Stephen Nissenbaum's *Salem Possessed* (1974), which connects the notorious witch trials to changes in community structure and economic base. Of the more recent works, see also Christine Heyrman's *Commerce and Culture* (1984),° Richard Melvoin's *New England Outpost: War and Society in Colonial Deerfield, Massachusetts* (1988),° Stephen Foster's *The Long Argument: English Puritanism and the Shaping of New England Culture 1570–1700* (1991). Francis J. Bremer's *Congregational Communion: Clerical Friendship in the Anglo-American Puritan Community, 1610–1692* (1994). Janice Knight's *Orthodoxies in Massachusetts: Rereading American Puritanism* (1994), and Stephen Innes's *Creating the Commonwealth: The Economic Culture of Puritan New England* (1995).

Broader in cultural interpretation are Richard S. Dunn's *Puritans and Yankees: The Winthrop Dynasty of New England, 1630–1717* (1962) and E. Digby Baltzell's *Puritan Boston and Quaker Philadelphia* (1979). For an interdisciplinary approach, see John Demos's *Entertaining Satan: Witchcraft and the Culture of Early New England* (1982).° Discussions of women in the New England colonies can be found in Laurel Ulrich's *Good Wives* (1982),° Joy Buel and Richard Buel's *The Way of Duty* (1984),° and Carol Karlsen's *The Devil in the Shape of a Woman: Witchcraft in Colonial New England* (1987).° Bernard Rosenthal challenges many myths concerning the Salem witch trials in *Salem Story: Reading the Witch Trials of 1692* (1993). John Demos describes family life in *A Little Commonwealth: Family Life in Plymouth Colony* (1970).°

Later generations of these colonists are described in Michael Zuckerman's *Peaceable Kingdoms: Massachusetts Towns in the Eighteenth Century* (1970), Robert A. Gross's *The Minutemen and Their World* (1976),° and Richard L. Bushman's *From Puritan to Yankee: Character and Social Order in Connecticut* (1976).°

For the social history of the southern colonies, see Allen Kulikoff's

°These books are available in paperback editions.

Tobacco and Slaves: The Development of Southern Cultures in the Chesapeake Colonies, 1680–1800 (1986) and *Colonial Chesapeake Society* (1988), edited by Lois Green Carr et al. Darrett B. Rutman and Anita H. Rutman's *A Place in Time* (2 vols., 1984)° is a community study of life in a Virginia county. Julia Cherry Spruill's *Women's Life and Work in the Southern Colonies* (1938) is the classic in that field. Family life along the Chesapeake is described in Gloria L. Main's *Tobacco Colony* (1982) and Daniel B. Smith's *Inside the Great House* (1980). For a closer look at the life of one of the great planters of the Chesapeake, see Kenneth Lockridge's *The Diary, and Life, of William Byrd II of Virginia, 1674–1744* (1987).°

The best southern social history is intertwined with analysis of the origins of slavery. Begin with Edmund S. Morgan's *American Slavery, American Freedom: The Ordeal of Colonial Virginia* (1975),° which examines Virginia's social structure, environment, and labor patterns in a biracial context. More specific on the racial nature of the origins of slavery are Winthrop D. Jordan's *White over Black: American Attitudes toward the Negro* (1986)° and David B. Davis's *The Problem of Slavery in Western Culture* (1966).° Philip D. Curtin's *The Atlantic Slave Trade* (1969)° is a valuable quantitative study. On the interaction of the cultures of blacks and whites, see Mechal Sobel's *The World They Made Together: Black and White Values in Eighteenth-Century Virginia* (1987). Black viewpoints are presented in two books on Virginia: Gerald W. Mullin's *Flight and Rebellion: Slave Resistance in Eighteenth Century Virginia* (1972)° and Timothy H. Breen and Stephen Innes's *"Myne Owne Ground": Race and Freedom on Virginia's Eastern Shore, 1640–1676* (1980).° David W. Galenson's *White Servitude in Colonial America* (1981) looks at the indentured labor force.

For patterns of trade during the colonial period, see Gary M. Walton and James F. Shepherd, *The Economic Rise of Early America* (1979). Trade connections with Europe are stressed in Ralph Davis's *The Rise of the Atlantic Economies* (1973) and Jacob M. Price's *France and the Chesapeake* (2 vols., 1973). The development of the Atlantic economy is further illuminated in Marcus Rediker's *Between the Devil and the Deep Blue Sea: Merchant Seamen, Pirates, and the Anglo-American Maritime World, 1700–1750* (1987). The interaction of trade and politics in America's first cities is the subject of Gary B. Nash's *The Urban Crucible* (1979).°

For the role of Indians and settlers in shaping the New World's ecology, see William Cronon's fine work *Changes in the Land* (1983)° and Albert E. Cowdrey's *This Land, This South* (1983). A number of books

---

°These books are available in paperback editions.

discuss colonial land policy. James T. Lemon explores land holding patterns in one county of Pennsylvania in *The Best Poor Man's Country* (1972).° The impact of land pressures and tenancy is explored in Sung Bok Kim's *Landlord and Tenant in Colonial New York* (1978). The political implications of land pressure are documented in Charles S. Grant's *Democracy in the Connecticut Frontier Town of Kent* (1961)° and Patricia U. Bonomi's *A Factious People* (1971),° a study of New York.

Henry F. May's *The Enlightenment in America* (1976) examines intellectual trends in eighteenth-century America. Lawrence A. Cremin's *American Education: The Colonial Experience, 1607–1783* (1970) surveys educational developments.

A concise introduction to the events and repercussions of the Great Awakening is J. M. Bumsted and John E. Van de Wetering's *What Must I Do to Be Saved?* (1976), but see also Edwin S. Gaustad's *The Great Awakening in New England* (1957) and Patricia U. Bonomi's *Under the Cope of Heaven* (1986). The political impact of the new religious enthusiasm is shown in Rhys Isaac's *The Transformation of Virginia, 1740–1790* (1982).° Perry Miller analyzes Jonathan Edwards's theological influence in *Jonathan Edwards* (1949)°; Patricia J. Tracy's *Jonathan Edwards, Pastor* (1980)° stresses the Northampton minister's relations to his community.

°These books are available in paperback editions.

4

THE IMPERIAL PERSPECTIVE

For the better part of the seventeenth century, the running struggle between Parliament and the Stuart kings prevented England from perfecting either a systematic colonial policy or effective agencies of imperial control. Intervention in colonial affairs was a matter of makeshift commissions, experimentation, and "muddling through," a practice at which the British had a certain skill and not a little luck. After the Restoration (1660), a plan of colonial administration slowly emerged, but even so it fell short of coherence and efficiency. As a result the Americans grew accustomed to rather loose imperial reins.

English Administration of the Colonies

Throughout the colonial period the king stood as the source of legal authority in America, and land titles derived ultimately from royal grants. All colonies except Georgia received charters from the king before the Glorious Revolution of 1688, when the crown lost supremacy to Parliament. The colonies therefore continued to stand as "dependencies of the crown," and the important colonial officials held office at the pleasure of the crown. After King George granted a group of investors a charter for the new colony of Georgia in 1732, its status conformed to the established practice.

The king exercised his power through the Privy Council, a body of some thirty to forty advisers appointed by and responsible solely to him, and this group became the first agency of colonial supervision. But the Privy Council was too large and too busy to keep track of the details. So in 1634 Charles I entrusted colonial affairs to eleven of its members, the Lords Commissioners for Plantations in General, with William Laud, archbishop of Canterbury, as its head. The Laud Commission grew in part out of the troubles following the dissolution of the Virginia

Company and in part out of Laud's design to impose political and religious conformity on New England. In 1638 his commission ordered Massachusetts to return its charter and answer charges that colonial officials had violated the provisions. Sir Ferdinando Gorges, appointed governor-general of New England, planned to subdue the region by force if necessary, and might have quashed the Puritan experiment except for the troubles at home that prevented further action. The Civil War in England, which lasted from 1641 to 1649, was followed by Cromwell's Puritan Commonwealth and Protectorate, and both developments gave the colonies a respite from efforts at royal control.

THE MERCANTILE SYSTEM   Cromwell showed little passion for colonial administration, but he had a lively concern for colonial trade, which had fallen largely to Dutch shipping during the upheavals in England. Therefore, in 1651 Parliament adopted a Navigation Act that excluded nearly all foreign shipping from the English and colonial trade. The act required that all goods imported into England or the colonies must arrive on English ships and that the majority of the crew must be English. In all cases colonial ships and crews qualified as English. The act excepted European goods, which might come in ships of the country that produced the goods, but only from the place of origin or the port from which they were usually shipped.

On economic policy, if nothing else, Restoration England under Charles II took its cue from Cromwell. The new Parliament quickly adopted the mercantile system he had effected. The mercantile system, or mercantilism, became in the seventeenth and eighteenth centuries the operative economic theory of all major European powers. It was based on a premise quite alien to modern economic theory. Mercantilism assumed that economies could not grow by themselves. A nation could gain wealth only at the expense of another country—by seizing its bullion and dominating its trade.

In a world of national rivalries, the reasoning went, power and wealth went hand in hand. A strong state must be wealthy. To be wealthy it must enlarge its stores of gold and silver. Mercantilists held that the total of the world's wealth, as reflected in the total stock of gold and silver, remained essentially fixed. All that changed was a nation's share of that stock. To get and keep gold and silver, the government should limit foreign imports and preserve a favorable balance of trade. This required the state to encourage manufacturers, through subsidies and monopolies if need be; it should also develop and protect its own shipping; and it should make use of colonies as sources of raw materials and markets for its own finished goods.

The Navigation Act of 1660 gave Cromwell's act of 1651 a new twist.

Ships' crews now had to be not just a majority but three-quarters English, and certain specified goods were to be shipped only to England or other English colonies. These were things needed but not produced by the mother country. The list of "enumerated" goods initially included tobacco, cotton, indigo, ginger, dyewoods, and sugar. Rice, naval stores, hemp, masts and spars, copper ores, and furs, among other items, were later added to the list. Not only did England (and the colonies) become the sole outlet for these colonial exports, but three years later the Navigation Act of 1663 sought to make England the funnel through which all colonial imports had to be routed. The act was sometimes called the Staple Act because it made England the staple (market or trade center) for all goods sent to the colonies. Everything shipped from Europe to America had to stop off in England, be landed, and duty paid on it before reshipment. There were few exceptions: only servants, horses, and provisions from Scotland; wine from Madeira and the Azores; and salt for fisheries. A third major act rounded out the trade system. The Navigation Act of 1673 (sometimes called the Plantation Duty Act) required that every captain loading enumerated articles give bond to land them in England, or if they were destined for another colony, that he pay on the spot a duty roughly equal to that paid in England.

ENFORCING THE NAVIGATION ACTS   The Navigation Acts supplied a convenient rationale for a colonial system: to serve the economic needs of the mother country. Yet enforcement was spotty. During the reign of Charles I a bureaucracy of colonial administrators began to emerge, but it took shape slowly and incompletely. After the Restoration of 1660, supervision of colonial affairs fell once again to the Privy Council, or rather to a succession of its committees. In 1675, however, Charles II introduced some order into the chaos when, as his father had done before, he designated certain privy councilors the Lords of Trade and Plantations, a name reflecting the overall importance of economic factors. The Lords of Trade were to make the colonies abide by the mercantile system and to seek out ways to make them more profitable to England and the crown. To these ends they served as the clearinghouse for all colonial affairs, building up an archive and a bureaucracy of colonial experts. By advice rather than by direct authority, at least in theory, the Lords of Trade named governors, wrote or reviewed the governors' instructions, and handled all reports and correspondence dealing with colonial affairs.

Within five years of the Plantation Duty Act, between 1673 and 1678, collectors of customs appeared in all the colonies, and shortly thereafter a surveyor general of the customs in the American colonies was named. The most notorious of these, insofar as resentful colonists were concerned, was Edward Randolph, the first man to make an entire career in

This view of eighteenth-century Boston shows the importance of shipping and its regulation in the colonies, especially in Massachusetts Bay.

the colonial service and the nemesis of insubordinate colonials for a quarter century.

Randolph arrived at Boston in 1676 to demand that Massachusetts answer complaints that it had usurped the proprietary rights in New Hampshire and Maine. More was at stake, however. Since the Restoration the colony had ignored gentle hints that it align its practices with fundamental elements of the Restoration compromise. Massachusetts had accepted the formality of conducting judicial proceedings in the king's name. It dragged its heels, however, on adopting an Oath of Allegiance, repealing laws counter to English law, allowing use of the Anglican *Book of Common Prayer,* or making property instead of church membership the voting test. The expanding commercial interests of New England counseled prudence and accommodation, but the Puritan leaders harbored a persistent distrust of Stuart designs on their utopia.

After a brief stay, Randolph submitted a report bristling with hostility. The Bay colony had not only ignored royal wishes, it had tolerated violations of the Navigation Acts, refused appeals from its courts to the Privy Council, and had operated a mint in defiance of the king's prerogative. Massachusetts officials had told him, Randolph reported, "that the legislative power is and abides in them solely to act and make laws by virtue" of their charter. Continuing intransigence from Massachusetts led the Lords of Trade to begin legal proceedings against the colonial charter in 1678, although the issue remained in legal snarls for another six years. Meanwhile Randolph returned in 1680 to establish the royal colony of New Hampshire, then set up shop as the king's collector of customs in Boston, whence he dispatched repeated accounts of colonial recalcitrance. Eventually, in 1684, the Lords of Trade won a court decision that annulled the charter of Massachusetts. The Puritan utopia was fast becoming a lost cause.

THE DOMINION OF NEW ENGLAND   Temporarily, the government of Massachusetts Bay was placed in the hands of a special royal commission. Then in 1685 Charles II died, to be succeeded by his brother, the duke of York, as James II, the first Catholic sovereign since the death of Queen Mary in 1558. Plans long maturing in the Lords of Trade for a general reorganization of colonial government fitted very well the autocratic notions of James II, who asserted his prerogatives more forcefully than his brother had. The new king therefore readily approved a proposal to create a Dominion of New England and to place under its sway all colonies south through New Jersey. Something of the sort might have been in store for Pennsylvania and the southern colonies as well if the reign of James II had lasted longer. In that case the English colonies might have found themselves on the same tight leash as the colonies of Spain or France.

The Dominion was to have a government named altogether by royal authority, a governor and council who would rule without any assembly. The royal governor, Sir Edmond Andros, appeared in Boston in 1686 to establish his rule, which he soon extended over Connecticut and Rhode Island, and in 1688 over New York and East and West New Jersey. Andros was a soldier, accustomed to taking—and giving— orders. He seems to have been honest, efficient, and loyal to the crown, but tactless in circumstances that called for the utmost diplomacy—the uprooting of long-established institutions in the face of popular hostility.

A rising resentment greeted Andros's measures, especially in Massachusetts. Taxation was now levied without the consent of the General Court, and when residents of one seaboard town protested against taxation without representation, a number of them were imprisoned or fined. Andros suppressed town governments, enforced the trade laws,

King James II (1685–1688).

and subdued smuggling with the help of Edward Randolph, that omnipresent servant of the crown. Most ominous of all, Andros and his lieutenants took over one of the Puritan churches for Anglican worship in Boston. Puritan leaders believed, with good reason, that he was conspiring to break their power and authority.

But the Dominion was scarcely established before word came from England of the Glorious Revolution of 1688. James II, like Andros in New England, had aroused resentment by instituting arbitrary measures and, what was more, by openly parading his Catholic faith. The birth of a son, sure to be reared a Catholic, put the opposition on notice that James's system would survive him. The Catholic son, rather than the Protestant daughters, Mary and Anne, would be next in line for the throne. Parliamentary leaders, their patience exhausted, invited Mary and her husband, the Dutch leader, William of Orange, to assume the throne as joint monarchs. James, his support dwindling, fled the country.

THE GLORIOUS REVOLUTION IN AMERICA   When news reached Boston that William had landed in England, Boston staged its own Glorious Revolution, as bloodless as that in England. Andros and his councilors were arrested, and Massachusetts reverted to its former government. In rapid sequence the other colonies that had been absorbed into the Dominion followed suit. All were permitted to retain their former status except Massachusetts and Plymouth which, after some delay, were united under a new charter in 1691 as the royal colony of Massachusetts Bay.

In New York, however, events took a different course. There, Andros's lieutenant-governor was deposed by a group led by a German immigrant, Jacob Leisler, who assumed the office of governor pending word from England. For two years he kept the province under his control with the support of the militia. Finally, in 1691, the king appointed a new governor. When Leisler hesitated to turn over authority, the new governor charged him with treason. Leisler and his son-in-law were hanged on May 16, 1691. Four years too late, in 1695, Parliament exonerated them of all charges. For years to come Leisler and anti-Leisler factions would poison the political atmosphere of New York.

The new monarchs made no effort to restore the Dominion of New England. But the crown salvaged a remnant of that design by bringing more colonies under royal control through the appointment of governors. Massachusetts was first, in 1691. New York kept the status of royal colony it had achieved upon the accession of James II. In Maryland after the Glorious Revolution, a local rebellion against the Catholic proprietor gave the occasion to appoint a royal governor in 1691. Maryland, however, reverted to proprietary status in 1715 after the fourth Lord Baltimore became Anglican. Pennsylvania had an even briefer career as a royal colony, 1692–1694, before reverting to Penn's proprietorship. New Jersey became royal in 1702, South Carolina in 1719, North Carolina in 1729, and Georgia in 1752.

The Glorious Revolution had significant long-term effects on American history in that the Bill of Rights and Toleration Act, passed in England in 1689, influenced attitudes and the course of events in the colonies. Even more significant, the overthrow of James II set an example and a precedent for revolution against the monarch. In defense of that action the philosopher John Locke published his *Two Treatises on Government* (1690), which had an enormous impact on political thought in the colonies. The *First Treatise* refuted theories of the divine right of kings. The more important *Second Treatise* set forth Locke's contract theory of government, which claimed that people were endowed with certain natural rights to life, liberty, and property. In a state of nature, prior to the implementation of a government, such rights went without safeguard. This led people to establish governments among themselves. Kings were parties to such agreements, and bound by them. They were obligated to protect the property and lives of their subjects. When they failed to do so, the people had the right—in extreme cases—to overthrow the monarch and change their government.

The idea that governments emerged by contract out of a primitive state of nature is of course hypothetical, not an account of actual events. But in the American experience governments had actually grown out of contractual arrangements such as Locke described: the Mayflower Compact, the Cambridge Agreement, the Fundamental Orders of Connecticut. The royal charters themselves constituted a sort of contract between the crown and the settlers. Locke's writings understandably appealed to colonial readers, and his philosophy probably had more influence in America than in England.

AN EMERGING COLONIAL SYSTEM   The accession of William and Mary to the English throne provoked a restatement and refinement of the existing Navigation Acts and administrative system. In 1696 two developments created at last the semblance, and to some degree the reality, of a coherent colonial system. First, the Navigation Act of 1696 required colonial governors to enforce the Navigation Acts, allowed customs officials to use "writs of assistance" (general search warrants that did not have to specify the place to be searched), and ordered that accused violators be tried in Admiralty Courts, which Edward Randolph had recommended because juries habitually refused to convict their peers. Admiralty cases were decided by judges whom the governors appointed.

Second, also in 1696, William III created the Board of Trade to take the place of the Lords of Trade and Plantations. Colonial officials were required to report to the board, and its archives constitute the largest single collection of materials on colonial relations with the mother country from that time on. The Board of Trade investigated the enforcement of the Navigation Acts and recommended ways to limit colonial manufactures and to encourage the production of raw materials. At the board's behest Parliament enacted a bounty for the production of naval stores, ship timber, masts, and hemp. Similar payments were later extended to encourage the production of rice, indigo, and other commodities. The board examined all colonial laws and made recommendations for their disallowance by the crown. In all, 8,563 colonial laws eventually were examined and 469 of them were actually disallowed. The board also made recommendations for official appointments in the colonies.

SALUTARY NEGLECT   From 1696 to 1725 the board met regularly and worked vigorously toward subjecting the colonies to a more efficient royal control. After the death of Queen Anne in 1725, however, its energies waned. The throne went in turn to the Hanoverian monarchs, George I (1714–1727) and George II (1727–1760), German princes who were next in the Protestant line of succession by virtue of descent from James I. Under these monarchs, the cabinet (a kind of executive committee in the Privy Council) emerged as the central agency of administration. Robert Walpole, as first minister (1721–1742), deliberately followed a policy that the philosopher Edmund Burke later called "a wise and salutary neglect." The board became chiefly an agency of political patronage, studded with officials who took an interest mainly in their salaries.

In the course of the eighteenth century other administrative agencies and offices became involved in certain aspects of colonial government. The most important of these was the secretary of state for the Southern Department. After about 1700 he was the chief administrative official with supervision over colonial matters. Royal governors were responsible to him for colonial defense and military matters. But none of the incumbents in this office showed much energy, except the elder William Pitt, who held the office while also first minister. The duke of Newcastle, who served (1727–1748) during the decades of salutary neglect, was, according to a contemporary, a man who lost an hour in the morning every day and spent the rest of the day running around trying to find it.

THE HABIT OF SELF-GOVERNMENT

Government within the colonies, like colonial policy, evolved without plan. In broad outline the governor, council, and assembly in each colony corresponded to the king, lords, and commons of the mother country. At the outset, all the colonies except Georgia had begun as projects of trading companies or feudal proprietors holding charters from the crown, but eight colonies eventually relinquished or forfeited their charters and became royal provinces. In these the crown named the governor. In Maryland, Pennsylvania, and Delaware the governor remained the choice of a proprietor, although each had an interim period of royal government. Connecticut and Rhode Island were the last of the corporate colonies; they elected their own governors to the end of the colonial period. In the corporate and proprietary colonies, and in Massachusetts, the charter served as a rough equivalent to a written constitution. Rhode Island and Connecticut in fact kept their charters as state constitutions after independence. Over the years certain anomalies appeared as colonial governments diverged from that of England. On the one hand the governors retained powers and prerogatives that the king had lost in the course of the seventeenth century. On the other hand the assemblies acquired powers, particularly with respect to appointments, that Parliament had yet to gain.

POWERS OF THE GOVERNORS   The crown never vetoed acts of Parliament after 1707, but the colonial governors still held an absolute veto and the crown could disallow (in effect, veto) colonial legislation on advice of the Board of Trade. With respect to the assembly, the governor still had the power to determine when and where it would meet, to prorogue (adjourn or recess) sessions, and to dissolve the assembly for new elections or to postpone elections indefinitely at his pleasure. The crown, however, had to summon Parliament every three years and call elections at least every seven, and could not prorogue sessions. The royal or proprietary governor, moreover, nominated for life appointment the members of his council (except in Massachusetts, where they were chosen by the lower house), and the council functioned as both the upper house of the legislature and the highest court of appeal within the colony. With respect to the judiciary, in all but the charter colonies the governor still held the prerogative of creating courts and of naming and dismissing judges, powers explicitly denied the king in England. The assemblies, however, generally made good their claim that courts should be created only by legislative authority, although the crown repeatedly disallowed acts to grant judges life tenure in order to make them more independent.

As chief executive the governor could appoint and remove officials, command the militia and naval forces, grant pardons, and as his commission often put it, "execute everything which doth and of right ought to belong to the governor"—which might cover a multitude of powers. In these respects his authority resembled the crown's, for the king still exercised executive authority and had the power generally to name all administrative officials. This often served as a powerful means of royal influence in Parliament, since the king could appoint members or their friends to lucrative offices. And while the arrangement might seem to another age a breeding ground for corruption or tyranny, it was often viewed in the eighteenth century as a stabilizing influence, especially by the king's friends. But it was an influence less and less available to the governors. On the one hand colonial assemblies nibbled away at their power of appointment; on the other hand the authorities in England more and more drew the control of colonial patronage into their own hands.

POWERS OF THE ASSEMBLIES   Unlike the governor and council, who were appointed by an outside authority, either king or proprietor, the colonial assembly was elected. Whether called the House of Burgesses (Virginia), of Delegates (Maryland), of Representatives (Massachusetts), or simply "assembly," the lower houses were chosen by popular vote in counties or towns or, in South Carolina, parishes. Although the English Toleration Act of 1689 did not apply to the colonies, religious tests for voting tended to be abandoned thereafter (the Massachusetts charter of 1691 so specified) and the chief restriction left was a property qualification, based on the notion that only men who held a "stake in society" could vote responsibly. Yet the property qualifications generally set low hurdles in the way of potential voters. Property holding was widespread, and a greater proportion of the population could vote in the colonies than anywhere else in the world of the eighteenth century.

Women, children, Indians, and blacks were excluded from the political process—as a matter of course—and continued to be excluded for the most part into the twentieth century, but the qualifications excluded few adult free white males. Virginia, which at one time permitted all freemen to vote, in the eighteenth century required only the ownership of twenty-five acres of improved land or one hundred acres of wild land, or the ownership of a "house" and part of a lot in town, or a service in a five-year apprenticeship in Williamsburg or Norfolk. Qualifications for membership in the assembly ran somewhat higher, and in an age that still held to habits of deference, officeholders tended to come from the more well-to-do—a phenomenon not unknown today—but there were exceptions. One unsympathetic colonist observed in 1744 that the New Jersey assembly "was chiefly composed of mechanicks and ignorant wretches; obstinate to the last degree." In any case, gentlefolk who ran for office found then as now that showing a certain respect for the sensibilities of humbler men paid off in votes.

Colonial politics of the eighteenth century mirrored English politics of the seventeenth. In one case there had been a tug-of-war between king and Parliament, ending with the supremacy of Parliament, confirmed by the Glorious Revolution. In the other case colonial governors were still trying to wield prerogatives that the king had lost in England. The assemblies knew this; they also knew the arguments for the "rights" and "liberties" of the people and their legislative bodies, and against the dangers of despotic power. A further anomaly in the situation was the undefined relationship of the colonies to Parliament. The colonies had been created by authority of the crown and their governmental connections ran to the crown, yet Parliament on occasion passed laws that applied to the colonies and were tacitly accepted by the colonies.

By the early eighteenth century the assemblies, like Parliament, held two important strands of power—and they were perfectly aware of the parallel. First, they held the power of the purse strings in their right to vote on taxes and expenditures. Second, they held the power to initiate legislation and not merely, as in the early history of some colonies, the right to act on proposals from the governor and council. These powers they used to pull other strands of power into their hands when the chance presented itself. Governors were held on a tight leash by the assembly's control of salaries, his and others, which were voted annually and sometimes not at all. Only in four southern colonies did governors have some freedom from this coercion. In South Carolina and Georgia they were paid from crown funds, and in North Carolina and Virginia out of permanent funds drawn from colonial revenues.

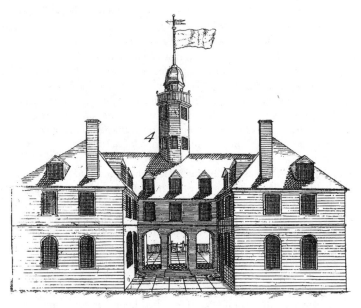

The Virginia Capitol, depicted here in the eighteenth century, "was an architectural representation of the British constitution as adapted for use in the colonies." In the upper story of one wing sat the King's Council, the upper legislative house. Immediately below, the governor and council sat as the General Court, the highest judicial body. Across from the Court sat the House of Burgesses, the body of elected representatives.

But even in those colonies the assemblies controlled other appropriations, and by refusing to vote money forced governors to yield up parts of the traditional executive powers. Assemblies, because they controlled finance, demanded and often got the right to name tax collectors and treasurers. Then they stretched the claim to cover public printers, Indian agents, supervisors of public works and services, and other officers of the government. By specifying how appropriations should be spent, they played an important role even in military affairs and Indian relations, as well as other matters. Indeed, in the choice of certain administrative officers they pushed their power beyond that of Parliament in England, where appointment remained a crown prerogative.

All through the eighteenth century the assemblies expanded their power and influence, sometimes in conflict with the governors, sometimes in harmony with them, and often in the course of routine business passing laws and setting precedents the collective significance of which neither they nor the imperial authorities fully recognized. Once established, however, these laws and practices became fixed principles, parts of the "constitution" of the colonies. Self-government became first a habit, then a "right."

SPANISH AMERICA IN DECLINE   By the start of the eighteenth century, the Spanish ruled over a huge colonial empire spanning North America. Yet in fact their settlements in the borderlands north of Mexico were a colossal failure when compared to the colonies of the other European powers. In 1821, when Mexico declared its independence without firing a shot and the Spanish withdrew from North America, the most populated Hispanic settlement, Santa Fe, had only 6,000 residents. The next largest, San Antonio and St. Augustine, totaled only 1,500 each.

The Spanish failed to create thriving North American colonies for several reasons. Perhaps the most obvious was that the region lacked the gold and silver as well as the large native populations that attracted Spanish priorities to Mexico and Peru. In addition, the Spanish were distracted by their need to control the perennial unrest in Mexico among the natives and *mestizos* (people of mixed Indian and European ancestry). Moreover, those Spaniards who led the colonization effort in the borderlands were so preoccupied with military and religious exploitation that they never devoted enough attention to the factors necessary for producing viable settlements with self-sustaining economies. Only rarely, for example, did the Spanish send many women to their colonies in North America. Even more important, they never understood that the main factor in creating successful communities was a thriving market economy. Instead they concentrated on building missions and forts and looking—in vain—for gold. Where the French and the English built their Indian policies around trading relationships (including firearms), Spain emphasized conversion to Catholicism and stubbornly adhered to an anachronistic mercantilism that forbade manufacturing within the colonies and strictly limited trade with the natives.

NEW FRANCE   Permanent French settlement in the New World differed considerably from the Spanish and English models. The French settlers were predominantly male but much smaller in number than the English and Spanish migrations. About 40,000 French colonists came to the New World over the seventeenth and eighteenth centuries. Interestingly enough, the relatively small French population proved to be an advantage in that their small numbers forced the French to develop cooperative relationships with the Indians. Unlike the English settlers, the French established trading outposts rather than farms, mostly along the St. Lawrence River, on lands not claimed by Indians. They thus did

Samuel de Champlain firing his arquebus at a group of Mohawks, killing two chiefs (1609).

not have to confront initial hostility. In addition, the French served as effective mediators between rival Great Lakes tribes. This diplomatic role gave them much more local authority and influence than their English counterparts along the Atlantic coast, who disdained such mediation. The heavily outnumbered and disproportionately male French settlers sought to integrate themselves with Indian culture rather than to displace it and encouraged the Indians to embrace Catholicism and hate the English. This more fraternal bond between the French and the Indians proved to be a source of strength in the wars with the English that enabled New France to survive until 1760, despite the lopsided disparity in numbers between the two colonial powers.

French exploration and colonization began the year after the Jamestown landing, far away in Québec, where the explorer Samuel de Champlain landed on the shores of the St. Lawrence River in 1608, and three years later at Port Royal, Acadia (later Nova Scotia). While Acadia remained a remote outpost, New France expanded well beyond Québec, from which Champlain pushed his explorations up the great river and into the Great Lakes as far as Lake Huron, and southward to the lake that still bears his name. There, in 1609, he joined a band of Huron and Ottawa allies in a fateful encounter, fired his harquebus into the ranks of their Iroquois foes, and kindled a hatred that pursued New France to the end. Shortly afterward the Iroquois had a more friendly meeting with Henry Hudson near Albany and soon acquired their own firearms from Dutch, and later English, traders. Thenceforth the Iroquois stood as a buffer against any French designs to move toward the English of the middle colonies and as a constant menace on the flank of the French waterways to the interior.

Until his death in 1635 Champlain governed New France under a sequence of trading companies, the last being the Company of a Hundred Associates, which the king's minister, Cardinal Richelieu, formed in 1627 of men chosen for their close loyalty to the crown. The charter imposed a fatal weakness that hobbled New France to its end. The company won a profitable monopoly of the fur trade, but it had to limit the population to French Catholics. Neither the enterprising, seafaring Huguenots (French Protestants) of coastal France nor foreigners of any faith were allowed to populate the country. Great land grants went to persons who promised to bring settlers to work the land under feudal tenure. The colony therefore remained a scattered patchwork of dependent peasants, Jesuit missionaries, priests, soldiers, officials, and *coureurs de bois* (literally, runners of the woods), who ranged the interior in quest of furs.

In 1663 King Louis XIV and his chief minister, Jean Baptiste Colbert, changed New France into a royal colony and pursued a plan of consolidation and stabilization. Colbert dispatched new settlers, including shiploads of young women to lure disbanded soldiers and *coureurs de bois* into settled matrimony. He sent out tools and ani-

An Iroquois warrior in an eighteenth-century French etching.

Sketch of Fort Rémy, built in 1671.

mals for farmers, nets for fishermen, and tried to make New France self-sufficient in foodstuffs. The population grew from about 4,000 in 1665 to about 15,000 in 1690. Still, Louis de Baude, Count Frontenac, who was governor from 1672 to 1682 and 1689 to 1698, held to a grand vision of French empire in the interior, spurring on the fur traders and missionaries and converting their outposts into military stations in the wilderness: Fort Detroit appeared at the far end of Lake Erie, Fort Michilimackinac at the far end of Lake Huron.

FRENCH LOUISIANA   From the Great Lakes French explorers moved southward. In 1673 Louis Joliet and Père Marquette, a Jesuit priest, ventured into Lake Michigan, up the Fox River from Green Bay, then down the Wisconsin to the Mississippi, and on as far as the Arkansas River. Satisfied that the great river flowed to the Gulf of Mexico, they turned back for fear of meeting with Spaniards. Nine years later Robert Cavalier, Sieur de La Salle, went all the way to the Gulf and named the country Louisiana after the king.

Settlement of the Louisiana country finally began in 1699 when Pierre le Moyne, Sieur d'Iberville, landed a colony at Biloxi, Mississippi. The main settlement then moved to Mobile Bay and in 1710 to the present site of Mobile, Alabama. For nearly half a century the driving force in Louisiana was Jean Baptiste le Moyne, Sieur de Bienville, a younger brother of d'Iberville. Bienville arrived with the first settlers in 1699, when he was only eighteen, and left the colony for the last time in 1743, when he was sixty-two. Sometimes called the "Father of Louisiana," he served periodically as governor or acting governor and always as adviser during those years. In 1718 he founded New Orleans, which shortly thereafter became the capital. Louisiana, first a proprietary and then a corporate colony, became a royal province in 1732.

In contrast to the English colonies, French Louisiana grew haltingly in the first half of the eighteenth century. Its population in 1732 was only 2,000 whites and about 3,800 slaves. The sweltering climate and mosquito-infested environment enticed few new settlers. Poorly administered, dependent on imports for its sustenance, and expensive to defend, it became and continued throughout the century to be a financial liability to the French government. It never became the thriving trade center with the Spanish that its founders had envisioned.

"France in America had two heads," the historian Francis Parkman wrote, "one amid the snows of Canada, the other amid the canebrakes of Louisiana." The French thus had one enormous advantage: access to the great water routes that led to the heartland of the continent. In the Illinois region, scattered settlers began farming the fertile soil, and courageous priests established missions at places such as Terre Haute ("high land") and Des Moines ("some monks"). Because of geography as well as deliberate policy, however, French America remained largely a howling wilderness traversed by a mobile population of traders, trappers, missionaries—and, mainly, Indians. In 1750 when the English colonials numbered about 1.5 million, the French population was no more than 80,000.

Yet in some ways the French had the edge on the British. They offered European goods in return for furs, encroached far less upon Indian lands, and so won allies against the English who came to possess the land. French governors could mobilize for action without any worry about quarreling assemblies or ethnic and religious diversity. The British may have had the greater population, but their separate colonies often worked at cross purposes. The middle colonies, for instance, protected by the Iroquois buffer, could afford to ignore the French threat—for a long time at least. Whenever conflict threatened, colonial assemblies seized the moment to extract new concessions from their governors. Colonial merchants, who built up a trade supplying foodstuffs to the French, persisted in smuggling supplies even in war time.

The Colonial Wars

French and British colonists clashed from the beginning of settlement. The Acadians fought with English settlers in Maine. Only a thin stretch of woods separated New England from Québec and Mon-

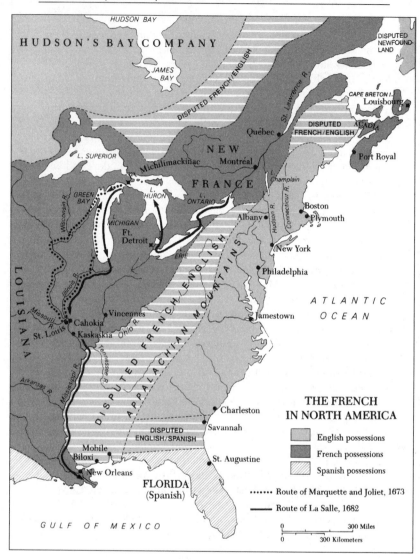

HUDSON BAY

HUDSON'S BAY COMPANY

JAMES BAY

DISPUTED NEWFOUND-LAND

DISPUTED FRENCH/ENGLISH

St. Lawrence R.

CAPE BRETON I.
Louisbourg

L. SUPERIOR

Québec

DISPUTED FRENCH/ENGLISH

ACADIA

Port Royal

Michilimackinac

NEW

Montréal

Champlain

GREEN BAY

L. HURON

FRANCE

L. ONTARIO

Wisconsin R.

L. MICHIGAN

Ft. Detroit

Boston

Albany

Plymouth

Hudson R.

Connecticut R.

ERIE

New York

Illinois R.

Philadelphia

Missouri R.

L O U I S I A N A

Vincennes

Cahokia

St. Louis

Kaskaskia

Ohio R.

Tennessee R.

Jamestown

**A T L A N T I C
O C E A N**

DISPUTED FRENCH/ENGLISH

APPALACHIAN MOUNTAINS

Arkansas R.

Mississippi R.

Charleston

Savannah

DISPUTED ENGLISH/SPANISH

Mobile

Biloxi

New Orleans

FLORIDA
(Spanish)

St. Augustine

**THE FRENCH
IN NORTH AMERICA**

English possessions

French possessions

Spanish possessions

······· Route of Marquette and Joliet, 1673

——— Route of La Salle, 1682

G U L F   O F   M E X I C O

| 0 | 300 Miles |
| 0 | 300 Kilometers |

tréal, and an English force briefly occupied Québec from 1629 to 1632. Between New York and Québec, Lake Champlain supplied an easy water route for invasion in either direction, but the Iroquois stood athwart the path. Farther south, the mountainous wilderness widened into an almost impenetrable buffer. On the northernmost flank, the isolated Hudson Bay Company offered British competition for the fur trade of the interior, and both countries laid claim to Newfoundland. On the southernmost flank, the British and French jockeyed for position in the Caribbean sugar islands.

But for most of the seventeenth century the two continental empires developed in relative isolation from each other, and for most of that century the homelands remained at peace with each other. After the Restoration, Charles II and James II pursued a policy of friendship with Louis XIV—and secretly took pensions from His Catholic Majesty. The Glorious Revolution of 1688, however, worked an abrupt reversal in English diplomacy. William III, the new king, as leader of the Dutch Republic had fought a running conflict against the ambitions of Louis XIV in the Netherlands and the German Palatinate. His ascent to the throne brought England almost immediately into a Grand Coalition against Louis in the War of the League of Augsburg, sometimes called the War of the Palatinate and known in the colonies simply as King William's War (1689–1697).

This was the first of four great European and intercolonial wars over the next sixty-four years: the War of the Spanish Succession (Queen Anne's War, 1701–1713), the War of the Austrian Succession (King George's War, 1744–1748), and the Seven Years' War (the French and Indian War, which lasted nine years in America, 1754–1763). In all except the last, which the historian Lawrence Gipson called the "Great War for Empire," the battles in America were but a sideshow to greater battles in Europe, where British policy riveted on keeping a balance of power against the French. The alliances shifted from one fight to the next, but Britain and France were pitted against each other every time.

Thus for much of the century after the great Indian conflicts of 1676 the colonies were embroiled in wars and rumors of wars. Some war contractors got rich, but the effect on much of the population was devastating. New England, especially Massachusetts, suffered probably more than the rest, for it was closest to the centers of French population. It is estimated that 900 Boston men (about 2.5 percent of the eligible males) died in the fighting. This meant that the city was faced with assisting a large population of widows and orphans. Even more important, these prolonged conflicts had profound consequences for Britain that later would reshape the contours of its relationship with America. The wars with France led the English government to incur an enormous debt, establish a huge navy and a standing army, and excite a jingoist sense of nationalism. During the early eighteenth century these changes in British financial policy and political culture provoked critics to charge that traditional liberties were being usurped by a tyrannical central

EUROPEAN WARS ALSO FOUGHT IN NORTH AMERICA

European War	Major Participants	Colonial War	Dates	Treaty
War of the League of Augsburg (War of the Palatinate)	England and Holland *vs.* France	King William's War	1689–1697	Treaty of Ryswick (1697)
War of the Spanish Succession	England, Austria, and Holland *vs.* France and Spain	Queen Anne's War	1701–1713	Peace of Utrecht (1713)
War of the Austrian Succession	England and Austria *vs.* France and Prussia	King George's War	1744–1748	Treaty of Aix-la-Chapelle (1748)
Seven Years' War	England and Prussia *vs.* France, Spain, Austria, and Russia	French and Indian War	1754–1763	Peace of Paris (1763)

government. After the French and Indian War, American colonists began making the same point.

KING WILLIAM'S WAR   In King William's War scattered fighting occurred in the Hudson Bay posts, most of which fell to the French, and in Newfoundland, which fell to a French force under d'Iberville, soon to be the founder of Louisiana. The French aroused their Indian allies to join in scattered raids along the northern frontier. In Massachusetts, Captain William Phips, who was about to become the first royal governor, got up an expedition that took Acadia. Various expeditions against French Canada failed to coalesce, and the war finally degenerated into a series of frontier raids. It ended ingloriously with the Treaty of Ryswick (1697), which returned the colonies to their prewar status.

QUEEN ANNE'S WAR   Fighting resumed only five years later. The War of the Spanish Succession was known to the colonists as Queen Anne's War. It saw the French and Spanish allied against the English. This time the Iroquois, tired of fighting the French, remained neutral. The French respected New York's immunity from attack, largely because New Yorkers were such good trading partners. The brunt of this war therefore fell on New England and South Carolina. Between 1706 and 1713 a sporadic border war raged between South Carolina and Spanish Florida, the English with Yemassee and Creek allies taking the war nearly to St. Augustine.

South Carolina's Indian allies in fact constituted most of a force that responded to North Carolina's call for help in the Tuscarora War (1711–1713). The Tuscaroras, a numerous people who had long led a settled life in the tidewater, suddenly found their lands invaded in 1709 by German and Swiss settlers. The war began when the Tuscaroras assaulted the new settlements. It ended when slave merchants of South Carolina mobilized their Indian allies, killed about 1,000 Tuscaroras and enslaved another 700. The survivors found refuge in the north, where they became the sixth nation of the Iroquois Confederacy.

In New England the exposed frontier from Maine to Massachusetts suffered repeated raids during Queen Anne's War. In the winter of 1704 French and Indian forces sacked several Massachusetts villages. The settlers were either slaughtered or taken on desperate marches through the snow to captivity among the Indians or the Canadians.

In the complex Peace of Utrecht (1713) Louis XIV recognized British title to the Hudson Bay, Newfoundland, Acadia (now Nova Scotia), and St. Christopher, as well as the British claim to sovereignty over the Iroquois. (Nobody consulted the Iroquois.) The French renounced any

A view of Québec, the spires of its cathedrals and seminaries soaring high (1740s).

claim to special privileges in the commerce of Spanish or Portuguese America. Spain agreed not to transfer any of its American territory to a third party, and granted to the British the *asiento,* a contract for supplying Spanish America 4,800 slaves annually over a period of thirty years and the right to send one ship a year to the great fair at Porto Bello in Panama—concessions that opened the door for British smuggling, a practice that grew into a major cause of friction and, eventually, of renewed warfare.

In the South the frontier flared up once more shortly after the war. The former Yemassee and Creek allies, outraged by the continuing advance of settlement, attacked the Charleston colony. The Yemassee War of 1715 was the southern equivalent of King Philip's War in New England, a desperate struggle that threatened the colony's very existence. Once again, however, the Indians were unable to present a united front. The Cherokees remained neutral for the sake of their fur trade, and the defeated Yemassees retired into Florida or mingled with the Creeks who retreated beyond the Chattahoochee River, leaving open the country in which the new colony of Georgia appeared eighteen years later.

KING GEORGE'S WAR   In the generation of nominal peace after Queen Anne's War, the European colonists jockeyed for position, plotted with the Indians, and set up fortified posts at strategic points in the wilderness. The third great international war began in 1739 with a preliminary bout between England and Spain, called the War of Jenkins' Ear in honor of an English seaman who lost an ear to a Spanish soldier and exhibited the shriveled member as part of a campaign to arouse London against Spain's rudeness to smugglers.

The war began with a great British disaster, a grand expedition against Porto Bello in Panama, for which thousands of colonists volunteered and in which many died of yellow fever. One of the survivors, Lawrence Washington of Virginia, memorialized the event by naming his estate Mount Vernon after the ill-starred but popular admiral in command. Along the southern frontier the new colony of Georgia, less than a decade old, now served its purpose as a military buffer. General James Oglethorpe staged a raid on St. Augustine and later fought off Spanish counterattacks, but Charleston remained secure.

In 1744 France entered the war, which merged with another general European conflict, the War of the Austrian Succession, or King George's War in the colonies. Once again border raids flared along the northern frontier. Governor William Shirley of Massachusetts mounted an expedition against French Canada and conquered Fort Louisbourg on Cape Breton after a long siege. It was a costly conquest, but the war ended in stalemate. In the Treaty of Aix-la-Chapelle (1748) the British exchanged Louisbourg for Madras, which the French had taken in India.

Thereafter, the focus of attention turned to the Ohio Valley. French traders had moved westward to the Great Lakes and down the Mississippi, but the Ohio, with short portages from Lake Erie to its headwaters, would make a shorter connecting link for French America. During the 1740s, however, fur traders from Virginia and Pennsylvania had also begun to exploit that disputed region. Not far behind were the Pennsylvania and Virginia land speculators. "The English," one French agent warned the Indians, "are much less anxious to take away your peltries than to become masters of your lands." Pennsylvania, because of the Quaker impulse, gave less support to its speculators than Virginia, which laid claim to the country through a quirk in the 1609 charter that described boundaries leading "westward and Northwestward" to the South Sea; it was their northern boundary, they said, that led "Northwestward." Virginians had organized several land companies, most conspicuously the Ohio Company, to which the king granted 200,000 acres along the upper Ohio in 1749, with a promise of 300,000 more. The company forthwith dispatched a Pennsylvania frontiersman to seek out the best lands.

The French resolved to act before the British advance became a dagger pointed at the continental heartland. In 1749 French scouts proceeded down the Allegheny and Ohio Rivers to spy out the land, woo the Indians, and bury leaden plates with inscriptions stating the French claim. Engravings hardly made the soil French, but in 1753 a new governor, the Marquis Duquesne, arrived in Canada and set about making good on the claim with a chain of forts in the region.

THE FRENCH AND INDIAN WAR When news of these trespasses reached Williamsburg, Governor Dinwiddie sent out an emissary to warn off the French. An ambitious young adjutant-general of the Virginia militia, Major George Washington, whose older brothers owned a part of the

Ohio Company, volunteered for the mission. With a few companions Washington made his way to Fort Le Boeuf and returned with a polite but firm French refusal. Dinwiddie then sent a small force to erect a fort at the strategic fork where the Allegheny and Monongahela Rivers meet to form the great Ohio. No sooner had the English started than a larger French force appeared, ousted them, and proceeded to build Fort Duquesne on the same strategic site.

Meanwhile, Washington had been organizing a force of volunteers, and in the spring of 1754 he went out with an advance guard and a few Indian allies. Near Great Meadows they skirmished with a French detachment. Who fired first is unknown, and perhaps irrelevant, but it marked the first bloodshed of a long—and finally decisive —war that reached far beyond America. Washington retreated with his prisoners and hastily constructed a stockade, Fort Necessity, which soon fell under siege by a larger force from Fort Duquesne. On July 4, 1754, Washington surrendered and was permitted to withdraw with his survivors. With that disaster in the backwoods a great world war had begun, but Washington came out of it with his reputation intact—and he was world famous at the age of twenty-two.

Back in London the Board of Trade already had taken notice of the growing conflict in the backwoods and had called a meeting in Albany, New York, of commissioners from all the colonies as far south as Maryland to confer on precautions. The Albany Congress (June 19 to July 10, 1754), which was sitting when the first shots sounded at Great Meadows, ended with little accomplished. The delegates conferred with Iroquois chieftains and sent them away loaded with gifts in return

Benjamin Franklin's symbol of the need to unite the colonies against the French in 1754 would become popular again twenty years later, when the colonies faced a different threat.

THE SEVEN YEARS' WAR:
MAJOR CAMPAIGNS, 1754-1760

★ Battle site

0   200 Miles

0   200 Kilometers

for some halfhearted promises of support. The congress is remembered mainly for the Plan of Union worked out by a committee under Benjamin Franklin and adopted by unanimous vote of the commissioners. The plan called for a chief executive, a kind of supreme governor to be called the President-General of the United Colonies, appointed and supported by the crown, and a supreme assembly called the Grand Council, with forty-eight members chosen by the colonial assemblies. This federal body would oversee matters of defense, Indian relations, and trade and settlement in the West and would levy taxes to support its programs.

It must have been a good plan, Franklin reasoned, since the assemblies thought it gave too much power to the crown and the crown thought it gave too much to the colonies. At any rate the assemblies either rejected or ignored the plan. Only two substantive results came out of the congress. Its idea of a supreme commander for British forces in America was adopted, as was its advice that a New Yorker who was a friend of the Iroquois be made British superintendent of the northern Indians.

In London the government decided to force a showdown in America. In 1755 the British fleet captured Nova Scotia and expelled most of its French population. Some 5,000–7,000 Acadians who refused to take an oath of allegiance to the British crown were scattered through the colonies from Maine to Georgia. Impoverished and homeless, many of them desperately found their way to French Louisiana, where they became the Cajuns (a corruption of "Acadians") whose descendants still preserve elements of the French language along the remote bayous and in many urban centers.

The backwoods, however, became the scene of one British disaster after another over the next three years. In 1755 a new British commander-in-chief, General Edward Braddock, arrived in Virginia with two regiments of regulars. With the addition of some colonial troops, including George Washington as a volunteer staff officer, Braddock hacked a road through the wilderness from the upper Potomac to the vicinity of Fort Duquesne. Hauling heavy artillery to surround the French fort, along with a wagon train of supplies, Braddock's men achieved a great feat of military logistics and were on the verge of success when, seven miles from Fort Duquesne, the surrounding woods suddenly came alive with Indians and Frenchmen in Indian costume. Beset on three sides by concealed enemies, the British forces panicked and retreated in disarray, abandoning most of their artillery and supplies. Braddock lost his life in the encounter, and his second in command directed the remaining British regulars to the safety of Philadelphia.

A WORLD WAR   For two years war raged along the frontier without becoming the cause of war in Europe. In 1756, however, the colonial war merged with what became the Seven Years' War in Europe. There, Empress Maria Theresa of Austria, still brooding over the loss of territory in the previous conflict, worked a diplomatic revolution by bringing Austria's old enemy France, as well as Russia, into an alliance against Frederick the Great of Prussia. Britain, ever mindful of the European balance of power, now deserted Austria to ally with Frederick. The onset of war brought into office a new British government with the eloquent William Pitt as war minister. Pitt's ability and assurance ("I know that I can save England and no one else can") instilled confidence at home and abroad. Pitt committed his main forces to the war for overseas empire while providing subsidies to Frederick, who was desperately fighting off attacks from three sides.

Soon the force of British sea power began to cut off French reinforcements and supplies to the New World—and the trading goods with which they bought Indian allies. Pitt improved the British forces, gave command to young men of ability, and carried the battle to the enemy. In 1758 the tides began to turn. Fort Louisbourg fell. The Iroquois,

Amherst's attack on Louisbourg, July 1758, depicted on a French map.

sensing the turn of fortunes, pressed their dependents, the Delawares, to call off the frontier attacks on English settlements.

In 1759 the war reached its climax in a three-pronged offensive against the French in Canada, along what had become the classic invasion routes: via Niagara, Lake Champlain, and up the St. Lawrence. British forces were earmarked for each. On the Niagara expedition the British were joined by a group of Iroquois, and they captured Fort Niagara, which virtually cut the French lifeline to the interior. On Lake Champlain, General Jeffrey Amherst took Fort George and Fort Ticonderoga, then paused to refortify and await reinforcements for an advance northward.

Meanwhile, the most decisive battle was shaping up at Québec. There, in a set battle more like the warfare of Europe than the skirmishes of the backwoods, British forces waited out the French advance until it was within close range, then loosed a simultaneous volley followed by one more that devastated the French ranks—and ended French power in North America for all time. News of the victory reached London along with similar reports from India, where English forces had reduced French outposts one by one and established the base for an expanding British control of India. It was the *annus mirabilis,* the miraculous year 1759, during which Great Britain secured an empire on which the sun never set.

The war dragged on until 1763, but the rest was a process of mopping up. In the South, where little significant action had occurred, the

The decisive British assault on Québec (1759).

Cherokee nation flared into belated hostility. A force of British regulars and provincials broke Cherokee resistance in 1761. In the North, just as peace was signed, a chieftain of the Ottawas, Pontiac, conspired to confederate all the Indians of the frontier and launched a series of attacks that were not completely suppressed until 1764, after the backwoods had been ablaze for ten years.

In 1760 King George II died, and his grandson ascended to the throne as George III. George III decided to take a more active role than his Hanoverian predecessors. He resolved to seek peace and forced Pitt out of office. Pitt had wanted to carry the fight to the enemy by declaring war on Spain before the French could bring that other Bourbon monarchy into the conflict. He was forestalled, but Spain belatedly entered in 1761 and during the next year met the same fate as the French: in 1762 British forces took Manila in the Philippines and Havana in Cuba.

THE PEACE OF PARIS   The Peace of Paris of 1763 brought an end to the war. It was a peace that ended French power in North America and all but eliminated it in India. In America, Britain took all French North American possessions east of the Mississippi River and all of Spanish Florida. The English split it into two administrative districts, West Florida and East Florida, separated by the Appalachicola and Chattahoochee Rivers. The English invited the Spanish settlers to remain and practice their Catholic religion, but few accepted the offer. The Spanish king ordered them to evacuate the colony and provided free transportation to Spanish possessions in the Caribbean.

Within a year most of the Spaniards sold their property at bargain prices to English speculators and began an exodus to Cuba and Mexico.

In compensation for the loss of Florida, Spain received Louisiana from France. Unlike the Spanish in Florida, however, few of the French settlers left Louisiana after 1763. The French government encouraged them to stay and work with their new Spanish governors to create a bulwark against further English expansion. Instead, the French sought to subvert Spanish authority. In 1768 the French revolted against their Spanish rulers. The Spanish governor and his small contingent of soldiers fled the region. Fearful of irritating their ally, French officials refused to reestablish their claim to the colony. A year later Spanish forces reasserted their control over the recalcitrant colony and arrested the rebel leaders. Spain would hold title to Louisiana for nearly four decades, but would never succeed in erasing its French roots. The French-born settlers always outnumbered the Spanish.

The loss of Louisiana left France with no territory on the continent of North America. In the West Indies, France gave up Tobago, Dominica,

With Québec in the background, France kneels before a victorious Britain (1763).

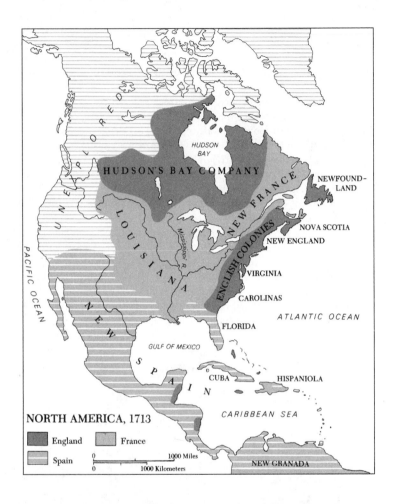

NORTH AMERICA, 1713

England   France

Spain

0   1000 Miles

0   1000 Kilometers

Grenada, and St. Vincent. British power reigned supreme over North America east of the Mississippi.

But a fatal irony would pursue the British victory. In gaining Canada the British government put in motion a train of events that would end twenty years later with the loss of all the rest of British North America. France, humiliated in 1763, thirsted for revenge. In London, Benjamin Franklin, agent for the colony of Pennsylvania (1764–1775), found the French minister inordinately curious about America and suspected him of wanting to ignite the coals of controversy. Less than three years after Franklin left London, and only fifteen years after the conquest of New France, he would be in Paris arranging an alliance on behalf of Britain's rebellious colonists.

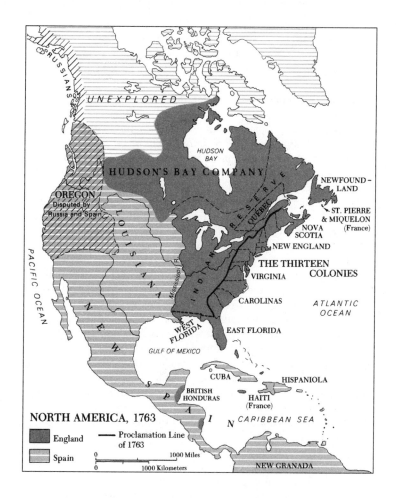

NORTH AMERICA, 1763

England

Spain

Proclamation Line of 1763

0   1000 Miles

0   1000 Kilometers

FURTHER READING

For greater depth on the structure of colonial government and the global context of colonial development, see the fourth volume of Charles M. Andrews's *The Colonial Period of American History* (4 vols., 1934–1938), which details the evolution of the British imperial system. Lawrence H. Gipson's *The British Empire before the American Revolution* (15 vols., 1936–1970) places the British colonies in the context of European imperial politics.

The economics motivating colonial policies are covered in John J. McCusker and Russell R. Menard's *The Economy of British America, 1607–1789* (1985).° The problems of colonial customs administration are explored in Michael G. Hall's *Edward Randolph and the American Colonies, 1676–1703* (1960).

The effect of imperial policies on colonial politics is covered in Alison G. Olson's *Anglo-American Politics, 1600–1775* (1973), which traces the rise of party-like factions on the provincial level. Jack P. Greene's *The Quest for Power* (1963)° describes the politics of the southern colonies, and Richard P. Johnson's *Adjustment to Empire* (1981) examines New England. The Andros crisis and related topics are treated in David S. Lovejoy's *The Glorious Revolution in America* (1972) and Jack M. Sosin's *English America and the Revolution of 1688* (1982). Stephen S. Webb's *The Governors-General* (1979) argues that the crown was more concerned with military administration than with commercial regulation, and Webb's *1676: The End of American Independence* (1984)° shows how the Indian wars undermined the autonomy of colonial governments.

Historians of early Indian wars have taken several different approaches to the topic. Richard Slotkin's *Regeneration through Violence* (1973)° links the colonists' treatment of Indians with later national character traits. Alden T. Vaughan defends the treatment of Indians by the Puritans in *New England Frontier: Puritans and Indians, 1620–1675* (1965).° Francis Jennings counters this thesis in *The Invasion of America* (1975).° See also Jennings's *The Ambiguous Iroquois Empire* (1984) and *Empire of Fortune: Crowns, Colonies and Tribes in the Seven Years War in America* (1988) and Richard Aquila's *The Iroquois Restoration: Iroquois Diplomacy on the Colonial Frontier* (1983). Gregory Evans Dowd describes the unification efforts of Indians east of the Mississippi in *A Spirited Resistance: The North American Indian Struggle for Unity, 1745–1815* (1992).

A good introduction to the imperial phase of the colonial conflicts is Howard H. Peckham's *The Colonial Wars, 1689–1762* (1964). More analytical is Douglas Leach's *Arms for Empire: A Military History of the British Colonies in North America* (1973). Fred Anderson's *A People's Army* (1984)° is a social history of the Seven Years' War. See also the majestic works of Francis Parkman, *France and England in North America;* the most rewarding single part is *Montcalm and Wolfe* (2 vols., 1884).

°These books are available in paperback editions.

5 &

FROM EMPIRE TO INDEPENDENCE

THE HERITAGE OF WAR

Seldom if ever since the days of Elizabeth had England thrilled with such pride as in the closing years of the Great War for Empire. In 1760 the vigorous, young George III ascended to the throne and confirmed once again the Hanoverian succession. And in 1763 the Peace of Paris, even though it brought England less than some would have liked, confirmed the possession of a great new empire spanning the globe. Most important, the Peace of Paris effectively ended the French imperial domain in North America. This in turn influenced the future development of the sprawling region between the Appalachian Mountains and the Mississippi River and from the Gulf of Mexico to Hudson's Bay. The maturing mainland colonies began to experience dynamic agricultural and commercial growth that enormously increased their importance to the British economy. Yet the North American colonies remained both extraordinarily diverse in composition and outlook and peculiarly averse to cooperative efforts. That they would manage to unify themselves and declare independence in 1775 was indeed surprising.

In 1763 the colonists shared in the ebullience of patriotism generated by the great victory over the French. But the moment of euphoria was all too brief. It served to mask festering resentments and new problems that were the heritage of the war. Underneath the pride in the British Empire an American nationalism was maturing. Ben Franklin foresaw a time, he said, when the capital of the British Empire would be on the Hudson instead of the Thames. Americans were beginning to think and speak of themselves more as Americans than as English or British. With a great new land to exploit, they could look to the future with confidence.

George III, at age thirty-three, the young king of a victorious empire.

Many Americans had a new sense of importance after starting and fighting a vast world war with such success. Some harbored resentment, justified or not, at the haughty air of British soldiers and slights received at their hands, and many in the early stages of the war lost their awe of British soldiers, who were at such a loss in frontier fighting. One Massachusetts soldier expressed some puzzlement that he should be expected to "stand still to be shot at" in the field rather than take cover.

Recent studies of the Seven Years' War reveal that many Americans became convinced as well of their moral superiority to their British allies. Ninety percent of the New England provincial soldiers were probably volunteers, and most of them were sons of moderately prosperous and tenaciously pious farm families. The proportion of volunteers was lower in New York and much lower in Virginia until pay rates and bounties were raised in a successful effort to boost recruitment.

At least one-third of military-age New England males participated in the fighting. For them, army life was both a revelation and an opportunity. From their isolated farms they converged to form huge army camps—hives of thousands of strangers living in overcrowded and disease-infested conditions. Although they admired the courage and discipline of British redcoats under fire, New Englanders abhorred the carefree cursing, whoring, and Sabbath breaking they observed among British troops. But most upsetting were the daily "shrieks and cries" resulting from the brutal punishments imposed by the British leaders on their wayward men. Minor offenses might earn hundreds of lashes, and a thousand was the standard punishment for desertion. One American soldier recorded in his diary in 1759 that "there was a man whipped to death belonging to the Light Infantry. They say he had twenty-five lashes after he was dead." The war thus heightened the New Englanders' sense of their separate identity and of their greater worthiness to be God's chosen people. The Puritan utopia might be a lost cause, but the Puritan ideal remained resilient.

Imperial forces nevertheless had borne the brunt of the war and had won it for the colonists, who had supplied men and materials, sometimes reluctantly, and who persisted in trading with the enemy. Molasses in the French West Indies, for instance, continued to draw New England ships like flies. The trade was too important for the colonists to give up, but was more than Pitt could tolerate. Along with naval patrols, one important means of disrupting this trade was the use of "writs of assistance," general search warrants that allowed officers to enter any place during daylight hours to seek evidence of illegal trade. In 1760 Boston merchants hired James Otis to fight the writs in the courts. He lost, but in the process advanced the provocative argument that any act of Parliament that authorized such "instruments of slavery" violated the British constitution and was therefore void. This was a very radical idea for its time. Otis sought to overturn a major tenet of the English legal system, namely that acts of Parliament were by their very nature constitutional.

Neither at Albany in 1754 nor later in the war had the colonies been able to form a concerted plan of action. They had relied on the imperial authorities to name a commander-in-chief, to formulate strategy, to bear most of the cost, and to set up superintendents of Indian affairs north and south. The assemblies had used the exigencies of war, though, to extract still more power from the governors and turn themselves more than ever into little parliaments.

The peace that secured an empire also laid upon the British ministry a burden of new problems. How should they manage the defense and governance of the new possessions? What should be done about the western lands inhabited by Indians but coveted by whites? How were they to service an unprecedented debt built up during the war and bear the new burdens of administration and defense? And—the thorniest problem of all, as it turned out—what role should the colonies play in all this? The problems were of a magnitude and complexity to challenge men of the greatest statemanship and vision, but those qualities were rare among the ministers of George III.

British Politics

In the British politics of the day nearly everybody called himself a Whig, even King George. Whig had been the name given to those who opposed James II, led the Glorious Revolution of 1688, and secured the Protestant Hanoverian succession in 1714. The Whigs were the champions of liberty and parliamentary supremacy, but with the passage of time Whiggism had drifted into complacency. The dominant group of landholding Whig families was concerned mostly with the pursuit of personal place and advantage and with local questions rather than great issues of statecraft. In the absence of party organization, parliamentary politics hinged on factions bound together by personal loyalties, family connections, and local interests, and on the pursuit of royal patronage.

In the administration of government, an inner "cabinet" of the king's ministers had been supplanting the unwieldy Privy Council as the center of power since the Hanoverian succession. The kings still had the prerogative of naming their ministers. They used it to form coalitions of men who controlled enough factions in the House of Commons to command majorities for the government's measures, though the king's ministers were still technically responsible to the king rather than to parliamentary majorities. George III resolved to take a more active role in the process than the first two Georges, who had abandoned initiative to the great Whig families—George I in part because he barely spoke English.

Throughout the 1760s the king turned first to one and then to another leader, ministries came and went, and the government fell into instability just as the new problems of empire required creative solutions. Ministries rose and fell because somebody offended the king or because somebody's friend failed to get a job. Colonial policy remained marginal to the chief concerns of British politics. The result was inconsistency and vacillation followed by stubborn inflexibility.

WESTERN LANDS

No sooner was peace arranged in 1763 than events thrust the problem of the western lands upon the government in an acute form. The Indians of the Ohio region, skeptical that their French friends were helpless and fully expecting the reentry of English settlers, grew restless and receptive to the warnings of Pontiac, chief of the Ottawas. In May 1763 Pontiac's effort to seize Fort Detroit was betrayed and failed, but the western tribes joined his campaign to reopen frontier warfare and within a few months wiped out every British post in the Ohio region except Detroit and Fort Pitt. A relief force lifted the siege of Fort Pitt and Pontiac abandoned the attack on Detroit, but the outlying settlements suffered heavy losses before British forces could stop the attacks. Pontiac himself did not agree to peace until 1766.

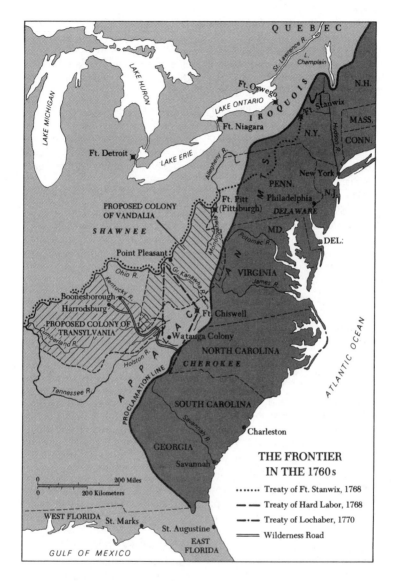

THE FRONTIER
IN THE 1760s

· · · · · · Treaty of Ft. Stanwix, 1768
— — Treaty of Hard Labor, 1768
—·— Treaty of Lochaber, 1770
═══ Wilderness Road

THE PROCLAMATION OF 1763   To keep the peace and to keep earlier promises to the Delawares and Shawnees, the ministers in London postponed further settlement. The immediate need was to stop Pontiac's warriors and reassure the Indians. There were influential fur traders, moreover, who preferred to keep the wilderness as a game preserve. The pressure for expansion into Indian-held territory might ultimately prove irresistible—British and American speculators were already dazzled by the prospects—but there would be no harm in a pause while things settled down and a new policy evolved. The king's ministers therefore brought forward, and the king signed, the Royal Proclamation of 1763. The order drew a Proclamation Line along the crest of the Appalachians beyond which settlers were forbidden to go and colonial governors were forbidden to authorize surveys or issue land grants. It also established the new British colonies of Quebec and East and West Florida, the last two consisting mainly of small settlements at St. Augustine and St. Marks, respectively, now peopled mainly by British garrisons.

The line did not long remain intact. In 1768 the chief royal agents for Indian affairs north and south negotiated two treaties (Fort Stanwix and Hard Labor) by which the Iroquois and Cherokees gave up their claims to lands in the Ohio region—a strip in western New York, a large area of southwestern Pennsylvania, and between the Ohio and Tennessee Rivers farther south. In 1770, by the Treaty of Lochaber, the Cherokees agreed to move the line below the Ohio River still farther westward. Land speculators, including Benjamin Franklin and a number of British investors, soon formed a syndicate and sought a vast domain covering most of present West Virginia and eastern Kentucky, where they proposed to establish the colony of Vandalia. The Board of Trade lent its support, but the formalities were not completed before Vandalia vanished in the revolutionary crisis.

SETTLERS PUSH WEST   Regardless of the formalities, hardy settlers pushed on over the Appalachian ridges; by 1770 the town of Pittsburgh had twenty log houses, and a small village had appeared on the site of Wheeling. In 1769 another colony was settled on the Watauga River by immigrants from southwestern Virginia, soon joined by settlers from North Carolina. The Watauga colony turned out to be within the limits of North Carolina, but so far removed from other settlements that it became virtually a separate republic under the Watauga Compact of 1772; North Carolina took it into the new district of Washington in 1776.

Another opening came south of the Ohio River into the dark and bloody ground of Kentucky, which had been something of a neutral hunting preserve shared by the northern and southern tribes. The Shawnees, who lived north of the Ohio, still claimed rights there despite the Iroquois and Cherokee concessions. In 1774 conflicts on the northwestern frontier of Virginia erupted into full-scale battles that forced the Shawnees to surrender their claims. Judge Richard Henderson of North Carolina formed a plan to settle the area. He organized the Transylvania Company in 1774, and in 1775 bought from the Cherokees a

Daniel Boone Escorting Settlers through the Cumberland Gap, *by George Caleb Bingham.*

dubious title to the land between the Kentucky and Cumberland Rivers. Next he sent out a band of men under the most famous frontiersman of them all, Daniel Boone, to cut the Wilderness Road from the upper Holston River via the Cumberland Gap in southwestern Virginia on up to the Kentucky River. Along this road settlers moved up to Boonesborough, and Henderson set about organizing a government for his colony of Transylvania. But his claim was weak. Transylvania sent a delegation to the Continental Congress, which refused to receive it, and in 1776 Virginia responded to a petition from the Harrodsburg settlers and organized much of present Kentucky into a county of Virginia.

GRENVILLE AND THE STAMP ACT

GRENVILLE'S COLONIAL POLICY Just as the Proclamation of 1763 was being drafted, a new ministry had begun to grapple with the problems of imperial finances. The new chief minister, George Grenville, first lord of the Treasury, was much like the king: industrious, honest, meticulous, and obtuse. Grenville took for granted the need for redcoats to defend the frontier, although the colonies had been left mostly to their own devices before 1754. He also wanted to keep a large army in America to avoid a rapid demobilization that would retire a large number of influential officers and thereby provoke political criticism at home. But he faced sharply rising costs for American defense, on top of an already

George Grenville, first lord of the Treasury, whose tax policy aroused colonial opposition.

staggering debt. He had already tried to find new revenues at home, one result being a cider tax so unpopular that it helped to drive him briefly out of office. It would not be the last time that British or American officials would learn that taxes on drink, fortified or otherwise, stirred deadly passions.

Because there was a large tax burden at home and a much lighter one in the colonies, Grenville reasoned that the Americans were obligated to share the cost of their own defense. He also learned that the American customs service was grossly inefficient. Evasion and corruption were rampant, and the service needed tightening. Grenville directed absentee customs agents to pack themselves off to America and cease hiring deputies. He issued stern orders to colonial officials and set the navy to patrolling the coasts. In Parliament he secured an Act for the Encouragement of Officers Making Seizures (1763), which set up a new maritime or vice-admiralty court in Halifax with jurisdiction over all the colonies, a court that had no juries of colonists sympathetic to smugglers. The old habits of salutary neglect in the enforcement of the Navigation Acts were coming to an end, causing no little annoyance to American shippers.

Strict enforcement of the old Molasses Act of 1733 posed a serious threat to New England's mercantile prosperity, which in turn created markets for British goods. The sixpence-per-gallon duty had been set prohibitively high, not for purposes of revenue but to prevent trade with the French sugar islands. Yet the rum distilleries consumed more molasses than the British West Indies provided, and as the governor of Massachusetts wrote to the king: "Even illegal trade, where the balance

is in favor of British subjects, makes its final return to Great Britain."
Grenville recognized that the sixpence duty, if enforced, would be
ruinous to a major colonial enterprise. So he put through a new Revenue Act of 1764, commonly known as the Sugar Act, which cut the
duty in half, from sixpence to three pence per gallon. This, he believed,
would reduce the temptation to smuggle or to bribe the customs officers. In addition the Sugar Act levied new duties on imports of foreign
textiles, wines, coffee, indigo, and sugar. The act, Grenville estimated,
would bring in about £45,000 a year that would go "toward defraying
the necessary expenses of defending, protecting, and securing, the said
colonies and plantations." For the first time Parliament had adopted
duties frankly designed to raise revenues in the colonies and not merely
intended to regulate trade.

Another of Grenville's new regulatory measures had an important
impact on the colonies: the Currency Act of 1764. The colonies faced a
chronic shortage of hard money, which kept going out to pay debts in
England. To meet the shortage, they resorted to issuing their own paper
money. British creditors, however, feared payment in such a depreciated currency. To alleviate their fears, Parliament in 1751 had forbidden
the New England colonies to make their currency legal tender. Now
Grenville extended the prohibition to all the colonies. The result was a

The Great Financier, or British Economy for the Years 1763, 1764, 1765.
*A cartoon critical of Grenville's tax policies. America, depicted as an
Indian (at left), groans under the burden of new taxes.*

decline in the value of existing paper money, since nobody was obligated to accept it in payment of debts, even in the colonies. The deflationary impact of the Currency Act, combined with new duties and stricter enforcement, delivered a severe shock to a colonial economy already suffering a postwar business decline.

THE STAMP ACT   But Grenville's new plan to make Americans pay for British expenses remained incomplete. The Sugar Act would defray only a fraction of the cost of maintaining the 10,000 soldiers to be stationed along the western frontier. He had in mind still another measure to raise money in America, a stamp tax. Early in 1765 he presented his plan to agents of the colonies in London. They protested unanimously, but had no response to his request for an alternative. And neither he nor they seemed to have any inkling of the storm it would arouse. Benjamin Franklin, representing four colonies, even proposed one of his friends as a stamp agent.

On February 13, 1765, Grenville laid his proposal before Parliament. It aroused little interest or debate. Only three speeches were delivered in opposition, but one of them included a fateful phrase. Colonel Isaac Barré, who had served with Wolfe at Québec, said that British agents sent out to the colonies had "caused the blood of these sons of liberty to recoil within them." Nevertheless the act passed the Commons easily. The act created revenue stamps and required that they be fixed to printed matter and legal documents of all kinds: newspapers, pamphlets, broadsides, almanacs, bonds, leases, deeds, licenses, insurance policies, ship clearances, college diplomas, even dice and playing cards. The requirement would go into effect on November 1, 1765.

In March 1765 Grenville completed his new system of colonial regulations when he put through the Quartering Act. In effect it was still another tax. This act required the colonies to supply British troops with provisions and to provide them with barracks or submit to their use of inns and vacant buildings. It applied to all colonies, but affected mainly New York, headquarters of the British forces.

THE IDEOLOGICAL RESPONSE   The cumulative effect of Grenville's measures raised colonial suspicions to a fever. Unwittingly, this plodding minister of a plodding king had stirred up a storm of protest and set in motion a profound exploration of English traditions and imperial relations. The radical ideas of the minority "Real Whigs" slowly began to take hold in the colonies. These ideas derived from various sources but above all from John Locke's justification of the Glorious Revolution, his *Two Treatises on Government* (1690). Locke and other "Real Whigs" viewed English history as a struggle by Parliament to preserve life, liberty, and property against royal tyranny.

Their religious heritage and what Patrick Henry called "the lamp of experience" also convinced them that human nature is corruptible and lusts after power. The safeguard against abuses, in the view of those in England who called themselves "Real Whigs," was not to rely on human goodness but to check power with power so as to preserve individual liberty. And the British constitution had embodied these principles in a mixed government of kings, lords, and commons, each serving as a check on the others. Even on the continent of Europe enlightened philosophers looked with admiration upon English liberties. A character in a Mozart opera announced: "I am an Englishwoman, born to freedom." The French writer Montesquieu, in his *Spirit of the Laws,* mingled the idea of a mixed government (king, lords, commons) with his own notion of the separation of powers (executive, legislative, judicial). The colonists, like Montesquieu, embraced the Enlightenment philosophy of natural law and natural rights. But if the Enlightenment found a place in their minds, the Real Whig interpretation of history and human nature was built into their bones. In the end it saved them from the facile optimism and the pursuit of utopia that would lure the French revolutionaries into the horrors of the Terror.

But in 1764 and 1765 the colonists felt that Grenville had loosed upon them the very engines of tyranny from which Parliament had rescued England in the seventeenth century, and by imposition of that very Parliament. A standing army was the historic ally of despots, and now with the French gone and Pontiac subdued, several thousand British soldiers remained in the colonies. For what purpose—to protect the colonists or to subdue them? It was beginning to seem clear that it was the latter. Among the fundamental rights of English people were trial by jury and the presumption of innocence, but the new vice-admiralty courts excluded juries and put the burden of proof on the defendant. Most important, Englishmen had the right to be taxed only by their elected representatives. Parliament claimed that privilege in England, and the colonial assemblies had long exercised it in America. Now Parliament was usurping the assemblies' power of the purse strings.

THE QUESTION OF REPRESENTATION   In a flood of colonial pamphlets, speeches, and resolutions, debate on the Stamp Act turned mainly on the point expressed in a slogan familiar to all Americans: "no taxation without representation," a cry that had been raised years before in response to the Molasses Act of 1733. In 1764 James Otis, now a popular leader in the Massachusetts assembly, set forth the argument in a pamphlet, *The Rights of the British Colonists Asserted and Proved.* Grenville had one of his subordinates prepare an answer, which developed the ingenious theory of "virtual representation." If the colonies had no vote in Parliament, neither did most Englishmen who lived in boroughs that had developed since the last apportionment. Large cities had grown up that had no right to elect a member, while old boroughs with little or no population still returned members. Nevertheless, each member of Parliament represented the interests of the whole country and indeed the whole empire. Charleston, South Carolina, for instance, had fully as much representation as Manchester, England.

Many colonial critics considered virtual representation nonsense, justified neither by logic nor by their own experience. In America, to be sure, the apportionment of assemblies failed to keep pace with the westward movement of population, but it was based more nearly on population and—in contrast to British practice—each member was expected to live in the district he represented. In a pamphlet widely circulated during 1765, Daniel Dulany, a young lawyer of Maryland, suggested that even if the theory had any validity for England, where the interests of electors might be closely tied to those of nonelectors, it had none for colonists 3,000 miles away, whose interests differed and whose distance made it impossible for them to influence members of Parliament.

PROTEST IN THE COLONIES   Soon after passage of the Stamp Act, Benjamin Franklin wrote from London to a radical friend in Philadelphia: "We might as well have hindered the sun's setting. But since 'tis down . . . let us make as good a night of it as we can." In reply, his friend predicted "the works of darkness" in the night. The Stamp Act became the chief target of colonial protest. Unlike the Sugar Act, which affected mainly New England, the Stamp Act imposed a burden on all the colonists who did any kind of business. And it affected most of all the articulate elements in the community: merchants, planters, lawyers, printer-editors—all strategically placed to influence opinion.

Through the spring and summer of 1765 popular resentment found outlet in mass meetings, parades, bonfires, and other demonstrations. To be sure, only a minority engaged in such public protests. They included farmers, artisans, laborers, businessmen, dock workers, and seamen alarmed at the disruption of business. Lawyers, editors, and merchants such as Christopher Gadsden of Charleston and John Hancock of Boston took the lead or lent support. North Carolina's governor reported the mobs to be composed of "gentlemen and planters." The militants began to assume a name adopted from Colonel Barré's speech: Sons of Liberty. They met underneath "Liberty Trees"—in Boston a great elm on Hanover Square, in Charleston a live oak. One day in mid-August, nearly three months before the effective date of the Stamp Act, an effigy of Boston's stamp agent swung from the Liberty Tree. In the evening a mob carried it through the streets, destroyed the stamp office, and used the wood to burn the effigy. Somewhat later another mob sacked the homes of Lieutenant-Governor Thomas

In protest of the Stamp Act, which was to take effect the next day, the
Pennsylvania Journal *appeared with the skull and crossbones on its*
masthead.

Hutchinson and the local customs officer. Thoroughly shaken, the
Boston stamp agent resigned his commission, and stamp agents
throughout the colonies were hounded out of office. Loyalists deplored
such riotous violence, arguing that the American rebels were behaving
more tyrannically than the British.

By November 1, its effective date, the Stamp Act was a dead letter.
Business went on without the stamps. Newspapers appeared with a skull
and crossbones in the corner where the stamp belonged. After passage
of the Sugar Act a movement had begun to boycott British goods. Now
colonists adopted non-importation agreements to exert pressure on
British merchants. Americans knew that they had become a major market for British products. By shutting off imports, they could exercise
real leverage. Homegrown sage and sassafras took the place of British
tea. Homespun garments became the fashion as symbols of colonial
defiance. In this regard, the non-importation movement offered landmark opportunities for women to participate in political agitation.

The widespread protests encouraged the idea of colonial unity, as
colonists discovered that they had more in common with each other
than with London. In May, long before the mobs went into action, the
Virginia House of Burgesses had struck the first blow against the Stamp
Act in the Virginia Resolves, a series of resolutions inspired by young
Patrick Henry's "torrents of sublime eloquence." Virginians, the
burgesses declared, were entitled to the rights of Englishmen, and En-

glishmen could be taxed only by their own representatives. Virginians, moreover, had always been governed by laws passed with their own consent. Newspapers spread the resolutions throughout the colonies, along with even more radical statements that were kept out of the final version, and other assemblies hastened to copy Virginia's example. In June, 1765, the Massachusetts House of Representatives issued a circular letter inviting the various assemblies to send delegates to confer in New York on appeals for relief from the king and Parliament.

Nine responded, and from October 7 to 25 the Stamp Act Congress of twenty-seven delegates conferred and issued expressions of colonial sentiment: a Declaration of the Rights and Grievances of the Colonies, a petition to the king for relief, and a petition to Parliament for repeal of the Stamp Act. The delegates acknowledged that the colonies owed a "due subordination" to Parliament and recognized its right to regulate colonial trade, but they questioned Parliament's right to levy taxes, which were a free gift granted by the people through their representatives.

REPEAL OF THE ACT   The storm had scarcely broken before Grenville's ministry was out of office, dismissed not because of the colonial turmoil but because they had fallen out with the king over the appointment of offices. In July 1765 the king installed a new minister, the marquis of Rockingham, leader of the "Rockingham Whigs," the "Old Whig" faction, which included people who sympathized with the colonists' views. Pressure from British merchants who feared the economic consequences of the non-importation movement bolstered Rockingham's resolve to repeal the Stamp Act, but he needed to move carefully in order to win a majority. Simple repeal was politically impossible without some affirmation of parliamentary authority. When Parliament assembled early in the year, William Pitt demanded that the Stamp Act be repealed "absolutely, totally, and immediately," but urged that Britain's authority over the colonies "be asserted in as strong terms as possible," except on the point of taxation. Rockingham steered a cautious course, and seized upon the widespread but false impression that Pitt accepted the principle of "external" taxes on trade but rejected "internal" taxes within the colonies. Benjamin Franklin, summoned before Parliament for interrogation in what was probably a rehearsed performance, helped to further the false impression that this was the colonists' view as well, an impression easily refuted by reference to the colonial resolutions of the previous year.

In March 1766 Parliament repealed the Stamp Tax, but at the same time passed the Declaratory Act, which asserted the full power of Parliament to make laws binding the colonies "in all cases whatsoever." It was a cunning evasion that made no concession with regard to taxes,

The Repeal, or the Funeral Procession of Miss America-Stamp *(1766)*.
Grenville carries the dead Stamp Act in its coffin. In the background,
trade with America starts up again.

but made no mention of them either. It left intact in the minds of many members the impression that a distinction had been drawn between "external" taxes on trade and "internal" taxes within the colonies, and that impression would have fateful consequences for the future. For the moment, however, the Declaratory Act seemed little if anything more than a gesture to save face. Amid the rejoicing and relief on both sides of the Atlantic there were no omens that the quarrel would be reopened within a year. To be sure, the Sugar Act remained on the books, but Rockingham reduced the molasses tax from three pence to a penny a gallon.

FANNING THE FLAMES

Meanwhile, the king continued to have his ministers play musical chairs. Rockingham fell because he lost the confidence of the king, and his own administration suffered a paralyzing fragmentation. The king invited Pitt to form a ministry including the major factions of Parliament. The ill-matched combination—which Edmund Burke compared to pigs gathered at a trough—would have been hard to manage even if Pitt had remained in charge, but the old warlord began to slip over the fine line between genius and madness. For a time in 1767 the guiding force in the ministry was Charles Townshend, chancellor of the Exchequer, whose "abilities were superior to those of all men," according to Horace Walpole, "and his judgement below that of any man." The erratic Townshend took advantage of Pitt's absence to reopen the question of colonial taxation and seized upon the notion that "external" taxes were tolerable to the colonies—not that he believed it for a moment.

THE TOWNSHEND ACTS   In May and June 1767 Townshend put his plan through the House of Commons, and in September he died, leaving behind a bitter legacy: the Townshend Acts. First, he sought to bring the New York assembly to its senses. That body had defied the Quartering Act and refused to provide billets or supplies for the king's troops. Parliament, at Townshend's behest, suspended all acts of the assembly until it yielded. New York protested but finally caved in, inadvertently confirming the British suspicion that too much indulgence had encouraged colonial bad manners. Townshend followed up with the Revenue Act of 1767, which levied duties ("external taxes") on colonial imports of glass, lead, paint, paper, and tea. Third, he set up a Board of Customs Commissioners at Boston, the colonial headquarters of smuggling. Finally, he reorganized the vice-admiralty courts, providing four in the continental colonies—at Halifax, Boston, Philadelphia, and Charleston.

The Townshend duties did increase government revenues, but the intangible costs were greater. The duties taxed goods exported from England, indirectly hurting British manufacturers, and had to be collected in colonial ports, increasing collection costs. But the greater cost was a new drift into ever-greater conflict. The Revenue Act of 1767 posed a more severe threat to colonial assemblies than Grenville's taxes, for Townshend proposed to apply these moneys to pay governors and other officers and release them from financial dependence on the colonial assemblies.

DICKINSON'S *LETTERS*   The Townshend Acts surprised the colonists, and this time the storm gathered more slowly than it had two years before. Once again citizens resolved to resist, to boycott British goods, to wear homespun, to develop their own manufactures. Once again the colonial press spewed out expressions of protest, most notably the essays of John Dickinson, a Philadelphia lawyer who hoped to resolve the dispute by persuasion. Late in 1767 his twelve *Letters of a Pennsylvania Farmer* (as he chose to style himself) began to appear in the *Pennsylvania Chronicle,* from which they were copied in other papers and in pamphlet form. His argument simply repeated with greater detail and more

John Dickinson, the Philadelphia lawyer who wrote the influential Letters of a Pennsylvania Farmer.

elegance what the Stamp Act Congress had already said. The colonists held that Parliament might regulate commerce and collect duties incidental to that purpose, but it had no right to levy taxes for revenue, whether they were internal or external. Dickinson used the language of moderation throughout. "The cause of Liberty is a cause of too much dignity to be sullied by turbulence and tumult," he argued. The colonial complaints should "speak at the same time the language of affliction and veneration."

SAMUEL ADAMS AND THE SONS OF LIBERTY   But the affliction grew and the veneration waned. British ministers could neither conciliate moderates like Dickinson nor cope with firebrands such as Samuel Adams of Boston, who was now emerging as the supreme genius of revolutionary agitation. Born in 1722, Adams, the son of moderately well off and sternly pious parents, was graduated from Harvard and soon thereafter inherited the family brewery, which he quickly ran into bankruptcy. The lure of monetary gain never intoxicated him. His distant cousin John Adams described Sam as a "universal good character," a "plain, simple, decent citizen, of middling stature, dress, and manners," who prided himself on his frugality and his distaste for ceremony and display. Politics, not profits, was his abiding passion, and he spent most of his time at midcentury and after debating political issues with sailors, roustabouts, and stevedores at local taverns. Often dressed in a dingy red coat and ink-stained shirt, he would bring his huge Newfoundland dog to the tavern and, while eating raw oysters and fish chowder, engage in animated

*Samuel Adams, an organizer of the
Sons of Liberty.*

discussions about British rule. Stubborn, cunning, courageous, pious, and impetuous, Adams grew obsessed with the conviction that Parliament had no right to legislate at all for the colonies, that Massachusetts must return to the spirit of its Puritan founders and defend itself from a new conspiracy against its liberties.

While other men tended their private affairs, Sam Adams was whipping up the Sons of Liberty and organizing protests in the Boston town meeting and the provincial assembly. Early in 1768 he and James Otis formulated another Massachusetts Circular Letter, which the assembly dispatched to the other colonies. The letter restated the illegality of parliamentary taxation, warned that the new duties would be used to pay colonial officials, and invited the support of other colonies. In London the earl of Hillsborough, just appointed to the new office of secretary of state for the colonies, only made matters worse. He ordered the assembly to withdraw the letter. The assembly refused and was dissolved. The consequence was simply more discussion of the need for colonial cooperation.

Among Townshend's legacies, the new Board of Customs Commissioners at Boston further confirmed Adams's suspicions of British intentions. Customs officers had been unwelcome in Boston since the arrival of Edward Randolph a century before. But the irascible Randolph had at least had the virtue of honesty. His successors cultivated the fine art of what one historian has called "customs racketeering." Under the Sugar Act, collectors profited from illegal cargoes and exploited technicalities. One ploy was to neglect certain requirements, then suddenly insist on a strict adherence. In May 1768, for example, they set a trap for Sam Adams's friend and patron John Hancock, a well-to-do merchant. On the narrow ground that Hancock had failed to post a bond before loading his sloop *Liberty* (previously he had always posted bond after loading), they seized the ship. A mob gathered to prevent its unloading. The commissioners towed the ship to Castle William in the harbor and called for the protection of British troops.

In September 1768 two regiments of redcoats arrived in Boston. Clearly they were not there to protect the frontiers. On the day the soldiers arrived, a convention of delegates from Massachusetts towns declared their "aversion to an unnecessary Standing Army, which they look upon as dangerous to their Civil Liberty." To members of Parliament the illegal convention smacked of treason, but it gave them little reason to believe that any colonial jury would ever convict the likes of Sam Adams. As a consequence, Parliament recommended that the king get information on "all treasons, or misprision of treason" committed in Massachusetts and return the accused to England for trial.

The king never acted on the suggestion, but the threat was unmistakable. In mid-May 1769 the Virginia assembly passed a new set of resolves reasserting its exclusive right to tax Virginians, challenging the constitutionality of an act that would take a man across the ocean for trial, and calling upon the colonies to unite in the cause. Virginia's governor promptly dissolved the assembly, but the members met independently, dubbed themselves a "convention" after Boston's example, and adopted a new set of non-importation agreements. Once again, as with the Virginia Resolves against the Stamp Act, most of the other assemblies followed the example.

In London, events across the Atlantic still evoked only marginal interest. The king's long effort to reorder British politics to his liking was coming to fulfillment, and that was the big news. In 1769 new elections for Parliament finally produced a majority of the "King's Friends." And George III found a minister to his taste in Frederick, Lord North, the plodding chancellor of the Exchequer who had replaced Townshend. In 1770 the king installed a cabinet of the King's Friends, with North as first minister. North, who venerated the traditions of Parliament, was no stooge for the king, but the two worked in harmony.

THE BOSTON MASSACRE   The impact of colonial boycotts on English commerce had persuaded Lord North to modify the Townshend Acts, just in time to halt a perilous escalation of conflict. The presence of soldiers in Boston had been a constant provocation. Bostonians copied the example of the customs officers and indicted soldiers on technical violations of local law. Crowds heckled and ridiculed the "lobster backs."

On March 5, 1770, in the square before the customs house, a group of rowdies began taunting and snowballing the sentry on duty. His call for help brought reinforcements. Then somebody rang the town firebell, drawing a larger crowd to the scene. At their head, or so the story goes, was Crispus Attucks, a runaway mulatto slave who had worked for

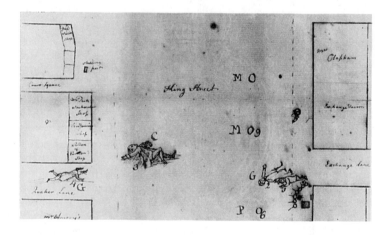

Paul Revere's partisan engraving of the Boston Massacre (top). Revere drew a plan of the Massacre (bottom) for use at the trial of the British soldiers. It shows the places where four of the dead fell.

some years on ships out of Boston. Finally one soldier was knocked down, rose to his feet, and fired into the crowd. When the smoke cleared, five people lay on the ground dead or dying, and eight more were wounded. The cause of resistance now had its first martyrs, and the first to die was Crispus Attucks. Governor Thomas Hutchinson, at the insistence of a mass meeting in Faneuil Hall, moved the soldiers out of town to avoid another incident. Those involved in the shooting were indicted for murder, but they were defended by John Adams, Sam's cousin, who thought they were the victims of circumstance, provoked, he said, by a "motley rabble of saucy boys, negroes and mulattoes, Irish teagues and outlandish Jack tars." All were acquitted except two, who were convicted of manslaughter and branded on their thumbs.

The so-called Boston Massacre sent shock waves up and down the colonies, and the unrest caught the attention of British officials. Late in April 1770 Parliament repealed all the Townshend duties save one. The cabinet, by a fateful vote of five to four, had advised keeping the tea tax as a token of parliamentary authority. Colonial diehards insisted that pressure should be kept on British merchants until Parliament gave in altogether, but the non-importation movement soon faded. Parliament, after all, had given up the substance of the taxes, with one exception, and much of the colonists' tea was smuggled in from Holland anyway.

For two years thereafter discontent simmered down and suspicions began to fade on both sides of the ocean. The Stamp Act was gone, as were all the Townshend duties except that on tea, and Lord Hillsborough disclaimed any intent to seek further revenues. But most of the Grenville-Townshend innovations remained in effect: the Sugar Act, the Currency Act, the Quartering Act, the vice-admiralty courts, the Board of Customs Commissioners. The redcoats had left Boston but they remained nearby, and the British navy still patrolled the coast. Each remained a source of irritation and the cause of occasional incidents. There was still tinder awaiting a spark, and the rebellious among the colonists promoted continuing conflicts. As Sam Adams stressed, "Where there is a spark of patriotick fire, we will enkindle it."

DISCONTENT ON THE FRONTIER

Many American colonists had no interest in the disputes over British regulatory policy raging along the seaboard. Parts of the backcountry stirred with quarrels that had nothing to do with the Stamp and Townshend Acts. Rival land claims to the east of Lake Champlain pitted New York against New Hampshire and the Green Mountain Boys led by Ethan Allen against both. Eventually the denizens of the area would simply set up shop on their own as the state of Vermont, created in 1777 although not recognized as a member of the Union until 1791. In Pennsylvania sporadic quarrels broke out with land claimants who held grants from Virginia and Connecticut, whose boundaries under their charters overlapped those granted to William Penn, or so they claimed.

A more dangerous division in Pennsylvania arose when a group of frontier ruffians took the law into their own hands. Outraged at the lack of frontier protection during Pontiac's rebellion because of Quaker influence in the assembly, a group called the "Paxton Boys" took revenge by massacring peaceful Conestoga Indians in Lancaster County; then they threatened the so-called Moravian Indians, a group of Moravian converts near Bethlehem. When the Moravian Indians took refuge in Philadelphia, some 1,500 Paxton Boys marched on the capital, where Benjamin Franklin talked them into returning home by promising that more protection would be forthcoming.

Farther south, frontier folk of South Carolina had similar complaints about the lack of settled government and the need for protection against horse thieves, cattle rustlers, and Indians. Backcountry residents organized societies called "Regulators" to administer vigilante justice in the region and refused to pay taxes until they gained effective government. In 1769 the assembly finally set up six new circuit courts in the region and revised the fees, but still did not respond to the backcountry's demand for representation in the legislature.

However, the South Carolina assembly also voted £1,500 for the radical Bill of Rights Society in England to pay the debts of the government's outspoken critic, John Wilkes. When the king's ministers instructed the governor and council to assert themselves in the matter, royal government in South Carolina reached an impasse. The assembly passed its last annual tax law in 1769, and after 1771 passed no legislation at all.

In North Carolina the protest was less over the lack of government than over the abuses and extortion inflicted by appointees from the eastern part of the colony. Farmers felt especially oppressed at the refusal either to issue paper money or to accept produce in payment of taxes, and in 1766 they organized to resist. Efforts of these Regulators to stop seizures of property and other court proceedings led to more disorders and an enactment of a bill that made the rioters guilty of treason. In the spring of 1771 Governor William Tryon led 1,200 militiamen into the Piedmont center of Regulator activity. There he met and defeated some 2,000 ill-organized Regulators in the Battle of Alamance, in which eight were killed on each side. One insurgent was executed on the battlefield, twelve others were convicted of treason, and six were hanged. While this went on, Tryon's men ranged through the backcountry, forcing some 6,500 Piedmont settlers to sign an oath of allegiance.

These internal disputes and revolts within the colonies illustrate the fractious diversity of opinion and outlook evident among Americans on the eve of the Revolution. Colonists were of many minds about many things, including British rule. The disputatious frontier in colonial America also helped convince British authorities that the colonies were inherently unstable. The colonies required even keener and firmer oversight, even to the extent of using military force to ensure civil stability.

A WORSENING CRISIS

Two events in June 1772 further eroded the colonies' fragile relationship with the mother country. Near Providence, Rhode Island, a British schooner, the *Gaspee,* patrolling for smugglers, accidentally ran aground. Under cover of darkness a crowd from the town boarded the ship, removed the crew, and set fire to the vessel. A commission of inquiry was formed with authority to hold suspects (for trial in England, it was rumored, under an old statute passed during the reign of Henry VIII), but no witnesses could be found. Four days after the burning, on June 13, 1772, Governor Thomas Hutchinson told the Massachusetts assembly that his salary thenceforth would come out of the customs revenues. Soon thereafter word came that judges of the Superior Court would be paid from the same source and no longer be dependent on the assembly for their income. The assembly expressed a fear that this portended "a despotic administration of government."

The existence of the *Gaspee* commission, which bypassed the courts of Rhode Island, and the independent salaries for royal officials in Mass-

Massachusetts governor Thomas Hutchinson found himself at the center of the imperial crisis in 1772 and 1773.

achusetts both suggested to the residents of other colonies that the same might be in store for them. The discussion of colonial rights and parliamentary encroachments regained momentum. To keep the pot boiling, in November 1772 Sam Adams convinced the Boston town meeting to form a Committee of Correspondence, which issued a statement of rights and grievances and invited other towns to do the same. Committees of Correspondence sprang up across Massachusetts and spread into other colonies. In March 1773 the Virginia assembly proposed the formation of such committees on an intercolonial basis, and a network of the committees spread across the colonies, mobilizing public opinion and keeping colonial resentments at a simmer. In unwitting tribute to their effectiveness, a Massachusetts Loyalist called the committees "the foulest, subtlest, and most venomous serpent ever issued from the egg of sedition."

THE BOSTON TEA PARTY   Lord North soon provided the colonists with the occasion to bring resentment from a simmer to a boil. In May 1773 he undertook to help some friends through a little difficulty. North's scheme was a clever contrivance, perhaps too clever, designed to bail out the East India Company, which was foundering in a spell of bad business. The company had in its British warehouses some 17 million pounds of tea. Under the Tea Act of 1773 the government would refund the British duty of twelve pence per pound on all that was shipped to the colonies and collect only the existing three-pence duty payable at the colonial port. By this arrangement colonists could get tea more cheaply than English buyers could. North, however, miscalculated in assuming that price alone would govern colonial reaction. Even worse, he permitted the East India Company to serve retailers directly through its own agents or consignees, bypassing the wholesalers who had handled it before. Once that kind of monopoly was established, colonial merchants began to wonder, how soon would the precedent apply to other commodities?

The Committees of Correspondence, backed by colonial merchants, alerted people to the new danger. The government, they said, was trying to purchase colonial acquiescence with cheap tea. Before the end of the year, large consignments of tea went out to major colonial ports. In New York and Philadelphia popular hostility forced company agents to resign. When no one received the tea, it went back to England. In Charleston it was unloaded into warehouses—and later sold to finance the Revolution. In Boston, however, Governor Hutchinson and Sam Adams engaged in a test of will. The ships' captains, alarmed by the radical opposition, proposed to turn back. Hutchinson, two of whose sons were among the consignees and stood to profit, refused permission until the tea was landed and the duty paid. On November 30, 1773, gathered

Americans throwing the Cargoes of the Tea Ships into the River, at Boston, *1773.*

in Old South Church, the Boston town meeting warned officials not to assist the landing of the tea. But they were legally bound to seize the cargo after twenty days in port, which in this case fell on December 16. On that night in December a group of men hastened to Griffin's Wharf where, thinly disguised as Mohawk Indians, they boarded the three ships and threw the tea overboard—cheered on by a crowd along the shore. Like those who had burned the *Gaspee,* they remained parties unknown—except to hundreds of Bostonians. One participant later testified that Sam Adams and John Hancock were there. About £15,000 worth of tea, a substantial sum in 1773, went to the fish.

Given a more deft response from London, the Boston Tea Party might easily have undermined the radicals' credibility. Many people, especially merchants, were aghast at the wanton destruction of property. A town meeting in Bristol, Massachusetts, condemned the action. Ben Franklin called on his native city to pay for the tea and apologize. But the British authorities had reached the end of their patience. They were now convinced that the very existence of the empire was at stake. The rebels in Boston had instigated what could become a widespread effort to evade royal authority and imperial regulations. A firm response was required. "The colonists must either submit or triumph," George III wrote to Lord North, and North strove to make the king's judgment a self-fulfilling prophecy.

THE COERCIVE ACTS   In April 1774 Parliament enacted four measures designed by North to discipline Boston. The Boston Port Act closed the port from June 1, 1774, until the city paid for the lost tea. An Act for the Impartial Administration of Justice let the governor transfer to England the trial of any official accused of committing an offense in the line of duty—no more redcoats would be tried on technicalities. A new Quartering Act directed local authorities to provide lodging for soldiers, in private homes if necessary. Finally, the Massachusetts Government Act made the colony's council and law-enforcement officers all appointive rather than elected; sheriffs would select jurors, and no town meeting could be held without the governor's consent, except for the annual election of town officers. In May, General Thomas Gage replaced Hutchinson as governor and assumed command of British forces. Massachusetts now had a military governor.

These actions were designed to isolate Boston and make an example of the colony. Instead they galvanized colonial unity and emboldened resistance. "Your scheme yields no revenue," Edmund Burke had warned Parliament; "it yields nothing but discontent, disorder, disobedience. . . ." At last, it seemed to the colonists, their worst fears were being confirmed. If these "Intolerable Acts," as the colonists labeled the Coercive Acts, were not resisted, they would eventually be applied to the other colonies.

Further confirmation of British designs came with news of the Que-

The Church Militant. *An anti-clerical view of the Anglican clergy eager to expand their authority to the American colonies.*

The Able Doctor, or America Swallowing the Bitter Draught. *This 1774 engraving shows Lord North, with the Boston Port Act in his pocket, pouring tea down America's throat. America spits it back.*

bec Act, passed in June. It set up a totally unrepresentative government to the north in Canada under an appointed governor and council and gave a privileged position to the Catholic church. The measure was actually designed to deal with the peculiar milieu of a predominantly French colony unused to representative assemblies, but it seemed merely another indicator of tyrannical designs for the rest of the colonies. In addition, colonists pointed out that they had lost many lives in an effort to liberate the trans-Appalachian West from the control of French Catholics. Now the British seemed to be protecting papists at the expense of their own colonists. What was more, the act placed within the boundaries of Quebec the western lands north of the Ohio River, lands that Pennsylvania, Virginia, and Connecticut claimed.

Meanwhile, colonists rallied to the cause of besieged Boston, taking up collections and sending provisions. In Williamsburg, when the Virginia assembly met in May, a young member of the Committee of Correspondence, Thomas Jefferson, proposed to set aside June 1, the effective date of the Boston Port Act, as a day of fasting and prayer in Virginia. The governor immediately dissolved the assembly, whose members retired to the Raleigh Tavern and drew up a resolution for a "Continental Congress" to make representations on behalf of all the colonies. Similar calls were coming from Providence, New York, Philadelphia, and elsewhere, and in June the Massachusetts assembly suggested a meeting at Philadelphia in September. Shortly before

George Washington left to represent Virginia at the gathering, he wrote to a friend: "the crisis is arrived when we must assert our rights, or submit to every imposition, that can be heaped upon us, till custom and use shall make us as tame and abject slaves, as the blacks we rule over with such arbitrary sway."

THE CONTINENTAL CONGRESS   On September 5, 1774, the First Continental Congress assembled in Philadelphia. There were fifty-five members, elected by provincial congresses or extralegal conventions, and representing twelve continental colonies, all but Georgia, Quebec, Nova Scotia, and the Floridas. Peyton Randolph of Virginia was elected president and Charles Thomson, "the Sam Adams of Philadelphia," became secretary, but not a member. The Congress agreed to vote by colonies, although Patrick Henry urged the members to vote as individuals on the grounds that they were not Virginians or New Yorkers or whatever, but Americans. In effect the delegates functioned as a congress of ambassadors, gathered to join forces on common policies and neither to govern nor to rebel but to adopt and issue a series of resolutions and protests.

The Congress gave serious consideration to a plan of union introduced by Joseph Galloway of Pennsylvania. His proposal followed closely the plan of the Albany Congress twenty years before: to set up a central administration of a governor-general appointed by the crown and a Grand Council chosen by the assemblies to regulate "general affairs." All measures dealing with America would require approval of both this body and Parliament. The plan was defeated only by a vote of six to five. Meanwhile a silversmith from Boston, Paul Revere, had come riding in from Massachusetts with the radical Suffolk Resolves, which the Congress proceeded to endorse. Drawn up by Joseph Warren and adopted by a convention in Suffolk County, the resolutions declared the Intolerable Acts null and void, urged Massachusetts to arm for defense, and called for economic sanctions against British commerce.

In place of Galloway's plan the Congress adopted a Declaration of American Rights, which conceded only Parliament's right to regulate commerce and those matters that were strictly imperial affairs. It proclaimed once again the rights of Americans as English citizens, denied Parliament's authority with respect to internal colonial affairs, and proclaimed the right of each assembly to determine the need for troops within its own province. In addition the Congress sent the king a petition for relief and issued addresses to the people of Great Britain and the colonies.

Finally the Continental Congress adopted the Continental Association of 1774, which recommended that every county, town, and city form committees to enforce a boycott on all British goods. These com-

WILLIAM COATS,

Takes this method of acquainting the P U B L I C in general, and his F R I E N D S
in particular, that he has for S A L E, at his S T O R E, at the sign of the
SUGAR-LOAF, contiguous to the PUBLIC WHARF, in FRONT-STREET, and near
POOL'S BRIDGE, WHOLESALE and RETAIL;

W EST-INDIA and PHILADELPHIA RUM,
Jamaica spirits, brandy, geneva, annifeed, cordials; Madeira, Lif-
bon, and Teneriff WI N E S ; lamp oil; loaf, lump and mufcovado
S U G A R S;molaffes ; green, fouchong, and bohea T E A ; chocolate, rice, oatmeal, ftarch, indigo, pepper, ginger, allfpice, cloves, mace, cinnamon, and nutmegs;

*Goods from around the world could be found in a Philadelphia shop in 1772:
Jamaica spirits, Madeira wines, molasses, souchong tea, cloves, Florence oil.*

mittees would become the organizational and communications network
for the Revolutionary movement, connecting every locality to the leadership. The Continental Association also included provisions for the
non-importation of British goods (implemented in December 1774) and
the nonexportation of American goods to Britain (to be implemented
in September 1775 unless colonial grievances were addressed).

In taking its bold stand, the Congress had adopted what later would
be called the dominion theory of the British Empire, a theory long
implicit in the assemblies' claim to independent authority but more
recently formulated in two widely circulated pamphlets by James Wilson of Pennsylvania *(Considerations on the Nature and Extent of the
Legislative Authority of the British Parliament)* and Thomas Jefferson
of Virginia *(Summary View of the Rights of British America)*. Each tract
had argued that the colonies were not subject to Parliament but merely
to the crown; each colony, like England itself, was a separate realm, a

The State Blacksmiths, Forging Fetters for the Americans. *A cartoon attacking parliamentary measures of 1775 and 1776.*

point further argued in the *Novanglus Letters* of John Adams, published in Massachusetts after the Congress adjourned.

In London the king fumed. In November 1774 he wrote his prime minister that the "New England colonies are in a state of rebellion," and "blows must decide whether they are to be subject to this country or independent." British critics of the American actions reminded the colonists that Parliament had absolute sovereignty. Power could not be shared. Parliament could not abandon its claim to authority in part without abandoning it altogether. Only a few members of Parliament were ready to comprehend, much less accept, the colonists' "liberal and expanded thought," as Jefferson called it. In the House of Commons, Edmund Burke, in a brilliant speech on conciliation, urged merely an acceptance of the American view on taxation as consonant with English principles. The real question, he argued, was "not whether you have the right to render your people miserable; but whether it is not your interest to make them happy."

But Parliament rejected the notion of compromise. Instead it declared Massachusetts in rebellion, forbade the New England colonies to trade with any nation outside the empire, and excluded New Englanders from the North Atlantic fisheries. Lord North's Conciliatory Resolution, adopted February 27, 1775, was as far as they would go. Under its terms, Parliament would refrain from any measures but taxes to regulate trade and would grant to each colony the duties collected within its boundaries, provided the colonies would contribute voluntarily to a quota for defense of the empire. It was a formula, Burke said, not for peace but for new quarrels.

SHIFTING AUTHORITY

Events were already moving beyond conciliation. All through late 1774 and early 1775 the patriot defenders of American rights were seizing the initiative. The uncertain and unorganized Loyalists, if they did not submit to non-importation agreements, found themselves confronted with persuasive committees of "Whigs," with tar and feathers at the ready. The Continental Congress urged each colony to mobilize its militia units. The militia, as much a social as a military organization in the past, now took to serious drill in formations, tactics, and marksmanship, and organized special units of Minute Men ready for quick mobilization. Everywhere royal and proprietary officials were losing control as provincial congresses assumed authority and colonial militias organized, raided military stores, and gathered arms and gunpowder. But British military officials remained smugly confident. Major John Pitcairn wrote home from Boston in March 1775: "I am satisfied that one active campaign, a smart action, and burning two or three of their towns, will set everything to rights."

LEXINGTON AND CONCORD   Pitcairn soon had his chance. On April 14, 1775, Gage received secret orders to suppress the "open rebellion" that existed in the colony. Leaders of the Provincial Congress, whom Gage was directed to arrest, were mostly beyond his reach, but he decided to move quickly against the militia's supply depot at Concord, about twenty miles away. On the night of April 18 Lieutenant-Colonel Francis Smith and Major Pitcairn gathered 700 men on Boston Common and set out by way of Lexington. But local patriots got wind of the plan, and Boston's Committee of Safety sent Paul Revere and William Dawes by separate routes on their famous ride to spread the alarm. Revere reached Lexington about midnight and alerted John Hancock and Sam Adams, who were hiding there. Joined by Dawes and Dr. Samuel Prescott, who had been visiting in Lexington, Revere rode on toward Concord. A British patrol intercepted the trio, but Prescott slipped through with the warning.

At dawn on April 19 the British advance guard found Captain John Parker and about seventy Minute Men lined up on the dewy Lexington green. Parker apparently intended only a silent protest, but Pitcairn rode onto the green, swung his sword, and brusquely yelled: "Disperse, you damned rebels! You dogs, run!" The Americans had already begun quietly backing away when somebody fired a shot, whereupon the British soldiers loosed a volley into the Minute Men, then charged them with bayonets, leaving eight dead and ten wounded. One American patriot, whose wife and son were watching the spectacle, was shot and crawled 100 yards to die on his front doorstep.

The British officers hastily brought their men under control and led them to Concord. There the Americans already had carried off most of their munitions, but the British destroyed what they could—including a Liberty Pole. At Concord's North Bridge the growing American forces inflicted fourteen casualties on a British platoon, and about noon Smith began marching his forces back to Boston. By then, however, the road back had turned into a gauntlet of death as the embattled farmers from "every Middlesex village and farm" sniped from behind stone walls, trees, barns, houses, all the way back to Charlestown peninsula. By nightfall the survivors were safe under the protection of the fleet and army at Boston, having suffered over 250 casualties along the way, and the Americans 93. A British official reported to London that the rebels had earned his respect: "Whoever looks upon them as an irregular mob will find himself much mistaken."

THE SPREADING CONFLICT   The war had begun. When the Second Continental Congress convened at Philadelphia on May 10, 1775, British-held Boston was under siege by the Massachusetts militia. On the very day that Congress met, Fort Ticonderoga in New York fell to a force of Green Mountain Boys under Ethan Allen of Vermont and Massachusetts volunteers under Benedict Arnold of Connecticut. The British yielded, Allen said, to his demand "in the name of the great Jehovah and the Continental Congress." Two days later the force took Crown Point, north of Ticonderoga.

The Continental Congress, with no legal authority and no resources, met amid reports of spreading warfare and had little choice but to assume the de facto role of a revolutionary government. The Congress accepted a request that it "adopt" the motley army gathered around Boston. On June 15 it named George Washington general and commander-in-chief of a Continental army. He accepted on the condition that he receive no pay. The Congress fastened on Washington because his service in the Seven Years' War made him one of the most experienced officers in America. The fact that he was from populous and influential Virginia heightened his attractiveness. To finance the enterprise the Congress resorted to a familiar colonial expedient, printing paper money.

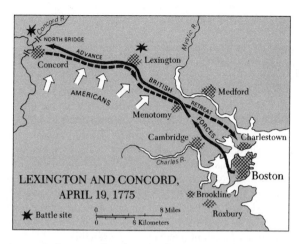

LEXINGTON AND CONCORD,
APRIL 19, 1775

★ Battle site

0   8 Miles
0   8 Kilometers

On June 17, the very day that Washington was commissioned, the colonials and British forces engaged in their first major fight, the Battle of Bunker Hill. While the Congress deliberated, both American and British forces in and around Boston had grown. Militiamen from Rhode Island, Connecticut, and New Hampshire joined in the siege. British reinforcements included three major-generals—Sir William Howe, Sir Henry Clinton, and John Burgoyne. On the day before the battle, American forces began to fortify the high ground of Charlestown peninsula, overlooking Boston. Breed's Hill was the battle location, nearer to Boston than Bunker Hill, the site first chosen (and the source of the battle's erroneous name).

The rebels were spoiling for a fight. As Joseph Warren, a dapper Boston physician, put it, "the British say we won't fight; by heavens, I hope I shall die up to my knees in blood!" He soon got his wish. With civilians looking on from rooftops and church steeples, Gage ordered a conventional frontal assault in the blistering heat, with 2,200 British troops moving in tight formation through tall grass. Numerous fences obstructed the assault and broke up the uniform lines. The Americans, pounded by naval guns, watched from behind their hastily built earthworks as the waves of brightly uniformed British troops advanced up the hill. Ordered not to fire until they could "see the whites of their eyes," the militiamen waited until the attackers came within fifteen to twenty paces, then loosed a shattering volley. Through the cloud of oily smoke the Americans could see fallen bodies "as thick as sheep in a fold." The militiamen cheered as they watched the greatest soldiers in the world retreating in panic.

Within a half hour, however, the British had reformed and attacked again. Another sheet of flame and lead greeted them, and the vaunted redcoats retreated a second time. Still, the proud British generals were determined not to let such ragtag rustics humiliate them. On the third attempt, when the colonials began to run out of gunpowder and were forced to throw stones, a bayonet charge ousted them. The British took the high ground, but at the cost of 1,054 casualties. Colonial losses were about 400. "A dear bought victory," recorded General Clinton; "another such would have ruined us." When Washington arrived to take charge, things had again reached a stalemate in Boston, and so remained through the winter.

The Battle of Bunker Hill had two profound effects. First, the high number of British casualties made the English generals more cautious in subsequent encounters with the Continental army. Second, Congress recommended after the battle that all able-bodied men enlist in the militia. This tended to divide the male population into Patriot and Loyalist camps. A middle ground was no longer tenable.

In early March 1776, American forces occupied Dorchester Heights to the south of Boston and brought the city under threat of bombardment with cannon and mortars. General William Howe, who had replaced Gage as British commander, retreated by water to Halifax, Nova Scotia. The last British forces, along with fearful American Loyalists, embarked on March 17, 1776. By that time British power had col-

The Retreat. *An American cartoon showing the retreat of British forces at Lexington and Concord, April 1775.*

The Battle of Bunker Hill and the burning of Charlestown peninsula.

lapsed nearly everywhere, and the British forces faced not the suppression of a rebellion but the reconquest of a continent.

While American forces held Boston under siege, the Continental Congress pursued the dimming hope of a compromise settlement. On July 5 and 6, 1775, the delegates issued two major documents: an appeal to the king thereafter known as the Olive Branch Petition, and a Declaration of the Causes and Necessity of Taking Up Arms. The Olive Branch Petition, written by John Dickinson, professed continued loyalty to George III and begged him to restrain further hostilities pending a reconciliation. The Declaration, also largely Dickinson's work, traced the history of the controversy, denounced the British for the unprovoked assault at Lexington, and rejected independence but affirmed the colonists' purpose to fight for their rights rather than submit to slavery. When the Olive Branch Petition reached London, the outraged king refused even to look at it. On August 22 he ordered the army at Boston to regard the colonists "as open and avowed enemies." The next day he issued a proclamation of rebellion.

Before the end of July 1775 the Congress authorized an attack on British troops in Quebec in the vain hope of rallying support from the French inhabitants in Canada. One force, under Richard Montgomery, advanced by way of Lake Champlain; another, under Benedict Arnold, struggled through the Maine woods. Together they held Quebec under siege from mid-September until their final attack was repulsed on December 30, 1775. Montgomery was killed in the battle and Arnold wounded.

In the South, Virginia's Governor Dunmore raised a Loyalist force, including slaves recruited on promise of freedom, but met defeat in December 1775. After leaving Norfolk he returned on January 1, 1776, and burned most of the town. In North Carolina, Loyalist Highland Scots, joined by some former Regulators, lost a battle with a patriot force at Moore's Creek Bridge. The Loyalists had set out for Wilmington to join an expeditionary force under Lord Cornwallis and Sir Henry Clinton. That plan frustrated, the British commanders decided to attack Charleston instead, but the patriot militia there had partially finished a palmetto log fort on Sullivan's Island (later named in honor of its commander, Colonel William Moultrie). When the British fleet attacked on June 28, 1776, the spongy palmetto logs absorbed the naval fire, and Fort Moultrie's cannon returned it with devastating effect. The fleet, with over 200 casualties and every ship damaged, was forced to retire. South Carolina honored the palmetto by putting it on the state flag.

As the fighting spread north into Canada and south into Virginia and the Carolinas, the Continental Congress assumed, one after another, the functions of government. As early as July 1775 it appointed commissioners to negotiate treaties of peace with Indian tribes and organized a Post Office Department with Benjamin Franklin as postmaster-general. In October it authorized formation of a navy, in November a marine corps. A committee appointed in November began to explore the possibility of foreign aid. In March 1776 the Continental navy raided Nassau in the Bahamas, and the Congress further authorized privateering operations against British vessels.

Still, the delegates continued to hold back from the seeming abyss of independence. Yet through late 1775 and early 1776 word came of one British action after another that proclaimed rebellion and war. In December 1775 a Prohibitory Act declared the colonies closed to all commerce. The king and cabinet also recruited mercenaries in Europe. Eventually almost 30,000 Germans served, about 17,000 of them from the principality of Hesse-Cassel, and "Hessian" became the name applied to them all. Parliament remained deaf to the warnings of members that the reconquest of America would not only be costly in itself but that the effort might lead to another great war with France and Spain.

COMMON SENSE   In January 1776 Thomas Paine's pamphlet *Common Sense* was published anonymously in Philadelphia. Paine had arrived there from England thirteen months before. Coming from a humble Quaker background, Paine had distinguished himself chiefly as a drifter, a failure in marriage and business. At age thirty-seven he set sail for America with a letter of introduction from Benjamin Franklin and the purpose of setting up a school for young ladies. When that did not work out, he moved into the political controversy as a freelance writer, and with *Common Sense* proved himself the consummate Revolutionary rhetorician. Until his pamphlet appeared, the squabble had been mainly with Parliament; few colonists considered independence an option. Paine, however, directly attacked allegiance to the monarchy, which had remained the last frayed connection to Britain, and refocused the hostility previously vented on Parliament. The common sense of the matter, it seemed, was that King George III and the King's Friends bore the responsibility for the malevolence toward the colonies. Monarchy, Paine boldly proclaimed, rested upon usurpation; its origins would not bear looking into. One honest man, he said, was worth more "than all the crowned ruffians that ever lived." Americans should consult their own interests, abandon George III, and declare their independence: "The blood of the slain, the weeping voice of nature cries, 'TIS TIME TO PART."

INDEPENDENCE

Within three months more than 150,000 copies of Paine's pamphlet were in circulation, an enormous number for the time. *"Common Sense* is working a powerful change in the minds of men," George Washington said. A visitor to North Carolina's Provincial Congress could "hear nothing praised but *Common Sense* and independence." One by one the provincial governments authorized their delegates in the Continental Congress to take the final step: Massachusetts in January 1776, South Carolina in March, Georgia and North Carolina in April, Virginia in May. On June 7 Richard Henry Lee of Virginia moved a resolution "that these United Colonies are, and of right ought to be, free and independent states. . . ." Lee's resolution passed on July 2, a date that "will be the most memorable epoch in the history of America," John Adams wrote to his wife, Abigail. The memorable date, however, became July 4, 1776, when the Congress adopted Thomas Jefferson's Declaration of Independence, a statement of political philosophy that retains its dynamic force to the present day.

JEFFERSON'S *DECLARATION*   Jefferson's summary of the prevailing political sentiment, prepared on behalf of a committee composed of John Adams, Benjamin Franklin, Roger Sherman, and Robert R. Livingston, was an eloquent restatement of John Locke's contract theory of government—the theory, in Jefferson's words, that governments derived

The Continental Congress votes Independence, July 2, 1776.

"their just Powers from the consent of the people," who were entitled to "alter or abolish" those that denied their "unalienable rights" to "life, Liberty, and the pursuit of Happiness." The appeal was no longer simply to "the rights of Englishmen" but to the broader "laws of Nature and Nature's God." But at the same time the Declaration implicitly supported the theory that the British Empire was a federation united only through the crown. Parliament, which had no proper authority over the colonies, was never mentioned by name. The enemy was a king who had "combined with others to subject us to a jurisdiction foreign to our constitution, and unacknowledged by our laws. . . ." The document set forth "a history of repeated injuries and usurpations, all having in direct object the establishment of an absolute Tyranny over these States." The "Representatives of the United States of America," therefore, declared the thirteen "United Colonies" to be "Free and Independent States."

"WE ALWAYS HAD GOVERNED OURSELVES"   So it had come to this, thirteen years after Britain acquired domination of North America. In explaining the causes of the Revolution, historians have advanced many theories and explanations: trade regulation, the restrictions on western lands, the tax burden, the mounting debts to British merchants, the fear of an Anglican bishop, the growth of a national consciousness, the lack of representation in Parliament, ideologies of Whiggery and the Enlightenment, the evangelistic impulse, the abrupt shift from a mercantile to an "imperial" policy after 1763, class conflict, revolutionary conspiracy.

Each of them separately and all of them together are subject to challenge, but each contributed something to collective grievances that rose to a climax in a gigantic failure of British statesmanship. A conflict between British sovereignty and American rights had come to a point of confrontation that adroit statesmanship might have avoided, side-stepped, or outflanked. Irresolution and vacillation in the British ministry finally gave way to the stubborn determination to force an issue long permitted to drift. The colonists, conditioned by the Whig interpretation of history, saw these developments as the conspiracy of a corrupted oligarchy—and finally, they decided, of a despotic king—to impose an "absolute Tyranny."

Perhaps the last word on how it came about should belong to an obscure participant, Levi Preston, a Minute Man from Danvers, Massachusetts. Asked sixty-seven years after Lexington and Concord about British oppressions, he responded, as his young interviewer reported later: " 'What were they? Oppressions? I didn't feel them.' 'What, were you not oppressed by the Stamp Act?' 'I never saw one of those stamps, and always understood that Governor Bernard put them all in Castle William. I am certain I never paid a penny for one of them.' 'Well, what then about the tea-tax?' 'Tea-tax! I never drank a drop of the stuff; the boys threw it all overboard.' 'Then I suppose you had been reading Har-

Thomas Jefferson's draft of the Declaration of Independence.

rington or Sidney and Locke about the eternal principles of liberty.' 'Never heard of 'em. We read only the Bible, the Catechism, Watts's Psalms and Hymns, and the Almanack.' 'Well, then, what was the matter? and what did you mean in going to the fight?' 'Young man, what we meant in going for those redcoats was this: we always had governed ourselves, and we always meant to. They didn't mean we should.' "

FURTHER READING

For a narrative survey of the events leading to the Revolution, see Edmund S. Morgan's *The Birth of the Republic, 1763–1789* (rev. ed., 1977),° and Edward Countryman's *The American Revolution* (1985).°

For the perspective of Great Britain on the imperial conflict, see Sir Lewis Namier's *England in the Age of the American Revolution* (2nd ed., 1961) and Ian Christie, *Crisis of Empire* (1966).

The intellectual foundations for revolt are traced in Bernard Bailyn's *The Ideological Origins of the American Revolution* (1967),° in the opening chapters of Gordon S. Wood's *The Creation of the American Republic, 1776–1787* (1969)°, and in John Phillip Reid's *Constitutional History of the American Revolution: The Authority of Rights* (1987). To understand how these views were connected to organized protest, see Pauline Maier's *From Resistance to Revolution: Colonial Radicals and the Development of American Opposition to Great Britain, 1765–1776* (1972). The transfer of allegiance from king to Congress is examined in Jerrilyn Marston's *King and Congress: The Transfer of Political Legitimacy, 1774–1776* (1987).

Profiles of the Revolutionary generation can be found in Bernard Bailyn's *Faces of Revolution: Personalities and Themes in the Struggle for Independence* (1990), in Pauline Maier's *The Old Revolutionaries: Political Lives in the Age of Samuel Adams* (1980),° and in A. J. Langguth's *Patriots: The Men Who Started the American Revolution* (1988). Other biographies include Merrill D. Peterson's *Thomas Jefferson and the New Nation* (1970), Dumas Malone's *Jefferson, the Virginian* (1948), Peter Shaw's *The Character of John Adams* (1976), and Eric Foner's *Tom Paine and Revolutionary America* (1976).° Jay Fliegelman's *Prodigals and Pilgrims* (1982) shows how changes in family structure predisposed colonists to revolution.

A number of books deal with specific events in the chain of crisis. Oliver M. Dickerson's *The Navigation Acts and the American Revolution* (1951) stresses the change from trade regulation to taxation in

°These books are available in paperback editions.

1764. Edmund S. Morgan and Helen M. Morgan's *The Stamp Act Crisis* (rev. ed., 1962)° gives the colonial perspective on that crucial event. Also valuable are Hiller B. Zobel's *The Boston Massacre* (1970), Benjamin W. Labaree's *The Boston Tea Party* (1964), and David Ammerman's *In the Common Cause* (1974), on the Coercive Acts. Thomas Doerfliner's *A Vigorous Spirit of Enterprise: Merchants and Economic Development in Revolutionary Philadelphia* (1986)° describes the role of that influential group in the imperial crisis. Carl L. Becker's *The Declaration of Independence* (1922)° remains the best introduction to the framing of that document. More interpretive on the contents of the Declaration is Garry Wills's *Inventing America: Jefferson's Declaration of Independence* (1978).°

For accounts of the imperial controversy at the colony level, see Patricia U. Bonomi's *A Factious People: Politics and Society in Colonial New York* (1971)° and Edward Countryman's *A People in Revolution* (1981),° both on New York; Richard D. Brown's *Revolutionary Politics in Massachusetts* (1970)° and Richard L. Bushman's *King and People in Provincial Massachusetts* (1985); James H. Hutson's *Pennsylvania Politics, 1746–1770* (1972); Rhys Isaac's *The Transformation of Virginia, 1740–1790* (1982)°; and A. Roger Ekirch's *"Poor Carolina": Politics and Society in Colonial North Carolina, 1729–1776* (1981).

Events west of the Appalachians are chronicled concisely by Jack M. Sosin in *The Revolutionary Frontier, 1763–1783* (1967). Military affairs in the early phases of the war are handled in John W. Shy's *Toward Lexington* (1965) and in other works listed in Chapter 6.

°These books are available in paperback editions.

PART TWO

BUILDING A NATION

The signing of the Declaration of Independence generated great excitement among the rebellious colonists. Yet a stern reality tempered their celebrations. It was one thing for Patriot leaders to declare American independence from British authority; it was quite another to win it on the battlefield. Barely a third of the colonists actively supported the Revolution. The political stability of the new nation was uncertain. And George Washington found himself in command of a poorly supplied, ragtag army.

Yet the Revolutionary movement would persevere and prevail. The skill and fortitude of Washington and his lieutenants enabled the American armies to exploit their geographic advantages. Equally important was the intervention of the French on behalf of the Revolutionary cause. The Franco-American Alliance proved to be decisive. After eight years of sporadic fighting and heavy human and financial losses, the British gave up the fight and their American colonies.

In the midst of the Revolutionary turmoil, the Patriots faced the daunting task of forming new governments for themselves. Their deeply engrained resentment of British imperial rule led them to decentralize power and place sovereignty in the individual states. As Thomas Jefferson declared, "Virginia, Sir, is my country." John Adams felt some loyalty for his native Massachusetts. Such local ties help explain why the colonists focused their attention on creating new state constitutions rather than a national government. The Articles of Confederation, ratified in 1781, provided only the semblance of national authority. All final power to make and execute laws remained with the states.

After the end of the Revolutionary War in 1783, the flimsy political bonds authorized by the Articles of Confederation proved inadequate to the needs of the new—and expanding—nation. This realization led to the calling of the Constitutional Convention in 1787. The process of drafting and ratifying the new constitution spawned a debate about the relative significance of national power, local control, and individual freedom that has provided the central theme of American political thought ever since.

The American Revolution, however, involved much more than the apportionment of political power. It also unleashed social forces and posed social questions that would help to reshape the very fabric of

American culture. What would be the role of women, blacks, and Native Americans in the new republic? How would the contrasting economies of the various regions of the new United States be developed? Who would control and facilitate access to the vast territories to the west of the original thirteen states? How would the new Republic relate to the other nations of the world?

These complex and controversial questions helped foster the creation of the first national political parties in the United States. During the 1790s, Federalists led by Alexander Hamilton and Democrat-Republicans led by Thomas Jefferson and James Madison engaged in a heated debate about the political and economic future of the new nation. With Jefferson's election as president in 1800, the Republicans gained the upper hand in national politics for the next quarter century. In the process they presided over a maturing American society that aggressively expanded westward at the expense of the Native Americans, ambivalently embraced industrial development, fitfully engaged in a second war with Great Britain, and ominously witnessed a growing sectional controversy over slavery.

6 ⁄⁊

THE AMERICAN REVOLUTION

Few foreign observers thought that the upstart American revolutionaries could win a war against the world's greatest empire—and the Americans did lose most of the battles of the Revolution. But they eventually forced the British to sue for peace and grant their independence, an unlikely result that reflects the tenacity of the Patriots as well as the peculiar difficulties facing the British as they tried to conduct a far-flung campaign thousands of miles from home. The costly military commitments they maintained elsewhere around the globe further complicated the British situation.

Fighting in the New World, however, was not an easy task for either side. The Americans had to create a military force from scratch, one capable of opposing the foremost army in the world. Recruiting, supplying, equipping, training and paying soldiers were monumental challenges, especially for a fledgling nation in the midst of forming its first governments. Yet the perseverance of the Revolutionaries bore fruit, as war-weariness and political dissension in London hampered British efforts to suppress the rebel forces.

Like all major military events, the Revolution had profound and unexpected consequences affecting political, economic, and social life. It not only secured American independence, generated a new sense of nationalism, and created a unique system of self-governance; it also began a process of societal definition and change that has yet to run its course. The turmoil of Revolution upset traditional class and social relationships and helped transform the lives of people who have long been relegated to the periphery of historical concern—blacks, women, and Indians. In important ways, then, the Revolution was much more than simply a war for independence. It was an engine for political experimentation and social change.

1776: WASHINGTON'S NARROW ESCAPE

On July 2, 1776, the day that Congress voted for independence, British redcoats landed on the undefended Staten Island. They were the vanguard of a gigantic effort to reconquer America and the first elements of an enormous force that gathered around New York Harbor over the next month. By mid-August General William Howe, with the support of a fleet under his older brother, Admiral Richard, Lord Howe, had some 32,000 men at his disposal, the largest single force ever mustered by the British in the eighteenth century. Washington had expected the move and transferred most of his men from Boston, but could gather only about 19,000 Continentals and militiamen. This was too small a force to defend New York, but Congress wanted it held. This forced Washington to expose his men to entrapments from which they escaped more by luck and Howe's caution than by any strategic genius of the American commander. Washington was still learning his trade, and the New York campaign afforded some expensive lessons.

FIGHTING IN NEW YORK AND NEW JERSEY   The first conflicts took place on Long Island. By invading and occupying New York, the British hoped to sever New England from the rest of the rebellious colonies. In late August, Howe inflicted heavy losses in early battles and forced Washington to evacuate Long Island to reunite his dangerously divided forces. A timely rainstorm, with strong winds and high tides, kept the British fleet out of the East River and made possible a withdrawal to Manhattan under cover of darkness.

Had Howe moved quickly, he could have trapped Washington's army in lower Manhattan. The main American force of 6,000 men, however, withdrew northward to mainland New York and then retreated slowly

General William Howe, commander-in-chief of His Majesty's forces in America.

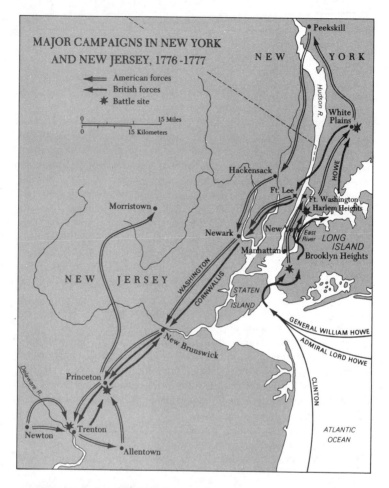

MAJOR CAMPAIGNS IN NEW YORK
AND NEW JERSEY, 1776-1777

⬅ American forces
⬅ British forces
✳ Battle site

0 _____ 15 Miles
0 _____ 15 Kilometers

NEW YORK

Peekskill

Hudson R.

White Plains

HOWE

Hackensack

Ft. Lee

Ft. Washington
Harlem Heights

Newark

New York

East River

LONG ISLAND

Manhattan

Brooklyn Heights

Morristown

NEW JERSEY

WASHINGTON

CORNWALLIS

STATEN ISLAND

GENERAL WILLIAM HOWE

ADMIRAL LORD HOWE

New Brunswick

CLINTON

Princeton

Delaware R.

Newton

Trenton

Allentown

ATLANTIC OCEAN

across New Jersey and over the Delaware River into Pennsylvania. In
the retreat marched a British volunteer, Thomas Paine. Having opened
an eventful year with his inspiring pamphlet *Common Sense,* he now
composed in Newark *The American Crisis,* in which he penned an
immortal line:

> These are the times that try men's souls: The summer soldier and the
> sunshine patriot will, in this crisis, shrink from the service of his country;
> but he that stands it NOW deserves the love and thanks of man and
> woman. Tyranny, like Hell, is not easily conquered. Yet we have this con-
> solation with us, that the harder the conflict, the more glorious the tri-
> umph.

The pamphlet, ordered read in the American army camps, bolstered the shaken morale of the Patriots—as events would soon do more decisively.

General Howe, firmly—and luxuriously—based in New York (which the British held throughout the war), established outposts in New Jersey and to the east at Newport, and settled down to wait out the winter. Washington, however, was not yet ready to go into winter quarters. Instead he seized the initiative. On Christmas night 1776, he slipped across the icy Delaware with some 2,400 men. Near dawn at Trenton, the Americans surprised a garrison of 1,500 Hessians (German mercenaries) still befuddled from too much holiday rum. It was a total rout from which only 500 royal soldiers escaped death or capture. Only six of Washington's men were wounded, one of whom was Lieutenant James Monroe, the future president. At nearby Princeton on January 3 the Americans repelled three regiments of British redcoats before taking refuge in winter quarters at Morristown, in the hills of northern New Jersey. The campaigns of 1776 had ended, after repeated defeats, with two minor victories that inspirited the Patriot cause. Howe had missed his great chance, indeed several chances, to bring the rebellion to a speedy end. Grumbled one British officer, the Americans had "become

George Washington at Princeton, *by Charles Willson Peale.*

a formidable enemy," even though they had yet to win a full-scale conventional battle.

AMERICAN SOCIETY AT WAR

THE LOYALISTS   After the British occupied New York, civilians had assumed that the rebellion was collapsing and thousands hastened to sign an oath of allegiance to the crown.

Opinion concerning the war divided in three ways: Patriots or Whigs (as the revolutionaries called themselves), Tories (as Patriots called the Loyalists, recalling the diehard defenders of royal prerogative in England), and an indifferent middle group swayed mostly by the better organized and more energetic radicals. That the Loyalists were numerous is evident from the departure during or after the war of roughly 100,000 of them, or more than 3 percent of the total population. But the Patriots were probably the largest of the three groups. There was a like division in British opinion. The aversion of so many Englishmen to the war was one reason for the government's hiring German mercenaries, the "Hessians."

Estimating how many Americans remained loyal to Britain was a central concern of English military planners, for they based many of their decisions on such figures. Through most of the war, in New Jersey and in other colonies, the British would be chasing the elusive Tory majority that Loyalists kept telling them was out there waiting only for British regulars to show the flag. Often they miscalculated. Generally, American Tories were concentrated in the seaport cities, but they came from all walks of life. Governors, judges, and other royal officials were almost totally loyal; most Anglican ministers also preferred the mother country; colonial merchants might be tugged one way or the other, depending on how much they had benefited or suffered from mercantilist regulation; the great planters were swayed one way by dependence on British bounties, another by their debts to British merchants. In the backcountry of New York and the Carolinas, many humble folk rallied to the crown. Where planter aristocrats tended to be Whig, as in North Carolina, backcountry farmers (many of them recently Regulators) leaned to the Tories.

In few places, however, were there enough Tories to assume control without the presence of British regulars, and nowhere for very long. Time and again the British forces were frustrated by both the failure of Loyalists to materialize in strength and the collapse of Loyalist militia units once regular detachments pulled out. Even more disheartening was what one British officer called "the licentiousness of the troops, who committed every species of rapine and plunder," and thereby converted

"One of those ubiquitous American frontiersmen-turned-soldier," second from right. Sketches of the American militia by a French soldier at Yorktown.

potential friends into enemies. British and Hessian regulars, brought up in a hard school of warfare, tended to treat all civilians as hostile. Loyalist militiamen, at the same time, were loath to let any rebel sympathizers slip back into passivity, and so prodded them into active hostility.

The inability of the British to use Loyalists effectively as pacification troops led them to abandon areas once they had conquered them. Because Patriot militias quickly returned whenever the British left an area, any Loyalists in the region faced a difficult choice: either accompany the British and leave behind their property or stay behind and face the wrath of the Patriots. In addition, the British policy of offering slaves their freedom in exchange for their loyalty and even arming many of them to fight against the Americans served to alienate large numbers of neutral or even Tory planters.

The Patriot militia kept springing to life whenever redcoats appeared nearby, and all adult white males, with few exceptions, were obligated under state law to serve when called. With time, even the most apathetic would be pressed into a commitment, if only to turn out for drill. And sooner or later nearly every colonial county experienced military action that would call for armed resistance. The war itself, then, whether through British and Loyalist behavior or the call of the militia, mobilized the apathetic into at least an appearance of support for the American cause. Once made, this commitment was seldom reversed.

MILITIA AND ARMY   American militiamen served two purposes. They constituted a home guard, defending their own communities, and they also helped augment the Continental army. In the backcountry, the militia engaged in the kind of fighting that had become habitual when they were colonists. Dressed in hunting shirts and armed with muskets with long, grooved barrels, they preferred to ambush their opponents or engage them in hand-to-hand combat rather than fight in traditional formations. They also tended to kill unnecessarily and torture prisoners. To repel an attack, the militia somehow materialized; the danger past, it evaporated, for there were chores to do at home. They "come in, you cannot tell how," George Washington said in exasperation, "go, you cannot tell when, and act you cannot tell where, consume your provisions, exhaust your stores, and leave you at last at a critical moment." All too often the green troops would panic in a formal line of battle. They therefore were usually placed in the front ranks in the hope that they would get off a shot or two before they fled.

The Continental army, by contrast, was on the whole well trained. As one British officer commented, the American forces displayed "a sort of implacable ardor and revenge, which happily are a good deal unknown in the prosecution of war in general." Unlike the professional soldiers in the British army, Washington's troops were citizen-soldiers, mostly poor native-born Americans, or immigrants who had been indentured servants or convicts. Many found camp life debilitating and combat horrifying. As General Nathanael Greene, Washington's ablest commander, pointed out, few had ever engaged in mortal combat, and they were hard pressed to "stand the shocking scenes of war, to march over dead men, to hear without concern the groans of the wounded."

Desertions grew as the war dragged on, and the army fluctuated in size from around 10,000 troops to as high as 20,000 and as low as 5,000. At times Washington could put only 2,000 to 3,000 men in the field. Regiments were organized state by state, and the states were supposed to keep them filled with volunteers, or conscripts if need be, but Washington could never be sure that his requisitions would be met. Local loyalties held sway, but participation in the Continental army led many veterans to develop a more national identity.

PROBLEMS OF FINANCE AND SUPPLY   The Congress found it difficult to supply the army. None of the states provided more than a part of its share, and Congress reluctantly let army agents take supplies directly from farmers in return for certificates promising future payment. Many of the states found a ready source of revenue in the sale of Loyalist estates. Nevertheless, the Congress and the states fell short of funding the war's cost, and resorted to printing paper money. In June 1775 Congress began the issuance of Continental currency and kept the printing presses running.

With goods scarce and money plentiful, prices in terms of "Continental" dollars rose sharply. At Valley Forge during the winter of 1777–1778, Washington's men would suffer terribly, less because of actual shortages than because farmers preferred to sell their produce for British gold and silver. Congress did better at providing munitions than at providing other supplies. In 1777 Congress established a government arsenal at Springfield, Massachusetts, and during the war states offered bounties for the manufacture of guns and powder. Still, most munitions were supplied either by capture during the war or by importation from France, where the government was all too glad to help rebels against its British archenemy.

During the harsh winter at Morristown (1776–1777), Washington's army very nearly disintegrated as enlistments expired and deserters fled the hardships. Only about 1,000 Continentals and a few militiamen stuck it out. With the spring thaw, however, recruits began arriving to claim the bounty of $20 and 100 acres of land offered by Congress to those who would enlist for three years or for the duration of the conflict, if less. With some 9,000 regulars Washington began

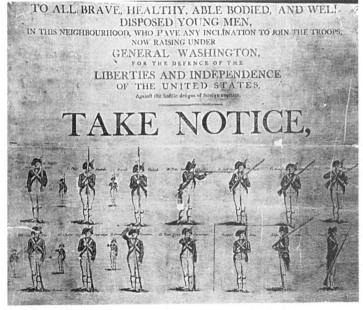

A poster recruiting soldiers for the Continental army. The Congress appealed to those interested in "viewing the different parts of this beautiful continent, in the honourable and truly respectable character of a soldier," and then returning home "with his pockets FULL of money and his head COVERED with laurels."

sparring and feinting with Howe in northern New Jersey. Howe had been making other plans, however, and so had other British officers.

1777: Setbacks for the British

Divided counsels, overconfidence, poor communications, and indecision plagued British planning for the campaigns of 1777. After the removal of General Gage during the siege of Boston, the vain-glorious "Gentleman Johnny" Burgoyne took command of the northern armies. Burgoyne proposed to bisect the colonies. His men would advance southward to the Hudson while another force moved eastward from Oswego down the Mohawk River Valley. Howe, meanwhile, would lead a third force up the Hudson from New York City. Howe in fact had proposed a similar plan, combined with an attack on New England. Had he stuck to it, he might have cut the colonies in two and delivered them a disheartening blow. But he changed his mind and decided to move against the Patriot capital, Philadelphia, expecting that the Pennsylvania Tories would then rally to the crown and secure the colony. Howe, it turned out, was wrong. Moreover, his decision to move on Philadelphia from the south, by way of Chesapeake Bay, put his forces even farther away from Burgoyne.

Howe's plan succeeded, up to a point. He took Philadelphia— or as Benjamin Franklin put it, Philadelphia took him. The Tories there proved fewer than he expected. Washington, sensing Howe's purpose, withdrew most of his men from New Jersey to meet the new threat. At Brandywine Creek, south of Philadelphia, Howe pushed Washington's forces back on September 11 and eight days later occupied Philadelphia. Washington counterattacked against a British encampment at Germantown on October 4, but reinforcements from Philadelphia under General Lord Cornwallis arrived in time to repulse the attack. Washington retired into winter quarters at Valley Forge while Howe and his men remained for the winter in the relative comfort of Philadelphia, twenty miles away. To the north, meanwhile, Burgoyne was stumbling into disaster.

SARATOGA   After concluding his marching orders by declaring "This Army must not Retreat," Burgoyne moved southward from Canada toward Lake Champlain in 1777 with about 7,000 men, his mistress, and a baggage train that included some 30 carts filled with his personal belongings and a large supply of champagne. Such heavily laden forces had a difficult time traversing the wooded and marshy terrain.

The American army in the north, like Washington's army at Morris-

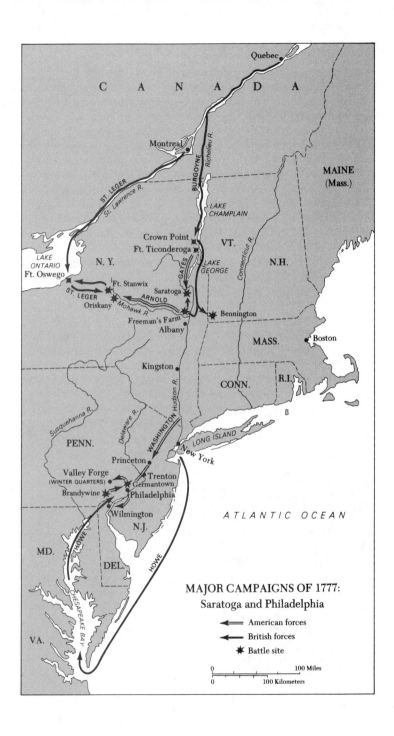

Quebec

C A N A D A

MAINE
(Mass.)

Montreal

ST. LEGER

St. Lawrence R.

Richelieu R.

BURGOYNE

LAKE
CHAMPLAIN

Crown Point
Ft. Ticonderoga

VT.

N.H.

Connecticut R.

LAKE
ONTARIO
Ft. Oswego

N. Y.

GATES

LAKE
GEORGE

ST. LEGER

Ft. Stanwix

Saratoga

ARNOLD

Oriskany

Mohawk R.

Freeman's Farm

Bennington

MASS.

Boston

Albany

Kingston

Hudson R.

CONN.

R.I.

Susquehanna R.

Delaware R.

WASHINGTON

PENN.

Princeton

Valley Forge
(WINTER QUARTERS)

Trenton
Germantown

Brandywine

Philadelphia

LONG ISLAND

New York

ATLANTIC OCEAN

Wilmington

N.J.

HOWE

MD.

DEL.

HOWE

CHESAPEAKE BAY

VA.

MAJOR CAMPAIGNS OF 1777:
Saratoga and Philadelphia

⟵ American forces
⟵ British forces
✹ Battle site

0   100 Miles

0   100 Kilometers

town, had dwindled during the winter. When Burgoyne brought his cannon to bear on Fort Ticonderoga, the Continentals prudently abandoned the fort, but with substantial loss of powder and supplies. An angry Congress thereupon fired the American commander and replaced him with Horatio Gates, a favorite of the New Englanders. Fortunately for the American forces, Burgoyne delayed at Ticonderoga, thereby enabling reinforcements to arrive from the south and New England.

The more mobile and seasoned Americans inflicted two serious reversals on the British forces. At Oriskany, New York, on August 6, 1777, a band of militia repulsed an ambush by Tories and Indians, and gained time for Benedict Arnold to bring a thousand Continentals to the relief of Fort Stanwix. The Indians, convinced they faced an even greater force than they actually did, deserted, and the Mohawk Valley was secured for the Patriot forces. To the east, at Bennington, Vermont (August 16), a body of New England militia led by Colonel John Stark repulsed a British foraging party with heavy losses. Stark had pledged that morning: "We'll beat them before night, or Molly Stark will be a widow." American reinforcements continued to gather, and after two sharp clashes at Freeman's Farm and Bemis Heights, Burgoyne pulled back to Saratoga, where General Horatio Gates's forces surrounded him.

On October 17, 1777, Burgoyne, resplendent in his scarlet, gold, and white uniform, surrendered to the plain, blue-coated Gates, and most of his 5,700 soldiers were imprisoned in Virginia. Gates allowed Burgoyne himself to go home, where he received an icy reception. Gates was ecstatic. He wrote his wife: "If old England is not by this lesson taught humility, then she is an obstinate old slut, bent upon her ruin."

The vainglorious General John Burgoyne, commander of England's northern forces. Burgoyne and most of his British troops surrendered to the Americans at Saratoga on October 17, 1777.

Horatio Gates in a portrait by Rembrandt Peale.

ALLIANCE WITH FRANCE   In early December 1777, news of the American triumph reached London and Paris, where it was celebrated almost as if it were a French victory. Its impact made Saratoga a decisive turning point in the war. The French foreign minister, the comte de Vergennes, had watched the developing Anglo-American crisis with great anticipation. In September 1775 he had sent a special agent to Philadelphia to encourage the colonists and hint at French aid. In November of that year the Continental Congress set up a Committee of Secret Correspondence, later called the Committee for Foreign Affairs, a forerunner of the State Department. The committee employed Massachusetts colonial agent Arthur Lee as its envoy in London. Then in March 1776 it sent Silas Deane, a Connecticut merchant, to buy French munitions and other supplies and inquire about French aid. In September 1776 the committee named Deane, Lee, and Benjamin Franklin its commissioners to France.

In May 1776 the French took their first step toward aiding the colonists. King Louis XVI provided a million livres to Pierre-Augustin Caron de Beaumarchais (author of *The Barber of Seville* and *The Marriage of Figaro*) for clandestine help to the Americans. Beaumarchais was soon sending fourteen ships with war matériel to America; most of

The British Lion Engaging Four Powers. *The American Revolution sparked a world war, as this British cartoon suggests: "Behold the Dutch and Spanish Currs, / Perfidious Gallus in his Spurs, / And Rattlesnake, with head upright, / The British Lion join to fight; / He scorns the Bark, the Hiss, the Crow, / That he's a Lion soon they'll know."*

the Continental army's powder in the first years of the war came from this source. The Spanish government added a donation, and soon established its own supply company. When the word of the American victory at Saratoga arrived in France, Beaumarchais got so carried away in his haste to tell Louis XVI that he wrecked his carriage.

Vergennes now saw his chance to strike a sharper blow at France's enemy and entered into serious negotiations with the American commissioners. On February 6, 1778, they signed two treaties: a Treaty of Amity and Commerce, in which France recognized the United States and offered trade concessions, including important privileges to American shipping, and a Treaty of Alliance. Under the latter both parties agreed, first, that if France entered the war, both countries would fight until American independence was won; second, that neither would conclude a "truce or peace" without "the formal consent of the other first obtained"; and third, that each guaranteed the other's possessions in America "from the present time and forever against all other powers." France further bound itself to seek neither Canada nor other British possessions on the mainland of North America.

By June 1778 British vessels had fired on French ships, and the two nations were at war. In 1779, after extracting French promises to help it regain territories taken by the British in previous wars, Spain entered the war as an ally of France, but not of the United States. In 1780 Britain declared war on the Dutch, who persisted in a profitable trade with the French and Americans. The embattled farmers at Lexington and Concord had indeed fired the "shot heard round the world." Like

Washington's encounter with the French in 1754, it was the start of another world war, and the fighting now spread to the Mediterranean, Africa, India, the West Indies, and the high seas.

1778: BOTH SIDES REGROUP

After Saratoga, Lord North knew that the war was unwinnable, but the king refused to let him either resign or make peace. On March 16, 1778, the House of Commons adopted a program that in effect granted all the American demands prior to independence. Parliament repealed the Townshend tea duty, the Massachusetts Government Act, and the Prohibitory Act, which had closed the colonies to commerce. The Congress refused to begin any negotiations until Britain recognized American independence or withdrew its forces.

Unbeknownst to the British peace commissioners, the crown had already authorized the evacuation of British troops from Philadelphia, a withdrawal that further weakened what little bargaining power they had. After Saratoga, General Howe had resigned his command and Sir Henry Clinton had replaced him, with orders to pull out of Philadelphia, and if necessary, New York, but to keep Newport. He was to supply troops for an expedition in the South, where the government believed a latent Tory sentiment in the backcountry needed only the British presence for its release. The ministry was right, up to a point, but the sentiment turned out once again, as in other theaters of war, to be weaker than it seemed.

For Washington's army at Valley Forge, the winter of 1777–1778 had been a season of suffering far worse than the previous winter at Morristown. The American force, encamped near Philadelphia, endured cold, hunger, and disease. Many soldiers deserted or resigned their commissions, leading Washington to warn Congress that unless substantial supplies were forthcoming, the army "must inevitably be reduced to one or other of these three things: starve, dissolve, or disperse." The winter witnessed dissension in Congress and the army. Some critics wanted to make Washington the scapegoat for the Patriots' plight, but there was never any concerted effort to replace him.

As winter drew to an end the army's morale stiffened when Congress promised extra pay and bonuses after the war. The good news from France helped as well. As General Clinton's British forces withdrew eastward toward New York, Washington pursued them across New Jersey. On June 28 he engaged the British in an indecisive battle at Monmouth Court House. But the Battle of Monmouth was significant for revealing Washington's temper and leadership qualities. In the midst of the fighting, he discovered that his potbellied subordinate, General

Charles Lee, was retreating rather than attacking as ordered. Infuriated, Washington swore at Lee "till the leaves shook the trees," at one point calling him a "damned poltroon." Then Washington rallied the troops just in time to stave off defeat. Clinton slipped away into New York while Washington took up a position at White Plains, north of the city. From that time on the northern theater, scene of the major campaigns and battles in the first years of the war, settled into a long stalemate, interrupted by minor and mostly inconclusive engagements.

ACTIONS ON THE FRONTIER   The one major American success of 1778 occurred far from the New Jersey battlefields. Out to the west the British at Forts Niagara and Detroit had incited frontier Tories and Indians to raid western settlements and offered to pay bounties for American scalps. To end such attacks, young George Rogers Clark took 175 frontiersmen and a flotilla of flatboats down the Ohio River early in 1778, marched through the woods, and on the evening of July 4 took Kaskaskia by surprise. The French inhabitants, terrified at first, "fell into transports of joy" at news of the French alliance. Within a month, and without bloodshed, Clark took Cahokia (opposite St. Louis), Vincennes, and some minor outposts in what he now called the county of Illinois in the state of Virginia. After the British retook Vincennes in December, Clark marched his men (almost half French volunteers) through icy rivers and

The Mohawk leader Thayendanegea (Joseph Brant), who fought against the Americans in the Revolution. Portrait painted by Gilbert Stuart in 1786.

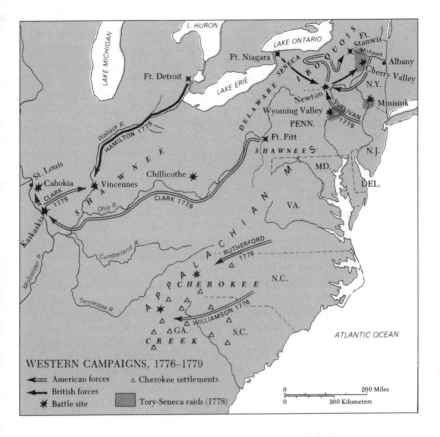

WESTERN CAMPAIGNS, 1776–1779

⟵ American forces △ Cherokee settlements

⟵ British forces

✶ Battle site   ▨ Tory-Seneca raids (1778)

0   200 Miles
0   200 Kilometers

flooded prairies, sometimes in water neck deep, and laid siege to an astonished British garrison there. Then Clark, the hardened woodsman, tomahawked Indian captives in sight of the fort to show that the British afforded them no protection. He spared the British captives when they surrendered, however. Clark is often credited with having conquered the West for the new nation, but there is no evidence that the peace negotiators in 1782 had yet heard of his exploits.

While Clark's captives traveled eastward, a much larger American expedition moved through western Pennsylvania to attack Iroquois strongholds in western New York. There the Tories and Indians terrorized frontier settlements all through the summer of 1778. Led by the charismatic and courageous Mohawk Joseph Brant, the Iroquois killed hundreds of militiamen along the Pennsylvania frontier. In response, Washington dispatched an expedition of 4,000 men under General John Sullivan. At Newton (now Elmira) on August 29, 1779, Sullivan defeated the only serious opposition and proceeded to carry out Washington's instruction that the Iroquois country be not "merely overrun but destroyed." The American force ruthlessly devastated about forty Seneca and Cayuga villages together with their orchards and food supplies. The action broke the power of the Iroquois federation for all time, but it did not completely pacify the frontier. Sporadic encounters with various tribes of the region continued to the end of the war.

In the Kentucky territory, Daniel Boone and his small band of settlers risked constant attack from the Shawnees and their British and Tory allies. During the Revolution, they survived frequent ambushes, at least seven skirmishes, and three pitched battles. In 1778 Boone and some thirty men, aided by their wives and children, held off an assault by more than 400 Indians at Boonesborough. Thereafter, Boone himself was twice shot and twice captured. Indians killed two of his sons, a brother, and two brothers-in-law. His daughter was captured and another brother was wounded four times. Despite such ferocious fighting and dangerous circumstances, the white settlers refused to leave Kentucky.

In early 1776 a delegation of northern Indians—Shawnees, Delawares, and Mohawks—talked the Cherokees into striking at frontier settlements in Virginia and the Carolinas. Swift retaliation followed. In August, South Carolina forces burned the lower Cherokee towns. Virginia and North Carolina militia brought a similar destruction upon the middle and upper towns. Once again, in 1780, a Virginia–North Carolina force wrought destruction on Cherokee towns lest the Indians go to the aid of General Cornwallis. By weakening the major Indian tribes along the frontier, the American Revolution, among its other results, cleared the way for rapid settlement of the trans-Appalachian West.

The War in the South

At the end of 1778 the focus of British action shifted suddenly to the south. The whole region from Virginia southward had been free from major action since 1776. Now the British would test King George's belief that a sleeping Tory power in the South needed only the presence of a few redcoats to awaken it. General Clinton decided to take Savannah, Georgia, and roll northward, gathering momentum from the Loyalist countryside. For a while the idea seemed to work, but it ran afoul of two developments: first, the Loyalist strength was less than estimated; and second, the British forces behaved so harshly as to drive even Loyalists into rebellion.

SAVANNAH AND CHARLESTON   In November 1778 Clinton dispatched units from New York and New Jersey to attack Savannah. So small was the defending force of Continentals and militia that the British quickly overwhelmed the Patriots, took the town, and brushed aside opposition in the interior. There followed a byplay of thrust and parry between British and South Carolinian forces until the redcoats finally drove toward Charleston, plundering plantation houses along the way.

The seesaw campaign took a major turn when General Clinton brought new naval and land forces southward to join a massive amphibious attack that bottled up General Benjamin Lincoln on the Charleston peninsula. On May 12, 1780, Lincoln surrendered the city and its 5,500 defenders, the greatest single American loss of the war. At this point Congress, against Washington's advice, turned to the victor of Saratoga,

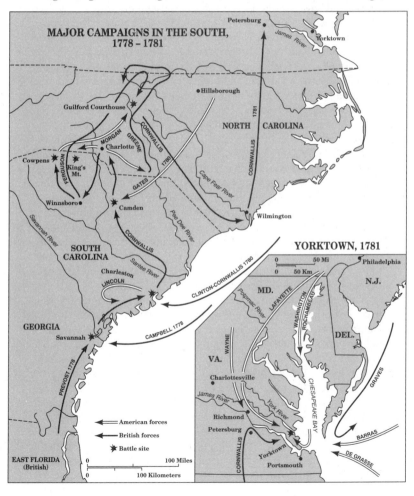

MAJOR CAMPAIGNS IN THE SOUTH, 1778–1781

YORKTOWN, 1781

Horatio Gates, to take command and sent him south. Charles Lord Cornwallis, dispatched with one of three columns to subdue the Carolina interior, surprised Gates's force at Camden, South Carolina, and routed his new army, which retreated all the way back to Hillsborough, North Carolina, 160 miles away. It had come to pass as Gates's friend and neighbor Charles Lee had warned after Saratoga: "Beware that your Northern laurels do not turn to Southern willows."

THE CAROLINAS   From the point of view of British imperial goals, the southern colonies were ultimately more important than the northern ones because they produced valuable staple crops such as tobacco, indigo, and naval stores. The war in the Carolinas eventually involved not only opposing British and American armies, but also degenerated into brutal guerrilla-style civil conflicts between local Loyalists and local Patriots. Such infighting brought chaos.

Cornwallis had South Carolina just about under control, but his subordinates Banastre Tarleton and Patrick Ferguson, who mobilized Tory militiamen, overreached themselves in their effort to subdue the Whigs. "Tarleton's Quarter" became bywords for savagery, because "Bloody Tarleton" gave little quarter to vanquished foes. Ferguson sealed his own doom when he threatened to march over the mountains and hang the leaders of the Watauga country. Instead the feisty "overmountain men" went after Ferguson and, allied with other backcountry Whigs, caught him and his Tories on King's Mountain, just inside South Carolina. There, on October 7, 1780, they devastated his force. By then feelings were so strong that American irregulars continued firing on Tories trying to surrender and later inflicted indiscriminate slaughter on Tory prisoners. King's Mountain was the turning point of the war in the South. By proving that the British were not invincible, it emboldened small farmers to join guerrilla bands under partisan leaders such as Frances Marion, "the Swamp Fox," and Thomas Sumter, "the Gamecock."

While the overmountain men were closing on Ferguson, Congress had chosen a new commander for the southern theater, General Nathanael Greene, the "fighting Quaker" of Rhode Island. A man of infinite patience, skilled at managing men and saving supplies, careful to avoid needless risks, he was suited to a war of attrition against the British forces. From Charlotte, where he arrived in December 1780, Greene moved his army eastward toward the Pee Dee River. As a diversion he sent General Daniel Morgan with about 700 men on a sweep to the west of Cornwallis's headquarters at Winnsboro.

Taking a position near Cowpens, Morgan found himself swamped by militia units joining him faster than he could provide for them. Tarleton caught Morgan and his men on January 17, 1781, with the rain-swollen Broad River at their backs—a position Morgan took deliberately to force the green militiamen to stand and fight. Once the battle was joined, Tarleton mistook a readjustment in the American line for a militia panic, and rushed his men into a destructive fire. Tarleton and a handful of cavalry escaped, but more than 100 of his men were killed and more than 700 taken prisoner.

Morgan then fell back into North Carolina, linked up with Greene's main force at Guilford Courthouse (now Greensboro), and then led Cornwallis on a wild goose chase up to the Dan River. Once the Americans had crossed, the British could not follow, for their supplies were running low. Cornwallis was forced to draw back to Hillsborough. When reinforcements of militiamen from Virginia and the Carolinas arrived, Greene returned to Guilford Courthouse and offered battle on March 15, 1781. There he placed his militiamen at the front of the line, asking them only to stand their ground long enough to fire three shots before they drew back. As he feared, they fled the field, but in the process drew the pursuing redcoats into a withering fire from either side. Having inflicted heavy losses, Greene prudently withdrew to fight another day. Cornwallis was left in possession of the field, but at a cost of nearly 100 men killed and more than 400 wounded. In London, when the word arrived, parliamentary leader Charles James Fox claimed that another "such victory and we are undone."

Cornwallis marched off toward the coast at Wilmington to lick his wounds and take on new supplies. Greene then resolved to go back into South Carolina in the hope of drawing Cornwallis after him or forcing the British to give up the state. There he joined forces with the guerrillas already active on the scene, and in a series of brilliant actions kept losing battles while winning the war: "We fight, get beat, rise, and fight again," he said. By September 1781 he had narrowed British control in the Deep South to Charleston and Savannah, although for more than a year longer Whigs and Tories slashed at each other "with savage fury" in the backcountry, where there was "nothing but murder and devastation in every quarter," Greene said.

Meanwhile Cornwallis had headed north away from Greene, reasoning that Virginia must be eliminated as a source of reinforcement before the Carolinas could be subdued. In May 1781 he marched north into Virginia. There, since December 1780, Benedict Arnold, now a British general, was engaged in a war of maneuver with American forces under Lafayette and von Steuben. Arnold, until September 1780, had been American commander at West Point. Overweening in ambition, lacking in moral scruples, and reckless in his spending on his fashionable wife, Arnold nursed a grudge against Washington over an official reprimand for his extravagances as commander of reoccupied Philadelphia. Traitors have a price, and Arnold soon found his: he crassly plotted to sell out the West Point garrison to the British, and he even suggested

A crowd parading through Philadelphia prior to burning an effigy of Benedict Arnold as "Spy Traytor" (1780).

how they might capture Washington himself. Only the fortuitous capture of the British go-between, Major John André, ended Arnold's plot. Forewarned that his plan had been discovered, Arnold joined the British in New York while the Americans hanged André as a spy.

YORKTOWN   When Cornwallis linked up with Arnold at Petersburg, their combined forces rose to 7,200, far more than the small American force there. The arrival of American reinforcements led Cornwallis to pick Yorktown as a defensible site. There appeared to be little reason to worry about a siege, since Washington's main land force seemed preoccupied with attacking New York and the British navy controlled American waters.

To be sure, there was a small American navy, but it was no match for the British fleet. Washington had started it with some fishing vessels during the siege of Boston, but American privateers, acting under state or Continental authority, proved far more troublesome. Most celebrated were the exploits of Captain John Paul Jones, who crossed the Atlantic in 1778 and gave the British navy some bad moments in its home waters. Off England's coast on September 23, 1779, Jones won a desperate battle with a British frigate, which he captured and occupied before his own ship sank. This was the occasion for his stirring and oft-repeated response to a British demand for surrender: "I have not yet begun to fight."

Still, such heroics were little more than nuisances to the British. But at a critical point, thanks to the French navy, the British lost control of the Chesapeake waters. Indeed, it is impossible to imagine an American victory in the Revolution without the assistance of the French. As long as the British navy maintained supremacy at sea, the Americans could not hope to force a settlement to their advantage. For three years Washington had waited to get some military benefit from the French alliance. In 1780 the French finally landed a force of about 6,000 at Newport, which the British had given up to concentrate on the South, but the French army under the comte de Rochambeau sat there for a year, blockaded by the British fleet.

Then, in 1781, the elements for combined action suddenly fell into place. In May, as Cornwallis moved into Virginia, Washington persuaded Rochambeau to join forces for an attack on New York. The two armies linked up in July, but before they could strike at New York, word came from the West Indies that Admiral De Grasse was bound for the Chesapeake with his entire French fleet and some 3,000 soldiers. Washington and Rochambeau immediately set out toward Yorktown, all the while preserving the semblance of a flank movement against New York.

On August 30 De Grasse's fleet reached Yorktown, and he landed his troops to join the American force already watching Cornwallis. On September 6, the day after a British fleet appeared, De Grasse gave battle and forced the British to give up the effort to relieve Cornwallis, whose fate was quickly sealed. De Grasse then sent ships up the Chesapeake to ferry down Washington's and Rochambeau's armies, which brought the total American and French forces to more than 16,000, or better than double the size of Cornwallis's army.

The siege began on September 28. At one point during the attack, Washington and his staff came under fire as they observed the action. A

British troops grounding their arms at the surrender at Yorktown in 1781.

worried aide suggested to the commanding general that perhaps he should "step back a little." Washington tersely replied: "Colonel Cobb, if you are afraid, you have the liberty to step back." On October 14 two major redoubts guarding the left of the British line fell to French and American attackers, the latter led by Washington's aide Alexander Hamilton. A British counterattack on October 16 failed to retake them. Later that day a squall forced Cornwallis to abandon a desperate plan to escape across the York River. On October 17, 1781, four years to the day after Saratoga, he sued for peace, and on October 19 the British force of almost 8,000 marched out, their colors cased, as the British band played somber tunes along with the English nursery rhyme "The World Turned Upside Down." Cornwallis himself claimed to be too "ill" to appear. His dispatch to his superior was telling: "I have the mortification to inform your Excellency that I have been forced to . . . surrender the troops under my command."

NEGOTIATIONS

Whatever lingering hopes of victory the British may have harbored vanished at Yorktown. "Oh God, it's all over," Lord North groaned at news of the surrender. On February 27, 1782, the House of Commons voted against continuing the war and on March 5 authorized the crown to make peace. On March 20 Lord North resigned. The new ministry included old friends of the Americans headed by the duke of Rockingham, who had brought about repeal of the Stamp Act. The new colonial minister, Lord Shelburne, became chief minister after Rockingham's death in September and directed negotiations with American commissioners.

The Continental Congress named a five-man commission to negotiate a peace treaty. Only three members of the commission were active, however: John Adams, who was on state business in the Netherlands; John Jay, minister to Spain; and Benjamin Franklin, already in Paris. Franklin and Jay did most of the work.

The French commitment to Spain complicated matters. Spain and the United States were both allied with France, but not with each other. America was bound by its alliance to fight on until the French made peace, and the French were bound to help the Spanish recover Gibraltar from England. Unable to deliver Gibraltar, or so the tough-minded Jay reasoned, the French might try to bargain off American land west of the Appalachians in its place. Jay's distrust quickened when the French minister's secretary informally suggested just such a bargain and left secretly for London. Fearful that the French were angling for a separate peace with the British, Jay persuaded Franklin to play the same game. Ignoring their instructions to consult fully with the French, they agreed to further talks with the British. On November 30, 1782, the talks produced a preliminary treaty with Great Britain. If it violated the spirit of the alliance, it did not violate the strict letter of the treaty with France, for the French minister was notified the day before it was signed, and final agreement still depended on a Franco-British settlement.

THE PEACE OF PARIS   Early in 1783 France and Spain gave up on Gibraltar and reached an armistice with Britain. The final signing of the Peace of Paris came on September 3, 1783. In accord with the bargain already struck, Great Britain recognized the independence of the United States and agreed to a Mississippi River boundary to the west. Both the northern and southern borders left ambiguities that would require further definition. Florida, as it turned out, passed back to Spain. The British further granted Americans the "liberty" of fishing off Newfoundland and in the St. Lawrence Gulf, and the right to dry

American Commissioners of the Preliminary Peace Negotiations with Great Britain, *A painting by Benjamin West. From left, John Jay, John Adams, Benjamin Franklin, Henry Laurens, and Franklin's nephew, William Temple Franklin (1782).*

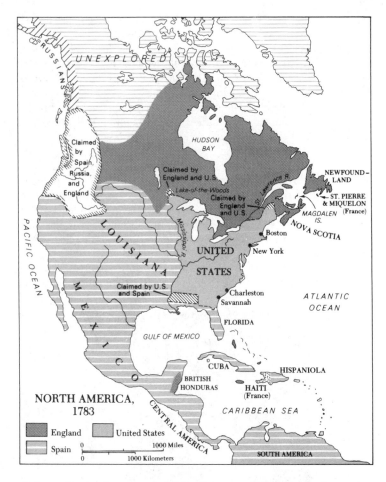

NORTH AMERICA, 1783

England | United States
Spain

0   1000 Miles
0   1000 Kilometers

Labels on the map:

RUSSIANS

UNEXPLORED

HUDSON BAY

Claimed by Spain, Russia, and England

Claimed by England and U.S.
Lake-of-the-Woods
Claimed by England and U.S.

NEWFOUND-LAND
ST. PIERRE & MIQUELON (France)
MAGDALEN IS.
NOVA SCOTIA

St. Lawrence R.

PACIFIC OCEAN

LOUISIANA

Mississippi R.

UNITED STATES

Boston
New York

MEXICO

Claimed by U.S. and Spain

Charleston
Savannah

ATLANTIC OCEAN

FLORIDA

GULF OF MEXICO

CUBA

HISPANIOLA

BRITISH HONDURAS

HAITI (France)

CENTRAL AMERICA

CARIBBEAN SEA

SOUTH AMERICA

their catches on the unsettled Atlantic coast of Canada. On the matter of debts, the best the British could get was a promise that British merchants should "meet with no legal impediment" in seeking to collect them. And on the tender point of Loyalists whose estates had been confiscated, the negotiators agreed that Congress would "earnestly recommend" to the states the restoration of confiscated property. Each of the last two points was little more than a face-saving gesture for the British.

On November 24 the last British troops left New York City, and on December 4 they evacuated Staten Island and Long Island. That same day Washington took leave of his officers in New York. On December 23 he appeared before the Continental Congress, meeting in Annapolis, to resign his commission. Before the end of the next day he was back at Mount Vernon, home in time for Christmas.

THE POLITICAL REVOLUTION

REPUBLICAN IDEOLOGY   The Americans had won their War for Independence. Had they undergone a political revolution as well? Years later, John Adams offered one answer: "The Revolution was effected before the war commenced. The Revolution was in the minds and hearts of the people. . . . This radical change in the principles, opinions, sentiments, and affections of the people, was the real American Revolution." Yet Adams's observation ignores the fact that the Revolutionary war itself served as the catalyst for a prolonged internal debate about what new forms of government would best serve an independent republic. The conventional British model of mixed government sought to balance monarchy, aristocracy, and the common people and thereby protect individual liberty. Because of the more democratic nature of their society, however, Americans knew that they must derive new political assumptions and institutions. They had no monarchy or aristocracy. Yet how could sovereignty reside in the common people? How could Americans ensure the survival and effectiveness of a republican form of government, long assumed to be the most fragile? The war thus provoked a spate of state constitution-making that remains unique in human history.

A struggle for the rights of English citizens became a fight for independence in which those rights found expression in governments that were new, yet deeply rooted in the colonial experience and the prevail-

America Triumphant and Britannia in Distress *(1782)*.

ing viewpoints of Whiggery and the Enlightenment. With the Loyalists displaced or dispersed, such ideas as the contract theory of government, the sovereignty of the people, the separation of powers, and natural rights found their way into the new frames of government that were devised while the fight went on—amid other urgent business.

The very idea of republican government was a radical departure in that day. The idea was rooted in that radical element of British Whiggery that a later historian labeled the eighteenth-century Commonwealthmen, a group that invoked the spirit of republican thinkers in classical antiquity. Drawing from such sources, Americans began to see themselves in a new light, no longer the rustic provincials in a backwater of European culture but rather the embodiment of the civic virtue deemed necessary to the success of a republican form of government. As free citizens of a republic, unshackled by dependence on the favor of the court, Americans would cast off the corruptions of the Old World and usher in a new reign of liberty and virtue, not only for themselves but for all peoples. The new American republic, in other words, would endure as long as the majority of the people were virtuous and willingly placed the good of society above the self-interests of individuals. Herein lay the hope and the danger of the new American experiment in popular government: even as leaders enthusiastically fashioned new state constitutions, they feared that their experiments in republicanism would fail because of a lack of civic virtue.

NEW STATE CONSTITUTIONS   Most of the political experimentation between 1776 and 1787 occurred at the state level. Innovations devised in the state constitutional conventions created the core principle of the American political system: representative government defined in written constitutions in which the people are sovereign and delegate limited authority to the government. In addition, the states initiated bills of rights guaranteeing particular individual rights, and fashioned procedures for constitutional conventions that have also remained an essential part of the American political system. In sum, the innovations at the state level during the Revolution created a reservoir of ideas and experience that formed the basis for the creation of the federal constitution in 1787.

At the onset of the fighting every colony saw the departure of governors and other officials, and usually the expulsion of Loyalists from the assemblies, which then assumed power as provincial "congresses" or "conventions." But they were acting as revolutionary bodies without any legal basis for the exercise of authority. In two of the states this presented little difficulty. Connecticut and Rhode Island, which had been virtually little republics as corporate colonies, simply purged their charters of any reference to colonial ties. Massachusetts followed their example until 1780.

In the other states the prevailing notions of social contract and popular sovereignty led to written constitutions that specified the framework and powers of government. One of the lessons of the Revolution was the danger of relying on the vague body of law and precedent that made up the unwritten constitution of Britain. Constitution-making in fact had begun even before independence. In May 1776 Congress advised the colonies to set up new governments "under the authority of the people." At first the authority of the people was exercised by legislatures, which simply adopted constitutions and promulgated them. But they had little more status than ordinary statutory law, it could be argued, since the people had no chance to express their wishes directly.

When the Massachusetts assembly hastily submitted a constitution to the towns for approval, however, it was rejected. Massachusetts thereupon invented what became a standard device for American constitution-making: a body separate from and superior to the legislature to exercise the people's sovereignty. In 1779–1780 Massachusetts elected a special convention, chosen for the specific purpose of making a constitution. The invention of the constitutional convention was an altogether original contribution to the art of government, and one that other states copied. The resultant document went out to the town meetings with the provision that two-thirds or more would have to ratify it, which they did. The Massachusetts Constitution of 1780 declared: "The body politic is formed by a voluntary association of individuals; it is a social compact, by which the whole people covenants with each citizen, and each with the whole people that all shall be governed by certain laws for the common good."

The first state constitutions varied mainly in detail. They formed governments much like the colonial governments, with elected governors and senates instead of appointed governors and councils. Generally they embodied, sometimes explicitly, a separation of powers as a safeguard against abuses. Most of them also included a Bill of Rights that protected the time-honored rights of petition, freedom of speech, trial by jury, freedom from self-incrimination, and the like. Most tended to limit the powers of governors and increase the powers of the legislatures, which had led the people in their quarrels with the colonial governors. Pennsylvania went so far as to eliminate the governor and upper house of the legislature altogether. It had an executive council of twelve, including a president, and operated until 1790 with a unicameral legislature limited only by a house of "censors" who reviewed its work every five years.

THE ARTICLES OF CONFEDERATION   The central government, like the state governments, grew out of an extralegal revolutionary body. The Continental Congress exercised governmental powers without any constitutional sanction before March 1781. Plans for a permanent frame of government were started very early, however. Richard Henry Lee's motion for independence included a call for a plan of confederation. As early as July 1776, a committee headed by John Dickinson produced a draft constitution, the "Articles of Confederation and Perpetual Union." For more than a year Congress debated the articles in between more urgent matters and finally adopted them in November 1777, subject to ratification by all the states. All states ratified promptly except Maryland, which stubbornly insisted that the seven states claiming western lands should cede them to the authority of Congress. Maryland did not relent until early 1781, when Virginia gave up its claims under the old colonial charter to the vast region north of the Ohio River. New York had already relinquished a dubious claim based on its "jurisdiction" over the Iroquois, and the other states eventually abandoned their charter claims, although Georgia did not until 1802.

When the Articles of Confederation became effective in March 1781, they did little more than legalize the status quo. "The United States in Congress Assembled" had a multitude of responsibilities but little authority to carry them out. The Congress was intended not as a legislature, nor as a sovereign entity unto itself, but as a collective substitute for the monarch. In essence, it was to be a plural executive rather than a parliamentary body. It had full power over foreign affairs and questions of war and peace; it could decide disputes between the states; it had authority over coinage, postal service, and Indian affairs, and responsibility for the government of the western territories. But it had no power to enforce its resolutions and ordinances upon either states or individuals. It also had no power to levy taxes, but had to rely on requisitions, which state legislatures could ignore at their will.

The states, after their battles with Parliament, were in no mood for a strong central government. The Congress in fact had less power than the colonists had once accepted in Parliament, since it could not regulate interstate and foreign commerce. For certain important acts, moreover, a "special majority" was required. Nine states had to approve measures dealing with war, privateering, treaties, coinage, finances, or the army and navy. Amendments to the articles required unanimous ratification by all the states. The Confederation had neither an executive nor a judicial branch; there was no administrative head of government (only the president of the Congress, chosen annually) and no federal courts.

For all its weaknesses, however, the Confederation government represented the most pragmatic structure for the new nation. After all, the Revolution on the battlefields had yet to be won, and America's statesmen could not risk the prolonged and divisive debates over the distribution of power that other forms of government would have provoked.

THE SOCIAL REVOLUTION

Americans forged a consensus on the general frame of government—the forms grew so naturally out of experience and the prevalent theories. On other points, however, there was sharp disagreement. Political revolutions easily spawn social revolutions. Just as the Great Awakening brought with it unintended social effects, the revolutionary turmoil allowed long-pent-up frustrations among the lower ranks to find expression. What did the Revolution mean to those workers, servants, farmers, and freed slaves who participated in the Stamp Act demonstrations, supported the boycotts, idolized Tom Paine, and fought with Washington and Greene?

Many laboring folk hoped that the Revolution would remove, not reinforce, the elite's traditional political and social advantages. The more conservative Patriots would have been content to replace royal officials with the rich, the well-born, and the able, and let it go at that. But more radical elements raised the question not only of home rule but who should rule at home.

EQUALITY AND ITS LIMITS   This spirit of equality found outlet in several directions, one of which was simply a weakening of old habits of deference. A Virginia gentleman told of being in a tavern when a rough group of farmers came in, spitting and pulling off their muddy boots without regard to the sensibilities of the gentlemen present: "The spirit of independence was converted into equality," he wrote, "and every one who bore arms, esteems himself upon a footing with his neighbors. . . . No doubt each of these men considers himself, in every respect, my equal." No doubt each did.

What was more, participation in the army or militia excited people who had taken little interest in politics before. The large number of new political opportunities afforded by the creation of state governments led more ordinary citizens into participation than ever before. The social base of the new legislatures was thus much broader than that of the old assemblies.

Men fighting for their liberty found it difficult to justify the denial to other white men of the rights of suffrage and representation. The property qualifications for voting, which already admitted an overwhelming majority of white males, were lowered still further. In Pennsylvania, Delaware, North Carolina, Georgia, and Vermont, any male taxpayer could vote, although officeholders usually had to meet higher property requirements. Men who had argued against taxation without representation now questioned the denial of proportionate representation for the backcountry, which generally enlarged its presence in the legislatures. More often than not the political newcomers were men of lesser

Benjamin Latrobe's watercolor of a tavern in Virginia. The dress of the billiards players suggests that "the spirit of independence was converted into equality."

property and little formal education. All states concentrated much power in a legislature chosen by a wide suffrage, but not even Pennsylvania, which adopted the most radical of the state constitutions, went quite so far as universal manhood suffrage.

New developments in land tenure that grew out of the Revolution extended the democratic trends of suffrage requirements. Confiscations resulted in the seizure of Tory estates by all the state legislatures. These properties, however, were of small consequence in contrast to the unsettled areas formerly at the disposal of crown and proprietors, now in the hands of popular assemblies, much of which was used for bonuses to veterans of the war. Western lands, formerly closed by the Proclamation of 1763 and the Quebec Act of 1774, were soon thrown open for settlers.

THE PARADOX OF SLAVERY   The revolutionary generation of leaders was the first to confront the issue of slavery and to consider abolishing it. The revolutionary principles of liberty and equality had clear implications for enslaved blacks. Jefferson's draft of the Declaration had indicted the king for having violated the "most sacred rights of life and liberty of a distant people, who never offended him, captivating them into slavery in another hemisphere," but the clause was deleted "in complaisance to South Carolina and Georgia." The clause was in fact inaccurate in completely ignoring the implication of American slaveholders and slave traders in the traffic. Before the Revolution, only Rhode Island, Connecticut, and Pennsylvania had halted the importation of slaves. After independence, all the states except Georgia stopped the traffic, although South Carolina later reopened it.

Black soldiers or sailors were present at most of the major battles, from Lexington to Yorktown; most were on the Loyalist side. Lord Dunmore, governor of Virginia, anticipated a general British policy in 1775 when he promised freedom to slaves, as well as indentured servants, who would bear arms for the Loyalist cause. Taking alarm at this, General Washington at the end of 1775 reversed the policy of excluding blacks from American forces—except the few already in militia companies—and Congress quickly approved. Only two states, South Carolina and Georgia, held out completely against the policy, but by a rough estimate few blacks, probably no more than about 5,000, were admitted to the total American forces of about 300,000, and most of those were free blacks from northern states. They served mainly in white units, although Massachusetts did organize two all-black companies and Rhode Island organized one.

Slaves who served in the cause of independence won their freedom and in some cases land bounties. But the British army, which carried off probably tens of thousands of slaves during the war, was a greater instrument of emancipation than the American forces. Most of the newly freed blacks found their way to Canada or to British colonies in the Caribbean. American Whigs showed no mercy to blacks who were caught aiding or abetting the British cause. A Charleston mob hanged and then burned Thomas Jeremiah, a free black who was convicted of telling slaves that the British "were come to help the poor Negroes." White Loyalists who were caught stirring up slave militancy were tarred and feathered.

In the northern states, which had fewer slaves than the southern states, the doctrines of liberty led swiftly to emancipation for all either during the fighting or shortly afterward. Vermont's Constitution of 1777 specifically forbade slavery. The Massachusetts Constitution of 1780 proclaimed the "inherent liberty" of all. In 1780 Pennsylvania provided that all children born thereafter to slave mothers would become free at age twenty-eight, after enabling their owners to recover their initial cost. In 1784 Rhode Island provided freedom for all children of slaves born thereafter, at age twenty-one for males, eighteen for females. New York lagged until 1799 in granting freedom to mature slaves born after enactment, but an act of 1817 set July 4, 1827, as the date for emancipation of all remaining slaves.

In the states south of Pennsylvania, emancipation was less popular. Yet even there slaveholders like Washington, Jefferson, Patrick Henry, and others expressed moral qualms. Jefferson wrote in his *Notes on Virginia* (1785): "Indeed I tremble for my country when I reflect that God is just; that his justice cannot sleep forever." But he, like many other white southerners, was riding the tiger and did not know how to dismount. The furthest antislavery sentiment carried the southern states was to relax the manumission laws under which owners might free their slaves as an individual act. It is estimated that some 10,000 slaves in Virginia were manumitted during the 1780s. A much smaller number would be shipped back to Africa during the early nineteenth century. By the outbreak of the Civil War in 1861, approximately half of the blacks living in Maryland were free.

Manumission, of course, freed slaves by the action of a white owner. But slaves, especially in the upper South, also earned freedom through their own actions during the Revolutionary era, frequently by running away. They often gravitated to the growing number of African American communities. Because of emancipation laws in the northern states, and with the formation of free black neighborhoods in the North and in several southern cities, runaways found refuges and the opportunities for new lives. Many of these free blacks used the egalitarian rhetoric spawned by the Revolution to speak out against the evils of slavery. It is estimated that 55,000 slaves fled to freedom during the Revolution.

THE STATUS OF WOMEN   The logic of liberty applied to the status of women as much as to that of blacks. Women in the colonies had remained essentially confined to the domestic sphere during the eighteenth century. They could not vote or preach or hold office. Few had access to formal education. Although both single and married women could own property and execute contracts, in several colonies married women could not legally own real or personal property—even their own

Elizabeth Freeman, born in Africa around 1742, was sold as a slave to a Massachusetts family. She won her freedom by claiming in court that the "inherent liberty" of all applied to slaves as well.

clothes—and they had no legal rights over their children. Divorces were extremely difficult to obtain.

Initially, women predicted that the Revolution would do little to improve their social status. Soon after the fighting started, Margaret Livingston of New York wrote her sister that "our Sex are doomed to be obedient in every stage of life so that we shant be gainers by this contest."

Yet the revolutionary ferment offered women new opportunities and engendered in many a new outlook. The war drew women at least temporarily into new pursuits. They plowed fields and melted down pots and pans to make shot. Esther Reed of Philadelphia organized a ladies' association that raised money to provide comforts for the troops. Women supported the armies in various roles, such as handling supplies, serving as couriers, and working as camp followers—cooking, cleaning, and nursing the soldiers. Wives often followed their husbands to camp, and on occasion took their places in the line, as Margaret Corbin did at Fort Washington when her husband fell at his artillery post, or Mary Ludwig Hays (better known as Molly Pitcher) did when hers collapsed of heat exhaustion. An exceptional case was that of Deborah Sampson, who joined a Massachusetts regiment as "Robert Shurtleff" and served from 1781 to 1783 by the "artful concealment" of her sex.

To be sure, most women retained the circumscribed domestic outlook that had long been their fate. But a few free-spirited reformers argued that only educated and independent mothers could raise children fit for republican citizenship. Some demanded equal treatment. In an essay entitled "On the Equality of the Sexes," written in 1779 and published in 1790, Judith Sargent Murray of Gloucester, Massachusetts, stressed the importance of mutuality in marriage: "Mutual esteem, mutual friendship, mutual confidence, begirt about by mutual forbearance." Murray and others insisted that women were perfectly capable of excelling outside the domestic sphere.

Early in the struggle, Abigail Adams, one of the most learned, spirited, and stubbornly independent women of the time, wrote to her husband John: "In the new Code of Laws which I suppose it will be necessary for you to make I desire you would remember the Ladies. . . . Do not put such unlimited power into the hands of the Husbands." Since men were "Naturally Tyrannical," she wrote, "why then, not put it out of the power of the vicious and the Lawless to use us with cruelty and indignity with impunity." Otherwise, "If particular care and attention is not paid to the Ladies we are determined to foment a Rebellion, and will not hold ourselves bound by any Laws in which we have no voice, or Representation."

Husband John expressed surprise that women might be discontented,

Frontispiece from Lady's Magazine, 1792. *"The Genius of the Ladies Magazine, accompanied by the Genius of Emulation, who carries in her hand a laurel crown, approaches Liberty, and kneeling, presents her with a copy of the Rights of Woman." The* Lady's Magazine *reprinted extensive extracts from Mary Wollstonecraft's* A Vindication of the Rights of Woman *(1792).*

but he clearly knew the privileges enjoyed by males and was determined to retain them: "Depend upon it, we know better than to repeal our Masculine systems." Thomas Jefferson was of one mind with Adams on this matter. When asked about women's voting rights, he replied that "the tender breasts of ladies were not formed for political convulsion."

The legal status of women did not improve dramatically as a result of the revolutionary ferment, even though in Pennsylvania and parts of New England divorces were somewhat easier to obtain after the Revolution. One Connecticut woman, for instance, successfully brought suit against her husband on the grounds that he "rendered her life miserable by frequent beating with brutal violence, almost constant intoxication and lascivious conduct with several lewd women." But married women in most of the states still forfeited control of their own property to their husbands, and women gained no permanent political rights. Under the 1776 New Jersey constitution, which neglected to specify an exclusively male franchise because the delegates apparently took the distinction for granted, women who met the property qualifications for voting exercised the right until they were denied access early in the nineteenth century.

FREEDOM OF RELIGION   The Revolution also set in motion a transition from the toleration of religious dissent to a complete freedom of religion in the separation of church and state. The Anglican church, established in five colonies and parts of two others, was especially vulnerable because of its association with the crown and because dissenters outnumbered Anglicans in most states except Virginia. And all but Virginia removed tax support for the church before the fighting was over. In 1776 the Virginia Declaration of Rights guaranteed the free exercise of religion, and in 1786 the Virginia Statute of Religious Freedom (written by Thomas Jefferson) declared that "no man shall be compelled to frequent or support any religious worship, place or ministry whatsoever," that none should in any way suffer for his religious opinions and beliefs, "that all men shall be free to profess, and by argument to maintain, their opinions in matters of religion." These statutes and the revolutionary ideology that spawned them helped shape the course that religion would take in the new United States: pluralistic and voluntary rather than state supported and monolithic.

New England, with its Puritan heritage, was in less haste to disestablish the Congregational church, although the rules were already being relaxed enough by the 1720s to let Quakers and Baptists assign their tax contributions to their own churches. New Hampshire finally discontinued tax support for its churches in 1817, Connecticut in 1818, Maine in 1820, and Massachusetts in 1833. Certain religious requirements for officeholding lingered here and there on the law books: Massachusetts and Maryland required a declaration of Christian faith; Delaware had a Trinitarian test; New Jersey and the Carolinas held that officeholders must be Protestants. But in most cases these requirements disappeared in a few years.

In churches as well as in government, the Revolution set off a period of constitution-making, as some of the first national church bodies emerged. In 1784 the Methodists, who at first were an offshoot of the Anglicans, came together in a general conference at Baltimore under Bishop Francis Asbury. The Anglican church, rechristened Episcopal, gathered in a series of meetings which by 1789 had united the various dioceses in a federal union; in 1789 also the Presbyterians held their first general assembly in Philadelphia. The following year, 1790, the Catholic church had its first bishop in the United States when John Carroll was named bishop of Baltimore. Other churches would follow in the process of coming together on a national basis.

EMERGENCE OF AN AMERICAN CULTURE

The Revolution generated a nascent sense of common nationality. At the time of the French and Indian War, an English traveler observed: "Fire and water are not more heterogeneous than the different colonies in North America. Nothing can exceed the jealousy . . . which they possess in regard to each other." But the Revolution taught at least some Americans to think "continentally," as Alexander Hamilton put it. As early as the Stamp Act Congress of 1765, Christopher Gadsden, leader of the Charleston radicals, had said: "There ought to be no New England man, no New Yorker, known on the Continent; but all of us Americans." In the First Continental Congress, Patrick Henry asserted that such a sense of identity had come to pass: "The distinc-

The Congregational church developed a national body in the early nineteenth century, and Lemuel Haynes, depicted here, was its first black preacher.

tions between Virginians, Pennsylvanians, New Yorkers, and New Englanders are no more. I am not a Virginian but an American."

The concrete experience of the war reinforced the rhetoric. Soldiers who went to fight in other states broadened their horizons. John Marshall, future chief justice, served first in the Virginia militia and then in the Continental army in the middle states and endured the winter of 1777–1778 at Valley Forge. He later wrote: "I found myself associated with brave men from different states who were risking life and everything valuable in a common cause. I was confirmed in the habit of considering America as my country and Congress as my government." The Revolution thus marked the start of a national consciousness and a national tradition.

ARTS IN THE NEW NATION   The marquis de Chastellux, a French aristocrat who fought in the cause, thought the Revolution in America had generated "more heroes than she [America] has marble and artists to commemorate them." The Revolution provided the first generation of native artists with inspirational subjects. It also filled them with high expectations that individual freedom would release creative energies and vitalize both commerce and the arts. In fact, the late eighteenth century did witness a sudden efflorescence of the arts.

Ironically, the best American painters of the time spent all or most of the Revolution in England, studying with Benjamin West of Pennsylvania and John Singleton Copley of Massachusetts, both of whom had set up shop in London before the outbreak. Even John Trumbull, who had served in the siege of Boston and the Saratoga campaign, somehow managed a visit to London during the war before returning to help supply the Continentals. Later he adopted patriotic themes in *The Battle of Bunker Hill,* and in his four panels in the Capitol Rotunda in Washington: *The Declaration of Independence, The Surrender of General Burgoyne, Surrender of Lord Cornwallis,* and *The Resignation of General Washington.* Charles Willson Peale, who fought at Trenton and Princeton and survived the winter at Valley Forge, produced a virtual portrait gallery of Revolutionary War figures. Over twenty-three years he painted George Washington seven times from life and produced in all sixty portraits of him. Peale's portrait of Washington after the battle of Princeton (painted in 1779; see page 243) is believed to be the most faithful representation of the general at the time of the War of Independence.

The poet John Trumbull (cousin of the painter) produced perhaps the most successful creative work on the Revolution in *M'Fingal* (1776), a mock heroic satire on American Tories. At the time its ironic tone suited the public temper less than *Common Sense,* but it went through many editions after the war. Joel Barlow, associated with Trumbull in a

Surrender of Lord Cornwallis. *John Trumbell completed his painting of the pivotal British surrender at Yorktown in 1794.*

literary group called the Hartford Wits, is best remembered for *The Hasty Pudding* (1796), a mock epic that celebrated American simplicity in contrast to Old World sophistication. The Revolution-era poems of Philip Freneau, such as his elegy "To the Memory of Brave Americans," "Eutaw Springs," and "The Memorable Victory of Paul Jones," capture better than any others the patriotic emotions of the war.

EDUCATION   The most lasting cultural effect of postwar nationalism may well have been its mark on education. In the colonies there had been a total of nine colleges, but once the Revolution was over, eight more sprang up in the 1780s and six in the 1790s. Several of the revolutionary state constitutions had provisions for state universities. Georgia's was the first chartered, in 1785, but the University of North Carolina (chartered in 1789) was the first to open, in 1795.

Even more important, the Revolution provided the initial impetus for state-supported public school systems. Many of the founders believed that the survival of the new nation depended upon instilling in the public an appreciation for the fragility of republican government and its utter dependence on private and civic virtue. They viewed public schools as the best institutions for such moral and civic development. In such schools, as Pennsylvania's Benjamin Rush maintained, American children not only would become literate but would also learn to choose the public good over all private interests and concerns.

Jefferson agreed that public education would serve as the very "keystone of our arch of government," and in 1779 he introduced his "Bill for the More General Diffusion of Knowledge" into the Virginia assembly. It included an elaborate plan for the state to fund elementary schools for all free persons, and higher education for the talented, up through a state university. Several years later Samuel Adams proposed the same in Massachusetts. Yet almost every one of these schemes for public schools came to naught. Wealthy critics opposed spending tax money on schools that would mingle their sons "in a vulgar and suspicious communion" with the masses. The spread of public schools would have to wait for a more democratic climate.

Education played an important role in broadening and deepening the sense of nationalism, and no single element was as important, perhaps, as the spelling book, an item of almost universal use. Noah Webster of Hartford, while teaching at Goshen, New York, prepared an elementary speller published in 1783. By 1890 more than 60 million copies of

A Class of Mohawk Children, *1786, shows the teacher and children in European-style clothing with traditional scalplock and earrings.*

his "Blue Back Speller" had been printed, and the book continued to sell well into the twentieth century. In his preface Webster issued a cultural Declaration of Independence: "The country," he wrote, "must in some future time, be as distinguished by the superiority of her literary improvements, as she already is by the liberality of her civil and ecclesiastical constitutions."

In a special sense American nationalism embodied a stirring idea. This first new nation, unlike the Old World nations of Europe, was not rooted in antiquity. Its people, except for the Indians, had not inhabited it over the centuries, nor was there any nation of a common ethnic descent. "The American national consciousness," one observer wrote, "is not a voice crying out of the depth of the dark past, but is proudly a product of the enlightened present, setting its face resolutely toward the future."

Many people, at least since the time of the Pilgrims, had thought America to be singled out for a special identity, a special mission. Jonathan Edwards said God had chosen America as "the glorious renovator of the world," and still later John Adams proclaimed the opening of America "a grand scheme and design in Providence for the illumination and the emancipation of the slavish part of mankind all over the earth." This sense of mission was neither limited to New England nor rooted solely in Calvinism. From the democratic rhetoric of Jefferson, to the pragmatism of Washington, to heady toasts bellowed in South Carolina taverns, Americans everywhere articulated a special American leadership role in human history. The mission was now a call to lead the world toward liberty and equality. Meanwhile, however, Americans had to come to grips with more immediate problems created by their new nationhood. The Philadelphia patriot doctor and scientist Benjamin Rush issued a prophetic statement in 1787: "The American war is over: but this is far from being the case with the American revolution. On the contrary, but the first act of the great drama is closed."

Further Reading

The Revolutionary War is the subject of many good surveys. Don Higginbotham's *The War of American Independence* (1971) and Robert Middlekauff's *The Glorious Cause: The American Revolution, 1763–1789* (1982),° are especially useful. Also see Jack P. Greene and J. R. Pole (eds.), *The Blackwell Encyclopedia of the American Revolution* (1991), Colin Bonwick's *The American Revolution* (1991),° and

°These books are available in paperback editions.

Gordon S. Wood's *The Radicalism of the American Revolution* (1991).°
David Hackett Fischer's *Paul Revere's Ride* (1994) details the events
surrounding the immediate outbreak of fighting, while Jeremy Black's
War for America: The Fight for Independence, 1775–1783 (1991) details
the war itself. Christopher Ward's *The War of the Revolution* (2 vols.,
1952) offers detailed accounts of maneuvers and clear maps. For the
first-person perspective provided by memoirs and reports by contemporaries, see *The Revolution Remembered* (1980),° edited by John C.
Dann. The British side of the conflict is handled well by Piers Mackesy
in *The War for America, 1775–1783* (1964). John Selby's *The Revolution in Virginia, 1775–1783* (1988) describes the war in that state.

Much good work has appeared recently on the social history of the
Revolutionary War. See John W. Shy's *A People Numerous and Armed*
(1976),° Charles Royster's *A Revolutionary People at War* (1979),°
Lawrence D. Cress's *Citizens in Arms* (1982), and E. Wayne Carp's *To
Starve the Army at Pleasure* (1984).

Biographical studies of the major American military figures include
James T. Flexner's *George Washington in the American Revolution,
1775–1783* (1968), Samuel E. Morison's *John Paul Jones: A Sailor's
Biography* (1959),° and Charles Royster's *Light-Horse Harry Lee*
(1984). For the British side, see Ira D. Gruber's *The Howe Brothers
and the American Revolution* (1972)° and Richard J. Hargrove's *General John Burgoyne* (1983).

Why some Americans remained loyal to the crown is the subject of
Bernard Bailyn's *The Ordeal of Thomas Hutchinson* (1974),° Robert M.
Calhoon's *The Loyalists in Revolutionary America, 1760–1781* (1973),
and Mary Beth Norton's *The British-Americans* (1972).° Paul H.
Smith's *Loyalists and Redcoats* (1964) traces the military role of the
Tories, and Wallace Brown's *The King's Friends* (1965) argues that the
Loyalists came from all classes of colonial society.

The effort to trace the social effects of the Revolution goes back at
least to J. Franklin Jameson's *The American Revolution Considered as a
Social Movement* (1926). More recently, Jackson Turner Main's *The
Social Structure of Revolutionary America* (1965) looks at the quantitative evidence for the emergence of social equality, while Rhys Isaac's
The Transformation of Virginia, 1740–1790 (1982)° examines the social
conflicts in that pivotal state. See also Gary Nash's *The Urban Crucible*
(1984).° The question of disestablishment and religious liberty is treated
in Sidney Mead's *The Lively Experiment* (1963). Relevant chapters in
Winthrop D. Jordan's *White over Black* (1968) address the issue of
emancipation during the revolutionary period. One of the few recent

°These books are available in paperback editions.

community-level studies of revolutionary change is Robert A. Gross's *The Minutemen and Their World* (1976). Mary Beth Norton's *Liberty's Daughters* (1980)° and Linda K. Kerber's *Women of the Republic* (1980)° document the role women played in securing independence. Joy D. Buel and Richard Buel's *The Way of Duty* (1984)° shows the impact of the Revolution on one New England family.

The standard introduction to the diplomacy of the revolutionary era is Jonathan R. Dull's *A Diplomatic History of the American Revolution* (1985). Richard B. Morris's *The Peacemakers* (1965) examines more closely the negotiations for the Peace of Paris.

°These books are available in paperback editions.

7

SHAPING A FEDERAL UNION

THE CONFEDERATION

In an address to fellow graduates at the Harvard commencement in 1787, young John Quincy Adams lamented "this critical period" when the country was "groaning under the intolerable burden of . . . accumulated evils." More than a century later the popular writer and lecturer John Fiske used the same phrase, the "critical period," as the title for a history of the United States under the Articles of Confederation. For many years it was the fashion among historians to dwell upon the weaknesses of the Confederation and the "accumulated evils" of the time to the neglect of major achievements.

The Congress of the Confederation, to be sure, had little if any more governmental authority than the United Nations would have 200 years later. "It could ask for money but not compel payment," as one historian wrote, "it could enter into treaties but not enforce their stipulations; it could provide for raising of armies but not fill the ranks; it could borrow money but take no proper measures for repayment; it could advise and recommend but not command." The Congress was virtually helpless to cope with problems of diplomacy and postwar depression that would have challenged the resources of a much stronger government. It was not easy to find men of stature to serve in such a body, and often hard to gather a quorum of those who did. Yet in spite of its handicaps, the Confederation Congress somehow managed to survive and to lay important foundations for the future. It concluded the Peace of Paris in 1783. It created the first executive departments. And it formulated principles of land distribution and territorial government that guided expansion all the way to the Pacific coast.

Throughout most of the War for Independence the Congress remained distrustful of executive power. It assigned administrative duties to its committees and thereby imposed a painful burden on con-scientious members. At one time or another John Adams, for instance, served on some eighty committees.

In 1781, however, anticipating ratification of the Articles of Confed-eration, Congress began to set up three departments: Foreign Affairs, Finance, and War. A Post Office Department had existed since 1775. Each was to have a single head responsible to Congress. For superin-tendent of finance Congress chose Robert Morris, a prominent Philadelphia merchant who by virtue of his business connections and a talent for financial sleight-of-hand brought a semblance of order into government accounts. The other departments had less success to their credit, and indeed lacked executive heads for long periods. Given time and stability, however, Congress and the department heads might have evolved something like the parliamentary cabinet system. As it turned out, these agencies were the forerunners of the government depart-ments that came into being later under the Constitution.

FINANCE As yet, however, there was neither president nor prime min-ister, only the presiding officer of Congress and its secretary, Charles Thomson, who served continuously from 1774 to 1789. The closest thing to an executive head of the Confederation was Robert Morris, who as superintendent of finance in the final years of the war became the most influential figure in the government. He wanted to make both himself and the Confederation more powerful. He envisioned a coher-ent program of taxation and debt management to make the government financially stable; "a public debt supported by public revenue will prove the strongest cement to keep our confederacy together," he confided to a friend. It would wed to the support of the federal government the powerful influence of the public creditors. Morris therefore welcomed the chance to enlarge the debt by issuing new government bonds in set-tlement of wartime claims. Because of the government's precarious finances, these securities brought only ten to fifteen cents on the dollar, but with a sounder treasury—certainly with a tax power—they could be expected to rise in value, creating new capital with which to finance banks and economic development.

In 1781, as part of his plan, Morris secured a congressional charter for the Bank of North America, which would hold government deposits, lend money to the government, and issue bank notes that would be a stable currency. Though a national bank, it was in part privately owned and was expected to turn a profit for Morris and other shareholders, in addition to performing a public service. But Morris's program depended ultimately on a secure income for the government, and it foundered on the requirement of unanimous approval for amendments to the Articles of Confederation. During the war he nearly got for Con-

Robert Morris, the most influential figure in the Confederation government, in a portrait by Charles Willson Peale.

gress the power to levy a 5 percent import duty, but Rhode Island's refusal to ratify the necessary amendment stood in the way. Once the war was over, the spur of military need was gone. Local interests and the fear of a central authority—a fear strengthened by the recent quarrels with king and Parliament—hobbled action.

To carry their point, Morris and his nationalist friends in 1783 risked a dangerous gamble. Washington's army, encamped at Newburgh on the Hudson River, had grown restless in the final winter of the war. Their pay was late as usual, and experience gave them reason to fear that claims to bounties and life pensions for officers might never be honored once their services were no longer needed. In January 1783 a delegation of officers appeared in Philadelphia with a petition for redress. Soon they found themselves drawn into a scheme to line up the army and public creditors with nationalists in Congress and confront the states with the threat of a coup d'état unless they yielded more power to Congress. Alexander Hamilton, congressman from New York and former aide to General Washington, sought to bring his old commander into the plan.

Washington sympathized with the purpose. If congressional powers were not enlarged, he had told a friend, "the band which at present holds us together, by a very feeble thread, will soon be broken, when anarchy and confusion must ensue." But Washington was just as deeply convinced that a military coup would be both dishonorable and dangerous. When he learned that some of the plotters had planned an unauthorized meeting of officers, he confronted the conspirators. Drawing his spectacles from his pocket, he began: "I have grown not only gray but blind in the service of my country." When he had finished his dramatic and emotional address, his officers unanimously adopted resolutions denouncing the recent "infamous propositions," and the so-called Newburgh Conspiracy came to a sudden end.

A body of Pennsylvania recruits provided a sorry aftermath to the quiet dispersal of troops at war's end. Their pay in arrears, about eighty militiamen mutinied, marched from Lancaster to Philadelphia, and with reinforcements from regiments there conducted a threatening demonstration in front of Independence Hall. When state authorities failed to provide a guard for fear the militia would join the mutiny, the Congress after three days fled to Princeton, later adjourned to Annapolis, then Trenton, and in 1785 finally settled in New York. Moving from place to place, often unable to muster a quorum, the Congress grew increasingly impotent. An amendment to give Congress power to levy duties for twenty-five years, proposed in 1783, met the same fate as the previous amendment. In 1784 Morris resigned as superintendent of finance, and a committee took charge once again.

The Confederation never did put its finances in order. The Continental currency had long since become a byword for worthlessness. It was never redeemed. The debt, domestic and foreign, grew from $11 million to $28 million as Congress paid off citizens' and soldiers' claims. Each year Congress ran a deficit on its operating expenses.

LAND POLICY   The one source from which Congress might hope ultimately to draw an independent income was the sale of western lands. Throughout the Confederation period, however, that income remained more a fleeting promise than an accomplished fact. The Confederation nevertheless dealt more effectively with the western lands than with anything else. There Congress had direct authority, at least on paper. Thinly populated by Indians, French settlers, and a growing number of American squatters, the region north of the Ohio River had long been the site of overlapping claims by colonies and speculators. The Revolution itself had been brought on in no small part by disagreement over western lands and British feelings that the colonies should be taxed for their administration and defense. In 1784 Virginia's cession of lands north of the Ohio was complete, and by 1786 all states had abandoned their claims in the area except for a 120-mile strip along Lake Erie, which Connecticut held until 1800 as its "Western Reserve," in return for giving up its claims in the Wyoming Valley of Pennsylvania.

As early as 1779 Congress had made a commitment in principle not to treat the western lands as colonies. The delegates resolved instead that western lands ceded by the states "shall be . . . formed into distinct Republican states," equal in all respects to other states. Between 1784 and 1787 policies for the development of the West emerged in three major ordinances of the Confederation Congress. These documents, which rank among its greatest achievements—and among the most important in American history—set precedents that the United States would follow in its expansion all the way to the Pacific. Thomas Jefferson in fact was prepared to grant self-government to western states at an

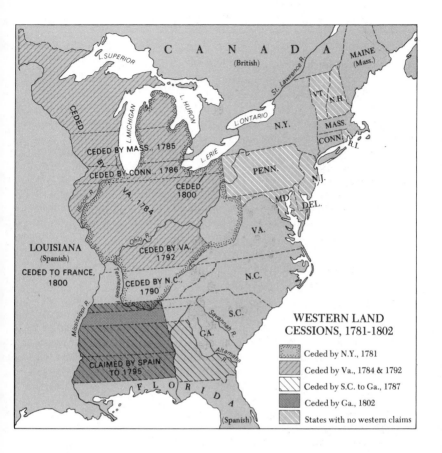

WESTERN LAND
CESSIONS, 1781-1802

Ceded by N.Y., 1781
Ceded by Va., 1784 & 1792
Ceded by S.C. to Ga., 1787
Ceded by Ga., 1802
States with no western claims

early stage, when settlers would meet and choose their own officials. Under Jefferson's ordinance of 1784, when the population equaled that of the smallest existing state, the territory would achieve full statehood.

In the Land Ordinance of 1785 the delegates outlined a plan of land surveys and sales that would eventually stamp a rectangular pattern on much of the nation's surface, a pattern still visible from the air in many parts of the country because of the layout of roads and fields. Wherever Indian titles had been extinguished, the Northwest was to be surveyed into townships six miles square along east-west and north-south lines. Each township in turn was divided into 36 lots (or sections) one mile square (or 640 acres). The 640-acre sections were to go at auction for no less than $1 per acre, or $640 total. Such terms favored land speculators, of course, since few common folk had that much money or were able to work that much land. In later years new land laws would make smaller plots available at lower prices, but in 1785 Congress was faced with an empty treasury. In each township, however, Congress did reserve the income from the sixteenth section for the support of schools—a significant departure at a time when public schools were rare.

In seven ranges to the west of the Ohio River, an area in which recent treaties had voided Indian titles, surveying began. But before any land sales occurred a group of speculators from New England presented Congress with a seductive offer. Organized in Boston, the group took the name of the Ohio Company and sent the Reverend Manasseh Cutler to present their plan. Cutler proved a persuasive lobbyist, and in 1787 Congress voted a grant of 1.5 million acres for about $1 million in certificates of indebtedness to Revolutionary War veterans. The arrangement had the dual merit, Cutler argued, of reducing the debt and encouraging new settlement and sales. Further, to ensure passage the lobbyist cut in several congressmen on another deal, the Scioto Company, which got an option on 5 million acres more.

In April 1788 the Ohio Company's first settlers floated downstream from Pittsburgh on a flatboat aptly named the *Mayflower* and established Marietta. The Scioto Company never took up its option, but that did not prevent its European agent from selling lands it did not own—with the help of an Englishman named, of all things, Playfair. In 1790 several hundred French settlers arrived, only to find that they had no title to the lands they had supposedly bought. A sympathetic Congress relieved their distress by voting them a grant of land. In 1788 a New Jersey speculator got an option on lands between the Great and the Little Miami Rivers and soon had Cincinnati and several other villages under way.

THE NORTHWEST ORDINANCE   Spurred by the plans for land sales and settlement, Congress drafted a more specific frame of territorial government to replace Jefferson's ordinance of 1784. The new plan backed off from Jefferson's recommendation of early self-government. Because of the trouble that might be expected from squatters who were clamoring for free land, the Northwest Ordinance of 1787 required a period of colonial tutelage. At first the territory fell subject to a governor, a secretary, and three judges, all chosen by Congress. Eventually there would be three to five territories in the region, and when any one had 5,000 free male adults it could choose an assembly, and Congress would name a council of five from ten names proposed by the assembly. The governor would have a veto, and so would Congress.

The resemblance to the old royal colonies is clear, but there were two significant differences. For one, the Ordinance anticipated statehood when any territory's population reached 60,000. At that point a convention could be called to draft a state constitution and apply to Congress for statehood. For another, it included a Bill of Rights that guaranteed religious freedom, representation in proportion to population, trial by jury, habeas corpus, and the application of common law. Finally, the

Ordinance excluded slavery permanently from the Northwest—a proviso Jefferson had failed to get accepted in his ordinance of 1784. This proved a fateful decision. As the progress of emancipation in the existing states gradually freed all slaves above the Mason-Dixon line, the Ohio River boundary of the Old Northwest extended the line between freedom and slavery all the way to the Mississippi.

The Northwest Ordinance had a larger importance beyond establishing a formal procedure for transforming territories into states. It represented a sharp break with the imperialistic assumption behind European expansion into the Western Hemisphere. The new states were to be admitted as equals into the American republic.

The lands south of the Ohio River followed a different line of development. Title to the western lands remained with Georgia, North Carolina, and Virginia for the time being, but settlement proceeded at a far more rapid pace during and after the Revolution, despite the Indians' fierce resentment of encroachments on their hunting grounds. Substantial centers of population grew up around Harrodsburg and Boonesboro in the Kentucky Blue Grass and along the Watauga, Holston, and Cumberland Rivers, as far west as Nashborough (Nashville). In the Old Southwest active movements for statehood arose early. North Carolina tentatively ceded its western claims in 1784, whereupon the Holston

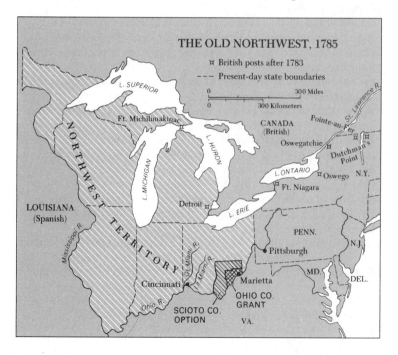

THE OLD NORTHWEST, 1785

settlers formed the short-lived state of Franklin, which became little more than a bone of contention between rival speculators until North Carolina reasserted control in 1789, shortly before the cession of its western lands became final.

Indian claims too were being extinguished. The Iroquois and Cherokees, badly battered during the Revolution, were in no position to resist encroachments. By the Treaty of Fort Stanwix (1784), the Iroquois were forced to cede land in western New York and Pennsylvania. In the Treaty of Hopewell (1785), the Cherokees gave up all claims in South Carolina, much of western North Carolina, and large portions of present-day Kentucky and Tennessee. Also in 1785 the major Ohio tribes dropped their claim to most of Ohio, except for a chunk bordering the western part of Lake Erie. The Creeks, pressed by the state of Georgia to cede portions of their lands in 1784–1785, went to war in the summer of 1786 with covert aid from Spanish Florida. When Spanish aid diminished, however, the Creek chief traveled to New York and in 1791 finally struck a bargain that gave the Creeks favorable trade arrangements with the United States but did not restore the lost lands.

TRADE AND THE ECONOMY   In its economic life, as in planning westward expansion, the young nation dealt vigorously with difficult problems. Congress had little to do with achievements in the economy, but neither could it bear the blame for an acute economic contraction between 1770 and 1790, the result primarily of the war and separation from the British Empire. Although farmers enmeshed in local markets maintained their livelihood during the Revolutionary era, commercial agriculture dependent upon trade with foreign markets suffered a severe downturn. The southern tidewater suffered a loss of slave labor, much of it carried off by the British. Chesapeake planters also lost their lucrative foreign markets. Tobacco was especially hard hit. The British decision to close its West Indian colonies to American trade devastated what had been a thriving trade in timber, wheat, and other foodstuffs. Returns from indigo and naval stores declined with the loss of British bounties.

Merchants suffered even more wrenching adjustments than the farmers. Cut out of the British mercantile system, they had to find new outlets for their trade. Circumstances that impoverished some enriched those who financed privateers, supplied the armies on both sides, and hoarded precious goods while demand and prices soared. By the end of the war, a strong sentiment for free trade had developed in both Britain and America. In the memorable year 1776, the Scottish economist Adam Smith brought out *The Wealth of Nations,* a classic manifesto against mercantilism. Some British statesmen embraced the new gospel, but the public and Parliament still clung to the conventional wisdom of mercantilism for many years to come.

A rare glimpse of a construction site in 1800, from William Birch's series The City of Philadelphia as It Appeared in the Year 1800.

After the war British trade with America did resume, and American ships were allowed to deliver American products and return to the United States with British goods. American ships could not carry British goods anywhere else, however. The pent-up demand for familiar goods created a vigorous market in exports to America, fueled by British credits and the hard money that had come into America from foreign aid, the expenditures of foreign armies, or wartime trade and privateering. The result was a quick cycle of postwar boom and bust, a buying spree followed by a money shortage and economic troubles that lasted several years.

In colonial days the chronic trade deficit with Britain had been offset by the influx of coins from trade with the West Indies. Now American ships found themselves excluded altogether from the British West Indies. The islands, however, still demanded wheat, fish, lumber, and other products from the mainland, and American shippers had not lost their talent for smuggling, at which the islanders connived. Already American shippers had begun exploring new outlets, and by 1787 their seaports were flourishing more than ever. Freed from colonial restraints, they now had the run of the seven seas. Trade treaties opened new markets with the Dutch (1782), Swedes (1783), Prussians (1785), and Moroccans (1787), and American shippers found new outlets on their own in Europe, Africa, and Asia. The most spectacular new

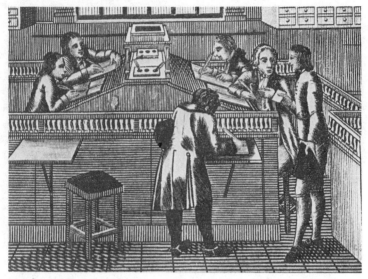

Merchants' Counting House. *Americans involved in overseas trade, such as the merchants depicted here, were sharply affected by the dislocations of war.*

development, if not the largest, was trade with China. It began in 1784–1785, when the *Empress of China* sailed from New York to Canton and back, around the tip of South America. Profits from its cargo of silks and tea encouraged the outfitting of other ships that carried ginseng root and other American goods to exchange for the luxury goods of East Asia.

By 1790 American commerce and exports had far outrun the trade of the colonies. Merchants had more ships than before the war. Farm exports were twice what they had been. Although most of the exports were the products of forests, fields, and fisheries, during and after the war more Americans had turned to small-scale manufacturing, mainly for domestic markets. By 1787 a summary of major American enterprises included dozens of products from ships and ironwork to shoes, textiles, and soap.

DIPLOMACY The achievements of the flourishing young nation are more visible in hindsight than they were then. Until 1787 the shortcomings and failures remained far more apparent—and the advocates of a stronger central government were extremely vocal on the subject. In diplomacy, there remained the nagging problems of relations with Great Britain and Spain, both of which still kept posts on American soil and conspired with Indians and white settlers in the West. The British, despite the peace treaty of 1783, held on to a string of forts along the Canadian border. From these they kept a hand in the fur trade and a degree of influence with the Indian tribes, whom they were suspected of stirring up to make sporadic attacks on the frontier. They gave as a reason for their continued occupation the failure of Americans to pay their prewar debts to British creditors. They conveniently ignored the point that the peace treaty had included only a face-saving gesture that committed Congress to recommend that the states place no legal impediment in the way of their collection. Impediments continued nonetheless. According to one Virginian, a common question in his state was: "If we are now to pay the debts due to British merchants, what have we been fighting for all this while?"

Another major irritant was the confiscation of Loyalist property. The peace treaty had encouraged Congress to stop confiscations, to guarantee immunity to Loyalists for twelve months, during which they could return and wind up their affairs, and to recommend that the states give back confiscated property. Persecutions, even lynchings, of Loyalists still occurred until after the end of the war. Some Loyalists returned unmolested, however, and once again took up their lives in their former homes. By the end of 1787, moreover, at the request of Congress,

The Savages Let Loose, or the Cruel Fate of the Loyalists. *A British comment on the treatment of Loyalists in the peace settlement of 1783.*

all the states had rescinded the laws that were in conflict with the peace treaty.

The British refused even to dispatch an ambassador to the new nation before 1791. As early as 1785, however, the United States took the initiative by sending over that confirmed rebel, John Adams, as ambassador to Great Britain. He spent three years in futile efforts to settle the points at issue: mainly the forts, debts, the property rights of Loyalists, and trade concessions in the British West Indies. Unknown to Adams, the British even toyed with the idea of annexing Vermont through intrigues with the Allen brothers, Ethan and Levi. Nothing came of it all, however, and Vermont became the fourteenth state in 1791.

With Spain the chief issues were the southern boundary and the right to navigate the Mississippi. According to the preliminary treaty with Britain, the United States claimed a line as far south as the 31st parallel; Spain held out for the line running eastward from the mouth of the Yazoo River (at 32°28′ N), which it claimed as the traditional boundary. The American treaty with Britain had also specified the right to navigate the Mississippi River to its mouth. Still, the international boundary ran down the middle of the river most of its length, and the Mississippi was entirely within Spanish Louisiana in its lower reaches. The right to navigation was a matter of importance because of the growing settlements in Kentucky and Tennessee, but in 1784 Louisiana's Spanish governor closed the river to American commerce and began to intrigue with the Creeks, Choctaws, Chickasaws, and other Indians of the Southwest against the American settlers and with the settlers against the United States. General James Wilkinson, a Kentucky land speculator, further enriched himself with Spanish gold in

John Adams, portrayed here while serving as United States ambassador to England.

return for his promise to conspire for secession of the West and perhaps its annexation by Spain. Wilkinson, however, was a professional conniver with an instinct for trouble, whose loyalties ran mainly to his own pocketbook. He was not the only man on the make who was double-dealing with the Spaniards.

In 1785 the Spanish government sent as its ambassador to the United States Don Diego de Gardoqui, who entered into long but fruitless negotiations with John Jay, the secretary for foreign affairs. Jay had instructions to get free navigation of the Mississippi and the Spanish acceptance of the 31° boundary; Gardoqui had instructions not to give them. But he did ply Jay and his wife with gifts and flattery. Finally, in hope of winning trade concessions with Spain, Jay sought permission from Congress to give up navigation of the Mississippi—an idea planted by Gardoqui in the knowledge that it would be divisive. It was granted, but only by a vote of seven to five, with the southern states holding out against such a sacrifice to the interest of northern merchants. Since ratification of a treaty required the vote of nine states, negotiations collapsed and the issues remained unsettled for nearly another decade.

THE CONFEDERATION'S PROBLEMS   The problems of trans-Appalachian settlers, however, seemed remote from the everyday concerns of most Americans. What touched them more closely were economic troubles and the currency shortage. Merchants who found themselves excluded from old channels of imperial trade began to agitate for reprisals. State governments, in response, laid special tonnage duties on British vessels and special tariffs on the goods they brought. State action alone, however, failed to work because of lack of uniformity. British ships could be diverted to states whose duties were less restrictive. The other states tried to meet this problem by taxing British goods that flowed across state lines, creating an impression that states were involved in commercial war with each other. Although these duties seldom affected American goods, there was a clear need, it seemed to commercial interests, for a central power to regulate trade.

Mechanics (skilled workers who made, used, or repaired tools and machines) and artisans (skilled workers who made products) were developing an infant industry. Their products ranged from crude iron nails to the fine silver bowls of Paul Revere. They wanted to go further. They wanted to take reprisals against British goods as well as British ships. They sought, and in various degrees obtained from the states, tariffs against foreign goods that competed with theirs. The country would be on its way to economic independence, they argued, if only the money that flowed into the country were invested in

American craftsmen, such as this cabinetmaker, were called "mechanics" in the eighteenth century. They sought tariffs against foreign goods that competed with theirs.

domestic manufactures instead of being paid out for foreign goods. Nearly all the states gave some preference to American goods, but again the lack of uniformity in their laws put them at cross purposes, and so urban mechanics along with merchants were drawn into the movement for a stronger central government in the interest of uniform regulation.

The shortage of cash and other economic difficulties gave rise to more immediate demands for paper currency as legal tender, for postponement of tax and debt payments, and for laws to "stay" the foreclosure of mortgages. Farmers, who had profited during the war, found themselves squeezed by depressed crop prices and mounting debts while merchants sorted out and opened up their new trade routes. Creditors demanded hard money, but it was in short supply—and paper money was almost nonexistent after the depreciation of the Continental currency. The result was an outcry for relief, and around 1785 the demand for new paper money became the most divisive issue in state politics. Debtors demanded such inflation as a means of easing repayment, and farmers saw it as a way to raise commodity prices. In Pennsylvania public creditors demanded paper as a device to collect their claims against the state. Paper, they reasoned, was better than nothing. Creditors elsewhere generally opposed such action, however, because it was likely to mean payment in a depreciated currency.

In 1785–1786 seven states (those named below plus Georgia and North Carolina) provided for issues of paper money. It served in five states—Pennsylvania, New York, New Jersey, South Carolina, and Rhode Island—as a means of credit to hard-pressed farmers through state loans on farm mortgages. It was variously used to fund state debts and to pay off the claims of veterans. In spite of the cries of calamity at the time, the money never seriously depreciated in Pennsylvania, New York, and South Carolina.

In Rhode Island, however, the debtor party ran wild. In 1786 the Rhode Island legislature issued more paper money than any other state in proportion to population, and declared it legal tender in payment of all debts. Creditors fled the state to avoid being paid in worthless paper, merchants closed their doors while mobs rioted against them, and a "forcing act" denied trial by jury and levied fines against anyone who refused to take the money at face value. Eventually a test case reached the state's supreme court, and in *Trevett v. Weeden* (1787) the court ruled the law unconstitutional. The case stands as a landmark, the first in which a court exercised the doctrine of judicial review in holding a state law unconstitutional. The forcing act was then repealed and the legal tender clause finally repealed in 1789.

Spinning and carding was work often assigned to women, as depicted in this early nineteenth-century engraving.

SHAYS'S REBELLION   Newspapers throughout the country ran accounts of the developments in Rhode Island. The little commonwealth, stubbornly independent since the days of Roger Williams, became the prime example of democracy run riot—until its riotous neighbor, Massachusetts, provided the final proof (some said) that the country was poised on the brink of anarchy: Shays's Rebellion. There, the trouble was not too much paper money but too little, as well as too much taxation. After 1780, Massachusetts had remained in the grip of a rigidly conservative regime, which levied ever-larger poll and land taxes to pay off a heavy war debt, held mainly by wealthy creditors in Boston. The taxes fell most heavily upon beleaguered farmers and the poor in general. When the Massachusetts legislature adjourned in 1786 without providing either paper money or any other relief from taxes and debts, three western counties erupted into spontaneous revolt. Armed bands closed the courts and prevented foreclosures, and a ragtag "army" of some 1,200 disgruntled farmers under Daniel Shays, a destitute farmer and war veteran, advanced upon the federal arsenal at Springfield, Massachusetts, in January 1787.

A small militia force, however, scattered the debtor army with a single volley that left four dead. General Benjamin Lincoln, a hero of the Revolution, arrived soon after with reinforcements from Boston and routed the remaining Shaysites. The rebel farmers nevertheless had a victory of sorts. The new state legislature included members sympathetic to the agricultural crisis. They omitted direct taxes the following year, lowered court fees, and exempted clothing, household goods, and tools from the debt process. But a more important consequence was the impetus the rebellion gave to conservatism and nationalism.

Rumors, at times deliberately inflated, greatly exaggerated the extent of this pathetic rebellion of desperate men. The rebels were linked to the conniving British and accused of seeking to pillage the wealthy. What was more, the uprising set an ominous example. "There are combustibles in every State," George Washington wrote, "which a spark might set fire to." Panic set in among the republic's elite. New York's Gouverneur Morris was typically blunt: "The mob begin to think and reason. Poor reptiles! They bask in the sun and ere noon they will bite, depend upon it. The gentry begin to fear this." In a letter to Jefferson, Abigail Adams was equally anxious. She tarred the Shaysites as "Ignorant, restless desperadoes, without conscience or principles . . . mobbish insurgents [who] are for sapping the foundation" of the struggling young government.

Jefferson disagreed. If Adams and others were overly critical of

Shays's Rebellion, Jefferson was, if anything, too complacent. From his post in Paris, where one of history's great civil bloodbaths would soon take place, he wrote to a friend back home: "The tree of liberty must be refreshed from time to time with the blood of patriots and tyrants." Abigail Adams was so infuriated by Jefferson's position that she stopped corresponding with him for months.

CALLS FOR A STRONGER GOVERNMENT   Well before the outbreaks in New England, the advocates of a stronger central authority had come to demand a convention to revise the Articles of Confederation. Noah Webster, the celebrated lexicographer, lamented in 1785 that "Our pretended union is but a name, and our confederation a cobweb." These nationalists gained momentum from the adversities of the times. Self-interest led bankers, merchants, and mechanics to promote a stronger central government. At the same time, many public-spirited men saw it as the only alternative to anarchy. Gradually people were losing the ingrained fear of a tyrannical central authority as they saw evidence that tyranny might come from other quarters, including the common people themselves.

By the mid-1780s, in fact, several prominent political spokesmen had become convinced that the new state governments were being run by uneducated entrepreneurs pursuing selfish economic and petty political interests. Men of humble origins and parochial points of view were allegedly displacing the "wise and virtuous" from seats of power. Such inexperienced and frequently uncouth legislators were passing an avalanche of legislation merely to serve particular interest groups and constituents rather than the general welfare. They were printing excessive amounts of paper money and passing "stay" laws preventing judicial action against debtors.

Such developments led many of the revolutionary leaders to revise their assessment of American character. "We have, probably," concluded George Washington in 1786, "had too good an opinion of human nature in forming our confederation." The following year James Madison reported to Jefferson that America was displaying "symptoms . . . truly alarming, which have tainted the faith of most orthodox republicans." People were stretching the meaning of liberty far beyond what he and others had envisioned. He found a "spirit of *locality*" rampant in the state legislature that was destroying the "aggregate interests of the community." Even worse, he saw people taking the law and other people's property into their own hands. Such developments led Madison and others to revise their assumptions about republican virtue. At any given time, they decided, only a distinct minority could be relied upon to set aside their private interests in favor of the common good.

These so-called Federalists concluded that the new republic must now depend for its success on the constant virtue of the few rather than the public-spiritedness of the many.

In March 1785 commissioners from Virginia and Maryland had met at Mount Vernon on Washington's invitation to promote commerce and economic development and to settle outstanding questions about the navigation of the Potomac and Chesapeake Bay. Washington had a personal interest in the river flowing by his door: it was a potential route to the West, with its upper reaches close to the upper reaches of the Ohio, where his military career had begun thirty years before. The delegates agreed on interstate cooperation, and Maryland suggested a further pact with Pennsylvania and Delaware to encourage water communication between the Chesapeake and the Ohio River; the Virginia legislature agreed, and at Madison's suggestion invited all thirteen states to send delegates for a general discussion of commercial problems. Nine states named representatives, but those from only five appeared at the Annapolis Convention in September 1786—neither the New England states nor the Carolinas and Georgia were represented. Apparent failure soon turned into success, however, when the alert Alexander Hamilton, representing New York, presented a resolution for still another convention in Philadelphia to consider all measures necessary "to render the constitution of the Federal Government adequate to the exigencies of the Union."

ADOPTING THE CONSTITUTION

THE CONSTITUTIONAL CONVENTION   After stalling for several months, Congress fell in line in February 1787, with a resolution endorsing a convention "for the sole and express purpose of revising the Articles of Confederation." By then five states had already named delegates; before the meeting, called to begin on May 14, 1787, six more states had acted. New Hampshire delayed until June, and its delegates arrived in July. Fearful of consolidated power, tiny Rhode Island kept aloof throughout. (Critics labeled the fractious little state "Rogue Island.") Virginia's Patrick Henry, an implacable foe of centralized government, claimed to "smell a rat" and refused to represent his state. Twenty-nine delegates from nine states began work on May 25. Altogether the state legislatures elected seventy-three men. Fifty-five attended at one time or another, and after four months, thirty-nine signed the Constitution they had drafted.

The durability and flexibility of that document testify to the remarkable quality of the men who made it. Thomas Jefferson, who was serving abroad as minister to France, later referred to the Convention as an

A Session of the Constitutional Convention with George Washington Presiding.

assembly of "demi-gods." The delegates were surprisingly young: forty-two was the average age. But they were even more surprisingly mature, audacious, and foresighted. Farmers, merchants, lawyers, bankers, many of them were widely read in history, law, and political philosophy. They were familiar with the writings of Locke and Montesquieu, aware of the confederacies of the ancient world, and at the same time practical men of experience, tested in the fires of the Revolution. Twenty-one had served in the conflict, seven had been state governors, most of them had been members of the Continental Congress, and eight had signed the Declaration of Independence. "Experience must be our only guide," Pennsylvania's John Dickinson said. "Reason may mislead us."

The magisterial Washington served as presiding officer, but participated little in the debates. Eighty-one-year-old Benjamin Franklin, the oldest delegate, also said little from the floor but did provide a wealth of experience, wit, and common sense behind the scenes. More active in the debates were James Madison, the ablest political philosopher in the group; Massachusetts's dapper Elbridge Gerry, a Harvard graduate who earned the nickname "Old Grumbletonian" because, as John Adams once said, he "opposed everything he did not propose"; George Mason, the irritable author of the Virginia Bill of Rights and a slave-owning planter with a deep-rooted suspicion of all government; the eloquent, arrogant New York aristocrat Gouverneur Morris, who harbored a venomous contempt for the masses; Marylander Luther Martin, the ardent spokesman for states' rights whose speeches were fueled by his fiery temper and frequent drunkenness; Scots-born James Wilson of Pennsylvania, one of the ablest lawyers in the new nation and next in importance at the convention only to Washington and Madison; and Roger Sherman of Connecticut, a self-trained lawyer adept at negotiating compromises. John Adams, like Jefferson, was serving abroad. Also conspicuously absent during most of the Convention was thirty-two-year-old Alexander Hamilton, the staunch nationalist who regretfully went home when the other two New York delegates walked out because of their states'-rights principles.

All the participants acknowledged that Madison emerged as the central figure at the Convention. Small of stature—barely over five feet tall—and frail in health, the thirty-six-year-old Madison was a studious bachelor descended from wealthy slave-owning Virginia planters. He suffered from chronic headaches and was painfully shy. Being jilted as a young man by his sixteen-year-old fiancée in favor of a medical student only heightened his natural aloofness. (She had sealed her farewell letter with rye dough as "a profession of indifference.") Crowds made him nervous, and he hated to use his high-pitched voice in public, much less in open debate.

But the Princeton graduate who had found the practice of law too "coarse and dry" possessed a keen, agile mind with a voracious appetite for learning, and the convincing eloquence of his arguments proved to be decisive. "Every person seems to acknowledge his greatness," wrote one delegate. Another commented that he possessed a "calm expres-

James Madison was only thirty-six when he assumed a major role in the drafting of the Constitution. This miniature is by Charles Willson Peale (c. 1783).

sion, blue eyes—and looked like a thinking man." Madison arrived in Philadelphia with trunks full of books and a head full of ideas. He had been preparing for the Convention for months and probably knew more about historic forms of government than any other delegate.

For the most part, the delegates' differences on political philosophy fell within a narrow range. On certain fundamentals they generally agreed: that government derived its just powers from the consent of the people, but that society must be protected from the tyranny of the majority; that the people at large must have a voice in their government, but that checks and balances must be provided to keep any one group from arrogating power; that a stronger central authority was essential, but that all power was subject to abuse. They assumed with Madison that if people were "angels, no government would be necessary." Even the best people were naturally selfish, and government, therefore, could not be founded altogether upon a trust in goodwill and virtue. Since governments existed to restrain people, Madison argued, their very existence was "a reflection upon human nature." Yet by a careful arrangement of checks and balances, by checking power with countervailing power, the Founding Fathers hoped to devise institutions that could constrain individual sinfulness and channel self-interest to benefit the public good.

THE VIRGINIA AND NEW JERSEY PLANS   At the outset the delegates unanimously elected Washington president of the Convention. One of the first decisions was to meet behind closed doors in order to discourage outside pressures and speeches to the galleries. The secrecy of the proceedings was remarkably well kept, and knowledge of the debates comes mainly from Madison's extensive notes. It was Madison, too, who drafted the proposals that set the framework of the discussions. These proposals, which came to be called the "Virginia Plan," embodied a revolutionary idea for the delegates to scrap their instructions to revise the Articles of Confederation and to submit an entirely new document to the states. The plan proposed separate legislative, executive, and judicial branches, and a truly national government to make laws binding upon individual citizens and upon states as well. Congress would be divided into two houses, a lower one chosen by popular vote and an upper house chosen by the lower house from nominees of the state legislatures. Congress could disallow state laws under the plan and would itself define the extent of its and the states' authority.

On June 15 delegates submitted the "New Jersey Plan," which proposed to keep the existing structure of equal representation of states in a unicameral Congress, but to give it power to levy taxes and regulate commerce and authority to name a plural executive (with no veto) and a Supreme Court. The different plans presented the Convention with two major issues: whether to amend the Articles or draft a new document, and whether to have congressional representation by states or by population. On the first point the Convention voted, June 19, to work toward a national government as envisioned by the Virginians. Regarding the powers of this government there was little disagreement save in detail. Experience with the Articles had persuaded the delegates that an effective central government, as distinguished from a confederation, needed the power to levy taxes, to regulate commerce, to raise an army and navy, and to make laws binding upon individual citizens. The lessons of the 1780s suggested to them, moreover, that in the interest of order and uniformity the states must be denied certain powers: to issue money, abrogate contracts, make treaties, wage war, levy tariffs, or export duties.

But furious disagreements then arose. The first clash in the Convention involved the issue of representation, and it was resolved by the "Great Compromise," sometimes called the "Connecticut Compromise," proposed by Roger Sherman, which gave both groups their way. The more populous states won apportionment by population in the House of Representatives; the states that sought to protect state power won equality in the Senate, but with the vote there by individuals and not by states.

An equally contentious struggle ensued between northern and southern delegates over slavery and the regulation of trade, an omen of sectional controversies to come. Slavery, Madison's secretary noted, was a "distracting question" to most of the delegates rather than a compelling moral dilemma. Few if any of the Framers even considered the notion of abolition, and they carefully avoided using the term "slavery" in the final document. In this they reflected the prevailing attitudes among white Americans. Most agreed with South Carolina's canny John Rutledge, described by the French minister as "the proudest and most imperious man in the United States," when he asserted: "Religion and humanity [have] nothing to do with this [slavery] question. Interest alone is the governing principle of nations."

The interest of southern delegates, with slaves so numerous in their states, dictated that slaves be counted as part of the population in determining the number of their representatives. Northerners were willing to have slaves counted in deciding each state's share of direct taxes, but not for purposes of representation. On this issue the Confederation Congress had supplied a handy precedent when it sought an amendment to make population rather than land values the standard for fiscal requisitions. The proposed amendment to the Articles would have counted three-fifths of the slaves for this purpose. The delegates, with little dissent, agreed to incorporate the same three-fifths ratio in the new Constitution as a basis for apportioning both representatives and direct taxes.

This cross-sectional view of the British slave ship Brookes
shows the abominably crowded conditions the "cargo"
endured in the international slave trade.

A more sensitive issue involved an effort to prevent the central government from stopping the Atlantic slave trade. Virginia's George
Mason, himself a slave owner, condemned the "infernal traffic," which
his state had already outlawed. He argued that the issue concerned "not

the importing states alone but the whole union." People in the western territories were "already calling out for slaves for their new lands." He feared that they would "fill the country" with slaves. Such a development would bring forth "the judgment of Heaven" on the country. Southern delegates were quick to challenge Mason's reasoning. South Carolina's Charles Cotesworth Pinckney insisted that the continued importation of slaves was not only vital to his state but to neighboring Georgia as well.

To resolve the question, the delegates established a time limit. "The morality or wisdom of slavery," said Oliver Ellsworth of Connecticut, "are considerations belonging to the states themselves." Congress could not forbid the foreign slave trade before 1808, but could levy a tax of $10 a head on all slaves imported. In both provisions, a sense of delicacy—and hypocrisy—dictated the use of euphemisms. The Constitution spoke of "free Persons" and "all other persons," of "such persons as any of the States Now existing shall think proper to admit," and of persons "held to Service of Labor." The odious word "slavery" did not appear in the Constitution until the Thirteenth Amendment (1865) abolished the "peculiar institution" by name.

The final decision on the slave trade was linked to a compromise on the question of the broader congressional power to regulate commerce. Northern states, where the merchant and shipping interests were most influential, were prepared to give Congress unlimited powers. The southerners, however, feared that navigation acts favoring American shipping might work at the expense of getting southern commodities to market by reducing foreign competition with northern shippers. Southerners therefore demanded that navigation acts be passed only by a two-thirds vote, but finally traded this demand for a prohibition on congressional power to levy export taxes and for a twenty-year, instead of a ten-year, delay on the power to prohibit the slave trade.

If the delegates found the slavery issue distracting, they considered irrelevant any discussion of the legal or political role of women under the new Constitution. The revolutionary rhetoric of liberty prompted some women to demand political equality. "The men say we have no business" with politics, Eliza Wilkinson of South Carolina observed as the Constitution was being framed, "but I won't have it thought that because we are the weaker sex as to bodily strength we are capable of nothing more than domestic concerns." Her complaint, however, fell on deaf ears. There was never any formal discussion of women's rights at the Convention. The new nationalism still defined politics and government as outside the realm of female endeavor.

The Constitution also said little about the processes of immigration and naturalization, and most of what it said was negative. In Article II, Section I, it prohibited any future immigrant from becoming president, limiting that office to a "natural born Citizen." In Article I, Sections 2 and 3, respectively, it stipulated that no person could serve in the House of Representatives who had not "been seven Years a Citizen of the United States" or in the Senate who had not "been nine years a citizen." On the matter of defining citizenship, the Constitution gave Congress the authority "to establish an uniform Rule of Naturalization," but offered no further guidance on the matter. As a result, naturalization policy has changed significantly over the years in response to fluctuating social attitudes and political moods. In 1790 the first Congress passed a naturalization law that allowed "free white persons" who had been in the country for as little as two years to be made naturalized citizens in any court. This meant that persons of African descent were denied federal citizenship. It was left to individual states to determine whether free blacks were citizens. And because Indians were not "free white persons," they were also treated as aliens rather than citizens. Not until 1924 would Congress grant citizenship to American Indians.

THE SEPARATION OF POWERS   The details of governmental structure, embedded in the Constitution, while causing disagreement, caused far less trouble than the basic issues pitting the large against the small states and the northern against the southern states. Existing state constitutions, several of which already separated powers among legislative, executive, and judicial branches, set an example that reinforced the Convention's resolve to disperse power with checks and balances. Although the Founding Fathers hated royal tyranny, most of them also feared the people and favored various mechanisms to check popular passions. Some delegates displayed a thumping disdain for any democratizing of the political system. Hamilton once called the people "a great beast," and Elbridge Gerry asserted that most of the nation's problems "flow from an excess of democracy." Roger Sherman likewise insisted that the people "should have as little to do as may be about the Government." Those without property, it was widely assumed, could not be trusted to exercise civic virtue. Instead they were likely to become dependent pawns in the hands of unscrupulous politicians. "Give the votes to the [poor]," Gouverneur Morris predicted, "and they will sell them to the rich."

These elitist views were accommodated by the Constitution's mixed legislative system, which acknowledged the "genius of the people," as George Mason phrased it. The lower house was designed to be closest to voters, who elected it every two years. It would be, according to Mason, "the grand repository of the democratic principle of the Government." House members should "sympathize with their constituents, should think as they think, & feel as they feel; and for these purposes should even be residents among them." The upper house, or Senate, its members elected by state legislatures, was intended to be more detached from the voters. Staggered six-year terms prevented the choice of a majority in any given year, and thereby further isolated senators from the passing fancies of public passion.

The decision that a single person be made the chief executive caused the delegates "considerable pause," according to Madison. George Mason protested that this would create a "fetus of monarchy." Indeed, the president was to be an almost kingly figure. Although presidents would be subject to election every four years, several of the chief executive's powers actually exceeded those of the British monarch. This was the sharpest departure from the recent experience in state government, where the office of governor had commonly been diluted because of the recent memory of struggles with the colonial executives. The president had a veto over acts of Congress, subject to being overridden by a two-thirds vote in each house, although the royal veto had long since fallen into complete disuse. The president was commander-in-chief of the armed forces and responsible for the execution of the laws. The chief executive could make treaties with the advice and consent of two-thirds of the Senate, and had the power to appoint diplomats, judges, and other officers with the consent of a Senate majority. The president was instructed to report annually on the state of the nation and was authorized to recommend legislation, a provision that presidents eventually would take as a mandate to form and promote extensive programs.

But the president's powers were limited in certain key areas. The chief executive could neither declare war nor make peace; those powers were reserved for Congress. Unlike the British king, moreover, the president could be removed. The House could impeach (indict) the chief executive—and other civil officers—on charges of treason, bribery, or "other high crimes and misdemeanors," and the Senate could remove an impeached president by a two-thirds vote upon conviction. The presiding officer at the trial of a president would be the chief justice, since the usual presiding officer of the Senate (the vice-president) would have a personal stake in the outcome.

The Convention's nationalists—men like Madison, James Wilson, and Hamilton—wanted to strengthen the independence of the executive by entrusting the choice to popular election. At least in this instance, the nationalists, often accused of being the aristocratic party, favored a bold new departure in democracy. But an elected executive was still too far beyond the American experience. Besides, a national election would have created enormous problems of organization and voter qualification. Wilson suggested instead that the people of each state choose presidential electors equal to the number of their senators and representatives. Others proposed that the legislators make the choice. Finally,

Signing the Constitution, September 17, 1787. *Thomas Pritchard Rossiter's painting shows George Washington presiding over what Thomas Jefferson called "an assembly of demi-gods."*

the Convention voted to let the legislature decide the method in each state. Before long nearly all the states were choosing the electors by popular vote, and the electors were acting as agents of party will, casting their votes as they had pledged before the election. This method diverged from the original expectation that the electors would deliberate and make their own choices.

On the third branch of government, the judiciary, there was surprisingly little debate. Both the Virginia and New Jersey plans had called for a Supreme Court, which the Constitution established, providing specifically for a chief justice of the United States and leaving up to Congress the number of other justices. The only dispute centered on courts "inferior" to the Supreme Court, and that too was left up to Congress. Although the Constitution nowhere authorized the courts to declare laws void when they conflicted with the Constitution, the power of judicial review was implied, and was soon exercised in cases involving both state and federal laws. Article VI declared the federal constitution, federal laws, and treaties to be the "supreme law of the land," state laws or constitutions to the contrary notwithstanding. At the time the advocates of states' rights thought this a victory, since it eliminated the proviso in the Virginia Plan for Congress to settle all conflicts with state authority. As it turned out, however, the clause became the basis for an important expansion of judicial review.

While the Constitution extended vast new powers to the national government, the delegates' mistrust of unchecked power is apparent in repeated examples of countervailing forces: the separation of the three branches of government, the president's veto, the congressional power of impeachment and removal, the Senate's power over treaties and appointments, the courts' implied right of judicial review. In addition the new frame of government specifically forbade Congress to pass bills of attainder (criminal condemnation by legislative act) or ex post facto laws (laws adopted after the event to make past deeds criminal). It also reserved to the states large areas of sovereignty—a reservation soon made explicit by the Tenth Amendment. By dividing sovereignty between the people and the government, the framers of the Constitution provided a distinctive contribution to political theory. That is, by vesting ultimate authority in the people, they divided sovereignty *within* the government. This constituted a dramatic break with the colonial tradition. The British had always insisted that the sovereignty of the king-in-Parliament was indivisible.

The most glaring defect of the Articles of Confederation, the rule of unanimity that defeated every effort to amend them, led the delegates to provide a less forbidding though still difficult method of amending the new Constitution. Amendments could be proposed either by two-thirds vote of each house or by a convention specially called, upon application of two-thirds of the legislatures. Amendments could be ratified by approval of three-fourths of the states acting through their legislatures or special conventions. The national convention has never been used, however, and state conventions have been called only once—to ratify the repeal of the Eighteenth Amendment, which had established Prohibition.

THE FIGHT FOR RATIFICATION   The old rule of unanimity under the Articles of Confederation, if applied to ratification of the Constitution itself, would almost surely have doomed its chances at the outset. The final article of the Constitution therefore provided that it would become effective upon ratification by nine states (not quite the three-fourths majority required for amendment). Conventions were specified as the proper agency for ratification, since legislatures might be expected to boggle at giving up any of their powers. The procedure, insofar as it bypassed the existing Articles of Confederation, was a constitutional revolution, but it was one in which the Confederation Congress joined. After fighting off efforts to censure the Convention for exceeding its authority, the Congress submitted its work to the states on September 28, 1787.

In the ensuing political debate, advocates of the new Constitution, who might properly have been called Nationalists because they preferred a strong central government, assumed the more reassuring name of Federalists. Opponents, who favored a more decentralized federal system, became Antifederalists. The initiative that the Federalists took in assuming their name was characteristic of the whole campaign. They got the jump on their critics. Their leaders had been members of the Convention and were already familiar with the document and the arguments on each point. They were not only better prepared but better organized, and on the whole, made up of the more articulate elements in the political community.

Historians have hotly debated the motivation of the advocates of the new Constitution. For more than a century the tendency prevailed to idolize the Founding Fathers, who created what one nineteenth-century British statesman called "the most wonderful work ever struck off at a given time by the brain and purpose of man." In 1913, however, Charles A. Beard's book *An Economic Interpretation of the Constitution* advanced the shocking thesis that the Philadelphia "assembly of demi-gods" was made up of men who had a selfish economic interest in the outcome.

Beard argued that the delegates represented an economic elite of speculators in western lands, holders of depreciated government securities, and creditors whose wealth was mostly in "paper": mortgages,

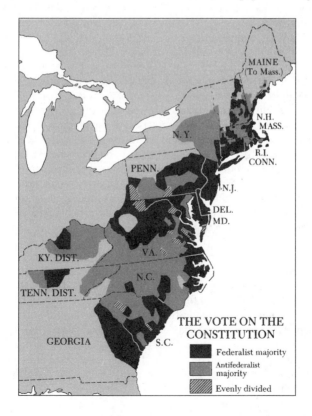

THE VOTE ON THE CONSTITUTION

■ Federalist majority

▨ Antifederalist majority

▨ Evenly divided

stocks, bonds, and the like. The holders of western lands and government bonds would benefit from a stronger government. Creditors generally stood to gain from the prohibitions against state currency issues and against the impairment of contract, provisions clearly aimed at the paper money issues and stay laws (granting stays, or postponements, on debt payments) then effective in many states.

Beard's thesis provided a useful antidote to unquestioning hero worship, and still contains a germ of truth, but he exaggerated. Most of the delegates, according to evidence unavailable to Beard, in fact had no compelling stake in paper wealth, and most were far more involved in landholding. Many prominent nationalists, including the "Father of the Constitution," James Madison himself, had no western lands, bonds, or much other personal property. Some opponents of the Constitution, on the other hand, held large blocks of land and securities. Economic interests certainly figured in the process, but they functioned in a complex interplay of state, sectional, group, and individual interests that turned largely on how well people had fared under the Confederation.

There is evidence, however, in the voting records and in the makeup of the ratifying conventions of divisions between "localist" and "cosmopolitan" elements, as the historian Jackson T. Main labeled them, who held to opposing worldviews because of their contrasting experiences. The localist tended to be a person "of narrow horizons—most often rural and sparsely educated—whose experience is limited to his own neighborhood," whereas the cosmopolitan was a person "of broad outlook, usually urban, urbane, and well-educated, who has traveled widely and has had extensive contacts with the world because of his occupation, the offices he has held, or his interests."

A large proportion of the localists were, to be sure, small farmers, but their leaders were often men of substance who were temperamentally or ideologically opposed to centralization. In general small farmers and frontier folk saw little to gain from the promotion of interstate commerce and much to lose from prohibitions on paper money and stay laws, and many of them feared that an expansive land policy was likely to favor speculators.

There were, however, some notable exceptions. Some farmers in New Hampshire and western Massachusetts, for instance, felt they had an interest in promoting interstate commerce up and down the Connecticut River. In Virginia the Shenandoah Valley, which runs northeastward, encouraged strong ties with Maryland and Pennsylvania. Some parts of the frontier looked to a stronger government for defense against Indians: in the state of Georgia, for instance, fear of the Creek Indians motivated unanimous ratification by a state convention eager to promote a stronger central government—which, as it turned out, soon reached an understanding with the Creeks.

Charles A. Beard hardly made a new discovery in finding that people are selfish, but it would be simplistic to attribute all human action to hidden economic interest. One must give some credence to the possibility that people mean what they say and are often candid about their motives, especially in large matters of public affairs. The most notable circumstance of the times in fact was that, unlike so many revolutions, the American Revolution led not to general chaos and terror but to "an outbreak of constitution-making." From the 1760s through the 1780s there occurred a prolonged debate over the fundamental issues of government, which in its scope and depth—and in the durability of its outcome—is without parallel.

THE FEDERALIST   Among the supreme legacies of that debate was *The Federalist,* a collection of essays originally published in the New York press between October 1787 and July 1788. Instigated by Alexander Hamilton, the eighty-five articles published under the name "Publius" included about fifty by Hamilton, thirty by James Madison, and five by John Jay. The authorship of some selections remains in doubt. Written in support of ratification, the essays defended the principle of a supreme national authority, but at the same time sought to reassure doubters that the people and the states had little reason to fear usurpations and tyranny by the new government.

In perhaps the most famous single essay, No. 10, Madison argued that the very size and diversity of the country would make it impossible for any single faction to form a majority that could dominate the government. This contradicted prevailing notions of republican forms of government. Republics, the conventional wisdom of the times insisted, could survive only in small, homogeneous countries like Switzerland and the Netherlands. Large republics, on the other hand, they would descend into anarchy and tyranny through the influence of factions. Quite the contrary, Madison insisted. Given a balanced federal polity, they could work in large and diverse countries probably better. "Extend the sphere," he wrote, "and you take in a greater variety of parties and interests; you make it less probable that a majority of the whole will have a common motive to invade the rights of other citizens."

The Federalists did try to cultivate a belief that the new union would contribute to prosperity, in part to link their movement with the economic recovery already under way. The Antifederalists, however, talked more of the dangers of power in terms that had become familiar during the long struggles with Parliament and the crown. They noted the absence of a Bill of Rights protecting the rights of individuals and states. They found the process of ratification highly irregular, as it was—indeed, illegal under the Articles of Confederation. Not only did Patrick Henry refuse to attend the Constitutional Convention, he demanded

View of Cons. on the Road to Philadelphia. *A 1790 cartoon opposing the Constitution.*

later (unsuccessfully) that it be investigated as a conspiracy. The Antifederalist leaders—George Mason, Henry, and Richard Henry Lee of Virginia, George Clinton of New York, Sam Adams and Elbridge Gerry of Massachusetts, Luther Martin of Maryland—were often men whose careers and reputations had been established well before the Revolution. The Federalist leaders, on the other hand, were more likely to be younger men whose careers had begun in the Revolution—men such as Hamilton, Madison, and Jay.

The disagreement between the two groups, however, was more over means than ends. Both sides, for the most part, agreed that a stronger national authority was needed, and that it required an independent income to function properly. Both were convinced that the people must erect safeguards against tyranny, even the tyranny of the majority. Few of its supporters liked the Constitution in its entirety, but they felt that it was the best obtainable; few of its opponents found it unacceptable in its entirety. Once the new government had become an accomplished fact, few diehards were left who wanted to undo the work of the Philadelphia convention.

THE DECISION OF THE STATES   Ratification gained momentum before the end of 1787, and several of the smaller states were among the first to act, apparently satisfied that they had gained all the safeguards they could hope for in equality of representation in the Senate. Massachusetts, still sharply divided in the aftermath of Shays's Rebellion, was the first state in which the outcome was close. There the Federalists carried the day by winning over two hesitant leaders of the popular party. They dangled before John Hancock the possibility of becoming vice-president, and won the acquiescence of Samuel Adams when they agreed to recommend amendments designed to protect human rights, including one that would specifically reserve to the states all powers not granted to the new government. Massachusetts approved by 187 to 168 on February 7, 1788.

New Hampshire was the ninth to ratify, and the Constitution could now be put into effect, but the union could hardly succeed without the approval of Virginia, the most populous state, or New York, with the third highest population, which occupied a key position geographically. Both states harbored strong opposition groups. In Virginia Patrick Henry became the chief spokesman of backcountry farmers who feared the powers of the new government, but wavering delegates were won over by the same strategem as in Massachusetts. When it was proposed that the Convention should recommend a Bill of Rights, Edmund Randolph, who had refused to sign the finished document, announced his conversion to the cause.

Virginia's convention ratified on June 25 by a vote of 89 to 79. In New York, as in New Hampshire, Hamilton and the other Federalists worked

RATIFICATION OF THE CONSTITUTION

Order of Ratification	State	Date of Ratification
1	Delaware	December 7, 1787
2	Pennsylvania	December 12, 1787
3	New Jersey	December 18, 1787
4	Georgia	January 2, 1788
5	Connecticut	January 9, 1788
6	Massachusetts	February 7, 1788
7	Maryland	April 28, 1788
8	South Carolina	May 23, 1788
9	New Hampshire	June 21, 1788
10	Virginia	June 25, 1788
11	New York	July 26, 1788
12	North Carolina	November 21, 1789
13	Rhode Island	May 29, 1790

for a delay, in the hope that action by New Hampshire and Virginia would persuade the delegates that the new framework would go into effect with or without New York. On July 26, 1788, they carried the day by the closest margin thus far, 30 to 27. North Carolina and Rhode Island remained the only holdouts, and North Carolina stubbornly withheld action until amendments comprising a Bill of Rights were actually submitted by Congress. On November 21, 1789, North Carolina joined the new government, which was already under way, 194 to 77. Rhode Island, true to form, continued to hold out, and did not relent until May 29, 1790. Even then the vote was the closest of all, 34 to 32.

Upon notification that New Hampshire had become the ninth state to ratify, the Confederation Congress began to draft plans for an orderly transfer of power. On September 13, 1788, it selected New York City as the seat of the new government and fixed the date for elections. March 4, 1789, was the date set for the meeting of the new Congress. Each state would set the date for electing the first members of Congress. On October 10, 1788, the Confederation Congress transacted its last business and passed into history.

"Our constitution is in actual operation," the elderly Ben Franklin wrote to a friend; "everything appears to promise that it will last; but in this world nothing is certain but death and taxes." George Washington was even more uncertain about the future under the new plan of government. He had told a fellow delegate as the Convention adjourned: "I do not expect the Constitution to last for more than twenty years."

The Constitution has lasted much longer, of course, and in the

Washington, holding the Constitution, and Franklin, with liberty cap, drive the Federal chariot as thirteen freemen, representing the states, pull it toward ratification (1788).

process it has provided a model of republican government whose features have been repeatedly borrowed by other nations through the years. Yet what makes the American Constitution so distinctive is not its specific provisions but its remarkable harmony with the particular "genius of the people" it governs. The Constitution has been neither a static abstraction nor a "machine that would go of itself," as the poet James Russell Lowell would later assert. Instead it has provided a flexible system of government that presidents, legislators, judges, and the people have adjusted to a fallible human nature and changing social, economic, and political circumstances. In this sense the Founding Fathers not only created "a more perfect Union" in 1787; they engineered a frame of government whose resilience has enabled later generations to continue to perfect their republican experiment. But the Framers of the Constitution failed in one significant respect. In skirting the issue of slavery so as to cement the union, they unknowingly allowed tensions over the "peculiar institution" to reach the point where there would be no political solution—only civil war.

FURTHER READING

A good overview of the Confederation period is Richard B. Morris's *The Forging of the Union, 1781–1789* (1987). Merrill Jensen's *The New Nation* (1950) presents the "consensus" view that downplays the extent of crisis under the Confederation. Another useful analysis of this period is Richard Buel, Jr.'s *Securing the Revolution: Ideology in American Politics. 1789–1815* (1974).° Relevant chapters of Gordon S. Wood's *The Creation of the American Republic, 1776–1787* (1969)° trace the changing contours of political philosophy during these years. The behavior of Congress is the subject of Jack N. Rakove's *The Beginnings of National Politics* (1979).° Also useful is Jackson Turner Main's *Political Parties before the Constitution* (1973).

David P. Szatmary's *Shays' Rebellion* (1980) covers that fateful incident. For a fine account of cultural change during the period, see Joseph J. Ellis's *After the Revolution: Profiles of American Culture* (1979)° and Oscar Handlin and Lilian Handlin's *A Restless People: America in Rebellion, 1770–1787* (1982).

Charles A. Beard's *An Economic Interpretation of the Constitution of the United States* (1913)° remained powerfully influential for more than a generation. More recent scholarship, however, has focused on the ideas, rather than the economic interests, of the founding period.

°These books are available in paperback editions.

Examples are Edmund S. Morgan's *Inventing the People* (1988), Michael Kammen's *Sovereignty and Liberty* (1988), and Forrest McDonald's *Novus Ordo Seclorum: The Intellectual Origins of the Constitution* (1985). Among the better collections of essays on the Constitution are *Toward a More Perfect Union* (1988), edited by Neil L. York; *The Framing and Ratification of the Constitution* (1987), edited by Leonard W. Levy and Dennis J. Mahoney; *Conceptual Change and the Constitution* (1988), edited by Terence Ball and J.G.A. Pocock; and *Essays on the Making of the Constitution* (2nd ed., 1987), edited by Leonard W. Levy. Also see Robert A. Goldwin and Robert A. Light (eds.), *The Spirit of the Constitution: Five Conversations* (1990). On the Constitutional Convention, see Christopher Collier and James Lincoln Collier's *Decision in Philadelphia* (1986).

Scholars treat both sides of the ratification argument. The best introduction to the Federalist viewpoint remains their own writings, edited by Benjamin F. Wright, *The Federalist* (1972).° Garry Wills's *Explaining America: The Federalist* (1981) provides an interpretation of what they wrote. Bruce Ackerman's *We the People: Foundations* (1990) examines Federalist political principles. Biographies of Federalist writers are also helpful, among them Jacob E. Cooke's *Alexander Hamilton* (1982), Forrest McDonald's *Alexander Hamilton: A Biography* (1979), and Irving Brant's *James Madison: The Nationalist, 1780–1787* (1948) and Jack N. Rakove's *James Madison and the Creation of the American Republic* (1990).° See also Richard B. Morris's *Witness at the Creation: Hamilton, Madison, Jay, and the Constitution* (1985) and James MacGregor Burns and Stewart Burns's *A People's Charter: The Pursuit of Rights in America* (1990).

Herbert J. Storing and Murray Dry compiled a multivolume compendium of the Antifederalist documents. Their slim but incisive introduction is *What the Anti-Federalists Were For* (1981). For the Bill of Rights that emerged from the ratification struggles, see Robert A. Rutland's *The Birth of the Bill of Rights, 1776–1791* (1955).

For discussions of the problem of slavery in forming the Constitution, see the relevant sections of Donald L. Robinson's *Slavery in the Structure of American Politics, 1765–1820* (1970)° and James MacGregor Burns's *The Vineyard of Liberty: The American Experiment* (1982).°

Michael Kammen's *A Machine that Would Go of Itself: The Constitution in American Culture* (1986) is a comprehensive cultural history of the Constitution that shows how it has become revered by the American public.

°These books are available in paperback editions.

8 ∕ℰ

THE FEDERALISTS:
WASHINGTON AND ADAMS

A New Nation

The framers of the Constitution sought to create a new federal government capable of administering a rapidly expanding territory and population. In 1789 the United States and the western territories covered an area from the Atlantic Ocean to the Mississippi River and included almost 4 million people. This vast area harbored distinct regional differences. New England remained a region of small farms and bustling seaports, but it was on the verge of developing a small-scale manufacturing sector. The Middle States boasted the most well-balanced economy, the largest cities, and the most diverse collection of ethnic and religious groups. The South was an agricultural region more ethnically homogeneous and increasingly dependent on slave labor. By 1790 the southern states were exporting as much tobacco as they had been before the Revolution, and new farm commodities such as grains, indigo, and hemp helped diversify the economy. Most important, however, was the surge in cotton production. Between 1790 and 1815 the annual production of cotton rose from less than 3 million pounds to 93 million pounds.

Overall, the United States in 1790 was predominantly a rural society. Eighty percent of households were involved in agricultural production. Only a few cities had more than 5,000 people. The first national census, taken in 1790, reported that there were 750,000 African Americans, almost one-fifth of the population. Most of the them lived in the five southernmost states. Less than 10 percent of the blacks lived outside the South. Most African Americans, of course, were slaves, but there

Venerate the Plough. *Medal of the Philadelphia Society for the Promotion of Agriculture (1786).*

were many free blacks as a result of the revolutionary turmoil. In fact, the proportion of free blacks to slaves was never higher than in 1790.

The 1790 census did not even include the many Indians still living east of the Mississippi River. Most Americans still viewed the Native Americans as those peoples whom the Declaration of Independence dismissed as "merciless Indian savages." It is estimated that there were over eighty tribes totaling perhaps as many as 150,000 persons in 1790. In the Old Northwest along the Great Lakes, the British continued to arm the Indians and encouraged them to resist American encroachments. Between 1784 and 1790 Indians killed or captured some 1,500 settlers in Kentucky alone. Such bloodshed generated a ferocious reaction. "The people of Kentucky," observed an official frustrated by his inability to negotiate a treaty between whites and Indians, "will carry on private expeditions against the Indians and kill them whenever they meet them, and I do not believe there is a jury in all Kentucky that will punish a man for it." In the South the five most powerful tribes—the Cherokees, Chickasaws, Choctaws, Creeks, and Seminoles—numbered between 50,000 and 100,000. They steadfastly refused to recognize

American authority and used Spanish-supplied weapons to thwart white settlement.

Only about 125,000 whites and blacks lived west of the Appalachians in 1790. But that was soon to change. The great theme of nineteenth-century American history would be the ceaseless stream of migrants flowing westward from the Atlantic seaboard. By foot, horse, boat, and wagon, pioneers and adventurers headed west. "A rage for emigrating to the western country prevails," noted New Yorker John Jay in 1785, "and thousands have already fixed their habitations in that wilderness. . . . The seeds of a great people are daily planting beyond the mountains." Kentucky, still a part of Virginia but destined for statehood in 1792, harbored 75,000 settlers in 1790. In 1776 there had been only 150 pioneers.

Rapid population growth, cheap land, and new economic opportunities fueled this phenomenon. Although immigrants contributed significantly to the rising numbers, the extraordinary growth rate resulted primarily from natural increase. The average white woman gave birth to eight children, and the white population doubled approximately once every twenty-two years. This made for a very young population on average. In 1790 almost half of all white Americans were under the age of sixteen.

A NEW GOVERNMENT   The men who drafted the Constitution and helped to gain its ratification were justifiably proud of their achievement. But they knew that many questions were left unanswered. And they feared that putting the new frame of government into practice would pose unexpected challenges. On the appointed date, March 4, 1789, the new Congress of the United States, meeting in New York, could muster only eight senators and thirteen representatives. A month passed before both chambers gathered a quorum. Only then could the temporary presiding officer of the Senate count the ballots and certify the foregone conclusion that George Washington, with sixty-nine votes, was the unanimous choice of the electoral college for president. John Adams, with thirty-four votes, the second-highest number, became vice-president.

Washington's journey from Mount Vernon to New York, where he was inaugurated on April 30, turned into a triumphal procession that confirmed the universal confidence he commanded and the hopeful expectancy with which the new experiment was awaited. But the fifty-seven-year-old Washington, by now grown gray-haired, partly deaf, and almost toothless, confessed to feeling like "a culprit who is going to his place of execution," burdened with dread that so much was expected of him. "I face an ocean of difficulties," he added. When Washington delivered the inaugural address, he trembled visibly and at times seemed barely able to make out the manuscript in front of him. The new nation, however, required not brilliant oratory but firm leadership, and Washington offered that in abundance.

SYMBOLS OF AUTHORITY   The task before the president and the Congress was to create a government anew. From the Confederation Washington inherited but the shadow of a bureaucracy: a foreign office with John Jay and two clerks; a Treasury Board with little or no treasury; a secretary of war with an army of 672 officers and men, and no navy at all; a dozen or so clerks who had served the old Congress; a heavy debt and almost no revenue, and no machinery for collecting one. There was the acute realization that anything done at the time would set important precedents for the future. Even the question of an etiquette suited to the dignity and authority of the new government occupied Congress to a degree that later Americans (and not a few at the time) would regard as absurd. A committee of Congress went so far as to suggest for a presidential title "His Highness, the President of the United States and Protector of Rights of the Same." A solemn discussion of the issue in Congress ended happily when the House of Representatives addressed the chief executive simply by his constitutional title: "President of the United States."

The Congress nevertheless agreed with one representative who said

Federal Hall, New York City, site of President Washington's inauguration, April 30, 1789.

on the floor of the House: "There are cases in which generosity is the best economy, and no loss is ever sustained by a decent support of the Magistrate. A certain appearance of parade and external dignity is necessary to be supported." To that end Congress set the president's salary at $25,000, an income far above that of any other official and probably all but a few Americans. The president obliged them with a show of pomp and circumstance. On public occasions he appeared in a coach drawn by four horses, sometimes six, escorted by liveried retainers. Seven slaves helped Martha Washington maintain the presidential mansion in New York. President Washington held formal dinners for "official characters and strangers of distinction," but accepted no invitations himself. Every Tuesday from 3 to 4 P.M. he held a formal reception, clothed in black velvet, his hair in full dress, powdered and gathered, wearing yellow gloves and a finely polished sword, holding a cocked hat with cockade and feather. Visiting in Boston, Washington stubbornly declined to meet Governor John Hancock until Hancock paid a call on him, thus making the point that a president takes precedence over a mere governor. Mixed emotions greeted the show of ceremony. Some members of Congress continued to fear that another president might make "that bold push for the throne" predicted by Patrick Henry. The antimonarchists did stop a move to stamp coins with the head of the incumbent president, preferring an emblem of Liberty instead.

GOVERNMENTAL STRUCTURE   More than matters of etiquette occupied the First Congress, of course. In framing the structure of government it was second in importance only to the Constitutional Convention itself. During the summer of 1789 Congress authorized executive departments corresponding in each case to those already formed under the Confederation. To head the Department of State, Washington named Thomas Jefferson, recently back from his mission to France. To head the Department of the Treasury, Washington picked his old wartime aide Alexander Hamilton, now a prominent lawyer in New York. The new position of attorney-general was occupied by Edmund Randolph, former governor of Virginia. Randolph headed no department but served as legal adviser to the government and on such a meager salary that he was expected to continue his private law practice on the side.

Almost from the beginning Washington routinely called these men to sit as a group for discussion and advice on matters of policy. This was the origin of the president's cabinet, an advisory body for which the Constitution made no formal provision—except insofar as it provided for the heads of departments. The office of vice-president also took on what would become its typical character. "The Vice-Presidency," John Adams wrote his wife Abigail, was the most "insignificant office . . . ever . . . contrived."

John Jay as Chief Justice of the Supreme Court (1794).

The structure of the court system, like that of the executive departments, was left to Congress, except for a chief justice and Supreme Court. Congress determined to set the membership of the highest court at six, the chief justice and five associate justices. There was some sentiment for stopping there and permitting state courts to determine matters of federal law, but the Congress decided in favor of thirteen federal district courts. From these, appeals might go to one of three circuit courts, composed of two Supreme Court justices and the district judge, meeting twice a year in each district. Members of the Supreme Court, therefore, became itinerant judges riding the circuit during a good part of the year. All federal cases originated in the district court, and if appealed on issues of procedure or legal interpretation, went to the circuit courts and from there to the Supreme Court. There were only two exceptions, both specified in the Constitution: the Supreme Court had original jurisdiction in cases involving either states or foreign ambassadors, ministers, and consuls.

As the first chief justice Washington named John Jay, who served until 1795. Born in New York City in 1745, Jay graduated from King's College (now Columbia University) in 1764. His distinction as a lawyer led New York to send him as its representative to the First and Second Continental Congresses. After serving as president of the Continental Congress in 1779, Jay became the American minister in Spain. While in Europe he helped John Adams and Benjamin Franklin negotiate the Treaty of Paris in 1783. After the Revolution Jay served as secretary of foreign affairs. He then joined Madison and Hamilton as co-author of the *The Federalist* and became one of the most effective champions of the Constitution.

THE BILL OF RIGHTS   In the new House of Representatives, James Madison made a Bill of Rights a top priority. The lack of such provisions had been one of the Antifederalists' major objections to the Constitution as originally proposed. At first Madison believed that the absence of a Bill of Rights made little difference. He later said that the proposals for a Bill of Rights were "unnecessary and dangerous." He feared that any list of rights would be incomplete. Madison and other Federalists also worried that specifying such rights might imply the existence of a parallel set of powers never meant to be delegated to the central government. Or, as Alexander Hamilton phrased it in the eighty-fourth paper of *The Federalist,* "Why declare things should not be done which there is no power to do?" Yet the fear of arbitrary federal power would not die. In the end, however, Madison recognized the need to allay the fears of Antifederalists and to meet the moral obligation imposed by those ratifying conventions that had approved the Constitution with the understanding that amendments would be offered.

Madison viewed the Bill of Rights as "the most dramatic single gesture of conciliation that could be offered the remaining opponents of the government." Those "opponents" included prominent statesmen such as Virginians George Mason and Richard Henry Lee as well as artisans, small traders, and backcountry farmers who expressed a profound egalitarianism. These "poor and middling" folk were skeptical that even the "best men" were capable of subordinating self-interest to the good of the Republic. Said one semiliterate Maine democrat: "I never wish to be in the power of any Sett of Men let them be never so good, but hope to be left in the hands of my Country." He and other anti-Federalists argued that no country could be founded on the premise that its leaders would possess an extraordinary degree of civic virtue. All people were prone to corruption. No one could be trusted. Therefore, a Bill of Rights must protect the liberties of all against the encroachments of a few.

In all, 210 amendments had been suggested in various state conventions. From the Virginia proposals Madison drew the first eight Amendments, modeled after the Virginia Bill of Rights that George Mason had written in 1776. These all provided safeguards for certain rights of individuals: freedom of religion, press, speech, and assembly; the right to keep and bear firearms; the right to refuse to house soldiers in private homes; protection against unreasonable searches and seizures; the right to refuse to testify against oneself; the right to a speedy public trial before an impartial jury and to have legal counsel present; and protection against cruel and unusual punishment.

The Ninth and Tenth Amendments addressed themselves to the demand for specific statements that the enumeration of rights in the Constitution "shall not be construed to deny or disparage others retained by the people" and that "powers not delegated to the United States by the Constitution, nor prohibited by it to the states, are reserved to the States respectively, or to the people." The Tenth

Amendment was taken almost verbatim from the Articles of Confederation. The House adopted, in all, seventeen amendments; the Senate, after conference with the House, adopted twelve; the states in the end voted separately on each proposed amendment and ratified ten, which constitute the Bill of Rights, effective December 15, 1791. The Bill of Rights provided no rights or legal protection to blacks.

RAISING A REVENUE   Revenue was the new federal government's most critical need. The Congress undertook a revenue measure as another of the first items of business. Madison proposed a modest tariff (tax on imports) for revenue only, but the demands of manufacturers in the northern states for higher duties to protect them from foreign competition forced a compromise that imposed higher tariffs on certain listed items. Madison linked the tariff to a proposal for a mercantile system that would levy extra tonnage duties on foreign ships, an especially heavy duty on countries that had no commercial treaty with the United States.

Madison's specific purpose was to wage economic war against Great Britain, which had no such treaty but had more foreign trade with the new nation than any other country. Northern businessmen, however, were in no mood for a renewal of economic pressures, for fear of disrupting the economy. Secretary of the Treasury Hamilton agreed with them. In the end the only discrimination built into the Tonnage Act of 1789 was between American and all foreign ships: American ships paid a duty of 6¢ per ton; American-built but foreign-owned ships paid 30¢; and foreign-built and -owned ships paid 50¢ per ton. The disagreements created by the trade measures were portents of quarrels yet to come. Should economic policy favor Britain or France? The more persistent question was whether tariff and tonnage duties should penalize farmers in the interest of northern manufacturers and shipowners. By imposing a tax on imports, tariffs and tonnage duties resulted in higher prices on goods bought by Americans, most of whom were tied to the farm economy. This raised a basic and perennial question: Should these rural consumers be forced to subsidize the nation's infant manufacturing sector? This issue became a sectional question of South versus North.

HAMILTON'S VISION OF AMERICA

But the tariff and tonnage duties, linked as they were to other issues, marked but the beginning of the effort to get the country on a sound fiscal basis. In finance, with all its broad implications for policy in general, it was thirty-four-year-old Alexander Hamilton who seized the initiative. The first secretary of the treasury was a protégé of the presi-

Alexander Hamilton, in a portrait by John Trumbull (1804).

dent, a younger man who had been Washington's aide during four years of the Revolution. Born out of wedlock on a Caribbean island and deserted by a ne'er-do-well father, Hamilton was left an orphan at thirteen by the death of his mother. With the help of friends and relatives, he found his way at seventeen to New York, attended King's College (later Columbia University), entered the revolutionary agitations as speaker and pamphleteer, and joined the army, where he came to the attention of the commander. "George Washington was an aegis essential to me," Hamilton wrote later, after the president's death. He studied law, passed the bar examination, established a legal practice in New York, and became a self-made aristocrat, serving as collector of revenues and member of the Confederation Congress. An early convert to nationalism, he had a major role in promoting the Constitutional Convention. Hamilton had been a hero of the siege of Yorktown, and he remained forever after a frustrated military genius, hungry for greater glory on the field of battle.

Shrewd, energetic, and determined, Hamilton was also quick to take offense and reluctant to forgive, impatient with critics and intolerant of error. When Jefferson once told him that he considered Francis Bacon, Isaac Newton, and John Locke the three greatest men who ever lived, Hamilton quickly countered: "The greatest man that ever lived was Julius Caesar." Hamilton indeed had Caesar's limitless ambition. As he recognized at age fourteen, "To confess my weakness, my ambition is prevalent."

In a series of classic reports submitted to Congress in the two years from January 1790 to December 1791, Hamilton outlined his program for government finances and the economic development of the United States. The reports were soon adopted, with some alterations in detail but little in substance. The last of the series, the Report on Manufactures, outlined a program of protective tariffs and other governmental supports of business. This eventually would become government policy, despite much brave talk of free enterprise and free trade.

ESTABLISHING THE PUBLIC CREDIT   Hamilton submitted the first and most important of his reports to the House of Representatives in January 1790 at the invitation of that body. This First Report on the Public Credit, as it has since been called, made two key recommendations: first, funding of the federal debt at face value, which meant that those citizens holding government bonds could exchange them for new interest-bearing bonds; and second, the federal government's assumption of state debts from the Revolution to the amount of $21 million. The funding scheme was controversial because many farmers and soldiers in immediate need of money had sold their securities for a fraction of their value to speculators who were eager to buy them up after reading Hamilton's First Report. These common folk argued that they should be reimbursed for their losses; otherwise, the speculators would gain a windfall from the new government's funding of bonds at face value. Hamilton sternly resisted such pleas. The speculators, he argued, had "paid what the commodity was worth in the market, and took the risks." Therefore, they should reap the benefits. In fact, Hamilton insisted, the government should do all it could to win over the financial community because it represented the bedrock of a successful nation.

The report provided the material for lengthy debates before its substance was adopted in August. Then in short order came three more reports: a Second Report on Public Credit, which included a proposal for an excise tax on distilled spirits to aid in raising revenue to cover the nation's debts (Hamilton meant this tax also to establish the precedent of an excise tax, and to rebuke elements that had been least friendly to his program). Another report recommended a national bank, a revival of the Robert Morris idea that had led to the Bank of North America. The secretary proposed a national mint—which was established in 1792. Finally, in December 1791, as the culmination of his basic reports, the Report on Manufactures proposed an extensive program of government aid and encouragement to the development of manufacturing enterprises.

Each of Hamilton's reports excited vigorous discussion and disagreement. His program was substantially the one Robert Morris had urged upon the Confederation a decade before, and which Hamilton had strongly endorsed at the time. "A national debt," he had written Morris in 1781, "if it is not excessive, will be to us a national blessing; it will be a powerful cement of our union. It will also create a necessity for keeping up taxation to a degree which without being oppressive, will be a spur to industry." Payment of the national debt, in short, would be not only a point of national honor and sound finance, ensuring the country's credit for the future; it would also be an occasion to assert a national taxing power and thus instill respect for the authority of the national government. Not least, the plan would win the new government the support of wealthy, influential creditors.

SECTIONAL DIFFERENCES EMERGE   It was on this point, however, that Madison, who had been Hamilton's close ally in the movement for a stronger government, broke with him for the second time (their first break had been over tonnage duties), and as in the first case the difference here had ominous overtones of sectionalism. Madison did not question that the debt should be paid; he was troubled, however, that speculators and "stock-jobbers" would become the chief beneficiaries. That the far greater portion of the debt was held north of the Mason-Dixon line further troubled him. Madison, whom Hamilton had expected to take the lead for his program in the House, therefore advanced an alternative plan to give a larger share to the first owners than to the later speculators. "Let it be a liberal one in favor of the present holders," Madison conceded. "Let them have the highest price which has prevailed in the market; and let the residue belong to the original sufferers." Madison's opposition touched off a vigorous debate, but Hamilton carried his point by a margin of three to one when the House brought it to a vote.

Madison's opposition to the assumption of state debts got more support, however, and set up a division more clearly along sectional lines. The southern states, with the exception of South Carolina, had whittled down their debts. New England, with the largest unpaid debts, stood to be the greatest beneficiary of the assumption plan. Rather than see Virginia victimized, Madison held out an alternative. Why not, he suggested, have the government assume state debts as they stood in 1783 at the conclusion of the peace? Debates on this point deadlocked the whole question of debt funding and assumption through much of 1790.

The stalemate finally ended when Hamilton accosted Thomas Jefferson on the steps of the president's home and suggested a compromise. The next evening, at a dinner arranged by Jefferson, Hamilton and Madison reached an understanding. In return for northern votes in favor of locating the permanent capital on the Potomac, Madison pledged to seek enough southern votes to pass the assumption, with the further arrangement that those states with smaller debts would get in effect outright grants from the federal government to equalize the difference. With these arrangements, enough votes were secured to carry Hamilton's funding and assumption schemes. The capital would be moved to Philadelphia for ten years, after which time it would be settled at a Federal City on the Potomac, the site to be chosen by the president. In August 1790 Congress finally passed the legislation for Hamilton's plan.

A NATIONAL BANK   By this vast program of funding and assumption, Hamilton had called up from nowhere, as if by magic, a great sum of capital. As he put it in his original report, a national debt "answers most of the purposes of money." Transfers of government bonds, once the debt was properly funded, would be "equivalent to payments in specie." This feature of the program was especially important in a country that had, from the first settlements, suffered a shortage of hard money. Having established the public credit, Hamilton moved on to a related measure essential to his vision of national greatness. He called for a national bank, which by issuance of bank notes (paper money) might provide a uniform currency. Government bonds held by the bank would back up the value of its new bank notes, needed as a medium of exchange because of the chronic shortage of specie. The national bank, chartered by Congress, would remain under governmental surveillance, but private investors would supply four-fifths of the $10 million capital and name twenty of the twenty-five directors; the government would pro-

The first Bank of the United States in Philadelphia. Proposed by Hamilton, the bank opened in 1791.

vide the other fifth of the capital and name five directors. Government bonds would be received in payment for three-fourths of the stock in the bank, and the other fourth would be payable in gold and silver.

The bank, Hamilton explained, would serve many purposes. Its notes would become a stable currency, uniform in value because redeemable in gold and silver upon demand. Moreover, the bank would provide a source of capital for loans to fund the development of business and commerce. Bonds, which might otherwise be stowed away in safes, would instead become the basis for a productive capital by backing up bank notes available for loan at low rates of interest, the "natural effect" of which would be "to increase trade and industry." What is more, the existence of the bank would serve certain housekeeping needs of the government: a safe place to keep its funds, a source of "pecuniary aids" in sudden emergencies, and the ready transfer of funds to and from branch offices through bookkeeping entries rather than shipment of metals.

Once again Madison rose to lead the opposition, arguing that he could find no basis in the Constitution for such a bank. He himself had proposed in the Constitutional Convention a grant of power to charter corporations, but no specific provisions had been adopted. That was enough to raise in President Washington's mind serious doubts as to the constitutionality of the measure, which Congress passed fairly quickly over Madison's objections. Before signing the bill into law, therefore, the president sought the advice of his cabinet and found there an equal division of opinion. The result was the first great and fundamental debate on constitutional interpretation. Should there be a strict or a broad construction of the document? Were the powers of Congress only those explicitly stated or were others implied? The argument turned chiefly on Article I, Section 8, which authorized Congress to "make all laws which shall be necessary and proper for carrying into execution the foregoing Powers."

Such language left room for disagreement and led to a confrontation between Jefferson, with whom Attorney-General Edmund Randolph agreed, and Hamilton, who had the support of Secretary of War Henry Knox. Jefferson pointed to the Tenth Amendment, which reserved to the states and the people powers not delegated to Congress. "To take a single step beyond the boundaries thus specially drawn around the powers of Congress, is to take possession of a boundless field of power, no longer susceptible of any definition." A bank might be a convenient aid to Congress in collecting taxes and regulating the currency, but it was not, as Article I, Section 8, specified, *necessary.*

Hamilton had not expected the constitutionality of the bank to become a divisive issue. His original report had neglected the point, but he was prepared to meet his opponents on their own ground. In a long report to the president, Hamilton insisted that the power to charter corporations was included in the sovereignty of any government, whether or not expressly stated. The word "necessary," he explained, often meant no more than "needful, requisite, incidental, useful, or conducive to." And in a classic summary, he expressed his criterion on constitutionality: "This criterion is the *end,* to which the measure relates as a *mean.* If the *end* be clearly comprehended within any of the specified powers, collecting taxes and regulating the currency, and if the measure have an obvious relation to that *end,* and is not forbidden by any particular provision of the Constitution, it may safely be deemed to come within the compass of the national authority."

The president, influenced by the fact that the matter came within the jurisdiction of the secretary of the treasury, accepted Hamilton's argument and signed the bill. In doing so, he had indeed, in Jefferson's words, opened up "a boundless field of power," which in coming years would lead to a further broadening of implied powers with the approval of the Supreme Court. Under John Marshall the Court would eventually adopt Hamilton's words almost verbatim. On July 4, 1791, the bank's stock was put up for sale and in what seemed to Jefferson a "delirium of speculation" sold out within a few hours, with hundreds of buyers turned away. It cost the government itself nothing until later, for its subscription of $2 million was immediately returned by the bank in a loan of the same amount, with ten years for repayment.

ENCOURAGING MANUFACTURES   Hamilton's imagination and his ambitions for the new country were as yet unexhausted. In the last of his great reports, the Report on Manufactures, he set in place the capstone of his design: the active encouragement of manufacturing to provide productive uses for the new capital created by his funding, assumption, and banking schemes. Hamilton believed that several advantages would flow from the development of manufactures: the diversification of labor in a country given over too much to farming; greater use of machinery; paid work for those not ordinarily employed outside the home, such as women and children; the promotion of immigration; a greater scope for the diversity of talents in business; more ample and various opportunities for entreprenurial activity; and a better domestic market for agricultural products.

To secure his ends Hamilton proposed to use the means to which other countries had resorted, and which he summarized: protective tariffs on foreign goods, or in Hamilton's words, "protecting duties," which in some cases might be put so high as to deter imports altogether; restraints on the export of raw materials; bounties and premiums to encourage certain industries; tariff exemptions for the raw materials needed for American manufacturing, or "drawbacks" (rebates) to man-

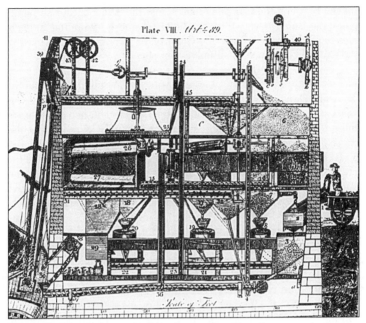

Hamilton's Report on Manufactures *proposed tariffs on foreign products to encourage American manufacturing and innovation, as represented by this mechanized grain elevator patented by a Delaware resident in 1795.*

ufacturers where duties had been levied for revenue or other purposes; encouragements to inventions and discoveries; regulations for the inspection of commodities; and finally, the encouragement of internal improvements in transportation, including the development of roads, canals, and navigable streams.

Some of Hamilton's tariff proposals were enacted in 1792. Otherwise the program was filed away—but not forgotten. It became an arsenal of arguments for the advocates of manufactures in years to come, in Europe as well as in America. A summary can hardly do justice to a complex state paper that anticipated and sought to demolish all counterarguments, among them the ominous question that kept arising with Hamilton's schemes, "ideas of a contrariety of interests between the northern and southern regions of the Union," which he found "in the Main as unfounded as they are mischievous." If, as seemed likely, the northern and middle states should become the chief scenes of manufacturing, they would create robust markets for agricultural products, some of which the southern states were peculiarly qualified to produce. North and South would both benefit, he argued, as more commerce moved between these regions than across the Atlantic, thus strengthening the Union: "every thing tending to establish *substantial* and *permanent order* in the affairs of a Country, to increase the total mass of industry and opulence, is ultimately beneficial to every part of it."

HAMILTON'S ACHIEVEMENT   Largely owing to the skillful Hamilton, the Treasury Department, which employed half or more of the civil servants at the time, largely as customs agents, was established on a basis of integrity and efficiency. The department began to retire the Revolutionary War debt, and a "Continental" became worth something after all (if only at a ratio of 100 to 1 in payments to the government), the credit of the government was secure, government securities sold at par, and foreign capital began to flow in once again. Prosperity, so elusive in the 1780s, began to flourish once again, although President Washington cautioned against attributing "to the Government what is due only to the goodness of Providence."

Yet suspicions lingered that Hamilton's program was designed to promote his personal interest. There is, however, no evidence that Hamilton benefited personally in any way from his program, although Assistant Treasury Secretary William Duer, unbeknownst to Hamilton, did leak word of the funding and assumption message to favored friends in time for them to reap a speculative harvest from the rise in values. Duer himself later became involved in deals that landed him in prison.

Hamilton was inclined toward a truly nationalist outlook, and he focused his energies on the rising power of commercial capitalism. In fact, he would have favored a much stronger central government, including a federal veto on state action, even a constitutional monarchy if that had been practicable. Hamilton believed that throughout history a minority of the strong dominated the weak. There was always a ruling group, perhaps military or aristocratic, and Hamilton had the foresight to see now the rising power of commercial capitalism. He was in many ways a classic Whig who, like Britain's ruling oligarchy of the eighteenth century, favored government by the rich and well-born. The mass of the people, he once said, "are turbulent and changing; they seldom judge or determine right." And once, under the influence of strong drink, he went further: "Your people, sir, is a great beast!" Aligning the government closely to the social elite, Hamilton believed, promoted good government and guarded the public order against the potential turbulence that always haunted him.

Hamilton's achievement, however, was to tie more closely to the government those who were already on its side—and to overlook, or even antagonize, those who had their doubts. Hamilton never understood or appreciated the people of the small villages and farms, the people of the frontier. They were foreign to his world, despite his own humble beginnings in the Caribbean islands. Along with the planters of the South, common folk would be at best only indirect beneficiaries of his programs. Below the Potomac the Hamiltonian vision excited little enthusiasm except in South Carolina, which had a large state debt to be assumed and a concentration of mercantile interests at Charleston. There were, in short, a vast number of people who were drawn into opposition to Hamilton's new engines of power. In part they were southern, in part backcountry, and in part a politically motivated faction opposing Hamilton in New York.

The Republican Alternative

This split over the Hamiltonian program provided the seeds of the first national political parties. Hamilton became the embodiment of the party known as the Federalists; Madison and Jefferson became the leaders of those who took the name Republican and thereby implied that the Federalists really aimed at a monarchy. Parties were slow in developing, or at least in being acknowledged as legitimate. All the political philosophers of the age deplored the spirit of party or faction. The concept of a loyal opposition, of a two-party system as a positive good, was yet to be formulated. Parties, or factions, as the eighteenth century knew them, were bodies of men bent upon self-aggrandizement through the favor of the government. They smelled of corruption. As Jefferson once declared, "If I could not go to heaven but with a party I would not go there at all."

Neither side in the disagreement over national policy deliberately set out to create a party system. But there were important differences of both philosophy and self-interest that simply would not dissolve. At the outset Madison, who had worked with Hamilton to build a national government, assumed leadership of Hamilton's opponents in the Congress. The states meant more to Madison than to Hamilton, who would just as soon have seen a consolidated central government. Madison, like Thomas Jefferson, was rooted in Virginia, where opposition to the funding schemes flourished.

In December 1790 the Virginia assembly bluntly protested Hamilton's funding schemes in a resolution drafted by Patrick Henry: "In an agricultural country like this . . . to erect, and concentrate, and perpetuate a large monied interest . . . must in the course of human events produce one or other of two evils, the prostration of agriculture at the feet of commerce, or a change in the present form of federal government, fatal to the existence of American liberty. . . . Your memorialists can find no clause in the Constitution authorizing Congress to assume the debts of the States!" To Hamilton this was "the first symptom of a spirit which must either be killed, or will kill the Constitution of the United States."

After the compromise that had assured the assumption of state debts, Madison and Jefferson moved into ever more resolute opposition to Hamilton's policies: his effort to place an excise tax on whiskey, which laid a burden especially on the trans-Appalachian farmers, whose grain was best transported in liquid form; his proposal for the bank; and his report on manufactures. Against the last two both men raised constitutional objections. As the differences built, hostility between Jefferson and Hamilton grew and festered, to the distress of President Washington. Jefferson, the temperamentally shy and retiring secretary of state, then emerged as the leader of the opposition to Hamilton's policies; Madison continued to direct the opposition in Congress.

JEFFERSON'S AGRARIAN VIEW   Thomas Jefferson, twelve years Hamilton's senior, was in most respects his opposite. In contrast to Hamilton, Jefferson was to the manor born, his father a successful surveyor and land speculator, his mother a Randolph, from one of the First Families in Virginia. Jefferson developed a breadth of cultivated interests that ranged perhaps more widely in science, the arts, and the humanities than those of any contemporary, even Franklin. Jefferson read or spoke seven languages. He was an architect of distinction (Monticello, the Virginia Capitol, and the University of Virginia are monuments to his talent), a man who understood mathematics and engineering, an inventor, an agronomist. In his *Notes on Virginia* (1785) he displayed a knowledge of geography, paleontology, zoology, botany, and archeology. He collected paintings and sculpture. He knew music and practiced the violin, although some wit said only Patrick Henry played it worse.

Philosophically, Hamilton and Jefferson represented polar visions of the character of the Union in the first generation under the Constitution and defined certain fundamental issues of American life that still echo two centuries later. Hamilton foresaw a diversified capitalistic economy, agriculture balanced by commerce and industry, and was thus the better prophet. Jefferson feared the growth of crowded cities divided into a capitalistic aristocracy on the one hand and a deprived proletariat on the other. Hamilton feared anarchy and loved order; Jefferson feared tyranny and loved liberty.

What Hamilton wanted for his country was a strong central government actively encouraging capitalistic enterprise. What Jefferson wanted was a republic made up primarily of small farmers: "Those who labor in the earth," he wrote, "are the chosen people of God, if ever he had a chosen people, whose breasts He has made His peculiar deposit for genuine and substantial virtue." Jefferson did not oppose all forms of

Thomas Jefferson. A portrait by Charles Willson Peale (1791).

manufacturing. What he feared was that the unlimited expansion of commerce and industry would produce a class of property less wage laborers who were dependent on others for their livelihood and therefore subject to political manipulation and economic exploitation.

Where Hamilton was the old-fashioned English Whig, Jefferson, who spent several years in France, was the enlightened *philosophe,* the natural radical and reformer who attacked the aristocratic relics of entail and primogeniture in Virginia, opposed an established church, proposed an elaborate plan for public schools, prepared a more humane criminal code, and was instrumental in eliminating slavery from the Old Northwest, although he kept the slaves he had inherited. On his tomb were finally recorded the achievements of which he was proudest: author of the Declaration of Independence and the Virginia Statute of Religious Freedom, and founder of the University of Virginia.

Jefferson set forth his vision of what America should be in his *Notes on Virginia:* "While we have land to labor then, let us never wish to see our citizens occupied at a work-bench, or twirling a distaff. . . . For the general operations of manufacture, let our workshops remain in Europe. It is better to carry provisions and materials to work-men there, than bring them to the provisions and materials, and with them their manners and principles. . . . The mobs of great cities add just so much to the support of pure government, as sores do to the strength of the human body."

PARTY DISPUTES   What Jefferson and Hamilton shared, it seemed, was mutual hatred, which began with disagreement in the cabinet and soon became widely visible in a journalistic war of words between two editors with the curiously similar names of Fenno and Freneau. John Fenno's *Gazette of the United States,* founded in 1789 "to endear the General Government to the people," became virtually the official administration organ. It extolled Hamilton and his policies at every opportunity and benefited from contracts for government printing. Philip Freneau, a poet and journalist, was enticed to Philadelphia from New York in 1791 to found the *National Gazette* and given a sinecure as translator for Jefferson's Department of State. Each man was compromised by his connection, but each loyally supported his benefactor out of real conviction.

In their quarrel Hamilton unwittingly identified Jefferson more and more in the public mind as the leader of the opposition to his policies; Madison was still a relatively obscure congressman whose central role in the Constitutional Convention was unknown. In the summer of 1791 Jefferson and Madison set out on a "botanizing" excursion up the Hudson, a vacation that many Federalists feared was a cover for consultations with Governor George Clinton, the Livingstons, and Aaron Burr, leaders of the faction in New York that opposed the aristocratic party of the DeLanceys, Van Rensselaers, and Philip Schuyler, Hamilton's father-in-law. While the significance of that single trip was blown out of proportion, there did ultimately arise an informal alliance of Jeffersonian Republicans in the south and New York that would become a constant if sometimes divisive feature of the party and its successor, the Democratic party.

Still, there was no opposition to Washington, who longed to end his exile from Mount Vernon and even began drafting a farewell address, but was urged by both Hamilton and Jefferson to continue in public life. He was the only man who could transcend party differences and hold things together with his unmatched prestige. In 1792 Washington was unanimously reelected, but in the scattering of second votes the Republican Clinton got fifty electoral votes to John Adams's seventy-seven.

CRISES FOREIGN AND DOMESTIC

In Washington's second term the problems of foreign relations came to center stage, brought there by the consequences of the French Revolution, which had begun during the first months of Washington's presidency. Americans followed the tumultuous events in France with almost universal sympathy, up to a point. By the spring of 1792, though, the experiment in liberty, equality, and fraternity had transformed itself into a monster. France plunged into war with Austria and Prussia. The Revolution began devouring its own children along with its enemies during the Terror of 1793–1794.

After the execution of King Louis XVI in January 1793, Great Britain entered into the coalition of monarchies at war with the French Republic. For the next twenty-two years Britain and France were at war, with only a brief respite, until the final defeat of the French forces under Napoleon in 1815. The war presented Washington, just beginning his second term, with an awkward decision. By the treaty of 1778 the United States was a perpetual ally of France, obligated to defend her possessions in the West Indies.

But Americans wanted no part of the war. They were determined to maintain their lucrative trade with both sides in the European conflict. Of course, the combatants resented and resisted America's profitable neutrality. For their part, Hamilton and Jefferson found in the neutrality policy one issue on which they could agree. Where they differed was in how best to implement the policy. Hamilton had a simple and direct answer to this problem: declare the alliance invalid because it was made with a government that no longer existed. Jefferson preferred to delay and use the alliance as a bargaining point with the British. In the end, however, Washington followed the advice of neither. Taking a middle course, on April 22, 1793, the president issued a neutrality proclamation that evaded even the word "neutrality." It simply declared the United States "friendly and impartial toward the belligerent powers" and warned American citizens that "aiding or abetting hostilities" or other un-neutral acts might be prosecuted.

CITIZEN GENÊT   At the same time, Washington accepted Jefferson's argument that the United States should recognize the new French government (becoming the first country to do so) and receive its new ambassador, Citizen Edmond Charles Genêt. Early in 1793 Citizen Genêt landed at Charleston, where he immediately organized a Jacobin Club to support that faction of French revolutionaries. Along the route to Philadelphia the enthusiasm of his sympathizers gave Genêt an inflated notion of his potential, not that he needed much encouragement. In Charleston he began to authorize privateers to bring in British prizes, and in Philadelphia he continued the process. He intrigued with frontiersmen and land speculators, including George Rogers Clark, with an eye to an attack on Spanish Florida and Louisiana.

Genêt quickly became an embarrassment even to his Republican friends. Jefferson decided that the French minister had overreached himself when he violated a promise not to outfit a captured British ship as a privateer. Such actions could have provoked a British declaration of war against the United States. When, finally, Genêt threatened in a moment of anger to appeal his cause directly to the American people over the head of their president, the cabinet unanimously agreed that he had to go, and in August 1793 Washington demanded his recall. Meanwhile a new party of radicals had gained power in France and sent over its own minister with a warrant for Genêt's arrest. Instead of returning to risk the guillotine, Genêt sought asylum, married the daughter of Governor Clinton, settled down as a country gentleman on the Hudson, and died years later an American citizen.

Genêt's foolishness and the growing excesses of the French radicals were fast cooling American support for their revolution. To Hamilton's followers it began to resemble their worst nightmares of democratic anarchy and infidelity. The French made it hard even for Republicans to retain sympathy, but they swallowed hard and made excuses. "The liberty of the whole earth was depending on the issue of the contest," the genteel Jefferson wrote, "and . . . rather than it should have failed, I would have seen half the earth devastated." Nor did the British make it easy for Federalists to rally to their side. Near the end of 1793 they informed the American government that they intended to occupy their northwestern posts indefinitely and announced Orders in Council under which they seized the cargoes of American ships with provisions for or produce from the French islands.

Despite the offenses by both sides, the French and British causes polarized American opinion. In the contest, it seemed, one either had to be a Republican and support liberty, reason, and France, or become a Federalist and support order, religious faith, and Britain. The division gave rise to some curious loyalties: slave-holding planters joined the cheers for Jacobin radicals who dispossessed aristocrats in France, and supported the protest against British seizures of New England ships; Massachusetts shippers still profited from the British trade and kept quiet. Boston, once a hotbed of revolution, became a bastion of Federalism.

JAY'S TREATY Early in 1794 the Republican leaders in Congress were gaining support for commercial retaliation to bring the British to their senses, when the British gave Washington a timely opening for a settlement. They announced abandonment of the Orders under which American brigs and schooners were being seized, and on April 16, 1794, Washington named Chief Justice John Jay as a special envoy to Great Britain. Jay left with instructions to settle all major issues: to get the British out of the western posts, to secure reparations for the losses of American shippers, compensation for slaves carried away in 1783, and a commercial treaty that would legalize American commerce with the British West Indies.

A 1794 watercolor of Fort Detroit, a major center of Indian trade that the British agreed to evacuate in Jay's Treaty.

Jay entered the negotiations with his bargaining power compromised by both Federalists and Republicans. In Philadelphia Hamilton indiscreetly told the British minister that the United States had no intention of joining the Armed Neutrality recently formed by Scandinavian countries to uphold neutral rights. In Paris the new American minister, James Monroe, spoke before the National Assembly and embraced both its president and its revolution. The British in turn demanded from Jay greater assurances that America would stay neutral.

To win his objectives, Jay was obliged to concede the British definition of neutral rights. He accepted the principles that naval stores were contraband, that provisions could not go in neutral ships to enemy ports, and the "Rule of 1756," by which trade with enemy colonies prohibited in peacetime could not be opened in wartime. Britain also gained most-favored-nation treatment in American commerce and a promise that French privateers would not be outfitted in American ports. Finally, Jay conceded that the British need not compensate Americans for the slaves who escaped during the war and that the old American debts to British merchants would be adjudicated and paid by the American government. In return for these concessions he won three important points: British evacuation of the northwestern posts by 1796, reparations for the seizures of American ships and cargoes in 1793–1794, and legalization of trade with the British West Indies. But the last of these (Article XII) was so hedged with restrictions that the Senate eventually struck it from the treaty.

Public outrage greeted the terms of the treaty. Even Federalist shippers, ready for settlement on almost any terms, were disappointed at the limitations on their privileges in the West Indies. But much of the outcry was simply expression of disappointment by Republican partisans who sought an escalation of conflict with "perfidious Albion." Some of it was the outrage of Virginia planters at the concession on debts to British merchants and the failure to get reparations for lost slaves. Given the limited enthusiasm of Federalists—Washington himself wrestled with doubts over the treaty—Jay remarked that he could travel across the country by the light of his burning effigies. Yet the Senate debated the treaty in secret, and in the end quiet counsels of moderation prevailed. Without a single vote to spare, Jay's Treaty got the necessary two-thirds majority on June 24, 1795, with Article XII (the provision regarding the West Indies) expunged.

Washington still hesitated but finally signed the treaty as the best he was likely to get and out of fear that a refusal would throw the United States into the role of a French satellite. In the House opponents went so far as to demand that the president produce all papers relevant to the treaty, but the president refused on the grounds that treaty approval was solely the business of the Senate. He thereby set an important precedent of executive privilege (a term not used at the time), and the House finally relented, supplying the money to fund the treaty by a close vote.

THE FRONTIER STIRS   Other events also had an important bearing on Jay's Treaty, adding force to the importance of its settlement of the Canadian frontier and strengthening Spain's conviction that it too needed to reach a settlement of long-festering problems along America's southwestern frontier. While Jay was haggling in London, frontier conflict with Indians was moving toward a temporary resolution. Washington named General Wayne, known as "Mad Anthony," to head an expedition into the Northwest Territory. In the fall of 1793 Wayne marched into Indian country with some 2,600 men, built Fort Greenville, and with reinforcements from Kentucky, went on the offensive in 1794. On August 4, 1794, some 2,000 Shawnee, Ottawa, Chippewa, and Potawatomi warriors, reinforced by some Canadian militia, attacked Wayne's force at the Battle of Fallen Timbers, but this time the Americans were ready and repulsed them. The Indians suffered heavy losses. American detachments then laid waste their fields and villages. Dispersed and decimated, they finally agreed to the Treaty of Greenville, signed in August 1795. In the treaty, at the cost of a $10,000 annuity, the United States bought from twelve tribes the rights to the southeastern quarter of the Northwest Territory (now Ohio and Indiana) and enclaves at the sites of Vincennes, Detroit, and Chicago.

THE WHISKEY REBELLION   Wayne's forces were still mopping up after the Battle of Fallen Timbers when the administration resolved on another show of strength in the backcountry against the so-called Whiskey Rebellion. Hamilton's excise tax on strong drink, levied in 1791, had excited strong feeling among frontier farmers because it taxed their staple crop. The frontiersmen considered the tax another part of Hamilton's scheme to pick the pockets of the poor to enrich fat speculators.

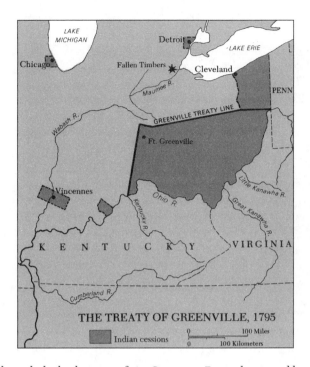

THE TREATY OF GREENVILLE, 1795

Indian cessions

0   100 Miles
0   100 Kilometers

All through the backcountry, from Georgia to Pennsylvania and beyond, the tax gave rise to resistance and evasion. In the summer of 1794 the rumblings of discontent broke into open rebellion in the four western counties of Pennsylvania, where vigilantes, mostly of Scottish or Irish descent, organized to terrorize revenues and taxpayers. They blew up the stills of those who paid the tax, robbed the mails, stopped court proceedings, and threatened an assault on Pittsburgh. On August 7, 1794, President Washington issued a proclamation ordering them home and calling out 12,900 militiamen from Virginia, Maryland, Pennsylvania, and New Jersey. Getting no response from the "Whiskey Boys," he issued a proclamation on September 24 for suppression of the rebellion.

Under the command of General Henry Lee, "a force larger than any Washington had ever commanded" in the Revolution marched out from Harrisburg across the Alleghenies with Hamilton in their midst, itching to smite the insurgents. But the rebels vaporized like corn mash when the heat was applied, and the troops met with little opposition. By dint of great effort and much marching, they finally rounded up twenty barefoot, ragged prisoners whom they paraded down Market Street in Philadelphia and clapped into prison. Eventually two of these were found guilty of treason, but were pardoned by Washington on the grounds that one was a "simpleton" and the other "insane." The government had made its point and gained "reputation and strength,"

Washington as commander-in-chief reviews the troops mobilized to quell the Whiskey Rebellion in 1794.

according to Hamilton, by suppressing a rebellion that, according to Jefferson, "could never be found." Hamilton's use of force came at the cost of creating or confirming new numbers of Republicans, who scored heavily in the next Pennsylvania elections. Nor was it the end of whiskey rebellions, which continued in an unending war of wits between moonshiners and revenuers down to the day of twentieth-century rumrunners in hopped-up stock cars.

PINCKNEY'S TREATY   While these stirring events were transpiring in the Keystone State, Spain was suffering some setbacks to its schemes farther south in Florida and Louisiana. Spanish intrigues among the Creeks, Choctaws, Chickasaws, and Cherokees were keeping up the same turmoil the British fomented along the Ohio. Washington had sought to buy peace with $100,000 and a commission as brigadier-general to the Creek chief, Alexander McGillivray, the half-Creek son of a Scottish trader, but it was to no avail. In 1793, therefore, some settlers from Eastern Tennessee took it upon themselves to teach the proud Cherokees a lesson by leveling a few of their villages, and in 1794 Tennesseeans from around Nashville attacked them again, burning and killing without pity.

The collapse of Spain's own designs in the west combined with Britain's concessions in the north to give some second thoughts to the Spanish, who were preparing to make peace with the French and switch sides in the European war. Among the more agreeable fruits of Jay's talks, therefore, were new parleys with the Spanish government. United States Minister Thomas Pinckney won acceptance of a boundary at the 31st parallel, free navigation of the Mississippi, the right to deposit goods at New Orleans for three years with promise of renewal, a commission to settle American claims against Spain, and a promise on each side to refrain from inciting Indian attacks on the other. Ratification of the Pinckney Treaty ran into no opposition. In fact, it was immensely popular, especially among westerners eager to use the Mississippi River to transport their crops to market.

Now that Jay and Pinckney had settled things with Britain and Spain, and General Wayne in the Northwest and the Tennessee settlers to the south had smashed the Indians, the West was open for a renewed surge of settlers. New lands, ceded by the Indians in the Treaty of Greenville, revealed Congress once again divided on land policy. There were two basic viewpoints on the matter, one that the public domain should serve mainly as a source of revenue, the other that it was more important to accommodate settlers with low prices, maybe free land, and get the country settled. In the long run the evolution of policy would be from the first toward the second viewpoint, but for the time being the government's need for revenue took priority.

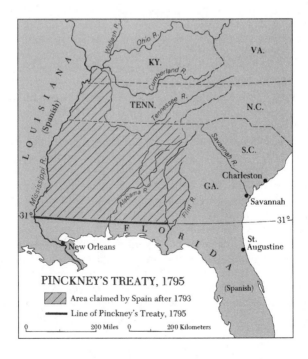

PINCKNEY'S TREATY, 1795

Area claimed by Spain after 1793

Line of Pinckney's Treaty, 1795

0   200 Miles   0   200 Kilometers

A newly cleared American farm.

Opinions on land policy, like other issues, separated Federalists from Republicans. Federalists involved in speculation might prefer lower land prices, but the more influential Federalists like Hamilton and Jay preferred to build the population of the eastern states first, lest the East lose political influence and lose a labor force important to the future growth of manufactures. Men of their persuasion favored high land prices to enrich the treasury, sale of relatively large parcels of land to speculators rather than small amounts to actual settlers, and the development of compact settlements. In addition to his other reports, Hamilton had put out one on the public lands, in which he emphasized the need for governmental revenues. Jefferson and Madison were reluctantly prepared to go along for the sake of reducing the national debt, but Jefferson expressed the hope for a plan by which the lands could be more readily settled. In any case, he suggested, frontiersmen would do as they had done before: "They will settle the lands in spite of everybody." The Daniel Boones of the West, always moving out beyond the settlers and surveyors, were already proving him right.

For the time, however, Federalist policy prevailed. In the Land Act of 1796 Congress resolved to extend the rectangular surveys ordained in 1785, but it doubled the price to $2 per acre, with only a year in which to complete payment. Half the townships would go in 640-acre sections, making the minimum cost $1,280, and alternate townships would be sold in blocks of eight sections, or 5,120 acres, making the minimum cost $10,240. Either was beyond the means of most ordinary settlers, and a bit much even for speculators, who could still pick up state lands at lower prices. By 1800 government land offices had sold fewer than 50,000 acres under the act. Continuing pressures from the West led to the Land Act of 1800, which reduced the minimum sale to 320 acres and spread the payments over four years. Thus with a down payment of $160 one could get a farm. All lands went for the minimum price if they did not sell at auction within three weeks. Under the Land Act of 1804 the minimum unit was reduced to 160 acres, which became the traditional homestead, and the price per acre went down to $1.64.

WASHINGTON'S FAREWELL   By 1796 President Washington had decided that two terms in office were enough. Tired of the political quarrels and the venom of the partisan press, he was ready to retire once and for all to Mount Vernon. He would leave behind a formidable record of achievement: the organization of a national government with demonstrated power, a secure national credit, the recovery of territory from Britain and Spain, a stable northwestern frontier, and the admission of three new states: Vermont (1791), Kentucky (1792), and Tennessee (1796). With the help of Jay and especially Hamilton, Washington set about preparing a valedictory address, using a draft prepared by Madison four years before.

Washington's Farewell Address, dated September 17, 1796, was not delivered as a speech. It was first published in the Philadelphia *Daily American Advertiser* two days later. It stated first his resolve to decline being considered for a third term. After that, most of the message dwelled on domestic policy, and particularly on the need for unity among the American people in backing their new government. Washington decried the spirit of sectionalism. "In contemplating the causes which may disturb our union," he wrote in one prescient passage, "it occurs as a matter of serious concern that any ground should have been furnished for characterizing parties by geographical discriminations—*Northern* and *Southern, Atlantic* and *Western*—whence designing men may endeavor to excite a belief that there is a real difference of local interests and views." He decried as strongly the spirit of party, while acknowledging a body of opinion that parties were "useful checks upon the administration of the government, and serve to keep alive the spirit of liberty." From the natural tendency of men there would always be enough spirit of party, however, to serve that purpose. The danger was partisan excess: "A fire not to be quenched, it demands a uniform vigilance to prevent its bursting into a flame, lest, instead of warming, it should consume."

In foreign relations, Washington said, America should show "good faith and justice toward all nations" and avoid either "an habitual hatred or an habitual fondness" for other countries. Europe, he noted, "has a set of primary interests which to us have none or a very remote rela-

The Washington family at Mount Vernon, with one of the family's slaves in the background, in a sketch by Latrobe (1797).

tion. Hence she must be engaged in frequent controversies, the causes of which are essentially foreign to our concerns." The United States should keep clear of those quarrels. It was, moreover, "our true policy to steer clear of permanent alliances with any portion of the foreign world." A key word here is "permanent." Washington enjoined against any further permanent arrangements like the one with France, still technically in effect. He did not speak of "entangling alliances"—that phrase would be used by Thomas Jefferson in his first inaugural address—and in fact specifically advised that "we may safely trust to temporary alliances for extraordinary emergencies." Washington's warning against permanent foreign entanglements thereafter served as a fundamental principle in American foreign policy until the early twentieth century.

Washington himself had not escaped the "baneful effects" of the party spirit, for during his second term the Republican press came to link him with the Federalist partisans. For the first time in his long career Washington was subjected to sustained, and often scurrilous, criticism. According to the editor of the Philadelphia *Aurora*, the president was "a man in his political dotage" and "a supercilious tyrant." Washington never responded to such abuse in public but in private he went into towering rages. This criticism hastened his resolve to retire. On the

eve of that event the *Aurora* proclaimed that "this day ought to be a
Jubilee in the United States. . . . If ever a nation was debauched by a
man, the American Nation has been debauched by Washington."

THE ADAMS YEARS

With Washington out of the race, the United States had its first
partisan election for president. The logical choice of the Federalists
would have been Washington's protégé Hamilton, the chief architect of
their programs. But like many a potential presidential candidate, Hamilton was not "available," however willing. His policies had left scars and
made enemies. Nor did he suffer fools gladly, a common affliction of
Federalist leaders, including the man on whom the choice fell. In
Philadelphia, a caucus of Federalist congressmen chose John Adams as
heir apparent with Thomas Pinckney of South Carolina, fresh from his

The Providential Detection. *An anti-Republican cartoon
shows the American eagle arriving just in time to stop
Thomas Jefferson from burning the Constitution on the
"Altar to Gallic Despotism."*

triumph in Spain, as nominee for vice-president. As expected, the Republicans drafted Jefferson and added geographical balance to the ticket with Aaron Burr of New York.

The rising strength of the Republicans, fueled by the smoldering resentment toward Jay's Treaty, very nearly swept Jefferson into office, and perhaps would have but for the public appeals of the French ambassador for his election—an action which, like the indiscretions of Citizen Genêt, backfired. Then, despite a Federalist majority among the electors, Alexander Hamilton thought up an impulsive scheme that very nearly threw the election away after all. Between Hamilton and Adams there had been no love lost since the Revolution, when Adams had joined the movement to remove Hamilton's father-in-law, General Schuyler, from command of the Saratoga campaign. Thomas Pinckney, Hamilton thought, would be more subject to influence than the strong-minded Adams. He therefore sought to have South Carolina Federalists withhold a few votes from Adams and bring Pinckney in first. The Carolinas more than cooperated—they divided their vote between Pinckney and Jefferson—but New Englanders got wind of the scheme and dropped Pinckney. The upshot of Hamilton's intrigue was to cut Pinckney out of both offices and elect Jefferson vice-president with sixty-eight votes, second to Adams's seventy-one.

Adams had behind him a distinguished career as a Massachusetts lawyer, a leader in the revolutionary movement and the Continental Congress, a diplomat in France, Holland, and Britain, and as vice-president. His political philosophy fell somewhere between Jefferson's and Hamilton's. He shared neither the one's faith in the common people nor the other's fondness for an aristocracy of "paper wealth." He favored the classic mixture of aristocratic, democratic, and monarchical elements, though his use of "monarchical" interchangeably with "executive" exposed him to the attacks of Republicans who saw a monarchist in every Federalist. Yet Adams's fondness for titles and protocol arose from a reasoned purpose, to exploit the human "thirst for distinction." He was always haunted by a feeling that he was never properly appreciated—and he may have been right. He tried to play the role of disinterested executive, which he outlined in his philosophy. And on the overriding issue of his administration, war and peace, he kept his head when others about him were losing theirs—probably at the cost of his reelection.

WAR WITH FRANCE Adams inherited from Washington his cabinet—the precedent of changing personnel with each new administration had not yet been set—and with them an intraparty division, for three of the department heads looked to Hamilton for counsel: Timothy Pickering at State, Oliver Wolcott at the Treasury, and Joseph McHenry at the War

John Adams.

Department. Adams also inherited a menacing quarrel with France, a by-product of the Jay Treaty. When Jay accepted the British position that food supplies and naval stores—as well as war matériel—were contraband subject to seizure, the French reasoned that American cargoes in the British trade were subject to the same interpretation and loosed their corsairs in the West Indies with even more devastating effect than the British had in 1793–1794. By the time of Adams's inauguration in 1797, the French had plundered some 300 American ships and had broken diplomatic relations. As ambassador to Paris James Monroe had become so pro-French and so hostile to the Jay Treaty that Washington had felt impelled to remove him for his indiscretions. France then had refused to accept Monroe's replacement, Charles Cotesworth Pinckney, and ordered him out of the country.

Adams immediately acted to restore relations in the face of an outcry for war from the "High Federalists," including Secretary of State Pickering. Hamilton agreed with Adams on this point and approved his last-ditch effort for a settlement. In October 1797 Charles C. Pinckney returned to Paris with John Marshall and Elbridge Gerry (a Massachusetts Republican) for further negotiations. After long, nagging delays, the three commissioners were accosted by three French counterparts (whom Adams labeled X, Y, and Z in his report to Congress), agents of Foreign Minister Talleyrand, a past master of the diplomatic shakedown. The three French diplomats delicately let it be known that negotiations could begin only if there were a loan of $12 million, a bribe of $250,000 to the five directors then heading the government, and suitable apologies for remarks recently made in Adams's message to Congress.

Such bribes were common eighteenth-century diplomatic practice—Washington himself had bribed a Creek chieftain and ransomed American sailors from Algerian pirates, each at a cost of $100,000—but Talleyrand's price was high merely for a promise to negotiate. The answer, according to the commissioners' report, was "no, no, not a sixpence." When the XYZ Affair broke in Congress and the public press, this was translated into the more stirring slogan first offered as a banquet toast by Robert Goodloe Harper: "Millions for defense but not one cent for tribute." Thereafter, the expressions of hostility toward France rose to a crescendo—even the most partisan Republicans were hard put to make any more excuses, and many of them joined a cry for war. Yet Adams resisted a formal declaration of war; the French would have to bear the onus for that. Congress, however, authorized the capture of armed French ships, suspended commerce with France, and renounced the alliance of 1778, which was already a dead letter.

In 1798 George Logan, a Pennsylvania Quaker, visited Paris at his own expense, hoping to head off war. He did secure the release of some American seamen and won assurances that an American minister would be welcomed. The fruits of his mission, otherwise, were widespread denunciation and passage of the Logan Act (1799), which still forbids private citizens to negotiate with foreign governments without official authorization.

Adams proceeded to strengthen American defenses. An American navy had ceased to exist at the end of the Revolution. Except for rev-

A cartoon indicating the anti-French feeling generated by the XYZ Affair. The three American ministers at left reject the "Paris Monster's" demand for money.

enue cutters of the Treasury Department, no armed ships were available when Algerian brigands began to war on American commerce in 1794. As a result Congress had authorized the arming of six ships. These were incomplete in 1796 when Washington bought peace with the Algerians, but Congress allowed work on three to continue: the *Constitution*, the *United States*, and the *Constellation*, all completed in 1797. In 1798 Congress authorized a new Department of the Navy. By the end of 1798 the number of naval ships had increased to twenty and by the end of 1799 to thirty-three. But before the end of 1798 an undeclared naval war had begun in the West Indies with the French capture of an American schooner.

While the naval war went on, a new army was authorized in 1798 as a 10,000-man force to serve three years. Adams called Washington from retirement to be its commander, agreeing to Washington's condition that he name his three chief subordinates. Washington sent in the names of Hamilton, Charles C. Pinckney, and Henry Knox. In the old army the three ranked in precisely the opposite order, but Washington insisted that Hamilton be his second in command. Adams relented, but resented the slight to his authority as commander-in-chief. The rift among Federalists thus widened further. Because of Washington's age, the choice meant that Hamilton would command the army in the field, if it ever took the field. But recruitment went slowly until well into 1799, by which time all fear of French invasion was dispelled. Hamilton continued to dream of imperial glory, though, planning the seizure of Louisiana and the Floridas to keep them out of French hands, and even the invasion of South America, but these remained Hamilton's dreams.

Peace overtures began to come from Talleyrand by the autumn of 1798, before the naval war was fully under way. Adams decided to act on the information and took it upon himself, without consulting the cabinet, to name the American minister to the Netherlands, William Vans Murray, as special envoy to Paris. The Hamiltonians, infected with a virulent attack of war fever, fought the nomination but finally compromised, in face of Adams's threat to resign, on a commission of three. After a long delay they left late in 1799 and arrived to find themselves confronting a new government under First Consul Napoleon Bonaparte. By the Convention of 1800 they won the best terms they could from the triumphant Napoleon. In return for giving up all claims of indemnity for American losses they got the suspension of the French alliance and the end of the quasi-war. The Senate ratified, contingent upon outright abrogation of the alliance, and the agreement became effective on December 21, 1801.

THE WAR AT HOME   The real purpose of the French crisis all along, the more ardent Republicans suspected, was to create an excuse to put down the domestic opposition. The Alien and Sedition Acts of 1798 lent credence to their suspicions. These four measures, passed in the wave of patriotic war fever, limited freedom of speech and the press and the liberty of aliens. Proposed by Federalists in Congress, they did not originate with Adams but had his blessing. Three of the four acts reflected hostility to foreigners, especially the French and Irish, a large number of whom had become active Republicans and were suspected of revolutionary intent. The Naturalization Act lengthened from five to fourteen years the residence requirement for citizenship. The Alien Act empowered the president to expel "dangerous" aliens on pain of imprisonment. The Alien Enemy Act authorized the president in time of declared war to expel or imprison enemy aliens at will. Finally, the Sedition Act defined as a high misdemeanor any conspiracy against legal measures of the government, including interference with federal officers and insurrection or riot. What is more, the law forbade writing, publishing, or speaking anything of "a false, scandalous and malicious" nature against the government or any of its officers.

Considering what Federalists and Republicans said about each other, the act, applied rigorously, could have caused the imprisonment of nearly the whole government. In practice, however, the purpose was transparently partisan, designed to punish Republicans, whom Federalists could scarcely distinguish from Jacobins and traitors. To be sure, partisan Republican journalists were resorting to scandalous lies and misrepresentations, but so were Federalists; it was a time when both sides seemed afflicted with paranoia. But the fifteen indictments brought under the act, with ten convictions, were all directed at Republicans, and some for trivial matters. In the very first case one unfortunate was fined $100 for wishing out loud that the wad of a salute cannon might hit President Adams in his rear. The most conspicuous targets of prosecution were Republican editors and a congressman, Matthew Lyon of Vermont, a rough-and-tumble Irishman who published censures of Adams's "continual grasp for power" and "unbounded thirst for ridiculous pomp, foolish adulation, and selfish avarice." For such libels Lyon got four months and a fine of $1,000, but from his cell he continued to write articles and letters for the Republican papers. The few convictions under the act only created martyrs to the cause of freedom of speech and the press, and exposed the vindictiveness of Federalist judges.

Lyon and the others based a defense on the unconstitutionality of the Sedition Act, but Federalist judges were scarcely inclined to entertain such notions. It ran against the Republican grain, anyway, to have federal courts assume the authority to declare laws unconstitutional. To offset the Alien and Sedition Acts, therefore, Jefferson and Madison conferred and brought forth drafts of what came to be known as the Kentucky and Virginia Resolutions. These passed the legislatures of the

Republican representative Matthew Lyon and the Connecticut Federalist Roger Griswald go at each other on the floor of the House (1798). Lyon soon became a target of the Sedition Act.

two states in November and December 1798, while further Kentucky Resolutions, adopted in November 1799, responded to counterresolutions from northern states. These resolutions, much alike in their arguments, denounced the Alien and Sedition Acts as unconstitutional and advanced what came to be known as the state-compact theory. Since the Constitution arose as a compact among the states, the resolutions argued, it followed logically that the states should assume the right to say when Congress had exceeded its powers. The Virginia Resolutions, drafted by Madison, declared that states "have the right and are in duty bound to interpose for arresting the progress of the evil." The second set of Kentucky Resolutions, in restating the states' right to judge violations of the Constitution, added: "That a nullification of those sovereignties, of all unauthorized acts done under color of that instrument, is the rightful remedy."

The doctrines of interposition and nullification, revised and edited by later theorists, were destined to be used for causes unforeseen by the authors of the Kentucky and Virginia Resolutions. (Years later Madison would disclaim the doctrine of nullification as developed by John C. Calhoun, but his own doctrine of "interposition" would resurface as late as the 1950s as a device to oppose racial integration.) At the time, it seems, both men intended the resolutions to serve chiefly as propaganda, the opening guns in the political campaign of 1800. Neither Kentucky nor Virginia took steps to nullify or interpose its authority against enforcement of the Alien and Sedition Acts. Instead both called upon the other states to help them win a repeal. Jefferson counseled against any thought of violence, which was "not the kind of opposition the American people will permit." He assured a fellow Virginian that "the reign of witches" would soon end, that it would be discredited by the arrival of the tax collector more than anything else.

In 1798 Congress had imposed a direct tax on houses, land, and slaves. The Alien and Sedition Acts touched comparatively few individuals, but the tax reached every property holder in the country. In eastern Pennsylvania during early 1799 the general discontent with the tax reached the stage of armed resistance in Fries's Rebellion, an incident that scarcely deserves so impressive a name. John Fries, a Pennsylvania Dutch auctioneer, had led a group of armed men to force the release of two tax evaders imprisoned at Bethlehem. To suppress this "insurrection" President Adams sent army regulars and militiamen into Northampton County. But like the Whiskey Rebellion five years before, the insurrection evaporated. The soldiers found not a rebellion but John Fries conducting an auction. He was arrested and brought to trial with two others on inflated charges of treason. The three men were found guilty twice, a second trial having been granted on appeal, and twice sentenced to hang. President Adams, however, decided that the men had not committed treason and granted them a pardon along with a general pardon to all participants in the affair.

REPUBLICAN VICTORY   Thus as the presidential election of 1800 approached, grievances were mounting against Federalist policies: taxation to support an army that had little to do but chase Pennsylvania farmers; the Alien and Sedition Acts, which cast the Federalists as anti-liberty; the lingering fears of "monarchism"; the hostilities aroused by Hamilton's programs; the suppression of the Whiskey Rebellion; and Jay's Treaty. When Adams decided for peace in 1800, he probably doomed his one chance for reelection, a wave of patriotic war fever with a united party behind him. His decision gained him much goodwill among the people at large, but left the Hamiltonians unreconciled and his party divided. In May 1800 the Federalists summoned enough unity to name as their candidates Adams and Charles C. Pinckney, brother of Thomas Pinckney, who had run in 1796; they agreed to cast all their electoral votes for both. But the Hamiltonians continued to snipe at Adams and his policies, and soon after his renomination Adams removed two of them from his cabinet. Hamilton struck back with a pamphlet questioning Adams's fitness to be president, citing his "disgusting egotism." Intended for private distribution among Federalist leaders, the pamphlet reached the hands of Aaron Burr, who put it in general circulation.

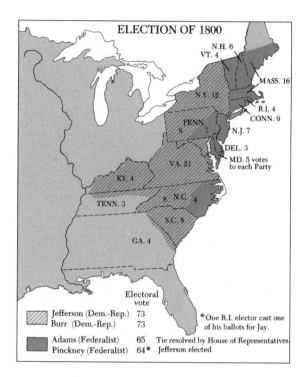

ELECTION OF 1800

N.H. 6
VT. 4
MASS. 16
N.Y. 12
R.I. 4
CONN. 9
PENN.
8   7
N.J. 7
DEL. 3
MD. 5 votes
to each Party
VA. 21
KY. 4
8   N.C. 4
TENN. 3
S.C. 8
GA. 4

Electoral
vote
Jefferson (Dem.-Rep.)   73   *One R.I. elector cast one
Burr (Dem.-Rep.)   73   of his ballots for Jay.

Adams (Federalist)   65   Tie resolved by House of Representatives.
Pinckney (Federalist)   64*   Jefferson elected

Jefferson and Burr, as the Republican candidates, once again represented the alliance of Virginia and New York. Jefferson, perhaps even
more than Adams, became the target of villification as a Jacobin and an
atheist. His election, Americans were warned, would bring "dwellings in
flames, hoary hairs bathed in blood, female chastity violated . . . children writhing on the pike and halberd." Jefferson kept quiet, refused
to answer the attacks, and directed the campaign by mail from his home
at Monticello. He was advanced as the farmers' friend, the champion
of states' rights, frugal government, liberty, and peace.

Adams proved more popular than his party, whose candidates generally fared worse than the president, but the Republicans edged him
out by seventy-three electoral votes to sixty-five. The decisive states
were New York and South Carolina, either of which might have given
the victory to Adams. But in New York Burr's organization won control
of the legislature, which cast the electoral votes. In South Carolina,
Charles Pinckney (cousin to the Federalist Pinckneys) won over the legislature by well-placed promises of Republican patronage. Still, the
result was not final, for Jefferson and Burr had tied with seventy-three
votes each, and the choice of the president was thrown into the House
of Representatives, where Federalist diehards tried vainly to give the
election to Burr. This was too much for Hamilton, who opposed Jefferson but held a much lower opinion of Burr. Eventually the deadlock

was broken when a confidant of Jefferson assured a Delaware congressman that Jefferson would refrain from wholesale removals of Federalists and uphold the new fiscal system. The representative resolved to vote for Jefferson, and several other Federalists agreed simply to cast blank ballots, permitting Jefferson to win without any of them actually having to vote for him.

Before the Federalists relinquished power to the Jeffersonian Republicans on March 4, 1801, their "lame-duck" Congress passed the Judiciary Act of 1801. Intended to ensure Federalist control of the judicial system, this act provided that the next vacancy on the Supreme Court should not be filled, created sixteen circuit courts with a new judge for each, and increased the number of attorneys, clerks, and marshals. Before he left office Adams named John Marshall to the vacant office of chief justice and appointed good Federalists to all the new positions, including forty-two justices of the peace for the new District of Columbia. The Federalists, defeated and destined never to regain national power, had in the words of Jefferson "retired into the judiciary as a stronghold." The election of 1800 marked a turning point in American political history. It was the first time that one political party, however ungracefully, relinquished power to the opposition party.

FURTHER READING

The best introduction to the early Federalists remains John C. Miller's *The Federalist Era, 1789–1800* (1960).° Other works analyze the ideological debates among the nation's first leaders. Richard Buel, Jr.'s *Securing the Revolution: Ideology in American Politics, 1789–1815* (1974),° Joyce Appleby's *Capitalism and a New Social Order* (1984), Drew McCoy's *The Elusive Republic: Political Economy in Jeffersonian America* (1982)° and Stanley Elkins and Eric McKitrick's *The Age of Federalism* (1993)° trace the persistence and transformation of ideas first fostered during the revolutionary crisis. John F. Hoadley's *Origins of American Political Parties, 1789–1803* (1986) is superb.

The 1790s may also be understood through the views and behavior of national leaders. Informative studies of Alexander Hamilton include Forrest McDonald's *Alexander Hamilton: A Biography* (1979)° and Gerald Stourzh's *Alexander Hamilton and the Idea of Republican Government* (1970). For the nation's first president, consult the two volumes by James T. Flexner, *George Washington and the New Nation, 1783–1793* (1970) and *George Washington: Anguish and Farewell,*

°These books are available in paperback editions.

1793–1799 (1972). Forrest McDonald's *The Presidency of George Washington* (1974), John R. Alden's *George Washington: A Biography* (1984)° and Richard Norton Smith's *Patriarch: George Wasington and the New American Nation* (1993) are also helpful. The second president is handled in Stephen G. Kurtz's *The Presidency of John Adams: The Collapse of Federalism, 1795–1800* (1957) and Joseph J. Ellis's *Passionate Sage: The Character and Legacy of John Adams* (1993).° For a female perspective on pre- and post-revolutionary America, see Phyllis Lee Levin's *Abigail Adams* (1991) and Edith B. Gelles's *Portia: The World of Abigail Adams* (1992). The opposition viewpoint is the subject of Lance Banning's *The Jeffersonian Persuasion: Evolution of a Party Ideology* (1978).°

Federalist foreign policy is explored in Jerald A. Combs's *The Jay Treaty* (1970), William C. Stinchcombe's *The XYZ Affair* (1980), and Felix Gilbert's *To the Farewell Address: Ideas of Early American Foreign Policy* (1961).° Albert H. Bowman's *The Struggle for Neutrality* (1974), on Franco-American relations, is more interpretive.

For specific domestic issues, see Thomas Slaughter's *The Whiskey Rebellion* (1986) and Harry Ammon's *The Genêt Mission* (1973).° Patricia Watlington's *The Partisan Spirit* (1972) examines the Kentucky Resolutions. The treatment of Indians in the Old Northwest is explored in Richard H. Kohn's *Eagle and Sword: The Federalists and the Creation of the Military Establishment in America, 1783–1802* (1975). For the Alien and Sedition Acts, consult James Morton Smith's *Freedom's Fetters: The Alien and Sedition Laws and American Civil Liberties* (1956) and Leonard W. Levy's *Legacy of Suppression: Freedom of Speech and Press in Early American History* (1960). Daniel Sisson's *The American Revolution of 1800* (1974) is useful on that important election.

Several recent books focus on social issues of the post-revolutionary period, including Paul A. Gilje and Howard B. Rock (eds.), *Keepers of the Revolution: New Yorkers at Work in the Early Republic* (1992),° Ronald Schultz's *The Republic of Labor: Philadelphia Artisans and the Politics of Class, 1720–1830* (1993), and Peter Way's *Common Labour: Workers and the Digging of North American Canals* (1993).

The African-American experience in the Revolutionary era is detailed in Mechal Sobel's *The World They Made Together: Black and White Values in Eighteenth-Century Virginia* (1988) and Gary B. Nash's *Forging Freedom: The Formation of Philadelphia's Black Community, 1720–1840* (1988).

°These books are available in paperback editions.

9

REPUBLICANISM:
JEFFERSON AND MADISON

A New Capital

On March 4, 1801, Thomas Jefferson, tall and thin, with ill-fitting clothes, chiseled features, red hair, and a ruddy complexion, became the first president to be inaugurated in the new federal city, Washington, District of Columbia. The location of the city on the Potomac had been the fruit of Jefferson and Madison's compromise with Hamilton on the assumption of state debts. Choice of the site had been entrusted to President Washington, who picked a location upstream from his home at Mount Vernon. In 1791 Major Pierre L'Enfant, a French engineer who had served in the Revolution, drew up the original plan for the district.

Work progressed on the public buildings and the city during the 1790s, and President Adams moved into his new home in September 1800. His wife Abigail arrived at the "great castle" in October. It was "in a beautiful situation" with a view of the Potomac and Virginia, but all the rooms were new and unfinished. By November the Adams family had to keep thirteen fires daily, she said, "or sleep in wet and damp places." Nearby Georgetown, D.C., where Abigail was obliged to market, was "the very dirtyest hole . . . for a place of any trade, or respectability of inhabitants."

When Jefferson took office, Washington was still a motley array of buildings around two centers, Capitol Hill and the Executive Mansion. Between them was a swampy wilderness traversed by the Tiber River and by Pennsylvania Avenue, still full of stumps and mudholes, but with

This Plan of the City of Washington *(1800) shows L'Enfant's detailed gridwork pattern of "Grand Avenues and Streets."*

a stone walkway that offered a vantage from which to shoot duck, snipe, and partridge. The Congress, having met in eight different towns and cities since 1774, had at last found a permanent home, but as yet enjoyed few amenities. There were only a few sad houses, "most of them small miserable huts," according to one resident. To a French acquaintance one senator wrote: "It is the best city in the world to live in—in the future." There were two places of amusement, one a racetrack, the other a theater filled with "tobacco smoke, whiskey breaths, and other stenches, mixed up with the effluvia of stables, and miasmas of the canal." Practically deserted much of the year, the town came to life only when Congress assembled.

JEFFERSON IN OFFICE

Jefferson's informal inauguration befitted the primitive surroundings. The new president left his lodgings and walked two blocks to the unfinished Capitol, entered the Senate chamber, took the oath from Chief Justice John Marshall, read his inaugural address in a barely audible voice, and returned to his boardinghouse for dinner with the guests at the common table. John Adams was absent. He had quietly slipped away, which was just as well according to his descendant, the historian Henry Adams, since "he would have seemed, in his successor's opinion, as little in place as George III would have appeared at the inauguration of President Washington." A tone of simplicity and conciliation ran through Jefferson's inaugural address, its seeming artlessness the product of three laborious drafts: "We are all Republicans—we are all Federalists. If there be any among us who would wish to dissolve this Union or to change its republican form, let them stand undisturbed as monuments of the safety with which error of opinion may be tolerated where reason is left free to combat it."

He then delivered a ringing affirmation of republican government: "I know, indeed, that some honest men fear that a republican government cannot be strong; that this government is not strong enough. But would the honest patriot, in the full tide of successful experiment, abandon a government which has so far kept us free and firm, on the theoretic and visionary fear that this government, the world's best hope, may by possibility want energy to preserve itself? I trust not. I believe this, on the contrary, the strongest government on earth. I believe it is the only one where every man . . . would meet invasions of the public order as his own personal concern."

Jefferson concluded with a summary of the "essential principles" that would guide his administration: "Equal and exact justice to all men . . . ; peace, commerce, and honest friendship with all nations, entangling alliances with none . . . ; freedom of religion; freedom of the press; and freedom of person, under the protection of the habeas corpus; and trial by juries impartially selected. . . . The wisdom of our sages and the blood of our heroes have been devoted to their attainment."

The deliberate display of republican simplicity at Jefferson's inauguration set the style of his administration. He took pains to avoid the occasions of pomp and circumstance that had characterized Federalist administrations and which to his mind suggested the trappings of kingship. Presidential messages went to Congress in writing lest they resemble the parliamentary speech from the throne. The practice also allowed Jefferson, a notoriously bad public speaker, to exploit his skill as a writer.

Jefferson discarded the coach and six in which Washington and Adams had gone to state occasions and rode about the city on horseback, often by himself. But this was, at least in part, therapy recommended by a doctor, and in part because Washington's rutted streets were hardly the place for a carriage. Dinners at the White House were held around a circular table, so that none should take precedence. At social affairs the new president simply ignored the rules of protocol for what he called the rule of *pele mele*, in which the only custom observed was that the ladies went ahead of the men. "When brought together in society, all are perfectly equal," Jefferson affirmed.

Jefferson liked to think of his election as the "Revolution of 1800," but the margin had been close and the policies that he followed were more conciliatory than revolutionary. His overwhelming reelection in 1804 attests to the popularity of his philosophy. Perhaps the most revolutionary thing about Jefferson's presidency was the orderly transfer of power in 1801, an uncommon event in the world of that day. "The changes of administration," a Washington lady wrote in her diary, "which in every age have most generally been epochs of confusion, villainy and bloodshed, in this our happy country take place without any species of distraction, or disorder."

Jefferson placed in policy-making positions men of his own party, and he was the first president to pursue the role of party leader, assiduously cultivating congressional support at his dinner parties and otherwise. It was a role he had not so much sought as fallen into; he still shared the eighteenth-century distrust of the party spirit. In the cabinet the leading fixtures were Secretary of State James Madison, a longtime neighbor and political ally, and Secretary of the Treasury Albert Gallatin, a Pennsylvania Republican whose financial skills had won him the respect of Federalists. In an effort to cultivate Federalist New England, Jefferson chose men from that region for the positions of attorney-general, secretary of war, and postmaster-general.

In lesser offices, however, Jefferson refrained from wholesale

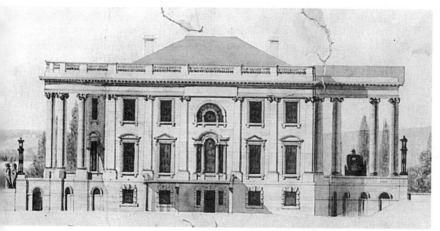

A watercolor of the president's house during Jefferson's term in office. Jefferson called it "big enough for two emperors, one pope, and the grand lama in the bargain."

removal of Federalists, preferring to wait until vacancies appeared, a policy which led to his rueful remark that vacancies obtained "by death are few; by resignation, none." But the pressure from Republicans was such that he often yielded and removed Federalists, trying as best he could to assign some other than partisan causes for the removals. In one area, however, he managed to remove the offices rather than the appointees. In 1802 Congress repealed the Judiciary Act of 1801, and so abolished the circuit judgeships and other offices to which Adams had made his "midnight appointments." A new judiciary act restored to six the number of Supreme Court justices, and set up six circuit courts, each headed by a justice.

MARBURY V. MADISON   Adams's "midnight appointments" sparked the case of *Marbury v. Madison*, the first in which the Supreme Court declared a federal law unconstitutional. The case involved the appointment of one William Marbury as justice of the peace in the District of Columbia. Marbury's appointment letter, or commission, signed by President Adams two days before he left office, was still undelivered when Madison took office as secretary of state, and Jefferson directed him to withhold it. Marbury then sued for a court order (a writ of mandamus) directing Madison to deliver his commission.

The Court's unanimous opinion, written by John Marshall, held that Marbury deserved his commission, but then denied that the Court had jurisdiction in the case. Section 13 of the Judiciary Act of 1789, which gave the Court original jurisdiction in mandamus proceedings, was unconstitutional, the Court ruled, because the Constitution specified that the Court should have original jurisdiction only in cases involving ambassadors or states. The Court, therefore, could issue no order in the case. With one bold stroke Marshall had chastised the Jeffersonians while avoiding an awkward confrontation with an administration that might have defied his order. At the same time he established the precedent that the Court could declare a federal law invalid on the grounds that it violated provisions of the Constitution.

PARTISAN SQUABBLES   The Court's decision, about which Jefferson could do nothing, confirmed his fear of the judges' tendency to "throw an anchor ahead, and grapple further hold for future advances of power." In 1804 Republicans finally determined to use the impeachment power against two of the most partisan Federalist judges, and succeeded in ousting one of the two. The Republican House brought impeachments against District Judge John Pickering of New Hampshire and Justice Samuel Chase. Pickering was clearly insane, which was not a high crime or misdemeanor, but he was also given to profane and drunken harangues from the bench, which the Senate quickly decided was an impeachable offense. In any event he was incompetent.

The case against Justice Chase was a more complicated and serious matter. That he was highhanded and intemperate there was no question. Chase had presided at the sedition trials of two Republican editors, ordering a marshal to strike off the jury panel "any of those creatures or persons called democrats." He once attacked the Maryland Constitution from the bench because it granted manhood suffrage, under which "our republican Constitution will sink into a mobocracy." But neither Jefferson nor the best efforts of John Randolph of Roanoke as prosecutor for the House could persuade two-thirds of the senators that Chase's vindictive partisanship constituted "high crimes and misdemeanors." His removal might have set off the partisanship of Republicans in a political carnival of reprisals. His acquittal discouraged further efforts at impeachment, however, which Jefferson pronounced a "farce," after the failure to remove Chase.

DOMESTIC REFORMS   Aside from this setback, however, Jefferson's first term was a succession of triumphs in both domestic and foreign affairs. He did not set out to dismantle Hamilton's program root and branch. Under Treasury Secretary Gallatin's tutoring, he learned to accept the national bank as an essential convenience, and did not push a measure for the bank's repeal which more dogmatic Republicans sponsored. It was too late of course to undo Hamilton's funding and debt assumption operations, but none too soon in the opinion of both Jefferson and Gallatin to begin retiring the resultant federal debt. At the same time, Jefferson won the repeal of the whiskey tax and other Federalist excises, much to the relief of backwoods distillers, drinkers, and grain farmers.

Without the excise taxes, frugality was all the more necessary to a government dependent for revenue chiefly on tariffs and the sale of western lands. Happily for Gallatin's treasury, both activities flourished. The European war brought a continually increasing traffic to American shipping and thus revenues to the federal Treasury. And settlers flocked into the western lands, which were coming more and more within their reach. The admission of Ohio in 1803 increased to seventeen the number of states.

By the "wise and frugal government" promised in the inaugural address, Jefferson and Gallatin reasoned, the United States could live within its income, like a prudent farmer. The basic formula was simple: cut back expenses on the military. A standing army menaced a free society anyway. It therefore should be kept to a minimum and the national defense left, in Jefferson's words, to "a well-disciplined militia, our best reliance in peace, and for the first moments of war, till regulars may relieve them." The navy, which the Federalists had already reduced

Cincinnati in 1800, twelve years after its founding. Though its population was only about 750, its inhabitants were already promoting Cincinnati as "the metropolis of the north-western territory."

after the quasi-war with France, ought to be reduced further. Coastal defense, Jefferson argued, should rely on fortifications and a "mosquito fleet" of small gunboats.

In 1807 the record of Jeffersonian reforms was crowned by an act that outlawed the foreign slave trade as of January 1, 1808, the earliest date possible under the Constitution. At the time South Carolina was the only state that still permitted the trade, having reopened it in 1803. But for years to come an illegal traffic would continue. By one informal estimate perhaps 300,000 slaves were smuggled into the United States between 1808 and 1861.

THE BARBARY PIRATES   Issues of foreign relations intruded on Jefferson early in his term, when events in the Mediterranean quickly gave him second thoughts about the need for a navy. On the Barbary Coast of North Africa the rulers of Morocco, Algeria, Tunis, and Tripoli had for years practiced piracy and extortion. After the Revolution, American shipping in the Mediterranean became fair game, no longer protected by British payments of tribute. The new American government yielded up protection money too, first to Morocco in 1786, then to the others in the 1790s. In May 1801, however, the pasha of Tripoli upped his demands and declared war on the United States by the symbolic gesture of chopping down the flagpole at the United States consulate. Rather than give in to this, Jefferson sent warships to blockade Tripoli.

A wearisome war dragged on until 1805, punctuated in 1804 by the notable exploit of Lieutenant Stephen Decatur, who slipped into Tripoli harbor by night and set fire to the frigate *Philadelphia*, which had been captured (along with its crew) after it ran aground. The pasha finally settled for $60,000 ransom and released the *Philadelphia*'s crew, whom he had held hostage for more than a year. It was still tribute, but less than the $300,000 the pasha had demanded at first, and much less than the cost of the war.

THE LOUISIANA PURCHASE   It was an inglorious end to a shabby affair, but well before it was over, events elsewhere had conspired to produce the greatest single achievement of the Jefferson administration. The Louisiana Purchase of 1803 more than doubled the territory of the United States. It included the entire Mississippi Valley west of the river itself. Louisiana, settled by the French, had been ceded to Spain in 1763. Since that time the dream of retaking Louisiana had stirred in French minds. In 1800 Napoleon Bonaparte secured its return in exchange for a promise (never fulfilled) to set up a Spanish princess and her husband in Italy as rulers of an enlarged Tuscany. When unofficial word of the deal reached Washington in 1801, Jefferson hastened Robert R. Livingston, the new minister to France, on his way. Spain in control of the Mississippi outlet was bad enough, but Napoleon in control could only mean serious trouble. "There is on the globe one single spot the possessor of which is our natural and habitual enemy," Jefferson wrote Livingston: "The day that France takes possession of New Orleans . . . we must marry ourselves to the British fleet and nation," an unhappy prospect for Jefferson.

But Spain still held the Floridas. Long and frustrating talks dragged out into 1803, while Spanish forces remained in control in Louisiana, awaiting the arrival of the French. Early that year James Monroe was sent to assist Livingston in Paris, but no sooner had he arrived than Napoleon's minister, Talleyrand, surprised Livingston by asking if the United States would like to buy the whole of Louisiana. Livingston, once he regained his composure, snapped up the offer.

Napoleon's motives in the whole affair can only be surmised. At first he seems to have thought of a New World empire, but that plan took an ugly turn in French Saint Domingue (later Haiti). There during the 1790s the revolutionary governments of France had lost control to a slave revolt. In 1802 Napoleon sent a force to subdue the island. By a ruse of war the French captured the black leader, Toussaint l'Ouverture, but then fell victim to guerrillas and yellow fever. Napoleon's plan may have been discouraged too by the fierce American reaction when the Spanish governor of Louisiana closed the Mississippi to American traffic in 1802, on secret orders from Madrid. In the end Napoleon's purpose seems to have been simply to cut his losses, turn a quick profit, mollify the Americans, and go back to reshaping the map of Europe.

By the treaty of cession, dated April 30, 1803, the United States obtained the Louisiana Territory for about $15 million. The treaty was vague in defining the boundaries of Louisiana. Its language could be stretched to provide a tenuous claim on Texas and a much stronger claim on West Florida, from Baton Rouge on the Mississippi past Mobile to the Perdido River on the east. When Livingston asked about the boundaries, Talleyrand responded: "I can give you no direction. You have made a noble bargain for yourselves, and I suppose you will make the most of it."

The turn of events had presented Jefferson with a noble bargain, a great new "empire of liberty," but also with a constitutional dilemma. Nowhere did the Constitution even mention the purchase of territory. By a strict construction, which Jefferson had professed, no such power existed. Jefferson at first thought to resolve the matter by offering an amendment, but his advisers argued against delay lest Napoleon change his mind. The power to purchase territory, they reasoned, resided in the power to make treaties. Jefferson relented, trusting, he said, "that the good sense of our country will correct the evil of loose construction when it shall produce ill effects." New England Federalists boggled at the prospect of new states that would probably strengthen the Jeffersonian party, and centered their fire on a proviso that the inhabitants be "incorporated in the Union" as citizens. In a reversal that anticipated many future reversals on constitutional issues, Federalists found themselves arguing strict construction of the Constitution while Republicans brushed aside such scruples in favor of implied power.

The Senate ratified the treaty by an overwhelming vote of 26 to 6, and on December 20, 1803, American officials took formal possession of Louisiana from a French agent who had taken over from Spanish authorities only three weeks before. For the time the Spanish kept West Florida, but within a decade that area would be ripe for the plucking. In 1808 Napoleon put his brother on the throne of Spain. With the Spanish colonial administration in disarray, American settlers in 1810 staged a rebellion in Baton Rouge and proclaimed the Republic of

In 1802 Toussaint L'Ouverture led the slave revolt on Saint Domingue (later Haiti) depicted in this engraving.

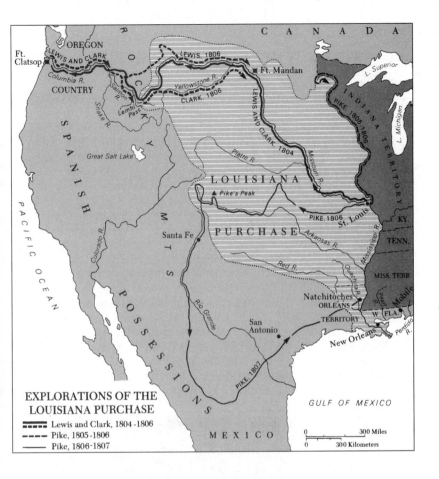

EXPLORATIONS OF THE
LOUISIANA PURCHASE

▬▬▬ Lewis and Clark, 1804-1806
▬ ▬ ▬ Pike, 1805-1806
▬▬▬ Pike, 1806-1807

0 _____ 300 Miles

0 _____ 300 Kilometers

West Florida, which was quickly annexed and occupied by the United
States as far eastward as the Pearl River. In 1812 the state of Louisiana
absorbed the region—still known today as the Florida parishes. In 1813,
with Spain itself a battlefield for French and British forces, Americans
took over the rest of West Florida, now the Gulf coast of Mississippi and Alabama. Legally, the American government has claimed
ever since, all these areas were included in the original Louisiana Purchase.

EXPLORING THE CONTINENT   As an amateur scientist long before he
was president, Jefferson had nourished an active curiosity about the
Louisiana country, its geography, its flora and fauna, its prospects for
trade and agriculture. In 1803 he asked Congress for money to send
an exploring expedition to the far northwest, beyond the Mississippi,

in what was still foreign territory. Congress approved and Jefferson assigned as commanders Meriwether Lewis, who as the president's private secretary had been groomed for the job, and another Virginian, William Clark, the much younger brother of George Rogers Clark.

In 1804 the "Corps of Discovery," numbering nearly fifty, set out from St. Louis to ascend the Missouri River. Forced to live off the land, they quickly adapted themselves to a new environment. Local Indians introduced them to new clothes made from deer hides and taught them new hunting techniques. Six months later, near the Mandan Sioux villages in what later became North Dakota, they built Fort Mandan and wintered there in relative comfort, sending back downriver a barge loaded with specimens such as the prairie dog, previously unknown to science, and the magpie, previously unknown in America. Jefferson kept the great horns of a wapiti (elk) to display at Monticello.

In the spring Lewis and Clark added to the main party a French guide, who was little help, and his remarkable Shoshone wife, Sacajawea ("Canoe Launcher"), who proved an enormous help as interpreter with the Indians of the region, and set out once again upstream. At the head of the Missouri they took the north fork, thenceforth the Jefferson River, crossed the Continental Divide at Lemhi Pass, and in dugout canoes descended the Snake and Columbia Rivers to the Pacific. Near the later site of Astoria at the mouth of the Columbia they built Fort

An American having struck a Bear but not killed him, escapes into a Tree

"Treed" by a grizzly bear, from a book of engravings of the Lewis and Clark expedition. (c. 1812).

Clatsop, in which they spent another winter. The following spring they headed back by almost the same route. After a swing through the Yellowstone country, the expedition returned to St. Louis in 1806, having been gone nearly two and a half years.

No longer was the Far West unknown country. Although it was nearly a century before a good edition of the *Journals of Lewis and Clark* appeared in print, many of their findings came out piecemeal, including an influential map in 1814. Convinced that they had found a practical route for the China trade, Lewis and Clark were among the last to hold out hope for a water route through the continent. Their reports of friendly Indians and abundant pelts quickly attracted traders and trappers to the region, and also gave the United States a claim to the Oregon country by right of discovery and exploration.

While Lewis and Clark were gone, Jefferson sent Lieutenant Zebulon Pike to find the source of the Mississippi River. He mistakenly picked a tributary, later discoveries showed, but contributed to knowledge of the upper Mississippi Valley. Then, during 1806–1807, he went out to the headwaters of the Arkansas River as far as Colorado. He discovered Pikes Peak but failed in an attempt to climb it, and made a roundabout return by way of Santa Fe, courtesy of Spanish soldiers who captured his party. Pike's account, while less reliable and less full than that of Lewis and Clark, appeared first and gave Americans their first overall picture of the Great Plains and Rocky Mountains. It also contributed to the widespread belief that the arid regions of the West constituted a Great American Desert, largely unfit for human habitation.

POLITICAL SCHEMES   Jefferson's policies, including the Louisiana Purchase, brought him almost solid support in the South and West. Even New Englanders were moving to his side. By 1809 John Quincy Adams, the son of the second president, would become a Republican! Die-hard Federalists read the handwriting on the wall. The acquisition of a vast new empire in the west would reduce New England to insignificance in political affairs, and along with it the Federalist cause. Under the leadership of Senator Thomas Pickering, a group of Massachusetts bitter-enders called the Essex Junto considered seceding from the Union, an idea that would simmer in New England circles for another decade.

Soon they hatched a scheme to link New York with New England and contacted Vice-President Aaron Burr, who had been on the outs with the Jeffersonians long since and who was, as ever, ready for subversive schemes. Their plan depended on Burr's election as governor of New York, but in April 1804, Burr was overwhelmed by the regular Republican candidate. The extreme Federalists, it turned out, could not

Aaron Burr.

even hold members of their own party to the plan, which Hamilton bitterly opposed on the grounds that Burr was "a dangerous man, and one who ought not to be trusted with the reins of government."

When Hamilton's remarks appeared in the public press, Burr's demand for an explanation led to a duel in 1804 at Weehawken, New Jersey. On a grassy ledge above the Hudson River, Burr shot Hamilton through the heart. Hamilton personally opposed dueling, but his romantic streak and sense of honor compelled him to demonstrate his courage, long since established beyond any question at Yorktown. He went to his death, as his son had done in a similar affair the previous year, determined not to fire at his opponent. Burr had no such scruples. The death of Hamilton ended both Pickering's scheme and Burr's political career—but not his intrigues.

Meanwhile the presidential campaign of 1804 got under way when a congressional caucus of Republicans renominated Jefferson and chose George Clinton for vice-president. Opposed by the Federalists Charles C. Pinckney and Rufus King, Jefferson and Clinton won 162 of 176 electoral votes. Jefferson's policy of conciliation had made him a national rather than a sectional candidate. With some pride, Jefferson said in his second inaugural address that he had carried out the general policies announced in the first: "The suppression of unnecessary offices, of useless establishments and expenses, enabled us to discontinue our internal taxes. . . . What farmer, what mechanic, what laborer ever sees a tax-gatherer of the United States?"

DIVISIONS IN THE REPUBLICAN PARTY

RANDOLPH AND THE *TERTIUM QUID*   "Never was there an administration more brilliant than that of Mr. Jefferson up to this period," said John Randolph of Roanoke. "We were indeed in the full tide of successful experiment." But freed from a strong opposition—Federalists made up only a quarter of the new Congress—the majority began to lose its cohesion. Cracks appeared in the Republican facade, portents of major fissures that would finally split the party as the Federalists faded into oblivion. Ironically, John Randolph, a Jeffersonian mainstay in the first term, became the most conspicuous of the dissidents. Randolph, apparently sexually impotent and given to fits of insanity in his later years, was a powerful combination of principle, eccentricity, and rancor. Famous for his venomous assaults delivered in a shrill soprano voice, the Virginian congressman strutted about the House floor with a whip in his hand, a symbol that he flourished best in opposition. Few colleagues had the stomach for his tongue-lashings.

Randolph, too much a loner for any leadership roles, became the crusty spokesman for a shifting group of "Old Republicans," whose adherence to party principles had rendered them more Jeffersonian than Jefferson himself. Their philosopher was John Taylor of Caroline, a Virginia planter-pamphleteer whose fine-spun theories of states' rights and strict construction had little effect at the time but delighted the secessionists of later years.

The mercurial John Randolph of Roanoke, in a silhouette drawn from life.

Neither Randolph nor Taylor could accept his leader's pragmatic gift for adjusting principle to circumstance.

Randolph first began to smell a rat in the case of the Yazoo Fraud, a
land scheme that originated in Georgia but entangled speculators from
all over. In 1795 the Georgia legislature had sold to four land companies, in which some of the legislators were involved, 35 million acres in
the Yazoo country (Mississippi and Alabama) for $500,000 (little more
than a penny an acre). A new legislature rescinded the sale the following
year, but not before some of the land claims had been sold to third parties. When Georgia finally ceded its western lands to federal authority in
1802, Jefferson sought a compromise settlement of the claims. But Randolph managed to block passage of the necessary measures and in the
ensuing quarrels was removed as Speaker of the House. The snarled
Yazoo affair plagued the courts and Congress for another decade.
Finally, in the case of *Fletcher v. Peck* (1810), Chief Justice Marshall
ruled that the original sale, however fraudulent, was a legal contract.
Marshall held that the repeal impaired the obligation of contract and
was therefore unconstitutional. Final settlement came in 1814 when
Congress awarded $4.2 million to the speculators.

Randolph's definitive break with Jefferson came in 1806, when the
president sought an appropriation of $2 million for a thinly disguised
bribe to the French to win their influence in persuading Spain to yield
the Floridas to the United States. "I found I might co-operate or be an
honest man—I have therefore opposed and will oppose them," Randolph said. Thereafter he resisted Jefferson's initiatives almost out of
reflex. Randolph and his colleagues were sometimes called "Quids," or
the *Tertium Quid* (the "third something"), and their dissents gave rise to
talk of a third party, neither Republican nor Federalist. But they never
got together. Some of the dissenters in 1808 backed James Monroe
against James Madison for the presidential succession, but the campaign
quickly fizzled. The failure of the Quids would typify the experience of
almost all third-party movements thereafter.

THE BURR CONSPIRACY   John Randolph may have got enmeshed in
dogma, but Aaron Burr was never one to let principle stand in the way.
Born of a distinguished line of Puritans, including grandfather Jonathan
Edwards, he cast off the family Calvinism to pursue the main chance—
and the women. Sheer brilliance and opportunism carried him to the
vice-presidency. With a leaven of discretion he might easily have
become heir apparent to Jefferson, but a taste for intrigue was the tragic
flaw in his character. Caught up in the dubious schemes of Federalist
die-hards in 1800 and again in 1804, he ended his political career once
and for all when he killed Hamilton. Even Hamilton's archenemies
abhorred Burr's act. "No one wished to get rid of Hamilton that way,"

John Adams muttered. Indicted in New York and New Jersey for murder and heavily in debt, the vice-president went first to Spanish-held Florida. Once the furor subsided, he boldly returned to Washington to preside over the Senate. As long as he stayed out of New York and New Jersey, he was safe. Groused one senator: "We are indeed fallen on evil times."

But Burr focused his attention less on the Senate than on a cockeyed scheme to carve out a personal empire for himself in the West. What came to be known as the Burr Conspiracy was hatched when Burr met with General James Wilkinson, an old friend with a tainted Revolutionary War record who was a spy for the Spanish. Just what he and Burr were up to probably will never be known. The most likely explanation is that they sought to organize a secession of Louisiana and set up an independent republic. Earlier Burr had solicited British support for his scheme to separate "the western part of the United States in its whole extent."

Whatever the goal, Burr succeeded in having Wilkinson appointed governor of the Louisiana Territory. In the summer of 1805 Burr himself sailed downriver from Pittsburgh on a lavishly outfitted flatboat, leaving behind him a wake of rumors. By the summer of 1806, he was in Lexington, Kentucky, recruiting adventurers. Meanwhile, rumors began to reach Jefferson, and in November 1806 so did a letter from General Wilkinson warning of "a deep, dark, wicked, and wide-spread conspiracy." Wilkinson had apparently developed cold feet and now feigned ignorance of the whole affair.

In early 1807, as Burr neared Natchez with his motley crew, he learned that Wilkinson had betrayed him and that Jefferson had ordered his arrest. He cut out cross-country for Pensacola, but was caught and taken off to Richmond for a trial, which, like the conspiracy, had a stellar cast. Charged with treason by the grand jury, Burr was brought for trial before Chief Justice Marshall. The case revealed both Marshall and Jefferson at their partisan worst. Marshall decided that the "hand of malignity" was grasping at Burr, while Jefferson, determined to get a conviction at any cost, published relevant affidavits in advance and promised pardons to conspirators who helped convict Burr. Marshall in turn was so indiscreet as to attend a dinner given by the chief defense counsel at which Burr himself was present.

The case established two major constitutional precedents. First, Jefferson ignored a subpoena requiring him to appear in court with certain papers in his possession. He refused, as Washington had refused, to submit papers to the Congress on grounds of executive privilege. Both believed that the independence of the executive branch would be compromised if the president were subject to a court writ. The second major precedent was the rigid definition of treason. On this Marshall adopted the strictest of constructions. Treason under the Constitution consists of "levying war against the United States or adhering to their enemies" and requires "two witnesses to the same overt act" for conviction. Since the prosecution failed to produce two witnesses to an overt act of treason by Burr, the jury found him not guilty.

Whether or not Burr escaped his just deserts, Marshall's strict construction of the Constitution protected the United States, as the authors of the Constitution clearly intended, against the capricious judgments of "treason" that governments through the centuries have used to terrorize dissenters. As to Burr, with further charges pending, he skipped bail and took refuge in France, but returned unmolested in 1812 to practice law in New York. He survived to a virile old age. At age eighty, shortly before his death, he was divorced on grounds of adultery.

WAR IN EUROPE

Oppositionists of whatever stripe were more an annoyance than a threat to Jefferson. The more intractable problems of his second term involved the renewal of the European war in 1803, which helped resolve the problem of Louisiana but put more strains on Jefferson's desire to avoid "entangling alliances" and the quarrels of Europe. In 1805 Napoleon's smashing defeat of Russian and Austrian forces at Austerlitz made him the master of western Europe. The same year, Nelson's defeat of the French and Spanish fleets in the Battle of Trafalgar secured Britain's control of the seas. The war resolved itself into a battle of elephant and whale, Napoleon dominant on land, the British dominant on the water, neither able to strike a decisive blow at the other, and neither restrained by an overly delicate sense of neutral rights or international law.

HARASSMENT BY BRITAIN AND FRANCE   For two years after the renewal of hostilities, American shippers reaped the benefits, taking over trade with the French and Spanish West Indies. But in the case of the *Essex* (1805), a British court ruled that the practice of shipping French and Spanish goods through American ports while on their way elsewhere did not neutralize enemy goods. Such a practice violated the British rule of 1756, under which trade closed in time of peace remained closed in time of war. Goods shipped in violation of the rule, the British held, were liable to seizure at any point under the doctrine of continuous voyage. In 1807 the commercial provisions of Jay's Treaty expired and James Monroe, ambassador to Great Britain, failed to get a renewal satisfactory to Jefferson. After that, the British interference with American shipping increased, not just to keep supplies from

Napoleon's continent but also to hobble competition with British merchant ships.

In a series of Orders in Council adopted in 1806 and 1807, the British ministry set up a paper blockade of Europe. Vessels headed for continental ports had to get licenses and accept British inspection or be liable to seizure. Napoleon retaliated with his "Continental System," proclaimed in the Berlin Decree of 1806 and the Milan Decree of 1807. In the first he declared a blockade of the British Isles and in the second he ruled that neutral ships that complied with British regulations were subject to seizure when they reached continental ports. The situation presented American shippers with a dilemma. If they complied with the demands of one side, they were subject to seizure by the other.

It was humiliating, but the prospects for profits were so great that shippers ran the risk. For seamen the danger was heightened by a renewal of the practice of impressment. The use of press gangs to kidnap men in British (and colonial) ports was a long-standing method of recruitment for the British navy. The seizure of British subjects from American vessels became a new source of recruits, justified on the principle that British subjects remained British subjects for life: "Once an Englishman, always an Englishman." Mistakes might be made, of course, since it was sometimes hard to distinguish British subjects from Americans; indeed a flourishing trade in fake citizenship papers arose in American ports. The humiliation of impressment was mostly confined to merchant vessels, but on at least two occasions before 1807, vessels of the American navy had been stopped on the high seas and seamen removed.

In the summer of 1807, the British *Leopard* accosted another American naval vessel, the frigate *Chesapeake,* just outside territorial waters off Norfolk. After the *Chesapeake*'s captain refused to be searched, the *Leopard* opened fire, killing three Americans and wounding eighteen. The *Chesapeake,* caught unready for battle, was forced to strike its colors. A British search party seized four men, one of whom was later hanged for desertion from the British navy. Soon after the *Chesapeake* limped back into Norfolk, the Washington *Federalist* editorialized: "We have never, on any occasion, witnessed . . . such a thirst for revenge. . . ." Public wrath was so aroused that Jefferson could have had war on the spot. Had Congress been in session, he might have been forced into war. But Jefferson, like Adams before him, resisted the war fever and suffered politically as a result. One Federalist called Jefferson a "dish of skim milk curdling at the head of our nation."

THE EMBARGO   Jefferson resolved to use public indignation as the occasion for an effort at "peaceable coercion." In December 1807, in response to his request, Congress passed the Embargo Act, which stopped all export of American goods and prohibited American ships

Preparation for War to Defend Commerce. *In 1806 and 1807 American shipping was caught in the crossfire of war between Britain and France.*

from clearing for foreign ports. The constitutional basis of the embargo was the power to regulate commerce, which in this case Republicans interpreted broadly as the power to prohibit commerce. "Let the example teach the world that our firmness equals our moderation," said the *National Intelligencer,* "that having resorted to a measure just in itself, and adequate to its object, we will flinch from no sacrifices which the honor and good of the nation demand from virtuous and faithful citizens."

Jefferson's embargo, however, failed from the beginning for want of the will to make the necessary sacrifices. The idealistic spirit that had made economic pressures effective in the prerevolutionary crises was lacking. Trade remained profitable despite the risks, and violation of the embargo was almost laughably easy. Lax enforcement and loopholes in the act permitted ships to clear port under the pretense of engaging in coastal trade or whaling, or under an amendment passed a few months after the act for the purpose of bringing home American property stored in foreign warehouses. Some 800 ships left on such missions, but few of them returned before the embargo expired. Trade across the Canadian border flourished. As it turned out, France was little hurt by the act. Napoleon in fact exploited it to issue the Bayonne Decree (1808), which ordered the seizure of American ships in continental ports on the pretext that they must be British ships with false papers. Or if they truly were American, Napoleon slyly noted, he would be helping Jefferson enforce the embargo. The lack of American cotton hurt some British manufacturers and workers, but they carried little weight with the government, and British shippers benefited. With American ports closed, they found a new trade in Latin American ports thrown open by the colonial authorities when Napoleon occupied the mother countries of Spain and Portugal.

The coercive effect was minimal, and the embargo revived the moribund Federalist party in New England, which renewed the charge that Jefferson was in league with the French. The embargo, one New Englander said, was "like cutting one's throat to cure the nosebleed." At the same time, agriculture in the South and West suffered for want of outlets for grain, cotton, and tobacco. After fifteen months of ineffectiveness, Jefferson finally accepted failure and in 1809 signed a repeal of the embargo shortly before he relinquished the "splendid misery" of the presidency.

In the election of 1808 the succession passed to another Virginian, Secretary of State James Madison. Clinton was again the candidate for

This 1807 Federalist cartoon compares Washington (left) *to Jefferson* (right). *Washington is flanked by the British lion and the American eagle, while Jefferson is flanked by a snake and a lizard. Below Jefferson are volumes by French philosophers.*

vice-president. The Federalists, backing Charles C. Pinckney and Rufus King of New York, revived enough as a result of the embargo to win 47 votes to Madison's 122.

THE DRIFT TO WAR   Madison's presidency was entangled in foreign affairs from the beginning. Still insisting on neutral rights and freedom of the seas, he pursued Jefferson's policy of "peaceful coercion" by different but no more effective means. In place of the embargo Congress had substituted the Non-Intercourse Act, which reopened trade with all countries except France and Great Britain and authorized the president to reopen trade with whichever of these gave up its restrictions. British minister David Erskine assured Madison's secretary of state that Britain would revoke its restrictions in 1809. With that assurance, Madison reopened trade with Britain, but Erskine had acted on his own and the foreign secretary, repudiating his action, recalled him. Non-intercourse resumed, but it proved as ineffective as the embargo. In the vain search for an alternative, Congress on May 1, 1810, reversed its ground and adopted a measure introduced by Nathaniel Macon of North Carolina, Macon's Bill Number 2, which reopened trade with the warring powers but provided that, if either dropped its restrictions, non-intercourse would be restored with the other.

This time Napoleon took a turn at trying to bamboozle Madison. Napoleon's foreign minister, the duc de Cadore, informed the American minister in Paris that he had withdrawn the Berlin and Milan Decrees, but the carefully worded Cadore letter had strings attached: revocation of the decrees depended on withdrawal of the British Orders in Council. The strings were plain to see, but either Madison misunderstood or, more likely, went along in hope of putting pressure on the British. In response to the Cadore letter, he restored non-intercourse with the British. The British refused to give in, but Madison clung to his policy despite Napoleon's continued seizure of American ships. The seemingly hopeless effort did indeed finally work. With more time, with more patience, with a transatlantic cable, Madison's policy would have been vindicated without resort to war. On June 16, 1812, the British foreign minister, facing economic crisis, announced revocation of the Orders in Council. Britain preferred not to risk war with the United States on top of its war with Napoleon. But on June 1 Madison had asked for war, and by mid-June the Congress concurred.

THE WAR OF 1812

CAUSES   The main cause of the war—the demand for neutral rights—seems clear enough. Neutral rights dominated Madison's war message and provided the salient reason for a mounting hostility toward the British. Yet the geographical distribution of the congressional vote for war raises a troubling question. The preponderance of the vote for war came from members of Congress representing the farm regions from Pennsylvania southward and westward. The maritime states of New York and New England, the region that bore the brunt of British attacks on American trade, gave a majority against the declaration of war. One explanation for this seeming anomaly is simple enough. The farming regions suffered damage to their markets for grain, cotton, and tobacco, while New England shippers made profits in spite of British restrictions.

Other plausible explanations for the sectional vote, however, include frontier Indian depredations, which were blamed on the British, western land hunger, and the desire for new lands in Canada and the Floridas. Indian troubles were endemic to a rapidly expanding West. Land-hungry settlers and speculators kept moving out ahead of government surveys and sales in search of fertile acres. The constant pressure to open new lands repeatedly forced or persuaded Indians to sign treaties they did not always understand, causing stronger resentment among tribes that were losing more and more of their lands. It was an old story, dating from the Jamestown settlement, but one that took a new turn with the rise of two Shawnee leaders, Tecumseh and his twin brother Tenskwatawa, "the Prophet."

Tecumseh, according to Governor William Henry Harrison of the Indiana Territory, was "one of those uncommon geniuses, which spring up occasionally to produce revolutions and overturn the order of things." Tecumseh saw with blazing clarity the consequences of Indian disunity, and he set out to form a confederation of tribes to defend Indian hunting grounds, insisting that no land cession was valid without the consent of all tribes, since they held the land in common. His brother supplied the inspiration of a religious revival, calling upon the

Tecumseh, the Shawnee leader who tried to unite the tribes in defense of their lands. He was killed in 1813 at the Battle of the Thames.

Indians to worship the "Master of Life," to resist the white man's liquor, and lead a simple life within their means. By 1811 Tecumseh had matured his plans and headed south to win the Creeks, Cherokees, Choctaws, and Chickasaws to his cause.

Governor Harrison gathered a force and set out to attack Tecumseh's capital, Prophet's Town, on the Tippecanoe River, while the leader was away. In early November 1811, the Indians attacked Harrison's encampment on the Tippecanoe River, although Tecumseh had warned against any fighting in his absence. The Shawnees lost a bloody engagement that left about a quarter of Harrison's men dead or wounded. Only later did Harrison realize that he had inflicted a defeat on the Indians, who had become demoralized and many of whom had fled to Canada. Harrison then burned their town and destroyed all its supplies. Tecumseh's dreams went up in smoke, and Tecumseh himself fled to British protection in Canada.

The Battle of Tippecanoe reinforced suspicions that the British were inciting the Indians. Actually the incident was mainly Harrison's doing. With little hope of help from war-torn Europe, Canadian authorities had steered a careful course, discouraging warfare but seeking to keep the Indians' friendship and fur trade. To eliminate the Indian menace, American frontiersmen reasoned, they needed to remove its foreign support, and they saw the province of Ontario as a pistol pointing at the United States. Conquest of Canada would accomplish a twofold purpose. It would eliminate British influence among the Indians and open a new empire for land-hungry Americans. It was also the only place, in case of war, where the British were vulnerable to American attack. East Florida, still under the Spanish flag, posed a similar threat. Spain was too weak or unwilling to prevent sporadic Indian attacks across the frontier. The British were also suspected of smuggling through Florida and intriguing with the Indians on the southwest border.

Such concerns helped generate a war fever. In the Congress that assembled in late 1811, a number of new members from southern and western districts began to clamor for war in defense of "national honor." Among them were Henry Clay of Kentucky, who became Speaker of the House, Richard M. Johnson of Kentucky, Felix Grundy of Tennessee, and John C. Calhoun of South Carolina. John Randolph of Roanoke christened these "new boys" the "War Hawks." After they entered the House, Randolph said, "We have heard but one word—like the whip-poor-will, but one eternal monotonous tone—Canada! Canada! Canada!"

PREPARATIONS   As it turned out, the War Hawks would get neither Canada nor Florida. For James Madison had carried into war a country that was ill-prepared both financially and militarily. In 1811, despite earnest pleas from Treasury Secretary Gallatin, Congress had let the twenty-year charter of the Bank of the United States expire. A combination of strict-constructionist Republicans and Anglophobes, who feared the large British interest in the bank, did it in. Also, many state banks were mismanaged, resulting in deposits lost through bankruptcy. Trade had approached a standstill and tariff revenues had declined. Loans were needed for about two-thirds of the war costs while Northeast opponents to the war were reluctant to lend money. Government bonds were difficult to float.

The military situation was almost as bad. War had been likely for nearly a decade, but Republican austerities had prevented preparations. When the war began the army numbered only 6,700 men, ill-trained, poorly equipped, and led by aging officers. Most of the senior officers were veterans of the Revolution. The ranking general, Henry Dearborn, was a veteran of Bunker Hill, sixty-one at the outbreak of war. One young Virginia officer named Winfield Scott, destined for military distinction, commented that most of the veteran commanders "had very generally slunk into either sloth, ignorance, or habits of intemperate drinking."

The navy, on the other hand, was in comparatively good shape, with able officers and trained men whose seamanship had been tested in the fighting against France and Tripoli. Its ships were well outfitted and seaworthy—all sixteen of them. In the first year of the war it was the navy that produced the only American victories in isolated duels with British vessels, but their effect was mainly an occasional lift to morale. Within a year the British had blockaded the coast, except for New England, where they hoped to cultivate antiwar feeling, and most of the little American fleet was bottled up in port.

THE WAR IN THE NORTH   The only place where the United States could effectively strike at the British was Canada. Only once, however, had a war in that arena proved decisive, late in the French and Indian War, when Wolfe took Quebec and strangled the French Empire in America. A similar instinct for the jugular was Madison's best hope: a quick attack on Québec or Montréal would cut Canada's lifeline, the St. Lawrence River. Instead, the old history of the indecisive colonial wars was repeated, for the last time.

The administration opted for a three-pronged drive against Canada: along the Lake Champlain route toward Montreal, with General Henry Dearborn in command; along the Niagara River, with forces under General Stephen Van Rensselaer; and into Upper Canada (north of Lake Erie) from Detroit, where General William Hull and some 2,000 men arrived in early July 1812. In Detroit, Hull, sickly and senile, procrastinated while his position worsened. The British commander cleverly played upon Hull's worst fears. Gathering what redcoats he could to parade in view of Detroit's defenders, he announced that thousands of Indian allies were at the rear and that once fighting began he would be unable to control them. Fearing massacre, Hull surrendered his entire force in August.

Along the Niagara front, General Van Rensselaer was more aggressive. On October 13 an advance party of 600 Americans crossed the Niagara River and worked their way up the bluffs on the Canadian side. The stage was set for a major victory, but the New York militia refused to reinforce Van Rensselaer's men, claiming that their military service did not obligate them to leave the country. They complacently remained on the New York side and watched their outnumbered countrymen fall to a superior force across the river.

On the third front, the old invasion route via Lake Champlain, the trumpet once more gave an uncertain sound. General Dearborn led his army north from Plattsburgh toward Montreal. He marched them up to the border, where the militia once again stood on its alleged constitutional rights and refused to cross, and then marched them down again.

Madison's navy secretary now pushed vigorously for American control of inland waters. At Presque Isle (Erie), Pennsylvania, twenty-eight-

John Bull stung to agony by the *Wasp* and *Hornet, two American ships with early victories in the War of 1812.*

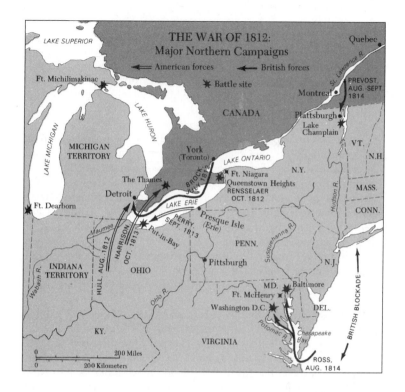

year-old Commodore Oliver H. Perry, already a fourteen-year veteran who had seen action against Tripoli, was fetching hardware up from Pittsburgh and building ships from the wilderness lumber. By the end of the summer Perry had superior numbers and set out in search of the British, whom he found at Lake Erie's Put-in-Bay, on September 10, 1813. After completing the preparations for battle, Perry told an aide: "This is the most important day of my life."

It was indeed. Two British warships used their superior weapons to pummel the *Lawrence,* Perry's flagship, at long distance. Blood flowed on the deck so freely that the sailors slipped and fell as they wrestled with the cannon. After four hours of intense shelling, none of the *Lawrence*'s guns was left working and 80 percent of the crew were dead or wounded. The British expected the Americans to turn tail, but Perry refused to quit. He transferred to another vessel, carried the battle to the enemy, and finally accepted surrender of the entire British squadron. Hatless, begrimed, and bloodied, Perry then sent to General William Henry Harrison the long-awaited message: "We have met the enemy and they are ours."

American naval control of waters in the region soon made Upper Canada untenable to the British. They gave up Detroit, and when they took a defensive stand at the Battle of the Thames (October 5), General Harrison inflicted a defeat that eliminated British power in Upper Canada and released the Northwest from any further threat. In the course of the battle Tecumseh fell, and his dream of Indian unity died with him.

THE WAR IN THE SOUTH   In the Southwest, too, the war flared up in 1813. On August 30 the Creeks attacked Fort Mims, on the Alabama River above Mobile, killing almost half the people in the fort. The news found Andrew Jackson home in bed recovering from a street brawl with Thomas Hart Benton, later a senator from Missouri. As major-general of the Tennessee militia, Jackson summoned about 2,000 volunteers and set out on a campaign that utterly crushed the Creek resistance. The decisive battle occurred on March 27, 1814, at the Horseshoe Bend of the Tallapoosa River, in the heart of the upper Creek country. In the Treaty of Fort Jackson signed that August, the Creeks ceded two-thirds of their lands to the United States, including part of Georgia and most of Alabama.

Four days after the Battle of Horseshoe Bend, Napoleon's empire collapsed. Now free to deal with America, the British developed a threefold plan of operations for 1814. They would launch a two-pronged invasion of America via Niagara and Lake Champlain to increase the clamor for peace in the Northeast; extend the naval blockade to New England, subjecting coastal towns to raids; and seize New Orleans to cut the Mississippi River, lifeline of the West. Uncertainties about the peace settlement in Europe, however, prevented the release of British veterans for a wholesale descent upon the New World. War weariness, after a generation of conflict, countered the British thirst for revenge against the former colonials. British plans were stymied also by the more resolute young commanders Madison had placed in charge of strategic areas by the summer of 1814.

MACDONOUGH'S VICTORY   The main British effort focused on a massive invasion via Lake Champlain. From the north General George Prevost, governor-general of Canada, advanced with the finest army yet assembled on American soil: fifteen regiments of regulars, plus militia and artillerymen, a total of about 15,000. The front was saved only by Prevost's vacillation and the superb ability of Commodore Thomas Macdonough, commander of the American naval squadron on Lake Champlain. A land assault might have taken Plattsburgh and forced Macdonough out of his protected position nearby, but England's army bogged down while its flotilla engaged Macdonough in a deadly battle on September 11.

The British concentrated their superior firepower on Macdonough's ship, the *Saratoga*. With his starboard battery disabled, Macdonough executed a daring maneuver known as "winding ship." He turned the *Saratoga* around while at anchor and brought its undamaged side into action with devastating effect. The *Saratoga* had to be scuttled, but the battle ended with the entire British flotilla either destroyed or captured. After reading the news, the duke of Wellington informed the British ministry: "That which appears to me to be wanting in America is not a general, or a general officer and troops, but a naval superiority on the Lakes." Lacking this advantage the duke thought the British had no right "to demand any concession of territory from America."

FIGHTING IN THE CHESAPEAKE   Meanwhile, however, American forces suffered the most humiliating experience of the war, the capture and burning of Washington, D.C. With attention focused on the Canadian front, the Chesapeake Bay offered the British a number of inviting targets, including Baltimore, now the fourth-largest city in America. A British force landed without opposition in June 1814 at Benedict, Maryland, and headed for Washington, forty miles away. To defend the capital the Americans had a force of about 7,000, including only a few hundred regulars and 400 sailors. At Bladensburg, Maryland, the American militia melted away in the face of the smaller British force.

On the evening of August 24, the British marched unopposed into Washington, where British officers ate a meal prepared for President and Mrs. Madison, who had joined the other refugees in Virginia. The

The British bombardment of Fort McHenry in Baltimore harbor, September 1814.

British then burned the White House, the Capitol, and all other government buildings except the Patent Office. A tornado the next day compounded the damage, but a violent thunderstorm dampened both the fires and the enthusiasm of the British forces, who left to prepare a new assault on Baltimore.

The attack on Baltimore was a different story. With some 13,000 men, chiefly militia, American forces fortified the heights behind the city. About 1,000 men held Fort McHenry, on an island in the harbor. When the British finally came into sight of the city on September 13, they halted in the face of American defenses. All through the following night the fleet bombarded Fort McHenry to no avail, and the invaders abandoned the attack on the city as too costly to risk. Francis Scott Key, a Washington lawyer, watched the siege from a vessel in the harbor. The sight of the flag still in place at dawn inspired him to draft the verses of "The Star Spangled Banner." Later revised and set to the tune of an English drinking song, it was immediately popular and eventually became the national anthem.

THE BATTLE OF NEW ORLEANS   The British failure at Baltimore followed by three days their failure on Lake Champlain, and their offensive against New Orleans had yet to run its course. Along the Gulf coast Andrew Jackson had been busy shoring up the defenses of Mobile and

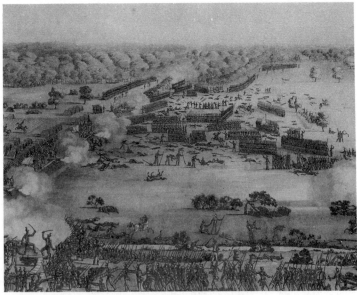

Andrew Jackson's defeat of the British at New Orleans, January 1815.

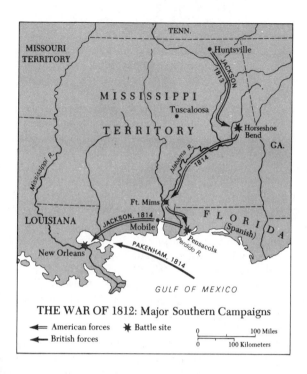

THE WAR OF 1812: Major Southern Campaigns

◀══ American forces ✹ Battle site

◀── British forces

0 ——— 100 Miles
0 ——— 100 Kilometers

New Orleans. In November, without authorization, he invaded Spanish Florida and took Pensacola to end British intrigues there. Back in Louisiana by the end of November, he began to erect defenses on the approaches to New Orleans, anticipating a British approach by the interior to pick up Indian support and control the Mississippi. Instead the British fleet, with some 7,500 European veterans under General Sir Edwin Pakenham, took up positions on a level plain on the banks of the Mississippi just south of New Orleans.

Pakenham's painfully careful approach—he waited until all his artillery was available—gave Jackson time to build earthworks bolstered by cotton bales for protection. It was an almost invulnerable position, but Pakenham, contemptuous of Jackson's motley array of frontier militiamen, Creole aristocrats, free blacks, and pirates, rashly ordered his veterans forward in a frontal assault at dawn on January 8, 1815. His redcoats ran into a murderous hail of artillery shells and deadly rifle fire. Before the British withdrew, about 2,000 had been wounded or killed, including Pakenham himself, whose body, pickled in a barrel of rum, was returned to the ship where his wife awaited news of the battle.

The Battle of New Orleans occurred after a peace treaty had already been signed. But this is not to say that it was an anticlimax or that it had no effect on the outcome of the war, for the treaty was yet to be ratified and the British might have exploited the possession of New Orleans had they won it. The battle did assure ratification of the treaty as it stood, and both governments acted quickly.

THE TREATY OF GHENT   Peace efforts had begun in 1812 even before hostilities got under way. The British, after all, had repealed their Orders in Council two days before the declaration of war and confidently expected at least an armistice. Secretary of State Monroe, however, told the British that they would have to give up the outrage of impressment as well. Meanwhile Czar Alexander of Russia offered to mediate the dispute, hoping to relieve the pressure on Great Britain, his ally against France. Madison then sent Albert Gallatin and James Bayard to join John Quincy Adams, American ambassador to Russia, in St. Petersburg. They arrived in July 1813, but the czar was at the war front, and they waited impatiently until January 1814. Then the British refused mediation and instead offered to negotiate directly. In February, Madison appointed Henry Clay and Jonathan Russell to join the other three commissioners in talks that finally got under way in the Flemish city of Ghent in August.

In contrast to the array of talent gathered in the American contingent, the British diplomats were nonentities, really messengers acting for the Foreign Office, which was more concerned with the effort to remake the map of Europe at the Congress of Vienna. The Americans had more leeway to use their own judgment, and sharp disagreements developed that had to be patched up by Albert Gallatin. The sobersided Adams and the hard-drinking, poker-playing Clay, especially, rubbed each other the wrong way. The American delegates at first were instructed to demand that the British abandon impressment and paper blockades, and to get indemnities for seizures of American ships. The British opened the discussions with demands for territory in New York and Maine, removal of American warships from the Great Lakes, an autonomous Indian buffer state in the Northwest, access to the Mississippi River, and abandonment of American fishing rights off Labrador and Newfoundland. If the British insisted on such a position, the Americans informed them, the negotiations would be at an end.

But the British were stalling, awaiting news of victories to strengthen their hand. They withdrew the demand for an Indian buffer state and substituted *uti possidetis* (retention of occupied territory) as a basis for settlement. This too was rejected. The Americans countered with a proposal for the *status quo ante bellum* (the situation before the war). The news of American victory on Lake Champlain arrived in October and weakened the British resolve. Their will to fight was further eroded by a continuing power struggle at the Congress of Vienna, by the eagerness of British merchants to renew trade with America, and by the war weariness of a tax-burdened public. The British finally decided that the game was not worth the cost. One by one demands were dropped on both sides until the envoys agreed to end the war, return the prisoners, restore the previous boundaries, and to settle nothing else. The questions of fisheries and disputed boundaries were referred to commissions for future settlement. The Treaty of Ghent was signed on Christmas Eve of 1814.

THE HARTFORD CONVENTION   While the diplomats converged on a peace settlement, an entirely different kind of meeting took place in Hartford, Connecticut. An ill-fated affair, the Hartford Convention represented the climax of New England's dissaffection with "Mr. Madison's war." New England had managed to keep aloof from the war and extract a profit from illegal trading and privateering. New England shippers monopolized the import trade and took advantage of the chance to engage in active trade with the enemy. After the fall of Napoleon, however, the British extended their blockade to New England, occupied Maine, and conducted several raids along the coast. Even Boston seemed threatened. Instead of rallying to the American flag, however, Federalists in the Massachusetts legislature on October 5, 1814, voted for a convention of New England states to plan independent action. The Constitution, they said, "has failed to secure to this commonwealth, and . . . to the Eastern sections of this Union, those equal rights and benefits which are the greatest objects of its formation."

On December 15 the Hartford Convention assembled with delegates chosen by the legislatures of Massachusetts, Rhode Island, and Connecticut, with two delegates from Vermont and one from New Hampshire: twenty-two in all. The convention included an extreme group, Timothy Pickering's "Essex Junto," who were prepared for secession from the Union, but it was controlled by a more moderate group led by Harrison Gray Otis, who wanted only a protest in language reminiscent of Madison's Virginia Resolutions of 1798. As the ultimate remedy for their grievances they proposed seven constitutional amendments designed to limit Republican influence: abolishing the three-fifths compromise, requiring a two-thirds vote to declare war or admit new states, prohibiting embargoes lasting more than sixty days, excluding the foreign-born from federal offices, limiting the president to one term, and forbidding successive presidents from the same state.

Their call for a later convention in Boston carried the unmistakable threat of secession if the demands were ignored. Yet the threat quickly evaporated. When messengers from Hartford reached Washington, they found the battered capital celebrating the good news from Ghent and New Orleans. The consequence was a fatal blow to the Federalist party, which never recovered from the stigma of disloyalty and narrow provincialism stamped on it by the Hartford Convention.

We Owe Allegiance to No Crown. *The War of 1812 generated a new feeling of nationalism.*

THE WAR'S AFTERMATH   For all the fumbling ineptitude with which the War of 1812 was fought, it generated an intense feeling of patriotism. Despite the standoff with which it ended at Ghent, the American public nourished a sense of victory, courtesy of Andrew Jackson and his men at New Orleans as well as the heroic exploits of American frigates in their duels with British ships. Under Republican leadership the nation had survived a "Second War of Independence" against the greatest power on earth, and emerged with new symbols of nationhood and a new gallery of heroes. The war also launched the United States toward economic independence, as the interruption of trade encouraged the growth of American manufactures. After forty years of independence, it dawned on the world that the new republic might be here to stay, and that it might be something more than a pawn in European power games.

As if to underline the point, Congress authorized a quick, decisive blow at the pirates of the Barbary Coast. During the War of 1812 the dey of Algiers had once again set about plundering American ships on the claim that he was getting too little tribute. On March 3, 1815, little more than two weeks after the Senate ratified the Peace of Ghent, Congress authorized hostilities against the pirates. On May 10 Captain Stephen Decatur sailed from New York with ten vessels. In the Mediterranean he first seized two Algerian ships and then sailed boldly into the harbor of Algiers. On June 30, 1815, the dey of Algiers agreed to cease molesting American ships and to give up all American prisoners. In July and August Decatur's show of force induced similar treaties from Tunis and Tripoli. This time there was no tribute; this time, for a change, the Barbary pirates paid indemnities for the damage they had done. This time victory put an end to the piracy and extortion in that quarter, permanently.

One of the strangest results of a strange war and its aftermath was a reversal of roles by the Republicans and Federalists. Out of the wartime experience the Republicans had learned some lessons in nationalism. Certain needs and inadequacies revealed by the war had "Federalized" Madison, or "re-Federalized" this Father of the Constitution. Perhaps, Madison reasoned, a peacetime army and navy would not be such an unmitigated evil. Madison now preferred to keep something more than a token force. The lack of a national bank had added to the problems of financing the war. Now Madison wanted it back. The rise of new industries during the war led to a clamor for increased tariffs. Madison went along. The problems of overland transportation in the West had revealed the need for internal improvements. Madison agreed, but on that point kept his constitutional scruples. He wanted a constitutional amendment. So while Madison embraced nationalism and broad construction of the Constitution, the Federalists took up the Jeffersonian's position of states' rights and stricts construction. It was the first great reversal of roles in constitutional interpretation. It would not be the last.

Further Reading

Marshall Smelser's *The Democratic Republic, 1801–1815* (1968) presents an overview of the Republican administration. James S. Young's *The Washington Community, 1800–1828* (1966)° provides an interesting look at both the mechanics of Jeffersonian politics and the design of the new national capital.

The standard biography of Jefferson is the multivolume work by

°These books are available in paperback editions.

Dumas Malone, *Jefferson and His Time* (6 vols, 1948–1981).° A one-volume biography which emphasizes Jefferson's public, political life is Noble Cunningham, Jr.'s *In Pursuit of Reason: The Life of Thomas Jefferson* (1987). Also valuable are Forrest McDonald's *The Presidency of Thomas Jefferson* (1976) and Merrill Peterson's *Thomas Jefferson and the New Nation* (1970). Jefferson's private life is described in Jack McLaughlin's *Jefferson and Monticello: The Biography of a Builder* (1988). Fawn Brodie's *Thomas Jefferson: An Intimate History* (1974)° offers a psychobiography. On the life of Jefferson's friend and successor see Ralph L. Ketcham's *James Madison* (1971) or Drew R. McCoy's *The Last of the Fathers: James Madison and the Republican Legacy* (1989). McCoy's *The Elusive Republic* (1982)° discusses the political economy of these years in the context of republicanism; Joyce Appleby's *Capitalism and a New Social Order* (1984)° deemphasizes the impact of republican ideology.

David Hackett Fischer's *The Revolution of American Conservatism: The Federalist Party in the Era of Jeffersonian Democracy* (1965), Shaw Livermore's *The Twilight of Federalism: The Disintegration of the Federalist Party* (1962), and Linda K. Kerber's *Federalists in Dissent* (1970) explore the Federalists while out of power.

The concept of judicial review and the courts can be studied in Richard E. Ellis's *The Jeffersonian Crisis* (1971). The most comprehensive work on John Marshall remains Albert J. Beveridge's *The Life of John Marshall* (4 vols., 1916–1919). Milton Lomask's two-volume *Aaron Burr: The Years from Princeton to Vice President, 1756–1805* (1979) and *The Conspiracy and the Years of Exile, 1805–1836* (1982) trace the career of that remarkable American.

For the Louisiana Purchase, consult Alexander De Conde's *This Affair of Louisiana* (1976). A detailed account of the explorations of Lewis and Clark may be found in David Lavender's *The Way to the Western Sea; Lewis and Clark Across the Continent* (1988). *The Journals of Lewis and Clark* (1953), edited by Bernard De Voto, and David F. Hawke's *Those Tremendous Mountains* (1980),° based on those journals, are both highly readable. Bernard W. Sheehan's *Seeds of Extinction* (1973) is more analytical about the Jeffersonians' Indian policy and the opening of the West. John C. Greene's *American Science in the Age of Jefferson* (1984) is a good summary of that topic.

Burton Spivak's *Jefferson's English Crisis: Commerce, the Embargo, and the Republican Revolution* (1979) discusses Anglo-American relations during Jefferson's administration; Clifford L. Egan's *Neither Peace nor War* (1983) covers Franco-American relations. A review of the

°These books are available in paperback editions.

events that brought on war in 1812 is presented in Robert A. Rutland's *Madison's Alternatives: The Jeffersonian Republicans and the Coming of War, 1805–1812* (1975). See also Roger H. Brown's *The Republic in Peril: 1812* (1964).* J. C. A. Stagg's *Mr. Madison's War* (1983) places the war in a larger historical context. Two works that concentrate on specific aspects of the war are Alan Lloyd's *The Scorching of Washington: The War of 1812* (1975) and William M. Fowler, Jr.'s *Jack Tars and Commodores* (1984), on the role of the navy.

*These books are available in paperback editions.

10

NATIONALISM AND SECTIONALISM

Economic Nationalism

When did the United States become a nation? There is no easy answer to the question, for a sense of nationhood develops slowly and is subject to crosscurrents of localism, sectionalism, and class interest. Americans of the colonies and the early republic by and large identified more closely with the local community and at most the province or state in which they resided than with any larger idea of empire or nation. Among the colonies there was no common tie equal to the connection between each and the mother country. The Revolution gave rise to a sense of nationhood, but that could hardly be regarded as the dominant idea of the Revolution. Men who, like Hamilton, were prepared to think continentally strengthened the federal Union by the Constitution, but Jefferson's "Revolution of 1800" revealed the countervailing forces of local and state interest. Jefferson himself, for instance, always spoke of Virginia as "my country."

Immediately after the War of 1812, however, Americans experienced a new surge of nationalism. An abnormal economic prosperity after the war fed a feeling of well-being and enhanced the prestige of the national government. Jefferson's embargo ironically had given impulse to the factories that he abhorred. His policy of "peaceful coercion," followed by the wartime constraints on trade, had caused capital in New England and the middle states to drift from commerce toward manufacturing. The idea spread that the country needed a more balanced economy of farming, commerce, and manufacturing. After a generation of war, shortages of farm products in Europe forced up the prices of American products and stimulated agricultural expansion, indeed, a wild speculation in farmlands. Southern cotton, tobacco, and rice came to account for about two-thirds of American exports. At the same time, planters and farmers could buy in a postwar market flooded with cheap

The Union Manufactories of Maryland in Patapsco Falls, Baltimore
County, c. 1815. *A textile mill begun during the embargo of 1807; by
1825 the Union Manufactories would employ over 600 people.*

English goods. The new American manufacturers would seek protection from this competition.

President Madison, in his first annual message to Congress after the
war, recommended several steps toward strengthening the government:
better fortifications, a permanent army and a strong navy, a new
national bank, effective protection of the new infant industries, a system of canals and roads for commercial and military use, and to top it
off, a great national university. "The Republicans have out-Federalized
Federalism," one New Englander remarked. Congress responded by
authorizing a standing army of 10,000 and strengthening the navy as
well.

THE BANK OF THE UNITED STATES   The trinity of economic nationalism—proposals for a second national bank, protective tariff, and internal
improvements—inspired the greatest controversies. After the national
bank expired in 1811, the country had fallen into a financial muddle.
State-chartered banks mushroomed with little or no control, and their
bank notes (paper money) flooded the channels of commerce with currency of uncertain value. Because hard money had been so short during
the war, many state banks had suspended specie (gold or silver) payments in redemption of their notes, thereby depressing their value. The
absence of the central bank had been a source of financial embarrassment to the government, which had neither a ready means of floating
loans nor a way of transferring funds across the country.

Madison and most younger Republicans salved their constitutional
scruples about a national bank with a dash of pragmatism. The issue,
Madison said, had been decided "by repeated recognitions . . . of the

validity of such an institution in acts of the legislative, executive, and judicial branches of the Government, accompanied by . . . a concurrence of the general will of the nation." In 1816 Congress adopted over the protest of Old Republicans provision for a new Bank of the United States. Modeled after Hamilton's bank, it differed chiefly in that it was capitalized at $35 million instead of $10 million. Once again the charter ran for twenty years, once again the government owned a fifth of the stock and named five of the twenty-five directors, and again the bank served as the government depository for federal funds. Its bank notes were accepted in payments to the government. In return for its privileges the bank had to take care of the government's funds without charge, lend the government $5 million on demand, and pay the government a cash bonus of $1.5 million.

The debate on the bank, then and later, was colorful and bitter, and it helped to set the pattern of regional alignment for most other economic issues. Missouri senator Thomas Hart Benton predicted that the currency-short western towns would be at the mercy of a centralized eastern bank. "They may be devoured by it any moment! They are in the jaws of the monster! A lump of butter in the mouth of a dog! One gulp, one swallow, and all is gone!"

The debate was also noteworthy because of the leading roles played by the great triumvirate of John C. Calhoun of South Carolina, Henry Clay of Kentucky, and Daniel Webster of New Hampshire, later of Massachusetts. Calhoun, still in his youthful phase as a War Hawk nationalist, introduced the measure and pushed it through, justifying its constitutionality by citing the congressional power to regulate the cur-

The second Bank of the United States.

rency, and pointing to the need for a uniform circulating medium. Clay, who had helped to kill Hamilton's bank in 1811, now confessed that he had failed to foresee the evils that resulted, and asserted that circumstances had made the bank indispensable. Webster, on the other hand, led the opposition of the New England Federalists, who did not want the banking center moved from Boston to Philadelphia. Later, after he moved from New Hampshire to Massachusetts, Webster would return to Congress as the champion of a much stronger national power, while events would carry Calhoun in the other direction.

A PROTECTIVE TARIFF   The shift of capital from commerce to manufactures, begun during the embargo of 1807, had speeded up during the war. Peace in 1815 brought a sudden renewal of cheap British imports and generated pleas for the protection of infant American industries. The self-interest of the manufacturers, who as yet had little political impact, was reinforced by a patriotic desire for economic independence from Britain. New England shippers and southern farmers opposed the movement, but both sections had sizable minorities who believed that the promotion of industry enhanced both sectional and national welfare.

The Tariff of 1816, the first intended more for the protection of industry against foreign competition than for revenue, easily passed in Congress. The South and New England registered a majority of their votes against the bill, but the middle states and Old Northwest cast only five negative votes altogether. Nathaniel Macon of North Carolina opposed the tariff and defended the Old Republican doctrine of strict construction. The power to protect industry, Macon said, like the power to establish a bank, rested on the idea that there were implied powers embedded in the Constitution; Macon worried that such implied powers might one day be used to abolish slavery. The minority of southerners who voted for the tariff, led by Calhoun, had good reason to expect that the South might itself become a manufacturing center. South Carolina was then developing a few textile mills. According to the census of 1810, the southern states had approximately as many manufacturers as New England. Within a few years New England moved ahead of the South, and Calhoun went over to Macon's views against protection. The tariff then became a sectional issue, with manufacturers, wool processors, and food, sugar, and hemp growers favoring higher tariffs, while planters and shipping interests favored lower duties.

INTERNAL IMPROVEMENTS   The third major issue of the time involved internal improvements: the building of roads and the development of water transportation. The war had highlighted the shortcomings of existing facilities. Troop movements through the western wilderness proved

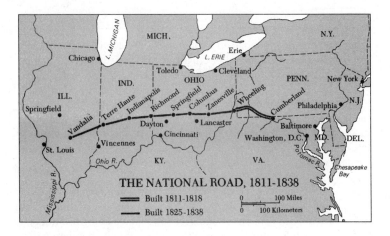

THE NATIONAL ROAD, 1811-1838

▬▬ Built 1811-1818
▬▬ Built 1825-1838

0 ___ 100 Miles
0 ___ 100 Kilometers

very difficult, and settlers found that unless they located near navigable waters, they were cut off from trade and limited to a frontier subsistence.

The federal government had entered the field of internal improvements under Jefferson, who went along with some hesitation. He and both of his successors recommended an amendment to give the federal government undisputed power in the field. But lacking that, the constitutional grounds for federal action rested mainly on provision for national defense and expansion of the postal system. In 1803, when Ohio became a state, Congress decreed that 5 percent of the proceeds from land sales in the state would go to building a National Road from the Atlantic coast into Ohio and beyond as the territory developed. In 1806 Jefferson signed a measure for a survey, and construction of the National Road began in 1811.

Originally called the Cumberland Road, it was the first federally financed interstate road network. By 1818 it was open from Cumberland, Maryland, to Wheeling on the Ohio River. Construction stopped temporarily during the business panic of 1819, but by 1838 the road extended all the way to Vandalia, Illinois. By reducing transportation costs and opening up new markets, the National Road and other privately financed turnpikes helped accelerate the commercialization of agriculture.

In 1817 John C. Calhoun put through the House a bill to place in a fund for internal improvements the $1.5 million bonus the Bank of the United States had paid for its charter, as well as all future dividends on the government's bank stock. Once again opposition centered in New England and the South, which expected to gain least, and support came largely from the West, which badly needed good roads. On his last day in office Madison vetoed the bill. While sympathetic to its purpose, he could not overcome his "insuperable difficulty . . . in reconciling the bill with the Constitution" and suggested instead a constitutional amendment. Internal improvements remained for another hundred years, with few exceptions, the responsibility of states and private enterprise. Then and later Congress supported river and harbor improvements, and scattered post roads, but nothing of a systematic nature. The federal government did not enter the field on a large scale until passage of the Federal Highways Act of 1916.

"GOOD FEELINGS"

JAMES MONROE   As Madison approached the end of a turbulent tenure, he, like Jefferson, turned to a fellow Virginian, another secretary of state, as his successor: James Monroe. In the Republican caucus Monroe won the nomination, then overwhelmed his Federalist opponent, Rufus King of New York, 183 to 34 in the electoral college. The "Virginia dynasty" continued. Like three of the four presidents before him, Monroe was a Virginia planter, but with a difference: he came from the small-planter group. At the outbreak of the Revolution he was just beginning college at William and Mary. He joined the army at the age of sixteen, fought with Washington at Trenton, and was a lieutenant-colonel when the war ended. Later he studied law with Jefferson.

Monroe never displayed the depth of his Republican predecessors in scholarship or political theory, but what he lacked in intellect he made up in dedication to public service. His soul, Jefferson said, if turned inside out, would be found spotless. Monroe served in the Virginia assembly, as governor of the state, in the Confederation Congress and United States Senate, and as minister to Paris, London, and Madrid.

James Monroe, portrayed as he entered the presidency in 1816.

Under Madison he had been secretary of state, and twice doubled as secretary of war. Tall, rawboned Monroe, with his powdered wig, cocked hat, and knee breeches, was the last of the revolutionary generation to serve in the White House and the last president to dress in the old style.

Firmly grounded in Republican principles, Monroe failed to keep up with the onrush of the new nationalism. He accepted as accomplished fact the bank and the protective tariff, but during his tenure there was no further extension of economic nationalism. Indeed, there was a minor setback. He permitted the National (or Cumberland) Road to be carried forward, but in his veto of the Cumberland Road Bill (1822) he denied the authority of Congress to collect tolls to pay for its repair and maintenance. Like Jefferson and Madison, he also urged a constitutional amendment to remove all doubt about federal authority in the field of internal improvements.

Whatever his limitations, Monroe surrounded himself with some of the ablest young Republican leaders. John Quincy Adams became secretary of state. William Crawford of Georgia continued as secretary of the treasury. John C. Calhoun headed the War Department after Henry Clay refused the job in order to stay on as Speaker of the House. The new administration found the country in a state of well-being: America was at peace and the economy was flourishing. Soon after his 1817 inauguration, Monroe embarked on a goodwill tour of New England. In Boston, lately a hotbed of wartime dissent, a Federalist paper com-

Election Day at the State House, *Philadelphia, 1818.*

mented on the president's visit under the heading "Era of Good Feelings." The label became a popular catchphrase for Monroe's administration, and one that historians seized upon later. Like many a maxim, it conveys just enough truth to be sadly misleading. A resurgence of factionalism and sectionalism erupted just as the postwar prosperity collapsed in the Panic of 1819.

For two years, however, general harmony reigned, and even when the country's troubles revived, little of the blame fell on Monroe. In 1820 he was reelected without opposition, even without needing nomination. The Federalists were too weak to put up a candidate, and the Republicans did not bother to call a caucus. Monroe won all the electoral votes except for three abstentions and one vote from New Hampshire for John Quincy Adams. The Republican party was dominant— for the moment. In fact, it was about to follow the Federalists into oblivion. Amid the general political contentment of the era, the first party system was fading away, but rivals for the succession soon commenced the process of forming new parties.

IMPROVING RELATIONS WITH BRITAIN   Adding to the prevailing contentment after the war was a growing rapprochement with the recent enemy. American shippers resumed trade with Britain (and India). The Peace of Ghent had left unsettled a number of minor disputes, but in the sequel two important compacts—the Rush-Bagot Agreement of 1817 and the Convention of 1818—removed several potential causes of irritation. In the first, effected by an exchange of notes between Acting Secretary of State Richard Rush and British Minister Charles Bagot, the threat of naval competition on the Great Lakes vanished with an arrangement to limit forces there to several revenue cutters. Although the exchange made no reference to the land boundary between the countries, its spirit gave rise to the tradition of an unfortified border, the longest in the world.

The Convention of 1818 covered three major points. The northern limit of the Louisiana Purchase was settled by extending the national boundary along the 49th parallel west from Lake of the Woods to the crest of the Rocky Mountains. West of that point the Oregon Country would be open to joint occupation by the British and Americans, but the boundary remained unsettled. The right of Americans to fish off Newfoundland and Labrador, granted in 1783, was acknowledged once again.

The chief remaining problem was Britain's exclusion of American ships from the West Indies in order to reserve that lucrative trade for British ships. The Commercial Convention of 1815 did not apply there, and after the War of 1812 the British had once again closed the door. This remained a chronic irritant, and the United States retaliated with several measures. Under a Navigation Act of 1817, importation of West Indian produce was restricted to American vessels or vessels belonging to West Indian merchants. In 1818 American ports were closed to all British vessels arriving from a colony that was legally closed to vessels of the United States. In 1820 Monroe approved an act of Congress that specified total non-intercourse—with British vessels, with all British colonies in the Americas, and even in goods taken to England and reexported. The rapprochement with Britain therefore fell short of perfection.

JACKSON TAKES FLORIDA   The year 1819 was one of the more fateful years in American history. Controversial efforts to expand American territory, a sharp financial panic, a tense debate over the extension of slavery, and several landmark Supreme Court cases combined to bring an unsettling end to the "Era of Good Feelings." The bumptious new nationalism reached a climax with the acquisition of Florida and the extension of the southwestern boundary to the Pacific, but nationalism quickly began to run afoul of domestic crosscurrents that would set up an ever-widening swirl in the next decades.

In the calculations of global power, it was perhaps long since reck-

Portrait of an escaped slave who lived with the Seminoles in Florida.

oned that Florida would someday pass to the United States. Spanish sovereignty was more a technicality than an actuality, and extended little beyond St. Augustine on the east coast and Pensacola and St. Marks on the Gulf. The thinly held province had been a thorn in the side of the United States during the recent war as a center of British intrigue; a haven for Creek refugees, who were beginning to take the name Seminole ("runaway" or "separatist"); and a harbor for runaway slaves and criminals. Florida also stood athwart the outlets of several important rivers flowing to the Gulf.

Spain, once dominant in the Americas, was now a declining power suffering from both internal and colonial revolt, unable to enforce its obligations under the Pinckney Treaty of 1795 to pacify the frontiers. In 1816 American forces clashed with a group of escaped slaves who had taken over a British fort on the Appalachicola River. Seminoles were soon fighting white settlers in the area, and in 1817 Americans burned a Seminole border settlement, killed five of its inhabitants, and dispersed the rest across the border into Florida.

At this point Secretary of War Calhoun authorized a campaign against the Seminoles, and he summoned General Andrew Jackson from Nashville to take command. Jackson's orders allowed him to pursue the offenders into Spanish territory, but not to attack any Spanish post. A frustrated Jackson pledged to President Monroe that if the United States wanted Florida, he could wind up the whole controversy in sixty days. All he needed was private, unofficial word, which might be sent through Tennessee representative John Rhea. Soon afterward Jackson indeed got a letter from Rhea, and claimed that it transmitted cryptically the required authority, although Monroe always denied any such intention. The truth about the Rhea letter, which Jackson destroyed (at Monroe's request, he said), remains a mystery.

In any case, when it came to Spaniards or Indians, few white Tennesseans—and certainly not Andrew Jackson—were likely to bother with technicalities. Jackson pushed eastward through Florida, reinforced by Tennessee volunteers and a party of friendly Creeks, taking a Spanish post and skirmishing with the Seminoles, destroying their settlements. Jackson hanged two of their leaders without any semblance of a trial. Having mopped up the region from the Appalachicola to the Suwannee, Jackson then turned west and seized Pensacola and returned home to Nashville. The whole episode had taken about four months; the Florida panhandle was in American hands by June 1818.

The news of Jackson's exploits aroused anger in Madrid and concern in Washington. Spain demanded the return of its territory, reparations, and the punishment of Jackson, but Spain's impotence was plain for all to see. Monroe's cabinet was at first prepared to disavow Jackson's action, especially his direct attack on Spanish posts. Calhoun, as secretary of war, was inclined, at least officially, to discipline Jackson for disregard of orders—a stand that caused bad blood between the two men later—but privately confessed a certain pleasure at the outcome. In any case a man as popular as Jackson was almost invulnerable. And he had one important friend at court, Secretary of State John Quincy Adams, who realized that Jackson had strengthened his hand in negotiations already under way with the Spanish minister. American forces withdrew from Florida, but negotiations resumed with the knowledge that the United States could take Florida at any time.

With the fate of Florida a foregone conclusion, Adams now turned his eye on a larger purpose, a definition of the western boundary of the Louisiana Purchase and—his boldest stroke—extension of a boundary to the Pacific coast. In lengthy negotiations Adams gradually gave ground on claims to Texas, but stuck to his demand for a transcontinental line. Agreement finally came early in 1819. Spain ceded all of Florida in return for American assumption of private American claims against Spain up to $5 million. The western boundary of the Louisiana Purchase would run along the Sabine River and then in stair-step fashion up to the Red River, along the Red, and up to the Arkansas River. From the source of the Arkansas it would go north to the 42nd parallel and thence west to the Pacific coast. A dispute over land claims held up ratification for another two years, but those claims were revoked and final ratifications were exchanged in 1821. Florida became a territory, and its first governor was briefly Andrew Jackson. In 1845 Florida achieved statehood.

Andrew Jackson, portrayed here at the time of his campaign against the Seminoles in Florida.

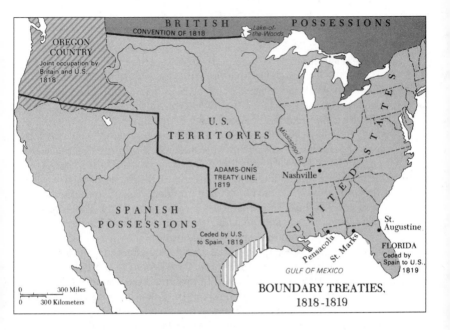

SPECULATION AND SLAVERY

THE PANIC OF 1819   Adams's Transcontinental Treaty was a triumph of foreign policy and the climactic event of the postwar nationalism. Even before it was signed in February 1819, however, two thunderclaps signaled the end of the brief "Era of Good Feelings" and gave warning of stormy weather ahead: the financial Panic of 1819 and the controversy over statehood for Missouri. The occasion for the panic was the sudden collapse of cotton prices in the English market. At one point in 1818 cotton had soared to 32 1/2¢ a pound. The pressure of high prices forced British manufacturers to turn away from American sources to cheaper East Indian cotton, and by 1819 cotton averaged only 14.3¢ per pound at New Orleans. The price collapse set off a decline in the demand for other American goods and suddenly revealed the fragility of the prosperity that had begun after the War of 1812.

Since 1815 a speculative bubble had grown, with expectations that expansion would go on forever. But American industry struggled to find markets for its goods. Even the Tariff of 1816 had not been enough to eliminate British competition. What was more, businessmen, farmers, and land jobbers had inflated the bubble with a volatile expansion of credit. The sources of this credit were both government and banks. Under the Land Law of 1800 the government extended four years' credit to those who bought western lands. After 1804 one could buy as little as 160 acres at a minimum price of $1.64 per acre (although in auctions the best lands went for more). In many cases speculators took up large tracts, paying only one-fourth down, and then sold them to settlers with the understanding that the settlers would pay the remaining installments. With the collapse of prices, and then of land values, both speculators and settlers found themselves caught short.

The reckless practices of state banks compounded the inflation of credit. To enlarge their loans they issued bank notes far beyond their means of redemption, and at first were under little pressure to promise redemption in specie. Even the second Bank of the United States, which was supposed to introduce some order to the financial arena, was at first caught up in the mania. Its first president yielded to the contagion of get-rich-quick fever that was sweeping the country. The proliferation of branches combined with little supervision from Philadelphia to carry the bank into the same reckless extension of loans that state banks had pursued. In 1819, just as alert businessmen began to take alarm, a case of extensive fraud and embezzlement in the Baltimore branch came to light. The disclosure prompted the appointment of Langdon Cheves, former congressman from South Carolina, as the bank's president and the establishment of a sounder policy.

Cheves reduced salaries and other costs, postponed dividends, restrained the extension of credit, and presented for redemption the state bank notes that came in, thereby forcing the state-chartered banks to keep specie reserves. Cheves rescued the bank from near-ruin, but only by putting heavy pressure on state banks. State banks in turn put pressure on their debtors, who found it harder to renew old loans or get new ones. In 1823, his job completed, Cheves relinquished his position to Nicholas Biddle of Philadelphia. The Cheves policies were the result rather than the cause of the Panic, but they were anathema to debtors, who found it all the more difficult to meet their obligations. Hard times lasted about three years, and the bank took much of the blame in the popular mind. The Panic passed, but resentment of the bank lingered. It never fully regained the confidence of the South and the West.

THE MISSOURI COMPROMISE   Just as the Panic spread over the country, another cloud appeared on the horizon, the onset of a sectional controversy over slavery. By 1819 the country had an equal number of slave and free states, eleven of each. The line between them was defined by the southern and western boundaries of Pennsylvania and the Ohio River. Although slavery still lingered in some places north of the line, it was on the way to extinction there. Beyond the Mississippi, however, no move had been made to extend the dividing line across the Louisiana Purchase territory, where slavery had existed from the days when France and Spain had colonized the area. At the time the Missouri Territory embraced all of the Louisiana Purchase except the state of

Louisiana (1812) and the Arkansas Territory (1819). In the westward rush of population, the old French town of St. Louis became the funnel through which settlers pushed on beyond the Mississippi. These were largely settlers from the South who brought their slaves with them.

In 1819 the House of Representatives was asked to approve legislation enabling Missouri to draft a state constitution, its population having passed the minimum of 60,000. At that point Representative James Tallmadge, Jr., a New York congressman, introduced a resolution prohibiting the further introduction of slaves into Missouri, which had some 10,000, and providing freedom at age twenty-five for those born after the territory's admission as a state. Tallmadge's motives remain obscure, but may have been very simply a moral aversion to slavery or perhaps a political aversion to having slavery and the three-fifths compromise extended any farther beyond the Mississippi River. After brief but fiery exchanges, the House passed the amendment on an almost strictly sectional vote. The Senate rejected it by a similar tally, but with several northerners joining in the opposition. With population at the time growing faster in the North, a balance between the two sections could be held only in the Senate. In the House, slave states had 81 votes while free states had 105; a balance was unlikely ever again to be restored in the House.

Congress adjourned in March 1819, postponing further debate until the regular session in December. When the debate erupted, it was remarkable for the absence of moral argument, although repugnance to slavery and moral guilt about it were never far from the surface. The debate turned on the constitutional issue. Congress, Rufus King of New York asserted, was empowered to forbid slavery in Missouri as the Confederation Congress had done in the Northwest Territory. William Pinkney of Maryland countered that the states were equal and that Congress could not bind a state. Southern leaders argued further that under the Fifth Amendment, slaveholders could not be denied the right to carry their property into the territory, which would be deprivation of property without due process of law. Henry Clay and others expressed a view, which Jefferson and Madison now shared, that the expansion and dispersal of slavery would ameliorate the condition of the slaves. Most of the constitutional arguments that would reverberate in later quarrels over slavery were already present in the argument over Missouri. But the moral issue of bondage had not yet reached the fevered condition it would later achieve, because few were yet prepared to defend slavery as a positive good. In fact, the general abhorrence of slavery was still strong enough that during 1820 Congress defined the illegal foreign slave trade as piracy, subjecting those engaged in it to the death penalty. This penalty, however, was not actually imposed until the outbreak of the Civil War.

Maine's application for statehood made it easier to arrive at an agree-

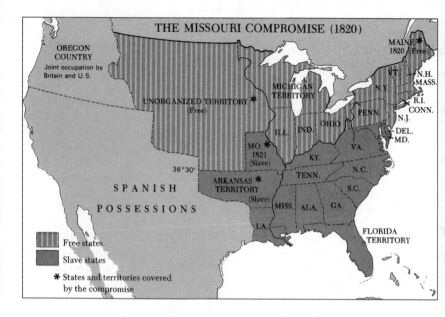

THE MISSOURI COMPROMISE (1820)

OREGON
COUNTRY
Joint occupation by
Britain and U.S.

MAINE *
1820 (Free)

VT.
N.H.
MASS.
N.Y.
R.I.
CONN.
N.J.
DEL.
MD.

MICHIGAN
TERRITORY

UNORGANIZED TERRITORY *
(Free)

ILL. IND. OHIO PENN

MO *
1821
(Slave)

VA.

KY.

36°30'

SPANISH

POSSESSIONS

ARKANSAS *
TERRITORY
(Slave)

TENN.

N.C.

S.C.

MISS. ALA. GA.

LA.

FLORIDA
TERRITORY

Free states

Slave states

* States and territories covered
by the compromise

ment. Since colonial times Maine had been the northern province of
Massachusetts. The Senate linked its request for separate statehood
with Missouri's and voted to admit Maine as a free state and Missouri as
a slave state, thus maintaining the balance in the Senate. An Illinois senator further extended the compromise by an amendment to exclude
slavery from the rest of the Louisiana Purchase north of 36°30′N, Missouri's southern border. Slavery thus would continue in the Arkansas
Territory and in the state of Missouri, and be excluded from the remainder of the area. But that was country that Zebulon Pike's reports had
persuaded the public was the Great American Desert, unlikely ever to
be settled. For this reason the arrangement seemed to be a victory for
the slave states. The House at first refused to accept the arrangement,
but the question went to a conference committee of the two houses for
which Speaker Henry Clay had carefully chosen malleable members.
They duly accepted the Senate compromise. By a very close vote it
passed the House on March 2, 1820.

Then another problem arose. The proslavery elements that dominated Missouri's constitutional convention inserted in the proposed new
state constitution a proviso excluding free blacks and mulattoes from
the state. This clearly violated the requirement of Article IV, Section 2,
of the Constitution: "The Citizens of each State shall be entitled to all
Privileges and Immunities of Citizens in the Several States." Free blacks
were citizens of many states, including the slave states of North Carolina and Tennessee where, until the mid-1830s, they also voted.

The renewed controversy threatened final approval of Missouri's

Henry Clay.

admission until Henry Clay, now beginning to earn his later title of the "Great Compromiser," formulated a "Second Missouri Compromise." Admission of Missouri as a state depended on assurance from the Missouri legislature that it would never construe the offending clause in such a way as to sanction denial of privileges that citizens held under the Constitution. It was one of the more artless dodges in American history, for it required the legislature to affirm that the state constitution did not mean what it clearly said, but the compromise worked. The Missouri legislature duly adopted the pledge, while denying that the legislature had any power to bind the people of the state. On August 10, 1821, President Monroe proclaimed the admission of Missouri as the twenty-fourth state. For the moment, the controversy subsided. "But this momentous question," the aging Thomas Jefferson wrote to a friend after the first compromise, "like a firebell in the night awakened and filled me with terror. I considered it at once as the knell of the Union."

JUDICIAL NATIONALISM

JOHN MARSHALL, CHIEF JUSTICE   Meanwhile nationalism still flourished in the Supreme Court, where Chief Justice John Marshall preserved Hamiltonian Federalism for yet another generation. Marshall, a survivor of the Revolution and a distant cousin of Thomas Jefferson, was among those who had been forever nationalized by the experience. In later years he said: "I was confirmed in the habit of considering America as my country and Congress as my government." The habit persisted through a successful legal career punctuated by service in Virginia's legislature and ratifying convention, as part of the "XYZ" mission to France, and as a member of Congress. Never a judge before he became chief justice in 1801, he established the power of the Supreme Court by his force of mind and crystalline logic.

During Marshall's early years on the Court (altogether he served thirty-four years), he affirmed the principle of judicial review. In *Marbury v. Madison* (1803) and *Fletcher v. Peck* (1810) the Court first struck down a federal law and then a state law as unconstitutional. In the cases of *Martin v. Hunter's Lessee* (1816) and *Cohens v. Virginia* (1821) the Court assumed the right to take appeals from state courts on the grounds that the Constitution, laws, and treaties of the United States could be kept uniformly the supreme law of the land only if the Court could review decisions of state courts. In the first case the Court overruled Virginia's confiscation of Loyalist property, because this violated treaties with Great Britain; in the second it upheld Virginia's right to forbid the sale of lottery tickets.

PROTECTING CONTRACT RIGHTS   In the fateful year 1819, Marshall and the Court made two more decisions of major importance in checking the states and building the power of the central government: *Dartmouth College v. Woodward* and *McCulloch v. Maryland.* The Dartmouth College case involved an attempt by the New Hampshire legislature to alter a provision in Dartmouth's charter, under which the college's trustees became a self-perpetuating board. In 1816 the state's Republican legislature, offended by this relic of monarchy and even more by the Federalist majority on the board, placed Dartmouth under a new board named by the governor. The original trustees sued, lost in the state courts, but with Daniel Webster as counsel won on appeal to

Chief Justice John Marshall, pillar of judicial nationalism.

the Supreme Court. The charter, Marshall said for the Court, was a valid contract that the legislature had impaired, an act forbidden by the Constitution. This implied a new and enlarged definition of *contract* that seemed to put private corporations beyond the reach of the states that chartered them. But thereafter states commonly wrote into charters and general laws of incorporation provisions making them subject to modification. Such provisions were then part of the "contract."

STRENGTHENING THE FEDERAL GOVERNMENT   Marshall's single most important interpretation of the constitutional system appeared in the case of *McCulloch v. Maryland.* McCulloch, a clerk in the Baltimore branch of the Bank of the United States, failed to affix state revenue stamps to bank notes as required by a Maryland law taxing the notes. Indicted by the state, McCulloch, acting for the bank, appealed to the Supreme Court, which handed down a unanimous judgment upholding the power of Congress to charter the bank and denying any right of the state to tax the bank. In a lengthy opinion Marshall rejected Maryland's argument that the federal government was the creature of sovereign states. Instead, he argued, it arose directly from the people acting through the conventions that ratified the Constitution. While sovereignty was divided between the states and the national government, the latter, "though limited in its powers, is supreme within its sphere of action."

Marshall then went on to endorse the doctrine of broad construction and implied powers set forth by Hamilton in his bank message of 1791. The "necessary and proper" clause, he argued, did not mean "absolutely indispensable." The test of constitutionality he summed up in almost the same words as Hamilton: "Let the end be legitimate, let it be within the scope of the constitution, and all means which are appropriate, which are plainly adapted to that end, which are not prohibited, but consistent with the letter and spirit of the constitution, are constitutional."

Maryland's effort to tax the national bank conflicted with the supreme law of the land. One great principle that "entirely pervades the constitution," Marshall wrote, was "that the constitution and the laws made in pursuance thereof are supreme: that they control the constitution and laws of the respective states, and cannot be controlled by them." The tax therefore was unconstitutional, for the "power to tax involves the power to destroy"—which was precisely what the legislatures of Maryland and several other states had in mind with respect to the bank.

REGULATING INTERSTATE COMMERCE   Marshall's last great decision, *Gibbons v. Ogden* (1824), established national supremacy in regulating interstate commerce. In 1808 Robert Fulton and Robert Livingston, who pioneered commercial use of the steamboat, got from the New

Deck Life on the *Paragon*, 1811–1812. *The* Paragon, *"a whole floating town," was the third steamboat operated on the Hudson by Robert Fulton and Robert R. Livingston. Fulton said the* Paragon *"beats everything on the globe, for made as you and I are we cannot tell what is in the moon."*

York legislature the exclusive right to operate steamboats on the state's waters. From them in turn Aaron Ogden received exclusive right to navigation across the Hudson between New York and New Jersey. Thomas Gibbons, however, operated a coastal trade under a federal license and came into competition with Ogden. On behalf of a unanimous Court, Marshall ruled that the monopoly granted by the state conflicted with the federal Coasting Act under which Gibbons operated. Congressional power to regulate commerce, the Court said, "like all others vested in Congress, is complete in itself, may be exercised to its utmost extent, and acknowledges no limitations other than are prescribed in the constitution."

The opinion stopped just short of stating an exclusive federal power over commerce, and later cases would clarify the point that states had a concurrent jurisdiction so long as it did not come into conflict with federal action. For many years there was in fact little federal regulation, so that in striking down the monopoly created by the state Marshall had opened the way to extensive development of steamboat navigation and, soon afterward, steam railroads. Economic expansion was often consonant with judicial nationalism.

NATIONALIST DIPLOMACY

THE NORTHWEST   In foreign affairs, too, nationalism continued to be an effective force. Within two years after final approval of Adams's Transcontinental Treaty, the secretary of state was able to draw another important transcontinental line. In 1819 Spain had abandoned its claim to the Oregon Country above the 42nd parallel. Russia, however, had claims along the Pacific coast as well. In 1741 Vitus Bering, in the employ of Russia, had explored the strait that now bears his name, and in 1799 the Russian-American Company had been formed to exploit the resources of Alaska. In 1821 the Russian czar claimed the Pacific coast as far south as 51°, which in the American view lay within the Oregon Country.

In 1823 Secretary of State Adams contested "the right of Russia to any territorial establishment on this continent." The American government, he informed the Russian minister, assumed the principle "that the American continents are no longer subjects for any new European colonial establishments." His protest resulted in a treaty signed in 1824 whereby Russia, which had more pressing concerns in Europe, accepted the line of 54°40′ as the southern boundary of its claim. In 1825 a similar agreement between Russia and Britain gave the Oregon Country clearly defined boundaries, although it was still subject to joint occupation by the United States and Great Britain under their agreement of 1818. In 1827 both countries agreed to extend indefinitely the provision for joint occupation, subject to termination by either power.

LATIN AMERICA   Adams's disapproval of further colonization also had clear implications for Latin America. One consequence of the Napoleonic wars and French occupation of Spain and Portugal had been a series of wars of liberation in Latin America. Within little more than a decade after the flag of rebellion was first raised in 1811, Spain had lost almost its entire empire in the Americas. All that was left were the islands of Cuba, Puerto Rico, and Santo Domingo. The only other European possessions in the Americas, 330 years after Columbus, were Russian Alaska, British Canada, British Honduras, and Dutch, French, and British Guiana.

That Spain could not regain her empire seems clear enough in retrospect. The British navy would not permit it, because Britain's trade with the area was too important. For a time, however, European victors over Napoleon sought to restore "legitimacy" everywhere. The great European peace conference, the Congress of Vienna (1814–1815), returned that continent, as nearly as possible, to its status before the French Revolution and set out to make the world safe for monarchy. To that end the major powers (Great Britain, Prussia, Russia, and Austria) set up the Quadruple Alliance (it became the Quintuple Alliance after France entered in 1818) to police the European continent. In 1821 the Alliance, with Britain dissenting, authorized Austria to put down liberal movements in Italy. The British government was no champion of liberal revolution, but neither did it feel impelled to police the entire continent. In 1822, when the allies met in the Congress of Verona, they authorized France to suppress the constitutionalist movement in Spain and to restore the monarchy.

THE MONROE DOCTRINE   In 1823 French troops crossed the Spanish border, put down the rebels, and restored the king to absolute authority. Rumors began to circulate that France would also try to restore the Spanish king's power over Spain's American empire. Monroe and Secretary of War Calhoun were alarmed at the possibility, although John Quincy Adams took the more realistic view that such action was unlikely. After breaking with the Quintuple Alliance, British foreign minister George Canning sought to reach an understanding with the American minister to London that the two countries would jointly undertake to forestall action by the Quadruple Alliance against Latin America.

Monroe at first agreed, with the support of his sage advisers Jefferson and Madison. Adams, however, urged upon Monroe and the cabinet the independent course of proclaiming a unilateral policy against the restoration of Spain's colonies. "It would be more candid," Adams said, "as well as more dignified, to avow our principles explicitly to Russia and France, than to come in as a cock-boat in the wake of the British man-of-war." Adams knew that the British navy would stop any action by the Quadruple Alliance in Latin America, and he suspected that the Alliance had no real intention to intervene anyway. The British, moreover, wanted the United States to agree not to acquire any more Spanish territory, including Cuba, Texas, or California, and Adams preferred to avoid such a commitment.

Monroe incorporated the substance of Adams's views in his annual message to Congress in December 1823. The Monroe Doctrine, as it was later called, comprised four major points: (1) that "the American continents . . . are henceforth not to be considered as subjects for future colonization by any European powers"; (2) the political system of European powers was different from that of the United States, which would "consider any attempt on their part to extend their system to any portion of this hemisphere as dangerous to our peace and safety"; (3) the United States would not interfere with existing European colonies; and (4) the United States would keep out of the internal affairs of European nations and their wars.

At the time the statement drew little attention either in the United States or abroad. The Monroe Doctrine, not even so called until 1852, became one of the cherished principles of American foreign policy, but for the time being it slipped into obscurity for want of any occasion to invoke it. In spite of Adams's affirmation, the United States came in as a cockboat in the wake of the British man-of-war after all, for the effectiveness of the doctrine depended on British naval supremacy. The doctrine had no standing in international law. It was merely a statement of intent by an American president to the Congress, and did not even draw enough interest at the time for European powers to renounce it.

ONE-PARTY POLITICS

Almost from the start of Monroe's second term the jockeying for the presidential succession had begun. Three members of Monroe's cabinet were active candidates: Secretary of War John Calhoun, Secretary of the Treasury William Crawford, and Secretary of State John Quincy Adams. Henry Clay, longtime Speaker of the House, hungered and thirsted after the office. And on the fringes of the Washington scene a new force appeared in the person of Andrew Jackson, the scourge of the British, Spaniards, Creeks, and Seminoles, the epitome of what every frontiersman admired, who was elected a senator from Tennessee in 1823. All were Republicans, for again no Federalist stood a chance, but they were competing in a new political world, complicated by the crosscurrents of nationalism and sectionalism. With only one party there was in effect no party, for there existed no generally accepted method for choosing a "regular" candidate.

PRESIDENTIAL NOMINATIONS   Selection by congressional caucus, already under attack in 1816, had disappeared in the wave of unanimity that reelected Monroe in 1820 without the formality of a nomination. The friends of Crawford sought in vain to breathe life back into "King Caucus," but only a minority of congressmen appeared in answer to the call. They duly named Crawford for president, but the endorsement was so weak as to be more a handicap than an advantage. Crawford was

The presidential "race" of 1824, with Clay and Jackson in the foreground, Adams at far right.

in fact the logical successor to the Virginia dynasty, a native of the state though a resident of Georgia. He had flirted with nationalism, but swung back to states' rights and strict construction, and assumed leadership of a faction, called the Radicals, that included Old Republicans and those who distrusted the nationalism of Adams and Calhoun. Crawford's candidacy floundered from the beginning, for the candidate had been stricken in 1823 by some unknown disease that left him half-paralyzed and half-blind. His friends protested that he would soon be well, but he never did fully recover.

Long before the rump caucus met in early 1824, indeed for two years before, the country had broken out in a rash of presidential endorsements by legislatures and public meetings. In 1822 the Tennessee legislature named Andrew Jackson. In 1824 a mass meeting of Pennsylvanians added their endorsement. Jackson, who had previously kept silent, responded that while the presidency should not be sought, it could not with propriety be declined. The same meeting named Calhoun for vicepresident, and Calhoun accepted. The youngest of the candidates, he was content to take second place and bide his time. Meanwhile, the

Kentucky legislature had named its favorite son, Henry Clay, in 1822. The Massachusetts legislature named Adams in 1824.

Of the four candidates, only two had clearly defined programs, and the outcome was an early lesson in the danger of being committed on the issues too soon. Crawford's friends emphasized his devotion to the "principles of 1798," states' rights and strict construction. Clay, on the contrary, took his stand for the "American System": he favored the national bank, the protective tariff, and a national program of internal improvements to bind the country together and build its economy. Adams was close to Clay, openly dedicated to internal improvements but less strongly committed to the tariff. Jackson, where issues were concerned, remained an enigma and carefully avoided commitment. His managers hoped that, by being all things to all men, Jackson could capitalize on his popularity as the hero of New Orleans.

THE "CORRUPT BARGAIN" The outcome turned on personalities and sectional allegiance more than on issues. Adams, the only northern candidate, carried New England, the former bastion of Federalism, and most of New York's electoral votes. Clay took Kentucky, Ohio, and Missouri. Crawford carried Virginia, Georgia, and Delaware. Jackson swept the Southeast, plus Illinois and Indiana, and, with Calhoun's support, the Carolinas, Pennsylvania, Maryland, and New Jersey. All candidates got scattered votes elsewhere. In New York, where Clay was strong, his supporters were outmaneuvered by the Adams forces in the legislature, which still chose the presidential electors.

The result was inconclusive in both the electoral vote and the popular vote, wherever the state legislature permitted the choice of electors by the people. In the electoral college Jackson had 99 votes, Adams 84, Crawford 41, Clay 37. In the popular vote the trend ran about the same: Jackson 154,000, Adams 109,000, Crawford 47,000, and Clay 47,000. Whatever might have been said about the outcome, one thing seemed apparent. It was a defeat for Clay's American System: New England and New York opposed him on internal improvements, the South and Southwest on the protective tariff. Sectionalism had defeated the national program.

Yet the advocate of the American System now assumed the role of president-maker, as the election was thrown into the House of Representatives, where Speaker Clay's influence was decisive. Clay had little trouble in choosing, since he regarded Jackson as unfit for the office. "I cannot believe," he muttered, "that killing 2,500 Englishmen at New Orleans qualifies for the various, difficult and complicated duties of the Chief Magistracy." He eventually threw his support to Adams. The final vote in the House, which was by state, carried Adams to victory with thirteen votes to Jackson's seven and Crawford's four.

It was a costly victory, for the result united Adams's foes and crippled his administration before it got under way. There is no evidence that Adams entered into any bargain with Clay to win his support. Still the charge was made and widely believed after Adams made Clay his secretary of state, and thus put him in the office from which three successive presidents had risen. Adams's Puritan conscience could never quite overcome a sense of guilt at the maneuverings that were necessary to gain his election, but a "corrupt bargain" was too much out of character for credence. Yet credence it had with a large number of people, and on that cry a campaign to elect Jackson next time was launched almost immediately after the 1824 decision. The Crawford people, including Martin Van Buren, the "Little Magician" of New York politics, soon moved into the Jackson camp. So too did the new vice-president, John Calhoun of South Carolina, who ran on both the Adams and the Jackson tickets but favored the general from Tennessee.

JOHN QUINCY ADAMS'S PRESIDENCY   John Quincy Adams was one of the ablest men, hardest workers, and finest intellects ever to enter the White House. Yet he lacked the common touch and the politician's gift for maneuver. He refused to play the game of patronage, arguing that it would be dishonorable to dismiss "able and faithful political opponents to provide for my own partisans." In four years he removed only twelve officeholders. His first annual message to Congress included a grandiose blueprint for national development, set forth in such a blunt way that it became a disaster of political ineptitude.

In the boldness and magnitude of its conception, the Adams plan outdid both Hamilton and Clay. The central government, the president proposed, should promote internal improvements, set up a national university, finance scientific explorations, build astronomical observatories ("lighthouses of the skies"), reform the patent laws, and create a new Department of the Interior. In general terms he proposed "laws promoting the improvement of the agriculture, commerce, and manufactures, the cultivation and encouragement of the mechanic and of the elegant arts, the advancement of literature, and the progress of the sciences, ornamental and profound."

To refrain from using broad federal powers "would be treachery to the most sacred of trusts." Officers of the government, he said, should not "fold up our arms and proclaim to the world that we are palsied by the will of our constituents." Whatever grandeur of conception the message to Congress had, it was obscured by an unhappy choice of language. For a minority president to demean the sovereignty of the voter was tactless enough. For the son of John Adams to cite the example "of the nations of Europe and of their rulers" was downright suicidal. At one fell swoop he had revived all the Republican suspicions of the

John Quincy Adams, a president of great intellect but without the common touch.

Adamses. To the aging Jefferson his message seemed like Federalism run riot, looking to "a single and splendid government of an aristocracy, founded on banking institutions, and moneyed incorporation under the guise and cloak of . . . manufactures, commerce, and navigation, riding and ruling over the plundered ploughman and beggared yeomanry." Jefferson did not see, though, that Adams's presidential message served to define a new party system. The minority who cast their lot with Adams and Clay were turning into National-Republicans; the opposition, the growing party of Jacksonians, were the Democratic-Republicans, who would eventually drop the name Republican and become Democrats.

Adams's headstrong plunge into nationalism and his refusal to play the game of politics condemned his administration to utter frustration. Congress ignored his domestic proposals, and in foreign affairs the triumphs that he had scored as secretary of state had no sequels. Before the year 1826 ended, Adams faced a showdown with the state of Georgia and meekly backed off. The affair began in 1825 when a federal Indian commissioner signed the fraudulent Treaty of Indian Springs with a group of Creek chieftains by which the Creeks lost 4.7 million acres in Georgia. Adams at first signed the treaty, but on further inquiry discovered that the Indian negotiators did not represent the prevailing sentiment among the Creeks. He thereupon withdrew it and worked out the somewhat less stringent Treaty of Washington in 1826. The Georgia legislature denounced this annulment of the previous treaty as invalid and, by some obscure reasoning, called it a violation of states' rights. The governor mobilized the Georgia militia and notified Adams that the state would repel with force any attempt to void the earlier treaty. At this the administration simply abandoned the Creeks to their fate. The Cherokees were next on the agenda, but by the time Georgia got around to them, there was a president who supported the land grabbers.

The climactic effort to discredit Adams came on the tariff issue. The Panic of 1819 had provoked calls for a higher tariff in 1820, but the effort failed by one vote in the Senate. In 1824 the advocates of protection renewed the effort, with greater success. The Tariff of 1824 favored the Middle Atlantic and New England manufacturers with higher duties on woolens, cotton, iron, and other finished goods. Clay's Kentucky won a tariff on hemp, and a tariff on raw wool brought the wool-growing interests to the support of the measure. Additional revenues were provided by duties on sugar, molasses, coffee, and salt. The tariff on raw wool was in obvious conflict with that on manufactured woolens, but the two groups got together and reached an agreement.

At this point Jackson's supporters saw a chance to advance their candidate through an awkward scheme hatched by John Calhoun. The plan was to present a bill with such outrageously high tariffs on raw materials that the manufacturers of the East would join the commercial interests there, and, with the votes of the agricultural South and Southwest, defeat the measure. In the process Jackson men in the Northeast could take credit for supporting the tariff, and Jackson men, wherever it fitted their interests, could take credit for opposing it—while Jackson himself remained in the background. Virginia's John Randolph saw through the ruse. The bill, he asserted, "referred to manufactures of no sort or kind, but the manufacture of a President of the United States."

The complicated scheme helped elect Jackson, but in the process Calhoun was hoist on his own petard. The high tariffs ended up becoming law. Calhoun calculated neither upon the defection of Van Buren, who supported a crucial amendment to satisfy the woolens manufacturers, nor upon the growing strength of manufacturing interests in New England. Daniel Webster, now a senator from Massachusetts, explained that he was ready to deny all he had said against the tariff because New England had built up her manufactures on the understanding that the protective tariff was a settled policy.

When the bill passed on May 11, 1828, it was Calhoun's turn to explain his newfound opposition to the gospel of protection, and nothing so well illustrates the flexibility of constitutional principles as the switch in positions by Webster and Calhoun. Back in South Carolina, Calhoun prepared the *South Carolina Exposition and Protest* (1828), which was issued anonymously along with a series of resolutions by the South Carolina legislature. In that document Calhoun declared that a state could nullify an act of Congress that it found unconstitutional.

JACKSON SWEEPS IN   Thus far the stage was set for the election of 1828, which might more truly be called a revolution than that of 1800. But if the issues of the day had anything to do with the election, they were hardly visible in the campaign, in which politicians on both sides reached depths of scurrilousness that had not been plumbed since 1800. Jackson was denounced as a hot-tempered and ignorant barbarian, a coconspirator with Aaron Burr, a participant in repeated duels and frontier brawls, a man whose fame rested on his reputation as a killer, a man whom Thomas Jefferson himself had pronounced unfit because of the rashness of his feelings—a remark inspired by Jackson's brief tenure in the Senate in 1797. In addition to that, his enemies dredged up the old story that Jackson had lived in adultery with his wife Rachel before they had been legally married; in fact they had lived together for two years in the mistaken belief that her divorce from a former husband was final. Rachel's worry over this humiliation and her probable reception in Washington may have contributed to an illness from which she died before her husband took office, and it was one thing for which Jackson could never forgive his enemies.

The Jacksonians, however, got in their licks against Adams, condemning him as a man who had lived his adult life on the public treasury, who had been corrupted by foreigners in the courts of Europe, and who had allegedly delivered up an American girl to serve the lust of Czar Alexander I while serving as minister to Russia. They called him a gambler and a spendthrift for having bought a billiard table and a chess set for the White House, and a puritanical hypocrite for despising the common people and warning Congress to ignore the will of its constituents. He had finally reached the presidency, the Jacksonians claimed, by a corrupt bargain with Henry Clay.

In the campaign of 1828 Jackson held most of the advantages. As a military hero he had some claim on patriotism. As a son of the West he was almost unbeatable there. As a planter and slaveholder he had the trust of southern planters. Debtors and local bankers who hated the national bank turned to Jackson. In addition, his vagueness on the issues protected him from attack by various interest groups. Not least of all, Jackson benefited from a spirit of democracy in which the common folk were no longer satisfied to look to their betters for leadership, as they had done in the lost world of Thomas Jefferson. It had become politically fatal to be labeled an aristocrat. Jackson's coalition now included even a seasoning of young Federalists eager to shed the stigma of aristocracy and get on in the world.

Jackson is to be President, and you will be HANGED. *This anti-Jackson cartoon, published during the 1828 campaign, shows him as a frontier ruffian.*

Since the Revolution and especially since 1800, white male suffrage had been gaining ground. The traditional story has been that a surge of Jacksonian Democracy came out of the West like a great wave, supported mainly by small farmers, leading the way for the East. But there were other forces working in the older states toward a wider franchise: the revolutionary doctrine of equality, and the feeling on the parts of the workers, artisans, and small merchants of the towns, as well as small farmers and landed gentry, that a democratic ballot provided a means to combat the rising commercial and manufacturing interests. From the beginning Pennsylvania had opened the ballot box to all adult males who paid taxes; by 1790 Georgia and New Hampshire had similar arrangements. Vermont, in 1791, became the first state with universal manhood suffrage, having first adopted it in 1777. Kentucky, admitted in 1792, became the second. Tennessee (1796) had only a light taxpaying qualification. New Jersey in 1807, and Maryland and South Carolina in 1810, abolished property and taxpaying requirements, and the new states of the West after 1815 came in with either white manhood suffrage or a low taxpaying requirement. Connecticut (1818), Massachusetts (1821), and New York (1821) all abolished their property requirements.

Along with the broadening of the suffrage went a liberalization of other features of government. Representation was reapportioned more nearly in line with population. An increasing number of officials, even judges, were named by popular vote. Final disestablishment of the Congregational church in New England came in Vermont (1807), New Hampshire (1817), Connecticut (1818), Maine (1820), and Massachusetts (1834). In 1824 six state legislatures still chose the presidential electors. By 1828 the popular vote prevailed in all but South Carolina and Delaware, and by 1832 in all but South Carolina.

The spread of the suffrage brought a new type of politician to the fore: the man who had special appeal to the masses or knew how to organize the people for political purposes, and who became a vocal advocate of the people's right to rule. Jackson fitted the ideal of this new political world, a leader sprung from the people rather than an aristocratic leader of the people, a frontiersman of humble origin who had scrambled up by will and tenacity. A defender of the liberties of the people, a man who made no pretense of profound learning, and who frequently let his emotions speak for him, Jackson suited the turbulent political temper of the time. "Adams can write," went one of the campaign slogans, "Jackson can fight." He could write too, but he once said that he had no respect for a man who could think of only one way to spell a word.

When the 1828 returns came in, Jackson won by a comfortable mar-

Jackson Forever!

The Hero of Two Wars and of Orleans!

The Man of the People!

HE WHO COULD NOT BARTER NOR BARGAIN FOR THE

PRESIDENCY!

Who, although "*A Military Chieftain*," valued the purity of Elections and of the Electors, **MORE** than the Office of **PRESIDENT** itself! Although the greatest in the gift of his countrymen, and the highest in point of dignity of any in the world,

BECAUSE

It should be derived from the

PEOPLE!

No Gag Laws! No Black Cockades! No Reign of Terror! No Standing Army or Navy Officers, when under the pay of Government, to browbeat, or

KNOCK DOWN

Old Revolutionary Characters, or our Representatives while in the discharge of their duty. To the Polls then, and vote for those who will support

OLD HICKORY

AND THE ELECTORAL LAW.

This 1828 handbill identifies Jackson, "The Man of the People," with the democratic impulse of the time.

ELECTION OF 1828

MAINE NR-8 DR-1
VT. 7
N.H. 8
MASS. 15
N.Y. DR-20 NR-16
R.I. 4
CONN. 8
MICHIGAN TERRITORY
PENN. 28
N.J. 8
OHIO 16
DEL. 3
ILL. 3 IND. 5
MD. NR-6 DR-5
VA. 24
MO. 3
KY. 14
N.C. 15
ARK. TERR.
TENN. 11
S.C. 11
MISS. 3 ALA. 5 GA. 9
LA. 5
FLORIDA TERRITORY

		Electoral vote	Popular vote
	A. Jackson (Democratic-Republican)	178	647,000
	J. Q. Adams (National-Republican)	83	509,000

gin. The electoral vote was 178 to 83, and the popular vote was about 647,000 to 509,000 (the figures vary). Adams won all of New England, except for one of Maine's nine electoral votes, sixteen of the thirty-six from New York, and six of the eleven from Maryland. All the rest belonged to Jackson.

FURTHER READING

The standard overview of the Era of Good Feelings remains George Dangerfield's *The Awakening of American Nationalism, 1815–1828* (1965),° but his *The Era of Good Feelings* (1952) is an elegant synthesis. The gathering sense of a national spirit, hindered by an equally growing sectionalism, can be traced in Daniel J. Boorstin's *The Americans: The Nationalist Experience* (1965).° William H. Pease and

°These books are available in paperback editions.

Jane H. Pease's *The Web of Progress* (1985) shows the emerging sectionalism through a look at two cities, Boston, Massachusetts, and Charleston, South Carolina.

For discussions of the American System, see Bray Hammond's *Banks and Politics in America from the Revolution to the Civil War* (1957) and George R. Taylor's *The Transportation Revolution, 1815–1860* (1951). For an overview of all the economic trends of the period, see Douglas C. North's *The Economic Growth of the United States, 1790–1860* (1961).°

The political temper of the times is treated in biographical studies of principal figures: Harry Ammon's *James Monroe: The Quest for National Identity* (1971), Clement Eaton's *Henry Clay and the Art of American Politics* (1957), Samuel F. Bemis's *John Quincy Adams and the Union* (1956), Richard N. Current's *John C. Calhoun* (1963), and Chase C. Mooney's *William H. Crawford, 1772–1834* (1974).

On diplomatic relations during James Monroe's presidency, see Williams Earl Weeks's *John Quincy Adams and American Global Empire* (1992). For relations after 1812, see Ernest R. May's *The Making of the Monroe Doctrine* (1975) and Dexter Perkins's *A History of the Monroe Doctrine* (1955).

Background on Andrew Jackson can be obtained from works cited in Chapter 11. The campaign that brought Jackson to the White House is analyzed in Robert V. Remini's *The Election of Andrew Jackson* (1963).°

°These books are available in paperback editions.

PART THREE

AN EXPANSIVE NATION

The election of Andrew Jackson signaled a new era in American history. By 1828 the United States was no longer an infant nation hugging the Atlantic coast. The maturing republic now included twenty-four states and almost thirteen million people. Many Americans were on the move during the early nineteenth century. Millions of them formed a relentless migratory stream that spilled over the Appalachian mountains, spanned the Mississippi River, and in the 1840s, reached the Pacific Ocean. Wagons, canals, flatboats, steamboats, and eventually railroads helped expedite the westward migration.

The feverish expansion of the United States into new western territories brought Americans into conflict with Native Americans, Mexicans, and the British. Only a few people, however, expressed moral reservations about displacing others. Most Americans believed it was the "manifest destiny" of the United States to spread across the entire continent—at whatever cost and at whomever's expense. Americans generally believed that they enjoyed the blessing of Providence in their efforts to consolidate the entire continent under their control.

While most Americans during the Jacksonian era continued to earn their living from the soil, textile mills and manufacturing plants began to dot the landscape and transform the nature of work and the pace of life. By mid-century the United States was emerging as one of the world's major industrial powers. In addition, the lure of cheap land and plentiful jobs, as well as the promise of political equality and religious freedom, attracted hundreds of thousands of immigrants from Europe. These newcomers, mostly from Germany and Ireland, faced ethnic prejudices, religious persecution, and language barriers that made assimilation into American culture all the more difficult.

All these developments gave to American life in the second quarter of the nineteenth century its dynamic and fluid quality. The United States, said the philosopher-poet Ralph Waldo Emerson, was "a country of beginnings, of projects, of designs, of expectations." A restless optimism seemed to characterize the period. People of lowly social status who heretofore had accepted their lot in life now strove to climb the social ladder and enter the political arena. The patrician democracy espoused by Jefferson and Madison gave way to the *frontier democracy promoted by the Jacksonians. Americans were no longer content to be governed by a small, benevolent aristocracy of talent and wealth. They began to demand—and obtain—government of, by, and for the people.*

The fertile economic environment during the antebellum era helped foster the egalitarian idea that individuals (except African Americans, Native Americans, and women) should have an equal opportunity to better themselves and should be granted political rights and privileges. In America, observed a journalist in 1844, "One has as good a chance as another according to his talents, prudence, and personal exertions."

The exuberant individualism embodied in such mythic expressions of economic equality and political democracy spilled over into the cultural arena during the Jacksonian era. The so-called Romantic movement applied democratic ideals to philosophy, religion, literature, and the fine arts. In New England, Ralph Waldo Emerson and Henry David Thoreau joined other Transcendentalists in espousing a radical individualism. Other reformers were motivated more by a sense of spiritual mission than democratic individualism. In striving to enhance personal morality and the general welfare, mostly middle-class reformers sought to introduce public-supported schools, abolish slavery, promote temperance, and improve the lot of the disabled, insane, and imprisoned. Their efforts helped ameliorate some of the problems created by the frenetic pace of economic growth and territorial expansion. But the reformers made little headway against slavery. It would take a brutal civil war to dislodge America's "peculiar institution."

11 ✺

THE JACKSONIAN IMPULSE

SETTING THE STAGE

The election of Andrew Jackson initiated a new era in American politics and social development. He was the first president not to come from a prominent colonial family. As a self-made soldier-politician-land speculator from the backcountry, he symbolized a sea change in the social temper. The nation he prepared to govern was vastly different from that led by Washington and Jefferson. In 1828 the United States boasted twenty-four states and nearly 13 million people, many of them recent arrivals from Germany and Ireland. An incredible surge in foreign demand for cotton and other goods, along with British investment in American enterprises, helped fuel a revolution in transportation and an economic boom. Textile factories sprouted like mushrooms across the New England countryside, their ravenous spinning looms fed by cotton grown in the newly cultivated lands of Alabama and Mississippi. This fluid new economic environment fostered a mad scramble for material gain and political advantage. People of all ranks and backgrounds engaged in a frenzied effort to acquire wealth and thereby gain social status and prestige. "The desire to grow suddenly rich has seized on all classes," exclaimed a character in one of James Fenimore Cooper's novels.

The Jacksonians sought to democratize economic opportunity and political participation. As Jackson frequently declared, the majority, the "great body of the people," would genuinely rule. Yet to call the Jacksonian era the "age of the common man," as many historians have done, is misleading. While political participation increased during the Jacksonian era, most of the common folk remained *common* folk. The period never produced true economic and social equality. Power and privilege, for the most part, remained in the hands of an "uncommon" elite. Jacksonians in power proved to be as opportunistic and manipulative as the patricians they displaced. And they never embraced the principle of material equality. "Distinctions in society will always exist under every just government," Andrew Jackson observed. "Equality of talents, or education, or of wealth cannot be produced by human institutions." He and other Jacksonians wanted every American to have an equal chance to compete in the economic marketplace and political arena, but they never sanctioned equality of results. "True republicanism," one commentator declared, "requires that every man shall have an equal chance—that every man shall be free to become as unequal as he can." But in the afterglow of Jackson's election victory, few observers troubled with such distinctions. It was time to celebrate the commoner's ascension to the presidency.

INAUGURATION   Inauguration day, March 4, 1829, was balmy after a bitterly cold winter. For days before, visitors had been crowding the streets and rooming houses of Washington in hope of seeing the people's hero take office. When Jackson, a sixty-one-year-old widower, emerged from his lodgings, dressed in black out of respect to his late wife Rachel, a great crowd filled both the east and west slopes of Capitol Hill. After Chief Justice Marshall administered the oath, the new president, plagued by a persistent cough and severe headaches, delivered his inaugural address in a voice so low that few in the crowd of 15,000 spectators could hear it. It mattered little, for Jackson's advisers had eliminated anything that might give offense. On the major issues of the tariff, internal improvements, and the Bank of the United States, Jackson remained vague. Only a few points foreshadowed policies that he would pursue: he favored retirement of the national debt, a proper regard for states' rights, a "just" policy toward Indians, and rotation in federal offices, which he pronounced "a leading principle in the republican creed"—a principle his enemies would dub the "spoils system."

To that point all proceeded with dignity. Francis Scott Key, who witnessed the spectacle, declared: "It is beautiful, it is sublime!" After his speech Jackson mounted his horse and rode to the White House, where a reception was scheduled for all who chose to come. The boisterous party that followed evoked the climate of turmoil that seemed always to surround Jackson. The revelers pushed into the White House, surged through the rooms, jostled the waiters, broke dishes, leaped onto the furniture—all in an effort to shake the president's hand or at least get a glimpse of him. Surrounded by a group of his friends, the president soon escaped through a side door and went back to his lodgings for the night. Somebody then had the presence of mind to haul tubs of punch out on the White House lawn, where the unruly crowd followed. To one observer, "the reign of 'King Mob' seemed triumphant."

As a fighter, horse trader, land speculator, and frontier lawyer,

Andrew Jackson was a symbol of the rugged new Western temperament. A fellow law student described him as a "most roaring, rollicking,
game-cocking, horse-racing, card-playing, mischievous fellow." His
father had died before he was born and his mother scratched out a
meager living as a housekeeper. Jackson grew to be proud, gritty, short-
tempered, and a good hater. During the Revolution, when he was a
young boy, his mother died, two of his brothers were killed by redcoats,
and the young Jackson suffered a scar that he carried with him for life
from a British officer's saber. He also carried with him the conviction
that it was not enough for a man to be right; he had to be tough as well,
a quality that inspired his soldiers to nickname him "Old Hickory."
During a duel with a man reputed to be the best shot in Tennessee,
Jackson nevertheless let his opponent fire first. For his gallantry Jackson received a bullet wedged next to his heart. But he straightened
himself, patiently took aim, and killed his aghast foe. "I should have hit
him," Jackson claimed, "if he had shot me through the brain." Daniel
Webster, one of Jackson's most ardent opponents, once observed that
the Tennessean "does what he thinks is right, and does it with all his
might."

APPOINTMENTS AND POLITICAL RIVALRIES   To the office seekers who
made up much of the restless crowd at the inaugural, Jackson held out
high expectations that he planned to "turn the rascals out" and let the
people rule. So it seemed when he set forth a reasoned defense of

All Creation Going to the White House. *The scene following Jackson's
inauguration as president, according to satirist Robert Cruikshank.*

Cartoon depicting Jackson as a demon dangling political plums before office seekers.

rotation in office. The duties of government were simple, he said. Democratic principles supported the idea that a man should serve a term in government, then return to the status of private citizen, for officeholders who stayed too long grew corrupt. And democracy, he argued, "is promoted by party appointments by newly elected officials."

Jackson hardly foresaw how these principles would work out in practice, and it would be misleading to link him too closely with the "spoils system," which took its name from an 1832 partisan assertion by Democratic Senator William L. Marcy of New York: "To the victor belong the spoils." Jackson in fact behaved with great moderation compared to the politicians of New York and Pennsylvania, where the spoils of office nourished extensive political machines. And a number of his successors made many more partisan appointments. During his first year in office Jackson replaced only about 9 percent of the appointed officials in the federal government, and during his entire term fewer than 20 percent.

Jackson relied very little on his cabinet, which therefore had little influence as an advisory group. More powerful was a coterie of men who had the president's ear and were soon dubbed his "Kitchen Cabinet." Among these, only Secretary of State Martin Van Buren headed a department, but most of the others were on the public payroll in some capacity. The most influential members seem to have been Amos Kendall of Kentucky, a former partisan of Clay; Duff Green, editor of the *United States Telegraph,* which had supported both Calhoun and Jackson; and Frank Blair, Sr., editor of the administration newspaper, the *Globe.*

Jackson's administration was from the outset a house divided between the partisans of Van Buren of New York and those of Vice-President Calhoun of South Carolina. Much of the political history of the next few years would turn upon the rivalry of the two, as each man jockeyed for position as Jackson's successor. It soon became clear that Van Buren held most of the advantages, foremost among them his skill at timing and tactics. As John Randolph put it, Van Buren always "rowed to his objective with muffled oars." Jackson, new to political administration, leaned heavily on him for advice and for help in soothing the ruffled feathers of rejected office seekers. Van Buren had perhaps more skill at maneuvering than Calhoun, and certainly more freedom to maneuver, because his home base of New York was more secure politically than Calhoun's base in South Carolina.

But Calhoun, a man of towering intellect, humorless outlook, and apostolic zeal, could not be taken lightly. "There is no *relaxation* with him," a frazzled friend once wrote. A visitor remarked after a three-hour discussion with the bushy-browed Calhoun, "I hate a man who makes

John C. Calhoun.

me think so much . . . and I hate a man who makes me feel my own inferiority." Perhaps Henry Clay described Calhoun best: "tall, careworn, with furrowed brow, haggard and intensely gazing, looking as if he were dissecting the last abstraction which sprung from a metaphysician's brain." Since returning from Washington to his South Carolina plantation in 1825, Calhoun had nurtured his crops and his ardent love for his native region. Now as vice-president he was determined to defend southern interests against the worrisome advance of northern industrialism and abolitionism.

THE EATON AFFAIR   In his battle with Calhoun over political power, Van Buren had luck on his side. Fate handed him a trump card: the succulent scandal of the Peggy Eaton affair. Peggy Eaton was a vivacious widow whose husband had supposedly committed suicide upon learning of her affair with Tennessee senator John Eaton. Her marriage to Eaton, three months before he became secretary of war, had scarcely made a virtuous woman of her in the eye of the proper ladies of Washington. Floride Calhoun, the vice-president's wife, pointedly snubbed her, and other cabinet wives followed suit.

Peggy's plight reminded Jackson of the gossip that had pursued his own Rachel, and he pronounced Peggy "chaste as a virgin." To a friend he wrote: "I did not come here to make a Cabinet for the Ladies of this place, but for the Nation." His cabinet members, however, were unable to cure their wives of what Van Buren dubbed "the Eaton Malaria." Van Buren, though, was a widower, and therefore free to lavish on poor Peggy all the attention that Jackson thought was her due. The amused John Quincy Adams looked on from afar and noted in his diary that Van Buren had become the leader of the party of the frail sisterhood. Mrs. Eaton herself finally wilted under the chill and withdrew from society. The outraged Jackson came to link Calhoun with what he called a conspiracy against her and drew even closer to Van Buren.

INTERNAL IMPROVEMENTS   While capital society weathered the chilly winter of 1829–1830, Van Buren prepared some additional blows to Calhoun. It was easy to bring Jackson into opposition to internal improvements and thus to federal programs with which Calhoun had long been identified. Jackson did not oppose road building per se, but he had the same constitutional scruples as Madison and Monroe about federal aid to local projects. In 1830 the Maysville Road Bill, passed by Congress, offered Jackson a happy chance for a dual thrust at both Calhoun and Clay. The bill authorized the government to buy stock in a road from Maysville to Clay's hometown of Lexington. The road lay entirely within the state of Kentucky, and though part of a larger scheme to link up with the National Road via Cincinnati, it could be

King Andrew the First.
Opponents considered Jackson's Maysville veto an abuse of power. This cartoon shows King Andrew Jackson trampling on the Constitution, internal improvements, and the U.S. bank.

viewed as a purely local undertaking. On that ground Jackson vetoed the bill as unconstitutional, to widespread popular acclaim.

Yet while Jackson continued to oppose federal aid to local projects, he supported interstate projects such as the National Road, as well as road building in the territories, and river and harbor bills, the "pork barrels" from which every congressman tried to pluck a morsel for his district. Even so, Jackson's attitude toward the Maysville Road set an important precedent, on the eve of the railroad age, for limiting federal initiative in internal improvements. Railroads would be built altogether by state and private capital at least until 1850.

NULLIFICATION

CALHOUN'S THEORY   There is a fine irony to Calhoun's plight in the Jackson administration, for Calhoun was now in midpassage from his early phase as a War Hawk nationalist to his later phase as a states'-rights sectionalist—and open to thrusts on both flanks. Conditions in his home state had brought on this change. Suffering from agricultural depression, South Carolina lost almost 70,000 people to emigration during the 1820s and was fated to lose nearly twice that number in the 1830s. Most South Carolinians blamed the protective tariff, which tended to raise the price of manufactured goods and, insofar as it discouraged the sale of foreign goods in the United States, reduced the ability of British and French traders to acquire the American money and bills of exchange with which to buy American cotton. This worsened problems of low cotton prices and exhausted lands. Compounding the South Carolinians' malaise was a growing reaction against the North's criticism of slavery. Hardly had the country emerged from the Missouri controversy when Charleston was thrown into panic by the Denmark Vesey slave insurrection of 1822, though the Vesey plot was put down before it got very far.

The unexpected passage of the Tariff of 1828 (called the "Tariff of Abominations" by its critics) left Calhoun no choice but to join those in opposition or give up his home base. Calhoun's *South Carolina Exposition and Protest* (1828), written in opposition to that tariff, actually had been an effort to check the most extreme states'-rights advocates with a fine-spun theory in which nullification stopped short of secession from the Union. The unsigned statement accompanied resolutions of the South Carolina legislature protesting the tariff and urging its repeal. Calhoun, it was clear, had not entirely abandoned his earlier nationalism. He wanted to preserve the Union by protecting the minority rights that the agricultural and slaveholding South claimed. The fine balance he struck between states' rights and central authority was actually not as far removed from Jackson's own philosophy as it might seem, but growing tension between the two men would complicate the issue. Jackson, in addition, was determined to draw the line at any defiance of federal law.

Nor would Calhoun's theory permit any state to take up such defiance lightly. The procedure of nullification, whereby a state could in effect repeal a federal law, would follow that by which the original thirteen states had ratified the Constitution. A special state convention, like the ratifying conventions embodying the sovereign power of the people, could declare a federal law null and void because it violated the Constitution, the original compact among the states. One of two outcomes would then be possible. Either the federal government would have to abandon the law, or it would have to get a constitutional amendment removing all doubt as to its validity. The immediate issue was the constitutionality of a tariff designed mainly to protect American industries against foreign competition. The South Carolinians argued that the Constitution authorized tariffs for revenue only.

THE WEBSTER-HAYNE DEBATE   South Carolina leaders had proclaimed their dislike for the tariff, but had postponed any action against its enforcement, awaiting with hope the election of 1828 in which antitariff Calhoun was the Jacksonian candidate for vice-president. There the issue stood until 1830, when the great Hayne-Webster debate sharpened the lines between states' rights and the Union.

The eloquent Massachusetts senator Daniel Webster stands to rebut the argument for nullification in the Webster-Hayne debate.

The immediate occasion for the debate, however, was the question of public lands. The federal government still owned immense tracts of unsettled land, and the issue of their fate elbowed its way onto center stage of sectional debate. Late in 1829 Senator Samuel A. Foot of Connecticut, an otherwise obscure figure, proposed that the federal government restrict land sales in the West. When the Foot Resolution came before the Senate in 1830, Thomas Hart Benton of Missouri denounced it as a sectional attack designed to hamstring the settlement of the West so that the East might maintain its supply of cheap factory labor. Robert Y. Hayne of South Carolina took Benton's side. Hayne saw in the issue a chance to strengthen the alliance of South and West that the vote for Jackson reflected. Perhaps by supporting a policy of cheap lands in the West, the southerners could gain western support for lower tariffs. The government, said Hayne, endangered the Union by imposing any policy that would cause a hardship on one section to the benefit of another. The use of public lands as a source of revenue to the central government would create "a fund for corruption—fatal to the sovereignty and independence of the states."

Daniel Webster of Massachusetts rose to defend the East. Possessed of a thunderous voice and a theatrical flair, Webster was widely recognized as the nation's foremost orator and lawyer. Legend had it that he could out-argue the devil, and his striking physical presence enhanced his rhetorical skills. Webster had the torso of a bull, and his huge head, with its craggy brows overhanging deep-set, lustrous black eyes, commanded attention. With the gallery hushed, Webster, attired in a buff-colored vest and dark blue coat with brass buttons, denied that the East had ever shown a restrictive policy toward the West. He then rebuked those southerners who, he said, "habitually speak of the Union in terms of indifference, or even of disparagement." Hayne had raised the false specter of "Consolidation!—That perpetual cry, both of terror and delusion—consolidation!" Federal revenue derived from land sales, Webster argued, was not a source of corruption but a source of improvement. At this point the issue of western lands vanished from sight. Webster had adroitly shifted the grounds of debate and lured Hayne into defending states' rights and upholding the doctrine of nullification instead of pursuing a coalition with the West.

Hayne took the bait. Himself an accomplished speaker, he launched into a defense of the *South Carolina Exposition,* appealed to the example of the Virginia and Kentucky Resolutions of 1798, and called attention to the Hartford Convention, in which New Englanders had taken much the same position against majority measures as South Carolina did. The Union constituted a compact of the states, he argued, and the federal government could not be the judge of its own powers, else its powers would be unlimited. Rather, the states remained free to judge when their agent had overstepped the bounds of its constitutional authority. The right of state interposition was "as full and complete as it was before the Constitution was formed."

In rebuttal to the state-compact theory, Webster defined a nationalistic view of the Constitution. From the beginning, he asserted, the American Revolution had been a crusade of the united colonies rather than of each separately. True sovereignty resided in the people as a whole, for whom both federal and state governments acted as agents in their respective spheres. If a single state could nullify a law of the general government, then the Union would be a "rope of sand," a practical absurdity. Instead the Constitution had created a Supreme Court with the final jurisdiction on all questions of constitutionality. A state could neither nullify a federal law nor secede from the Union. The practical outcome of nullification would be a confrontation leading to civil war.

Hayne may have had the better of the argument historically in advancing the state-compact theory, but the Senate galleries and much of the country at large thrilled to the eloquence of "the God-like Daniel." Webster's closing statement became an American classic, reprinted in school texts and committed to memory by schoolchild orators: "When my eyes shall be turned to behold, for the last time, the sun in heaven, may I not see him shining on the broken and dishonored fragments of a once glorious Union. . . . Let their last feeble and lingering glance, rather, behold the gorgeous ensign of the republic . . . blazing on all its ample folds, as they float over the sea and over the land . . . Liberty and Union, now and forever, one and inseparable." In the practical world of coalition politics Webster had the better of the argument, for the Union and majority rule meant more to westerners, including Jackson, than the abstractions of state sovereignty and nullification. As for the public lands, the Foot Resolution was soon defeated anyway. And whatever one might argue about the origins of the Union, its evolution would more and more validate Webster's position.

THE RIFT WITH CALHOUN   As yet, however, the enigmatic Jackson had not spoken out on the issue. Jackson, like Calhoun, was a slaveholder, albeit a westerner, and might be expected to sympathize with South Carolina, his native state. Soon all doubt was removed, at least on the point of nullification. On April 13, 1830, the Jefferson Day Dinner was held in Washington to honor the birthday of the former president. It was a party affair, but the Calhounites controlled the arrangements with an eye to advancing their own doctrine. Jackson and Van Buren were invited as a matter of course, and the two agreed that Jackson should present a toast proclaiming his opposition to nullification. When his turn came, after twenty-four toasts, many of them extolling states' rights, Jackson raised his glass, pointedly stared at Calhoun, and announced: "Our Union—It must be preserved!" (At the behest of Senator Hayne the first words were later published as "Our Federal Union.") Calhoun, who followed, trembled so that he spilled some of the amber fluid from his glass (according to Van Buren), but tried quickly to retrieve the situation with a toast to "The Union, next to our liberty most dear! May we all remember that it can only be preserved by respecting the rights of the States and distributing equally the benefit and the burden of the Union!" But Jackson had set off a bombshell that exploded the plans of the states'-righters.

Nearly a month afterward a final nail was driven into the coffin of Calhoun's presidential ambitions. On May 12, 1830, Jackson first saw a letter containing final confirmation of reports that had been reaching him of Calhoun's stand in 1818, when as secretary of war Calhoun had proposed to discipline Jackson for his Florida invasion. A tense correspondence between Jackson and Calhoun followed, and ended with a curt note from Jackson cutting it off. "Understanding you now," Jackson wrote two weeks later, "no further communication with you on this subject is necessary."

As a result of the growing rift between the two proud men, Jackson resolved to remove all Calhoun partisans from the cabinet. Before the end of the summer of 1831 the president had a new cabinet entirely loyal to him. He then named Van Buren, who had resigned from the cabinet, minister to Great Britain, and Van Buren departed for Lon-

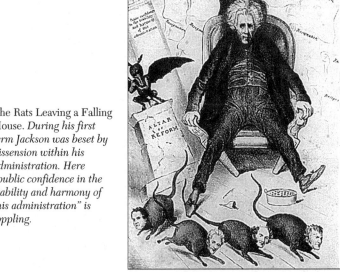

The Rats Leaving a Falling House. *During his first term Jackson was beset by dissension within his administration. Here "public confidence in the stability and harmony of this administration" is toppling.*

don. The friends of Van Buren now urged Jackson to repudiate his previous intention of serving only one term. It might be hard, they felt, to get the nomination in 1832 for the New Yorker, who had been charged with intrigues against Calhoun, and the still-popular Carolinian might yet carry off the prize.

Jackson relented and in the fall of 1831 announced his readiness for one more term, with the idea of returning Van Buren from London in time to win the presidency in 1836. But in January 1832, when the Senate reconvened, Van Buren's enemies opposed his appointment as minister, and gave Calhoun, as vice-president, a chance to reject the nomination by a tie-breaking vote. "It will kill him, sir, kill him dead," Calhoun told Senator Thomas Hart Benton. Benton disagreed: "You have broken a minister, and elected a Vice-President." So, it turned out, he had. Calhoun's vote against Van Buren provoked popular sympathy for the New Yorker, who returned from London in June and would soon be nominated to succeed Calhoun.

Now that his presidential hopes were blasted, Calhoun came forth as the public leader of the nullificationists. These South Carolinians thought that, despite Jackson's gestures, tariff rates remained too high. Jackson accepted the principle of using tariffs to protect new American industries from foreign competition. Nevertheless, he had called upon Congress in 1829 to modify duties by reducing tariffs on goods "which cannot come in competition with our own products." Late in the spring of 1830 Congress lowered duties on such consumer products as tea, coffee, salt, and molasses. That and the Maysville veto, coming at about the same time, mollified a few South Carolinians, but nullifiers regarded the two actions as "nothing but sugar plums to pacify children." By the end of 1831 Jackson was calling for further reductions to take the wind out of the nullificationists' sails, and the Tariff of 1832, pushed through by John Quincy Adams (back in Washington as a congressman), cut rates again. But rates on cottons, woolens, and iron remained high.

THE SOUTH CAROLINA ORDINANCE   In the South Carolina state elections of 1832, attention centered on the nullification issue. The nullificationists took the initiative in organization and agitation, and the Unionist party was left with a distinguished leadership but only small support, drawn chiefly from the merchants of Charleston and the small farmers of the up-country. A special session of the legislature called for the election of a state convention, which assembled at Columbia and overwhelmingly adopted an ordinance of nullification, which repudiated the tariff acts of 1828 and 1832 as unconstitutional and forbade collection of the duties in the state after February 1, 1833. The reassembled legislature then provided that any citizen whose property was seized by federal authorities for failure to pay the duty could get a state court order to recover twice its value. The legislature also chose Hayne as governor and elected Calhoun to succeed him as senator. Calhoun promptly resigned as vice-president in order to defend nullification on the Senate floor.

JACKSON'S FIRM RESPONSE   In the crisis South Carolina found itself standing alone, despite the sympathy expressed elsewhere. The Georgia legislature called for a southern convention, but dismissed nullification as "rash and revolutionary." Alabama pronounced it "unsound in theory and dangerous in practice"; Mississippi stood "firmly resolved" to put down nullification. Jackson's response was measured and firm, but not rash—at least not in public. In private he threatened to hang Calhoun and all other traitors—and later expressed regret that he had failed to hang at least Calhoun. In his annual message on December 4, 1832, Jackson announced his firm intention to enforce the tariff, but once again urged Congress to lower the rates.

On December 10 Jackson followed up with his Nullification Proclamation, which characterized the doctrine of nullification as an "impractical absurdity." He said in part: "I consider, then, the power to annul a law in the United States, assumed by one state, incompatible with the existence of the Union, contradicted expressly by the letter of the Constitution, unauthorized by its spirit, inconsistent with every principle on which it was founded, and destructive of the great object for which it was formed." He appealed to the people of his native state not to follow false leaders: "The laws of the United States must be executed. I have no discretionary power on the subject; my duty is emphatically pronounced in the constitution. Those who told you that you might peaceably prevent their execution, deceived you; they could not have been deceived themselves. . . . Their object is disunion. But be not deceived by names. Disunion by armed force is treason."

CLAY'S COMPROMISE   Jackson sent General Winfield Scott to Charleston Harbor with reinforcements of federal soldiers, who were kept carefully isolated in the island posts at Fort Moultrie and Castle Pinckney to avoid incidents. A ship of war and seven revenue cutters appeared in the harbor, ready to enforce the tariff before ships had a chance to land their cargoes. The nullifiers mobilized the state militia while unionists in the state organized a volunteer force. In January 1833 the president requested from Congress a "Force Bill" specifically authorizing him to use the army to compel compliance with federal law in South Carolina. Under existing legislation he already had such authority, but this affirmation would strengthen his hand. At the same time he supported a bill in Congress that would have lowered tariff duties substantially within two years.

The nullifiers postponed enforcement of their ordinances in anticipation of a compromise. Passage of the bill depended on the support of Henry Clay, who finally yielded to those urging him to save the day. On February 12, 1833, he brought forth a plan to reduce the tariff gradually until 1842, by which time the rate on cotton would be cut in half. It was less than South Carolina would have preferred, but it got the nullifiers out of the corner into which they had painted themselves.

On March 1, 1833, the compromise tariff and the Force Bill were passed by Congress, and the next day Jackson signed both. The South Carolina convention then met and rescinded its nullification. In a face-saving gesture, it then nullified the Force Bill, for which Jackson no longer had any need. Both sides were able to claim victory. Jackson had upheld the supremacy of the Union, and South Carolina had secured a reduction of the tariff. Calhoun, worn out by the controversy, returned to his plantation. "The struggle, so far from being over," he ominously wrote, "is not more than fairly commenced."

JACKSON'S INDIAN POLICY

During the 1820s and 1830s the United States was fast becoming a multicultural nation of many peoples from many different countries. As economic growth reinforced the institution of slavery and accelerated westward expansion, policy makers struggled to preserve white racial homogeneity and hegemony. "Next to the case of the black race within our bosom," declared former president James Madison, "that of the red [race] on our borders is the problem most baffling to the policy of our country."

Andrew Jackson, however, saw nothing baffling about Indian policy. His attitude toward Indians was the typically western one, that they were barbarians and better off out of the way. Jackson had already done his part in the Creek and Seminole Wars to chastise Indians and separate them from their lands. By the time of his election in 1828 he was fully in accord with the view that a "just, humane, liberal policy toward Indians" dictated moving them onto the plains west of the Mississippi River. The policy was by no means new or original with Jackson; the idea had emerged gradually after the Louisiana Purchase in 1803. It had been formally set forth in 1823 by Calhoun, as secretary of war. By now it was generally accepted that a permanent solution to the Indian "problem" would involve their removal and resettlement in the "Great American Desert," which white settlers would never covet, since it was thought fit mainly for horned toads and rattlesnakes.

INDIAN REMOVAL   In response to a request by Jackson, Congress in 1830 approved the Indian Removal Act and appropriated $500,000 for the purpose. Jackson's presidency saw some ninety-four removal treaties negotiated. By 1835 he was able to announce that the policy had been carried out or was in process of completion for all but a handful of Indians. The policy was effected with remarkable speed, but even that was too slow for state authorities in the South and Southwest. Unlike the Ohio Valley–Great Lakes region, where the flow of white settlement had constantly pushed the Indians westward before it, in the Old Southwest, settlement moved across Kentucky and Tennessee and down the Mississippi, surrounding the Creeks, Choctaws, Chickasaws, Seminoles, and Cherokees. These tribes had over the years taken on many of the features of white society. The Cherokees even had such appurtenances of "white civilization" as a constitution, a written language, and black slaves.

Most of the northern tribes were too weak to resist the offers of Indian commissioners who, if necessary, used bribery and alcohol to woo the chiefs, and there was, on the whole, remarkably little resistance. In Illinois and Wisconsin Territory an armed clash sprang up from April to August 1832, which came to be known as the Black Hawk War, when the Sauk and Fox under Chief Black Hawk sought to reoccupy some lands they had abandoned in the previous year. Facing famine and hostile Sioux west of the Mississippi, they were simply seeking a place to raise a corn crop. The Illinois militia mobilized to expel them, chased them into Wisconsin Territory, and massacred women and children as they tried to escape across the Mississippi. The Black Hawk War came to be remembered later, however, less because of the atrocities inflicted on the Indians than because the participants included two native Kentuckians later pitted against each other: Lieutenant Jefferson Davis of the regular army and Captain Abraham Lincoln of the Illinois volunteers.

In the South two nations, the Seminoles and Cherokees, put up a stubborn resistance. The Seminoles of Florida fought a protracted guerilla war in the Everglades from 1835 to 1842. But most of the vigor went out of their resistance after 1837, when their leader, Osceola, was seized by treachery under a flag of truce, imprisoned, and left to die at Fort Moultrie near Charleston Harbor. After 1842 only a few hundred Seminoles remained, hiding out in the swamps. Most of the rest had been banished to the West.

THE CHEROKEES' TRAIL OF TEARS   The Cherokees had by the end of the eighteenth century fallen back into the mountains of northern Georgia and western North Carolina, onto land guaranteed to them in 1791 by treaty with the United States. But when Georgia ceded its western lands in 1802, it did so on the ambiguous condition that the United States extinguish all Indian titles within the state "as early as the same can be obtained on reasonable terms." In 1827 the Cherokees, relying

Elias Boudinot (1802–1839), editor of the Cherokee Phoenix, *signed the Indian removal treaty in 1835 and was subsequently murdered.*

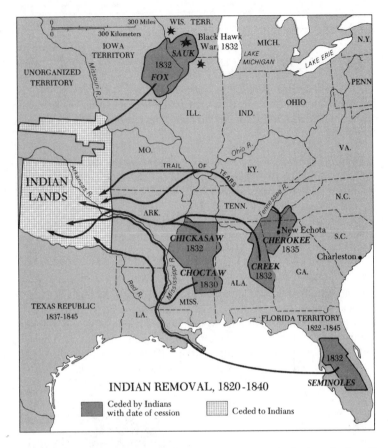

Ceded by Indians
with date of cession
Ceded to Indians

on their treaty rights, adopted a constitution in which they declared pointedly that they were not subject to any other state or nation. In 1828 Georgia responded with a law stipulating that after June 1, 1830, the authority of state law would extend over the Cherokees living within the boundaries of the state.

The discovery of gold in 1829 whetted the whites' appetite for Cherokee lands and brought bands of rough prospectors into the country. The Cherokees sought relief in the Supreme Court, but in *Cherokee Nation v. Georgia* (1831) John Marshall ruled that the Court lacked jurisdiction because the Cherokees were a "domestic dependent nation" rather than a foreign state in the meaning of the Constitution. Marshall added, however, that the Cherokees had "an unquestionable right" to their lands "until title should be extinguished by voluntary cession to the United States." In 1830 a Georgia law had required whites in the territory to get licenses authorizing their residence there, and to take an oath of allegiance to the state. Two New England missionaries among the

Indians refused and were sentenced to four years at hard labor. On appeal their case reached the Supreme Court as *Worcester v. Georgia* (1832), and the Court held that the Cherokee Nation was "a distinct political community" within which Georgia law had no force. The Georgia law was therefore unconstitutional.

Six years earlier Georgia had faced down President Adams when he tried to protect the rights of the Creeks. Now Georgia faced down the Supreme Court with the tacit consent of another president. Jackson is supposed to have said privately: "Marshall has made his decision, now let him enforce it!" Whether or not he put it so bluntly, Jackson did nothing to enforce the decision. In the circumstances there was nothing for the Cherokees to do but give in and sign a treaty, which they did in 1835. They gave up their lands in the Southeast in exchange for tracts in the Indian Territory west of Arkansas, $5 million from the federal government, and expenses for transportation.

By 1838 the Cherokees had departed on the "Trail of Tears" westward, following the Choctaws, Chickasaws, Creeks, and Seminoles on a journey marked by the cruelty and neglect of soldiers and private contractors, and scorn and pilferage by whites along the way. A few held out in the mountains and acquired title to federal lands in North Carolina; thenceforth they were the "Eastern Band" of the Cherokees. Some Seminoles were able to hide out in the Everglades, and a scattered few of the others remained in the Southeast, especially mixed-blood Creeks who could pass for white.

The Bank Controversy

THE BANK'S OPPONENTS   The overriding national issue in the campaign of 1832 was neither Jackson's Indian policy nor South Carolina's obsession with nullification. It was the question of rechartering the Bank of the United States. On the bank issue, as on others, Jackson had made no public commitment, but his personal opposition to the bank was already formed. Jackson had absorbed the western attitude of hostility toward the bank after the Panic of 1819, and held to a conviction that it was unconstitutional no matter what Marshall had said in *McCulloch v. Maryland*. Banks in general had fed a speculative mania, and Jackson, suspicious of all banks, preferred a hard-money policy. The general knew that the bank was wrong and felt that he did not need to form his opinions out of an intimate knowledge of banking. He was in fact blissfully ignorant of the subject.

Under the management of Nicholas Biddle, the Bank of the United States had prospered and grown. Coming from a well-to-do Philadelphia family, Biddle had previously little acquaintance with business when Monroe appointed him a government director of the bank, but he proved a quick study. By the time he became president of the bank in 1823 Biddle was well versed in banking.

The bank had facilitated business expansion and supplied a stable currency by forcing state banks to keep a specie reserve (gold or silver) behind their notes. But arrayed against the bank were powerful enemies: some of the state and local banks that had been forced to reduce their note issues, debtor groups that suffered from the reduction, and businessmen and speculators "on the make," who wanted easier credit. States'-rights groups questioned the bank's constitutionality, though Calhoun, who had sponsored the original charter and valued the bank's function of regulating the currency, was not among them. Financiers on New York's Wall Street resented the supremacy of the bank on Philadelphia's Chestnut Street.

Many westerners and workingmen, like Jackson, felt in their bones that the bank was, in Thomas Hart Benton's word, a "Monster," a monopoly controlled by a few of the wealthy with power that was irreconcilable with a democracy. "I think it right to be perfectly frank with you," Jackson told Biddle in 1829. "I do not dislike your Bank any more than all banks. But ever since I read the history of the South Sea Bubble I have been afraid of banks." This struck Biddle as odd, since he regarded his conservative policies as a safeguard against speculative manias like the eighteenth-century "South Sea Bubble," in which thousands of British investors had been fleeced. Jackson was perhaps right in his instinct that the bank lodged too much power in private hands, but mistaken in his understanding of the bank's policies.

Biddle at first tried to conciliate Jackson and appointed a number of Jackson men to branch offices of the bank. In his first annual message (1829), though, Jackson questioned the bank's constitutionality and asserted (whatever the evidence to the contrary) that it had failed to maintain a sound and uniform currency. Jackson talked of a compromise, perhaps a bank completely owned by the government with its operations confined chiefly to government deposits, its profits payable to the government, and its authority to set up branches in any state, dependent on the state's wishes. But Jackson would never commit himself on the precise terms of compromise. The defense of the bank was left up to Biddle.

BIDDLE'S RECHARTER EFFORT   The bank's twenty-year charter would run through 1836, but Biddle could not afford the uncertainty of waiting until then for a renewal. He pondered whether to force the issue of recharter before the election of 1832 or after. On this point, leaders of the National-Republicans, especially Clay and Webster (who was legal counsel to the bank as well as a senator), argued that the time to move

Jackson battling the hydra-headed bank.

was before the election. Clay, already the candidate of the National-Republicans, proposed to make the bank the central issue of the presidential canvass. Friends of the bank held a majority in Congress, and Jackson would risk loss of support in the election if he vetoed a renewal. But they failed to grasp the depth of prejudice against the bank, and succeeded mainly in handing to Jackson a popular issue on the eve of the election.

Both houses passed the recharter by comfortable margins, but without the two-thirds majority needed to override a veto. On July 10, 1832, Jackson vetoed the bill, sending it back to Congress with a ringing denunciation of monopoly and special privilege. Jackson argued that the bank was unconstitutional, whatever the Court and Congress said. "Each public officer who takes an oath to support the Constitution swears that he will support it as he understands it, and not as it is understood by others. . . . The opinion of the judges has no more authority over Congress than the opinion of Congress had over the judges, and on that point the President is independent of both." Besides, there were substantive objections aside from the question of constitutionality. Foreign stockholders in the bank had an undue influence. The bank had shown favors to members of Congress and exercised an improper power over state banks. The bill, he argued, demonstrated that "Many of our rich men have not been content with equal protection and equal benefits, but have besought us to make them richer by act of Congress." An effort to overrule the veto failed in the Senate; a vote of twenty-two to nineteen for the bank fell far short of the needed two-thirds majority. Thus the stage was set for a nationwide financial crisis.

CAMPAIGN INNOVATIONS   The presidential campaign, as usual, was under way early, the nominations having been made before the bank veto, two in fact before the end of 1831. For the first time a third party entered the field. The Anti-Masonic party was, like the bank, the object of strong emotions then sweeping the new democracy. The group had grown out of popular hostility toward the Masonic order, members of which were suspected of having kidnapped and murdered a New Yorker for revealing the "secrets" of his lodge. Opposition to a fraternal order was hardly the foundation on which to build a lasting party, but the Anti-Masonic party had three important "firsts" to its credit: in addition to being the first third party, it was the first party to hold a national nominating convention and the first to announce a platform, all of which it accomplished in September 1831 when it nominated William Wirt of Maryland for president.

The major parties followed its example by holding national conventions of their own. In December 1831 the delegates of the National-Republican party assembled in Baltimore to nominate Henry Clay for president and John Sergeant of Pennsylvania, counsel to the bank and

George Caleb Bingham's Verdict of the People *depicts the increasingly democratic politics of the early to middle nineteenth century.*

chief advocate of the recharter strategy, for vice-president. Jackson endorsed the idea of a nominating convention for the Democratic party (the name "Republican" was now formally dropped) to demonstrate popular support for its candidates. To that purpose the convention, also meeting at Baltimore, adopted the two-thirds rule for nomination (which prevailed until 1936, when it became a simple majority), and then named Martin Van Buren as Jackson's running mate. The Democrats, unlike the other two parties, adopted no formal platform at their first convention, and relied to a substantial degree on hoopla and the personal popularity of the president to carry their cause.

The outcome was an overwhelming endorsement of Jackson in the electoral college by 219 votes to 49 for Clay, and a less overwhelming but solid victory in the popular vote, by 688,000 to 530,000. William Wirt carried only Vermont, with several electoral votes. South Carolina, preparing for nullification and unable to stomach either Jackson or Clay, delivered its eleven votes to Governor John Floyd of Virginia.

REMOVAL OF GOVERNMENT DEPOSITS   Jackson interpreted the election as a mandate to proceed further against the bank. He asked Congress to investigate the safety of government deposits in the bank, since one of the current rumors told of empty vaults, carefully concealed. After a committee had checked, the Calhoun and Clay forces in the House of Representatives passed a resolution affirming that government deposits were safe and could be continued. The resolution passed on March 2, 1833, by chance the same day that Jackson signed the compromise tariff and the Force Bill. With the nullification issue out of the way, however, Jackson was free to wage his unrelenting war on the bank, that "hydra of corruption," which still had nearly four years to run on its charter. Despite the House study and resolution, Jackson now resolved to remove all government deposits from the bank.

When Secretary of the Treasury Louis McLane opposed removal of the government deposits and suggested a new and modified version of the bank, Jackson again shook up his cabinet. He kicked McLane upstairs to head the State Department, which Edward Livingston left to become minister to France. To take McLane's place at the Treasury he chose William J. Duane of Philadelphia, but by some oversight Jackson failed to explore Duane's views fully or advise him of the presidential expectations. Duane was antibank, but he was consistent in his convictions. Dubious about banks in general, he saw no merit in removing deposits from the Monster for redeposit in countless state banks. Jackson might well have listened to Duane's warnings that such action would lead to speculative inflation, but the old general's combative instincts were too much aroused. He summarily dismissed Duane and moved Attorney-General Roger Taney to the Treasury, where the new

The Downfall of Mother Bank. *In this pro-Jackson cartoon, the bank crumbles and Jackson's opponents flee in the face of the heroic president's removal of government deposits.*

secretary gladly complied with the presidential wishes, which corresponded to his own views.

Taney continued to draw on governmental accounts with Biddle's bank, and to deposit all new federal receipts in state banks. By the end of 1833 there were twenty-three state banks that had the benefit of governmental deposits, "pet banks" as they came to be called. Jackson's headlong plunge into finance, it soon turned out, produced the precise opposite of what he had sought. As so often happens with complex public issues, dissatisfaction had become focused on a symbol. In this case the symbol was the "Monster of Chestnut Street," the Bank of the United States in Philadelphia, which had been all along the one institution able to maintain some degree of order in the financial world. Jackson's action forced Biddle's bank to contract credit to shore up its defenses against the loss of deposits. By 1834 the tightness of credit was creating complaints of business distress, which was probably exaggerated by both sides in the bank controversy for political effect: Biddle to show the evil consequences of the withdrawal of deposits, Jacksonians to show how Biddle abused his power.

The bank's contraction policy quickly gave way, however, to a speculative binge encouraged by the deposit of government funds in the pet banks. With the restraint of Biddle's bank removed, the state banks gave full rein to their wildcat tendencies. (The term "wildcat," used in this sense, originated in Michigan, where one of the fly-by-night banks featured a panther, or wildcat, on its worthless notes.) New banks mushroomed, printing bank notes with abandon for the purpose of lending to speculators. Sales of public lands rose from 4 million acres in 1834 to 15 million in 1835 and to 20 million in 1836. At the same time the states plunged heavily into debt to finance the building of roads and canals, inspired by the success of New York's Erie Canal. By 1837 total state indebtedness had soared to $170 million, a very large sum for this time. The supreme irony of Jackson's war on the bank was that it sparked a speculative mania that dwarfed even the South Sea Bubble.

FISCAL MEASURES   The new bubble reached its greatest extent in 1836, when events combined suddenly to deflate it. Most important among these were the Distribution Act and the Specie Circular. Distribution of the government's surplus funds to the states had long been a pet project of Henry Clay. One of its purposes was to eliminate the federal surplus, thus removing one argument for cutting the tariff. Much of the surplus, however, resulted from the "land office business" in western real estate, and was therefore in the form of bank notes that had been issued to speculators. Many westerners thought that the solution to the surplus was simply to lower the price of land; southerners preferred to lower the tariff—but such action would now upset the compromise achieved in the Tariff of 1833. For a time the annual surpluses could be applied to paying off the government debt, but the debt, reduced to $7 million by 1832, was entirely paid off by January 1835.

Still the federal surplus continued to mount. Clay again proposed distribution, but Jackson had constitutional scruples about the process. Finally, a compromise was worked out whereby the government would distribute most of the surplus as loans to the states. To satisfy Jackson's scruples the funds were technically "deposits," but in reality they were never demanded back. Distribution was to be in proportion to each state's representation in the two houses of Congress, and was to be paid out in quarterly installments, beginning January 1, 1837.

The Specie Circular, issued by the secretary of the treasury at Jackson's order, applied the president's hard-money conviction to the sale of public lands. According to his order, the government would accept only gold or silver in payment for land after August 15. The purposes declared in the circular were to "repress frauds," to withhold support "from the monopoly of the public lands in the hands of speculators and capitalists," and to discourage the "ruinous extension" of bank notes and credit.

Irony dogged Jackson to the end on this matter. Since few actual settlers could get their hands on specie, they were now left all the more at the mercy of speculators for land purchases. Both the Distribution Act and the Specie Circular put many state banks in a precarious plight. The distribution of the surplus to the state governments resulted in federal funds being withdrawn from the state banks. In turn, the state banks had to call in a large part of their loans in order to make the transfer of federal funds to the state governments. This caused greater disarray among the already chaotic state banking community. At the same time, the new requirement that only hard money be accepted for federal land purchases put an added strain on the supplies of gold and silver.

BOOM AND BUST   But the boom and bust cycle of the 1830s had causes larger even than Andrew Jackson, causes that were beyond his control. The inflation of mid-decade was rooted not so much in a prodigal expansion of bank notes, as it seemed at the time, but in an increase of specie payments from England and France, and especially from Mexico, for investment and for the purchase of American cotton and other products. At the same time, British credits enabled Americans to buy British goods without having to export specie. Meanwhile, the flow of hard cash to China, where silver had been much prized, decreased. The Chinese now took in payment for their goods British credits, which they could in turn use to cover rapidly increasing imports of opium from British India.

Contrary to appearances, therefore, the reserves of specie in American banks kept pace with the increase of bank notes, despite reckless behavior on the part of some banks. But by 1836 a tighter British economy caused a decline in British investments and in British demand for American cotton just when the new western lands were creating a rapid

Broadway and Canal Street, New York City, 1836. New York's economy, and that of the nation, was strongly affected by world events in the mid-1830s.

increase in cotton supply. Fortunately for Jackson, the Panic of 1837 did not break until he was out of the White House and safely back at the Hermitage, his plantation near Nashville, Tennessee. His successor would serve as the scapegoat.

In May 1837 New York banks suspended specie payments on their bank notes, and fears of bankruptcy set off runs on banks around the country, many of which were soon overextended. A brief recovery followed in 1838, stimulated in part by a bad wheat harvest in England, which forced the British to buy American wheat. But by 1839 that stimulus had passed. The same year a bumper cotton crop overloaded the market, and a collapse of cotton prices set off a depression from which the economy did not fully recover until the mid-1840s.

VAN BUREN AND THE NEW PARTY SYSTEM

THE WHIG COALITION Before the crash, however, the Jacksonian Democrats reaped a political bonanza. Jackson had downed the dual monsters of nullification and the bank, and the people loved him for it. But out of the political wreckage that Jackson had inflicted on his opponents, they began in 1834 to pull together a new coalition of diverse elements united chiefly by their hostility to Jackson. The imperious demeanor of that champion of democracy had given rise to the name of "King Andrew I". His followers therefore were "Tories," supporters of the king, and his opponents became "Whigs," a name that linked them to the patriots of the American Revolution. This diverse coalition clustered around its center, the National-Republican party of John Quincy Adams, Clay, and Webster. Into the combination came remnants of the Anti-Masons and Democrats who for one reason or another were alienated by Jackson's stands on the bank or states' rights. Of the forty-one Democrats in Congress who had voted to recharter the bank, twenty-eight joined the Whigs by 1836.

Whiggery always had about it an atmosphere of social conservatism and superiority. The core Whigs were the supporters of Henry Clay, men who supported his "American System." In the South the Whigs enjoyed the support of the urban banking and commercial interests, as well as their planter associates, owners of most of the slaves in the region. In the West, farmers who valued internal improvements joined the Whig ranks. Most states'-rights supporters eventually dropped away, and by the early 1840s the Whigs were becoming more clearly the party of Henry Clay's nationalism, even in the South. Unlike the Democrats, who attracted Catholics from Germany and Ireland, Whigs tended to be native-born and British-American evangelical Protestants—Presbyterians, Baptists, and Congregationalists—who were active in promoting social reforms such as abolitionism and temperance. Throughout their two decades of strength, the Whigs were a national party, strong both north and south, and a cohesive force for Union.

THE ELECTION OF 1836   By the presidential election of 1836 a new two-party system was emerging out of the Jackson and anti-Jackson forces, a system that would remain in fairly even balance for twenty years. In May 1835, eighteen months before the election, the Democrats held their second national convention and nominated Jackson's handpicked successor, Vice-President Martin Van Buren. The Whig coalition, united chiefly in its opposition to Jackson, held no convention but adopted a strategy of multiple candidacies, hoping to throw the election into the House of Representatives.

The result was a free-for-all reminiscent of 1824, except that this time one candidate stood apart from the rest. It was Van Buren against the field. The Whigs put up three favorite sons: Daniel Webster, named by the Massachusetts legislature; Hugh Lawson White, chosen by anti-Jackson Democrats in the Tennessee legislature; and William Henry Harrison of Indiana, nominated by a predominantly Anti-Masonic convention in Harrisburg, Pennsylvania. In the South the Whigs made heavy inroads on the Democratic vote by arguing that Van Buren would be soft on antislavery advocates and that the South could trust only a

Jackson urging on his hand-picked successor, Martin Van Buren, in his battle with William Henry Harrison, 1836.

Martin Van Buren, the "Little Magician."

southerner—that is, White—as president. In the popular vote Van Buren outdistanced the entire Whig field, with 765,000 votes to 740,000 votes for the Whigs, most of which were cast for Harrison. Van Buren had 170 electoral votes, Harrison 73, White 26, and Webster 14.

Martin Van Buren, the eighth president, was the first of Dutch ancestry and at the age of fifty-five the first born under the Stars and Stripes. Son of a tavernkeeper in Kinderhook, New York, he had been schooled in a local academy, read law, and entered politics. Although he kept up a limited legal practice, he had been for most of his adult life a professional politician, so skilled in the arts of organization and manipulation that he came to be known as the "Little Magician." In 1824 he supported Crawford, then switched to Jackson in 1828, but continued to look to the Old Republicans of Virginia as the southern anchor of his support. After a brief tenure as governor of New York, he resigned to join the cabinet, and because of Jackson's favor became vice-president.

THE PANIC OF 1837   Van Buren owed much of his success to good luck. But once he had climbed to the top of the greased pole, luck suddenly deserted him. Van Buren had inherited Jackson's favor and many of his followers, but he also inherited a financial panic. An already precarious economy was tipped over into crisis by depression in England, which resulted in a drop in the price of cotton from 17 1/2¢ to 13 1/2¢ a pound, and caused English banks and investors to cut back their commitments in the New World and refuse extensions of loans. This was a particularly hard blow, because much of America's economic expansion depended on European—and mainly English—capital. On top of every-

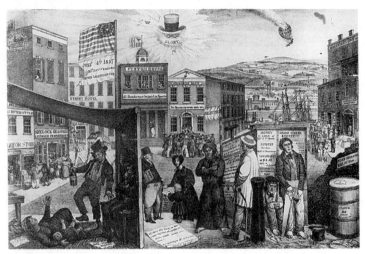

The Times. *This anti-Jacksonian cartoon depicts the effects of the depression of 1837: a panic at the bank, beggars in the street.*

thing else, in 1836 there had been a failure of the wheat crop, the export of which in good years helped offset the drain of payments abroad. As creditors hastened to foreclose, the inflationary spiral went into reverse. States curtailed ambitious plans for roads and canals, and in many cases felt impelled to repudiate their debts. In the crunch a good many of the wildcat banks succumbed, and the government itself lost some $9 million it had deposited in pet banks.

The working classes, as always, were particularly hard hit during the economic slump, and they largely had to fend for themselves. By the fall of 1837, one-third of the work force was jobless, and those still fortunate enough to have jobs saw their wages cut by 30–50 percent within two years. At the same time, prices for food and clothing soared. As winter approached in 1837, a journalist reported that in New York City there were 200,000 people "in utter and hopeless distress with no means of surviving the winter but those provided by charity." Indeed, there was no government aid; churches and voluntary societies were the major source of support for the indigent.

Van Buren's advisers and supporters were inclined to blame speculators and bankers, but at the same time to expect that the evildoers would get what they deserved in a healthy shakeout that would bring the economy back to stability. Van Buren did not believe that he or the government had any responsibility to rescue hard-pressed farmers or businessmen or to provide public relief. He did feel obliged to keep the government itself in a healthy financial situation, however. To that end he called a special session of Congress in September 1837, which quickly voted to postpone indefinitely the distribution of the surplus because of a probable upcoming deficit, and also approved an issue of Treasury notes to cover immediate expenses.

AN INDEPENDENT TREASURY   But Van Buren devoted most of his message to his idea that the government cease risking its deposits in shaky banks and set up an independent treasury. Under this plan the government would keep its funds in its own vaults and do business entirely in hard money. Van Buren observed that the founders of the republic had "wisely judged that the less government interferes with private pursuits the better for the general prosperity." Webster's response typified the Whig reaction: "I feel . . . as if this could not be America when I see schemes of public policy proposed, having for their object the convenience of Government only, and leaving the people to shift for themselves." The Whiggish approach, presumably, would have been some kind of Hamiltonian program of government promotion of economic development, perhaps in the form of tariff or currency legislation. Good Jacksonians disapproved of such programs, at least when they were run from Washington.

The Independent Treasury Act provoked opposition from a combination of Whigs and conservative Democrats who feared deflation. It took Van Buren several years of maneuvering to get what he wanted. Calhoun signaled a return to the Democratic fold, after several years of flirting with the Whigs, when he came out for the Independent Treasury. Van Buren gained western support by backing a more liberal land policy. He finally got his Independent Treasury on July 4, 1840. Although it lasted little more than a year before the Whigs repealed it in 1841, it would be restored in 1846.

The drawn-out hassle over the Treasury was only one of several that kept Washington preoccupied through the Van Buren years. A flood of petitions for Congress to abolish slavery and the slave trade in the District of Columbia brought on tumultuous debate, especially in the House of Representatives. Border incidents growing out of a Canadian insurrection in 1837 and a dispute over the Maine boundary kept British-American animosity at a simmer, but General Winfield Scott, the president's ace troubleshooter, managed to keep the hotheads in check along the border. The spreading malaise of the time was rooted in the depressed condition of the economy, which lasted through Van Buren's entire term. Fairly or not, the administration became the target of growing discontent. The president won renomination easily enough, but could not get the Democratic convention to agree on his vice-presidential choice, which the convention left up to the Democratic electors.

THE "LOG CABIN AND HARD CIDER" CAMPAIGN   The Whigs got an early start on their campaign when they met at Harrisburg, Pennsylvania, on December 4, 1839, to choose a candidate. Clay expected 1840 to be his year and had soft-pedaled talk of his American System in the interest of building broader support. Although he led on the first ballot, the convention was of a mind to look for a Whiggish Jackson, as it were, a military hero who could enter the race with few known political convictions or enemies. One possibility was Winfield Scott, but the delegates finally turned to William Henry Harrison. His credentials were impressive: victor at the Battle of Tippecanoe against the Shawnees in 1811, former governor of the Indiana Territory, briefly congressman and senator from Ohio, more briefly minister to Colombia. Another advantage of Harrison's was that the Anti-Masons liked him. To rally their states'-rights wing, the Whigs chose for vice-president John Tyler of Virginia, a close friend of Clay.

The Whigs had no platform. That would have risked dividing a coalition united chiefly by opposition to the Democrats. But they had a slogan, "Tippecanoe and Tyler too," that went trippingly on the tongue. And they soon had a rousing campaign theme, which a Democratic paper unwittingly supplied them when the Baltimore *Republican* declared sardonically "that upon condition of his receiving a pension of $2,000 and a barrel of cider, General Harrison would no doubt consent to withdraw his pretensions, and spend his days in a log cabin on the banks of the Ohio." The Whigs seized upon the cider and log cabin sym-

The Whigs prevailed in their "Log Cabin and Hard Cider" campaign of 1840.

bols to depict Harrison as a simple man sprung from the people. Actually, he sprang from one of the first families of Virginia and lived in a commodious farmhouse.

Substituting spectacle for argument, the Whig "Log Cabin and Hard Cider" campaign featured such sublime irrelevancy as the country had never seen before. Portable log cabins rolled through the streets along with barrels of potable cider to the tune of catchy campaign songs in support of

> The iron-armed soldier, the true-hearted soldier,
> The gallant old soldier of Tippecanoe.

Harrison's sweating supporters rolled huge victory balls along the highways to symbolize the snowballing majorities. All the devices of hoopla were mobilized: placards, emblems, campaign buttons, floats, effigies, great rallies, and a campaign newspaper, *The Log Cabin*. Building on the example of the Jacksonians' campaign to discredit John Quincy Adams, the Whigs pictured Van Buren, who unlike Harrison really did come from humble origins, as an aristocrat living in luxury at "the Palace":

> Let Van from his coolers of silver drink wine,
> And lounge on his cushioned settee;
> Our man on his buckeye bench can recline
> Content with hard cider is he!

The campaign left one lasting heritage in the American language, the expression "O.K.," a usage now virtually worldwide. It apparently grew out of a newspaper fad in the late 1830s for inventing comical abbreviations. Editors across the country vied with each other in perpetrating such absurdities as "G. t. d. h. d.," meaning "Give the devil his due," or "O.W.," meaning "all right," as if spelled "oll wright." On March 23, 1839, the Boston *Morning Post* carried the earliest usage of "O.K." yet found, and explained that it meant "all correct," with the spelling "oll korrect" implied.

Other newspapers spread it across the country, and Democrats picked it up as an abbreviation for "Old Kinderhook," an affectionate name for Van Buren, whose supporters began to organize "O.K. Clubs." The Whigs, however, gave the initials a new turn when they credited them to Andrew Jackson's creative spelling. He had marked papers that crossed his desk that way, they said, to signify they were "oll korrect." Thereafter Whig cider barrels carried the same seal of approval.

"We have taught them to conquer us!" the *Democratic Review* lamented. The Whig party had not only learned its lessons well, it had

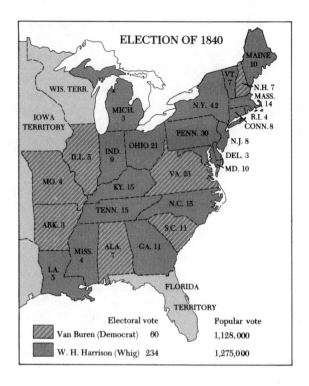

ELECTION OF 1840

	Electoral vote	Popular vote
Van Buren (Democrat)	60	1,128,000
W. H. Harrison (Whig)	234	1,275,000

learned to improve on its teachers in the art of campaigning. "Van! Van! Is a Used-up Man!" went one of the campaign refrains, and down he went by the thumping margin of 234 votes to 60 in the electoral college. In the popular vote it was closer: 1,275,000 for Old Tip, 1,128,000 for Van Buren.

ASSESSING THE JACKSON YEARS

The Jacksonian impulse had altered American politics permanently. Long-standing ambivalence about political parties had been purged in the fires of political conflict, and mass political parties had arrived to stay. They were now widely justified as a positive good. By 1840 both parties were organized down to the precinct level, and the proportion of adult white males who voted in the presidential election tripled, from 26 percent in 1824 to 78 percent in 1840. That much is beyond dispute, but the phenomenon of Jackson, the great symbol for an age, has inspired among historians conflicts of interpretation as spirited as those among his supporters and opponents at the time.

Jackson's personality itself seemed a compound of contradictions. His first major biographer discovered in different accounts that Jackson "was a patriot and a traitor. He was one of the greatest of generals, and wholly ignorant of the art of war. . . . The first of statesmen, he never devised, he never framed a measure. He was the most candid of men, and was capable of the profoundest dissimulation. A most law-defying, law-obeying citizen. A stickler for discipline, he never hesitated to disobey his superior. A democratic aristocrat. An urbane savage. An atrocious saint."

Interpretations of his policies, their sources, and their consequences have likewise differed. The earliest historians of the Jackson era belonged largely to an eastern elite nurtured in a "Whiggish" culture, men who could never quite forgive Jackson for the spoils system, which in their view excluded the fittest from office. A later school of "progressive" historians depicted Jackson as the leader of a vast democratic movement that welled up in the West and mobilized a farmer-labor alliance to sweep the "Monster" bank into the dustbin of history. Some historians have recently focused attention on local power struggles in which the great national debates of the time often seemed empty rhetoric or at most snares to catch the voters. One view of Jackson makes him out to be essentially a frontier nabob, an opportunist for whom democracy "was good talk with which to win the favor of the people."

Another interpretive school has emphasized the importance of cultural-ethnic identity in deciding party loyalties. Jackson, according to this view, revitalized the Jeffersonian alliance of Virginia and New York, of individualistic southern planters and those elements of the North who stood outside the straitlaced Yankee culture created mainly by peo-

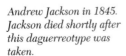
Andrew Jackson in 1845. Jackson died shortly after this daguerreotype was taken.

ple of English origin. Though the political effects of ethnic identities were complex, in large measure such out-groups as the Scotch-Irish and the Catholic Irish felt more comfortable with the more tolerant Democratic party. If valid for the northern states, however, the cultural-ethnic interpretation needs qualification in the light of southern experience. Ethnic identities in the South had faded with the decline of immigration after the Revolution, but the South developed in the 1840s as vigorous a party division as the North. Southern Whigs, mostly wealthy planters and members of the urban commercial elite, disdained the egalitarian rhetoric of Jacksonian Democrats and supported internal improvements to facilitate economic development.

There seems little question that, whatever else Jackson and his supporters had in mind, they followed an ideal of republican virtue, of returning to the Jeffersonian vision of the Old Republic in which government would leave people largely to their own devices. In the Jacksonian view the alliance of government and business was always an invitation to special favors and an eternal source of corruption. The national bank was the epitome of such evil. The right policy for government, at the national level in particular, was to refrain from granting special privileges and to let free competition in the marketplace regulate the economy.

In the bustling world of the nineteenth century, however, the idea of a return to agrarian simplicity was a futile exercise in nostalgia. Instead, free enterprise policies opened the way for a host of aspiring entrepreneurs eager to replace the established economic elite with a new order of free enterprise capitalism. And in fact there was no great conflict in the Jacksonian mentality between the farmer or planter who delved in the soil and the independent speculator and entrepreneur who won his way by other means. Jackson himself was all these things. What the Jacksonian mentality could not foresee was the degree to which, in a growing country, unrestrained enterprise could lead to new economic combinations, centers of gigantic power largely independent of governmental regulation. But history is forever pursued by unintended consequences. Here the ultimate irony would be that the laissez-faire rationale for republican simplicity eventually became the justification for the growth of unregulated centers of economic power far greater than any ever wielded by Biddle's bank.

FURTHER READING

A survey of events covered in the chapter can be found in Glyndon Van Deusen's *The Jacksonian Era, 1828–1848* (1959). A recent interpretation is Harry L. Watson's *Liberty and Power: The Politics of*

Jacksonian America (1990). Arthur M. Schlesinger, Jr.'s *The Age of Jackson* (1945)° emphasizes the role played by antibusiness interests in the agrarian South and the urban North. Richard Hofstadter's *The American Political Tradition and the Men Who Made It* (1948)° challenges this thesis. Lee Benson's *The Concept of Jacksonian Democracy* (1961) examines the ethnocultural basis for New York's politics of the common man. Edward Pessen's *Jacksonian America: Society, Personality, and Politics* (rev. ed., 1978) surveys these arguments.

An introduction to the development of political parties of the 1830s can be found in Richard P. McCormick's *The Second Party System* (1966).° In addition to the work by Benson, illuminating case studies include Ronald P. Formisano's *The Birth of Mass Political Parties* (1971), on Michigan; Formisano's *The Transformation of Political Culture* (1983), on Massachusetts; and Harry L. Watson's *Jacksonian Politics and Community Conflict: The Emergence of the Second American Party System in Cumberland County, North Carolina* (1981). Amy Bridges's *A City in the Republic* (1984) is about New York City politics. For an outstanding analysis of women in New York City during the Jacksonian period, see Christine Stansell's *City of Women* (1986). In *Chants Democratic* (1984) Sean Wilentz analyzes the social basis of working-class politics.

Biographies of Jackson include Robert V. Remini's *Andrew Jackson* (1966), which can serve as a good introduction. Also consult the three-volume biography by Remini: *Andrew Jackson and the Course of American Empire, 1767–1821* (1977), *Andrew Jackson and the Course of American Freedom, 1822–1832* (1981), and *Andrew Jackson and the Course of American Democracy, 1833–1845* (1984). On Jackson's successor, consult John Niven's *Martin Van Buren* (1983); Donald B. Cole's *Martin Van Buren and the Political System* (1984) is more critical. Studies of other major figures of the period include John Niven's *John C. Calhoun and the Price of Union* (1988) and Merrill Peterson's *The Great Triumvirate: Webster, Clay, and Calhoun* (1987). For a recent scholarly biography of Clay, see Robert Remini's *Henry Clay: Statesman for the Union* (1992).

The political philosophies of those who came to oppose Jackson are treated in Daniel W. Howe's *The Political Culture of American Whigs* (1979). William P. Vaughn's *The Antimasonic Party in the United States, 1826–1843* (1983) discusses that group of Jackson's opponents.

Two studies of the impact of the bank controversy are William G. Shade's *Banks or No Banks: The Money Question in the Western States,*

°These books are available in paperback editions.

1832–1865 (1972) and James R. Sharp's *The Jacksonians versus the Banks: Politics in the States after the Panic of 1837* (1970). Daniel Feller's *The Public Lands in Jacksonian Politics* (1985) is a good introduction to that important topic.

An outstanding book on the nullification issue is William W. Freehling's *Prelude to Civil War: The Nullification Controversy in South Carolina, 1816–1836* (1966).° John M. Belohlavek's *"Let the Eagle Soar!": The Foreign Policy of Andrew Jackson* (1985) is a thorough study of Jacksonian diplomacy. Ronald N. Satz's *American Indian Policy in the Jacksonian Era* (1974) surveys that tragedy; Michael P. Rogin's *Fathers and Children: Andrew Jackson and the Subjugation of the American Indian* (1975) is a psychological interpretation of Jackson's Indian policy. The question of rising inequality in American cities is treated in Edward Pessen's *Riches, Class, and Power before the Civil War* (1973).

°These books are available in paperback editions.

12 ❧

THE DYNAMICS OF GROWTH

The Jacksonian-era political debate between democratic and aristocratic elements was rooted in a profound transformation of American social and economic life. Between 1815 and 1850 the United States expanded all the way to the Pacific coast. An industrial revolution in the Northeast began to reshape the contours of the economy and propel an unrelenting process of urbanization. In the West an agricultural empire began to emerge based upon the foundation of corn, wheat, and cattle. In the South cotton became king, and its reign came to depend on an expanding institution of slavery. At the same time, innovations in transportation—horse-drawn wagons, canals, steamboats, and railroads—conquered time and space and knit together a national market. An economy based primarily on small-scale farming and local commerce matured into a far-flung capitalist marketplace entwined with world markets. These economic developments in turn generated changes in every other area of American life, from politics to the legal system, from the family to social values.

AGRICULTURE AND THE NATIONAL ECONOMY

COTTON   The first stage of industrialization brought with it an expansive commercial and urban outlook that by the end of the century would supplant the agrarian philosophy espoused by Thomas Jefferson and many others. "We are greatly, I was about to say fearfully, growing," John C. Calhoun told his congressional colleagues in 1816, and many other statesmen shared his ambivalent outlook. Would the republic retain its virtue and cohesion amid the turmoil of commercial development? In the brief period of good feelings after the War of 1812, however, such a troublesome question was easily brushed aside. Economic opportunities seemed available to Americans everywhere, and nowhere more than in Calhoun's native South Carolina. The reason was cotton, the new staple crop of the South, which was spreading from South Carolina and Georgia into the new lands of Mississippi, Alabama, Louisiana, and Arkansas.

Cotton had been used from ancient times, but the Industrial Revolution and its spread of textile mills created a rapidly growing market for the fluffy staple. Cotton had remained for many years rare and expensive because of the need for hand labor to separate the lint from the tenacious seeds. But by the mid-1780s in coastal Georgia and South Carolina a long-fiber Sea Island cotton was being grown commercially that could easily be separated from its shiny black seeds by squeezing it through rollers. Sea Island cotton, like the rice and indigo of the colonial tidewater, had little chance, though, in the soil and climate of the upcountry. And the green seed of the upland cotton clung to the lint so stubbornly that the rollers crushed the seed and spoiled the fiber. One person working all day could manage to separate little if any more than a pound by hand. Cotton could not yet be king.

The rising cotton kingdom of the lower South came to birth at a plantation called Mulberry Hill in coastal Georgia, the home of Mrs. Nathanael Greene, widow of the Revolutionary War hero. At Mulberry Hill discussion often turned to the promising new crop and to speculation about better ways to remove the seeds. In 1792, on the way to a job as a tutor in South Carolina, young Eli Whitney, recently graduated from Yale, visited fellow graduate Phineas Miller, who was overseer at Mulberry Hill. Catharine Greene noticed her visitor's mechanical aptitude, which had been nurtured in boyhood by the needs of a Massachusetts farm. When she suggested that young Whitney devise a mechanism for removing the seed from upland cotton, he mulled it over and solved the problem in ten days. In the spring of 1793, his job as a tutor quickly forgotten, Whitney had a working model of a cotton gin (short for engine).

By chance one of Mrs. Greene's daughters had bought some iron wire for a birdcage. Whitney used the wire to make iron pins, which he inserted into a cylinder. When rotated, the cylinder passed cotton fiber through slots in an iron guard, and the seeds dropped into a box below. Rotating brushes on the other side removed the fiber as it passed through. With it one person could separate fifty times as much cotton as could be done by hand. The device was an "absurdly simple contrivance," too much so as it turned out. A simple description was all any skilled worker needed to make a copy, and by the time Whitney and Miller had secured a patent in 1794, a number of copies were already in use. As a consequence, the two men were never able to make good on the promise of riches that the gin offered, and spent most of their modest gains in expensive lawsuits. Improved models soon appeared. The

Whitney's cotton gin revolutionized the South's economy and breathed new life into slavery.

use of a saw-toothed cylinder proved more effective than the original pins, and that device—which had occurred to Whitney at the start— appeared on the market as one of many designs contesting for patent rights.

Although Whitney realized little profit from his idea, he had unwittingly begun a revolution. Green-seed cotton first engulfed the up-country hills of South Carolina and Georgia, and after the War of 1812 migrated into the former Creek, Choctaw, and Chickasaw lands to the west. Cotton production soared, and in the process planters found a new and profitable use for slavery. Planters migrated westward with their gangs of workers in tow, and a profitable trade began to develop in the sale of slaves from the coastal South to the West. The cotton culture became a way of life that tied the Old Southwest to the coastal Southeast in a common interest.

Not the least of the cotton gin's revolutionary consequences, although less apparent at first, was that cotton became almost immediately a major export commodity. Cotton exports averaged about $9 million in value from 1803 to 1807, about 22 percent of the value of all exports; from 1815 to 1819 they averaged over $23 million, or 39 percent of the total; and from the mid-1830s to 1860 they accounted for more than half the value of all exports. For the national economy as a whole, one historian asserted, "Cotton was the most important proximate cause of expansion." The South supplied the North both raw materials and markets for manufactures. Income from the North's role in handling the

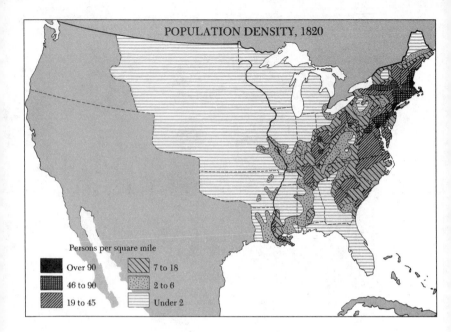

POPULATION DENSITY, 1820

Persons per square mile

Over 90   7 to 18

46 to 90   2 to 6

19 to 45   Under 2

cotton trade then provided surpluses for capital investment. It was once assumed that the South supplied the Old Northwest with markets for foodstuffs, but recent research shows the cotton belt to have been self-sufficient in foodstuffs. The more likely explanation of growth in the Old Northwest now seems to be its own growing urban markets for foodstuffs, which supplemented the export market for grain.

FARMING THE WEST   The westward flow of planters and their slaves to Alabama and Mississippi during these flush times mirrored another migration through the Ohio Valley and the Great Lakes region, where the Indians had been steadily pushed westward. "Old America seems to be breaking up and moving westward," an English traveler observed in 1817 as he watched the migrants make their way along westward roads in Pennsylvania. Family groups, stages, light wagons, and riders on horseback made up "a scene of bustle and business, extending over three hundred miles, which is truly wonderful." In 1800 some 387,000 settlers were counted west of the Atlantic states; by 1810, 1,338,000 lived over the mountains; by 1820, 2,419,000. By 1860 more than half the nation's expanded population resided in trans-Appalachia, and the restless movement had long since spilled across the Mississippi and touched the shores of the Pacific.

North of the expanding cotton belt in the Gulf states, the fertile woodland soils, riverside bottom lands, and black loam of the prairies drew farmers from the rocky lands of New England and the leached,

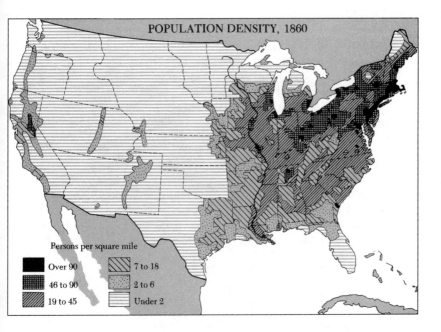

POPULATION DENSITY, 1860

Persons per square mile

Over 90

46 to 90

19 to 45

7 to 18

2 to 6

Under 2

exhausted soils of the Southeast. A new land law of 1820, passed after the Panic of 1819, eliminated the credit provisions of the 1800 act but reduced the minimum price from $1.64 to $1.25 per acre and the minimum plot from 160 to 80 acres. The settler could get a place for as little as $100, and over the years the proliferation of state banks made it possible to continue buying on credit. Even that was not enough for westerners, who began a long—and eventually victorious—agitation for further relaxation of the land laws. They favored preemption, the right of squatters to purchase land at the minimum price, and graduation, the progressive reduction of the price on lands that did not sell.

Congress eventually responded with two bills. Under the Preemption Act of 1830, a renewable law made permanent in the Preemption Act of 1841, squatters could stake out claims ahead of the land surveys and later get 160 acres at the minimum price of $1.25 per acre. In effect the law recognized a practice enforced more often than not by frontier vigilantes. Under the Graduation Act of 1854, which Senator Thomas Hart Benton had promoted since the 1820s, prices of unsold lands were to go down in stages until the lands could sell for 12 1/2¢ per acre after thirty years.

The progress of settlement followed the old pattern of clearing trees, grubbing out the stumps and underbrush, and settling down at first to a crude subsistence. The development of effective iron plows greatly eased the backbreaking job of breaking up the soil. As early as 1797 an American inventor had secured a patent on an iron plow, but a superstition that iron poisoned the soil prevented much use until after 1819, when Jethro Wood of New York developed an improved version with separate parts that could be replaced without buying a whole new plow complete. The prejudice against iron suddenly vanished, and the demand for plows grew so fast that Wood, like Whitney, could not supply the need and spent much of his remaining fifteen years fighting against patent infringements. The iron plow was a special godsend to those farmers who first ventured into the sticky black loams of the treeless prairies. Further improvements would follow, including John Deere's steel plow (1837) and the chilled-iron and steel plow of John Oliver (1855).

By the 1840s new mechanical seeders replaced the need to sow seed by hand. Even more important, Cyrus Hall McCormick of Virginia invented a primitive grain reaper in 1834, a development as significant to the agricultural economy of the Old Northwest as the cotton gin was to the South. After tinkering with his machine for almost a decade, McCormick applied for a patent in 1841. Six years later he moved to Chicago and built a manufacturing plant for his reapers and mowers. Within a few years he had sold thousands of new machines, transforming the scale of American agriculture. Using a hand-operated sickle, a farmer could harvest half an acre of wheat a day; with a McCormick reaper two people could work twelve acres a day.

McCormick's success attracted other manufacturers and inventors, and soon there were mechanical threshers to separate the grains of wheat from the straw. Farming remained, as it still is, a precarious vocation, subject to the whims of climate, the assault of insects, and the fluctuations of foreign markets, but by the 1850s it had become a major commercial activity. As the volume of agricultural products soared,

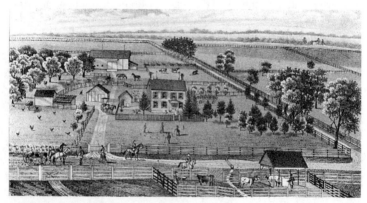

Farm Residence, Putnam County, Illinois. *Through the early decades of the nineteenth century migrants transformed midwestern plains to farmland.*

prices dropped, income rose, and the standard of living for many farm families in the Old Northwest improved.

TRANSPORTATION AND THE NATIONAL ECONOMY

NEW ROADS   Transportation improvements helped spur the development of a national market. As settlers moved west, there developed a stronger demand for better roads. In 1795 the Wilderness Road, along the trail blazed by Daniel Boone twenty years before, was opened to covered-wagon and stagecoach traffic, thereby easing the route through the Cumberland Gap into Kentucky and along the Knoxville and Old Walton Roads, completed the same year, into Tennessee. Even so, travel was difficult at best. Stagecoaches crammed with as many as a dozen people crept along at four miles per hour. One early stage rider said he alternately walked and rode and "though the pain of riding exceeded the fatigue of walking, yet . . . it refreshed us by varying the weariness of our bodies." South of these roads there were no such major highways. South Carolinians and Georgians pushed westward on whatever trails or rutted roads had appeared.

To the northeast a movement for graded and paved roads (macadamized with crushed stones packed down) gathered momentum after completion of the Philadelphia-Lancaster Turnpike in 1794 (the term derives from a pole or pike at the tollgate, turned to admit the traffic). By 1821 some 4,000 miles of turnpikes had been completed, mainly connecting eastern cities. Western traffic moved along the Frederick Pike to Cumberland and thence along the National Road, completed to Wheeling on the Ohio River in 1818, and to Vandalia, Illinois, by about mid-century. Another route went along the old Forbes Road from Philadelphia to Pittsburgh. Another used the Mohawk and Genesee Turnpike from the Massachusetts state line through Albany to Buffalo, whence one could take ship for points on the Great Lakes.

WATER TRANSPORT   Once turnpike travelers had reached the Ohio River, they could float westward in comparative comfort. At Pittsburgh, Wheeling, and other points the emigrants could buy flatboats, commonly of two kinds: an ark with room for living quarters, possessions, and perhaps some livestock; or a keelboat—similar but with a keel. For large flatboats—a capacity of forty tons was common—crews were available for hire. At the destination the boat could be used again or sold for lumber. In the early 1820s an estimated 3,000 flatboats went down the Ohio every year, and for many years after that the flatboat remained the chief conveyance for heavy traffic downstream.

By the early 1820s the turnpike boom was giving way to new devel-

opments in water transportation: the river steamboat and the canal barge, which carried bulk commodities far more cheaply than did covered wagons on the National Road. As early as 1787 one inventor had launched a steamboat on the Delaware River, but no commercially successful steamboat appeared until Robert Fulton and Robert R. Livingston sent the *Clermont* up the Hudson River to Albany in 1807. Thereafter, the use of the steamboat spread rapidly to other eastern rivers and to the Ohio and Mississippi, opening nearly half a continent to water traffic.

By 1836, 361 steamboats navigated the western waters, reaching ever farther up the tributaries that connected to the Mississippi. By the 1840s shallow-draft, steam-powered ships that traveled *on* rather than *in* the water became the basis of the rivermen's boast that they could navigate a heavy dew, that the boats were "so built that when the river is low and the sandbars come out for air, the first mate can tap a keg of beer and run the boat four miles on the suds." These boats ventured into far reaches of the Mississippi Valley, up such rivers as the Wabash,

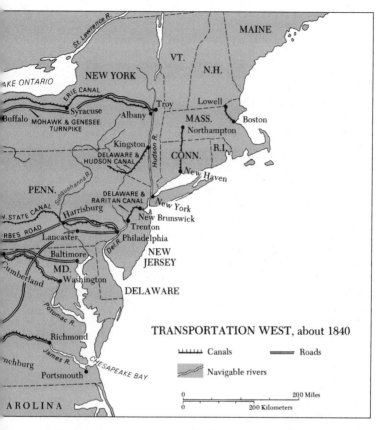

TRANSPORTATION WEST, about 1840

Canals   Roads   Navigable rivers

0   200 Miles
0   200 Kilometers

the Monongahela, the Cumberland, the Tennessee, the Missouri, and the Arkansas.

The miracle of these floating palaces became one of the romantic epics of America. The tradition was fixed early. In 1827 a lyrical writer for Cincinnati's *Western Monthly Review* let himself go with a description of the "fairy structures of oriental gorgeousness and splendor . . . rushing down the Mississippi . . . or plowing up between the forests . . . bearing speculators, merchants, dandies, fine ladies, everything real and everything affected in the form of humanity, with pianos, and stocks of novels, and cards, and dice, and flirting, and love-making, and drinking, and champagne, and on the deck, perhaps, three hundred fellows, who have seen alligators and neither fear whiskey, nor gunpowder. A steamboat, coming from New Orleans, brings to the remotest villages of our streams, and the very doors of the cabins, a little Paris, a section of Broadway, or a slice of Philadelphia, to a ferment in the minds of our young people, the innate propensity for fashions and finery."

The durable flatboat, however, still carried to market most of the western wheat, corn, flour, meal, bacon, ham, pork, whiskey, soap and candles (the by-products of slaughterhouses), lead from Missouri, copper from Michigan, wood from the Rockies, and ironwork from Pittsburgh. But the steamboat, by bringing two-way traffic to the Mississippi Valley, created a continental market and an agricultural empire that became the new breadbasket of America. Farming evolved from a subsistence level to the ever greater production of valuable staples. Along with the new farmers came promoters, speculators, and land-boomers. Villages at strategic trading points along the streams evolved into centers of commerce and urban life. The port of New Orleans grew in the 1830s and 1840s to lead all others in exports.

But by then the Erie Canal was drawing eastward much of the trade that once went down to the Gulf, and this would have major economic and political consequences, tying together the West and East while further isolating the Deep South. In 1817 the New York legislature endorsed Governor De Witt Clinton's dream of connecting the Hudson River with Lake Erie. Eight years later, in 1825, the canal was open for its entire 350 miles from Albany to Buffalo; branches soon put most of the state within reach of the canal. After 1828 the Delaware and Hudson Canal linked New York with the anthracite fields of northeastern Pennsylvania. The speedy success of the New York system inspired a mania for canals that lasted more than a decade and resulted in the

Steamers at the levee at St. Paul, Minnesota, 1859.

The Erie Canal at Lockport, 1840.

completion of about 3,000 miles of waterways by 1837. But no canal ever matched the spectacular success of the Erie, which rendered the entire Great Lakes region an economic tributary to the port of New York. With the further development of canals spanning Ohio and Indiana from north to south, much of the upper Ohio Valley also came within the economic sphere of New York.

RAILROADS   The Panic of 1837 and the subsequent depression cooled the canal fever. Some states that had borrowed heavily to finance canals had to repudiate their debts. The holders of repudiated bonds had no recourse. Meanwhile, a new and more versatile form of transportation was gaining on the canal: the railroad. Vehicles that ran on iron rails had long been in use, especially in mining, but now came a tremendous innovation—the use of steam power—as the steam locomotive followed soon after the steamboat. As early as 1814 the first practical steam locomotive was built in England. In 1825, the year the Erie Canal was completed, the world's first commercial steam railway began operations in England. By the 1820s the port cities of Baltimore, Charleston, and Boston were alive with schemes to tap the hinterlands by rail.

On July 4, 1828, Baltimore got the jump on other cities when Charles Carroll, the last surviving signer of the Declaration of Independence, laid the first stone in the roadbed of the Baltimore and Ohio (B&O)

WANTED!
3,000 LABORERS

On the 12th Division of the
ILLINOIS CENTRAL RAILROAD

Wages, $1.25 per Day.

Fare, from New-York, only - - $4)5

By Railroad and Steamboat, to the work in the
State of Illinois.

Constant employment for two years or more
given. Good board can be obtained at two
dollars per week.

This is a rare chance for persons to go
West, being sure of permanent employment
in a healthy climate, where land can be
bought cheap, and for fertility is not surpassed
in any part of the Union.

Men with families preferred.

Advertisement (1853) for laborers on the Illinois Central Railroad, "a rare chance for persons to go West, . . . sure of permanent employment in a healthy climate, where land can be bought cheap, and for fertility is not surpassed in any part of the Union."

Railroad. Four years later the road reached seventy-three miles west of Baltimore. The Charleston and Hamburg Railroad, started in 1831 and finished in 1833, was at that time the longest railroad under single management in the world. It reached westward 136 miles to the hamlet of Hamburg, opposite Augusta, where Charleston merchants hoped to divert traffic from the Savannah River. By 1836 Boston had fanned out three major lines to Lowell, Worcester, and Providence.

By 1840 the railroads, with a total of 3,328 miles, had outdistanced the canals by just two miles. Over the next twenty years, though, railroads grew nearly tenfold to cover 30,626 miles; more than two-thirds of this total was built in the 1850s. Several major east-west lines appeared, connecting Boston to Albany and Albany with Buffalo; combined in 1853, these lines became the New York Central. In 1851 the Erie Railroad spanned southern New York; by 1852 the Pennsylvania Railroad connected Philadelphia and Pittsburgh; in 1853 the B&O finally reached Wheeling on the Ohio. By then New York had connections all the way to Chicago, and in two years to St. Louis. Before 1860 the Hannibal and St. Joseph had crossed the state of Missouri. Farther south, despite Charleston's early start on both canals and railroads and despite the brave dream of a line to tap western commerce at Cincinnati, the network of railroads still had many gaps in 1860. By 1857 Charleston, Savannah, and Norfolk connected by way of lines into Chattanooga and thence along a single line to Memphis, the only southern route that connected the east coast and the Mississippi. In 1860 the North and South had only three major links: at Washington, Louisville, and Cairo, Illinois.

The proliferation of trunk lines had by then supplemented the earlier canals to create multiple ties between the Old Northwest and Northeast. But it was still not until the eve of the Civil War that railroads surpassed canals in total haulage: in 1859 they carried a little over 2 billion ton compared to 1.6 billion tons that the canals carried.

Travel on the early railroads was a risky venture. Iron straps on top of wooden rails, for instance, tended to work loose and curl up into "snakesheads" that sometimes pierced railway coaches. The solution was the iron T-rail, introduced in 1831 and soon standard equipment on the best roads, but the strap-iron rail remained common because wood was so cheap. Wood was used for fuel too, and the sparks often caused fires along the way or damaged passengers' clothing. An English traveler reported seeing a lady's shawl ignited on one trip. She found in her own gown thirteen holes "and in my veil, with which I saved my eyes, more than could be counted." Creation of the "spark arrester" and the use of coal alleviated but never overcame the hazard. Before 1860 brakes had to be operated manually, crude pin-and-link couplings were used, and adequate springs were unknown. Different track widths often forced passengers to change trains until a standard gauge became national in 1882. Land travel, whether by stagecoach or train, was a jerky, bumpy, wearying ordeal.

Water travel, where available, offered far more comfort, but railroads gained supremacy over other forms of transport because of their economy, speed, and reliability. They averaged ten miles per hour, more than twice as fast as stagecoaches and four times as fast as water travel. By 1859 railroads had reduced the cost of transportation services by $150 million to $175 million, accounting for a social saving that amounted to some 4 percent of the gross national product. By 1890 the saving would run up to almost 15 percent. Railroads provided indirect benefits by encouraging settlement and the expansion of farming. During the antebellum period the reduced costs brought on by the railroads aided the expansion of farming more than manufacturing, since manufacturers in the Northeast, especially New England, had better access to water transportation. The railroads' demand for rail iron and equipment of various kinds, however, did provide an enormous market for the

THE GROWTH
OF RAILROADS,
1850

——— Railroads in 1850

industries that made these capital goods. And the ability of railroads to operate year round in all kinds of weather gave them an advantage in carrying finished goods, too.

OCEAN TRANSPORT   For oceangoing traffic, the start of service on regular schedules was the most important change of the early 1800s. In the first week of 1818 ships of the Black Ball Line inaugurated a weekly transatlantic packet service between New York and Liverpool. Beginning with four ships in all, the Black Ball Line thereafter had one ship leaving each port monthly at an announced time. With the business recovery in 1822 the packet business grew in a rush. Runs to London and Le Havre were added, and by 1845 some fifty two transatlantic lines ran square-riggers on schedule from New York, with three regular sailings per week. Many others ran in the coastwise trade, to Charleston, Savannah, New Orleans, and elsewhere.

The same year, 1845, witnessed a great innovation with the launching of the first clipper ship, the *Rainbow.* Built for speed, the sleek clippers were the nineteenth-century equivalent of the supersonic jetliner. They doubled the speed of the older merchant vessels, and trad-

THE GROWTH
OF RAILROADS,
1860

——— Railroads in 1860
——— Principal east-west lines

ing companies rushed to purchase them. Long and lean, with taller masts and more sails, they cut dashing figures during their brief but colorful career, which lasted less than two decades. What provoked the clipper boom was the lure of Chinese tea, a drink long coveted in America but in scarce supply. The tea leaves were a perishable commodity that had to reach market quickly, and the new clippers now made this possible. Even more important, the discovery of California gold in 1848 lured thousands of prospectors and entrepreneurs from the Atlantic seaboard. These new settlers generated an urgent demand for goods, and the clippers met the need. In 1854 the *Flying Cloud* took eighty-nine days and eight hours to make the distance from New York to San Francisco, around Cape Horn, a speed that steamships took several decades to equal. But clippers, while fast, lacked ample cargo space, and after the Civil War would give way to the steamship.

THE ROLE OF GOVERNMENT   The massive internal improvements of the era were the product of both state government and private initiatives, sometimes undertaken jointly and sometimes separately. Private investment accounted for nearly all the turnpikes in New England and the middle states. Elsewhere states invested heavily in turnpike companies and in some cases, notably South Carolina and Indiana, themselves built and owned the turnpikes. Canals were to a much greater extent the product of state investment, and more commonly state owned and operated. The Panic of 1837, however, caused states to pull back and leave railroad development mainly to private corporations. Most of the railroad capital came from private sources. Still, government had an enormous role in railroad development. Several states of the South and West built state-owned lines, although they generally looked to private companies to handle actual operations and in some cases sold the lines. States and localities along the routes invested in railroad corporations and granted loans; states were generous in granting charters and tax concessions.

The federal government helped too, despite the constitutional scruples of some officials against direct involvement. The government bought stock in turnpike and canal companies, and after the success of the Erie, extended land grants to several western states for the support of canal projects. Congress provided for railroad surveys by government engineers, and reduced the tariff duties on iron used in railroad construction. In 1850 Senator Stephen A. Douglas of Illinois and others prevailed on Congress to extend a major land grant to support a north-south line connecting Chicago with Mobile, Alabama. Grants of three square miles on alternate sides for each mile of railroad subsidized the building of the Illinois Central and the Mobile and Ohio Railroads. Regarded at the time as a special case, the 1850 grant set a precedent for other bounties that totaled about 20 million acres by 1860—a small amount compared to the grants for transcontinental lines in the Civil War decade.

Clipper ship at the New York docks, 1840s.

THE GROWTH OF INDUSTRY

While the South and West developed the agricultural basis for a national economy, the Northeast was laying foundations for an industrial revolution. Technology in the form of the cotton gin, the harvester, and improvements in transportation had quickened agricultural development and to some extent decided its direction. But technology altered the economic landscape even more profoundly by giving rise to the factory system.

EARLY TEXTILE MANUFACTURES   At the end of the colonial period manufacturing remained in the household or handicraft stage of development, or at most the "putting-out" stage, in which the merchant capitalist would distribute raw materials (say, leather patterns for shoes) to be worked up at home, then collected and sold. In 1815 the town of Mount Pleasant, Ohio, with a population of barely over 500, supported some thirty-eight handicraft shops, including blacksmiths and bakers, and eight more shops engaged in tanning, textile production, and rail-making. Farm families themselves had to produce much of what they needed in the way of crude implements, shoes, and clothing, and in their simple workshops inventive genius was sometimes nurtured. As a boy Eli Whitney had set up a forge to make nails in his father's rural workshop. The transition from such production to the factory was slow, but one for which a base had been laid before 1815.

In the eighteenth century Great Britain had jumped out to a long head start in industrial production. The foundations of Britain's advantage were the development of iron smelting by coke when sufficient wood was lacking; the invention of the steam engine in 1705 and its improvement by James Watt in 1765; and a series of inventions that mechanized the production of textiles, including John Kay's flying shuttle (1733), James Hargreaves's spinning jenny (1764), Richard Arkwright's "water frame" (1769), and Samuel Crompton's spinning mule (1779). The water frame was a water-powered spinning machine that twisted carded cotton into thread. The spinning mule could do the work of 200 spinners. Britain also carefully guarded its hard-won secrets, forbidding the export of machines or descriptions of them, even restricting the departure of informed mechanics. But the secrets could not be kept. In 1789 Samuel Slater arrived in America from England with the plan of a water frame in his head. He contracted with an enterprising merchant-manufacturer in Rhode Island to build a mill in Pawtucket, and in this little mill, completed in 1790, nine children turned out a satisfactory cotton yarn, which was then worked up by the putting-out system.

The beginnings in textile production were slow and faltering until Jefferson's embargo in 1807 stimulated domestic production. Policies

New England Factory Village, 1830. *Mills and factories gradually transformed the New England landscape in the early nineteenth century.*

adopted during the War of 1812 restricted imports and encouraged the merchant capitalists of New England to switch their resources into manufacturing. New England, it happened, had the distinct advantage that its many rivers provided waterpower and water transportation. In 1813 Francis Cabot Lowell and a group of wealthy merchants known as the Boston Associates formed the Boston Manufacturing Company. At Waltham, Massachusetts, they built the first factory in which the processes of spinning and weaving by power machinery were brought under one roof, mechanizing every process from raw material to finished cloth. By 1815 textile mills numbered in the hundreds. A flood of British imports after the War of 1812 dealt a temporary setback to the infant industry, but the foundations of textile manufacture were laid, and they spurred the growth of garment trades and a machine-tool industry to build and service the mills.

TECHNOLOGY IN AMERICA Meanwhile, American ingenuity was adding other bases for industrial growth. Oliver Evans of Philadelphia was a frustrated pioneer who had the misfortune to be ahead of his time. As a teenager on a Delaware farm he had been fascinated by steam engines but could not find the backing to pursue his ideas for steamboats and locomotives. As early as 1785 he built an automatic mill in which grain introduced at one end came out flour at the other, but could not get millers interested in trying it. Success eluded him until 1804, when he developed a high-pressure steam engine adapted to a variety of uses in ships and factories.

The practical bent of Americans was one of the outstanding traits noted by foreign visitors. In Europe, where class consciousness prevailed, Alexis de Tocqueville wrote, people confined themselves to "the arrogant and sterile researches of abstract truths, whilst the social condition and institutions of democracy prepare them [Americans] to seek immediate and useful practical results of the sciences." In 1814 Dr. Jacob Bigelow, a Harvard botanist, began to lecture on "The Elements of Technology," a word he did much to popularize. In his book of the same title he argued that technology constituted the chief superiority of moderns over the ancients, effecting profound changes in ways of living.

One of the most striking examples of the connection between pure research and innovation, however, was in the work of Joseph Henry, a Princeton physicist. His research in electromagnetism provided the basis for Samuel F. B. Morse's invention of the telegraph and for electrical motors later on. In 1846 Henry became head of the new Smithsonian Institution, founded with a bequest from the Englishman James Smithson "for the increase and diffusion of knowledge among men." The year 1846 also saw the founding of the American Association for the Advancement of Science.

It would be difficult to exaggerate the importance of science and technology in changing the ways people live. All aspects of life—the social, cultural, economic, and political—were and are shaped by it. To cite but a few examples: improved transportation and a spreading market economy combined with innovations in canning and refrigeration to provide people a more healthy and varied diet. Fruit and vegetables, heretofore available only during harvest season, could be shipped in much of the year. Scientific breeding of cattle helped make meat and milk more abundant.

Technological advances also helped improve living conditions: houses were larger, better heated, and better illuminated. Although working-class residences remained Spartan, with few creature comforts, the affluent were able to afford indoor plumbing, central heating, gas lighting, bathtubs, iceboxes, and sewing machines. Even the lower classes were able to afford new coal-burning cast-iron cooking stoves that facilitated the preparation of more varied meals and improved heating. The first sewer systems began to help rid city streets of human and animal waste, while underground water lines enabled fire companies to use hydrants rather than bucket brigades. Machine-made clothes fit better and were cheaper than homespun; newspapers and magazines were more abundant and affordable, as were clocks and watches. Invention often brought about completely new enterprises, the steamboat and the railroad being the most spectacular, without which the pace of development would have been slowed immeasurably.

Eli Whitney, whose cotton gin had deeply influenced the development of the South, also developed a basic principle that promoted the industrial growth of the North—mass production. In 1799 he won a government contract for the manufacture of muskets, and in his shop at New Haven developed machine tools to make parts with such precision as to be virtually identical. In a shop twenty miles away, Simeon North began the same year with a contract for pistols. No one can say with assurance which man was the inventor. It was in fact more an evolution in machine tools than an invention, and the original idea seems to have been French. Its perfection, however, was an original American contribution.

Most basic inventions were imports from Europe. Preservation of food by canning, for instance, was unknown before the early nineteenth century, when Americans learned of a new French discovery that food stayed fresh when cooked in airtight containers. By 1820 major canneries were in existence in Boston and New York. At the end of the 1830s glass containers were giving way to the "tin can" (tin-plated steel) brought in from England, and these were eventually used to market Gail Borden's new invention—a process for condensed milk.

A spate of inventions in the 1840s generated dramatic changes in American life. In 1844 Charles Goodyear patented a process for vulcanizing rubber, which made it stronger and more elastic. In the same year the first intercity telegraph message was transmitted from Baltimore to Washington on the device Morse had invented back in 1832. The telegraph was slow to catch on at first, but seventeen years after that demonstration, with the completion of connections to San Francisco, an entire continent had been wired for instant communication. In 1846 Elias

"In this Field, July 25, 1831, will be Tried a new Patent Grain Cutter, worked by horsepower, invented by C. H. McCormick."

Howe invented the sewing machine, soon improved by Isaac Merritt Singer. The sewing machine, incidentally, actually slowed the progress of the factory. Since it was adapted to use in the home, it gave the "putting-out" system a new lease on life in the clothing industry.

Examples can do no more than hint at the magnitude of change in technology and manufacturing. A suggestive if flawed measure was the growing number of patents issued. During the first twenty-one years of the Patent Office, 1790–1811, the number issued averaged only 77 per year; from 1820 to 1830 the average was up to 535; during the 1840s it was 646; and during the 1850s the number suddenly quadrupled to an average of 2,525 per year.

THE LOWELL SYSTEM   Before the 1850s the factory still had not become typical of American industry. Handicraft and domestic production (putting-out) remained common. In many industries they stayed for decades the chief agencies of growth. Hatmaking in Danbury, Connecticut, and shoemaking in eastern Massachusetts, for instance, grew mainly by the multiplication of small shops and their gradual enlargement. Not until the 1850s did either begin to adopt power-driven machinery, usually a distinctive feature of the factory system.

The factory system sprang full-blown upon the American scene at Waltham, Massachusetts, in 1813, in the plant of the Boston Manufacturing Company. In 1822 its promoters, the Boston Associates, developed a new center at a village, renamed Lowell, where the Merrimack River fell thirty-five feet. At this "Manchester of America" the Merrimack Manufacturing Company developed a new plant similar to the Waltham mill. Another sprang up in 1823 at Chicopee, and before 1850 textile mills appeared at many other places in Massachusetts, New Hampshire, and Maine. By 1850, as good waterpower locations were occupied, steam power was becoming common in textile manufacture. Companies organized on the Waltham plan produced by 1850 a fifth of the nation's total output of cotton cloth. The chief features of this plan were large capital investment, the concentration of all processes in one plant under unified management, and specialization in a relatively coarse cloth requiring minimum skill by the workers.

The founders of the enterprise sought to establish at Lowell an industrial center compatible with republican values of plain living and high thinking. During the early decades of the nineteenth century, Jefferson and others had claimed that urban-industrial development threatened a republican form of government rooted in self-reliant agrarianism. Sensitive to this view, Lowell's owners insisted that they could design model factory centers and communities that would strengthen rather than corrupt the social fabric. To avoid the drab, crowded, and wretched life of English mill villages, they located American mills in the countryside and established an ambitious program of paternal supervision for the workers.

The operatives in the Lowell factories were mostly young women from New England farm families. Employers preferred women because they could pay them less than men. Moreover, by the 1820s there was a surplus of females in the region because so many men had migrated westward in search of cheap land and new economic opportunities. As many of the household goods produced by daughters gave way to the "store-bought" goods of a market economy, young farm women faced diminishing prospects for employment as well as for marriage. The chance to escape the routine of farm life and to earn cash money to help the family or improve their own circumstances also drew many women workers to the Lowell mills. As one female mill worker explained, she was working because of "a father's debts . . . to be paid, an aged mother to be supported, a brother's ambition to be aided." Another stressed in a letter to her parents the greater excitement and fellowship afforded by life in Lowell: "You may think me unkind but how can you blame me for wanting to stay here. I have but one life to live and I want to enjoy myself as well as I can."

In the early 1820s a steady stream of single women began flocking toward Lowell and the other mill towns cropping up across the region. To reassure worried parents, the mill owners promised to provide the "Lowell girls" with tolerable work, prepared meals, secure and comfortable housing, moral discipline, and a variety of educational and cultural opportunities such as lectures and evening classes. Kentucky statesman Henry Clay asserted that the Lowell experiment "will tell whether the manufacturing system is compatible with the social virtues."

Initially the "Lowell idea" worked pretty much according to plan. Visitors commented on the well-designed mills with their lecture halls and libraries. The laborers appeared "healthy and happy." One appreciative worker, in fact, described the new community as demonstrating that "corporations should have souls, and should exercise a paternal influence over the lives of their operatives." Lowell was certainly paternalistic. The women workers lived in dormitories staffed by matronly supervisors who rigidly enforced mandatory church attendance, temperance regulations, and curfews.

Despite their twelve-hour day and seventy-two-hour week tending the knitting looms, some of the women found the time and energy to form study groups, publish a literary magazine, and attend lectures by Ralph Waldo Emerson and other luminaries of the era. But Lowell soon lost its innocence as it experienced mushrooming growth. By 1840 there were thirty-two mills and factories in operation, and the blissful rural town had become a bustling, grimy, bleak industrial city.

The cotton mills at Lowell, Massachusetts, 1852.

Other factory centers began sprouting up across New England, displacing forests and farms and engulfing villages, filling the air with smoke, noise, and stench. As early as 1832 the writer Washington Irving lamented that the "march of mechanical invention is driving everything poetical before it." Between 1820 and 1840 the number of Americans engaged in manufactures increased eightfold, and the number of city dwellers more than doubled.

Booming growth transformed the Lowell experiment in industrial republicanism. By 1846 a concerned worker told those young farm women thinking about taking a job in a factory that they would do well not to leave their "homes in the country. It will be better for you to stay at home on your fathers' farms than to run the risk of being ruined in a manufacturing village." The problem of the degeneration of morals attributed to life in the factory towns was accompanied by the emergence of class consciousness and labor unrest among the supposedly contented workers.

During the 1830s, as textile prices and mill wages dropped, relations between workers and managers rapidly deteriorated. A new generation of owners and foremen paid little heed to the original paternalistic philosophy and began stressing efficiency and profit margins over community values. They worked their machines and operatives at a faster pace, and the women workers organized strikes to protest deteriorating working conditions. In 1834, for instance, they unsuccessfully "turned out" (struck) against the mills after learning of a sharp cut in their wages. Visitors noted the growing similarity between Lowell and the dismal factory towns of England immortalized in Dickens's *Hard Times.*

The "Lowell girls" drew attention less because they were typical than because they were special. An increasingly common pattern for industry was the family system, sometimes called the Rhode Island or Fall River system, which prevailed in textile manufactures outside of northern New England. The Rhode Island factories, which relied on waterpower, often were built in unpopulated areas, and part of their construction included tenements or mill villages. Whole families might be hired, the men for heavy labor, the women and children for the lighter work. Like the Lowell model, the Rhode Island system promoted paternalism. Employers dominated the life of the mill villages, often setting rules of good behavior. Wages under the system are hard to establish, for employers frequently paid in goods from the company store. The hours of labor often ran from sunup to sunset, and longer in winter—a sixty-eight- to seventy-two-hour week. Such hours were common on the farms of the time, but in factories the work was more intense and offered no seasonal letup. The labor of children, common on the farm, excited little censure from communities still close to the soil. A common opinion at the time regarded the provision of gainful employment for the women and children of the "lower orders" as a community benefit.

CORPORATIONS AND INDUSTRY   Early American manufacturing firms usually took the form of individual proprietorships, family enterprises, or partnerships. However, the growing scale and complexity of business affairs led more and more firms to "incorporate" ownership. The success of the Boston Associates at Waltham and Lowell, and the growth of larger units, particularly in textiles, brought the corporate form into greater use. But until 1860 most manufacturing was carried on by unincorporated enterprises.

The corporate organization was more common for banking, turnpike, canal, and railroad companies, since many people then believed that the form should be reserved for such quasi-public and quasi-monopolistic functions. The irregular practices of wildcat banks also gave corporations a bad name in local communities throughout the period. Corporations were regarded with suspicion as the beneficiaries of special privileges, as threats to individual enterprises. "The very object of the act of incorporation is to produce inequality, either in rights, or in the division of property," one observer wrote in 1820. "*Prima facie,* therefore, all money corporations, are detrimental to national health. They are always for the benefit of the rich, and never for the poor." It would be years before corporations were widely regarded as agencies of free enterprise.

Banks of the time supplied mainly short-term commercial loans and long-term secured loans, but even before 1815 some of them had become active as investment banks—that is, they would take government or private securities in wholesale lots and put them on the market. The New York Stock Exchange, started in 1817, soon became the chief exchange for these securities, and the Boston Stock Exchange (1834) was the one on which manufacturing securities were traded before the Civil War. Most of the capital that financed new factories through the purchase of securities came from profits made earlier in commerce. New England's head start in commerce fueled its head start in factories. Foreign investments were important in building the canals and railroads, but contributed little to manufacturing. The same was true of investments by the states.

Still, most of the country remained wedded to agriculture. Industry was heavily concentrated in the Northeast. In southern New England, especially its coastal regions, and along the Hudson and Delaware Rivers, the concentration of industry rivaled that in any of the industrialized parts of Britain and exceeded that in most parts of Europe.

In the 1860 census of manufactures, cotton textiles stood ahead of all other categories in rank order of value added (value of product minus value of raw material). Recognizing the primacy of the fiber in exports as well, the census report began with these words: "The growth of the culture and manufacture of cotton in the United States constitutes the

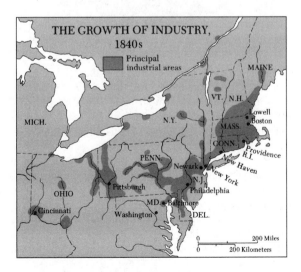

A photograph of Boston in 1860 made from an aerial balloon.

most striking feature of the industrial history of the last fifty years." In all, American industry in 1860 employed 1,311,000 workers in 140,000 establishments; with a capital investment of just over $1 billion, output amounted to $1.9 billion (up significantly from 1810's total output of $149 million), of which the value added by manufacturing was $854 million.

INDUSTRY AND CITIES The rapid growth of commerce and industry impelled a rapid growth of cities. Using the census definition of "urban" as places with 8,000 inhabitants or more, the proportion of urban population grew from 3.3 percent in 1790 to 16.1 percent in 1860. Modern cities have served three major economic functions: they have been centers of trade and distribution, centers of manufacturing, and centers of administration. Until near the mid-nineteenth century American cities

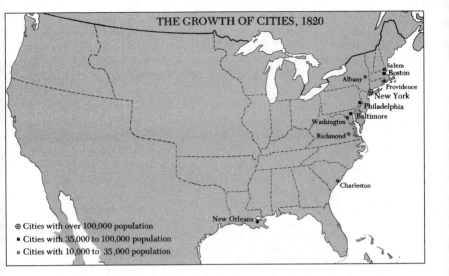

THE GROWTH OF CITIES, 1820

Salem
Boston
Albany
Providence
New York
Philadelphia
Baltimore
Washington
Richmond
Charleston
New Orleans

⊙ Cities with over 100,000 population
■ Cities with 35,000 to 100,000 population
○ Cities with 10,000 to 35,000 population

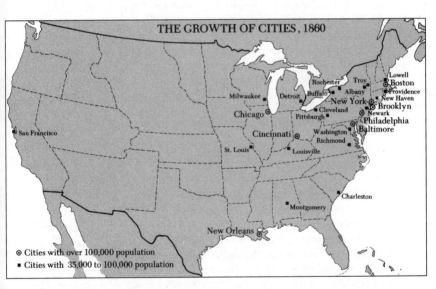

THE GROWTH OF CITIES, 1860

Rochester   Troy   Lowell
Buffalo   Albany   Boston
Milwaukee   Detroit   Providence
                New York   New Haven
Chicago   Cleveland   Brooklyn
        Pittsburgh   Newark
                Philadelphia
Cincinnati   Washington   Baltimore
St. Louis   Richmond
        Louisville
San Francisco

Charleston
Montgomery

New Orleans

⊙ Cities with over 100,000 population
■ Cities with 35,000 to 100,000 population

grew mainly in response to the circumstances of transportation and trade. Because of their strategic locations the four great Atlantic seaports of New York, Philadelphia, Baltimore, and Boston held throughout the pre–Civil War period the relative positions of leadership they had gained by the end of the Revolution. New Orleans became the nation's fifth-largest city from the time of the Louisiana Purchase. Its focus on cotton exports, to the neglect of imports, however, eventually caused it to lag behind its eastern competitors. New York outpaced all its competitors and the nation as a whole in its population growth. By 1860 it was the first American city to reach a population of more than a million, largely because of its superior harbor and its unique access to commerce.

Pittsburgh, at the head of the Ohio River, was already a center of iron production by 1800, and Cincinnati, at the mouth of the Little Miami, soon surpassed all other meatpacking centers, with pork a specialty. Louisville, because it stood at the falls of the Ohio, became an important stop for trade and remained so after the short Louisville and Portland Canal bypassed the falls in 1830. On the Great Lakes the leading cities also stood at important breaking points in water transportation: Buffalo, Cleveland, Detroit, Chicago, and Milwaukee. Chicago was well located to become a hub of both water and rail transportation on into the trans-Mississippi West. During the 1830s St. Louis tripled in size mainly because most of the trans-Mississippi fur trade was funneled down the Missouri River. By 1860 St. Louis and Chicago were positioned to challenge Boston and Baltimore for third and fourth places.

Before 1840 commerce dominated the activities of major cities, but early industry often created new concentrations of population at places convenient to waterpower or raw materials. During the 1840s and 1850s, however, the stationary steam engine and declining transportation costs more and more offset the advantages of locations near waterpower and resources, and the attractions of older cities were enhanced: pools of experienced labor, capital, warehousing and trading services, access to information, the savings of bulk purchasing and handling, and the many amenities of city life. Urbanization thus was both a consequence of economic growth and a positive force in its promotion.

IMMIGRATION

Amid all the new economic growth, one condition of American life carried over beyond the mid-nineteenth century: land remained plentiful and relatively cheap, while labor was scarce and relatively dear. A decline in the birth rate coinciding with the onset of industry and urbanization reinforced this condition. The United States remained a strong magnet for immigrants, offering them chances to take up farms in the country or jobs in the cities. Glowing reports from early arrivals who made good reinforced romantic views of American opportunity and freedom. "Tell Miriam," one immigrant wrote back, "there is no sending children to bed without supper, or husbands to work without dinner in their bags." A German immigrant in Missouri applauded the "absence of overbearing soldiers, haughty clergymen, and inquisitive tax collectors."

During the forty years from the outbreak of the Revolution until the end of the War of 1812, immigration had slowed to a trickle. The wars of the French Revolution and Napoleon restricted travel until 1815.

Within a few years, however, packet lines had begun to cross the north Atlantic, and competing shippers who needed westbound payloads kept the transatlantic fares as low as $30 per person. One informed estimate revealed that from 1783 to 1819 total arrivals numbered about 250,000, or something under 7,000 per year. Thereafter the pace followed just behind the growth of business. For two decades the numbers rose steadily: 10,199 in 1825; 23,322 in 1830; 84,066 in 1840. After 1845 the tempo picked up rapidly. During the 1830s total arrivals had numbered fewer than 600,000. In the 1840s almost three times as many, or 1.7 million, immigrated, and during the 1850s 2.6 million more came. The years from 1845 to 1854 saw the greatest proportionate influx of immigrants in American history, 2.4 million, or about 14.5 percent of the total population in 1845.

During the early 1800s most European immigrants entered the United States through the Port of New York. Ships would discharge passengers at wharves, and the newcomers would immediately have to fend for themselves in their alien environment. Before long thieves, thugs, and wily con men began preying upon the new arrivals. The infectious diseases that many of the immigrants brought with them also aroused popular concern.

By 1855 the problems associated with the immigrants' arrival in America provoked the New York state legislature to lease Castle Garden, at the southern tip of Manhattan, for use as an immigration receiving center. Inside the depot, clerks would record the names, nationalities, and destinations of the new arrivals, physicians would give them a cursory physical exam, and labor bureau representatives would assist them in seeking jobs.

THE IRISH   In 1860 America's population was 31 million, with more than one of every eight foreign born. The largest groups among them were 1.6 million Irish, 1.2 million Germans, and 588,000 British (mostly English). The Irish had a long-standing reason for migrating from their country: resentment of British rule, British landlords, British Protestantism, and British taxes. But what caused so many Irish to flee their homeland in the nineteenth century was the onset of a prolonged depression that brought immense social hardship. The most densely populated country in Europe, Ireland was so ravaged by the economic collapse that in rural areas the average age at death declined to nineteen.

By the 1830s the number of Irish migrants to America was growing quickly, and after an epidemic of potato rot in 1845 brought famine to rural Ireland that killed upwards of a million peasants, the flow of Irish immigrants to Canada and the United States rose to a flood. Horrible conditions at home made Irish peasants attentive to the recruiting efforts of shipping companies and American employers searching for

Steerage Accommodation Unequalled for Ventilation, Light, and Care for Passengers' Comfort.

Passengers cannot do better than take their Tickets from our Agents before leaving home.

WHITE STAR LINE

UNITED STATES — MAIL STEAMERS.

BRITANNIC.   CELTIC.   GERMANIC.   ADRIATIC.   BALTIC.
REPUBLIC.   OCEANIC.   GAELIC.   BELGIC.

THESE WELL-KNOWN, FAST MAIL STEAMERS SAIL FROM

LIVERPOOL TO NEW YORK,
EVERY THURSDAY,

GERMANIC,	Thursday, Aug. 31	BRITANNIC,	Thursday, Oct. 26
CELTIC,	„ Sept. 7	GERMANIC,	„ Nov. 9
BRITANNIC,	„ 21	CELTIC,	„ 16
GERMANIC,	„ Oct. 5	BRITANNIC,	„ 30
CELTIC,	„ 12		

Calling at QUEENSTOWN on the Following Day.

These splendid, full-powered, First-class Iron Screw Steamers are among the largest and most powerful vessels afloat, and are distinguished for the shortness and regularity of their passages, and the completeness and comfort of their passenger accommodation.

SALOON PASSAGE, 15, 18, AND 21 GUINEAS EACH BERTH,
According to State Room selected, all having equal Privileges in Saloon. Children under Twelve Years, Half-Fare. Infants Free.
Return Tickets, available for one year, issued at Reduced Rates,

STEERAGE FARE to NEW YORK, BOSTON, or PHILADELPHIA,
Six Guineas (£6 6s.) including a plentiful supply of cooked Provisions.
Children under Eight years Half Fare, and Infants under 12 months £1 1s.

AN EXPERIENCED SURGEON IS CARRIED BY EACH STEAMER
STEWARDESSES IN STEERAGE TO ATTEND THE WOMEN AND CHILDREN. NO FEES OR EXTRA CHARGES

Passage can be engaged and Tickets obtained from any Agent of the "White Star" Line, or by sending name, age, and occupation, together with a deposit of One Pound in each berth, to

Wells & Holohan, Railway Agents, 6 Eden-quay, and 9

In 1847, nearly 214,000 Irish emigrated to the United States and Canada aboard ships of the White Star Line and other companies. Thirty percent of these immigrants died on board, despite company promises of "unusually spacious, well lighted, ventilated, and warmed" steerage accommodations.

cheap laborers. A popular emigrant song expressed the mythic image of America:

> They say there's bread and work for all,
> And the sun always shines there.

But dreaming of a new life in America was one thing; getting there was another. Thousands died of dysentery, typhus, and malnutrition during the six-week ocean crossing. In 1847 alone, 40,000 Irish perished aboard the overcrowded ships. "If crosses and tombs could be erected on water," lamented the United States commissioner for immigration, "the whole route of the emigrant vessels from Europe to America would long since have assumed the appearance of a crowded cemetery."

In 1847 Irish arrivals numbered above 100,000, and they stayed above that level for eight years, reaching a peak of 221,000 in 1851. By 1850 the Irish constituted 43 percent of the foreign-born population in the United States. Unlike the German immigrants, who were predominantly male, the Irish newcomers were more evenly apportioned by sex; in fact a slight majority of them were women, most of them single young adults. Most of the Irish arrivals had been tenant farmers, but their rural sufferings left them little taste for farm work and little money to travel or buy land in America. Great numbers of the men hired on with construction gangs building the canals and railways—about 3,000 set to work on the Erie Canal as early as 1818. Others worked in iron foundries, steel mills, warehouses, and shipyards. Many Irish women found jobs as domestic servants, laundresses, or textile mill workers in New England. In 1845 the Irish constituted only 8 percent of the work force in the Lowell mills; by 1860 they made up 50 percent. Although there were substantial Irish communities in New Orleans, Vicksburg, and Memphis, relatively few immigrants during the Jacksonian era found their way into the South, where land was expensive and industries scarce. The widespread use of slaves also left few opportunities in the region for free manual laborers.

Too poor to move inland, most of the destitute Irish congregated in the eastern cities, in or near their port of entry. By the 1850s the Irish made up over half the populations of Boston and New York City, and they were almost as prominent in Philadelphia. They clustered in murky slums and around Catholic churches, both of which became familiar features of the urban scene. Life in America beat starvation at home, but their new situation was anything but comfortable. Irish newcomers crowded into filthy, poorly ventilated tenements, plagued by high rates of crime, infectious disease, prostitution, alcoholism, and infant mortality. The archbishop of New York City at midcentury described the Irish as "the poorest and most wretched population that can be found in the world."

With few skills and little education, most of the new arrivals to the cities could find work only as manual laborers or servants. Although wages were significantly higher than in Ireland, Irish workingmen frequently toiled at the docks or in warehouses fifteen hours a day, seven days a week. Servant girls rose at dawn and worked sixteen hours a day to earn $1.50 per week. One immigrant commented on the working conditions in his new country in a letter to his father back in Ireland: "Believe me, there is no idle bread to be had here. If you get a dollar a day, you have got to earn it *well*."

But many enterprising Irish immigrants seized opportunities in their new environment to forge remarkable success stories. Twenty years after arriving in New York, Alexander T. Stewart became the owner of America's largest department store and thereafter accumulated vast real-estate holdings in Manhattan. Michael Cudahy, who began work in a Milwaukee meatpacking business at age fourteen, became head of the Cudahy Packing Company and developed the process for the summer curing of meats under refrigeration. Dublin-born Victor Herbert emerged as one of America's most revered composers, and Irish dancers and playwrights came to dominate the American stage. Irishmen were equally successful in the boxing arena and on the baseball diamond.

These accomplishments did little to quell the acute anti-Irish sentiments prevalent in nineteenth-century America. Irish immigrants confronted demeaning stereotypes and intense anti-Catholic prejudices. It was commonly assumed that the Irish were ignorant, filthy, clannish folk incapable of assimilation. George Templeton Strong, a prominent New York civic leader, expressed the contempt felt by many of his peers toward the Irish when he said: "Our Celtic fellow citizens are almost as remote from us in temperament and constitution as the Chinese." Even Theodore Parker, the esteemed minister and social reformer, dismissed the Irish as "the worst people in Europe to make colonists of." Many employers felt the same way, and "No Irish Need Apply" signs sprouted in every eastern city. But the Irish could be equally contemptuous of other groups, such as free African Americans who competed with them for low-status jobs. In 1850 the New York *Tribune* expressed consternation at the fact that the Irish, having themselves escaped from "a galling, degrading bondage" in their homeland, typically voted against any proposal for equal rights for the Negro and frequently arrived at the polls shouting, "Down with the Nagurs! Let them go back to Africa, where they belong." For their part, many African Americans viewed the Irish with equal disdain. In 1850 a slave expressed a common sentiment: "My Master is a great tyrant, he treats me badly as if I were a common Irishman."

Anti-immigrant cartoon showing drunken Irish and German immigrants making off with a ballot box.

In part because of the hostility they faced, the Irish communities in American cities retained much of their ethnic and cultural identity. Neighborhood newspapers, churches, political groups, saloons, volunteer fire companies, and fraternal associations such as the Friendly Sons of St. Patrick bolstered a sense of community. Especially popular were Irish militia companies with colorful names: the Jasper Greens, Napper Tandy Light Artillery, and Irish Rifles. The Hibernian Society and the Shamrock Society aided Irish immigrants, and Irish newspapers such as the Boston *Pilot* remain in circulation today.

Experienced at organized resistance to rent and tax collectors in their homeland, the Irish after becoming naturalized citizens formed powerful blocs of voters and found their way into American politics more quickly than any other immigrant group. Drawn mainly to the party of Jackson, they set a crucial pattern of identification with the Democrats that other ethnic groups by and large followed. In Jackson the Irish immigrants found a hero. Himself the son of Irish colonists, he was also popular for having defeated the hated British at New Orleans. In addition, the Irish loathing of aristocracy, which they associated with British rule, attracted them to the party claiming to represent "the common man." Although property requirements initially kept most Irish-Americans from voting, a New York state law extended the franchise in 1821, and five years later the state removed the property qualification altogether. In 1828 masses of Irish voters made the difference in the election between Jackson and John Quincy Adams. One newspaper expressed alarm at this new force in politics: "Every thing in the shape of an Irishman was drummed to the polls and their votes made to pass. . . . It was emphatically an Irish triumph. The foreigners have carried the day." Although women, African Americans, and Native Americans still could not vote, the Irish newcomers were able to use the franchise to exert a remarkable political influence.

Perhaps the greatest collective achievement of the Irish immigrants was stimulating the growth of the Catholic church in the United States. "In this country," wrote an Irish teacher in 1840, "the idea of Catholicity and Ireland is so blended in the minds of the American people, as to be in a manner inseparable." Years of persecution had instilled in Irish Catholics a fierce loyalty to the doctrines of the church, leading one Irish-American to proclaim that religion "overrides all other sovereigns, and has the supreme authority over all the affairs of the world." Such passionate attachment to Catholicism generated both community cohesion among Irish-Americans and fears of Romanism among American Protestants. By 1860 Catholics had become the largest single denomination in the United States.

THE GERMANS   During the eighteenth century, Germans had responded to William Penn's offer of free religious expression and cheap, fertile land by coming in large numbers to America. As a consequence, when a new wave of German migration formed in the 1830s, there were still large enclaves of Germans in Pennsylvania and Ohio who had preserved their language and cultures, and in the Old World style had clustered in agricultural villages.

The new German migration took on a markedly different cast. It peaked in 1854, just a few years after the crest of Irish arrivals, when 215,000 Germans disembarked in American ports. These immigrants included a large number of learned, cultured professional people—doctors, lawyers, teachers, engineers—some of them refugees from the failed German revolutions of 1830 and 1848. In addition to an array of political opinions ranging from laissez-faire conservatism to Marxism, the Germans at midcentury and after also brought with them a variety of religious preferences. A third of the new arrivals were Catholic, most were Protestants (usually Lutherans), and a significant number were Jewish or freethinking atheists or agnostics. By the end of the century some 250,000 German Jews had emigrated to America.

Unlike the Irish, the Germans settled more in rural areas than cities, and they included fair numbers of independent farmers, skilled workers, and shopkeepers who arrived with some means to get themselves established in skilled jobs or on the land. More so than the Irish, they migrated in families and groups rather than as individuals, and this clannish quality helped them better sustain elements of German language and culture in their New World environment. More of them also tended to return to their homeland. About 14 percent of the Germans eventually went back to their homeland, compared to 9 percent of the Irish.

Among the German immigrants who prospered in the New World were Ferdinand Schmacher, who began peddling oatmeal in glass jars in Ohio and eventually formed the Quaker Oats Company; Heinrich Steinweg, a piano-maker from Lower Saxony, who in America changed his name to Steinway and became famous for the quality of his pianos; and Levi Strauss, a Jewish tailor who followed the gold rushers to California and began making long-wearing work pants that later were dubbed blue jeans or Levi's. Carl Schurz, another German immigrant, became a general in the Union army, represented Missouri in the Senate, and served as secretary of the interior under President Hayes. Major centers of German settlement developed in Missouri and southwestern Illinois (around St. Louis), in Texas (near San Antonio), in Ohio, and in Wisconsin (especially around Milwaukee). The larger German communities developed traditions of bounteous food, beer, and music along with German *Turnvereine* (gymnastic societies), sharpshooter clubs, fire engine companies, and kindergartens.

THE BRITISH, SCANDINAVIANS, AND CHINESE   Among the British immigrants too were large numbers of professionals, independent farmers, and skilled workers. Some British workers, such as Samuel Slater, helped transmit the technology of British factories into the United States. Two other groups that began to arrive in some number during the 1840s and 1850s were just the vanguard of greater numbers to come. Annual arrivals from Scandinavia did not exceed 1,000 until 1843, but by 1860 a total of 72,600 Scandinavians lived in America. The Norwegians and Swedes gravitated to Wisconsin and Minnesota, where the climate and woodlands reminded them of home. By the 1850s the sudden development of California was bringing in Chinese who, like the Irish in the East, did the heavy work of construction. Infinitesimal in numbers until 1854, the Chinese in America numbered 35,500 by 1860.

NATIVISM   America had always been a land of immigrants, but the welcome accorded them had often been less than cordial. For many natives these waves of strangers in the land posed a threat of unknown languages and mysterious customs. The flood of Irish and German Catholics aroused Protestant hostility to "popery." A militant Protestantism growing out of the revivals in the early nineteenth century heated up the climate of opinion. There were fears of radicalism among the Germans and of voting blocs among the Irish, but above all hovered the menace of unfamiliar religious practices. Catholic authoritarianism was widely perceived as a threat to hard-won liberties, religious and political. Because the Catholic church in most places remained small enough to be attacked with impunity, it was a convenient target for political adventurers and fanatics.

In the 1830s nativism was conspicuously on the rise. Pointing to the Catholic missions sponsored by European groups and to the pope's trappings of monarchy in Italy, overheated patriots envisioned conspiracy and subversion in America. Samuel F. B. Morse, already at work on his telegraph, took time out from his painting and inventing to write two books demonstrating his theory that Catholicism in America was a plot of foreign monarchs to undermine American liberty before its revolutionary message affected their own people. In 1836 he ran for mayor of New York on a Native American ticket, and his books went through numerous editions. But the literature of conspiracy could scarcely compete with a profitable trade in other anti-Catholic books which, in the guise of attacking evil, exploited salacious fantasies of sex in Catholic convents.

At times this hostility rekindled the spirit of the wars of religion. In 1834 a series of anti-Catholic sermons by Lyman Beecher, a popular Congregational minister who served as president of Lane Seminary in Cincinnati, aroused feelings to the extent that a mob attacked and burned the Ursuline Convent in Charlestown, Massachusetts. In 1844 armed clashes between Protestants and Catholics in Philadelphia ended with about 20 killed and 100 injured. Sporadically, the nativist spirit took organized form in groups that proved their patriotism by hating foreigners and Catholics.

As early as 1837 a Native American Association was formed at Washington, but the most significant such group was the Order of the Star Spangled Banner, founded in New York in 1849. Within a few years this group had grown into a formidable third party. In July 1854 delegates from thirteen states gathered to form the American party, which had the trappings of a secret fraternal order. Members pledged never to vote for any foreign-born or Catholic candidate. When asked about the organization, they were to say "I know nothing." In popular parlance the American party became the Know-Nothing party. For a season it seemed that the American party might achieve major-party status. In state and local campaigns during 1854 the Know-Nothings carried one election after another. In November they swept the Massachusetts legislature, winning all but two seats in the lower house. That fall they elected more than forty congressmen. For a while they threatened to control New England, New York, and Maryland, and showed strength elsewhere, but the anti-Catholic movement subsided when slavery became the focal issue of the 1850s, (it would be exploited again by the new Republican party).

The Know-Nothings demanded the exclusion of immigrants and Catholics from public office and extension of the period for naturalization from five to twenty-one years, but the party never gathered the political strength to effect such legislation. Nor did Congress act during the period to restrict immigration in any way. The first federal law on immigration, passed in 1819, enacted only safety and health regulations regarding supplies and the number of passengers on immigrant ships. This and subsequent acts designed to protect immigrants from overcrowding and unsanitary conditions were, however, poorly enforced.

IMMIGRANT LABOR   After 1840 waves of immigration contributed to economic growth and demand, whether the newcomer took up land or went into the city. By meeting the demand for cheap, unskilled labor, immigrants made a twofold contribution: they moved into jobs vacated or bypassed by those who went into the factories, and they themselves made up a pool of labor from which in time factory workers were drawn.

By 1860 immigrants made up more than half the labor force in New England mills. Even so, their pay was generally higher than that of the women and children who worked to supplement family incomes. The

A Know-Nothing cartoon showing the Catholic Church attempting through Irish immigration to control American religious and political life.

flood of immigration never rose fast enough to stop the long-term rise in wages. So factory labor continued to draw people from the countryside. Work in the cities offered higher real wages than work on the farm. Labor costs encouraged factory owners to seek ever more efficient machines in order to increase production without hiring more workers. In addition, the owners' desire to control the upward pressure on wage rates accelerated the emphasis on mass production. By stressing high production and low prices, owners helped workers afford to buy the items they made. Artisans who emphasized quality and craftsmanship for a custom trade found it hard to meet such competitive conditions. Many artisans in fact found that their skills were going out of style. Some took work as craftsmen in factories, while others went into small-scale manufacturing or shopkeeping, and some bought homesteads to practice their skills in the West.

ORGANIZED LABOR

EARLY UNIONS   Few workers of the period belonged to unions, but in the 1820s and 1830s a growing fear that they were losing status led artisans of the major cities into intense activity in labor politics and unions. As early as the colonial period craftsmen had formed fraternal and mutual-benefit societies, much like the medieval guilds, through which they regulated a system for training apprentices. These organizations continued to flourish well into the national period. After the Revolution, however, organizations of journeymen carpenters, masons, shipfitters, tailors, printers, and cordwainers (as shoemakers were called) became concerned with wages, hours, and working conditions and began to back up their demands with such devices as the strike and the closed shop (in which only union members could work). These organizations were local, often largely social in purpose, and frequently lasted only for the duration of the dispute.

Early labor unions faced serious legal obstacles. Unions were prosecuted as unlawful conspiracies. In 1806, for instance, Philadelphia shoemakers were found guilty of a "combination to raise their wages." The decision broke the union. Such precedents were used for many years to hamstring labor organizations until the Massachusetts Supreme Court made a landmark ruling in the case of *Commonwealth v. Hunt* (1842). In this case the court ruled that forming a trade union was not in itself illegal, nor was a demand that employers hire only members of the union.

Until the 1820s labor organizations took the form of local trade unions, confined to one city and one craft. During the ten years from 1827 to 1837 organization on a larger scale began to take hold. Philadelphia, in 1827, had the first city central, a collection of separate unions,

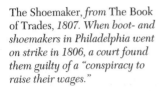

The Shoemaker, *from* The Book of Trades, *1807. When boot- and shoemakers in Philadelphia went on strike in 1806, a court found them guilty of a "conspiracy to raise their wages."*

formed after the carpenters had lost a strike for the ten-hour day. The Mechanics' Union of Trade Associations included carpenters, shoemakers, bricklayers, glaziers, and other groups. In the mid-1830s still wider organizations were attempted. In 1834 the National Trades' Union was set up in the effort to federate the city societies. At the same time national craft unions were established by the shoemakers, printers, combmakers, carpenters, and hand-loom weavers, but all the national groups and most of the local ones vanished in the economic collapse of 1837.

LABOR POLITICS With the removal of property qualifications for voting nearly everywhere, labor politics flourished briefly. In this, as in other respects, Philadelphia was in the forefront. A Working Men's party, formed there in 1828, gained the balance of power in the city council that fall. This success inspired other Working Men's parties in New York, Boston, and about fifteen states. In 1829 the New York party elected the head of the carpenters' union to the state legislature. The Working Men's parties were broad reformist groups devoted to the interests of labor. But they admitted to their ranks many who were not workers by any strict definition, and their leaders were mainly reformers and small businessmen. The labor parties faded quickly for a variety of reasons: the inexperience of labor politicians, which left the parties prey to manipulation by political professionals; the fact that some of their causes were espoused also by the major parties; and their vulnerability to attack on grounds of extreme radicalism or dilettantism. In addition, they often splintered into warring fractions which limited their effectiveness.

Once the parties had faded, however, many of their supporters found their way into a radical wing of the Jacksonian Democrats. This wing became the Equal Rights party and in 1835 acquired the name "Loco-focos" when their opponents from New York City's regular Democratic organization, Tammany Hall, turned off the gas lights at one of their meetings and the Equal Rights supporters produced candles, lighting them with the new friction matches known as Locofocos. The Locofocos soon faded as a separate group, but endured as a radical faction within the Democratic party.

While the labor parties elected few candidates, they did succeed in drawing notice to their demands, many of which attracted the support of middle-class reformers. Above all they carried on an agitation for free public education and the abolition of imprisonment for debt, causes that won widespread popular support. The labor parties and unions actively promoted the ten-hour day. In 1836 President Jackson established the ten-hour day at the Philadelphia Navy Yard in response to a strike, and in 1840 President Van Buren extended the limit to all government offices and projects. In private jobs the ten-hour day became increasingly common, although by no means universal, before 1860. Other reforms put forward by the Working Men's parties included mechanics' lien laws, to protect workers against nonpayment of wages; reform of a militia system that allowed the rich to escape service with fines but forced the poor to face jail terms; the abolition of "licensed monopolies," especially banks; measures to ensure hard money and to protect workers against inflated bank-note currency; measures to restrict competition from prison labor; and the abolition of child labor.

LABOR AND REFORM   After the Panic of 1837 the nascent labor movement went into decline, and during the 1840s the focus of its radical spirit turned toward the promotion of cooperative societies. During the 1830s there had been sporadic efforts to provide self-employment through producers' cooperatives, but the movement began to catch on after the iron molders of Cincinnati set up a successful shop in 1848. Soon the tailors of Boston had a cooperative workshop that employed thirty to forty men. New York was an especially strong center, with cooperatives among tailors, shirtmakers, bakers, shoemakers, and carpenters. Consumer cooperatives became much more vigorous and involved more people. The New England Protective Union, formed in 1845, organized a central purchasing agency for co-op stores and by 1852 was buying more than $1 million worth of goods while affiliated stores were doing in excess of $4 million in trade.

Most people were drawn to the producers' and consumers' movement for practical reasons: to reduce their dependence on employers or to reduce the cost of purchases. After peaking in the early 1850s, however, the cooperatives went into decline. The high mobility of

Americans and the heterogeneous character of the population as immigration increased created unfavorable conditions. Insufficient capital and weak, inexperienced management also plagued the cooperative movement.

THE REVIVAL OF UNIONS   The high visibility of reform efforts, however, should not obscure the continuing activity of unions, which began to revive with improved business conditions in the early 1840s. Still, the unions remained local, weak, and given to sporadic activity. Often they came and went with a single strike. The greatest single labor dispute before the Civil War came on February 22, 1860, when shoemakers at Lynn and Natick, Massachusetts, walked out for higher wages. Before the strike ended it had spread through New England, involving perhaps twenty-five towns and 20,000 workers. It stood out also because it was a strike the workers won. Most of the employers agreed to wage increases, and some also agreed to recognize the union as a bargaining agent.

This reflected the growing tendency of workers to view their unions as permanent. Workers began to emphasize the importance of union recognition and regular collective-bargaining agreements. They also shared a growing sense of solidarity. In 1852 the National Typographical Union revived the effort to organize skilled crafts on a national scale. Others followed, and by 1860 about twenty such organizations had appeared, although none was strong enough as yet to do much more than hold national conventions and pass resolutions.

JACKSONIAN INEQUALITY

During the years before the Civil War the United States had begun to develop a distinctive working class, most conspicuously in the factories and the ranks of common labor, often including many Irish or German immigrants. More and more craftsmen, aware that they were likely to remain wage earners, joined unions to protect their interests. But the American legend of "rags to riches," the image of the self-made man, was a durable myth. Speaking to the Senate in 1832, Henry Clay claimed that almost all the successful factory owners he knew were "enterprising self-made men, who have whatever wealth they possess by patient and diligent labor." The legend had just enough basis in fact to gain credence. John Jacob Astor, the wealthiest man in America, worth more than $20 million at his death in 1848, came of humble if not exactly destitute origins. Son of a minor official in Germany, he arrived in 1784 with little or nothing, made a fortune first on the western fur trade, then parlayed that into a large fortune in New York real estate. But his and similar cases were more exceptional than common.

Research by social historians on the rich in major eastern cities show that while men of moderate means could sometimes run their inheritances into fortunes by good management and prudent speculation, those who started with the handicaps of poverty and ignorance seldom made it to the top. In 1828 the top 1 percent of New York's families (owning $34,000 or more) held 40 percent of the wealth, and the top 4 percent held 76 percent. Similar circumstances prevailed in Philadelphia, Boston, and other cities.

A supreme irony of the times was that "the age of the common man," "the age of Jacksonian Democracy," seems actually to have been an age of increasing social rigidity. Years before, the colonists had brought to America conceptions of a social hierarchy that during the eighteenth century corresponded imperfectly with the developing reality. In the late eighteenth century, slavery aside, American society probably approached equality more closely than any population its size anywhere else in the world. During the last half of the 1700s, one historian has argued, social mobility was higher than either before or since. By the time popular egalitarianism caught up with reality, reality was moving back toward greater inequality.

Why this happened is difficult to say, except that the boundless wealth of the untapped frontier narrowed as the land was occupied and claims on various opportunities were staked out. Such developments took place in New England towns even before the end of the seventeenth century. But despite growing social distinctions, it seems likely that the white population of America, at least, was better off than the general run of European peoples. New frontiers, geographical and technological, raised the level of material well-being for all.

FURTHER READING

On economic development in the nation's early decades, see Stuart W. Bruchey's *Enterprise: The Dynamic Economy of a Free People* (1990) and W. Elliot Brownlee's *Dynamics of Ascent: A History of the American Economy* (2nd ed., 1979). Older, yet still valuable, are Douglass C. North's *The Economic Growth of the United States, 1790–1860* (1961)° and Thomas C. Cochran and William Miller's *The Age of Enterprise: A Social History of Industrial America* (rev. ed., 1961).°

The resilient classic on transportation and economic growth is George

°These books are available in paperback editions.

R. Taylor's *The Transportation Revolution, 1815–1861* (1951). Concurrent with transportation innovations was industrial growth. Thomas C. Cochran's *Frontiers of Change: Early Industrialism in America* (1981) is a useful survey. The business side of industrial growth can be studied in Elisha P. Douglass's *The Coming of Age of American Business* (1971). The impact of technology is traced in David J. Jeremy's *Transatlantic Industrial Revolution: The Diffusion of Textile Technologies between Britain and America* (1981) and Merritt R. Smith's *Harper's Ferry Armory and the New Technology: The Challenge of Change* (1977).

Richard D. Brown's *Modernization: The Transformation of American Life, 1600–1865* (1976) assesses the impact of technology on living patterns. How American values were affected by the new industrial system is assessed in John F. Kasson's *Civilizing the Machine: Technology and Republican Values in America, 1776–1900* (1976)° and Leo Marx's *The Machine in the Garden: Technology and the Pastoral Ideal in America* (1964).° Paul Johnson's *A Shopkeepers Millennium: Society and Revivals in Rochester, New York, 1815–1837* (1978) studies the role religion played in the emerging industrial order.

The attitude of the worker during this time of transition is surveyed in Joseph G. Rayback's *A History of American Labor* (rev. ed., 1966). Edward E. Pessen's *Most Uncommon Jacksonians: The Radical Leaders of the Early Labor Movement* (1967) concentrates on political reactions. Detailed case studies of working communities include Anthony F. C. Wallace's *Rockdale: The Growth of an American Village in the Early Industrial Revolution* (1978)°; Thomas Dublin's *Women at Work: The Transformation of Work and Community in Lowell, Massachusetts, 1826–1860* (1979)°; Stephen Thernstrom's *Poverty and Progress* (1964),° on Newburyport, Massachusetts; and Sean Wilentz's *Chants Democratic* (1984), on New York City. Walter Licht's *Working for the Railroad* (1983) is rich in detail.

For introductions to urbanization, see Sam Bass Warner, Jr.'s *The Urban Wilderness* (1972) and Richard C. Wade's *The Urban Frontier* (1959). A recent valuable case study is Edward K. Spann's *The New Metropolis: New York City, 1840–1857* (1981). Studies of the origins of immigration include Oscar Handlin's classic *The Uprooted* (2nd ed., 1973)° and Marcus Lee Hansen's *The Atlantic Migration, 1607–1860* (1940). Charles Dickens's *American Notes* (1842)° gives an Englishman's view of mid-nineteenth-century America.

°These books are available in paperback editions.

13 ⤸

AN AMERICAN RENAISSANCE:
ROMANTICISM AND REFORM

RATIONAL RELIGION

The American novelist Nathaniel Hawthorne once lamented "the difficulty of writing a romance about a country where there is no shadow, no antiquity, no mystery, no picturesque and gloomy wrong." Unlike nations of the Old World, rooted in shadow and mystery, entwined in historic cultures and traditions, the United States was an infant nation swaddled in the ideas of the Enlightenment. Those ideas, most vividly set forth in Jefferson's Declaration, had in turn a universal application. In the eyes of many if not most citizens, the "first new nation" had a mission to stand as an example to the world, much as John Winthrop's "city upon a hill" had once stood as an example to erring humanity. The concept of America as having a special mission in fact still carried spiritual overtones, for the religious fervor quickened in the Great Awakening had reinforced the idea of national purpose. In turn the sense of high calling infused the national character with an element of perfectionism—and an element of impatience when reality fell short of expectations. The combination brought major reforms and advances in human rights. It also brought disappointments that at times festered into cynicism and alienation.

DEISM   The currents of the Enlightenment and the Great Awakening, now mingling, now parting, flowed on into the nineteenth century and in different ways eroded the remnants of Calvinist orthodoxy. As time passed, the orthodox image of a just but stern God promising predestined hellfire and damnation gave way to a more optimistic religious outlook. Enlightenment rationalism increasingly stressed humankind's inherent goodness rather than depravity, and it encouraged a belief in social progress and the promise of individual perfectibility.

Many leaders of the Revolutionary War era, such as Jefferson and Franklin, became deists, even while nominally attached to existent churches. Deism, which arose in eighteenth-century Europe, carried the logic of Sir Isaac Newton's image of the world as a smoothly operating machine to its logical conclusion. The God of the deist had planned the universe, built it, set it in motion, and then left it to its own fate. By the use of reason people might grasp the natural laws governing the universe. Thomas Paine in *The Age of Reason* (1794) defined religious duties as "doing justice, loving mercy and endeavoring to make our fellow creatures happy," a message of Quaker-like simplicity. But ever the controversialist, Paine felt obliged to assail the "superstition" of the Scriptures and the existing churches—"human inventions set up to terrify and enslave mankind and monopolize power and profit."

Orthodox believers could hardly distinguish such doctrine from atheism, but Enlightenment rationalism soon began to make deep inroads into American Protestantism. The old Puritan churches around Boston proved most vulnerable to the logic of the Enlightenment. A strain of rationalism had run through Puritan belief in its stress on the need for right reason to interpret the Scriptures. Boston's progress—or some would say degeneration—from Puritanism to prosperity had persuaded many rising families that they were anything but sinners in the hands of an angry God. Drawn toward more consoling and less strenuous doctrines, some went back to the traditional rites of the Episcopal church. More of them simply dropped or qualified their adherence to Calvinism while remaining in the Congregational churches.

UNITARIANISM AND UNIVERSALISM   By the end of the eighteenth century many New Englanders were drifting into Unitarianism, a belief that emphasized the oneness and benevolence of God, the inherent goodness of humankind, and the primacy of reason and conscience over established creeds and confessions. People were not inherently depraved, Unitarians stressed; they were capable of doing tremendous good, and *all* were eligible for salvation. One stale jest had it that Unitarians believed in the fatherhood of God, the brotherhood of man, and the neighborhood of Boston. Boston was very much the center of the movement, and it flourished chiefly within Congregational churches that kept their standing in the established order until controversy began to smoke them out. During the early nineteenth century, more and more liberal churches accepted the name of Unitarian.

William Ellery Channing of Boston's Federal Street Church emerged as the most inspiring Unitarian leader. "I am surer that my rational nature is from God," he said, "than that any book is an expression of his will." A "Conference of Liberal Ministers," formed in 1820, became in 1826 the American Unitarian Association with 125 churches (all but 5 of them in Massachusetts), including 20 of the 25 oldest Calvinist churches in the United States. That same year, when the Presbyterian minister Lyman Beecher moved to Boston, he lamented: "All the literary men of Massachusetts were Unitarian; all the trustees and professors of Harvard College were Unitarian; all the elite of wealth and fashion crowded Unitarian churches."

A parallel movement, Universalism, attracted a different social group: working-class people of more humble status. In 1779 John Murray, who had come from England as a missionary for the new doctrine, founded the first Universalist church at Gloucester, Massachusetts. In 1794 a Universalist convention in Philadelphia organized the sect. Universalism stressed the salvation of all men and women, not just a predestined few. God, they taught, was too merciful to condemn anyone to eternal punishment. The unregenerate would suffer in proportion to their sins, but eventually all souls would come into harmony with God. "Thus, the Unitarians and Universalists were in fundamental agreement," wrote one historian of religion, "the Universalists holding that God was too good to damn man; the Unitarians insisting that man was too good to be damned."

THE SECOND GREAT AWAKENING

By the end of the eighteenth century, Enlightenment secularism had made deep inroads into American thought. In 1799 only a handful of Yale undergraduates professed a belief in religion, and the following year there was only one church member in the graduating class. Yet for all the impact of rationalism, Americans remained a profoundly religious people—as they have ever since. There was, the perceptive French visitor Alexis de Tocqueville observed, "no country in the world where the Christian religion retains a greater influence over the souls of men than in America." Around 1800 fears that secularism was indeed taking root sparked a revival that soon grew into a Second Awakening.

An early exemplar of the movement, Timothy Dwight, became president of Yale College in 1795 and struggled to purify a place which, in Lyman Beecher's words, had turned into "a hotbed of infidelity," where students openly discussed French radicalism, deism, and perhaps things even worse. Like his grandfather, Jonathan Edwards, "Pope Timothy" had the gift of moving both mind and spirit, of reaching both the lettered and the unlettered. The result was a series of revivals that swept the student body and spread to all of New England as well. "Wheresoever students were found," wrote a participant in the 1802 revival, "the reigning impression was, 'surely God is in this place.' "

After its founding in 1808, Jedediah Morse's Andover Seminary reinforced orthodoxy and the revival spirit so forcefully that its location came to be known as "Brimstone Hill." Morse lambasted "the insidious encroachments of *innovation*—that evil and beguiling spirit which is now stalking to and fro in the earth, seeking whom it may devour." To avoid Harvard's fate, Morse and his associates made professors assent to an Andover Creed of double-distilled Calvinism. The religious intensity and periodic revivals at Andover and Yale had their counterparts in many colleges for the next fifty years, since most were under the control of evangelical denominations.

REVIVALS ON THE FRONTIER   In its frontier phase the Second Awakening, like the first, generated great excitement and strange manifestations. It gave birth, moreover, to a new institution, the camp meeting, in which the fires of faith were repeatedly rekindled. Missionaries found ready audiences among lonely frontier folk hungry for spiritual intensity and a sense of community. Among the established sects, the Presbyterians were entrenched among the Scotch-Irish from Pennsylvania to Georgia. They gained further from the Plan of Union worked out in 1801 with the Congregationalists of Connecticut and later with other states. Since the two groups agreed on doctrine and differed mainly on the form of church government, they were able to form unified congregations and call a minister from either church. The result through much

While Methodist preachers address the crowd at this revivalist camp meeting, a man in the foreground is overcome with religious ecstasy.

of the Old Northwest was that New Englanders became Presbyterians by way of the "Presbygational" churches.

The Baptists embraced a simplicity of doctrine and organization that appealed especially to the common people of the frontier. Their theology was grounded in the infallibility of the Bible and the recognition of humankind's innate depravity. But they replaced the Calvinist notion of predestination with the concept of universal redemption and highlighted the ritual of adult baptism. They also explicitly stressed the equality of all men and women before God, regardless of one's wealth, social standing, or educational training. Since each congregation was its own highest authority, a frontier congregation need appeal to no hierarchy before setting up shop and calling a minister or naming one of its own. Sometimes whole congregations moved across the mountains as a body. As Theodore Roosevelt later described it: "Baptist preachers lived and worked exactly as their flocks. . . . they cleared the ground, split rails, planted corn, and raised hogs on equal terms with their parishioners."

But the Methodists, who shared with Baptists an emphasis on salvation by free will but established a much more centralized church structure, may have developed the most effective evangelical method of all, the circuit rider who sought out people in the most remote areas with the message of salvation as a gift free for the taking. The system began with Francis Asbury, an aggressive, fervent, and tireless British-born revivalist who scoured the trans-Appalachian frontier for lost souls, preaching some 25,000 sermons all the while defying hostile Indians and suffering through harsh winters. "When he came to America," a biographer wrote, "he rented no house, he hired no lodgings, he made no arrangements to board anywhere, but simply set out on the Long Road, and was traveling forty-five years later when death caught up with him." Asbury thus established a mobile evangelism perfectly suited to the frontier environment and the new democratic age.

Peter Cartwright emerged as the most successful Methodist "circuit rider," and this sturdy, fearless preacher grew justly famous for his highly charged sermons. He recalled stopping at a decaying Baptist church in frontier Kentucky: "While I was preaching, the power of God fell on the assembly, and there was an awful shaking among the dry bones. Several fell to the floor and cried for mercy. . . . I believe if I had opened the doors of the Church then, all of them would have joined the Methodist Church." Cartwright typified the Methodist disdain for an educated clergy, at one point arguing that it was "the illiterate Methodist preachers [who] actually set the world on fire." He was right. By the 1840s the Methodists had grown into the largest Protestant church in the country.

The Great Revival spread quickly through the West and into more settled regions back east. Camp meetings were held typically in late summer or fall, when farm work slackened. People came from far and wide, camping in wagons, tents, or crude shacks. Mass excitement swept up even the most skeptical onlookers, and infusions of the spirit moved participants to strange manifestations. Some went into cataleptic trances; others contracted the "jerks," laughed the "holy laugh," babbled in unknown tongues, or got down on all fours and barked like dogs to "tree the Devil." More sedate and prudent believers thought such excitements might be the work of the devil, out to discredit the true faith.

But to dwell on the bizarre aspects of the camp meetings would be to distort an institution that offered a social outlet to an isolated people. This was especially true for women, for whom the camp meetings provided an alternative to the rigors and isolation of frontier domesticity. Camp meetings also brought a more settled community life through the churches they spawned, and they helped spread a more democratic faith among the frontier people.

THE "BURNED-OVER DISTRICT"   Regions swept by such revival fevers might be compared to forests devastated by fire. In the single year 1830–31 alone, the number of churches in New England grew by one-third. Lyman Beecher called the awakening of 1831 "the greatest work of God, and the greatest revival of religion, that the world has ever seen." Western New York from Lake Ontario to the Adirondacks and including Rochester experienced such intense levels of evangelical activity that it was labeled the "Burned-Over District."

The most successful evangelist in the "Burned-Over District" was a lawyer named Charles Grandison Finney. In 1839 he preached for six months in Rochester and helped generate 100,000 conversions. He arrived at his intense religious convictions through a circuitous route. Raised in the backwoods of New York, he never heard the name of God mentioned in his home except in profanity. He left home to study law and then began his legal practice in Adams, New York. While visiting the local Presbyterian church, he scoffed when he heard the parishioners praying for revival. This led several young adults in the congregation, including the woman he would marry, to begin praying for him. Finney's conscience began to gnaw at him. He could not eat or sleep. Finally, one evening in 1821, he fled to the woods on the edge of town and a "mighty baptism of the Holy Ghost overwhelmed him." The spirit went through him "in waves and waves of liquid love," he remembered, and the next day he announced a new profession: "I have a retainer from the Lord Jesus Christ to plead his case," he told a caller. In 1823 Finney was ordained and for the next decade he subjected the Burned-Over District to yet another scorching.

An engraving depicting Charles Finney's conversion in the woods outside Adams, New York, 1821.

Finney went on to become the greatest single exemplar of evangelical Protestantism and, some would argue, the very inventor of professional revivalism. He wrestled with an age-old question that had plagued Protestantism for centuries: what role can the individual play in earning salvation? Orthodox Calvinists had long argued that people could neither earn nor choose salvation on their own accord. Grace was a gift of God, a predetermined decision incapable of human understanding or control. In contrast, Finney insisted that the only thing preventing conversion was the individual. And what most often discouraged individual conversion was the terrifying loneliness of the decision. Finney sought to combat such discomfort and bolster the courage of the ambivalent. He transformed revivals into collective conversion experiences in which spectacular public events displaced private communion and the unregenerate were brought into intense and public contact with praying Christians. Group prayer generated a sense of trust and common purpose among the community of strangers. The saving of souls did not have to wait for a miracle, Finney argued; it could come from careful planning.

Nor did Finney shrink from comparing his methods to those of politicians who used advertising and showmanship to get attention. The revivalist planned carefully to arouse excitement, not for its own sake but to rivet attention on the Word. "New measures are necessary from time to time to awaken attention and bring the gospel to bear on the public mind." To those who challenged such use of emotion Finney had a frank answer: "The results justify my methods." He carried the methods of the frontier revival into the cities of the East and as far as Great Britain.

Untrained in theology, Finney read the Bible, he said, as he would a law book, and worked out his own theology of free will. His gospel combined faith and good works: one led to the other. "All sin consists in selfishness," he said, "and all holiness or virtue, in disinterested benevolence." Regeneration therefore was "a change from selfishness to benevolence, from having a supreme regard to one's own interest to an absorbing and controlling choice of the happiness and glory of God's Kingdom."

In 1835 Finney took the chair of theology in the new Oberlin College, founded by pious New Englanders in Ohio's Western Reserve. Later he served as its president. From the start Oberlin radiated a spirit of reform predicated on faith; it was the first college in America to admit either women or blacks, and it was a hotbed of antislavery doctrine. Finney himself, however, held that people must be reformed from within, and cautioned against political action. In this, he held to a view that deeply influenced American social thought and action, a view that one historian has called romantic perfectionism: "Since social evils were simply individual acts of selfishness compounded, . . . it followed that . . . deep and lasting reform . . . meant an educational crusade based on the assumption that when a sufficient number of individual Americans had seen the light, they would automatically solve the country's social problems."

On the other hand, the ardor aroused by revivals led to narrow sectarian bickerings, repeated schisms, and the phenomenon known as "come-outism," which further multiplied the sects—a result almost always noted by foreign travelers. Revivals created a tremendous demand for preachers, which was met by ordaining men who lacked proper educational credentials. Independent congregations sprang up that recognized no other authority than the Bible. A movement arose independently in western Pennsylvania in 1809 led by Thomas and Alexander Campbell. The Campbellites adopted the name "Christian" and the practice of baptism by immersion. In 1832 a movement started in Lexington, Kentucky, to unite these churches as the Disciples of Christ.

THE MORMONS The Burned-Over District gave rise to several new religious departures, of which the most important was the Church of Jesus Christ of Latter Day Saints, or the Mormons. The founder, Joseph Smith, Jr., born in Vermont, was the fourth child of wandering parents who finally settled in the village of Palmyra, New York. In 1820 young Smith (then fourteen) had a vision of "two Personages, whose brightness and glory defy all description." They identified themselves as the Savior and God the Father and cautioned him that all existing beliefs were false. About three years later, Smith claimed, an angel led him to a hill where he found the Book of Mormon engraved on golden tablets in "reformed Egyptian." Later, with the aid of magic stones, he rendered into English what he found to be a lost section of the Bible. This was the story of ancient Hebrews who had inhabited the New World and to whom Jesus had made an appearance.

On the basis of this revelation, Smith began forming his own church in 1830, and within a few years he had gathered converts by the thousands. They found in Mormonism the promise of a pure kingdom of Christ in America and an alternative to the social turmoil and the degrading materialism of the era. From the outset the Mormon saints upset the "gentiles" with their close-knit community and their assurance of righteousness. In their search for a refuge from persecution, the Mormons moved from New York to Ohio, then to several places in Missouri, and finally in 1839 to Commerce, Illinois, which they renamed Nauvoo. There they settled and grew in number for some five years. In 1844 a crisis arose when dissidents accused Smith of justifying polygamy and published in the *Nauvoo Expositor* an exposé of polygamy in theory and practice. Smith's efforts to suppress the paper provoked a schism in the church. Non-Mormons in the neighboring counties attacked Nauvoo, and Smith and his brother Hyrum were arrested. On June 27, 1844, an anti-Mormon lynch mob stormed the feebly defended jail and shot both Joseph and Hyrum Smith.

In Brigham Young, successor to Joseph Smith, the Mormons found a leader of uncommon qualities: strong-minded, intelligent, and decisive.

The Mormon temple sits atop the highest hill in Nauvoo, Illinois, which the Mormons built into a city of 20,000 inhabitants in the early 1840s.

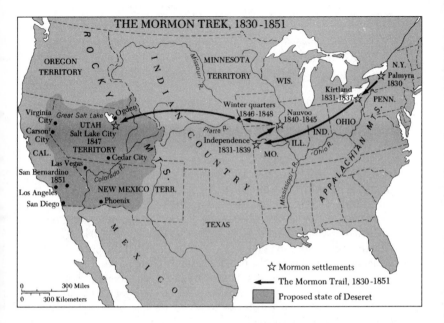

THE MORMON TREK, 1830-1851

☆ Mormon settlements

← The Mormon Trail, 1830-1851

Proposed state of Deseret

0   300 Miles

0   300 Kilometers

After the murder of the founder, Young patched up an unsure peace with the neighbors by promising an early exodus from Nauvoo. Before the year was out Young had chosen a new land from promotional literature on the West. It lay near the Great Salt Lake in Utah, then part of Mexico, guarded by mountains to the east and north, deserts to the west and south, yet itself fed by mountain streams——"Truly a bucolic region," in John Charles Frémont's words. Despite its isolation it was close enough to the Oregon Trail for the saints to prosper by trade with passing gentiles.

Brigham Young trusted God, but made careful preparations—no wandering in the wilderness for the Mormon Moses. As a result, the Mormon trek was better organized and less burdensome than most of the overland migrations of the time. Early in 1846 a small band of courageous believers crossed the frozen Mississippi into Iowa to set up the Camp of Israel, the first in a string of way stations along the route. By the fall of 1846 all 15,000 of the migrants had reached the prepared winter quarters on the Missouri River, where they paused until the first bands set out the next spring for the Promised Land.

The first arrivals at Salt Lake in July 1847 found only "a broad and barren plain hemmed in by mountains . . . the paradise of the lizard, the cricket and the rattlesnake." But by the end of 1848 the Mormons had developed an efficient irrigation system, and over the next decade, by cooperative labor, they brought about the greening of the desert. The Mormons had scarcely arrived when their land became part of the

United States. They organized at first their own state of Deseret (meaning "land of the honey bee," according to Young) with ambitious boundaries that reached the Pacific in southern California. But the Utah Territory, which Congress created, afforded them almost the same control, with Governor Young the chief political and theocratic authority.

MILLENNIALISM   In the 1840s the Burned-Over District was once more swept by religious fervor, this time centered on millennialism and spiritualism. One William Miller, a Baptist farmer-preacher in upstate New York near the Vermont line, had become persuaded that the signs of the times pointed to an early Second Advent of Christ. The year 1843, which Miller called the last sure "year of time," brought widespread excitement and religious delusions. Miller had set no exact date, but when 1843 passed, some of his followers set October 22, 1844, as the date of Christ's second coming. Even after that final disappointment Miller and others held to the belief that the millennium was near, however wrong their mathematics. In 1845 a loose organization was formed, which grew into the Advent Christian Association, from which in 1846 the Seventh Day Adventists broke away over the question of observing the Jewish Sabbath instead of the new Lord's Day.

Hard on the heels of the Millerite frenzy came the craze of "spirit-

A satirical depiction of William Miller and his followers ascending to heaven at the millennium.

rapping," which began with Kate and Margaret Fox, daughters of a farmer near Rochester. In 1848 strange knocking sounds in the house began to keep their family awake. The girls soon identified the sounds as messages from the spirit world. As the word spread, the curious gathered to hear about their revelations, and the Fox sisters were launched on a professional career of demonstrations as far away as England. Before long hundreds of spirit mediums were staging séances, communicating with the dead, and promoting their activities through spiritualist magazines.

This revival of faith reflected and reinforced the rising democratic belief in the power and wisdom of the common folk, with its preference for heart over head. No one expressed the hopefulness of this belief better than the future president, Andrew Johnson, political scourge of the Tennessee aristocrats:

> I believe that man can be elevated; man can become more and more endowed with divinity; and as he does he becomes more God-like in his character and capable of governing himself. Let us go on elevating our people, perfecting our institutions, until democracy shall reach such a point of perfection that we can acclaim with truth that the voice of the people is the voice of God.

ROMANTICISM IN AMERICA

The revival of piety during the early 1800s represented a widespread tendency throughout the Western world to accentuate the stirrings of the spirit over the dry logic of reason and the allure of material gain. Another great victory of heart over head was the romantic movement in thought, literature, and the arts. By the 1780s a revolt was brewing in Europe against the well-ordered world of the Enlightened thinkers. Were there not, after all, more things in this world than reason and logic could box up and explain: moods, impressions, feelings; mysterious, unknown, and half-seen things? After all, a clear and lucid idea, organized and understandable, might well be superficial. Americans also took readily to the romantics' emphasis on individualism, idealizing now the virtues of common people, now the idea of original or creative genius in the artist, the author, or the great personality.

Where the Enlightened thinkers of the eighteenth century had scorned the Middle Ages, the romantics now looked back to the period with fascination. America, lacking a feudal history, nonetheless had an eager audience for the novels of Sir Walter Scott and copied the Gothic style in architecture. Even more congenial to the American scene were the new themes in art. In contrast to well-ordered classical scenes,

Kaaterskill Falls, *1826, by Thomas Cole.*

romantic artists such as Thomas Cole (1801–1848) and Thomas Doughty (1793–1856) preferred wild and misty landscapes that often evoked more than they showed.

The German philosopher Immanuel Kant gave the worldwide romantic movement a summary definition in the title of his *Critique of Pure Reason* (1781), an influential book that emphasized the limits of human science and reason in explaining the universe. People have innate conceptions of conscience and beauty, the romantics believed, and religious impulses too strong to be dismissed as illusions. In those areas in which science could neither prove nor disprove concepts, people were justified in having faith. The impact of such ideas elevated intuitive knowledge at the expense of rational knowledge.

TRANSCENDENTALISM   The most intense expression of such thought was the Transcendentalist movement of New England, which drew its name from its emphasis on those things which transcended (or rose above) the limits of reason. Transcendentalism, said one of its chroniclers, assumed "certain fundamental truths not derived from experience, not susceptible of proof, which transcend human life, and are perceived directly and intuitively by the human mind." If transcendentalism drew much from Kant, it was also rooted in New England Puritanism, to which it owed a pervasive moralism. It also had a close affinity with the Quaker doctrine of the inner light. The inner light, a gift from God's grace, was transformed into intuition, a faculty of the mind.

An element of mysticism had always lurked in Puritanism, even if viewed as a heresy—Anne Hutchinson, for instance, had been banished for claiming direct revelations from God. The reassertion of mysticism had something in common, too, with the meditative religions of Asia— with which New England now had a flourishing trade. Transcendentalists steeped themselves in the teachings of the Buddha, the Mohammedan Sufis, the Upanishads, and the Bhagavad Gita.

In 1836 an informal discussion group soon named the Transcendental Club began to meet at the homes of members in Boston and Concord. It drew at different times clergymen such as Theodore Parker, George Ripley, and James Freeman Clarke; writers such as Henry Thoreau, Bronson Alcott, Nathaniel Hawthorne, and Orestes Brownson; and learned women such as Elizabeth and Sophia Peabody and Margaret Fuller. Fuller edited the group's quarterly review, *The Dial* (1840–1844), for two years before the duty fell to Ralph Waldo Emerson, soon to become the acknowledged high priest of transcendentalism.

EMERSON   More than any other person, Emerson spread the Transcendentalist gospel. Sprung from a line of New England ministers, he set out to be a Unitarian parson, then quit the "cold and cheerless" denomination before he was thirty. After travel to Europe, where he met England's great literary lights, Emerson settled in Concord to take up the life of an essayist, poet, and popular speaker on the lecture circuit, preaching the good news of optimism, self-reliance, and the individual's unlimited potential. Having found pure reason "cold as a cucumber" and discovered that the "ideal is truer than the actual," he was determined to *transcend* the limitations of inherited conventions and of rationalism in order to penetrate the inner recesses of the self. As he once explained, transcendentalism meant a belief in a realm "a little beyond" the rational world.

Emerson's lectures and writings hold the core of the Transcendentalist worldview. His notable lecture, "The American Scholar," delivered at Harvard in 1837, essentially summarized his first book, *Nature,* pub-

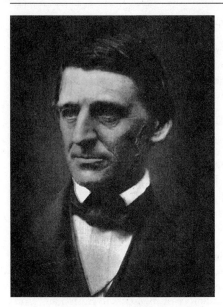

*Ralph Waldo Emerson,
author of* Nature, *America's
"intellectual Declaration of
Independence."*

lished the previous year. In that lecture he urged the audience to put
aside their awe of European culture and explore their own new world. It
was "our intellectual Declaration of Independence," said one observer.

Emerson's lecture on "The Over-soul" set forth a kind of pantheism,
in which the souls of all individuals commune with the great universal
soul, of which they are part and parcel. His essay on "Self-Reliance"
(1841) has a timeless appeal to youth with its message of individualism
and the cultivation of one's personality. Like most of Emerson's writings, it is crammed with quotations:

> Whoso would be a man, must be a nonconformist. . . . Nothing is at last
> sacred but the integrity of your own mind. . . . It is easy in the world to live
> after the world's opinion; it is easy in solitude to live after our own; but the
> great man is he who in the midst of a crowd keeps with perfect sweetness
> the independence of solitude. . . . A foolish consistency is the hobgoblin
> of little minds, adored by little statesmen and philosophers and divines. . . .
> Speak what you think now in hard words and tomorrow speak what tomor-
> row thinks in hard words again, though it contradict everything you said
> today. . . . To be great is to be misunderstood.

THOREAU   Emerson's young friend and Concord neighbor, Henry
David Thoreau, practiced the reflective self-reliance that Emerson
preached. "I like people who can do things," Emerson stressed, and

Thoreau, fourteen years his junior, could do many things well—carpentry, masonry, painting, surveying, sailing, gardening. Thoreau, Emerson noted, was "as ugly as sin, long-nosed, queer-mouthed," and possessed of "uncouth and somewhat rustic manners." But the philosophical son of a pencil-maker father and domineering, abolitionist mother displayed a sense of uncompromising integrity, outdoor vigor, and tart individuality that Emerson found captivating. "If a man does not keep pace with his companions," Thoreau wrote, "perhaps it is because he hears a different drummer."

Thoreau himself marched to a different drummer all his life. After Harvard, where he exhausted the resources of the library in gargantuan bouts of reading, and after a brief stint as a teacher in which he got in trouble for refusing to cane students, Thoreau settled down to eke out a living through his family's cottage industry of pencil making. But he made frequent escapes to drink in the beauties of nature. He showed no interest in the contemporary scramble for wealth. It too often corrupted

Henry David Thoreau, author of the American classics Walden *and "Civil Disobedience."*

the pursuit of happiness. "The mass of men," he wrote, "lead lives of quiet desperation."

Determined himself to practice plain living and high thinking, Thoreau boarded with the Emersons for a time and then embarked on an experiment in self-reliance. On July 4, 1845, he took to the woods to live in a cabin he had built on Emerson's land beside Walden Pond. He wanted to see how far he could free himself from the complexities and hypocrisies of modern commercial life, and to devote his time to observation, reflection, and writing. His purpose was not to lead a hermit's life. He frequently walked the mile or so to town to dine with his friends, and he often welcomed guests at his cabin. "I went to the woods because I wished to live deliberately," he wrote in *Walden, or Life in the Woods* (1854), "and not, when I came to die, discover that I had not lived."

While Thoreau was at Walden Pond, the Mexican War erupted. Believing it an unjust war to advance the cause of slavery, he refused to pay his state poll tax as a gesture of opposition, for which he was put in jail (only for one night; an aunt paid the tax). The incident was so trivial as to be almost comic, but out of it grew the classic essay "Civil Disobedience," (1849) which was later to influence the passive-resistance movements of Mahatma Gandhi in India and Martin Luther King in the American South. "If the law is of such a nature that it requires you to be an agent of injustice to another," Thoreau wrote, "then, I say, break the law. . . ."

The broadening ripples of influence more than a century after Thoreau's death show the impact a contemplative person can have on the world of action. Although both men lent their voices to worthy causes, Thoreau, like Emerson, shied away from involvement in public life. The Transcendentalists primarily supplied the force of an animating idea: people must follow their consciences. Though these thinkers attracted only a small following among the public at large in their own time, they inspired reform movements and were the quickening force for a generation of writers that produced the first great classic age of American literature.

The half-decade of 1850–1855 saw the publication of *Representative Men* by Emerson, *Walden* by Thoreau, *The Scarlet Letter* and *The House of the Seven Gables* by Nathaniel Hawthorne, *Moby-Dick* by Herman Melville, and *Leaves of Grass* by Walt Whitman. As the critic F. O. Mathiessen wrote in his book *American Renaissance:* "You might search all the rest of American literature without being able to collect a group of books equal to these in imaginative quality."

The Flowering of American Literature

HAWTHORNE   Nathaniel Hawthorne, the supreme artist of the New England group, never shared the sunny optimism of his neighbors or

Nathaniel Hawthorne, author of
The Scarlet Letter.

their perfectionist belief in reform. A sometime resident of Concord, but a native and longtime inhabitant of Salem, he was haunted by the knowledge of evil bequeathed to him by his Puritan forebears—one of whom had been a judge at the Salem witchcraft trial. After college at Bowdoin, he worked for some time in obscurity in Salem, gradually began to sell a few stories, and finally earned a degree of fame with his collection of *Twice-Told Tales* (1837). In these, as in most of his later work, he presented powerful moral allegories. His central themes examined sin and its consequences: pride and selfishness, secret guilt, selfish egotism, the impossibility of rooting sin out of the human soul. His greatest novels explored such burdens. In *The Scarlet Letter* (1850) Hester Prynne, an adulteress tagged with a badge of shame by the Puritan authorities, won redemption by her suffering, while the Reverend Arthur Dimmesdale was destroyed by his gnawing guilt and Roger Chillingworth by his obsession with vengeance.

DICKINSON   The flowering of New England featured, too, a foursome of poets who shaped the American imagination in a day when poetry was still accessible to a wide public: Henry Wadsworth Longfellow, John Greenleaf Whittier, Oliver Wendell Holmes, Sr., and James Russell Lowell. A fifth poet, Emily Dickinson, the most original and powerful of the lot, remained a white-gowned recluse in her second-story bedroom in Amherst, Massachusetts. As she once prophetically wrote, "Success is counted sweetest / By those who ne'er succeed." Only two of her almost 1,800 poems had been published (anonymously) before her death in 1886, and the full corpus of her work remained unknown for years thereafter. Born in Amherst in 1830, the child of a prominent, stern father and gentle mother, she received a first-rate secondary education and then attended the new Mount Holyoke Female Seminary.

Neither she nor her sister married, and they both lived out their lives in their parents' home.

Perhaps it was Emily's severe eye trouble during the 1860s that induced her solitary withdrawal from the larger society; perhaps it was the aching despair generated by her unrequited love for a married minister. Whatever the reason, her intense isolation led her to focus her writings on her own shifting psychic state. Her themes were elemental: life, death, fear, loneliness, nature, and, above all, God, a "Force illegible," a "distant, stately lover."

IRVING AND COOPER   A noted British critic asked in 1820: "In the four quarters of the Globe, who reads an American book?" Quoted out of context, the question rubbed Americans the wrong way, but the critic, an admirer of American institutions, foresaw a future flowering in the new country. He did not have long to wait, for within a year Washington Irving's *The Sketch Book* (1820), James Fenimore Cooper's *The Spy* (1821), and William Cullen Bryant's *Poems* (1821) were drawing wide notice in Britain as well as in America. Bryant's energies were drawn into journalism by his need to earn a living. As editor of the New York *Evening Post* he wielded an important influence in American life. Irving and Cooper went on to greater literary triumphs, and made New York for a time the national literary capital.

Irving in fact stood as a central figure in the American literary world from the time of his satirical *Diedrich Knickerbocker's A History of New York* (1809) until his death fifty years later. He showed that an American could, after all, make a career of literature, and was a confidant and advocate of numerous other writers. During those years a flood of histories, biographies, essays, and stories poured from his pen. A talented writer, Irving was the first to show that authentic American themes could draw a wide audience. Yet, as Melville later noted, he was less a creative genius than an adept imitator. Even the most "American" of his stories, "Rip Van Winkle" and "The Legend of Sleepy Hollow," drew heavily on German folk tales.

Cooper, a country gentleman, got his start as a writer on a bet with his wife that he could write a better novel than one they had just read. *Precaution* (1820) was an imitative story of manners in English high society, but the following year he brought out *The Spy* (1821), an historical romance based on a real incident of the American Revolution. In 1823 Cooper in *The Pioneers* introduced Natty Bumppo, an eighteenth-century frontiersman destined to be the hero of five novels collectively labeled *The Leather-Stocking Tales*. Natty Bumppo, a crack shot also known as Hawkeye, and his Indian friend Chingachgook, the epitome of the noble savage, took a place among the most unforgettable heroes of world literature. The tales of man pitted against nature in the backwoods, of hairbreadth escapes and gallant rescues, were the first successful romances of frontier life, and they served as models for the later cowboy novels and movies set in the Far West. In addition to the backwoods tales, Cooper also was the virtual creator of the sea novel in *The Pilot* (1823), another romance of the Revolution.

POE AND THE SOUTH   By the 1830s and 1840s new major talents had come on the scene. Edgar Allan Poe, born in Boston but reared in Virginia, was arguably America's most inventive genius in the first half of the century, and probably the most important American writer of the times. Poe's success had many dimensions. As a critic, he argued that the object of poetry was beauty (not truth) and that the writer should calculate his effect on the reader with precision. To that end he favored relatively short poems and stories, and wrote only one novel in his brief career. His poems, such as "The Raven," exemplified his theory, and although relatively few in number, won great fame. The tormented, heavy-drinking Poe was moreover a master of Gothic horror in the short story and the inventor of the detective story and its major conventions. He judged prose by its ability to provoke emotional tension, and since he considered fear to be the most powerful emotion, he focused his efforts on making the grotesque and supernatural seem disturbingly real to his readers. Anyone who has read "The Tell-Tale Heart" or "The Pit and the Pendulum" can testify to his success.

If Poe hardly fit Americans' image of the proper man of letters, neither did a group of southern writers who came to be called the southwestern humorists. With stories of the backwoods from Georgia westward they exploited frontier tall tales and the raw, violent life of the region. Their number included Davy Crockett, a sort of real-life Natty

Edgar Allan Poe, perhaps the most inventive American writer of the period.

Bumppo; George Washington Harris, whose hero, Sut Lovingood, lived up to his name; and Johnson Jones Hooper, author of *Some Adventures of Captain Simon Suggs* (1845), about a peerless con man whose motto became a national joke: "It is good to be shifty in a new country." Augustus Baldwin Longstreet, author of *Georgia Scenes* (1835), would hardly be remembered but for his stories about Ransy Sniffle and other examples of backwoods low life. Dismissed at the time as subliterary amusement, southwestern humor was later raised to the level of high art by Mark Twain.

Among southern authors, William Gilmore Simms best exemplified the genteel man of letters. Editor and writer in many genres, he had a prodigious output of poems, novels, histories, biographies, essays, short stories, and drama. He gained a wide audience with *Guy Rivers* (1834), first of a series of "Border Romances" set in frontier Georgia, but the peak of his achievement was in two novels published in 1835: *The Yemassee,* a story of Indian war in 1715, and *The Partisan,* first of seven novels about the Revolution in South Carolina. In his own time Simms was the preeminent southern author and something of a national figure, but he finally dissipated his energies in politics and the defense of slavery. He went down steadily in critical esteem, and most critics would agree with his own epitaph, that he had "left all his better works undone."

The duc de La Rochefoucauld-Liancourt, who visited the South in the 1790s, noted some cultural characteristics that continued to prevail in the nineteenth century: "In spite of the Virginian love for dissipation, the taste for reading is commoner there among men of the first class than in any other part of America; but the populace is perhaps more ignorant there than elsewhere." The readers of "the first class," however, tended to take their cues in literary and aesthetic matters from London or New York. They usually read English and northern authors to the neglect of their own, and preferred northern rather than southern magazines. And "men of the first class" who read widely tended to look upon literature as ornamental and a less praiseworthy activity than the high arts of oratory and statesmanship.

MELVILLE   Those southerners who followed the literary preferences of the North passed over the work of Herman Melville, whose literary reputation went into a decline after his initial successes. In the twentieth century Melville's good reputation was dramatically revived, elevating him into the literary pantheon occupied by only the finest American authors. Born of distinguished ancestry on both sides, Melville suffered a sharp reversal of fortunes when his father died a bankrupt. After taking various odd jobs, he shipped out as a seaman at age twenty. Some time later, after eighteen months aboard a whaler, he arrived in the

Harpooning sperm whales off the Hawaiian Islands, 1833.

South Seas and jumped ship with a companion in the Marquesas Islands. After several weeks spent with a friendly tribe in the valley of the Typees, he signed on to an Australian whaler, jumped ship again in Tahiti, and finally returned home as a seaman aboard a frigate of the United States Navy. An embroidered account of his exotic adventures in *Typee* (1846) became an instant popular success, which he repeated in *Omoo* (1847), based on his stay in Tahiti.

So many readers took his accounts as fictional (as in part they were) that Melville was inspired to write novels of nautical adventures, and he produced one of the world's great novels in *Moby-Dick* (1851). In the story of Captain Ahab and his obsessive quest for the white whale that had caused the loss of his leg, Melville explored the darker recesses of the soul just as his good friend Hawthorne had done. The book was aimed at two audiences. On one level it was a ripping good yarn of adventure on the high seas. But Ahab's single-minded mission to slay the evildoer turned the captain himself into a monster of destruction who sacrificed his ship, his crew, and himself to his folly, leaving as the one survivor the narrator of the story. Unhappily, neither the public nor the critics at the time accepted the novel on either level. After that Melville's career wound down into futility. He supported himself for years with a job in the New York Custom House and turned to poetry, much of which, especially the Civil War *Battle-Pieces* (1866), gained acclaim in later years.

WHITMAN   The most provocative American writer during the antebellum period was Walt Whitman, a remarkably vibrant personality who disdained inherited conventions and artistic traditions. There was something elemental in Whitman's character, something bountiful and generous and compelling— even his faults and inconsistencies were ample. Born on a Long Island farm, he moved with his family to Brooklyn and from the age of twelve worked mainly as a handyman and journalist, frequently taking the ferry across the river to booming, bustling Manhattan. The city fascinated him, and he gorged himself on the urban spectacle—shipyards, crowds, factories, shop windows. From such material he drew his editorial opinions and poetic inspiration, but he remained relatively obscure until the first edition of *Leaves of Grass* (1855) caught the eye and aroused the ire of readers. Emerson found it "the most extraordinary piece of wit and wisdom that America has yet contributed," but more conventional critics shuddered at Whitman's explicit sexual references and groused at his indifference to rhyme and meter as well as his buoyant egotism.

The jaunty Whitman, however, refused to conform to genteel notions of art, and he spent most of his career working on his gargantuan *Leaves of Grass,* enlarging and reshaping it in successive editions. The growth of the book he identified with the growth of the country, which he proclaimed in all its variety. "I hear America singing," he wrote, "the varied carols I hear." He sounded his "barbaric yawp over the roofs of the world," and wrote unabashedly:

> Do I contradict myself?
> Very well then I contradict myself,
> (I am large, I contain multitudes.)

While he celebrated America, Whitman also set out to "celebrate myself and sing myself." To his generation he was a startling figure with his frank sexual references and homoerotic overtones. He also stood out from the pack of fellow writers in rejecting the idea that a woman's proper sphere was in a supportive and dependent role.

Later, during the Civil War, Whitman went to Washington to see his injured brother. The injury was slight, but "the good gray poet" stayed on to visit the sick and wounded, to serve as attendant and nurse when needed. Out of his wartime service came *Drum Taps* (1865), containing his masterpiece of the 1860s, an elegy on the death of Lincoln: "When lilacs last in the dooryard bloom'd." In much of his prose Whitman vig-

Walt Whitman.

orously defended democracy and summoned Americans to higher goals than materialism.

FEMININE FICTION   In both poetry and fiction the antebellum reading public most loved edifying poems or "romances" that celebrated pious domestic life. Between 1830 and 1850 over 1,000 fictional works were published in the United States, and most of them revolved around domestic topics—courtship, marriage, religion, home management, child-rearing, and education. Such hearthside literature, redolent with an evangelical moralism and glazed with a meringue of sentimentalism, was intended to shore up the eroding strength of orthodox religious beliefs and conventional social and gender roles. The most popular of these novels were written by women, many of whom unapologetically viewed their fictions as idealizing sermons. As one of them confessed, "I mean always to write a good, pure, natural story, such as mothers are willing their daughters should read and such as will do good instead of harm."

Such saccharine fiction appealed not only to thousands of women readers but also to anxious male moralists who eagerly enlisted the aid of women in restoring the stabilizing social influence of the church and the family. They also wanted to channel female energies toward their "proper sphere" and away from organized efforts to promote political and legal equality for women or to allow women into the male work-place. One male editor advised that "it is far more important to the nation . . . that women should be good wives and mothers, than that they should excel in any one art or science which men can achieve as well as they." The patriarchal message was clear: women were to accept their role as self-denying, submissive protectors of the hearth now that husbands were too busy with commercial affairs to attend to such traditional priorities.

Some of the "damned mob of scribbling women," as Hawthorne once enviously and angrily labeled the popular female writers, openly rebelled against what Louisa May Alcott called the "twaddle" about a separate "woman's sphere" and about "sturdy oaks and clinging vines and man's chivalric protection of woman. Let woman find out her own limitations." But Alcott was in the minority; overall the explicit message of women writers during the antebellum era was one of acceptance of the "cult of domesticity." Their writings contained tears and prayers because they themselves experienced familial grief, practiced spiritual devotion, and sought imaginative escape.

THE POPULAR PRESS   The renaissance in literature coincided with a massive expansion in the popular press. The steam-driven Napier press, introduced from England in 1825, could print 4,000 sheets of newsprint in an hour. Richard Hoe of New York improved on it, inventing in 1847 the Hoe rotary press, which printed 20,000 sheets an hour. Like many advances in technology, this was a mixed blessing. The high cost of such a press made it harder for a person of small means to break into publishing. On the other hand it expedited production of cheap newspapers, magazines, and books—which were often cheap in more ways than one.

The New York *Sun*, in 1833 the first successful penny daily, and others like it often ignored the merely important in favor of scandals and sensations, true or false. James Gordon Bennett, a native of Scotland, perfected this style on the New York *Herald*, which he founded in 1835. His innovations drew readers by the thousands: the first Wall Street column, the first society page (which satirized the well-to-do until it proved more gainful to show readers their names in print), pictorial news, telegraphic news, and great initiative in getting scoops. Eventually, however, the *Herald* suffered from dwelling so much on crime, sex, and depravity in general.

The chief beneficiary of a rising revulsion against the gutter press was the New York *Tribune*, founded as a Whig organ in 1841. Horace Greeley, who became the most important journalist of the era, announced that it would be a cheap but decent paper avoiding the "matters which have been allowed to disgrace the columns of our leading Penny

Getting the News, California, 1850.

Papers." And despite occasional lapses, Greeley's "Great Moral Organ"
typically amused its readers with wholesome human-interest stories.
Greeley also won a varied following by plugging the reforms of the day.
Socialism, land reform, feminism, abolitionism, temperance, the protective tariff, internal improvements, improved methods of agriculture,
vegetarianism, spiritualism, trade unions—all got a share of attention.
The *Tribune*, moreover, set a new standard in reporting literary news.
Margaret Fuller briefly served as critic; in 1856 the *Tribune* became the
first daily to have a regular book-review column. For a generation it was
probably the most influential paper in the country. By 1860 its weekly
edition had a national circulation of 200,000. Meanwhile, the number of
newspapers around the country grew from about 1,200 in 1833 to some
3,000 in 1860.

Magazines found a growing market too. *Niles' Weekly Register*

(1811–1849) of Baltimore and Washington, founded by the printer Hezekiah Niles, was an earlier version of the twentieth-century news magazine. Niles provided accurate reports on the War of 1812 and made a reputation for good and unbiased coverage of public events—all of which make it a basic source for historians. The *North American Review* of Boston (1815–1940), started by a young Harvard graduate, achieved high standing among scholarly readers. Its editor adorned the journal with materials on American history and biography. It also featured coverage of European literature.

Harpers' Magazine (1850–present), originally the organ of the publishers Harper and Brothers, pirated the output of popular English writers in the absence of an international copyright agreement. Gradually, however, faced with an outcry against the practice, *Harpers'* began paying for fresh contributions and published original material by American authors. *Frank Leslie's Illustrated Newspaper* (1855–1922) in New York used large and striking pictures to illustrate its material, and generally followed its founder's motto: "Never shoot over the heads of the people." *Leslie's* and a vigorous competitor of somewhat higher quality, *Harper's Illustrated Weekly* (1857–1916), appeared in time to provide a thoroughgoing pictorial record of the Civil War.

The boom in periodicals gave rise to more journals directed to specialized audiences. Worthy of mention, among others, are such magazines as *Godey's Lady's Book* (1830–1898), *The Southern Literary Messenger* (1834–1864), *Hunt's Merchants' Magazine* (1839–1870), *DeBow's Commercial Review of the South and West* (1846–1880), and *The American Farmer* (1819–1897), the first important agricultural journal. The new methods of production and distribution boosted the book market as well. The publisher Samuel Goodrich estimated gross sales of books in America at $2 million in 1820, $12 million in 1850, and nearly $20 million in 1860. From 1820 to 1850, he estimated, books by American authors doubled their share of the market from about a third to about two-thirds.

EDUCATION

EARLY PUBLIC SCHOOLS   Literacy in Jacksonian America was surprisingly widespread, given the condition of public education. By 1840, according to census data, some 78 percent of the total population and 91 percent of the white population could read and write. Ever since the colonial period, in fact, Americans had had the highest literacy rate in the Western world. Most children learned their letters from church or private "dame" schools, from formal tutors, or from their families. When Abraham Lincoln came of age, he said, he did not know much. "Still, somehow, I could read, write and cipher to the rule of three, but that was all." At that time, about 1830, no state had a school system in the modern sense, although Massachusetts had for nearly two centuries required towns to maintain schools. Some major cities had the resources to develop real systems on their own. For instance, the Public School Society of New York, established in 1805, built a model system of free schools in the city, with state aid after 1815. By 1853 when the state took over its properties the society had provided schooling for more than 600,000 pupils.

A scattered rural population, however, did not lend itself so readily to the development of schools. In 1860, for instance, Louisiana had a population density of 11 per square mile and Virginia 14, while Massachusetts had 127. In many parts of the country, as in South Carolina after 1811, the state provided some aid to schools for children of indigent parents, but such institutions were normally stigmatized as "pauper schools," to be shunned by the better sort.

By the 1830s the demand for public schools was rising fast. Reformers argued that popular government presupposed a literate and informed electorate. With the lowering of barriers to the ballot box, the argument carried all the more force. Workers wanted free schools to give their children an equal chance to pursue the American dream. In 1830 the Working Men's party of Philadelphia called for "a system of education that shall embrace equally all the children of the state, of every rank and condition." Education, it was argued, would improve manners and at the same time lessen crime and poverty. Opposition was minor, mostly from taxpayers who held education to be a family matter and from those church groups that maintained schools at their own expense.

Horace Mann of Massachusetts stood out in the early drive for statewide school systems. Trained as a lawyer, he sponsored through the legislature the creation of a state board of education, which he then served as secretary. Mann went on to sponsor many reforms in Massachusetts, including the first state-supported "normal school" for the training of teachers, a state association of teachers, and a minimum school year of six months. He repeatedly defended the school system as the way to social stability and equal opportunity. It had never happened, he argued, and never could happen, that an educated people could be permanently poor. "Education then, beyond all other devices of human origin, is a great equalizer of the conditions of men—the balance wheel of the social machinery."

In the South the state of North Carolina led the way toward state-supported education. There Calvin H. Wiley played a role like that of Mann, building from a law of 1839 that provided support to localities willing to tax themselves for the support of schools. As the first state

FOOD FOR THOUGHT 35

THIRD READER. 35

7. He found the little boy, whose name was Joe, sitting by the table, on which he was making marks with a piece of chalk.

Charles asked him whether he was drawing pictures.

8. "No, I am trying to write," said little Joe, "but I know only two words. Those I saw upon a sign, and I am trying to write them."

9. "If I could only learn to read and write," said he, "I should be the happiest boy in the world."

Learning to read, from McGuffey's 3d Eclectic Reader, 1837.

superintendent of public instruction he traveled to every county, drumming up support for the schools. By 1860, as a result of his activities, North Carolina enrolled more than two-thirds of its white school population for an average term of four months. But the educational pattern in the South continued to reflect the aristocratic pretensions of the region: the South had a higher percentage of college students than any other region, but a lower percentage of public school students. And the South had some 500,000 white illiterates, more than half the total number in the country.

For all the effort to establish state-supported schools, conditions for public education were seldom ideal. Funds were insufficient for buildings, books, and equipment; teachers were poorly paid, and often so poorly prepared as to be little ahead of their charges in the ability to read, write, and do arithmetic. In many a rural schoolhouse the teacher's first task was to thrash the huskiest youth in the class in order to establish authority. The teachers, consequently, were at first mostly men, often young men who did not regard teaching as a career but as a means of support while preparing for a career as a lawyer or preacher, or as part-time work during slack seasons on the farm. With the encouragement of educational reformers, however, teaching was beginning to be regarded as a profession. As the schools multiplied and the school term lengthened, women increasingly entered the field.

Given the condition of their preparation, teachers were heavily dependent on textbooks, and publishers were happy to oblige them. The most common texts were Noah Webster's *Blue Back Speller* and a series of six graded *Eclectic Readers* that William Holmes McGuffey, a professor and university president in Ohio, began to bring out in 1836 and completed in 1857. His books taught children to recite "Twinkle, Twinkle, Little Star," and the patriotic words of Washington, Patrick Henry, Webster, and Clay. The *Readers* were replete with parables designed to instill thrift, morality, and patriotism. At the same time they carried selections from the masters of English prose and verse.

Most students going beyond the elementary grades went to private academies, often subsidized by church and public funds. Such schools, begun in colonial days, multiplied until there were in 1850 more than 6,000 of them. In 1821 the Boston English High School opened as the first free public secondary school, set up mainly for students not going on to college. By a law of 1827 Massachusetts required a high school in every town of 500; in towns of 4,000 or more the school had to offer Latin, Greek, rhetoric, and other college preparatory courses. Public high schools became well established in school systems only after the Civil War. In 1860 there were barely 300 in the whole country.

POPULAR EDUCATION   Beyond the schools there grew up many societies and institutes to inform the general public: mechanics' and workingmen's "institutes," "young men's associations," "debating societies," "literary societies," and such. Outstanding in the field was the Franklin Institute, founded at Philadelphia in 1824 to inform the public mainly in the fields of science and industry. Similar institutes were sponsored by major philanthropists such as Francis Cabot Lowell in Boston, George Peabody in Baltimore, and Peter Cooper in New York. Some cities offered evening classes to those who could not attend day schools. The most widespread and effective means of popular education, however, was the lyceum movement, which aimed to diffuse knowledge through public lectures. Professional agencies provided speakers and performers of all kinds, in literature, science, music, humor, travel, and other fields.

Akin to the lyceum movement and ultimately reaching more people was the movement for public libraries. Benjamin Franklin's Philadelphia Library Company (1731) had given impulse to the growth of subscription or association libraries. In 1803 Salisbury, Connecticut, opened a free library for children and in 1833 Peterborough, New Hampshire, established a tax-supported library open to all. The opening of the Boston Public Library in 1851 was a turning point. By 1860 there were approximately 10,000 public libraries (not all completely free) housing some 8 million volumes.

HIGHER EDUCATION   The postrevolutionary proliferation of colleges continued after 1800 with the spread of small church schools and state universities. Nine colleges had been founded in the colonial period, all of which survived; but not many of the fifty that sprang up between 1776 and 1800 lasted. Among those that did were Hampden-Sydney, Charleston, Bowdoin, and Middlebury, all of which went on to long and fruitful careers. Of the seventy-eight colleges and universities in 1840, fully thirty-five had been founded after 1830, almost all as church schools. A postrevolutionary movement for state universities flourished in those southern states that had had no colonial university. Federal policy abetted the spread of universities into the West. When Congress granted statehood to Ohio in 1803, it set aside two townships for the support of a state university and kept up that policy in other new states.

The coexistence of state and religious schools, however, set up conflicts over funding and curriculum. Beset by the need for funds, as colleges usually were, denominational schools often competed with tax-

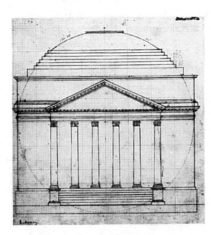

Jefferson's design for the rotunda at the University of Virginia, founded in 1819.

Greek Class at the Western Reserve Eclectic Institute at Hiram, Ohio, 1853. *At front right are the young James A. Garfield and his future wife, Lucretia Randolph.*

supported schools. Regarding curricula, many of the church schools emphasized theology at the expense of science and the humanities. On the other hand, America's development required broader access to education and programs geared to vocations. The University of Virginia, "Mr. Jefferson's University," founded in 1819 within sight of Monticello, introduced in 1826 a curriculum modeled after Jefferson's own view that education ought to combine pure knowledge with "all the branches of science useful *to us,* and *at this day."* The model influenced the other new state universities of the South and West.

Technical education grew slowly. The United States Military Academy at West Point, founded in 1802, and the Naval Academy at Annapolis, opened in 1845, trained a limited number of engineers. More learned technical skills through practical experience with railroad and canal companies, and apprenticeship to experienced technologists. Similarly, most aspiring lawyers went to "read law" with an established attorney, and doctors served their apprenticeships with practicing physicians. The president of Brown University remarked that there were forty-two theological schools and forty-seven law schools, but none to provide "the agriculturalist, the manufacturer, the mechanic, and the merchant with any kind of professional preparation." There were few schools of this sort before 1860, but a promise for the future came in 1855 when Michigan and Pennsylvania each established an agricultural and mechanical college, now Michigan State and Pennsylvania State.

Elementary education for girls met with general acceptance, but training beyond that level did not. Many men and women thought higher education unsuited to a woman's destiny in life. Some did argue that education would produce better wives and mothers, but few were ready yet to demand equality on principle. Progress began with the academies, some of which taught boys and girls alike. Good "female seminaries" like those founded by Emma Willard at Troy, New York (1824), and Mary Lyon at Mount Holyoke, Massachusetts (1836), prepared the way for women's colleges. Many of them, in fact, grew into such colleges, but Georgia Female College (later Wesleyan College) at Macon, chartered in 1836, first offered women the A.B. in 1840. The curricula in female seminaries usually differed from the courses in men's schools, giving more attention to the social amenities and such "embellishments" as music and art. Vassar, opened at Poughkeepsie, New York, in 1865, is usually credited with being the first women's college to give priority to academic standards. Oberlin College in Ohio, founded in 1833, opened as both a biracial and a coeducational institution. Its first women students were admitted in 1837. In general the West gave the greatest impetus to coeducation, with state universities in the lead. But once admitted, women students remained in a subordinate status. At Oberlin, for instance, they were expected to clean male students' rooms and were not allowed to speak in class or recite at graduation exercises. Coeducation did not mean equality.

SOME MOVEMENTS FOR REFORM

Alexis de Tocqueville, the French traveler who wrote a classic report on American society, *Democracy in America* (1835), commented on many things, including the role of education in the United States. Another matter caught his special attention: nothing, he wrote, "in my view, more deserves attention than the intellectual and moral associations in America." During his extended visit in 1831 he heard that 100,000 men had pledged to abstain from alcohol. At first he thought it was a joke. Why should these abstinent citizens not quietly drink water by their own firesides? Then he understood that "Americans of all ages, all stations to life and all types of dispositions are forever forming associations. There are not only commercial and industrial associations in which all take part, but others of a thousand different types—religious, moral, serious, futile, very general and very limited, very large and very minute."

Emerson spoke for his generation, as he so often did, when he asked: "What is man born for, but to be a Reformer, a Remaker of what man has made?" The urge to eradicate evil from nineteenth-century America had its roots in the widespread sense of mission, which in turn drew upon rising faith in human perfectibility. Belief in perfectibility had both evangelical and liberal bases. Transcendentalism, the spirit of which infected even those unfamiliar with the philosophy, offered a romantic faith in the individual and the belief that human intuition led to right thinking.

Few areas of life escaped the attention of the reformers, however trivial or weighty: observance of the Sabbath, dueling, crime and punishment, the hours and conditions of work, poverty, vice, care of the handicapped, pacifism, foreign missions, temperance, women's rights, the abolition of slavery. Some crusaders challenged a host of evils; others focused on pet causes. One Massachusetts reformer, for example, insisted that "a vegetable diet lies at the basis of all reforms." The greatest dietary reformer of the age, however, was Sylvester Graham, who started as a temperance speaker in 1830 and moved on to champion a natural diet of grains, vegetables, and fruits, and abstinence from alcohol, coffee, tea, tobacco, and many foods. The Graham cracker is one of the movement's legacies to later times. Graham's ideas evolved into a way of life requiring proper habits of dress, hygiene, sex, and mind. The movement became a major industry, sponsoring health clubs, camps, sanitariums, magazines, and regular lecture tours by Graham.

TEMPERANCE   The temperance crusade, at which Tocqueville marveled, was perhaps the most widespread of all, with the possible exception of the public school movement. The cause drew its share of prigs, but it also drew upon concern over a real problem. The census of 1810 reported some 14,000 distilleries producing 25 million gallons of spirits each year. With a hard-drinking population of just over 7 million, the "alcoholic republic" was producing well over three gallons per year for every man, woman, and child, not counting beer, wine, and cider. And the census takers no doubt missed a few stills. William Cobbett, an English reformer who traveled in the United States, noted in 1819 that one could "go into hardly any man's house without being asked to drink wine or spirits, even *in the morning.*"

The temperance movement rested on a number of arguments. First and foremost was the religious concern that "soldiers of the cross" lead blameless lives. The bad effects of distilled beverages on body and mind were noted by the respected physician Benjamin Rush as early as 1784. The dynamic new economy, with factories and railroads moving on strict schedules, made tippling by the labor force a far greater problem than it had been in a simple economy. Humanitarians emphasized the relations between drinking and poverty. Much of the movement's propaganda focused on the sufferings of innocent mothers and children. "Drink," said a pamphlet from the Sons of Temperance, "is the prolific source (directly or indirectly) of nearly all the ills that afflict the human family."

In 1826 a group of ministers in Boston organized the American Society for the Promotion of Temperance. The society worked through lecturers, press campaigns, prize essay contests, and the formation of local and state societies. A favorite device was to ask each person who took the pledge to put by his or her signature a T for Total Abstinence. With that a new word entered the language: "teetotaler."

In 1833 the society called a national convention in Philadelphia, where the American Temperance Union was formed. The convention revealed internal tensions, however: Was the goal moderation or total

The Way of Good & Evil. *Intemperance was one of the steps on the way of evil, leading to "everlasting punishment."*

abstinence, and if the latter, abstinence merely from liquor or also from wine, cider, and beer? Should activists work by persuasion or by legislation? Like nearly every movement of the day, temperance had a wing of perfectionists who rejected prudence. They would brook no compromise with Demon Rum and carried the day with a resolution that the liquor traffic was morally wrong and ought to be prohibited by law. The union, at its spring convention in 1836, called for abstinence from all alcoholic beverages—a costly victory that caused moderates to abstain from the movement instead.

The demand for the prohibition of alcoholic beverages led in the 1830s and thereafter to experiments with more stringent regulations and local option laws. In 1838 Massachusetts forbade the sale of spirits in lots of less than fifteen gallons, thereby cutting off sales in taverns and to the poor—who could not handle it as well as their betters, or so their betters thought. After repeal of the law in 1840, prohibitionists in Massachusetts turned to the towns, about a hundred of which were dry by 1845. In 1839 Mississippi restricted sales to no less than a gallon, but the movement went little further in the South. In 1846 Maine enacted a law against sales of less than twenty-eight gallons; five years later Maine forbade the manufacture or sale of *any* intoxicants. By 1855 thirteen states had such laws. Rum-soaked New England had gone legally dry, along with New York and parts of the Midwest. But most of the laws were poorly drafted and vulnerable to court challenge. Within a few years they survived only in northern New England. Still, between 1830 and 1860 the temperance agitation drastically reduced Americans' per-capita consumption of alcohol.

PRISONS AND ASYLUMS   The sublime optimism of the age, the liberal belief that people were innately good and capable of improvement, brought major changes in the treatment of prisoners, the handicapped, and dependent children. Public institutions arose dedicated to the treatment and cure of social ills. Earlier these had been "places of last resort," David Rothman wrote in *The Discovery of the Asylum.* Now they "became places of first resort, the preferred solution to the problems of poverty, crime, delinquency, and insanity." Removed from society, the needy and deviant could be made whole again. Unhappily, this ideal kept running up against the dictates of convenience and economy. The institutions had a way of turning into breeding grounds of brutality and neglect.

In the colonial period prisons were usually places for brief confinement before punishment, which was either death or some kind of pain or humiliation: whipping, mutilation, confinement in stocks, branding, and the like. A new attitude began to emerge after the Revolution. American reformers argued against the harshness of the penal code and

The Pennsylvania Hospital was one of the few in eighteenth-century America to care for the mentally ill. It is depicted here in 1767.

asserted that the certainty of punishment was more important than its severity. Society, moreover, would benefit more from the prevention than the punishment of crime. The Philadelphia Society for Alleviating the Miseries of Public Prisons, founded in 1787, took the lead in spreading the new doctrines. Gradually the idea of the penitentiary developed. It would be a place where the guilty experienced penitence and underwent rehabilitation, not just punishment.

An early model of the new system, widely copied, was the Auburn Penitentiary, commissioned by New York in 1816. The prisoners at Auburn had separate cells and gathered for meals and group labor. Discipline was severe. The men were marched out in lockstep and never put face to face or allowed to talk. But prisoners were at least reasonably secure from abuse by other prisoners. The system, its advocates argued, had a beneficial effect on the prisoners and saved money since the workshops supplied prison needs and produced goods for sale at a profit. By 1840 there were twelve prisons of the Auburn type.

It was still more common, and the persistent curse of prisons, for inmates to be thrown together willy-nilly. In an earlier day of corporal punishments jails housed mainly debtors. But as practices changed, debtors found themselves housed with convicts. Without provision for food, furniture, or fuel, the debtors would have expired but for charity. The absurdity of the system was so obvious that the tardiness of reform seems strange. New York in 1817 made $25 the minimum for which one could be imprisoned, but no state eliminated the practice altogether until Kentucky acted in 1821. Other states gradually fell in line, but it was still more than three decades before debtors' prisons became a thing of the past.

The reform impulse naturally found outlet in the care of the insane. The Philadelphia Hospital (1752), one of the first in the country, had a provision in its charter that it should care for "lunaticks," but before 1800 few hospitals provided care for the mentally ill. One notable exception was the hospital opened in Williamsburg in 1759 specifically for treatment of the mentally ill. The insane were usually confined at home with hired keepers or in jails and almshouses. In the years after 1815, however, asylums that housed the disturbed separately from criminals began to appear. Early efforts led to such optimism that a committee reported to the Massachusetts legislature in 1832 that with the right treatment "insanity yields with more readiness than ordinary diseases." These high expectations gradually faded with experience.

The most important figure in arousing the public conscience to the plight of these unfortunates was Dorothea Lynde Dix. A pious, withdrawn, almost saintly Boston schoolteacher, she was called upon to instruct a Sunday-school class at the East Cambridge House of Correction in 1841. There she found a roomful of insane persons completely neglected and left without heat on a cold March day. She then commenced a two-year investigation of jails and almshouses in Massachusetts. In a memorial to the state legislature in 1843 she reported on "the *present* state of insane persons confined within the Commonwealth, in *cages, closets, cellars, stalls, pens! Chained, naked, beaten with rods, and lashed into obedience!*" Keepers of the institutions dismissed her charges as "slanderous lies," but she won the support of leading reformers and garnered a large appropriation. From Massachusetts she carried her campaign throughout the country and abroad. By 1860 she had

Dorothea Dix.

persuaded twenty states to heed her advice. Of Dorothea Dix it was truly said that "Few persons have ever had such far-reaching effect on public policy toward reform."

WOMEN'S RIGHTS   While Dorothea Dix stood out as an example of the opportunity reform gave middle-class women to enter public life, Catharine Beecher, a leader in the education movement and founder of women's schools in Connecticut and Ohio, published a guide prescribing the domestic sphere for women. *A Treatise on Domestic Economy* (1841) became the leading handbook of what historians have labeled the "cult of domesticity." While Beecher upheld high standards in women's education, she also accepted the prevailing view that the "woman's sphere" was the home and argued that young women should be trained in the domestic arts. Her guide, designed for use also as a textbook, led prospective wives and mothers through the endless rounds from Monday washing to Saturday baking, with instructions on health, food, clothing, cleanliness, care of domestics and children, gardening, and hundreds of other household details. Such duties, Beecher emphasized, should never be taken as "petty, trivial or unworthy" since "no statesman . . . had more frequent calls for wisdom, firmness, tact, discrimination, prudence, and versatility of talent."

The social custom of assigning the sexes different roles, of course, did not spring full-blown into life during the nineteenth century. In earlier agrarian societies gender-based functions were closely tied to the household and often overlapped. As the more complex economy of the nineteenth century matured, economic production came to be increasingly separated from the home, and the home in turn became a refuge from the cruel world outside, with separate and distinctive functions. Some have argued that the home became a trap for women, a prison that hindered fulfillment. But others have noted that it often gave women a sphere of independence in which they might exercise a degree of initiative and leadership. The so-called cult of domesticity idealized a woman's moral role in civilizing husband and family.

The official status of women during this period remained much as it had been in the colonial era. Legally, a woman was unable to vote and, after marriage, was denied control of her property and even of her children. A wife could not make a will, sign a contract, or bring suit in court without her husband's permission. Her legal status was like that of a minor, a slave, or a free black. Gradually, however, women began to protest their status, and men began to listen. The organized movement for women's rights had its origins in 1840, when the American antislavery movement split over the question of women's right to participate. American women decided then that they needed to organize on behalf of their own emancipation too.

In 1848 two prominent moral reformers and advocates of women's rights, Lucretia Mott, a fifty-five-year-old Philadelphia Quaker, and Elizabeth Cady Stanton, a thirty-two-year-old graduate of Troy Seminary who refused to be merely "a household drudge," decided to call a convention to discuss "the social, civil, and religious condition and rights of women." The hastily organized Seneca Falls Convention, the first of its kind, issued on July 19, 1848, a clever paraphrase of Jefferson's Declaration, the Declaration of Sentiments, mainly the work of Mrs. Stanton, who was also the wife of a prominent abolitionist and the mother of seven.

The document proclaimed the self-evident truth that "all men and women are created equal," and the attendant resolutions said that all laws that placed women "in a position inferior to that of men, are contrary to the great precept of nature, and therefore of no force or authority." Such language was too strong for most of the thousand delegates, and only about a third of them signed it. Ruffled male editors lampooned the women activists as being "love-starved spinsters" and "petticoat rebels." Yet the Seneca Falls gathering represented an important first step in the evolving campaign for women's rights.

From 1850 until the Civil War the women's-rights leaders held annual conventions and carried on a program of organizing, lecturing,

An English print advises women of the early nineteenth century. "To Avoid Many Troubles Which Others Endure: Keep Within Compass and You Shall Be Sure."

funds and antifeminist women and men. Its success resulted from the work of a few undaunted women who refused to be overawed by the odds against them. Susan B. Anthony, already active in temperance and antislavery groups, joined the crusade in the 1850s. At age seventeen she had angrily noted, "What an absurd notion that women have not intellectual and moral faculties sufficient for anything else but domestic concerns!" Unlike Stanton and Mott, Anthony was unmarried and therefore able to devote most of her attention to the women's crusade. As one observer put it, Mrs. Stanton "forged the thunderbolts and Miss Anthony hurled them." Both were young when the movement started and both lived into the twentieth century, focusing after the Civil War on demands for women's suffrage. Many of the feminists like Stanton, Lucretia Mott, and Lucy Stone had supportive husbands, and the movement won prominent male champions such as Emerson, Whitman, William Ellery Channing, and William Lloyd Garrison.

The fruits of the movement ripened slowly. Women did not gain the ballot, but there were some legal gains. The state of Mississippi, seldom regarded as a hotbed of reform, was in 1839 the first to grant married women control over their property; by the 1860s eleven more states had such laws.

Still, the only jobs open to educated women in any numbers were nursing and teaching, both of which extended the domestic roles of health care and nurture into the world outside. Both brought relatively lower status and pay than "man's work" despite the skills, training, and responsibility involved. Against the odds, a hardy band of women carved out professional careers. With the rapid expansion of schools, women

Elizabeth Cady Stanton (left) and Susan B. Anthony. Mrs. Stanton "forged the thunderbolts and Miss Anthony hurled them."

Margaret Fuller, one of the great American intellectuals of her time.

moved into the teaching profession first. If women could be teachers, Susan Anthony asked, why not lawyers or doctors?

Harriet Hunt of Boston was a teacher who, after nursing her sister through a serious illness, set up shop in 1835 as a self-taught physician and persisted in medical practice although twice rejected by Harvard Medical School. Voted into Geneva Medical College in western New York as a joke, Elizabeth Blackwell of Ohio had the last laugh when she finished at the head of her class in 1849. She founded the New York Infirmary for Women and Children and later had a long career as a professor of gynecology in the London School of Medicine for Women.

An intellectual prodigy among women of the time—the derisory term was "bluestocking"—was Margaret Fuller. A precocious child, she was force-fed education by a father who set her at Latin when she was six. As a young adult she moved confidently in the literary circles of Boston and Concord, edited *The Dial* for two years, and became literary editor and critic for Horace Greeley's New York *Tribune.* From 1839 to 1844 she conducted "conversations" with the cultivated ladies of Boston. From this classroom-salon emerged many of the ideas that went into her book *Woman in the Nineteenth Century* (1845), a plea for removal of all intellectual and economic disabilities. Minds and souls were neither masculine nor feminine, she argued. Genius had no sex. "What woman needs," Fuller contended, "is not as a woman to act or rule, but as a nature to grow, as an intellect to discern, as a soul to live freely and unimpeded, to unfold such powers as were given her when we left our common home."

UTOPIAN COMMUNITIES   Amid the pervasive climate of reform during the Jacksonian era, the quest for utopia flourished. "We are all a little mad here with numberless projects of social reform," Emerson wrote in 1840. "Not a reading man but has a draft of a new community in his pocket." Plans for new communities had long been an American passion, at least since the Puritans set out to build a Wilderness Zion. The visionary communes of the nineteenth century often had purely economic and social objectives, but those rooted in religion proved most durable.

An early instance, an offshoot of the Mennonites in 1732, the Ephrata Community in Pennsylvania practiced an almost monastic life into the early nineteenth century. Founder Johann Conrad Beissel's emphasis on music left a lasting imprint on American hymnology. In 1803 George Rapp led about 600 Lutheran come-outers from Württemberg to Pennsylvania. They took the Bible literally, and like Beissel's group, renounced sex. Since the millennium was near they had to keep ready. No quarrel went unsettled overnight, and all who had sinned confessed to Rapp before sleeping. Industrious and disciplined, the Rappites prospered, and persevered to the end of the century.

More than a hundred utopian communities sprang up between 1800 and 1900. Among the most durable were those founded by the Shakers, officially the United Society of Believers in Christ's Second Appearing. Ann Lee Stanley (Mother Ann) reached New York State with eight followers in 1774. Believing religious fervor a sign of inspiration from the Holy Ghost, Mother Ann and her followers had strange fits in which they saw visions and prophesied. These manifestations later evolved into a ritual dance—hence the name Shakers. Shaker doctrine held God to be a dual personality: in Christ the masculine side was manifested, in

A Shaker sewing desk with drawers on the front and side, so two Sisters could share in the work.

Mother Ann the feminine element. Mother Ann preached celibacy to prepare Shakers for the perfection that was promised them. The church would first gather in the elect, and eventually in the spirit world convert and save all humankind.

Mother Ann died in 1784, but the group found new leaders. From the first community at Mount Lebanon, New York, the movement spread to new colonies in New England, and soon afterward into Ohio and Kentucky. By 1830 about twenty groups were flourishing. In Shaker communities all property was held in common. Governance of the colonies was concentrated in the hands of select groups chosen by the ministry, or "Head of Influence" at Mount Lebanon. To outsiders this might seem almost despotic, but the Shakers emphasized equality of labor and reward, and members were free to leave at will. The Shakers' farms yielded a surplus for the market. They were among the leading sources of garden seed and medicinal herbs, and many of their manufactures, including clothing, household items, and especially furniture, were prized for their simple beauty. By the mid-twentieth century, however, few members remained alive; they had reached the peak of activity in the years 1830–1860.

John Humphrey Noyes, founder of the Oneida Community, was the son of a Vermont congressman. Educated at Dartmouth and then Yale Divinity School, he discovered true religion at one of Charles G. Finney's revivals and entered the ministry. He was forced out, however, when he concluded that with true conversion came perfection and a complete release from sin. In 1836 he gathered a group of "Perfectionists" around his home in Putney, Vermont. Ten years later Noyes announced a new doctrine of complex marriage, which meant that every man in the community was married to every woman and vice versa. "In a holy community," he claimed, "there is no more reason why sexual intercourse should be restrained by law, than why eating and drinking should be." Authorities thought otherwise, and Noyes was arrested for practicing his "free love" theology. He fled to New York and in 1848 established the Oneida Community, which numbered more than 200 by 1851.

The communal group eked out a living with farming and logging until the mid-1850s, when the inventor of a new steel trap joined the community. Oneida traps were soon known as the best in the country. The community then branched out into sewing silk, canning fruits, and making silver spoons. The spoons were so popular that, with the addition of knives and forks, tableware became the Oneida specialty. In 1879, however, the community faced a crisis when Noyes fled to Canada to avoid prosecution for adultery. The members then abandoned universal marriage, and in 1881 decided to convert into a joint-stock company, the Oneida Community, Ltd., which remains today a successful flatware company.

In contrast to these religious-based communities, Robert Owen's New Harmony was based on a secular principle. A British capitalist who worried about the social effects of the factory system, Owen built a model factory town, supported labor legislation, and set forth a scheme for a model community in his pamphlet *A New View of Society* (1813). Later he snapped at a chance to buy the Rappites' town of Harmony, Indiana, and promptly christened it New Harmony. In Washington an audience including President Monroe crowded the hall of the House of Representatives to hear Owen tell about his high hopes.

In 1825 a varied group of about 900 colonists gathered in New Harmony for a period of transition from Owen's ownership to the new system of cooperation. The group began to run the former Rappite industries, and after only nine months' trial Owen turned over management of the colony to a town meeting of all residents and a council of town officers. The high proportion of learned participants generated a certain intellectual electricity about the place. Schools sprang up quickly. Owen's two sons started a sprightly paper, the *New Harmony Gazette.* There were frequent lectures and social gatherings with music and dancing.

For a time it looked like a brilliant success, but New Harmony soon fell into discord. The *Gazette* complained of "grumbling, carping, and murmuring" members and others who had the "disease of laziness." The problem, it seems, was a problem common to reform groups. Every idealist wanted his or her own patented plan put into practice. In 1827 Owen returned from a visit to England to find New Harmony insolvent. The following year he dissolved the project and sold or leased the lands on good terms, in many cases to the settlers. All that remained he turned over to his sons, who stayed and became American citizens.

The 1840s brought a flurry of interest in the ideas of Fourieristic socialism. Charles Fourier, a Frenchman, proposed to reorder society into small units, or "phalanxes," ideally of 1,620 members. All property would be held in common and each phalanx would produce that for which it felt itself best suited; the joy of work and communal living would supply the incentive. By example the phalanxes would eventually cover the earth and displace capitalism. Fourier remained a prophet without honor in his own country, but Arthur Brisbane's book *The Social Destiny of Man* (1840) brought Fourierism before the American public, and Horace Greeley's New York *Tribune* kept it there.

Greeley was in such a hurry to try out the idea, however, that Brisbane thought him rash. Brisbane was right. The first community, the Sylvania Phalanx in northern Pennsylvania, founded with Greeley's help in 1842, lasted but a year. Sylvania picked up 2,300 acres of remote and infertile land at little cost. During their only season about 100 members produced just eleven bushels of grain on the four acres of arable land.

Greeley lost $5,000. In all some forty or fifty phalanxes sprang up, but lasted on the average about two years.

Brook Farm was surely the most celebrated of all the utopian communities because it had the support of Emerson, Fuller, and countless other well-known literary figures of New England. Nathaniel Hawthorne, a member, later memorialized its failure in his novel *The Blithedale Romance* (1852). George Ripley, a Unitarian minister and Transcendentalist, conceived of Brook Farm as a kind of early-day "think tank," combining high thinking and plain living. The place survived, however, mainly because of an excellent community school that drew tuition-paying students from outside. In 1844 Brook Farm converted itself into a phalanstery, but when a new central building burned down on the day of its dedication in 1846, the community spirit expired in the embers.

Utopian communities, with few exceptions, quickly ran into futility. Soon after Hawthorne left Brook Farm he wrote: "It already looks like a dream behind me." His life there was "an unnatural and unsuitable, and therefore an unreal one." Such experiments, performed in relative isolation, had little effect on the real world outside, where reformers wrestled with the sins of the multitudes. Among all the targets of reformers' wrath, one great evil would finally take precedence over the others—human bondage. The paradox of American slavery coupled with American freedom, of "the world's fairest hope linked with man's foulest crime," in Herman Melville's words, would inspire the climactic crusade of the age, abolitionism, one that would ultimately move to the center of the political stage and sweep the nation into an epic struggle.

FURTHER READING

Few single-volume works cover the diversity of early American reform and culture. A good start is Perry Miller's *The Life of the Mind in America: From the Revolution to the Civil War* (1965),° on the intellectual evolution which ran concurrently with reformist activity. Russel B. Nye's *Society and Culture in America, 1830–1860* (1974) provides a wide-ranging survey. On reform itself, consult Ronald G. Walter's *American Reformers, 1815–1860* (1978).°

Sydney E. Ahlstrom's *A Religious History of the American People* (1972) provides a solid survey of antebellum religious movements and developments. More interpretive is Martin E. Marty's *Righteous Empire: The Protestant Experience in America* (1970). Revivalist reli-

°These books are available in paperback editions.

gion is discussed in Whitney R. Cross's *The Burned-Over District* (1950)* and John B. Boles's *The Great Revival* (1972). Donald G. Mathews, in *Religion in the Old South* (1977), assesses the evangelical temperament.

For splinter sects, the scholarship is most voluminous on the Mormons. See Klaus J. Hansen's *Mormonism and the American Experience* (1981), Leonard J. Arrington's *Brigham Young: American Moses* (1985), and Richard L. Bushman's *Joseph Smith and the Beginnings of Mormonism* (1984). See also Wallace E. Stegner's *The Gathering of Zion: The Story of the Mormon Trail* (1964).

The best introduction to Transcendentalist thought are the writings of the Transcendentalists themselves, collected in Perry Miller (ed.), *The Transcendentalists* (1950).* Also see Paul Boller's *American Transcendentalism, 1830–1860* (1974) and Anne Rose's *Transcendentalism as a Social Movement* (1981). On the foremost Transcendentalist, see Gay Wilson Allen's *Waldo Emerson: A Biography* (1981)* and Joel Porte's *Representative Man: Ralph Waldo Emerson in His Time* (1979). For Emerson's protégé, consult Robert D. Richardson, Jr.'s *Henry Thoreau: A Life of the Mind* (1986). A fine biography of the poet Whitman is Justin Kaplan's *Walt Whitman: A Life* (1980).* A solid introduction to antebellum newspapers is Frank L. Mott's *American Journalism* (3rd ed., 1962). Barbara Novak's *Nature and Culture: American Landscape and Painting, 1825–1875* (1980)* provides an overview of the Hudson River School. A different aspect of the nineteenth-century intellectual community is described in Robert V. Bruce's *The Launching of Modern American Science, 1846–1876* (1987).

Several good works describe various aspects of the antebellum reform movement. For temperance, see W. J. Rorabaugh's *The Alcoholic Republic: An American Tradition* (1979)* and Barbara Leslie Epstein's *The Politics of Domesticity: Women, Evangelism, and Temperance in Nineteenth-Century America* (1981). Stephen Nissenbaum's *Sex, Diet, and Debility in Jacksonian America* (1980) looks at health reform. On prison reform and other humanitarian projects, see David J. Rothman's *The Discovery of the Asylum* (1971),* Gerald N. Grob's *Mental Institutions in America* (1973), and Charles Rosenberg's *The Care of Strangers: The Rise of America's Hospital System* (1987). For the religious context of reform, consult Carroll Smith-Rosenberg's *Religion and the Rise of the American City: The New York Mission Movement* (1971).

Lawrence A. Cremin's *American Education: The National Experience, 1783–1876* (1980) traces early school reform. For other views, see

*These books are available in paperback editions.

Stanley K. Schultz's *The Culture Factory: Boston Public School, 1789–1860* (1973) and Carl F. Kaestle's *Pillars of the Republic* (1983).

The literature on women's history is both voluminous and diverse. Three surveys of women's history that include the antebellum period are Carl N. Degler's *At Odds: Women and Family in America from the Revolution to the Present* (1980),° Gerda Lerner's *The Woman in American History* (1971), and Mary P. Ryan's *Womanhood in America* (3rd ed., 1983).° More particular to the antebellum period are Nancy F. Cott's *The Bonds of Womanhood: "Women's Sphere" in New England, 1780–1835* (1977)° and Ellen C. DuBois's *Feminism and Suffrage: The Emergence of an Independent Women's Movement in America, 1848–1869* (1978). Also valuable are Shirley Samuels's *The Culture of Sentiment: Race, Gender, and Sentimentality in 19th Century America* (1992), Jeanne Boydston's *The Limits of Sisterhood: The Beecher Sisters on Women's Rights and Woman's Sphere* (1988) and Mary P. Ryan's *Women in Public: Between Banners and Ballots, 1825–1880* (1990). Biographical studies include Alma Lutz's *Susan B. Anthony* (1959), Lois W. Banner's *Elizabeth Cady Stanton* (1980), Charles Capper's *Margaret Fuller: An American Romantic Life* (1992), and Jean H. Baker's *Mary Todd Lincoln: A Biography* (1987).

A small but growing literature on ideals of masculinity and changing roles of men in the nineteenth century includes David Leverenz's *Manhood and the American Renaissance* (1989), Mark C. Carnes's *Secret Ritual and Manhood in Victorian America* (1989), Mary Ann Clawson's *Constructing Brotherhood: Class, Gender, and Fraternalism* (1989), and E. Anthony Rotundo's *American Manhood: Transformations in Masculinity from the Revolution to the Modern Era* (1993). Changing ideals of the family in the nineteenth century are described in Steven Mintz and Susan Kellog's *Domestic Revolutions: A Social History of American Family Life* (1988). Further perspectives on the family at this time can be gleaned from Milton A. Rugoff's *The Beechers* (1981) and Mary P. Ryan's *Cradle of the Middle Class* (1981).°

Michael Fellman's *The Unbounded Frame: Freedom and Community in Nineteenth Century Utopianism* (1973) surveys the utopian movements. Specific experiments are treated in Robert D. Thomas's *The Man Who Would Be Perfect* (1977), on John Humphrey Noyes; J. F. C. Harrison's *Quest for the New Moral World* (1969), on Robert Owen; Maren L. Carden's *Oneida* (1969); and Henri Desroche's *The American Shakers from Neo-Christianity to Pre-Socialism* (1971). Lawrence Foster's *Religion and Sexuality* (1981) discusses the Oneida, Shaker, and Mormon communities.

°These books are available in paperback editions.

14

MANIFEST DESTINY

During the 1840s the westering impulse, the quest for a better chance and more living room, continued to excite the American imagination. "If hell lay to the west," one pioneer declared, "Americans would cross heaven to get there." That may or may not have been true, but millions of Americans were willing to cross the Mississippi River and experience unrelenting hardships in order to conquer new frontiers and express their "providential destiny" to subdue the entire continent. By 1860 some 4.3 million people had settled in the trans-Mississippi West.

Of course, most of these settlers and adventurers wanted to exploit the many economic opportunities afforded by the new lands. Trappers and farmers, miners and merchants, hunters, ranchers, teachers, domestics, and prostitutes, among others, headed west seeking their fortunes. Others sought religious freedom or new converts to Christianity. Whatever the reason, they formed an unceasing migratory stream flowing across the Great Plains and the Rocky Mountains. The Indian and Mexican inhabitants of the region soon found themselves swept aside by successive waves of American settlement. In 1858 President James Buchanan could report that the nation was bound east and west "by a chain of Americans which can never be broken."

THE TYLER YEARS

When William Henry Harrison took office in 1841, elected like Jackson mainly on the strength of his military record and his lack of a public stand on key issues, the Whig leaders expected him to be a figurehead, a tool in the hands of Webster and Clay. Webster became secretary of state. Clay, who preferred to stay in the Senate, saw the cabinet filled with his friends. Within a few days of the inauguration, signs of strain appeared between Harrison and Clay, whose disappointment at missing the nomination had made him peevish. But the quarrel never had a chance to develop, for Harrison served the shortest term of any president—after the longest inaugural address. At the inauguration, held on a chilly and rainy day, he caught cold. The pleadings of office seekers in the following month filled his days and sapped his strength. On April 4, 1841, exactly one month after the inauguration, he died of pneumonia.

Thus John Tyler of Virginia, the first vice-president to succeed on the death of a president, served practically all of Harrison's term. And if there was ambiguity about where Harrison stood, there was none about Tyler's convictions. At age fifty-one the thin, fragile Virginian was the youngest president to date, but he already had a long career behind him as legislator, governor, congressman, and senator, and his opinions on all the important issues had been forcefully stated and were widely known. Although officially a Whig, at an earlier time he might have been called an Old Republican; he was stubbornly opposed to everything associated with Clay's American System—protective tariffs, a national bank, and internal improvements at national expense—and in favor of strict construction and states' rights.

When asked about the concept of nationalism, Tyler replied that he had "no such word in my political vocabulary." Once a Democrat, he had broken with the party over Jackson's stand on a state's right to nullify federal laws and Jackson's imperious use of executive authority. Tyler had been chosen to "balance" the ticket, with no expectation that he would wield power. Acid-tongued John Quincy Adams said that Tyler was "a political sectarian of the slave-driving, Virginian, Jeffersonian school, principled against all improvement, with all the interests and passions and vices of slavery rooted in his moral and political constitution—with talents not above mediocrity, and a spirit incapable of expansion to the dimensions of the station upon which he has been cast."

DOMESTIC AFFAIRS   Given more finesse on Clay's part, he might have bridged the divisions among the Whigs over financial issues. But for once, driven by disappointment and ambition, the "Great Compromiser" lost his instinct for compromise. When Congress met in special session at the end of May 1841, Clay introduced a series of resolutions designed to supply the platform that the party had evaded in the previous election. The chief points were repeal of the Independent Treasury, establishment of a third Bank of the United States, distribution to the states of proceeds from public land sales, and a higher tariff. Clay then set out to push his program through Congress. "Tyler dares not resist me. I will drive him before me," he said.

Tyler, it turned out, was not easily driven. Although he agreed to allow the repeal of the Independent Treasury and signed a higher tariff bill in 1842, Tyler vetoed Clay's bill for a new national bank. This provoked Tyler's entire cabinet, with the exception of Webster, to resign, in an unprecedented action. Tyler replaced the defectors with anti-Jackson Democrats like himself who had become Whigs. By 1842 Clay's program was in ruins. Even his successes were temporary—a Democratic Congress and president in 1846 restored the Independent Treasury and cut the tariff, leaving preemption (which legalized the frontier tradition of "squatter's rights") as the only major permanent achievement of the Whigs, something that had been no part of Clay's original scheme. If the program was in ruins, however, Clay's leadership of his party was fixed beyond question, and Tyler had become a president without a party.

FOREIGN AFFAIRS   In foreign relations, on the other hand, developments of immense significance were taking place. Several unsettled issues had arisen to trouble relations between Britain and the United States. In 1837 Canadian militia seized the American steamboat *Caroline* and set it afire. In the course of the incident, one American was killed. The British ignored all protests, but President Van Buren sent federal troops to prevent frontier violations in either direction. The issue faded until 1840, when Alexander McLeod, a Canadian, was arrested and brought to trial in New York State after he boasted of his participation in the incident and his responsibility for the killing. The British government now admitted that it had ordered destruction of the vessel and argued that McLeod could not be held personally responsible. The incident fortunately was closed when McLeod proved to have an airtight alibi—he was miles away and his story had been nothing but barroom braggadocio.

Another issue between the two nations involved the suppression of the African slave trade, which both the United States and Britain had outlawed in 1808. Congress failed to provide funds for American participation in the African slave patrol. In 1841 Prime Minister Palmerston asserted the right of British patrols off the coast of Africa to board and search vessels flying the American flag to see if they carried slaves. But the American government, mindful of the impressments and seizures during the Napoleonic Wars, refused to accept it. Relations were further strained late in 1841 when American slaves on the *Creole,* bound from Hampton Roads to New Orleans, mutinied and sailed into Nassau, where the British set them free. Secretary of State Webster demanded that the slaves be returned as American property, but the British refused.

Fortunately at this point a new British ministry decided to accept Webster's overtures for negotiations and sent Lord Ashburton to Wash-

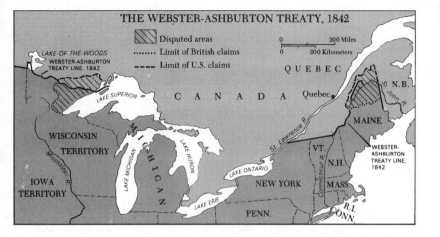

THE WEBSTER-ASHBURTON TREATY, 1842

Disputed areas
Limit of British claims
Limit of U.S. claims

0   200 Miles
0   200 Kilometers

LAKE-OF-THE-WOODS
WEBSTER-ASHBURTON
TREATY LINE, 1842

QUEBEC

Quebec

N.B.

St. John R.

MAINE

CANADA

LAKE SUPERIOR

WISCONSIN
TERRITORY

Mississippi R.

LAKE MICHIGAN

M I C H I G A N

LAKE HURON

St. Lawrence R.

WEBSTER-
ASHBURTON
TREATY LINE,
1842

VT.

Connecticut R.

N.H.

IOWA
TERRITORY

LAKE ONTARIO

NEW YORK

MASS.

R.I.

LAKE ERIE

PENN.

CONN.

ington. The Maine boundary was settled in what Webster later called "the battle of the maps." Webster settled for about seven-twelfths of the contested lands along the Maine boundary, and except for Oregon, which remained under joint occupation, he settled the other border disputes by accepting the existing line between the Connecticut and St. Lawrence Rivers, and by compromising on the line between Lake Superior and the Lake-of-the-Woods. The Webster-Ashburton Treaty (1842) also provided for joint patrols off Africa to suppress the slave trade.

MOVING WEST

In the early 1840s the American people were no more stirred by the quarrels of Tyler and Clay over such issues as banking, tariffs, and distribution, important as they were, than students of history would be at a later date. What stirred the blood was the mounting evidence that the "empire of freedom" was hurdling the barriers of the "Great American Desert" and the Rocky Mountains, reaching out toward the Pacific coast. In 1845 John Louis O'Sullivan, editor of the *United States Magazine and Democratic Review,* gave a name to this bumptious spirit of expansion. "Our manifest destiny," he wrote, "is to overspread the continent allotted by Providence for the free development of our yearly multiplying millions." At its best this much-trumpeted notion of "Manifest Destiny" offered a moral justification for American expansion, a prescription for what an enlarged United States could and should be. At its worst it was a cluster of flimsy rationalizations for naked greed and imperial ambition.

Most of the western pioneers during the second quarter of the nineteenth century were American-born whites from the upper South and

Midwest. A few free blacks joined in the migration. One settler remembered seeing "a Negro woman . . . tramping along through the heat and dust, carrying a cast iron black stove on her head, with her provisions and a blanket piled on top . . . bravely pushing on for California." Although some emigrants traveled by sea to California, most went overland. Between 1841 and 1867, some 350,000 men, women, and children made the arduous trek to California or Oregon, while hundreds of thousands of others settled along the way in Colorado, Texas, Arkansas, and other areas.

As they crossed the Mississippi River and made their way westward, American pioneers entered not only a new environment but a new culture as well. The Great Plains and the Far West were already occupied by Indians and Mexicans, peoples who had lived in the region for centuries and had established their own distinctive customs and ways of life. Now they were joined by Americans of diverse ethnic origin and religious persuasion. It made for a volatile mix.

THE INDIAN AND SPANISH FRONTIER

WESTERN INDIANS   Historians estimate that over 325,000 Indians inhabited the Southwest, the Great Plains, California, and the Pacific Northwest in 1840, when the great migration of white settlers began to pour into the region. These Native Americans were divided into more than 200 different tribes, each with its own language, religion, economic base, kinship practices, and system of governance. Some were primarily farmers who tended peach orchards or raised corn and beans in the fertile river valleys. Others were nomadic hunters who preyed upon game animals as well as other Indians.

Some twenty-three tribes resided in the Great Plains, a vast grassland stretching from the Mississippi River west to the Rocky Mountains and from Canada to Mexico. This region had been virtually devoid of a human presence until the Spaniards introduced the horse and gun in the late sixteenth century. Prior to the advent of horses, Indians relied upon dogs as their beast of burden—other than women, who carried whatever the dogs could not. A horse could carry seven times as much weight as a dog. Even more important, a horse dramatically increased the mobility and hunting ability of the Plains Indians. Indians from the Midwest were able to leave their villages and follow the great buffalo herds. The buffalo offered Indians virtually a self-sufficient livelihood. They used the meat for food and transformed the skins into clothing, bedding, and tipi coverings. The bones and horns served as tools and utensils. Even buffalo manure could be dried and used for fuel.

Plains Indians such as the Arapaho, Blackfoot, Cheyenne, Kiowa, and

Blacksmith shop in Zuni pueblo, 1853.

Sioux were horse-borne nomads; they moved across the grasslands with the buffalo herds, carrying their tipis with them. About fifteen feet in diameter, a tipi was a remarkably efficient and mobile dwelling. It typically consisted of a network of sticks covered by buffalo hides tied in place and staked to the ground. A smoke flap at the top enabled residents to build fires inside. Three beds were usually placed inside, along with firewood and other articles of equipment.

Disputes over buffalo and hunting grounds provoked clashes between rival tribes, which helps explain the cult of the warrior among the Plains Indians. Scalping or killing an enemy would earn praise from elders and feathers for their ceremonial headdresses. The most revered chiefs were allowed to wear eagle-feather warbonnets. Yet chiefs exercised only modest authority over their followers. As Chief Low Horn, a Blackfoot, explained, the chiefs "could not restrain their young men . . . their young men were wild, and ambitious, in their turn to be braves and chiefs. They wanted by some brave act to win the favor of their young women, and bring scalps and horses to show their prowess."

Several quite different Indian tribes lived to the south and west of the Plains Indians. In the arid region including what is today Arizona, New Mexico, and southern Utah were the peaceful Pueblo tribes— Acoma, Hopi, Laguna, Taos, Zia, Zuni. They were sophisticated farmers who lived in adobe villages along rivers that they used to irrigate their crops of corn, beans, and squash. The word *pueblo* comes from the Spanish term for "village." Their rivals were the Apache and Navajo, warlike hunters who roamed the countryside in small bands and preyed upon the Pueblos. They, in turn, were periodically harassed by their powerful enemies, the Comanches.

To the north, in the Great Basin between the Rocky Mountains and the Sierra Nevada range, Indians such as the Paiutes and Gosiutes struggled to survive in the harsh, arid region of what is today Nevada, Utah, and eastern California. They traveled in family groups and subsisted on berries, pine nuts, insects, and rodents. West of the mountains, along the California coast, the Indians lived in small villages. They gathered wild plants and acorns and were quite adept at fishing in the rivers and bays. More than 100,000 Indians lived in coastal California in the 1840s.

The Indian tribes living along the northwest Pacific Coast—the Nisqually, Spokane, Yakima, Chinook, Klamath, and Nez Percé (pierced noses)—enjoyed the most abundant natural resources and the most temperate climate. The ocean and rivers provided bountiful supplies of seafood—whales, seals, salmon, crabs. The lush forests just east of the coast harbored game, berries, and nuts. And the majestic stands of fir, redwood, and cedar offered wood for cooking and shelter.

All these Indian tribes eventually felt the unrelenting pressure of white expansion. Because Indian life on the plains depended on the buffalo, the influx of white settlers posed a direct threat to their cultural survival. In an 1846 petition to President Polk, the Sioux protested that "for several years past the Emigrants going over the Mountains from the United States, have been the cause that Buffalo in great measure left our hunting grounds, thereby causing us to go into the Country of Our Enemies to hunt, exposing our lives daily for the necessary subsistence of our wives and children and getting killed on several occasions." But the federal government turned a deaf ear to such pleas for assistance. It continued to build a string of frontier forts to protect the advancing settlers, and it sought to use treaties to gain control of new lands. When officials of the Indian Bureau could not coerce, cajole, or confuse Indian leaders into selling title to their tribal lands, fighting ensued. And after the discovery of gold in California in 1848, the tidal wave of white expansion flowed all the way to the west coast.

THE SPANISH WEST   As American settlers moved westward they also encountered Spanish-speaking peoples. Many whites were as contemptuous of these people as they were of Indians. Senator Lewis Cass, the expansionist from Michigan, expressed the sentiment of many Americans during a debate over the annexation of New Mexico. "We do not

Church interior, Las Trampas, New Mexico, constructed around 1760.

want the people of Mexico," he declared, "either as citizens or as subjects. All we want is a portion of territory . . . with a population, which would soon recede, or identify itself with ours." He viewed Mexicans as ignorant, indolent, and conniving. The vast majority of the Spanish-speaking people in what is today the American Southwest resided in New Mexico. Most of these were of mixed Indian and Spanish blood and were poor ranch hands or small farmers and herders.

The Spanish had been less successful in colonizing Arizona and Texas than they had been in New Mexico and Florida. The Yuma and Apache Indians in Arizona and the Comanches and Apaches in Texas thwarted efforts to establish Catholic missions. After years of fruitless missionary efforts among the Pueblo Indians, one Spaniard complained that "most" of them "have never forsaken idolatry, and they appear to be Christians more by force than to be Indians who are reduced to the Holy Faith."

In eastern Texas during the first half of the eighteenth century, French traders from Louisiana undermined the authority and influence of the Spanish missions. The French furnished the Indians with guns, ammunition, and promises of protection. "We do not have a single gun," lamented one Franciscan friar, "while we see the French giving hundreds of arms to the Indians." Several of the Texas missions were abandoned and reestablished near San Antonio in 1731. By 1750 the Pawnees, Wichitas, Comanches, and Apaches were using Spanish horses and French rifles to raid Spanish settlements in Texas. One Spanish commander reported that "the enemy is so superior . . . in firearms as well as in numbers, that our destruction seems probable."

Such conditions help explain why Texas was one of the most sparsely populated provinces on the northern frontier of New Spain. By 1790, the Hispanic population in Texas numbered only 2,510 while in New Mexico it exceeded 20,000.

THE MEXICAN REVOLUTION   In 1807 French forces occupied Spain and imprisoned the king. This created both consternation and confusion throughout Spain's colonial possessions, including Mexico. Miguel Hidalgo y Costilla, a *creole* (Europeans born in the New World) Mexican priest, took advantage of the fluid situation to organize a revolt of Indians and *mestizos* (people of mixed Indian and white ancestry) against Spanish rule. But the poorly organized uprising failed miserably. In 1811 Spanish troops captured Hidalgo and executed him. Other Mexicans, however, continued to yearn for independence. In 1820, a revolt by liberals in Spain greatly weakened the authority of the monarch, and Mexican creoles seized the opportunity to again liberate themselves from Spanish authority. By then, the Spanish forces in Mexico had lost much of their cohesion and dedication. Facing a growing revolt, the last Spanish officials withdrew from Mexico in 1821, and it became an independent nation.

Mexican independence unleashed tremors throughout the Southwest. In New Mexico and Arizona, American fur traders streamed into the region and developed a lucrative commerce in beaver pelts. A semi-literate Missouri trader reported that "the mackeson [Mexican] province Has de Clared Independence of the mother Cuntry and is desirous of a traid with the people of the united States." Soon thereafter, wagon trains carrying American settlers began to make their way along the Santa Fe Trail. In California, American entrepreneurs also flooded into the now-Mexican province and soon became a powerful force for change. By 1848 Americans made up half of the non-Indian population. In Texas, American adventurers decided to promote their own independence from a newly independent—and chaotic—Mexican government. Suddenly, it seemed, the Southwest was a ripe new frontier for American exploitation and settlement.

REACHING THE ROCKIES   The Santa Fe traders had pioneered more than a new trail. They showed that heavy wagons could cross the plains and the mountains, and they developed the technique of organized caravans for common protection. They also began to discover the weakness of Mexico's control over its northern borderlands, and to implant in American minds their contempt for the "mongrel" population of the region. From the 1820s on, however, that population had begun to include a few Americans who lingered in Santa Fe or Taos, using them as jumping-off points for hunting and trapping expeditions northward and westward.

George Caleb Bingham's Fur Traders Descending the Missouri *(1845).*

The more important avenue for the fur trade, however, was the Missouri River with its many tributaries. The heyday of the mountain fur trade began in 1822 when a Missouri businessman sent his first trading party to the upper Missouri. By the mid-1820s there developed the "rendezvous system," in which trappers, traders, and Indians from all over the Rocky Mountain country gathered annually at some designated place, usually in or near the Grand Tetons, in order to trade. But by 1840 the great days of the western fur trade were over. The streams no longer teemed with beavers.

During the 1820s and 1830s the fur trade had sired a uniquely reckless breed of "mountain men" who deserted civilization for the pursuit of the beaver and reverted to a primitive existence in the wilderness, sometimes in splendid isolation, sometimes in the shelter of primitive forts, and sometimes among the Indians. They were the first to find their way around in the Rocky Mountains, and they pioneered the trails over which settlers by the 1840s were beginning to flood the Oregon Country and trickle across the border into California.

THE OREGON COUNTRY   Beyond the mountains the Oregon Country stretched from the 42nd parallel north to 54°40′, between which Spain and Russia had given up their rights, leaving Great Britain and the United States as the only claimants. Under the Convention of 1818 the two countries had agreed to "joint occupation." Until the 1830s, however, joint occupation had been a legal technicality, because the only American presence was the occasional mountain man who wandered into the Pacific slope or the infrequent trading vessel from Boston, Salem, or New York.

WAGON TRAILS WEST

0   300 Miles

0   300 Kilometers

Word of Oregon's fertile soil, temperate climate, and magnificent forests gradually spread eastward. By the late 1830s, in the midst of economic hard times after the Panic of 1837, a trickle of emigrants was flowing along the Oregon Trail. Soon, "Oregon Fever" spread like a contagion. In 1841 and 1842 the first sizable wagon trains made the trip, and in 1843 the movement became a mass migration. That year about a thousand overlanders followed the trail westward from Independence, Missouri, along the North Platte River into what is now Wyoming, through South Pass down to Fort Bridger (abode of a celebrated mountain man, Jim Bridger), then down the Snake River to the Columbia and along the Columbia to their goal in the fertile Willamette Valley. By 1845 there were about 5,000 settlers in the region.

EYEING CALIFORNIA   California was also becoming an alluring attraction for new settlers and entrepreneurs. It first felt the influence of European culture in 1769, when Spain grew concerned about Russian fur and seal traders moving south along the Pacific coast from their base in Alaska. To thwart Russian intentions, Spain sent a naval expedition to explore and settle the region. The Spanish discovered San Francisco Bay and constructed presidios (military garrisons) at San Diego and Monterey. Even more important, Franciscan friars led by Junipero Serra established a mission at San Diego.

Over the next fifty years Franciscans built twenty more missions, spaced a day's journey apart along the coast from San Diego to San Francisco. There they converted Indians to their faith and established thriving agricultural estates. As in Mexico, the Spanish monarchy awarded huge land grants in California to a few ex-soldiers and colonists, who turned the grants into profitable cattle ranches. The Indians were left with the least valuable land, and most of them subsisted as farmers or artisans serving the missions. By 1803, 40 percent of California's Native American population had embraced Catholicism. Friars encouraged the piety and diligence of these "Mission Indians" with whippings, causing some to flee the jurisdiction of the church. Within three decades infectious diseases transmitted by European settlers ravaged the Indian population, leaving only a third as many by 1833 as in 1803.

For all of its rich natural resources, California remained thinly populated by Indians and mission friars well into the nineteenth century. It was a simple, almost feudal, agrarian society, without schools, industry, or defenses. In 1821, when Mexico wrested its independence from Spain, Californians took comfort in the fact that Mexico City was so far away that it would exercise little effective control over its farthest state. During the next two decades Californians, including many recent Amer-

Ferriage of the Platte, July 1849. *The Mormons did a thriving business ferrying emigrants bound for Oregon across the Platte River. This sketch shows overlanders improvising their own ferry.*

ican arrivals, staged ten revolts against the governors dispatched to lord over them.

Yet Mexican rule did produce a dramatic change in California history. In 1824, Mexico passed a colonization act that granted hundreds of huge "rancho" estates to Mexican settlers. With free labor extracted from Indians, who were treated like slaves, the *rancheros* lived a life of self-indulgent luxury and ease, roaming their lands, gambling, horseracing, bull-baiting, and dancing. These freebooting *rancheros* soon cast covetous eyes on the vast estates controlled by the Franciscan missions. In 1833–1834, they convinced the Mexican government to confiscate the California missions, exile the Franciscan friars, release the Indians from church control, and make the mission lands available to new settlement. Within a few years some 700 huge new rancho grants of 4,500 to 50,000 acres were issued along the coast from San Diego to San Francisco. Organized like feudal estates, these California ranches resembled southern plantations. But the death rate for Indian workers was twice as high as that of slaves in the Deep South.

Few accounts of life in California, however, took note of the brutalities inflicted on the Indians. Instead they portrayed the region as a proverbial land of milk and honey, ripe for development. Such a natural paradise could not long remain a secret, and Americans had already been visiting the Pacific coast in search of profits and land. By the late 1820s American trappers wandered in from time to time, and American ships began to enter the "hide and tallow" trade. The ranchos of California produced cowhide and beef tallow in large quantity, and both products enjoyed a brisk demand, cowhides mainly for shoes and the tallow chiefly for candles. Ships from Boston, Salem, or New York, well stocked with trade goods, struggled southward around Cape Horn and northward to the customs office at the California capital of Monterey. From there the ships worked their way down the coast, stopping to sell their goods and take on return cargoes. Richard Henry Dana's *Two Years Before the Mast* (1840), a classic account of his adventures as a seaman in the trade, brought the scene vividly to life for his many readers and focused their attention on the romance and the potential of California.

By the mid-1830s shippers began setting up representatives in California to buy the hides and store them until a company ship arrived. One of these agents, Thomas O. Larkin at Monterey, would play a leading role in the American acquisition of California. Larkin stuck pretty much to his trade, operating a retail business on the side, while others branched out and struck it rich in ranching. The most noteworthy of the traders, however, was not American, but Swiss. John A. Sutter had tried the Santa Fe trade first, then found his way to California via Oregon, Hawaii, and Alaska. In Monterey he persuaded the Mexi-

Sutter's Fort, renamed Fort Sacramento during the Mexican War.

can governor to give him land on which to plant a colony of Swiss émigrés.

At the juncture of the Sacramento and American Rivers (later the site of Sacramento) Sutter built an enormous enclosure that guarded an entire village of settlers and shops. At New Helvetia (Americans called it Sutter's Fort), completed in 1843, no Swiss colony materialized, but the baronial estate became the mecca for Americans bent on settling the Sacramento country. It stood at the end of what became the most traveled route through the Sierras, the California Trail, which forked off the Oregon Trail and led through the mountains near Lake Tahoe. By the start of 1846 there were perhaps 800 Americans in California, along with some 8,000–12,000 Californios of Spanish descent.

LIFE ON THE OVERLAND TRAIL   The settlers bound for Oregon and California traveled mostly in family groups, and they came from all over the United States. They usually left Missouri in late spring, completing the grueling 2,000-mile trek in six months. Traveling in ox-drawn, canvas-covered wagons nicknamed "prairie schooners," they jostled their way across the dusty or muddy trails and traversed rugged mountains at the rate of about fifteen miles per day. The first wagon trains departed in 1841. By 1845 some 5,000 people made the arduous journey annually. The discovery of gold in California in 1848 brought some 30,000 pioneers along the Oregon Trail in 1849. By 1850, the peak year of travel along the trail, the number had risen to 55,000.

Contrary to popular myth, the Indians rarely attacked wagon trains. Less than four percent of the fatalities associated with the overland trail experience were the result of Indian depredations. More often, the Indians either allowed the settlers to pass through their tribal lands unmolested or demanded payment. The Sioux were especially shrewd toll keepers, who "in every case get the best of the bargain," observed one overlander. Many wagon trains never encountered a single Indian, and others received generous aid from Indians who served as guides, advisers, or traders. The Indians, one woman pioneer noted, "proved better than represented." To be sure, as the number of pioneers increased dramatically during the 1850s, tensions between overlanders and Indians increased, but never to the degree portrayed in Western novels and films.

Still, the journey west was incredibly difficult. Few who embarked on their western quest were adequately prepared for the ordeals they were to face. The carcasses of mules, oxen, and wagons from previous groups signaled the difficulties they would confront. The diary of Amelia Knight, who set out for Oregon in 1853 with her husband and their seven children, reveals the mortal threats along the trail: "Chatfield quite sick with scarlet fever. A calf took sick and died before breakfast. Lost one of our oxen; he dropped dead in the yoke. I could hardly help shedding tears. Yesterday my eighth child was born." Cholera claimed many lives. On average there was one grave every eighty yards along the trail between the Missouri River and the Willamette Valley. Some 20,000 pioneers died in all.

The never-ending routine of necessary chores and grinding physical labor on the overland trail took its toll on once-buoyant spirits. This was especially true for women, whose labors went on day and night. Uprooting their families and journeying west placed a special burden on wives and mothers, especially those accustomed to the comforts of middle-class domesticity. The hardships of trail life shattered the conventional notion of the settled home as the family's moral center and nursery. The diary of one woman settler records with great poignancy the trail's wearying regimen: "I have done a washing. Stewed apples, made pies and a rice pudding, and mended our wagon cover. Rather tired." The next day brought more of the same: "Baked biscuits, stewed berries, fried meat, boiled and mashed potatoes, and made tea for supper, afterward baked bread. Thus you see I have not much rest." Another woman complained that, unlike the men, who smoked and talked together after supper, we *have no time for sociability.*" All was "hurry scurry." There "is no rest in such a journey."

Initially, the pioneers along the Overland Trail adopted the same division of labor used back East. Women cooked, washed, sewed, and monitored the children while men drove the wagons, tended the horses and cattle, and handled the heavy labor. But the unique demands of the trail soon dissolved such neat distinctions and posed new tasks. Women found themselves gathering buffalo dung for fuel, pitching in to help liberate a wagon mired in mud, helping to construct a makeshift bridge,

Life on the trail: "Father & Mother went into St. Joseph's bought another tent, heavy canvas for the boys and men to sleep in, using the other tent for an eating place. They also bought a small sheet iron stove, cut a hole in the tent for the pipe, then when it was raining, we could warm up a pot of beans, make a kettle of soup or a pot of coffee, sometimes a pot of mush." Mary Hite, age 13, 1853.

or a variety of other unladylike activities. Yet only rarely did menfolk assume conventional female roles. Most of the older women strove to keep distinct the traditional boundaries between men's and women's work, and quarrels frequently erupted. One woman reported that there was "not a little fighting" in their group, "invariably the outcome of disputes over divisions of labor." Mary Ellen Todd, a teenaged girl, revealed the tensions that younger women felt in defining their roles within this new society on wheels. Having taken great delight in learning to use a bullwhip, she was crestfallen to overhear her mother tell her father that " 'I am afraid it isn't a very lady-like thing for a girl to do.' After this, while I felt a secret joy in being able to have a new power that set things going, there was also a sense of shame over this new accomplishment."

The hard labor of the trail understandably provoked tensions within families and powerful yearnings for home. Many a tired pioneer could identify with the following comment in a girl's journal: "Poor Ma said only this morning, 'Oh, I wish we had never started.' She looks so sorrowful and dejected." Another woman wondered "what had possessed my husband, anyway, that he should have thought of bringing us away out through this God forsaken country." Some turned back, but most continued on. And once in Oregon or California they set about establishing stable communities. Noted one settler:

> Friday, October 27.—Arrived at Oregon City at the falls of the Willamette.
> Saturday, October 28.—Went to work.

THE DONNER PARTY   The most tragic story along the Overland Trail involved the party led by George Donner, a prosperous sixty-two-year-old farmer from Illinois, who led his family and a train of other settlers along the Oregon Trail in 1846. They made every mistake possible. They started too late in the year, overloaded their wagons, and took a foolish shortcut to California across the Wasatch Mountains in the Utah Territory. In the Wasatch, the Donner party was joined by another group of thirteen pioneers, bringing the total to eighty-seven. Finding themselves lost on their "shortcut," they had to backtrack before finally finding their way across the Wasatch and into the desert leading to the Great Salt Lake. Crossing the desert exacted a terrible toll. They lost over 100 oxen and were forced to abandon several wagons and their precious supplies. Tempers flared as the tired and hungry travelers trudged on. One leader of the party killed a young teamster and was expelled, leaving his wife and children behind.

By the time the Donner party reached Truckee Lake at the base of Truckee Pass, the last mountain barrier before reaching the Sacramento Valley, the group had grown surly. They knew that they must cross the pass before the next major snowfall hemmed them in, but they were too late. A two-week-long snowfall trapped them in two separate camps. By December eighty-one settlers, half of them children, were marooned, and there was only enough meat to last through the end of the month. Seventeen of the strongest members decided to cross the pass on their own, only to be trapped by more snow on the western slope. Two members died of exposure and starvation. Just before he died, Uncle Billy Graves urged his daughters to eat his body. The daughters were appalled by the prospect of cannibalism, but a day later they saw no other choice. The group struggled on, and, when two more died, they, too, were consumed. Only seven lived to reach the Sacramento Valley.

Four search parties were then dispatched to save the rest of the Donner party. Back at the main camps at Alder Creek and Truckee Lake, the survivors slaughtered and ate the last of the livestock, then proceeded to boil hides and bones. One family killed their dog. When the rescue party finally reached them, they discovered a grisly scene. Thirteen people had died, and cannibalism had become so commonplace that one pioneer noted casually in his diary that "Mrs. Murphy said here yesterday that she thought she would commence on Milt and eat him. It is distressing. Saturday the 27th a beautiful morning." As the rescuers led the forty-seven survivors over the pass, George Donner, so weakened that he was unable to walk, stayed behind to die. His wife chose to remain with him.

THE PATHFINDER   Despite the hardships and dangers of the overland crossing, the Far West proved an irresistible attraction. The premier press agent for California, and the Far West generally, was John Charles Frémont, "the Pathfinder"—who mainly found paths that the mountain men showed him. Born in Savannah, Georgia, and raised in the South, he had a relentless love of the outdoors and an exuberant, charismatic personality. Frémont studied at the College of Charleston before being commissioned a second lieutenant in the United States Topographical Corps in 1838. In the early 1840s his new father-in-law, Missouri senator Thomas Hart Benton, arranged the explorations toward Oregon that made Frémont famous. In 1842 he mapped the Oregon Trail—and met Christopher "Kit" Carson, one of the most knowledgeable of the mountain men, who became his frequent associate and the most famous frontiersman after Daniel Boone. In 1843–1844 Frémont, typically clad in deerskin shirt, blue army trousers, and moccasins, went on to Oregon, then made a heroic sweep down the eastern slopes of the Sierras, headed southward through the central valley of California, bypassed the

John Charles Frémont, the Pathfinder.

mountains in the south, and returned via Great Salt Lake. His reports on both expeditions, published together in 1845, gained a wide circulation and helped excite the interest of easterners.

American presidents, beginning with Jackson, tried to acquire at least northern California, down to San Francisco Bay, by purchase from Mexico. Jackson reasoned that as a free state California could balance the future admission of Texas as a slave state. But Jackson's agent had to be recalled after a clumsy effort to bribe Mexican officials. Tyler's minister to Mexico resumed talks, but they ended abruptly after a bloodless comic-opera conquest of Monterey by the commander of the American Pacific Fleet, who had heard a false rumor of war.

Rumors flourished that the British and French were scheming to grab California, though neither government actually had such intentions. Political conditions in Mexico left the remote territory in near anarchy much of the time, as governors came and went in rapid succession. Amid the chaos substantial Californios reasoned that they would be better off if they cut ties to Mexico altogether. Some favored an independent state, perhaps under French or British protection. A larger group, led by a Sonoma cattleman, admired the balance of central and local authority in the United States and felt their interests might best be served by American annexation. By the time the Americans were ready to fire the spark of rebellion in California, there was little will in Mexico to resist.

Annexing Texas

AMERICAN SETTLEMENTS   America's lust for land was most clearly at work in the most accessible of all the Mexican borderlands, Texas. More Americans resided there than in all the other coveted regions combined. Many claimed in fact, if with little evidence, that Texas had been part of the Louisiana Purchase, abandoned only when John Quincy Adams had accepted a boundary at the Sabine River in 1819. Adams himself, as president, tried to make up for the loss by offering to buy Texas for $1 million, but Mexico refused both that and a later offer of $5 million from Jackson. Meanwhile, however, Texas was rapidly turning into an American province, for Mexico welcomed American settlers there as a means of stabilizing the border.

First and foremost among the promoters of Anglo-American settlement was Stephen F. Austin, a Missouri resident who gained from Mexico a huge land grant originally given to his father by Spanish authorities. Before Mexican independence from Spain was fully won, he had started a colony on the lower Brazos River late in 1821, and by 1824 more than 2,000 hardy souls had settled on his lands. In 1825, under a

National Colonization Law, the state of Coahuila-Texas offered large tracts to *empresarios,* large ranchers, who promised to sponsor immigrants. Most of the newcomers were southern farmers drawn to rich new cotton lands going for only a few cents an acre. As a young woman settler recalled, "I was a young thing then, but 5 months married, my husband . . . failed in Tennessee. . . . I ready to go anywhere . . . freely consented. . . . Texas fever rose then . . . there we must go. There without much reflection, we did go." By 1830 the coastal region of eastern Texas had about 20,000 white settlers and 1,000 black slaves brought in to work the cotton.

At that point the Mexican government grew alarmed at the flood of strangers threatening to engulf the province, and it forbade further immigration. Troops moved to the frontier to enforce the law, but illegal American immigrants moved across the long border as easily as illegal Mexican immigrants would later cross over in the other direction. By 1835 the American population had grown to around 30,000, about ten times the number of Mexicans in Texas. Friction mounted in 1832 and 1833 as Americans organized conventions to demand a state of their own. Instead of granting the request, General Santa Anna, who had seized power in Mexico, dissolved the national congress late in 1834, abolished the federal system, and became dictator of a centralized state. Texans rose in rebellion and summoned a convention which, like the earlier Continental Congress, adopted a "Declaration of Causes" for taking up arms. On March 2, 1836, however, the Texans declared their independence as Santa Anna approached with an army of conquest.

INDEPENDENCE FROM MEXICO   The Mexican army delivered its first blow at San Antonio, where it assaulted a small garrison of Texans and American volunteers holed up behind the adobe walls of an abandoned mission, the Alamo. Among the most celebrated of the volunteers was Davy Crockett, the Tennessee frontiersman and soldier who had fought Indians under Andrew Jackson and then served as a congressman. Full of bounce and brag, he was thoroughly expert at killing with his trusty rifle, "Old Betsy." As he once told his men, "Pierce the heart of the enemy as you would a feller that spit in your face, knocked down your wife, burnt up your houses, and called your dog a skunk! Cram his pesky carcass full of thunder and lightning like a stuffed sassidge . . . and bite his nose off into the bargain."

On February 23, 1836, Santa Anna demanded that the 185 defenders at the Alamo surrender. They answered with a cannon shot. The 4,000 Mexicans then launched a series of frontal assaults. For twelve days they were repulsed with fearful losses. At one point, during a lull in the fighting, Colonel William B. Travis, the garrison commander from South Carolina, drew a line on the ground with his sword as he addressed his men: "Those prepared to give their lives in freedom's cause," he said in a trembling voice, "come over to me." Every man crossed the line. The notorious slave smuggler, Indian fighter, and inventor of the Bowie knife, Colonel James Bowie, bedridden with pneumonia, asked that his cot be carried over.

In the chilly, predawn hours of March 6, the defenders of the Alamo were awakened by the sound of Mexican bugles playing the dreaded "Deguello" ("no mercy to the defenders"). Soon thereafter Santa Anna's men attacked from every side. They were twice repulsed, but on the third try, as the defenders ran low on ammunition, the Mexicans broke through the battered north wall and swarmed through the breach. Colonel Travis was killed by a bullet to the forehead. Davy Crockett and the other frontiersmen used their muskets as clubs, but they too were slain. Jim Bowie, his pistols emptied, his famous knife bloodied, and his body riddled by Mexican bullets, lay dead on his cot. Santa Anna ordered the wounded Americans put to death and their bodies burned with the rest. All but one of the defenders was killed. The survivor persuaded his Mexican captors that he had been forced to fight against his will. It was a complete victory for the Mexicans, but a costly one. The defenders of the Alamo gave their lives at the cost of 1,544 Mexicans, and their heroic stand inspired the rest of Texas to fanatical resistance.

The commander-in-chief of the Texas forces was Sam Houston, a Tennessee frontiersman who had learned war under the tutelage of Andrew Jackson at Horseshoe Bend, had later represented the Nashville district in Congress, and had moved to Texas only three years before. Houston beat a strategic retreat eastward, gathering reinforcements as he went, including volunteer recruits from the United States.

Sam Houston.

Just west of the San Jacinto River he finally paused near the site of the city that later bore his name, and on April 21, 1836, surprised a Mexican encampment there. The Texans charged, yelling "Remember the Alamo," overwhelmed the Mexican force within fifteen minutes, and took Santa Anna prisoner. The Mexican dictator bought his freedom for the price of a treaty recognizing Texan independence, with the Rio Grande as the boundary. The Mexican Congress repudiated the treaty, but the war was at an end.

THE MOVE FOR ANNEXATION   The Lone Star Republic then drafted a constitution, made Houston its first president, and voted almost unanimously for annexation to the United States as soon as the opportunity arose. Houston's old friend Jackson was still president, but even Old Hickory could be discreet when delicacy demanded it. The addition of a new slave state at a time when Congress was beset with abolitionist petitions threatened a serious sectional quarrel that might endanger the election of Van Buren, his hand-picked successor. Worse than that, it raised the specter of war with Mexico. Jackson kept his counsel and even delayed recognition of the Texas Republic until his last day in office. Van Buren shied away from the issue of annexation during his entire term as president.

Rebuffed in Washington, Texans turned their thoughts to a separate destiny. Under President Mirabeau Bonaparte Lamar, elected in 1838, they began to talk of expanding to the Pacific as a new nation that would rival the United States. France and Britain extended recognition and began to develop trade relations. Texas supplied them with an independent source of cotton, new markets, and promised also to become an obstacle to American expansion. The British, who had emancipated the slaves in their colonies in 1833, hoped Texans might embrace abolition in exchange for British protection against any Mexican effort to reassert its sovereignty over Texas.

Most Texans, however, had never abandoned their hopes of annexation. Reports of growing British influence in Texas created anxieties in the United States government and among southern slaveholders, who became the chief advocates of annexation. Secret negotiations with Texas began in 1843, and that April John C. Calhoun, Tyler's secretary of state, completed a treaty that went to the Senate for ratification.

Calhoun chose this moment also to send the British minister a letter instructing him on the blessings of slavery and stating that annexation of Texas was needed to foil the British abolitionists. Publication of the note fostered the claim that annexation was planned less in the national interest than to promote the expansion of slavery. It was so worded, one observer wrote Jackson, as to "drive off every northern man from the support of the measure." Sectional division, plus fear of a war with Mexico, contributed to the Senate's overwhelming rejection of the treaty. Solid Whig opposition was the most important factor behind its defeat.

POLK'S PRESIDENCY

THE ELECTION OF 1844   Prudent leaders in both political parties had hoped to keep this divisive issue out of the 1844 campaign. Clay and Van Buren, the leading candidates, had reached the same conclusion about Texas: when the treaty was submitted to the Senate, they both wrote letters opposing annexation because it would create the danger of war. Both letters, dated three days apart, appeared in separate Washington newspapers on April 27, 1844. Clay's "Raleigh letter" (written while he was on a southern tour) added that annexation was "dangerous to the integrity of the Union . . . and not called for by any general expression of public opinion." The outcome of the Whig convention in Baltimore seemed to bear out his view. Party leaders showed no qualms about Clay's stance. The convention nominated him unanimously, and the Whig platform omitted any reference to Texas.

The Democratic convention was a different story. Van Buren's southern supporters, including Jackson, abandoned him because of his opposition to Texas annexation. With the convention deadlocked, on the eighth ballot expansionist forces brought forward James K. Polk of Tennessee, and on the ninth ballot he became the first "dark horse" candidate to win a major-party nomination. The party platform took an unequivocal stand favoring expansion, and to win support in the North and West as well as in the South, it linked the questions of Oregon and Texas: "our title to the whole of the territory of Oregon is clear and unquestionable," the party proclaimed, and called for "the reoccupation of Oregon and the reannexation of Texas."

The combination of southern and western expansionism offered a winning strategy, so popular that Clay began to hedge his statement on Texas. While he still believed the integrity of the Union was the chief consideration, he had "no personal objection to the annexation of Texas" if it could be achieved "without dishonor, without war, with the common consent of the Union, and upon just and fair terms." His explanation seemed clear enough, but prudence was no match for spread-eagle oratory and the emotional pull of Manifest Destiny. The net result of Clay's stand was to turn more antislavery votes to the Liberty party, which increased its count from about 7,000 in 1840 to more than 62,000 in 1844. In the western counties of New York the Liberty party drew enough votes away from the Whigs to give the state to Polk. Had he carried New York, Clay would have won the election by seven electoral votes. Polk won a narrow plurality of 38,000 popular

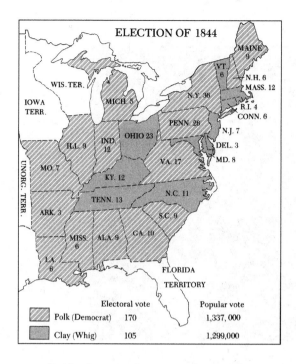

ELECTION OF 1844

	Electoral vote	Popular vote
Polk (Democrat)	170	1,337,000
Clay (Whig)	105	1,299,000

votes nationwide (the first president since John Quincy Adams to win without a majority) but a clear majority of the electoral college, 170 to 105.

"Who is James K. Polk?" the Whigs scornfully asked in the campaign. But the man was not as obscure as they implied. He was a dark horse only in the sense that he was not a candidate before the convention. Born near Charlotte, North Carolina, trained in mathematics and the classics at the University of North Carolina, Polk had moved to Tennessee as a young man. A successful lawyer and planter, he had entered politics early, served fourteen years in Congress (four as Speaker of the House) and two as governor of Tennessee.

Young Hickory, as his partisans liked to call him, was a short, slender man with a shock of long, grizzled hair, probing gray eyes, and a seemingly permanent grimace. He had none of Jackson's charisma, but shared Jackson's prejudices and made up for his lack of color by stubborn determination and hard work, which destroyed his health during four years in the White House. March 4, 1845, was dark and rainy; Polk delivered his inaugural address to "a large assemblage of umbrellas," as John Quincy Adams described it. The speech was as colorless as the day, a recitation of Jeffersonian and Jacksonian principles in which Polk denounced protective tariffs, national banks, and implied powers, and again claimed title to Oregon.

James K. Polk.

POLK'S PROGRAM   In domestic affairs "Young Hickory" Polk hewed to the principle of the old hero, but the new Jacksonians subtly reflected the growing influence of the slaveholding South within the party. Abolitionism, Polk warned, could bring the dissolution of the Union. Antislavery northerners had already begun to drift away from the Democratic party, which they complained was coming to represent the slaveholding interest.

Polk's major objectives were tariff reduction, reestablishment of the Independent Treasury, settlement of the Oregon question, and the acquisition of California. He gained them all. The Walker Tariff of 1846, in keeping with Democratic tradition, reduced the tariff to an average level of about 26 percent. In the same year Polk persuaded Congress to restore the Independent Treasury, which the Whigs had eliminated. Twice Polk vetoed internal-improvements bills. In each case his blows to the American System of Henry Clay's Whigs satisfied the urges of the slaveholding South, but at the cost of annoying northern protectionists and westerners who needed internal improvements.

THE STATE OF TEXAS   But Polk's chief concern remained geographic expansion. He privately vowed to acquire California, and New Mexico as well, preferably by purchase. The acquisition of Texas was already under way when Polk took office. In his final months in office President Tyler, taking Polk's election as a mandate to act, asked Congress to accomplish annexation by joint resolution, which required only a simple majority in each house and avoided the two-thirds Senate vote needed to ratify a treaty. Congress had read the election returns too, and after a bitter debate over slavery, the resolution passed by votes of 27 to 25 in the Senate and 120 to 98 in the House. Tyler signed the resolution on March 1, 1845, offering to admit Texas to statehood. The new state would keep its public lands but pay its own war debt, and with its own consent might be divided into as many as five states in the near future. A Texas convention accepted the offer in July, the voters of Texas ratified the action in October, and the new state formally entered the Union on December 29, 1845.

OREGON   Meanwhile, the Oregon issue heated up as expansionists aggressively insisted that Polk abandon previous offers to settle on the 49th parallel and stand by the platform pledge to take all of Oregon. The bumptious expansionists were prepared to risk war with Britain while relations with Mexico were simultaneously moving toward the breaking point. "Fifty-four forty or fight," they intoned. "All of Oregon or none." In his inaugural address Polk declared the American title to Oregon "clear and unquestionable," but privately he favored a prudent

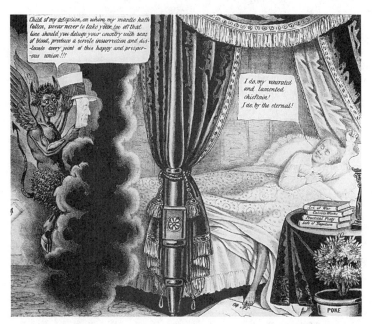

The devil advising Polk to pursue 54° 40′ even if "you deluge your country with seas of blood, produce a servile insurrection, and dislocate every joint of this happy and prosperous union."

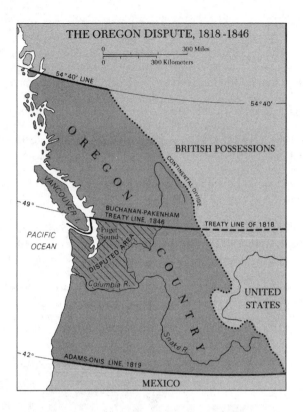

THE OREGON DISPUTE, 1818-1846

54°40′ LINE

54°40′

BRITISH POSSESSIONS

OREGON

VANCOUVER I.

49°

BUCHANAN-PAKENHAM
TREATY LINE, 1846

CONTINENTAL DIVIDE

TREATY LINE OF 1818

PACIFIC
OCEAN

Puget
Sound

DISPUTED AREA

COUNTRY

Columbia R.

UNITED
STATES

Snake R.

42°

ADAMS-ONIS LINE, 1819

MEXICO

compromise. War with Mexico was brewing; the territory up to 54°40′
seemed of less importance than Puget Sound or the ports of California,
on which the British also were thought to have an eye. Since Monroe
each administration had offered to extend the boundary along the 49th
parallel. In July 1845 Polk renewed the offer, only to have it refused by
the British minister, Richard Pakenham.

Polk withdrew the offer and went back to his claim to all of Oregon.
In the annual message to Congress at year's end, he asked for permission to give a year's notice that joint occupation would be abrogated,
and revived the Monroe Doctrine with a new twist: "The people of *this
continent* alone have the right to decide their own destiny." After a long
and bitter debate, Congress adopted the resolution, but Polk was playing a bluff game. War with Mexico seemed increasingly certain, and
Secretary of State James Buchanan privately assured the British government that any new offer would be submitted to the Senate.

Fortunately for Polk the British government had no enthusiasm for
war over that remote wilderness at the cost of profitable trade relations
with the United States. From the British viewpoint, the only land in dispute all along had been between the 49th parallel and the Columbia
River. Now the fur trade of the region was a dying industry. In early

June 1846 the British government submitted a draft treaty to extend the border along the 49th parallel and through the main channel south of Vancouver Island. On June 15 Buchanan and British minister Pakenham signed it, and three days later it was ratified in the Senate, where the only opposition came from a group of bitter-end expansionists representing the Old Northwest who wanted more. Most of the country was satisfied. Southerners cared less about Oregon than about Texas, and northern business interests valued British trade more than they valued Oregon. Besides, the country was already at war with Mexico.

THE MEXICAN WAR

THE OUTBREAK OF WAR   Relations with Mexico had gone from bad to worse. On March 6, 1845, two days after Polk took office, the Mexican ambassador broke off relations and left for home to protest the annexation of Texas. When an effort at negotiation failed, Polk focused his efforts on unilateral initiatives. Already he was egging on American intrigues in California. On October 17, 1845, he had written Consul Thomas O. Larkin in Monterey that the president would make no effort to induce California into the Union, but "if the people should desire to unite their destiny with ours, they would be received as brethren." Larkin, who could take a hint, began to line up Americans and sympathetic Californios. Meanwhile Polk ordered American troops under General Zachary Taylor to take up positions on the Rio Grande in the new state of Texas. These positions lay in territory that was doubly disputed: Mexico recognized neither the American annexation of Texas nor the Rio Grande boundary.

The last hope for peace died when John Slidell, sent to Mexico City to negotiate a settlement, finally gave up on his mission in March 1846. Polk then resolved that he could achieve his purposes only by force. He sought and got the cabinet's approval of a war message to Congress. That very evening, May 9, the news arrived that Mexicans had attacked American soldiers north of the Rio Grande. Eleven Americans were killed, five wounded, and the remainder taken prisoner. Polk's provocative scheme had worked.

In his war message Polk could now take the high ground that the war was a response to aggression, a recognition that war had been forced upon the United States. "The cup of forbearance had been exhausted" before the incident; now, he said, Mexico "has passed the boundary of the United States, has invaded our territory, and shed American blood upon the American soil." The Congress quickly passed the war resolution, and Polk signed the declaration of war on May 13, 1846. But support for the war was guarded. In the House twenty-seven members had favored an amendment stating that the resolution should not be construed as approval of Polk's moving troops into the disputed area between the Nueces River and the Rio Grande. The House authorized a call for 50,000 volunteers and a war appropriation of $10 million, but sixty-seven Whigs voted against that measure, another token of rising opposition to the war.

OPPOSITION TO THE WAR   In the Mississippi Valley, where expansion fever ran high, the war was immensely popular. In New England, however, there was less enthusiasm for "Mr. Polk's War." Whig opinion ranged from lukewarm to hostile. John Quincy Adams, who voted against participation, called it "a most unrighteous war." An obscure one-term congressman from Illinois named Abraham Lincoln, upon taking his seat in 1847, began introducing "spot resolutions," calling on Polk to name the spot where American blood had been shed on American soil, implying that American troops may, in fact, have been in Mexico when fired upon.

Many New Englanders believed that the war was the work of "Land-Jobbers and Slave-Jobbers." As the Massachusetts poet James Russell Lowell put it in his *Biglow Papers:*

> They just want this Californy
> So's to lug new slave-states in
> To abuse ye, an' to scorn ye,
> An' to plunder ye like sin.

Some New Englanders, including Lowell, were ready to separate from the slave states, and the Massachusetts legislature formally pronounced the conflict a war of conquest. But before the war ended some antislavery men had a change of heart. Mexican territory seemed so unsuited to plantation staples that they endorsed expansion in hope of enlarging the area of free soil. Manifest Destiny exerted a potent influence even on those who opposed the war. *The Harbinger,* house organ of the Transcendental community at Brook Farm, managed to have it both ways. "This plundering aggression," the paper editorialized, "is monstrously iniquitous, but after all it seems to be completing a more universal design of Providence of extending the power and intelligence of advanced civilized nations."

PREPARING FOR BATTLE   Both the United States and Mexico approached the war ill prepared. American policy had been incredibly reckless, risking war with both Britain and Mexico while doing nothing to strengthen the armed forces until war came. At the outset of war the regular army numbered barely over 7,000, in contrast to the Mexican force of 32,000. Before the war ended the American force grew to 104,000, of whom about 31,000 were regular army troops and marines. Most of these were six- and twelve-month volunteers from the West. Volunteer militia companies, often filled with frontier toughs, made up as raunchy a crew as ever graced the American military—devoid of uniforms, standard equipment, and discipline alike. One observer watched a band of such recruits with "torn and dirty shirts—uncombed heads—unwashed faces" trying to drill, "all hollowing, cursing, yelling like so many incarnate fiends." Repeatedly, despite the best efforts of the commanding generals, these undisciplined forces engaged in plunder, rape, and murder.

Nevertheless, being used to a rough-and-tumble life, the motley American troops outmatched larger Mexican forces, which had their own problems with training, discipline, and munitions. Many of the Mexicans were pressed into service or recruited from prisons, and they made less than enthusiastic fighters. Mexican artillery pieces were generally obsolete, and the powder was so faulty that American soldiers could often dodge cannonballs that fell short and bounced ineffectively along the ground.

The United States entered the war without even a tentative plan of action. One had to be worked out hastily, and politics complicated things. What Polk wanted, Thomas Hart Benton wrote later, was "a small war, just large enough to require a treaty of peace, and not large enough to make military reputations, dangerous for the presidency." Winfield Scott, general-in-chief of the army, was a politically ambitious Whig. Nevertheless Polk named him at first to take charge of the Rio Grande front. When Scott quarreled with Polk's secretary of war, the exasperated president withdrew the appointment. Scott, already known as "Old Fuss and Feathers" for his insistence on proper uniform, had also a genius for absurd turns of phrase. He began an indignant reply to the secretary of war with the remark that he got the secretary's letter as he "sat down to take a hasty plate of soup."

There seemed now a better choice. Zachary Taylor's men had scored two victories over Mexican forces north of the Rio Grande, at Palo Alto (May 8) and Resaca de la Palma (May 9). On May 18 Taylor crossed the river and occupied Matamoros, which a demoralized and bloodied Mexican army had abandoned. These quick victories brought Taylor instant popularity, and the president responded willingly to the demand that he be made commander for the conquest of Mexico. "Old Rough and Ready" Taylor, a bowlegged, squatty, and none-too-handsome man of sixty-one, seemed unlikely stuff from which to fashion a hero and impressed Polk as less of a political threat than Scott. Taylor acted at least as cautiously as Scott, awaiting substantial reinforcements and sup-

Zachary Taylor.

plies before moving any deeper into Mexico. Yet without a major battle he had achieved Polk's main objective, the conquest of Mexico's northern provinces.

ANNEXATION OF CALIFORNIA   Along the Pacific coast, conquest was under way before definite news of the Mexican war arrived. Near the end of 1845 John C. Frémont brought out a band of sixty frontiersmen, ostensibly on another exploration of California and Oregon. "Frémont's conduct was extremely mysterious," John A. Sutter wrote. "Flitting about the country with an armed body of men, he was regarded with suspicion by everybody." When the Mexican commandant at Monterey ordered him out of the Salinas Valley, Frémont defied the Mexicans to oust him, but soon changed his mind and headed for Oregon. In 1846 he and his men moved south into the Sacramento Valley. Americans in the area fell upon Sonoma on June 14, proclaimed the "Republic of California," and hoisted the hastily designed Bear Flag, a grizzly bear and star painted on white cloth—a version of which became the state flag.

Frémont endorsed the Bear Flag Republic and set out for Monterey. Before he arrived, the commodore of the Pacific Fleet, having heard of the outbreak of hostilities with Mexico, sent a party ashore to raise the American flag and proclaim California a part of the United States. The Republic of California had lasted less than a month, and most Californians of whatever origin welcomed a change that promised order in preference to the confusion of the unruly Bear Flaggers.

Before the end of July a new commodore, Robert F. Stockton, began preparations to move against southern California. As senior officer on the scene, Stockton enlisted Frémont's band as the California Battalion and gave Frémont the rank of major. Stockton sent this group down to San Diego but they were too late to overtake the fleeing Mexican loyalists. In a more leisurely fashion, Stockton occupied Santa Barbara and Los Angeles. By mid-August resistance had dissipated. On August 17 Stockton declared himself governor, with Frémont as military commander in the north.

By August another expedition was closing on Santa Fe. On August 18 Stephen Kearny and his men entered the Mexican town, whence an irresolute governor had fled with its defenders. After setting up a civilian governor, Kearny divided his remaining force, leading 300 dragoons west toward California in late September. On October 6 they encountered a band of frontiersmen under Frémont's old helper, Kit Carson, who was riding eastward with news that California had already fallen. Kearny sent 200 of his men back and with the remaining 100 pushed west with Carson serving as a reluctant guide.

But after Carson's departure from the coast, the picture had changed. In southern California, where most of the poorer Mexicans and Mexicanized Indians resented American rule, a rebellion broke out. By the end of October the rebels had ousted the token American force in southern California. Kearny walked right into this rebel zone when he arrived. At San Diego he met up with Stockton and joined him in the reconquest of southern California, which they achieved after two brief clashes when they entered Los Angeles on January 10, 1847. Rebel forces capitulated on January 13.

TAYLOR'S BATTLES   Both California and New Mexico had been taken before General Zachary Taylor fought his first major battle in northern Mexico. Having waited for more men and munitions, he finally moved out of his Matamoros base in September 1846 and headed southward

The Battle of the Plains of Mesa took place just before American forces entered Los Angeles. This sketch was made at the scene.

THE MEXICAN WAR:
MAJOR CAMPAIGNS

◄━━ U.S. forces ◄━ Mexican forces
★ Battle site
━·─·─ Line set by Treaty of Guadalupe Hidalgo, 1848

0 ———————— 400 Miles
0 ———————— 400 Kilometers

toward the heart of Mexico. His first goal was the fortified city of Monterrey, which he took after a five-day siege. Polk, however, was none too happy with the easy terms of surrender to which Taylor agreed, or with Taylor's growing popularity. The whole episode merely confirmed the president's impression that Taylor was too passive to be trusted further with the major campaign. Besides, his victories, if flawed, were leading to talk of Taylor as the next Whig candidate for president.

Yet Polk's grand strategy was itself flawed. Having never seen the Mexican desert, he wrongly assumed that Taylor could live off the country and need not depend on resupply. Polk therefore misunderstood the general's reluctance to strike out across several hundred miles of barren land in front of Mexico City. On another point the president was simply duped. The old dictator Santa Anna, forced out in 1844, got word to Polk from his exile in Havana that in return for the right considerations he could bring about a settlement of the war. Polk in turn assured the Mexican leader that Washington would pay well for any territory taken through a settlement. In August 1846, after another change in the Mexican government, Santa Anna was permitted to pass through the American blockade into Vera Cruz. Soon he was again in command of the Mexican army and then was named president once more. Polk's intrigue unintentionally put perhaps the ablest Mexican general back in command of the enemy army, where he busily organized his forces to strike at Taylor.

By then another American front had been opened, and Taylor was ordered to wait in place. In October 1846 Polk and his cabinet decided to move against Mexico City by way of Vera Cruz. Polk would have preferred a Democratic general, but for want of a better choice named Winfield Scott to the field command. In January 1847 Taylor was required to give up most of his regulars to Scott's force gathering at Tampico. Taylor, miffed at his reduction to a minor role, disobeyed orders and advanced beyond Saltillo.

There, near the hacienda of Buena Vista, Santa Anna met Taylor's untested volunteers with a large but ill-trained and tired army. The Mexican general invited the outnumbered Americans to surrender. "Tell him to go to hell," Taylor replied. In the hard-fought Battle of Buena Vista (February 22–23, 1847), Taylor saw his son-in-law, Colonel Jefferson Davis, the future president of the Confederacy, lead a regiment that broke up a Mexican cavalry charge. Neither side could claim victory on the strength of the outcome, but Taylor was convinced that only his lack of regulars prevented him from striking a decisive blow. In any case it was the last major action on the northern front, and Taylor was granted leave to return home.

SCOTT'S TRIUMPH   Meanwhile, the long-planned assault on the enemy capital had begun on March 9, 1847, when Scott's army landed on the beaches south of Vera Cruz. It was the first major amphibious operation by American military forces, and was carried out without loss. Vera Cruz surrendered on March 27 after a week-long siege. Scott then set out on the route taken by Cortés more than 300 years before. Santa Anna tried to set a trap for him at the mountain pass of Cerro Gordo, but Scott's men took more than 3,000 prisoners, large quantities of equipment and provisions, and the Mexican president's personal effects.

On May 15 Scott's men entered Puebla, the second-largest Mexican city. There Scott lost about a third of his army because men whose twelve-month enlistments had expired felt free to go home, leaving Scott with about 7,000 troops in all. There was nothing to do but hang on until reinforcements and new supplies came up from the coast. Finally, after three months, with his numbers almost doubled, Scott set out on August 7 through the mountain passes into the valley of Mexico, cutting his supply line to the coast. The aging duke of Wellington, following the campaign from afar, predicted Scott "is lost—he cannot capture the city and he cannot fall back upon his base."

Scott, however, directed a brilliant flanking operation around the lakes and marshes that guarded the eastern approaches to Mexico City. After a series of battles in which they overwhelmed Mexican defenses, American forces entered Mexico City on September 13, 1847, and within three days mopped up the remnants of resistance. At the National Palace a battalion of marines ran up the American flag and occupied the "halls of Montezuma."

THE TREATY OF GUADALUPE HIDALGO   After the fall of the capital, Santa Anna resigned and a month later left the country. Meanwhile Polk had appointed as chief peace negotiator Nicholas P. Trist, chief clerk of the State Department and a Virginia Democrat of impeccably partisan credentials. Trist was frustrated for want of anybody to negotiate with. There was as yet no government to replace the departed Santa Anna. In October Polk decided that the Mexican delays required a stronger stand and ordered Trist recalled, but before the message reached Mexico City things had changed. On November 11 the Mexican Congress elected an interim president, and on November 22 the new administration told Trist it had named commissioners to deal with him. Trist, having just received the recall notice, decided to go ahead with negotiations anyway. A sixty-five-page letter of justification did nothing to persuade Polk that he was anything but an "impudent and unqualified scoundrel," but Trist reasoned that it was better to continue than to risk a return of the war party or the disintegration of all government in Mexico.

Formal talks got under way on January 2, 1848, at the village of Guadalupe Hidalgo just outside the capital, and dragged on through the month. Finally Trist, fearing stronger orders from Washington at any time, threatened to end the negotiations, and the Mexicans yielded. By the Treaty of Guadalupe Hidalgo, signed on February 2, 1848, Mexico gave up all claims to Texas above the Rio Grande and ceded California and New Mexico to the United States. In return the United States agreed to pay Mexico $15 million and assume the claims of American citizens against Mexico up to a total of $3 1/4 million.

Miffed that Trist had ignored his orders, Polk nevertheless had little choice but to submit the treaty to the Senate. A growing movement to annex all of Mexico had impelled him to hold out for more. But as Polk confided to his diary, rejecting the treaty would be too risky. If he should reject a treaty made in accord with his own original terms in order to gain more territory, "the probability is that Congress would not grant either men or money to prosecute the war." In that case he might eventually have to withdraw the army and lose everything. The treaty went to the Senate, which ratified it on March 10, 1848. By the end of July the last remaining American soldiers had boarded ship in Vera Cruz.

THE WAR'S LEGACIES   The seventeen-month-long Mexican War had cost the United States 1,721 killed, 4,102 wounded, and far more—11,155—dead of disease. The military and naval expenditures totaled $98 million. For this price, and payments made under the treaty, the United States acquired more than 500,000 square miles of territory (more than a million counting Texas), including the great Pacific harbors of San Diego, Monterey, and San Francisco, with uncounted millions in mineral wealth. Except for a small addition by the Gadsden Purchase of 1853, these annexations rounded out the continental United States. After the treaty was ratified, Polk wrote in his diary: "There will be added to the United States an immense empire, the value of which twenty years hence it would be difficult to calculate." A prominent Mexican, Porfirio Díaz, later to become president of Mexico, expressed a different view: "Alas, poor Mexico! So far from God and so close to the United States!"

Several important "firsts" are associated with the Mexican War: the first successful offensive war, the first major amphibious operation, the first occupation of an enemy capital, the first in which martial law was declared on foreign soil, the first in which West Point graduates played a major role, and the first reported by modern war correspondents. It was also the first significant combat experience for a group of junior officers who would later serve as leading generals during the Civil War: Robert E. Lee, Ulysses S. Grant, Thomas "Stonewall" Jackson, George B. McClellan, George Pickett, Braxton Bragg, George Meade, and others.

Initially, the victory in Mexico provoked a surge of national pride. American triumphs "must elevate the *true* self-respect of the American people," Walt Whitman exclaimed. Others were not so sure. Ralph Waldo Emerson rejected war "as a means of achieving America's destiny," but he then accepted the annexation of new territory by force with the explanation that "most of the great results of history are brought about by discreditable means." As the years passed the Mexican War somehow never became entrenched in the national legends. It was increasingly seen as a war of conquest provoked by a president bent on expansion. One might argue that Polk merely hastened, and possibly achieved at less cost in treasure and human misery, what the march of the restless frontier would soon have achieved anyway. During one term in office he annexed to Jefferson's "empire of liberty" more land than Jefferson himself, but the imperishable glamor that shone about the names of Caesar, Cortés, or Napoleon never brightened the name of Polk. For a brief season, however, the glory of conquest did add luster to the names of Zachary Taylor and Winfield Scott. Despite Polk's best efforts, he had manufactured the next, and last, two Whig candidates for president. One of them, Taylor, would replace him in the White House, with the storm of sectional conflict already on the horizon.

FURTHER READING

For background on Whig programs and ideas, see Glyndon Van Dusen's *The Jacksonian Era, 1828–1848* (1959), Richard P. McCormick's *The Second American Party System* (1966), William R. Brock's *Parties and Political Conscience* (1979), and Daniel W. Howe's *The Political Culture of the American Whigs* (1979).

Several works help interpret the concept of Manifest Destiny. Frederick Merk's *Manifest Destiny and Mission in American History* (1963) remains a classic. Merk takes a more diplomatic slant in *The Monroe Doctrine and American Expansionism, 1843–1849* (1966). A more recent treatment of expansionist ideology is Thomas R. Hietala's *Manifest Design: Anxious Aggrandizement in Late Jacksonian America* (1985). Reginald Horsman's *Race and Manifest Destiny* (1981) highlights racial assumptions behind expansionism. For an excellent survey of western expansion that gives special attention to the role of the federal government, see Richard White's *"It's Your Misfortune and None of My Own": A New History of the American West* (1991).° Henry Nash Smith's *Virgin Land* (1950) is an interpretation of the role of the West in the American imagination.

Ray A. Billington's *Westward Expansion* (5th ed., 1982), John D. Unruh's *The Plains Across: The Overland Emigrants and the TransMississippi West, 1840–1860* (1979),° and John Mack Faragher's *Women and Men on the Overland Trail* (1979)° narrate well the story of pioneer movement. Bernard De Voto's *The Wide Missouri* (1947)° concentrates on the fur trappers and the mountain men.

California was the promised land for many, and several scholars have concentrated on that area. Kevin Starr's *Americans and the California Dream, 1850–1915* (1973)° is a fine introduction. See also Earl Pomeroy's *The Pacific Slope: A History* (1965), which analyzes the early history of Oregon. A more focused treatment of the Oregon migration is Malcolm Clark, Jr.'s, *Eden Seekers: The Settlement of Oregon, 1812–1862* (1982).

The controversy over the annexation of Texas is analyzed in David M. Pletcher's *The Diplomacy of Annexation: Texas, Oregon, and the Mexican War* (1973) and Frederick Merk's *Slavery and the Annexation of Texas* (1972).

°These books are available in paperback editions.

Gene M. Brack's *Mexico Views Manifest Destiny, 1821–1846* (1975) takes Mexico's viewpoint on American designs on the West. On James K. Polk, see John H. Schroeder's *Mr. Polk's War* (1973). A survey of the military conflict is provided in K. Jack Bauer's *The Mexican War, 1846–1848* (1974). For a different perspective, see Robert W. Johannsen's *To the Halls of the Montezumas: The Mexican War in the American Imagination* (1984).

PART FOUR

A House Divided and Rebuilt

Of all the regions of the United States during the first half of the nineteenth century, the South was the most distinctive. Southern society remained fundamentally rural and agricultural long after the rest of the nation embraced the urban-industrial revolution. By 1860 a southern white was only one-third as likely as a northern white to work at a non-farm job, live in a city, or be foreign born. Likewise, the southern elite's tenacious desire to preserve and expand the institution of slavery muted social reform impulses in the South and ignited a prolonged political controversy that would end in civil war.

The rapid and relentless settlement of the western territories set in motion a ferocious competition between North and South for political influence in the burgeoning West. Would the new states in the West be "slave" or "free"? The issue of allowing slavery into the new territories involved more than humanitarian concern for the plight of enslaved blacks. By the 1840s, North and South had developed quite different economic interests. The North wanted high tariffs on imported manufactures to "protect" its infant industries from foreign competition. Southerners, on the other hand, favored free trade because they wanted to import British goods in exchange for the cotton they provided British textile mills.

A series of ingenious political compromises glossed over the fundamental differences between the sections during the first half of the nineteenth century. But abolitionists refused to give up their crusade against slavery. Moreover, a new generation of national political leaders emerged in the 1850s, men from both North and South who were less willing to seek political compromises. The continuing debate over allowing slavery into the new western territories kept sectional tensions at a fever pitch. By the time Abraham Lincoln was elected in 1860, many Americans had decided with the new president that the nation could not survive half-slave and half-free; something had to give.

In a last ditch effort to preserve the institution of slavery, eleven southern states seceded from the union and created a separate Confederate nation. This, in turn, prompted northerners such as Lincoln to support a civil war to preserve the Union. No one realized in 1861 how prolonged and costly the war between the states would become. Over 600,000 soldiers and sailors died of wounds or disease.

The colossal carnage caused even the most seasoned observers to blanch in disbelief. As President Lincoln confessed in his second inaugural address, no one expected the war to become so "fundamental and astonishing."

Nor did people envision how sweeping the war's effects would be on the future of the country. The northern victory in 1865 restored the Union and in the process helped to accelerate America's transformation into a modern nation-state. National power and a national consciousness began to displace the sectional emphases of the antebellum era. A Republican-led Congress pushed through legislation to foster industrial and commercial development and western expansion. In the process, the United States began to leave behind the Jeffersonian dream of a decentralized agrarian republic.

The Civil War also ended slavery. Yet the actual status of the three million freed blacks remained precarious. How would they fare in a society built on slavery? In 1865 the daughter of a Georgia planter expressed her concern about such issues when she wrote in her diary that "there are sad changes in store for both races. I wonder the Yankees do not shudder to behold their work" ahead in trying to "reconstruct" the defeated South.

The former slaves found themselves legally free, but most were without property, homes, education, or training. Although the Fourteenth Amendment (1867) set forth guarantees for the civil rights of African Americans and the Fifteenth Amendment (1870) provided that black males could vote, local authorities found ingenious—and often violent—ways to avoid the spirit and letter of these new laws.

The restoration of the former Confederate states to the Union did not come easily. Much bitterness and resistance remained among the vanquished. Although Confederate leaders were initially disenfranchised, they continued to exercise considerable authority in political and economic matters. Indeed, in 1877 the last federal troops were removed from the occupied South, and former Confederates gleefully declared themselves "redeemed" from the stain of occupation. By the end of the nineteenth century, most states of the former Confederacy had devised a system of legal discrimination that recreated many aspects of slavery.

15

THE OLD SOUTH:
AN AMERICAN TRAGEDY

MYTH, REALITY, AND THE OLD SOUTH

SOUTHERN MYTHOLOGY   Southerners, a North Carolina editor once wrote, are "a mythological people, created half out of dream and half out of slander, who live in a still legendary land." Most Americans, including southerners, carry in their minds an assorted baggage of myths about the South. But the main burden of southern mythology is carried in those especially pernicious images of the Old South set during the nineteenth-century sectional conflict: the idealized picture of kindly old massa with his mint julep on the white-columned porch, happy "darkies" singing in fields, coquettish belles wooed by slender gallants underneath the moonlight and magnolias. The legend of the Southern Cavalier seemed to fulfill some psychic need for an American counterweight to the mental image of the grasping, money-grubbing Yankee.

There are other elements in the traditional myth. Off in the piney woods and erosion-gutted red clay hills, away from the plantation elite, dwelt a depraved group known as the poor white trash: the crackers; hillbillies; sand-hillers; squatters; rag, tag, and bobtail. Somewhere in the myth the respectable small farmer so often praised by Jefferson and Jackson was lost from sight, perhaps neither romantic enough nor outrageous enough to fit in. He was absent too from the image of the Benighted South, in which the plantation myth simply appeared in reverse, as a pattern of corrupt opulence resting on human exploitation. Gentle old massa became the arrogant, haughty, imperious potentate, the very embodiment of sin, the central target of antislavery attack. He kept a slave mistress; he bred blacks like cattle and sold them "down the river" to certain death in the sugar mills, separating families if that suited his purpose, while southern women suffered in silence the guilty knowledge of their men's infidelity. The "happy darkies" in this picture became white men in black skins, an oppressed people longing for freedom, the victims of countless atrocities, forever seeking a chance to follow the North Star to freedom. The masses of the white folks were, once again, poor whites, relegated to ignorance and degeneracy by the slavocracy.

THE SOUTHERN CONDITION   Everyone recognizes these pictures as overdrawn stereotypes, but myths are hard to shake, partly because they have roots in reality. To comprehend the distinctiveness of the Old South we must first identify the forces and factors that gave it a sense of unity. Efforts to do so usually turn on two lines of thought: the causal effects of environment (geography and climate), and the causal effects of human decisions and actions. The hot, humid weather fostered the growing of staple crops, and thus encouraged the plantation system and black slavery. These things in turn brought sectional conflict and civil war.

Yet while geography was and is a key determinant of southern folkways, explanations that involve human agency are more persuasive. In the 1830s many observers found the origins of southern distinctiveness in the institution of slavery. The resolve of slaveholders to retain control of their socioeconomic order created a sense of racial unity that muted class conflict among whites. In the long run, however, the biracial character of the population influenced far more. In shaping patterns of speech and folklore, of music, religion, literature, and recreation, black southerners immeasurably influenced and enriched the region's development.

The South differed from other sections too in its high proportion of native population, both white and black. Despite a great diversity of origins in the colonial population, the South drew few immigrants after the Revolution. One reason was that the main shipping lines went to northern ports; another, that the prospect of competing with slave labor deterred immigrants. After the Missouri Controversy of 1819–1821 the South became more and more a conscious minority, its population growth lagging behind that of other sections, its "peculiar institution" of slavery more and more an isolated and odious thing in Western civilization. Attitudes of defensiveness strongly affected its churches. The religious culture of the white South retreated from the liberalism of the Revolutionary War era into orthodoxy, which provided one line of defense against new doctrines of any kind, while black southerners found in a similar religious culture a refuge from the hardships of their lot, a promise of release on some future day of Jubilee.

Slave quarters, a South Carolina plantation.

The South also differed in its architecture, its penchant for fighting, for guns, and for the military, and its country-gentlemen ideal. The preponderance of farming remained a distinctive regional characteristic, whether pictured as the Jeffersonian small farmer living by the sweat of his brow or the lordly planter dispatching his slave gangs. In an agricultural society such as the South, there tended to be a greater "personalness" of human relations in contrast to the organized and contractual nature of relations in a more complex urban environment. But in the end what made the South distinctive was its people's belief, and other people's belief, that they *were* distinctive. Southernism, one historian asserted, defied a clear definition. "Poets," he wrote, "have done better in expressing the oneness of the South than historians in explaining it."

STAPLE CROPS   The idea of the Cotton Kingdom is itself something of a mythic stereotype. Although cotton was the most important of the staple, or market, crops, it was a latecomer. Tobacco, the first staple crop, had earlier been the mainstay of Virginia and Maryland, and common in North Carolina. After the Revolution, pioneers carried it over the mountains into Kentucky and as far as Missouri. Indigo, an important crop in colonial South Carolina, vanished with the loss of British bounties for this source of a valuable blue dye, but rice growing continued in a coastal strip that lapped over into North Carolina and Georgia. Rice growing was limited to the tidewater because it required frequent flooding and draining of the fields, and along that sector of the coast the tides rose and fell six or seven feet. Since rice growing required substantial capital for floodgates, ditches, and machinery, its plantations were large and relatively few in number.

Sugar, like rice, called for a heavy capital investment in machinery to grind the cane, and was limited in extent because the cane was extremely susceptible to frost. An influx of refugees from the revolution in Haiti helped the development of a sugar belt centered along the Mississippi River above New Orleans. Some sugar grew in a smaller belt of eastern Texas, but it was always something of an exotic growth, better suited to a tropical climate. Since it needed the prop of a protective tariff, it produced the anomaly in southern politics of pro-tariff congressmen from Louisiana. Hemp had something of the same effect in the Kentucky Blue Grass region and northwestern Missouri. Both flax and hemp were important to backcountry farmers at the end of the colonial era. Homespun clothing was most apt to be linsey-woolsey, a combination of linen and wool. But flax never developed more than a limited commercial market, and that mostly for linseed oil. Hemp, on the other hand, developed commercial possibilities in rope and cotton baling cloth, and canvas for sails, although it suffered heavy competition from a higher-quality Russian product.

Cotton, the last of the major staples, eventually outpaced all the others put together. At the end of the War of 1812 annual cotton production was estimated at less than 150,000 bales; in 1860 it was reported at 3.8 million. Two things accounted for the growth: the voracious market for American cotton in British and French textiles, and the cultivation of new lands in the Southwest. Much of the story of the southern people—white and black—from 1820 to 1860 was their movement to fertile cotton lands farther west. The crop flourished best in the hot growing season of the Deep South. By 1860 the center of the cotton belt stretched from eastern North Carolina through the fertile Alabama-Mississippi black belts (so called for color of the soil), on to Texas, and up the Mississippi Valley as far as southern Illinois. Cotton prices fell sharply after the Panic of 1837, and remained below 10¢ a pound through most of the 1840s, but they advanced above 10¢ late in 1855 and stayed there until 1860, reaching 15¢ in 1857—despite a business setback and a constantly increasing supply.

AGRICULTURAL DIVERSITY   The focus on cotton and the other cash crops has obscured the degree to which the South fed itself from its own fields. With 30 percent of the country's area in 1860, and 39 percent of its population, the slave states produced 52 percent of the nation's corn, 29 percent of the wheat, 19 percent of the oats, 19 percent of the rye,

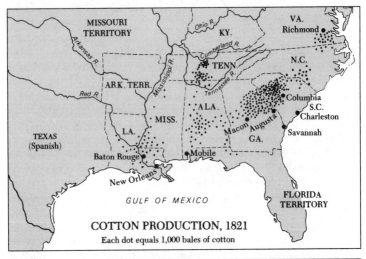

COTTON PRODUCTION, 1821

Each dot equals 1,000 bales of cotton

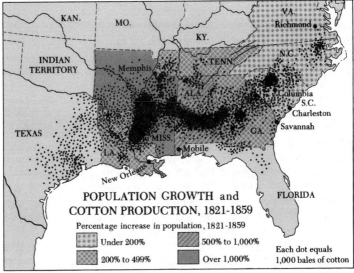

**POPULATION GROWTH and
COTTON PRODUCTION, 1821-1859**

Percentage increase in population, 1821-1859

Under 200%   500% to 1,000%

200% to 499%   Over 1,000%

Each dot equals
1,000 bales of cotton

10 percent of the white potatoes, and 94 percent of the sweet potatoes. The upper South in many areas practiced general farming in much the same way as the Northwest. Cyrus McCormick first tested his harvester in the wheatfields of Virginia. Corn grew everywhere, but went less into the market than into local consumption, as feed and fodder, as hoecake and grits. On many farms and plantations the rhythms of the growing season permitted the labor force to alternate attention between the staples and the food crops.

Livestock added to the diversity of the farm economy. In 1860 the South had half of the nation's cattle, over 60 percent of the swine, nearly 45 percent of the horses, 52 percent of the oxen, 90 percent of the mules, and nearly a third of the sheep, the last mostly in the upper South. Cattle herding prevailed on the southern frontier at one time, and persisted in areas less suited to farming, such as the piney woods of the coastal plains, the Appalachians, and the Ozarks and their foothills. Plantations and farms commonly raised livestock for home consumption.

Yet the picture was hardly one of unbroken prosperity. The South's staple crops quickly exhausted the soil, and open row crops such as tobacco, cotton, and corn left the bare ground in between subject to leaching and erosion. By 1800 much of eastern Virginia had abandoned tobacco, and in some places had turned to scrabbling wheat from the soil for the northern market. One ex-slave later recalled what he saw as a slave trader carried him across Virginia about 1805: "For several days we traversed a region, which had been deserted by the occupants— being no longer worth culture—and immense thickets of young red cedars now occupied the fields." In low-country South Carolina Senator Robert Y. Hayne spoke of "Fields abandoned; and hospitable mansions of our fathers deserted." The older farming lands had trouble competing with the newer soils farther west. But western lands too began to show wear and tear. By 1855 an Alabama senator noted: "Our small planters, after taking the cream off their lands . . . are going further west and south in search of other virgin lands which they may and will despoil and impoverish in like manner." This of course happened all along the frontier.

So the Southeast and then the Old Southwest faced a growing sense

Planting sweet potatoes on the Hopkinson plantation, Edisto Island, South Carolina, April 1862.

of economic crisis as the century advanced. Proposals to deal with it followed two lines. Some argued for agricultural reform and others for diversification through industry and trade. Edmund Ruffin of Virginia stands out as perhaps the greatest of the reformers. After studying the chemistry of soils, he reasoned that most exhausted soils of the upper South had acid conditions, which needed to be neutralized before they could become productive again. He turned his plantations into laboratories in which he discovered that marl from a shell deposit in eastern Virginia did the trick. Ruffin published the results in his *Essay on Calcareous Manures* (1832). Such publications and farm magazines in general, however, reached but a minority of farmers, mostly the larger and more successful planters. The same was true of the agricultural associations that sprang up in the Old South. However, some of these sponsored experimental farms and agricultural fairs, which became common by the 1840s and 1850s, reaching farmers with examples put before their very eyes.

MANUFACTURING AND TRADE   By 1840 many thoughtful southerners concluded that by staking everything on agriculture the region had wasted chances in manufacturing and trade. The census of 1810 had shown the South with more various and numerous manufactures than New England. The War of 1812 provided the South some stimulus for manufacturing, but the momentum ebbed in the postwar flood of British imports. Then cotton growing swept everything before it. The proliferation of textile manufacturing in Britain led to a seemingly limitless demand for American cotton. As the cotton mania deflected concern with industry, the South became increasingly dependent on northern manufacturing and trade. Cotton and tobacco were exported mainly in northern vessels. In 1830 southern ship tonnage of 109,000 was less than a third of the North's 360,000; by 1860 the South's 855,000 was little more than a fifth of the North's 4 million. Southerners also relied on connections in the North for imported goods. The South became, economically if not formally, a kind of colonial dependency of the North. The merchants of northern cities, a southerner said, "export our . . . valuable productions, and import our articles of consumption and from this agency they derive a profit which has enriched them . . . at our expense."

Along with the call for direct trade in southern ships went a movement for a more diversified economy, for native industries to balance agriculture and trade. Southern publicists called attention to the section's great resources: its raw materials, labor supply, waterpower, wood and coal, and markets. In Richmond, Virginia, the Tredegar Iron Works grew into the most important single manufacturing enterprise in the Old South. It used mostly slave labor to produce cannon, shot, and shell,

The Tredegar Iron Works in Richmond, Virginia.

axes, saws, bridge materials, boilers, and steam engines, including loco-motives.

Daniel Pratt of Alabama built Prattville, which grew into a model of diversified industry. Prattville ultimately had a gristmill, a shingle mill, a carriage factory, foundries, a tin mill, and a blacksmith shop. Pratt then launched into the iron business and coal mining, while on the side experimenting with vineyards and truck farming. He used both black and white labor, but his appraoch was paternalistic. Profits from his company store went into churches, schools, a library, an art gallery, and a printing establishment—and into handsome dividends.

Pratt and others directed a program of industry that gathered momentum in the 1850s, and in its extent and diversity belied the common image of a strictly agricultural South. Manufactures were sup-plemented by important extractive industries such as coal, iron, lead, copper, salt, and gold, the last chiefly in North Carolina and Georgia. In manufacturing, the slave states altogether in 1860 had 22 percent of the country's plants, 17 percent of its labor, 20 percent of the capital invested, 17 percent of the wages generated, and 16 percent of the out-put—an impressive showing but still not up to the South's 30 percent of the population. Also, southern industry was concentrated in the border states, where economic conditions resembled those of neighboring states to the north—cheap labor, raw materials, capital investment, urban markets, and good transportation.

ECONOMIC DEVELOPMENT   During the antebellum years, there were two major explanations generally put forward for the lag in southern industrial development. First, blacks were presumed unsuited to fac-tory work, perhaps because they supposedly could not adjust to the dis-cipline of work by the clock. Second, the ruling orders of the Old South were said to have developed a lordly disdain for the practice of trade, because a certain aristocratic prestige derived from owning land and slaves, and from conspicuous consumption. But any argument that black labor was incompatible with industry simply flew in the face of the evidence, since factory owners bought or hired slave operatives for just about every kind of manufacture. Given the opportunity, a number of blacks displayed managerial skills as overseers. Nor should one take at face value the legendary indifference of aristocratic planters to profits. On the southwestern frontiers of the cotton kingdom, those who did fit that description became pathetic objects of humor, pushed aside by the hustlers.

More often than not the successful planter was a driving newcomer bent on maximizing profits. While the profitability of slavery has been a long-standing subject of controversy, in recent years economic historians have concluded that slaves on the average supplied about a 10 percent return on their cost. Then, as now, this was an enticing profit margin. Slave ownership was, moreover, a reasonable speculation, for slave prices tended to move upward. By a strictly hardnosed and hardheaded calculation, investment in slaves and cotton lands was the most profitable investment available at the time in the South, and it remained a lucrative activity through much of the region when the Civil War erupted. Some slaveholders, particularly in the newer cotton lands of the Southwest, were rich beyond the dreams of avarice.

The notion that the South was economically backward emerged from the sectional quarrels of the times, in which southerners took a poorer-than-thou attitude, so to speak, in order to bolster their claims of northern exploitation. Antislavery elements also contributed to this notion by arguing the failure of a slave economy. It was true that in any comparison of the South with the North, the South usually came off second best. But in comparison with the rest of the world, the South as a whole was well off: its average per capita income in 1860 ($103) was about the same as that of Switzerland, and was exceeded only by Australia, the North, and Great Britain, in that order.

WHITE SOCIETY IN THE SOUTH

If an understanding of the Old South must begin with a knowledge of social myths, it must end with a sense of tragedy. White southerners had won short-term gains at the costs of both long-term development and moral isolation in the eyes of the world. The concentration on land and slaves, and the paucity of cities and immigrants, deprived the South of the dynamic bases of innovation. The slaveholding South hitched its wagon not to a star, but to the world (largely British) demand for cotton, which had not slackened from the start of the Industrial Revolution.

During the late 1850s, it seemed that prosperity would never end. The South, "safely entrenched behind her cotton bags . . . can defy the world—for the civilized world depends on the cotton of the South," said a Vicksburg newspaper in 1860. "No power on earth dares to make war upon it," said James H. Hammond of South Carolina. "Cotton is king." The only perceived threat to King Cotton was the growing antislavery sentiment. What southern boosters could not perceive was an imminent slackening of the cotton market. The heyday of expansion in British textiles was over by 1860, but by then the Deep South was locked into cotton production for generations to come.

THE PLANTERS   Although great plantations were relatively few in number, they set the tone of economic and social life in the South. What distinguished the plantation from the farm, in addition to its size, was the use of a large labor force, under separate control and supervision, to grow primarily staple crops (cotton, rice, tobacco, and sugarcane) for profit. A clear-cut distinction between management and labor set the planter apart from the small slaveholder, who often worked side by side with his or her slaves at the same tasks.

If, to be called a planter, one had to own 20 slaves, the South in 1860 numbered only 46,274 planters. Fewer than 8,000 owned 50 or more slaves, and the owners of over 100 numbered 2,292. The census enumerated only 11 with 500 and just 1 with as many as 1,000 slaves. Yet this small, privileged elite tended to think of its class interest as the interest of the entire South, and to perceive themselves as community leaders in much the fashion of the English gentry. The planter group, making up only 4 percent of the adult white males in the South, owned more than half the slaves, produced most of the cotton, tobacco, and hemp, and all of the sugar and rice. The total number of slaveholders was only 383,637, out of a total white population of 8 million. But assuming that each family numbered five people, the whites with some proprietary interest in slavery came to 1.9 million, or roughly one-fourth of the white population. While the preponderance of southern whites belonged to the small-farmer class, the presumptions of the planters were seldom challenged. Too many small farmers aspired to become planters themselves.

Often the planter did live in the splendor that legend attributed to him, with the wealth and leisure to cultivate the arts of hospitality, good manners, learning, and politics. More often the scene was less charming. Some of the mansions on closer inspection turned out to be modest houses with false fronts. A style of housing derived from the frontier log cabin grew to be surprisingly common. The one-room cabin would expand by the building of a second room with a sheltered open "dog trot" in the middle. As wealth increased, larger houses evolved from the

Photographs front and rear of the Stirrup Branch plantation, Bishopville, South Carolina, June 1857. Posed in front of the house is the family of Capt. James Rembert, the plantation owner. Assembled by rank at the rear of the house are the family slaves, with uniformed house servants, a foreman named Nero, two yard keepers, and a cook.

plain log cabin, and the dog trot grew into a central hall from the front to the rear of the house. In larger houses, halls to one or both sides might be added.

The planter commonly had less leisure than legend would suggest, for he in fact managed a large enterprise. At the same time he often served as the patron to whom workers appealed the actions of their foremen. The quality of life for the slaves was governed far more by the attitude of the master than by the formal slave codes, which were seldom enforced strictly except in times of troubles.

THE PLANTATION MISTRESS   The mistress of the plantation, like the master, seldom led a life of idle leisure. She supervised the domestic household in the same way the planter took care of the business, overseeing food, linens, housecleaning, the care of the sick, and a hundred other details. Mary Boykin Chesnut of South Carolina complained that "there is no slave like a wife."

The wives of all but the most wealthy planters were expected to supervise all the domestic activities of the household and manage the slaves to boot. A transplanted New Yorker living on a plantation in North Carolina observed that her mother-in-law "works harder than any Northern farmer's wife I know." The son of a Tennessee slaveholder remembered that his mother and grandmother were "the busiest women I ever saw." One of the most frustrating realities for the plantation mistress was the lack of personal freedom and leisure occasioned by the complex demands of her "separate sphere" of genteel domesticity. "These women have less chance to live their own lives than if they were African missionaries," wrote Chesnut. "They have a swarm of blacks about them like children under their care." One white woman, having stayed up all night helping deliver a slave baby, complained to a friend about her relentless routine: "It is the slaves who own me. Morning, noon, and night, I'm obliged to look after them, to doctor them, and attend to them in every way."

White women living within a slave-owning culture also confronted a double standard in terms of moral and sexual behavior. While they were expected to behave as chaste exemplars of Christian piety and sexual discretion, their husbands, brothers, and sons followed an unwritten rule of self-indulgent hedonism. "God forgive us," Mary Chesnut wrote in her diary, "but ours is a monstrous system. Like the patriarchs of old, our men live all in one house with their wives and their concubines; and the mulattos one sees in every family partly resemble the white children. Any lady is ready to tell you who is the father of all the mulatto children in everybody's household but her own. Those, she seems to think, drop from the clouds."

Such a double standard both illustrated and reinforced the arrogant authoritarianism displayed by many male planters. Chesnut said that her father-in-law lorded over his plantation household. He was "as absolute a tyrant as the Czar of Russia . . . or the Sultan of Turkey." Another white woman complained that the men in her family had become so accustomed to practicing a paternalistic absolutism that they treated everyone else as lesser people. "I can see it in Father—in Brother John—in Brother Patrick." Yet for all of their complaints and burdens, few plantation mistresses engaged in public criticism of the prevailing social order and racist climate.

THE MIDDLE CLASS   Overseers on the largest plantations generally came from the middle class of small farmers or skilled workers, or were younger sons of planters. Most aspired to become slaveholders themselves, and sometimes rose to that status, but others were constantly on the move in search of better positions. Their interests did not always coincide with the long-term interests of the planter. "Overseers are not interested in raising negro children, or meat, in improving land, or improving productive qualities of seed or animals," a Mississippi planter complained. "Many of them do not care whether property has depreciated or improved, so they make a crop to boast of." Occasionally there were black overseers, but the highest management position to which a slave could aspire was usually that of driver, placed in charge of a small group of slaves with the duty of getting them to work without creating dissension.

The most numerous white southerners were the small farmers (yeomen), those who lived with their families in modest two-room cabins rather than columned mansions. They raised a few hogs and chickens, grew some corn and cotton, and traded with neighbors more than stores. The men in the family focused their energies on outdoor labors. Women also worked in the fields during harvest time, but most of their days were spent attending to domestic chores. As a Tennessee farmer explained, he and his father "did all kinds of farm work [while] my mother cooked, sewed, spun thread, wove clothes, and clothed the family of eleven children." Many of these "middling" farmers owned a handful of slaves, but most owned none. The most prosperous of these small farm families generally lived in the mountain-sheltered valleys from the Shenandoah of Virginia down to northern Alabama, areas with rich soil but without ready access to markets, and so less suitable for staple crops or slave labor. But most of the South's small farms were located in the midst of the plantation economy.

In North Carolina in 1860, for instance, 70 percent of the farmers held less than 100 acres, and they were scattered throughout the state.

These and other southern farmers were typically mobile folk, willing to pull up stakes and move west or southwest in pursuit of better land. They tended to be fiercely independent and suspicious of government authority, and they overwhelmingly identified with the party of Andrew Jackson and the spiritual fervor of evangelical Protestantism. Some southern farmers resented the planter elite because it controlled the most fertile land, the commodity markets, and the political machinery. Most of them, however, admired and envied the slaveholding aristocracy. And even though only a minority of the middle-class farmers owned slaves, most of them supported the slave system. They feared that the slaves, if freed, would compete with them for land, and they also enjoyed the priviliged status that racially based slavery afforded them. As one farmer told a northern traveler, "Now suppose they [the slaves] was free. You see they'd all think themselves as good as we." Such sentiments pervaded the border states as well as the Deep South. Kentucky, for example, held a popular referendum on the issue of slavery in 1849, and the voters, most of whom owned no slaves, resoundingly endorsed the "peculiar institution."

THE "POOR WHITES" Outside observers often had trouble telling yeomen apart from the true "poor whites," a degraded class crowded off onto the least desirable land. Stereotyped views of southern society had prepared many travelers to see only planters and "poor whites," and many a small farmer living in rude comfort, his wealth concealed in cattle and swine off foraging in the woods, was mistaken for "white trash." The type was a familiar one from the frontier days, living on the fringes of polite society. One observer wrote in 1860: "There is no . . . method by which they can be weaned from leading the lives of vagrom-men, idlers, and squatters, useless to themselves and to the rest of mankind." The "poor whites" were characterized by a pronounced lankness and sallowness, given over to hunting and fishing, to hound dogs and moonshine whiskey.

Speculation had it that they were descended from indentured servants or convicts transported to the colonies, or that they were the weakest of the frontier population, forced to take refuge in the sand land, the pine barrens, and the swamps after having been pushed aside by the more enterprising and successful. But the problem was less heredity than environment, the consequence of infections and dietary deficiencies that gave rise to a trilogy of "lazy diseases": hookworm, malaria, and pellagra, all of which produced an overpowering lethargy. Many poor whites displayed a morbid craving to chew clay, from which they got the name "dirt eaters"; the cause was a dietary deficiency, although a folklore grew up about the nutritional and medicinal qualities of certain clays. Around 1900 modern medicine discovered the causes and cures for these diseases. By 1930 they had practically disappeared, taking with them many stereotypes of poor whites.

PROFESSIONALS AND OTHERS   Professional people, including lawyers, doctors, and editors, stood in close relationship to the planter and merchant classes that they served and to which they sometimes belonged. Manufacturers held their own with the planters, as did merchants, often called brokers or factors, who handled the planters' crops and acted as purchasing agents for their needs, supplying credit along the way. Many professionals bought their way into the slaveholding class, and many eventually acquired farms of their own.

There was a degree of fluidity and social mobility in the class structure of the white South. Few indeed were the "cotton snobs" who lorded over the lower orders. Planters were acknowledged as the social models and natural leaders. Yet those who aspired to public office, especially, could not afford to take a lordly attitude, for every southern state by 1860 allowed universal white male suffrage. The voters, while perhaps showing deference to their "betters," could nevertheless pick and choose among them at election time.

Other groups stood farther from the mainstream. The mountain people of Appalachia engaged in subsistence farming, employed few or no slaves, and in attitude stood apart from the planter society, sometimes in open hostility toward it. Scattered in many of the flatland counties were small groups who sometimes fell even below the poor whites in the social scale. In some places the advance of the frontier had left behind pockets of Indians with whom passing whites and escaped slaves eventually mingled. The triple admixture of races produced islands of peoples known variously as brass ankles, Turks, redbones, yellow hammers, and Melungeons (derived apparently from "mélange," mixture).

BLACK SOCIETY IN THE SOUTH

"FREE PERSONS OF COLOR"   In the Old South, "free persons of color" occupied an uncertain status, balanced somewhere between slavery and freedom, subject to legal restrictions not imposed on whites. State laws prohibited them from serving on juries or testifying against whites. In the seventeenth century a few blacks had been freed on the same basis as indentured servants. Over the years some slaves were able to purchase their freedom, while some gained freedom as a reward for service in American wars. Others were simply freed by conscien-

Yarrow Mamout was an African Muslim who was sold into slavery, purchased his freedom, acquired property, and settled in Georgetown (now part of Washington, D.C.). Charles Willson Peale executed this portrait of Mamout in 1819, when Mamout was over one hundred years old.

tious masters, either in their wills, as in the case of George Washington, or during their lifetimes, as in the case of John Randolph. In one incredible case, an African prince captured in warfare turned up as a slave in Natchez, and after some years managed to get a letter in Arabic to the sultan of Morocco, who intervened in his favor. In 1827, after thirty-nine years of slavery, he gained his freedom and returned to Africa.

The free persons of color included a large number of mulattoes. In urban centers like Charleston and especially New Orleans, "colored" society became virtually a third caste, a new people who occupied a status somewhere between black and white. Some of them built substantial fortunes and even became slaveholders. They often operated inns serving a white clientele. Jehu Jones, for instance, was the "colored" proprietor of one of Charleston's best hotels, which he bought in 1815 for $13,000. In Louisiana a mulatto, Cyprien Ricard, bought an estate that had ninety-one slaves for $250,000. In Natchez William Johnson, son of a white father and mulatto mother, operated three barbershops and owned 1,500 acres of land and several slaves.

William Ellison, a freed slave of partial white ancestry who lived in Stateburg, South Carolina, prospered as a cotton-gin maker. In 1816, at the age of twenty-six, he purchased his own freedom from his white master (who may have been his father). By the start of the Civil War he had become the wealthiest free black in South Carolina, owner of a thriving business, an 800-acre plantation, and some sixty slaves. He was so indifferent to the plight of his fellows of African descent that he commonly sold his slaves' female babies because he believed they were

A badge, issued in Charleston, South Carolina, to be worn by free blacks.

unprofitable in his business. Like other successful mulattoes, Ellison distanced himself from the slaves and displayed a snobbish preoccupation with gradations of color. As a member of Charleston's "brown aristocracy," he looked down upon black people. During the Civil War Ellison supported the Confederacy.

Black slaveholders were a tiny minority. The 1830 census revealed that only 3,775 free blacks, about 2 percent of the total free black population, owned 12,760 slaves. Although most of these black slave owners were in the South, some also lived in Rhode Island, Connecticut, Illinois, New Jersey, New York, and the border states. Many blacks owned slaves for humanitarian purposes. One minister, for instance, bought slaves and then enabled them to purchase their freedom from him on easy terms. Most often, black slaveholders were free blacks who bought their own family members with the express purpose of later freeing them. But many blacks engaged in slavery for purely selfish rather than humanitarian reasons. Like their white counterparts, they participated in slave auctions and advertised for the return of runaways.

Most free blacks were not slave owners. Men were usually skilled artisans (blacksmiths, carpenters, cobblers), farmers, or common laborers. The increase in their numbers slowed as southern legislatures put more and more restrictions on the right to free slaves, but by 1860 there were 262,000 free blacks in the slave states, a little over half the national total of 488,000. They were most numerous in the upper South. In Maryland the number of free blacks very nearly equaled the number still held in slavery; in Delaware free blacks made up 91.7 percent of the black population.

THE TRADE IN SLAVES   The slaves stood at the bottom of the social hierarchy. Some Indians, themselves subject to brutal discrimination, owned African slaves. In fact, the practice became so widespread that

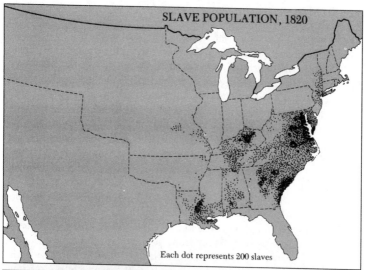

SLAVE POPULATION, 1820

Each dot represents 200 slaves

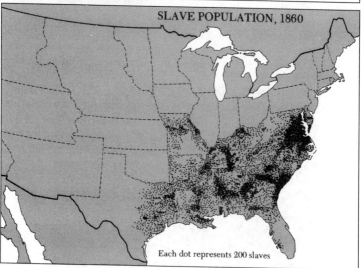

SLAVE POPULATION, 1860

Each dot represents 200 slaves

when the Civil War erupted, most southern tribes supported the Confederacy. From the first census in 1790 to the eighth in 1860, the number of slaves had grown from 698,000 to almost 4 million. The rise in the slave population occurred mainly through a natural increase, the rate of which was very close to that of whites at the time. When the African slave trade was outlawed in 1808, it seemed to many a step toward the extinction of slavery, but the expansion of the cotton belt, with its voracious appetite for workers, soon created such a vested interest in slaves as to dash such hopes. Shutting off the import of slaves only added to the value of those already present. Prices for prime fieldhands ranged between $300 and $400 in the 1790s, rose to $1,000–$1,300 in the 1830s, peaked just before the onset of depression in 1837, and rose again in the great prosperity of the 1850s to $1,500–$2,000. Slaves with special skills cost even more.

The rise in slave value tempered some of the harsher features of the peculiar institution. Valuable slaves, like valuable livestock, justified some minimal standards of care. "Massa was purty good," one ex-slave recalled later. "He treated us jus' 'bout like you would a good mule." Another said his master "fed us reg'lar on good, 'stantial food, jus' like you'd tend to you hoss, if you had a real good one." Some owners hired wage laborers, often Irish immigrants, for ditching and other danger-ous work rather than risk the lives of the more valuable slaves.

The end of the foreign slave trade gave rise to a flourishing domestic trade, with slaves moving mainly from the used-up lands of the South-east into the booming new country of the Old Southwest. The trade peaked just before 1837, then slacked off, first because of depression, then because agricultural reform and recovery renewed the demand for slaves in the upper South. Many slaves moved south and west with their owners, but there also developed an organized business with brokers, slave pens, and auctioneers. Franklin and Armfield, the leading traders,

The offices of Price, Birch & Co., dealers in slaves, Alexandria, Virginia.

had their offices and collecting pens in Alexandria, Virginia, where they fattened and spruced up slaves for the auction block. From Alexandria slave traders moved overland through the Ohio Valley or down the Piedmont, making sales along the way. Other groups went out by sea to Wilmington, Charleston, Savannah, or directly to Mobile, New Orleans, and on to Natchez, a leading market for the new districts.

While the mainstream of the trade moved southwestward, every town of any size had public auctioneers and dealers willing to buy and sell slaves—along with other merchandise—or handle sales on a commission. The worst aspect of the slave trade was the dissolution of families. Only Louisiana and Alabama (from 1852) forbade selling a child under ten from its mother, and no state forbade separation of husband from wife. Many such sales are matters of record, and although the total number is controversial, it took only a few to damage the morale of all.

PLANTATION SLAVERY Most slaves labored on plantations. The preferred jobs were those of household servants and skilled workers, including blacksmiths, carpenters, and coopers. Others might get special assignments as, say, boatmen or cooks. Fieldhands were usually housed in simple one- or two-room wooden shacks with dirt floors, some without windows. Of food there was usually a rough sufficiency, but one slave recalled that "de flour dat we make the biscuits out of wus de third-grade shorts." A set of clothes was distributed twice a year, but shoes were generally provided only in winter. On larger plantations there was sometimes an infirmary and regular sick call, but most planters resorted to doctors mainly in cases of severe sickness. Based on detailed records from eleven plantations in the lower South during the antebellum era, scholars have calculated that more than half of all slave babies died in the first year of life, a mortality rate more than twice that of whites.

To some extent, chiefly in the rice and tobacco belts, work was parceled out to slaves by the task. But more commonly fieldhands worked long hours from dawn to dusk, or "from kin [see] to kaint." The slave codes gave little protection from long hours. South Carolina's limit of fifteen hours in winter and sixteen in summer exceeded the hours of daylight most of the year. The slave codes adopted in each state concerned themselves mainly with the owner's interests, and subjected the slaves not only to his governance but to surveillance by patrols of county militiamen, who struck fear into the slave quarters by abusing slaves found at large. Evidence suggests that a majority of both planters and small farmers used the whip, which the slave codes authorized. The difference between a good owner and a bad one, according to one ex-slave, was the difference between one who did not "whip too much" and one who "whipped till he's bloodied you and blistered you."

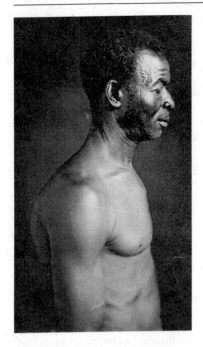

Jack (Driver), Guinea.
Plantation of B.F. Taylor, Esq.
Columbia, S.C. *1850.*

A male slave's ultimate recourse was rebellion or flight, but most recognized the futility of such measures, with whites wielding most of the power and weapons. Female slaves rarely saw escape as an option, concerned as they were with pregnancies and child-raising responsibilities. "Slavery is terrible for men; but it is far more terrible for women," declared Harriet Jacobs, a North Carolina slave. In the nineteenth century only three slave insurrections drew much notice, and two of those were betrayed before they got under way. In 1800 a slave named Gabriel on a plantation near Richmond hatched a plot involving perhaps a thousand others to seize key points in Richmond and start a general slaughter of whites. Twenty-five of the slave conspirators were executed and ten others deported to the West Indies.

The Denmark Vesey plot in Charleston, discovered in 1822, was probably the plan of a free black to fall upon the white population of the town, seize ships in the harbor, and head for Santo Domingo. In this case thirty-five slave rebels were executed and thirty-four deported. The Vesey insurrection, however, remains an enigma. Some contemporaries in Charleston and historians since believed it had less to do with insurrection than with white hysteria, which fabricated a plot from rumors and the testimony of frightened slaves out to save their own skins by incriminating others.

Only the Nat Turner insurrection of 1831 in rural Southampton County, Virginia, got beyond the planning stage. Turner, a black overseer, was also a religious exhorter who professed a divine mission in leading the movement. The revolt began when a small group killed those in Turner's master's household and set off down the road repeating the process at other farmhouses, where other slaves joined in. Before it ended at least fifty-five whites were killed. Eventually trials resulted in seventeen hangings and seven deportations, but the militia killed large numbers of slaves indiscriminately in the process of putting down the rebels.

Slaves more often retaliated against oppression by malingering or by outright sabotage. There were constraints on such behavior, however, for laborers would likely eat better on a prosperous plantation than on one they had reduced to poverty. And the shrewdest slaveholders knew that they would more likely benefit from holding out rewards than from inflicting pain. Plantations based on the profit motive fostered between slaves and owners mutual dependency as well as natural antagonism. And in an agrarian society where personal relations counted for much, blacks could win concessions that moderated the harshness of slavery, permitting them a certain degree of individual and community development.

FORGING THE SLAVE COMMUNITY To generalize about slavery is to miss elements of diversity from place to place and from time to time. The experience could be as varied as people are. Historians of slavery in recent years have transferred their perspectives from the institutional aspects of slavery to the human aspects: what it was like to be held in bondage. At its worst, the historian Stanley M. Elkins has argued, slavery, like the concentration camps of Nazi Germany, dehumanized its victims, and turned them into dependent people who internalized their masters' image of them. The slave thus actually became what he seemed to whites to be, a "Sambo" who in Elkins's words "was docile but irresponsible, loyal but lazy, humble but chronically given to lying and stealing," an adult "full of infantile silliness" and "utter dependence and childlike attachment." Some slaves were no doubt so beaten down as to fit the description, but slave lore was too full of stories about "puttin' on ole massa" to permit the belief that "Sambo" was often anything more than a protective mask put on to meet the white folks' expectations—and not all slaves would demean themselves in that way.

Slaves were victims, there was no question about that. But to stop with so obvious a perception would be to miss an important story of endurance and achievement. If ever there was a melting pot in American history, the most effective may have been that in which Africans from a variety of ethnic, linguistic, and tribal origins fused into a new community and a new culture as African Americans.

Recent scholarship on slavery has looked inside the slave community, once thought inaccessible, mainly by taking seriously firsthand accounts previously discounted as unreliable. Most useful among these have been the slave narratives, life stories of slaves and former slaves published in the 1800s. Among the more interesting are *The Narrative of the Life of Frederick Douglass* (1845), *Twenty Years a Slave* (1853) by Solomon Northrup, a free man in the North who was kidnapped and sold south into slavery, and Harriet Jacobs's *Incidents in the Life of a Slave Girl, Written by Herself* (1861). Born in slavery in Edenton, North Carolina, Jacobs eventually escaped and became a leading activist in the abolitionist movement.

Members of the slave community were bound together in helping and protecting one another, which in turn created a sense of cohesion and pride. Slave culture incorporated many African survivals, especially in areas where whites were few. Among the Gullah blacks of the South Carolina and Georgia coast, a researcher found as late as the 1940s more than 4,000 words still in use from the languages of twenty-one African tribes. But the important point, as another researcher put it, was not survivals that served "as quaint reminders of an exotic culture sufficiently alive to render the slaves picturesquely different but little more." The point was one of transformations in a living culture. Elements of African cultures thus "have continued to exist . . . as dynamic, living, creative parts of life in the United States," and have interacted with other cultures in which they came in contact.

SLAVE RELIGION AND FOLKLORE   Among the most important manifestations of slave culture was its religion, a mixture of African and Christian elements. In this slaves could find both balm for the soul and release for their emotions. Most Africans brought with them a concept of a Creator, or Supreme God, whom they could recognize in Jehovah, and lesser gods whom they might identify with Christ, the Holy Ghost, and the saints, thereby reconciling their earlier beliefs with the new Christian religion. Alongside the church they maintained beliefs in spirits (many of them benign), magic, and conjuring. Belief in magic is in fact a common human response to conditions of danger or helplessness. Conjurors plied a brisk trade in the slave community, and often exercised considerable influence by promising protection against floggings, separations, and other dangers.

Yet slaves found greater comfort in the church. Masters sought to instill lessons of Christian humility and obedience, but blacks could identify their plight with that of the Israelites in Egypt or of the God who suffered as they did. And the ultimate hope of a better world gave solace in this one. Some owners encouraged religious meetings among their slaves, many of them believing that a Christian slave would be a better slave. "Church was what they called it," one former slave remembered, "but all that [white] preacher talked about was for us slaves to obey our masters and not to lie and steal."

Such a manipulated Christianity alienated many slaves, and most sought to create a genuine faith that spoke to their own spiritual and human needs. This required many of them to worship in secret, stealing away from their quarters to hold "bush meetings." A slave preacher explained that the "way in which we worshiped is almost indescribable. The singing helped provoke a certain ecstasy of emotion, clapping of hands, tossing of heads, which would continue without cessation about half an hour. The old house partook of the ecstasy; it rang with their jubilant shouts, and shook in all its joints."

The preachers and exhorters who sprang up in the slave world commonly won the acceptance of the owners if only because efforts to get rid of them proved futile. The peculiar cadences of their exhortations, chants, and spirituals were to the whites at best exotic but fundamentally mystifying. The ecstatic "ring shout," in which the celebrants moved rhythmically in a circle, was not a dance—as whites tended to believe—because, the worshippers said, they never crossed their feet. Because whites so widely misperceived slave religion, one historian has called it the "invisible institution" of the antebellum South.

Slaves found the Bible edifying in its tributes to the poor and oppressed, and they embraced its promise of salvation through Jesus. Likewise, the lyrics in religious "spirituals" helped slaves endure the strain of field labor and provided them a code with which to express their own desire for freedom on earth. As one of the spirituals promised,

> In that morning, true believers,
> In that morning,
> We will sit aside of Jesus,
> In that morning,
> If you should go fore I go,
> In that morning,
> True believers, where your tickets
> In that morning,
> Master Jesus got your tickets
> In that morning.

Frederick Douglass stressed that "slaves sing most when they are most unhappy," and such spirituals offered them deliverance from their worldly woes.

"African culture was much more resistant to the bludgeon of slavery than historians have hitherto suspected," one historian has written.

African cultural forms influenced a music of great rhythmic complexity, forms of dance and body language, spirituals and secular songs, and folk tales. Among oppressed peoples humor often becomes a means of psychological release, and there was a lively humor in the West African "trickster tales" of rabbits, tortoises, or Anansi the spider—relatively weak creatures who outwitted stronger animals. African American folklore tended to be realistic in its images of wish fulfillment. Until after emancipation there were few stories of superhuman heroes, except for tales about captive Africans who escaped slavery by flying back home across the ocean. For the most part whites remained strangely blind and deaf to the black culture around them.

THE SLAVE FAMILY   Whites showed much the same ambivalence toward the slaves' instinct for family life. Slave marriages had no legal status, but slaveowners generally seem to have accepted marriage as a stabilizing influence on the plantation. Sometimes they performed marriages themselves or had a minister celebrate a formal wedding with all the trimmings. A common practice was the "broomstick wedding," in which the couple jumped over a broomstick, a custom of uncertain origin. But whatever the formalities, the norm for the slave community as for the white was the nuclear family of parents and children, with the father regarded as head of the family. Slaves also displayed a lively awareness

Several generations of a family raised in slavery. Plantation of J. J. Smith, Beaufort, South Carolina, 1862.

of the extended family of cousins. Most slave children were socialized into their culture through the nuclear family, which afforded some degree of independence from white influence.

Slaves were not always allowed to realize this norm. In some cases the matter of family arrangements was ignored or left entirely up to the slaves on the assumption that black females were simply promiscuous—a convenient rationalization for sexual exploitation, to which the presence of many mulattoes attested. The census of 1860 reported 412,000 persons of mixed ancestry in the United States, or about 10 percent of the black population, probably a drastic undercount. Planters and their sons often took sexual advantage of female slaves. They sometimes clumsily defended such abuse on the grounds that the practice protected the chastity of white women.

THE CULTURE OF THE SOUTHERN FRONTIER

There were substantial social and cultural differences within the South during the three decades before the Civil War. The antebellum southern frontier, for example, was a quite different region from the more settled areas in the states along the Atlantic seaboard. Of all the many frontiers that have combined to produce a distinctive American culture, the Old Southwest is perhaps the least well known and studied. It included the states and territories west of the Georgia-Alabama border—Alabama, Mississippi, Louisiana, Texas, and Arkansas—as well as the frontier areas in Tennessee, Kentucky, and Florida.

Largely unsettled until the 1820s, this region bridged the South and the West, exhibiting characteristics of both areas. Raw and dynamic, filled with dangers, uncertainties, and opportunities, it served as a powerful magnet, luring thousands of settlers from Virginia and the Carolinas when the seaboard economy faltered during the 1820s and 1830s. The agricultural economy of the upper South suffered from depressed commodity prices and soil exhaustion by the Jacksonian era. Large farm families, especially, struggled to provide each child with sufficient land and resources to subsist and maintain the family legacy. As the international market for cotton soared in the early nineteenth century, the sons of seaboard planters began heading to the Southwest, eager to exploit a splendid new "land of promise." By the 1830s, the bulk of cotton production was occurring in the lower South. The migrating southerners carved out farms, built churches, raised towns, and eventually brought culture and order to a raw frontier. As they took up new lives and occupations, these southern pioneers transplanted many practices and institutions from the coastal states. But they also fashioned a distinct new set of cultural values and social customs.

THE DECISION TO MIGRATE   Young white men aspiring to be planters, usually in their twenties, responded to the siren call of fertile soil in the Southwest. Several factors prompted their decision to move. The dwindling economic opportunities available in the Carolinas and Virginia, and restrictive kinship ties played a major role. As one young pioneer explained, he did not want to "creep and crawl in North Carolina like a poor sloth" when he could amass a fortune in the Southwest. Fathers were living longer; the best lands were already occupied and often exhausted of nutrients; the professions were overpopulated. Like their northern counterparts, restless southern sons of the planter and professional elite wanted to make it on their own, to be "self-made men," economically self-reliant and socially independent. To them speculative profit-seeking was more enticing than family stability. They refused to be "kept back" from economic gain and social status by the "prejudices" of the old men governing their families. A North Carolinian expected to "rise and soar like an eagle" in the Southwest because he would be freed from the strictures of his family circle. Many sons of seaboard planters also believed that they could prove their masculinity more readily on the southwestern frontier than in the more settled society along the Atlantic coast. A South Carolinian longed to prove his mettle on the frontier's "busy battle ground—to meet opposition—to trample it underfoot. I feel that the West is the land for me."

Women were underrepresented among migrants to the Old Southwest. Few were interested in relocating to a disease-ridden, violent, and primitive frontier. The new region did not offer them independence or adventure. And their never-ending routine of domestic tasks would only increase in the frontier environment. In general, women regretted more than men the loss of kinship ties that migration would entail. To them a stable family life was more important than the prospect of material gain. As a Carolina woman prepared to depart for Alabama, she confided to a friend that "you *cannot* imagine the state of despair that I am in." Another said that "my heart bleeds within me" at the thought of the "many tender cords [of kinship] that are now severed forever." Others feared that life on the frontier would produce a "dissipation" of morals. They heard vivid stories of frontier lawlessness, drunkenness, gambling, and miscegenation.

Slaves had many of the same reservations about moving west. Almost a million captive blacks joined in the migration to the Southwest during the antebellum era, most of them making the journey in the 1830s. Like the white women, they feared the harsh working conditions and torpid heat and humidity of the Southwest. They also were despondent at the breaking up of their family ties. As Frederick Douglass observed, the "removal" of a slave to the Southwest was considered a form of psychological "death." Departures were seared with emotional anguish. When a young slave girl left Virginia for the Southwest, her mother ran after the wagon, eventually fell down and rolled "over on de groun' jes' acryin'." She never saw her daughter again.

JOURNEY AND SETTLEMENT   Most of the migrants to the Southwest headed for the fertile lands of Alabama, Mississippi, and central Tennessee. The typical trek was about 500 miles. Along rough roads and trails, the pioneers averaged fifteen miles per day, occasionally staying overnight in taverns, more often camping in the open air amid panthers, bears, and wolves. At times the route was clogged with people. One traveler said that often he would see "an uninterrupted line of walkers, wagons, and carriages." For slaves the journey was especially dangerous. Most traveled on foot, tied or chained together. Many drowned while fording rivers; others contracted mortal illnesses along the way.

Once in the Southwest the pioneers bought land that had been appropriated from the Indians. Parcels of 640 acres sold for as little as two dollars an acre. Land in Alabama's black belt brought higher prices. As cotton prices soared in the 1830s, aspiring planters bought as much land and as many slaves as possible. As a result, the average size of farms and plantations in the Southwest was larger than that in the Carolinas and Virginia. For many, it seems, the new region lived up to its images as a land of fertile possibilities. One new arrival pronounced Alabama to be "a glorious farming country." Another expressed his delight that he was finally on his own. "I never felt more independent & cheerful in my life."

But the Southwest was not utopia. The region was much more unhealthy than the Carolina Piedmont. The hot climate, contaminated water, and poor sanitation spawned an epidemic of diseases. Malaria was especially endemic to the region. Women and slaves also found their harsh new surroundings uninviting. Life in tents and rude log cabins made many newcomers yearn for the material comforts they had left behind. A male settler reported that "all the men is very well pleased but the women is not very satisfied." The physical and social isolation on the frontier was a disheartening new reality. People usually settled far from relatives. The kinship networks that had provided them with practical assistance and emotional fulfillment disintegrated. After starting a homestead in Alabama, Mary Drake regretted the loss of her "large and respectable circle of relations" in North Carolina. Many decided to return home or move farther west.

A MASCULINE CULTURE   The southern frontier environment provoked important changes in sex roles, and relations between men and women became even more inequitable. Frontier life lent itself to the psychology of "manly independence" that many male pioneers eagerly sought.

Young adult males indulged themselves in activities that would have generated disapproval in the more settled seaboard society. They drank, gambled, fought, and indulged their sexual desires. According to one disheartened observer, the typical young male settler, his "desires and appetites . . . unrestrained," became an embarrassment and source of sorrow to his family back east. In 1834 a South Carolina migrant urged his brother to move west and join him because "you can live like a fighting cock with us." A few years later he implored another brother to leave the seaboard because he had too much potential "to hang around Mother and drivel away your life."

Alcohol consumption hit new heights along the southwestern frontier. Most plantations had their own stills to manufacture whiskey, and alcoholism ravaged frontier families. Masculine violence was also commonplace. A Virginian who settled in Mississippi fought in fourteen duels and killed ten men in the process. The frequency of fights, stabbings, shootings, and murders shocked visitors. So, too, did the propensity of white men to take sexual advantage of slave women. An Alabama woman married to a lawyer and politician was outraged by the "beastly passions" of the white men who fathered slave children and then sold them like livestock. She also recorded in her diary instances of men regularly beating their wives with whips and drinking to excess. Wives, it seems, had little choice but to endure such mistreatment because, as one woman wrote about a friend whose husband abused her, she was "wholly dependent upon his care."

CELIA   Occasionally a single historical incident can encapsulate the larger web of laws and customs within a society. Such is the case with the story of a teenaged slave girl named Celia. Robert Newsom migrated from Virginia to the Southwest in the early 1820s and eventually established a prosperous 800-acre homestead. He owned a half dozen slaves, including Celia. Newsom told his family that he had bought her to serve as a domestic servant. But immediately after purchasing Celia, while driving her back to his farm, Newsom raped her. For the next five years he treated Celia as his mistress. During that time she gave birth to two children, presumably his offspring. In a fit of tortured generosity, Newsom built Celia a separate, comfortable brick cabin fifty yards from the main house. But the anguish and humiliation she suffered took its toll. When Celia privately appealed to Newsom's two grown daughters to intervene on her behalf and put a stop to their father's sexual advances, they turned a deaf ear.

Desperate for relief from her tormentor, Celia resolved in 1855 to resist his next assault, with words if possible, with a club if necessary. Soon thereafter, Newsom again entered her cabin, ignored her impassioned appeal, and kept advancing until she struck him on the head.

TO BE SOLD,
A likely ſtrong Negro
Girl, abcut 17 Years of Age ; fold
by Reaſon that a Boy would ſuit
the Owner better. Enquire at
R. & S. *Draper*'s Printing Office

Notice for the sale of a seventeen-year-old female slave.

After he fell to the floor, she clubbed him to death. As she later explained, "the Devil got into me, and I struck him with the stick until he was dead." Celia then burned the body, pulverized the bones, and convinced one of Newsom's grandsons to help her discard the ashes. She eventually was accused of the crime and confessed. Her attorneys, all of them slaveowners, argued that the right of white women to defend their sexual honor against assault should be extended to slaves as well. The judge and jury, however, disagreed, and Celia was hanged.

ANTISLAVERY MOVEMENTS

EARLY OPPOSITION TO SLAVERY   From the Revolution to the early 1830s few southern whites showed much disposition to defend the peculiar institution. But in the oft-used figure of speech, they had the wolf by the ears and could not let go. The specter of racial intermarriage and possible race war convinced many whites that slavery must be maintained despite its evils. Such scattered antislavery groups and publications as existed in those years in fact were found mainly in the upper South. In 1821 Benjamin Lundy established in Ohio the *Genius of Universal Emancipation,* later published at Greenville, Tennessee, and Baltimore. In 1827 Lundy counted 106 emancipation societies, with 5,150 members, in the slave states and only 24, with 1,475 members, in the free states. The North Carolina Manumission Society held meetings as late as 1834. These groups and publications urged masters to free their slaves voluntarily.

The emancipation movement had accelerated with the formation of the American Colonization Society in 1817. The society proposed to colonize freed slaves in Africa, or as one historian put it, "more truly, away from America." Its supporters included such prominent figures as James Madison, James Monroe, Henry Clay, John Marshall, and Daniel

Webster, and it appealed to diverse opinions. Some backed it as an anti-slavery group, while others saw it as a way to bolster slavery by getting rid of potentially troublesome free blacks. Articulate elements of the free black community denounced it from the start. About a month after the group's founding, when James Forten, a successful sailmaker and Revolutionary War veteran, called upon the assembled free blacks of Philadelphia to vote on the proposition, he got a long, tremendous "No" which, he wrote, "seemed as if it would bring down the walls of the building." America, the blacks insisted, was now their native land.

In 1821, nevertheless, agents of the society acquired from local chieftains in West Africa a parcel of land that became the nucleus of a new country. In 1822 the first freed slaves arrived there, and twenty-five years later the society relinquished control to the independent republic of Liberia. But given its uncertain purpose, the colonization movement received only meager support from either antislavery or proslavery elements. In all, up to 1860 only about 15,000 blacks migrated to Africa, approximately 12,000 with the help of the Colonization Society. The number was infinitesimal compared to the number of slave births.

FROM GRADUALISM TO ABOLITIONISM   Meanwhile in the early 1830s the antislavery movement took a new departure. Its initial efforts to promote a gradual end to slavery through prohibiting it in the territories and encouraging manumission gave way to demands for immediate abolition. Three dramatic events marked this transition. In 1829 a pamphlet appeared in Boston: *Walker's Appeal . . . to the Colored Citizens of the World*. Its author, David Walker, born a free black in North Carolina, preached insurrection and violence as a proper response to the wrongs that blacks suffered. Over the next few years Walker circulated the pamphlet widely among blacks and white sympathizers. While free blacks in parts of the South were known to have read it, the message appears to have reached few slaves.

Two other major events followed in close sequence during 1831. On January 1, William Lloyd Garrison began publication in Boston of a new antislavery newspaper, *The Liberator*. Garrison, who rose from poverty in Newburyport, Massachusetts, had been apprenticed to a newspaperman and had edited a number of papers. For two years he worked on Benjamin Lundy's *Genius of Universal Emancipation* in Baltimore, but became restless with Lundy's moderation. In the first issue of his new paper he renounced "the popular but pernicious doctrine of gradual emancipation" and vowed: "I will be as harsh as truth, and as uncompromising as justice. On this subject, I do not wish to think, or speak, or write, with moderation. . . . I am in earnest—I will not equivocate—I will not excuse—I will not retreat a single inch AND I WILL BE HEARD." And he was heard, mainly at first because his language pro-

William Lloyd Garrison.

voked outraged retorts from slaveholders who publicized the paper more than his own supporters did. Circulation in fact was never very large, but copies went to papers with much wider circulations. In the South, literate blacks would more likely encounter Garrison's ideas in the local papers than in the few copies of *The Liberator* that found their way to them.

Slaveholders' outrage mounted higher after the Nat Turner insurrection in August 1831. Garrison, they assumed, bore a large part of the responsibility for the affair, but there is no evidence that Nat Turner had ever heard of him, and Garrison said that he had not a single subscriber in the South at the time. What is more, however violent his language, Garrison was a pacifist, opposed to the use of physical violence.

THE AMERICAN ANTI-SLAVERY SOCIETY   A period of organization followed these events. In 1832 Garrison and his followers set up the New England Anti-Slavery Society. In 1833 two wealthy New York merchants, Arthur and Lewis Tappan, founded a similar group in their state and the same year took the lead in starting a national society with the help of Garrison and a variety of other antislavery people. They hoped to exploit the publicity gained by the British antislavery movement, which that same year had induced Parliament to end slavery, with compensation to slaveholders, throughout the British Empire.

The American Anti-Slavery Society conceded the right of each state to legislate on its domestic institutions, but set a goal of convincing fellow citizens "that Slaveholding is a heinous crime in the sight of God, and that the duty, safety, and best interests of all concerned, require its *immediate abandonment*, without expatriation." The society went beyond the issue of emancipation to argue that blacks should "share an equality with the whites, of civil and religious privileges."

The group issued a barrage of propaganda for its cause, including periodicals, tracts, agents, lecturers, organizers, and fund-raisers. Probably its most effective single agent was Theodore Dwight Weld of Ohio, a convert and disciple of the great evangelist Charles Grandison Finney. In 1834 Weld led a group of students at Lane Theological Seminary in Cincinnati in a protracted discussion of abolition. Efforts of its president, Lyman Beecher, and the trustees to repress this interruption of normal routine led to a mass secession from Lane and the start of a new theological school at the recently opened Oberlin College. The move won the financial and moral support of the Tappans.

Weld and a number of the "Lane rebels" set out to evangelize the country for abolition. Weld earned the reputation of troublemaker and "the most mobbed man in the United States," but at the same time he displayed a genius for turning enemies into disciples. In 1836 Weld conducted a New York training school for lecturers from which seventy apostles went out two by two to weave a network of abolitionist organizations across the North. Publications by Weld included *The Bible Against Slavery* (1837) and *American Slavery as It Is: Testimony of a Thousand Witnesses* (1839), the latter including examples of atrocities against slaves gathered from news accounts. The book sold 100,000 copies in its first year.

THE MOVEMENT SPLITS   As the movement spread, debates over tactics inevitably grew. The Garrisonians, mainly New Englanders, were radicals who felt that American society had been corrupted from top to bottom and needed universal reform. Garrison embraced just about every important reform movement that came down the pike in those years: antislavery, temperance, pacifism, and women's rights. Deeply affected by the perfectionism of the times, he refused to compromise principle for expediency, to sacrifice one reform for another. Abolition was not enough. He opposed colonization of freed slaves and stood for equal rights. He broke with the organized church, which to his mind was in league with slavery. The federal government, with its Fugitive Slave Law, was all the more so. The Constitution, he said, was "a covenant with death and an agreement with hell." Garrison therefore refused to vote. He was, however, prepared to collaborate with those who did, or with those who disagreed with him on other matters.

Other reformers saw American society as fundamentally sound and concentrated their attention on purging it of slavery. Garrison struck them as an impractical fanatic. A showdown came in 1840 on the issue of women's rights. Women had joined the abolition movement from the start, but largely in groups without men. The activities of the Grimké sisters brought the issue of women's rights to center stage.

Sarah and Angelina Grimké, daughters of a prominent South Carolina family, had broken with their parents and moved north to embrace antislavery, feminism, and other reforms. Their publications included Angelina's *Appeal to the Christian Women of the South* (1836), calling on southern women to speak and act against slavery, and Sarah's *Letter on the Equality of the Sexes and the Condition of Women* (1838). Having attended Theodore Weld's school for antislavery apostles in New York (Angelina later married Theodore), they set out speaking to women in New England and slowly widened their audiences to "promiscuous assemblies" of both men and women. Such unseemly behavior inspired the Congregational clergy of Massachusetts to chastise the Grimké sisters for engaging in unfeminine activity. And it provoked Catharine Beecher to remind the activist sisters that women occupied "a subordinate relation in society to the other sex" and should therefore limit their activities to the "domestic and social circle." Angelina Grimké rejected such conventional arguments. "It is a woman's right," she insisted, "to have a voice in all laws and regulations by which she is to be governed, whether in church or in state."

The debate over the role of women in the antislavery movement crackled and simmered until it finally exploded at the Anti-Slavery Society's meeting in 1840. There the Garrisonians insisted on the right of women to participate equally in the organization, and carried their point. They did not commit the group to women's rights in any other way, however. Contrary opinion, mainly from the Tappans' New York group, ranged from outright antifeminism to simple fear of scattering shots on too many reforms. The New Yorkers broke away to form the American and Foreign Anti-Slavery Society. Weld, who had probably done more than anybody else to build the movement, declined to go with either group. Like the New Yorkers, he preferred to focus on slavery as the central evil of the times, but he could not accept their "anti-woman" attitude, as he saw it. Discouraged by the bickering, he drifted away from the movement he had done so much to build and into a long-term teaching career.

BLACK ANTISLAVERY   White antislavery men also balked at granting full recognition to black abolitionists of either sex. Often blindly patronizing, white leaders expected African Americans to take a back seat in the movement. Not all blacks were easily manipulated, however, and most became exasperated at whites' tendency to value purity over results, to strike a moral posture at the expense of action. But despite the invitation to form separate black groups, black leaders were active in the white societies from the beginning. Three attended the organizational meeting of the American Anti-Slavery Society in 1833, and some became outstanding agents for the movement, notably the former slaves who could speak from firsthand experience. Garrison pronounced such

Frederick Douglass (left) *and Sojourner Truth* (right) *were both leading abolitionists.*

men as Henry Bibb and William Wells Brown, both escapees from Kentucky, and Frederick Douglass, who fled Maryland, "the best qualified to address the public on the subject of slavery."

Douglass, blessed with an imposing frame and a gift of eloquence, became the best-known black man in America. "I appear before the immense assembly this evening as a thief and a robber," he told a Massachusetts group in 1842. "I stole this head, these limbs, this body from my master, and ran off with them." Fearful of capture after publishing his *Narrative of the Life of Frederick Douglass* (1845), he left for an extended lecture tour of the British Isles and returned two years later with enough money to purchase his freedom. He then started an abolitionist newspaper for blacks, the *North Star,* in Rochester, New York.

Douglass's *Narrative* was but the best known among a hundred or more such accounts. Escapees often made it out on their own—Douglass borrowed a pass from a free black seaman—but many were aided by the Underground Railroad, which grew in legend into a vast system to conceal runaways and spirit them to freedom, often over the Canadian border. Levi Coffin, a North Carolina Quaker who moved to Cincinnati and did help many fugitives, was the reputed president. Actually, there seems to have been more spontaneity than system about the matter, and blacks contributed more than was credited in the legend. Experience had conditioned escapees to distrust whites. One escapee recalled later: "We did not dare ask [for food], except when we found a slave's or a free colored person's house remote from any other, and then we were never refused, if they had food to give." A few intrepid refugees actually ventured back into slave states to organize escapes. Harriet Tubman, the most celebrated, went back nineteen times.

Equally courageous was the articulate black female abolitionist Sojourner Truth. Born in New York State in 1797, Isabella Baumfree renamed herself in 1843 after experiencing a mystical conversation with God, who told her "to travel up and down the land" preaching the sins of slavery. She did just that, crisscrossing the country during the 1840s and 1850s, exhorting audiences about abolitionism and women's rights. Having been a slave until she fled to freedom in 1827, Sojourner Truth was able to speak with added conviction and knowledge about the evils of the "peculiar institution" and the inequality of women. As she told a gathering of the Ohio Women's Rights Convention in 1851, "I have plowed, and planted, and gathered into barns, and no man could head me—and ar'n't I a woman? I have borne thirteen children, and seen 'em mos' all sold off into slavery, and when I cried out with a mother's grief, none but Jesus heard—and ar'n't I a woman?" Through such compelling testimony, Sojourner Truth demonstrated the powerful intersection of abolitionism and women's-rights agitation, and in the process she displayed and tapped the distinctive energies that women brought to reformist causes. "If the first woman God ever made was strong enough to turn the world upside down all alone," she concluded her address to the Ohio gathering, "these women together ought to be able to turn it back, and get it right side up again!"

REACTIONS TO ANTISLAVERY   Even the road north, many blacks found to their dismay, did not lead to the Promised Land. North of slavery, they encountered much of the discrimination and segregation that freed slaves would later encounter in the southern states. When Prudence Crandall of Connecticut admitted a black girl to her private school in 1833, she lost most of her white pupils. She held out in the face of insults, vandalism, and a law that made her action illegal, but closed the school after eighteen months and left the state. Garrison, Douglass, Weld, and other abolitionists had to face down hostile crowds who disliked blacks or found antislavery agitation bad for business. In 1837 a hostile mob in Alton, Illinois, killed the antislavery editor Elijah P. Lovejoy, giving the movement a martyr to both abolition and freedom of the press.

By then proslavery southerners, by seeking to suppress discussion of emancipation, had already given abolitionists ways to link antislavery with the cause of civil liberties for whites. In the summer of 1835 a mob destroyed several sacks of abolitionist literature in the Charleston post office. The postmaster had announced that he would not try to deliver such matter. Bitter debates in Congress ensued. President Jackson wanted a law against handling "incendiary literature," but Congress failed to oblige him. The postmaster-general, nevertheless, did nothing about forcing delivery.

One shrewd political strategy, promoted by Weld, was to deluge Congress with petitions for abolition in the District of Columbia. Most such petitions were presented by former president John Quincy Adams, elected to the House from Massachusetts in 1830. In 1836, however, the House adopted a rule to lay abolition petitions automatically on the table, in effect ignoring them. Adams, "Old Man Eloquent," stubbornly fought this "gag rule" as a violation of the First Amendment, and hounded its supporters until the gag rule was finally repealed in 1844.

Meanwhile, in 1840, the year of the schism in the antislavery movement, a small group of abolitionists called a convention in Albany, New York, and launched the Liberty party, with James G. Birney, one-time slaveholder of Alabama and Kentucky, as its candidate for president. Birney, converted to the cause by Weld, had tried without success to publish an antislavery paper in Danville, Kentucky. He then moved it to Ohio and in 1837 became executive secretary of the American Anti-Slavery Society. In the 1840 election he polled only 7,000 votes, but in 1844 his vote rose to 60,000, and from that time forth an antislavery party contested every national election until Abraham Lincoln won the presidency.

THE DEFENSE OF SLAVERY   Birney was but one among a number of southerners propelled north during the 1830s by the South's growing hostility to emancipationist ideas. Antislavery in the upper South had its last stand in 1831–1832 when the Virginia legislature debated a plan of gradual emancipation and colonization, then rejected it by a vote of 73 to 58. Thereafter, leaders of southern thought worked out an elaborate intellectual defense of slavery, presenting it as a positive good rather than, in the words of Tennessee's constitutional convention of 1834, "a great evil" that "the wisest heads and most benevolent hearts" had not been able to dispose of.

In 1832 Professor Thomas R. Dew of the College of William and Mary published the most comprehensive defense of slavery produced to that time, his *Review of the Debate of the Virginia Legislature of 1831 and 1832*. In it he made the practical argument that the natural increase of the slave population would outrun any colonization effort. But he went on to justify slavery as required by the circumstances of southern life and the condition of human inequality, citing as authorities the Bible, Aristotle, and Edmund Burke, the eighteenth-century English conservative philosopher.

The biblical argument became one of the most powerful. The evangelical churches, which had widely condemned slavery at one time, gradually turned proslavery. Ministers of all denominations joined in the argument. Had not the patriarchs of the Old Testament held people in bondage? Had not Noah, upon awakening from a drunken stupor, cursed Canaan, son of Ham, from whom the Negroes were descended? Had not Saint Paul advised servants to obey their masters and told a fugitive servant to return to his master? And had not Jesus remained silent on the subject, at least so far as the Gospels reported his words? In 1843–1844 disputes over slavery split two great denominations along sectional lines and led to the formation of the Southern Baptist Convention and the Methodist Episcopal Church, South. Presbyterians, the only other major denomination to split, did not divide until the Civil War.

Another, and more fundamental, feature of the proslavery argument stressed the intrinsic inferiority of blacks. Most whites, blind and deaf to the complexity of black culture, assumed that the evidence of their eyes and ears confirmed their own superiority. The weight of scientific opinion, which was not above prejudice on such matters, was on their side, but it is doubtful that many felt the need of science to prove what seemed so obvious to them. Stereotyping the poor and powerless as inferior is an old and seemingly ineradicable human habit. There was in fact a theory championed by a physician from Mobile, Alabama, that blacks were the product of a separate creation, but this challenged orthodox faith in the biblical account of creation and was generally rejected.

Other arguments took a more "practical" view of slavery. Not only was slavery profitable, it was a matter of social necessity. Jefferson, for instance, in his *Notes on Virginia* (1785), had argued that emancipated slaves and whites could not live together without risk of race war growing out of the recollection of past injustices. What is more, it seemed clear that blacks could not be expected to work under conditions of freedom. They were too shiftless and improvident, the argument went, and in freedom would be a danger to themselves as well as to others. White workmen, on the other hand, feared their competition. Whites were also struck with fear by the terrible example of the bloody rebellion in Santo Domingo.

In 1856 William J. Grayson of Charleston published a long poem, *The Hireling and the Slave,* which defended slavery as better for the worker than the "wage slavery" of northern industry. George Fitzhugh of Virginia developed the same argument, among others, in two books: *Sociology for the South; or, The Failure of a Free Society* (1854) and *Cannibals All! or, Slaves Without Masters* (1857). Few if any socialists ever waxed more eloquent over the evils of industrial capitalism than these proslavery theorists. The factory system had brought abuses and neglect far worse than those of slavery. Slavery, Fitzhugh argued, was the truest form of socialism, for it provided security for the workers in sickness and old age, whereas workers in the North were exploited for profit and then cast aside without compunction. Men were not born equal, he insisted: "It would be far nearer the truth to say that some were born with saddles on their backs, and others booted and spurred to ride them—and the riding does them good." Fitzhugh argued for an organic, hierarchical society, much like the family, in which each had a place with both rights and obligations. Calhoun endorsed slavery with the more popular argument that it freed masters from drudgery to pursue higher things, and thus made possible a Greek democracy— or what one historian has more aptly tagged a "Herrenvolk [master-race] democracy."

Within one generation such ideas had triumphed in the white South over the postrevolutionary apology for slavery as an evil bequeathed by the forefathers. Opponents of the orthodox faith in slavery as a positive good were either silenced or exiled. Freedom of thought in the Old South had become a victim of the nation's growing obsession with slavery.

FURTHER READING

Those interested in the problem of discerning myth and reality in the southern experience should consult *Myth and Southern History* (1974), edited by Patrick Gerster and Nicholas Cords, for various essays on the topic. William R. Taylor's *Cavalier and Yankee: The Old South and American National Character* (1961) remains helpful. W. J. Cash's *The Mind of the South* (1941)° is a classic on the subject. Two new works make substantial contributions to the renewed effort to understand the mind of the Old South and its defense of slavery: Eugene D. Genovese's *The Slaveholders' Dilemma: Freedom and Progress in Southern Conservative Thought, 1820–1860* (1992) and Eric H. Walther's *The Fire-Eaters* (1992).

The dominance of the plantation system is analyzed in Ulrich B. Phillips's *Life and Labor in the Old South* (1929). Frank L. Owsley's *Plain Folk of the Old South* (1949) argues that yeoman farmers were dominant in many aspects of antebellum agriculture. Bruce Collins's *White Society in the Antebellum South* (1985) sees broad consensus among all classes of whites. Contrasting analyses of the plantation system are Eugene D. Genovese's *The World the Slaveholders Made* (1969) and Gavin Wright's *The Political Economy of the Cotton South* (1978).° Why southern industry lagged behind agriculture is treated in

---

°These books are available in paperback editions.

relevant chapters of Genovese's *The Political Economy of Slavery* (1965).

Other works on southern culture and society include Bertram Wyatt-Brown's *Southern Honor* (1982), Elizabeth Fox-Genovese's *Within the Plantation Household: Black and White Women of the Old South* (1988), Suzanne Lebsock's *Free Women of Petersburg* (1984), Catherine Clinton's *The Plantation Mistress: Woman's World in the Old South* (1982), Anne Firor Scott's *The Southern Lady: From Pedestal to Politics* (1970), Joan Cashin's *A Family Venture: Men and Women on the Southern Frontier* (1991), and Theodore Rosengarten's *Tombee: Portrait of a Cotton Planter* (1987). William J. Cooper, Jr.'s *Liberty and Slavery* (1983)° and Robert F. Durden's *The Self-Inflicted Wound* (1985) cover southern politics of the era. For a look at the role of religion in southern political life, see Mitchell Snay's *Gospel of Disunion: Religion and Separatism in the Antebellum South* (1993).

The historiography of slavery and racism contains some of the most exciting and controversial scholarship in American letters. A provocative discussion of the psychology of black slavery can be found in Stanley M. Elkin's *Slavery: A Problem in American Intellectual Life* (3rd ed., 1976).° More recent scholarship emphasizes the self-generative, dynamic character of black society under slavery. John W. Blassingame's *The Slave Community: Plantation Life in the Antebellum South* (rev. ed., 1979),° Eugene D. Genovese's *Roll, Jordon, Roll: The World the Slaves Made* (1974),° and Herbert G. Gutman's *The Black Family in Slavery and Freedom, 1750–1925* (1976)° all stress the theme of a persisting and identifiable slave culture. The diversity of the experience of slavery may be seen in studies of slavery in particular places, such as John C. Inscoe's *Mountain Masters, Slavery, and the Sectional Crisis in Western North Carolina* (1989) and Randolph B. Campbell's *An Empire for Slavery: The Peculiar Institution in Texas, 1821–1865* (1989).

On the question of slavery's profitability, see Robert W. Fogel and Stanley L. Engerman's *Time on the Cross: The Economics of Negro Slavery* (2 vols., 1974),° which argues that not only did planters benefit from bondage, but the slaves themselves incorporated a Victorian work ethic based on incentives. Herbert G. Gutman reviewed this controversy in *Slavery and the Numbers Game* (1975). See also Robert Fogel's conclusions on the subject in *Without Consent or Contract* (1992).°

Other recent works on slavery include Lawrence W. Levine's *Black Culture and Black Consciousness: Afro-American Folk Thought from Slavery to Freedom* (1977), Albert J. Raboteau's *Slave Religion: The*

°These books are available in paperback editions.

"Invisible Institution" in the Antebellum South (1978),° Joel Williamson's *New People: Miscegenation and Mulattoes in the United States* (1980), Dorothy Sterling's *We Are Your Sisters* (1984), Sterling Stuckey's *Slave Culture: Nationalists Theory and the Foundations of Black America* (1987), Jacqueline Jones's *Labor of Love, Labor of Sorrow: Black Women, Work and the Family from Slavery to Present* (1985), Deboray Gray White's *Ar'nt I a Woman? Female Slaves in the Plantation South* (1985), Charles B. Dew's *Bond of Iron: Master and Slave at Buffalo Forge* (1994), and Joel Williamson's *The Crucible of Race* (1985). For an oral history of slavery, see *Slave Testimony* (1977), edited by John W. Blassingame. Charles Joyner's *Down by the Riverside* (1984) offers a vivid reconstruction of one slave community.

Useful surveys of abolitionism include Ronald G. Walters's *The Antislavery Appeal* (1976)° and James B. Stewart's *Holy Warriors: The Abolitionists and American Slavery* (1976).°

Numerous biographies of the leading abolitionists contribute to an understanding of the movement: John L. Thomas's *The Liberator: William Lloyd Garrison* (1963), Gerda Lerner's *The Grimké Sisters from South Carolina: Rebels against Slavery* (1967), Bertram Wyatt-Brown's *Lewis Tappan and the Evangelical War against Slavery* (1969), and Robert H. Abzug's *Passionate Liberator: Theodore Dwight Weld and the Dilemma of Reform* (1980).°

On the role of free blacks in the antislavery movement, see Benjamin Quarles's *Black Abolitionists* (1969)°, R. J. M. Blackett's *Building an Antislavery Wall: Black Americans in the Abolitionist Movement, 1830–1860* (1983), Shirley J. Yee's *Black Women Abolitionists: A Study in Activism* (1992), Carleton Mabee's *Sojourner Truth: Slave, Prophet, Legend* (1993), and Jane H. Pease and William H. Pease's *They Who Would Be Free* (1974). William S. McFeely's *Frederick Douglass* (1990) portrays the most eminent black abolitionist. For a captivating first-person account, see *The Autobiography of Frederick Douglass* (1967).°
Surveys of black history for the period include John B. Boles's *Black Southerners, 1619–1869* (1983), Leon F. Litwack's *North of Slavery: The Negro in the Free States, 1790–1860* (1961), and Ira Berlin's *Slaves without Masters* (1974), on southern free blacks. See also Michael P. Johnson and James L. Roark's *Black Masters: A Free Family of Color in the Old South* (1984). For primary source material of black abolitionists see Peter Ripley, Roy E. Finkenbine, Michael F. Hembree, and Donald Yacovone's *Witness for Freedom: African American Voices on Race, Slavery, and Emancipation* (1993).

For the proslavery argument as it developed in the South, see Larry

---

°These books are available in paperback editions.

Tise's *Proslavery: A History of the Defense of Slavery in America* (1988), William J. Cooper's *The South and the Politics of Slavery, 1828–1856* (1978), James Oakes's *The Ruling Race: A History of American Slave- holders* (1982),° and *Slavery Defended* (1963), edited by Eric L. McK- itrick, the last a collection of proslavery writings. The problems south- erners had in justifying slavery are explored in Drew G. Faust's *A Sacred Circle: The Dilemma of the Intellectual in the Old South, 1840–1860* (1977), Kenneth S. Greenberg's *Masters and Statesmen: The Political Culture of American Slavery* (1985), and Carl N. Degler's *The Other South: Southern Dissenters in the Nineteenth Century* (1974). George M. Fredrickson's *The Black Image in the White Mind* (1971) examines a variety of racial stereotypes held by white southerners.

°These books are available in paperback editions.

16 ⤸

THE CRISIS OF UNION

SLAVERY IN THE TERRITORIES

John C. Calhoun and Ralph Waldo Emerson had little else in common, but both men sensed in the Mexican War the omens of a greater disaster. Mexico was "the forbidden fruit; the penalty of eating it would be to subject our institutions to political death," Calhoun warned. "The United States will conquer Mexico," Emerson conceded, "but it will be as the man swallows the arsenic. . . . Mexico will poison us." Wars, as both men knew, have a way of corrupting ideals and breeding new wars, often in unforeseen ways. Like Britain's conquest of New France, America's winning of the Southwest gave rise in turn to quarrels over newly acquired lands. In each case the quarrels set in train a series of disputes: Britain's eighteenth-century crisis of empire had its counterpart in America's nineteenth-century crisis of union.

THE WILMOT PROVISO   The Mexican War was less than three months old when the seeds of a new conflict began to sprout. On August 8, 1846, a sweltering House of Representatives reassembled to clear its calendar for adjournment. Polk had sent Congress that noon a hurried request for $2 million to expedite negotiations with Mexico. He expected little hindrance, since party discipline had already whipped through most of his program. But the House, resentful of Polk's triumphs, was ripe for revolt when a freshman Democrat from Pennsylvania, David Wilmot, stood up. He favored expansion, Wilmot explained, even the annexation of Texas as a slave state. But slavery had come to an end in Mexico, and if new territory should be acquired, "God forbid that we should be the means of planting this institution upon it." Drawing upon the words of the Northwest Ordinance, he offered a fateful amendment to Polk's appropriations bill: in lands acquired from Mexico, "neither slavery nor involuntary servitude shall ever exist in any part of said territory."

Within ten minutes an otherwise obscure congressman had immortalized his name. The Wilmot Proviso, although never a law, politicized slavery once and for all. For a generation, since the Missouri controversy of 1819–1821, the issue had been lurking in the wings, kept there most of the time by politicians who feared its disruptive force. From that day forth, for two decades the question would never be far from center stage.

The first flurry of excitement passed quickly, however. The House immediately adopted the Wilmot Proviso, but the Senate refused to concur, and Congress adjourned without giving Polk his $2 million. When Congress reconvened in December 1846, Polk prevailed on Wilmot to withhold his amendment when he asked for the money again, but by then others were ready to take up the cause. When a New York congressman revived the proviso, he signaled a revolt by the Van Burenites in concert with the antislavery forces of the North. Once again the House approved the amendment. Once again the Senate refused. In March the House finally gave in, but in one form or another Wilmot's idea kept cropping up. Abraham Lincoln later recalled that during one term as congressman, 1847–1849, he voted for it "as good as forty times."

John Calhoun meanwhile devised a thesis to counter the proviso and set it before the Senate in four resolutions on February 19, 1847. The Calhoun Resolutions, which never came to a vote, argued that since the territories were the common possession of the states, Congress had no right to prevent any citizen from taking slaves into them. To do so would violate the Fifth Amendment, which forbade Congress to deprive any person of life, liberty, or property without due process of law, and slaves were property. By this clever stroke of logic, Calhoun took that basic guarantee of liberty, the Bill of Rights, and turned it into a basic guarantee of slavery. The irony was not lost on his critics, but the point became established southern dogma—echoed by his colleagues and formally endorsed by the Virginia legislature.

Senator Thomas Hart Benton of Missouri, himself a slaveholder but also a Jacksonian nationalist, found in Calhoun's resolutions a set of abstractions "leading to no result." Wilmot and Calhoun between them, he said, had fashioned a pair of shears. Neither blade alone would cut very well, but joined together they could sever the ties of union. Within another year Benton was complaining that the slavery issue had become like the plague of frogs in Pharaoh's Egypt, with "this black question, forever on the table, on the nuptial couch, everywhere."

POPULAR SOVEREIGNTY   Many others, like Benton, refused to be polarized, seeking to bypass the brewing conflict. President Polk was among the first to suggest extending the Missouri Compromise dividing free and slave territory at latitude 36°30′ all the way to the Pacific. Senator Lewis Cass of Michigan suggested that the citizens of a territory "regulate their own internal concerns in their own way," like the citizens of a state. Such an approach would combine the merits of expediency and democracy. It would take the issue out of the national arena and put it in the hands of those directly affected.

Popular sovereignty, or squatter sovereignty, as the idea was also called, had much to commend it. Without directly challenging the slaveholders' access to the new lands, it promised to open them quickly to non-slaveholding farmers who would almost surely dominate the territories. With this tacit understanding the idea prospered in Cass's Old Northwest, where Stephen A. Douglas of Illinois and other prominent Democrats soon endorsed it. Popular sovereignty, they hoped, might check the magnetic pull toward the opposite poles of Wilmot and Calhoun and thereby preserve the Union.

When the Mexican War ended in 1848, the question of bondage in the new territories was no longer hypothetical—unless one reasoned, as many did, that their arid climate excluded plantation crops and therefore excluded slavery. For Calhoun, who leaned to that opinion, that was beside the point, since the right to carry slaves into the territories was the outer defense line of the peculiar institution, not to be yielded without opening the way to further assaults. In fact, there is little reason in retrospect to credit the argument that slavery had reached its natural limits of expansion. Slavery had been adapted to occupations other than plantation agriculture. Besides, on irrigated lands, cotton later became a staple crop of the Southwest.

Nobody doubted that Oregon would become free soil, but it too was drawn into the growing controversy. Territorial status, pending since 1846, was delayed because its provisional government had excluded slavery. To concede that provision would imply an authority drawn from the powers of Congress, since a territory was created by Congress. Finally, a Senate committee proposed to let Oregon exclude slavery but to deny the territories of California and New Mexico any power to legislate at all on the subject, thus passing the issue to the courts. The question of slavery, previously outlawed under Mexican rule, could rise on appeal to the Supreme Court and thus be kept out of the political arena. The Senate accepted this but the House rejected it, and finally an exhausted Congress let Oregon organize without slavery, but postponed decision on the Southwest. Polk signed the bill on the principle that Oregon was north of 36°30′.

Polk had promised to serve only one term; exhausted and having reached his major goals, he refused to run again in 1848. At the Democratic convention Lewis Cass won the presidential nomination, but the party refused to endorse the "squatter sovereignty" plan. Instead it simply denied the power of Congress to interfere with slavery in the states and criticized all efforts to bring the question before Congress. The Whigs devised an even more artful shift. Once again, as in 1840, they passed over their party leader, Clay, for a general, Zachary Taylor, whose fame and popularity had grown since the Battle of Buena Vista. He was a legal resident of Louisiana who owned more than a hundred slaves, an apolitical figure who had never voted in a national election. Once again, as in 1840, the party adopted no platform at all.

THE FREE-SOIL COALITION   But the antislavery impulse was not easily squelched. Wilmot had raised a standard to which a broad coalition could rally. People who shied away from abolitionism could readily endorse the exclusion of slavery from the territories. The Northwest Ordinance and the Missouri Compromise supplied honored precedents. By doing so, moreover, one could strike a blow for liberty without caring about slavery itself, or about the slaves. One might simply want free soil for white farmers, while keeping the unwelcome blacks far away in the South, where they belonged. Free soil, therefore, rather than abolition, became the rallying point—and also the name of a new party.

Three major groups entered the free-soil coalition: rebellious Democrats, antislavery Whigs, and members of the Liberty party, which dated from 1840. Disaffection among the Democrats centered in New York, where the Van Burenite "Barnburners" squared off against the pro-administration "Hunkers" in a factional dispute that had as much to do with personal ambitions as with local politics. Each group gave the other its name, the one for its alleged purpose to rule or ruin like the farmer who burned his barn to get rid of the rats, the other for hankering or "hunkering" after office.   •

As their conflict grew, however, the Barnburners seized on the free-soil issue as a means of winning support. When the Democratic convention voted to divide the state's votes between contesting delegations, they bolted the party and named Van Buren as their candidate for president on a free-soil platform. Other Wilmot Democrats, including Wilmot himself, joined the revolt. Revolt among the Whigs centered in Massachusetts where a group of "Conscience" Whigs battled the "Cotton" Whigs. The latter, according to Charles Sumner, belonged to a coalition of northern businessmen and southern planters, "the lords of the lash and the lords of the loom." Conscience Whigs rejected the slaveholder, Taylor. The third group in the coalition, the abolitionist Liberty party, had already nominated Senator John P. Hale of New Hampshire for president.

In August these groups—Barnburners, Conscience Whigs, and Liberty party followers—organized the Free Soil party in a convention at

Buffalo. Its presidential nomination went to Martin Van Buren, while the vice-presidential nomination went to Charles Francis Adams, a Conscience Whig. The old Jacksonian and the son of John Quincy Adams made strange bedfellows indeed! The Liberty party was rewarded with a platform plank that pledged the government to abolish slavery whenever such action became constitutional, but the party's main principle was the Wilmot Proviso, and it entered the campaign with the catchy slogan of "free soil, free speech, free labor, and free men."

Its impact on the election was mixed. The Free Soilers split the Democratic vote enough to throw New York to Taylor, and the Whig vote enough to give Ohio to Cass, but Van Buren's total of 291,000 votes was far below the popular totals of 1,361,000 for Taylor and 1,222,000 for Cass. Taylor won with 163 to 127 electoral votes, and both major parties retained a national following. Taylor took eight slave states and seven free; Cass just the opposite, seven slave and eight free.

THE CALIFORNIA GOLD RUSH   Meanwhile a new dimension had been introduced into the question of the territories. On January 24, 1848, gold was discovered in California. The word spread quickly, and Polk's confirmation of the discovery in his last annual message, on December 5, 1848, turned the gold fever into a worldwide contagion. Word of limitless gold deposits in California, Polk said, "would scarcely command belief were they not corroborated by authentic reports." Throughout the rest of the nation, men quit their jobs or sold their businesses and headed west in 1849 and after. These "forty-niners" were often termed "Argonauts," after the band of adventurers in Greek mythology who went in search of the Golden Fleece. The influential editor Horace Greeley encouraged such fantasies. In his *New York Daily Tribune,* he declared that "We are on the brink of an Age of Gold." In California, "fortune lies abroad upon the surface of the earth as plentiful as mud in our streets." Only a few commentators expressed concern about the gold mania. Henry David Thoreau, for instance, saw the gold fever as a symptom of America's materialistic priorities and moral bankruptcy. California, he said, was "three thousand miles nearer to hell."

During 1849, by the best estimates, more than 80,000 gold seekers reached California, half of them Americans. Most went overland; the rest went by way of Panama or Cape Horn. Along the western slopes of the Sierra Nevada they thronged the valleys and canyons. The village of San Francisco, located near the harbor entrance Frémont had aptly named Golden Gate, grew rapidly into a city, mushrooming from 459 to 20,000 residents in a few months. The influx quickly reduced the 14,000 Mexicans in 1849 to a minority, and sporadic conflicts with the Indians of the Sierra Nevada foothills decimated the native peoples. In 1850 Americans already accounted for 68 percent of the population, and

Grand Patent India-Rubber Air Line Railway to California. *Gold-seekers on their way to California, 1840s.*

there was a cosmopolitan array of "Sydney Ducks" from Australia, "Kanakas" from Hawaii, "Limies" from London, "Paddies" from Ireland, "Coolies" from China, and "Keskydees" from France (who were always asking "Qu'est-ce qu'il dit?"—"What did he say?").

THE MINING FRONTIER   Of all the many frontiers in the American experience, the mining frontier was perhaps the most exceptional and unstable. Unlike the land-hungry pioneers who traversed the overland trails, the miners were mostly unmarried young men from a variety of places and representing a wide spectrum of ethnic and cultural backgrounds. Few miners were interested in permanent settlement. They wanted to strike it rich and return home. The mining camps in California valleys, canyons, and along creek beds thus sprang up like mushrooms and disappeared almost as rapidly. Several settlements were named for Ophir, the Biblical site of King Solomon's wealth. Others were called Long Bar, Poverty Bar, or Missouri Bar, after the gravel or sand bars where gold was found. As soon as rumors of a new strike made the rounds, miners converged on the area, joined soon thereafter by a hodgepodge of merchants and camp followers who made their living servicing the Argonauts. Then, when no more gold was found, they picked up and moved on. Said one miner: "There is an excitement connected with the pursuit of gold which renders one restless and uneasy—ever hoping to do something better."

The mining shantytowns were disorderly and often lawless communities where vigilante justice prevailed and leisure time revolved around saloons and gambling halls. One newcomer reported that "in the short space of twenty-four days, we have had murders, fearful accidents, bloody deaths, a mob, whippings, a hanging, an attempt at suicide, and a fatal duel." Women were as rare as liquor was abundant. In 1850 less than 8 percent of California's total population was female, and even fewer women hazarded life in the mining camps. Those who did could demand quite a premium for their work as cooks, laundresses, entertainers, and prostitutes. "A smart woman can do very well in this country," one woman reported to a friend back east. "It is the only country I ever was in where a woman received anything like just compensation for work." One woman arrived in Sacramento to discover that a biscuit could be sold for $10. That night she dreamed of getting rich herself by feeding the miners, imagining "crowds of bearded miners striking gold from the earth with every blow of the pick, each one seeming to leave a share for me." Women from back east who rarely had a suitor suddenly found themselves smothered with attention in the mining country. Another female immigrant noted that she had "men come forty miles over the mountains, just to look at me, and I never was called a handsome woman, in my best days, even by my most ardent admirers."

In the polyglot mining camps, the Americans often looked with disdain upon the Hispanics ("greasers") and Chinese ("chinks"), who were most often employed as wage laborers to help in the panning process,

An Indian woman doing domestic chores, Yosemite Valley, 1870.

Indian Woman Panning Out Gold.

separating gold from sand and gravel. But the Americans focused their contempt on the Indians. In the mining culture it was not a crime to kill Indians or work them to death. American miners tried several times to outlaw foreigners in the mining country but had to settle for a tax on foreign miners that was applied to Mexicans in express violation of the treaty ending the Mexican War.

CALIFORNIA STATEHOOD   As civic leaders emerged within the burgeoning California population, they grew increasingly frustrated by the inability of military authorities to maintain law and order. In this context the new president, Zachary Taylor, thought he saw an ideal opportunity to use California statehood as a lever to end the stalemate in Congress caused by the slavery issue. Born in Virginia, raised in Kentucky, he had been a soldier most of his adult life, with service in the War of 1812, the Black Hawk and Seminole Wars, and in Mexico. Constantly on the move, he had acquired a home in Louisiana and a plantation in Mississippi. Southern Whigs had rallied to his support, expecting him to uphold the cause of slavery. Instead they had turned up a southern man with Union principles, who had no more use for Calhoun's proslavery abstractions than Jackson had for his nullification doctrine. Innocent of politics Taylor might be, and to southern Whigs it was ominous that the antislavery William H. Seward had his ear, but "Old Rough and Ready" had the direct mind of the soldier he was. Slavery should be upheld where it existed, he felt, but he had little patience with abstract theories about slavery in territories where it probably could not exist. Why not make California and New Mexico into states immediately, he reasoned, and bypass the whole issue?

But the Californians, in need of organized government, were already ahead of him. By December 1849, without consulting Congress, California had a free-state government in operation. New Mexico responded more slowly, but by June 1850 Americans there had adopted another free-state constitution. The Mormons around Salt Lake, meanwhile, drafted a basic law for the imperial state of Deseret, which embraced most of the Mexican cession, including a slice of the coast from Los Angeles to San Diego.

In Taylor's annual message on December 4, 1849, he endorsed immediate statehood for California and enjoined Congress to "abstain from . . . those exciting topics of sectional character which have hitherto produced painful apprehensions in the public mind." The new Congress, however, was in no mood for simple solutions.

THE COMPROMISE OF 1850

THE GREAT DEBATE   The spotlight fell on the Senate, where a stellar cast enacted one of the great dramas of American politics, the Compromise of 1850: the triumvirate of Clay, Calhoun, and Webster, with a supporting cast that included William Seward, Stephen A. Douglas, Jefferson Davis, and Thomas Hart Benton. Seventy-three-year-old Henry Clay once again took the role of "Great Compromiser," which he had played in the Missouri and nullification controversies. In January 1850 he presented a package of eight resolutions that wrapped up solutions to all the disputed issues. He proposed to (1) admit California as a free state, (2) organize the remainder of the Southwest without restriction as to slavery, (3) deny Texas its extreme claim to a Rio Grande boundary up to its source, (4) compensate Texas for this by assuming the Texas debt, (5) uphold slavery in the District of Columbia, but (6) abolish the slave trade across its boundaries, (7) adopt a more effective fugitive slave act, and (8) deny congressional authority to interfere with the interstate slave trade. His proposals, in substance, became the Compromise of 1850, but only after a prolonged debate, the most celebrated, if not the greatest, in the annals of Congress—and the final great debate for Calhoun, Clay, and Webster. Calhoun, already dying, would be gone on March 31, and Clay and Webster two years later, in 1852.

On February 5–6 Clay summoned all his eloquence in a defense of the settlement. In the interest of "peace, concord and harmony," he called for an end to "passion, passion—party, party—and intemperance." California should be admitted on the terms that its own people had approved. As to the remainder of the new lands, he told northerners: "You have got what is worth more than a thousand Wilmot provisos. You have nature on your side." Secession, he warned southerners, would inevitably bring on war. Even a peaceful secession, however unlikely, would gain none of the South's demands. Slavery in the territories and the District, the return of fugitives—all would be endangered.

The debate continued sporadically through February, with Sam Houston rising to the support of Clay's compromise, Jefferson Davis defending the slavery cause on every point, and none rising to any effective defense of President Taylor's straightforward plan. Then on March 4 Calhoun left his sickbed to sit in the Senate chamber, a gaunt figure with his cloak draped about his shoulders, as a colleague read the "sentiments" he had "reduced to writing."

"I have, Senators, believed from the first that the agitation of the subject of slavery would, if not prevented by some timely and effective measure, end in disunion," said Calhoun. Neither Clay's compromise nor Taylor's efforts would serve the Union. The South needed but an acceptance of its rights: equality in the territories, the return of fugitive slaves, and some guarantee of "an equilibrium between the sections." The last, while not spelled out in the speech, referred to Calhoun's notion of a "concurrent majority" by which each section could gain security through a veto power, perhaps through a dual executive, an idea that would be elaborated in his posthumously published *Discourse on the Constitution*.

Three days later Calhoun returned to hear Daniel Webster. The "Godlike Daniel," long since acknowledged the supreme orator of an age of superb oratory, no longer possessed the thunderous voice of his youth, nor did his shrinking frame project its once magisterial aura, but he remained a formidable presence. His weathered face showed signs of worry and sorrow as he addressed the hushed Senate. He chose as his central theme the preservation of the Union: "I wish to speak today, not as a Massachusetts man, not as a Northern man, but as an American. . . . I speak today for the preservation of the Union. Hear me for my cause." The extent of slavery was already determined, he insisted, by the Northwest Ordinance, by the Missouri Compromise, and in the new lands by the law of nature. The Wilmot Proviso was superfluous: "I would not take pains to reaffirm an ordinance of nature nor to re-enact

Daniel Webster, in a daguerreotype made around the time of the 1850 Compromise.

the will of God." Both sections, to be sure, had legitimate grievances: on the one hand the excesses of "infernal fanatics and abolitionists" in the North; and on the other hand southern efforts to expand slavery and heap southern slurs on northern workingmen. But "Secession! Peaceable secession! Sir, your eyes and mine are never destined to see that miracle." Instead of looking into such "caverns of darkness," let "men enjoy the fresh air of liberty and union. Let them look to a more hopeful future."

The March 7 speech was a supreme gesture of conciliation, and Webster had knowingly brought down a storm upon his head. New England antislavery leaders lambasted this new "Benedict Arnold" who had betrayed his region. John Greenleaf Whittier lamented in "Ichabod":

> So fallen! so lost! the light withdrawn
> Which once he wore!
> The glory from his gray hairs gone
> Forevermore!

But Webster had also revived hopes of compromise in both North and South. Agreement, wrote one observer, "will be mainly owing to the conciliatory tone taken by Mr. Webster." Georgia's Senator Toombs found "a tolerable prospect for a proper settlement of the slavery question, probably along the lines backed by Webster."

On March 11 William Seward, freshman Whig senator from New York, gave the antislavery reply to Webster. As the confidant of Taylor he might have been expected to defend the president's program. Instead he stated his own view that compromise with slavery was "radically wrong and essentially vicious." There was, he said, "a higher law than the Constitution," thus leaving some doubt, whether he was floor leader for Zachary Taylor or for God.

In mid-April a select Committee of Thirteen bundled Clay's suggestions (insofar as they concerned the Mexican cession) into one comprehensive bill, which the committee reported to the Senate early in May. The measure was quickly dubbed the "Omnibus" bill because it resembled the contemporary vehicle that carried many riders. Taylor continued to oppose Clay's compromise, and the two men came to an open break that threatened to split the Whig party wide open. Another crisis loomed when word came near the end of June that a convention in New Mexico was applying for statehood, with Taylor's support, and with boundaries that conflicted with the Texas claim to the east bank of the Rio Grande.

TOWARD A COMPROMISE On July 4, 1850, friends of the Union staged a grand rally at the base of the unfinished Washington Monument. Taylor went to hear the speeches, lingering in the hot sun. Back at the White House he quenched his thirst with iced water and milk, ate some cherries, cucumbers, or cabbage, and contracted cholera morbus (a gastrointestinal affliction). Five days later he was dead. The outcome of the sectional quarrel, had he lived, probably would have been different, whether for better or worse one cannot know. In a showdown Taylor had put everyone on notice that he would be as resolute as Jackson. "I can save the Union without shedding a drop of blood," he said. On the other hand a showdown might have provoked civil war ten years before it came, years during which the northern states gained in population and economic strength.

Taylor's sudden death, however, strengthened the chances of compromise. The soldier in the White House was followed by a politician, Millard Fillmore. The son of a poor farmer in upper New York, Fillmore had come up through the school of hard knocks. Largely self-educated, he had made his own way in the profession of law and the rough-and-tumble world of New York politics. Experience had taught him caution, which some thought was indecision, but he had made up his mind to support Clay's compromise and had so informed Taylor. It was a strange switch. Taylor, the Louisiana slaveholder, had been ready to make war on his native region; Fillmore, who southerners thought was antislavery, was ready to make peace.

At this point young Senator Stephen A. Douglas of Illinois, a rising star of the Democratic party, rescued Clay's faltering compromise. Short and stocky, brash and brilliant, Douglas was known as the "Little Giant." His strategy was in fact the same one that Clay had used to pass the Missouri Compromise thirty years before. Reasoning that nearly

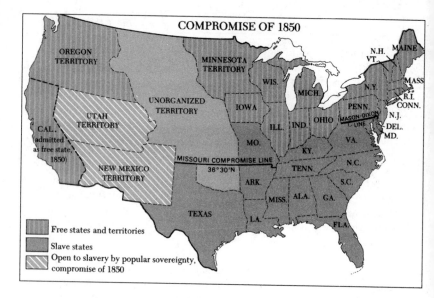

COMPROMISE OF 1850

- Free states and territories
- Slave states
- Open to slavery by popular sovereignty, compromise of 1850

everybody objected to one or another provision of the Omnibus, Douglas worked on the principle of breaking it up into six (later five) separate measures. Few members were prepared to vote for all of them, but from different elements Douglas hoped to mobilize a majority for each.

It worked. Thomas Hart Benton described the sequel. The separate items were like "cats and dogs that had been tied together by their tails four months, scratching and biting, but being loose again, every one of them ran off to his own hole and was quiet." By September 17 it was over, and three days later Fillmore had signed the last of the five measures into law. The Union had muddled through, and the settlement went down in history as the Compromise of 1850. For the time it defused an explosive situation and settled each of the major points at issue.

First, California entered the Union as a free state, ending forever the old balance of free and slave states. *Second*, the Texas and New Mexico Act made New Mexico a territory and set the Texas boundary at its present location. In return for giving up its claims east of the Rio Grande Texas was paid $10 million, which secured payment of the Texas debt and brought a powerful lobby of bondholders to the support of compromise. *Third*, the Utah Act set up another territory. The territorial act in each case omitted reference to slavery except to give the territorial legislature authority over "all rightful subjects of legislation" with provision for appeal to federal courts. For the sake of agreement the deliberate ambiguity of the statement was its merit. Northern congressmen could assume that territorial legislatures might act to exclude slavery on the unstated principle of popular sovereignty. Southern congressmen assumed that they could not.

Fourth, a new Fugitive Slave Act put the matter wholly under federal jurisdiction and stacked the cards in favor of slave-catchers. Fifth, as a gesture to antislavery forces, the slave trade, but not slavery itself, was abolished in the District of Columbia. The spectacle of chained-together slaves passing through the streets of the capital was brought to an end. Calling these five measures the Compromise of 1850 was an afterthought. Actually they were the result less of a sectional bargain than of a legislative maneuver. They were nevertheless an accomplished fact, and a large body of citizens welcomed the outcome, if not with joy, at least with relief.

Millard Fillmore's message to Congress in December 1850 pronounced the measures "a final settlement." Still, doubts lingered that either North or South could be reconciled to the measures permanently. In the South the disputes of 1846–1850 had transformed the abstract doctrine of secession into a movement animated by such fire-eaters as Robert Barnwell Rhett of South Carolina, William Lowndes Yancey of Alabama, and Edmund Ruffin of Virginia.

But once the furies aroused by the Wilmot Proviso were spent, the compromise left little on which to focus a proslavery agitation. The state of California was an accomplished fact, and, ironically, tended to elect proslavery men to Congress. New Mexico and Utah were far away, and in any case at least hypothetically open to slavery. Both in fact adopted slave codes, but the census of 1860 reported no slaves in New Mexico and only twenty-nine in Utah. The Fugitive Slave Law was something else again. It was the one clear-cut victory for the cause of slavery, but a Pyrrhic victory if ever there was one.

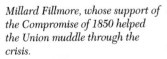

Millard Fillmore, whose support of the Compromise of 1850 helped the Union muddle through the crisis.

THE FUGITIVE SLAVE LAW   Southern insistence on the Fugitive Slave Law had presented abolitionists their greatest gift since the gag rule, a new focus for agitation and one that was far more charged with emotion. The Fugitive Slave Law did more than strengthen the hand of slave-catchers; it offered a strong temptation to kidnap free blacks. The law denied alleged fugitives a jury trial and provided that special commissioners got a fee of $10 when they certified delivery of an alleged slave but only $5 when they refused certification. In addition federal marshals could require citizens to help in enforcement; violators could be imprisoned for up to six months and fined $1,000. A Massachusetts man said it fixed the value of a Carolina slave at $1,000, of a Yankee soul at $5.

"This filthy enactment was made in the nineteenth century, by people who could read and write," Emerson marveled in his journal. He advised neighbors to break it "on the earliest occasion." The occasion soon arose in many places, if not in Emerson's Concord. Within a month of the law's enactment claims were filed in New York, Philadelphia, Harrisburg, Detroit, and other cities. Trouble soon followed. In Detroit only military force stopped the rescue of an alleged fugitive by an outraged mob in October 1850.

There were relatively few such incidents, however. In the first six

A notice to the free blacks of Boston to avoid the "watchmen and police officers" who "are empowered to act as kidnappers and slave catchers," 1851.

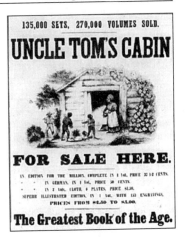

"*The Greatest Book of the Age.*" Uncle Tom's Cabin, *as this advertisement indicates, was a tremendous commercial success.*

years of the fugitive act, only three fugitives were forcibly rescued from the slave-catchers. On the other hand probably fewer than 200 were returned to bondage during the same years. More than that were rescued by stealth, often through the Underground Railroad. Still, the Fugitive Slave Act had tremendous effect in widening and deepening the antislavery impulse in the North.

UNCLE TOM'S CABIN   Antislavery forces found their most persuasive appeal not in the Fugitive Slave Act but in the fictional drama of Harriet Beecher Stowe's *Uncle Tom's Cabin* (1852), a combination of unlikely saints and sinners, stereotypes, and melodramatic escapades—and a smashing commercial success. The long-suffering Uncle Tom, the villainous Simon Legree, the angelic Eva, the desperate Eliza taking her child to freedom across the icy Ohio River—all became stock characters of the American imagination. Slavery, seen through Mrs. Stowe's eyes, subjected its victims either to callous brutality or, at the hands of spendthrift masters, to the indignity of bankruptcy. It took time for the novel to work its effect on public opinion, however. Neither abolitionists nor fire-eaters fought for their sections at the time. The country was enjoying a surge of prosperity, and the course of the presidential campaign in 1852 reflected a common desire to lay sectional quarrels to rest.

FOREIGN ADVENTURES

The Democrats, despite a fight over the nomination, had some success in papering over the divisions within their party. As their nominee for president they turned finally to Franklin Pierce of New Hampshire. The platform pledged the Democrats to "abide by and adhere to a faithful execution of the acts known as the Compromise measures." The candidates and the platform generated a surprising reconciliation of the party's factions. Pierce rallied both the Southern Rights men and the Van Burenite Barnburners, who at least had not burned their bridges with the Democrats. The Free Soilers, as a consequence, mustered only 156,000 votes for John P. Hale in contrast to the 291,000 they got for Van Buren in 1848.

The Whigs were less fortunate. They repudiated the lackluster Fillmore, who had faithfully supported the Compromise, and once again tried to exploit martial glory. It took fifty-three ballots, but the convention finally chose Winfield Scott, the hero of Mexico City, a native of Virginia backed mainly by northern Whigs. The convention dutifully endorsed the Compromise, but with some opposition from the North. Scott, an able commander but politically inept, had gained a reputation for antislavery and nativism, alienating German and Irish ethnic voters. In the end Scott carried only Tennessee, Kentucky, Massachusetts, and Vermont. Pierce overwhelmed him in the electoral college 254 to 42, although the popular vote was close: 1.6 million to 1.4 million.

Pierce, an undistinguished but handsome and engaging figure, a former congressman, senator, and brigadier in Mexico, was, like Polk, touted as another "Young Hickory." But he turned out to be made of more pliable stuff, unable to dominate the warring factions of his party, trying to be all things to all people, but looking more and more like a "Northern man with Southern principles."

"YOUNG AMERICA"   Foreign diversions now distracted attention from domestic quarrels. After the Mexican War the spirit of Manifest Destiny took on new life in an amorphous movement called "Young America." The Spirit of Young America exuded spread-eagle bombast, buoyant optimism, and enthusiasm for economic growth and territorial expansion. The dynamic force of American institutions would somehow transform the world. On February 21, 1848, just two days after word of the Mexican treaty reached Washington, an uprising in Paris signaled the Revolutions of 1848, which set Europe ablaze. The Young Americans greeted that new dawn with all the ardor Jeffersonians had lavished on the first French Revolution. And when it all collapsed, the result seemed to confirm the belief that Europe was, in the words of Stephen A. Douglas, "antiquated, decrepit, tottering on the verge of dissolution . . . a vast graveyard."

CUBA   Closer to home, Cuba, one of Spain's earliest and one of its last possessions in the New World, continued to be an object of American desire. In the early 1850s a crisis arose over expeditions launched against Cuba from American soil. Spanish authorities retaliated against these provocations by harassment of American ships. In 1854 the Cuban crisis expired in one final outburst of braggadocio, the Ostend Manifesto. That year the Pierce administration instructed Pierre Soulé, the minister in Madrid, to offer $130 million for Cuba, which Spain peremptorily spurned. Soulé then joined the American ministers to France and Britain in drafting the Ostend Manifesto. It declared that if Spain, "actuated by stubborn pride and a false sense of honor refused to sell," then the United States must ask itself, "does Cuba, in the possession of Spain, seriously endanger our internal peace and existence of our cherished Union?" If so, "then, by every law, human and divine, we shall be justified in wresting it from Spain. . . ." Publication of the supposedly confidential dispatch left the administration no choice but to disavow what northern opinion widely regarded as a "slaveholders' plot." The last word on this and other such episodes perhaps should go to the staid London *Times,* which commented near the end of 1854: "The diplomacy of the United States is certainly a very singular profession."

So was the practice of filibustering, a term referring to American adventurers seeking to gain control of foreign lands. In practice, filibustering was more bluster than action. Little wonder the word has come to suggest gas bag as well as freebooter, and the double meaning is appropriate for its use in the 1850s. William Walker, a Tennessean by birth who went to California and began to fancy himself a new Cortés, reached his supreme moment in 1855 when this "grey-eyed man of destiny" sailed with sixty followers, "the immortals," to mix in a Nicaraguan civil war. Before the year was out he had made himself president of a republic that Franklin Pierce promptly recognized. Walker was deposed in 1857, and in 1860 was executed by a firing squad in Honduras.

DIPLOMATIC GAINS IN THE PACIFIC   In the Pacific, however, American diplomacy scored some important achievements. American trade with China dated from 1785, but was allowed only through the port of Canton. In 1844 the United States and China signed the Treaty of Wanghsia, which opened four ports, including Shanghai, to American trade and for the first time granted America "extraterritoriality," or special privileges, including the right of Americans in China to remain subject to their own law. The Treaty of Tientsin (1858) opened eleven more ports and granted Americans the right to travel and trade throughout China. American Protestant missionaries also developed a keen interest in China. About fifty were already there by 1855, and for nearly a century China remained far and away the most active mission field for Americans.

Japan meanwhile had remained for two centuries closed to American trade. Moreover, American whalers wrecked on the shores of Japan

A Japanese view of Commodore Perry's landing in Yokohama Harbor.

had been forbidden to leave the country. Mainly in their interest President Fillmore entrusted a special Japanese expedition to Commodore Matthew Perry, who arrived in Tokyo in July 1853. Japan's actual ruler, the Tokugawa shogun, was already under pressure from merchants and the educated classes to seek wider contacts in the world. He agreed to deliver Perry's letter to the emperor. Negotiations followed, and in the Treaty of Kanagawa (March 31, 1854) Japan agreed to an American consulate, promised good treatment to castaways, and permitted visits in certain ports for supplies and repairs. Broad commercial relations came after the first envoy, Townsend Harris, negotiated the Harris Convention of 1858, which opened five ports to American trade and made certain tariff concessions. In 1860 a Japanese diplomatic mission, the first to enter a Western country, visited the United States for three months.

THE KANSAS-NEBRASKA CRISIS

During the 1850s the only land added to the United States was a barren stretch of some 30,000 square miles south of the Gila River in present New Mexico and Arizona. This Gadsden Purchase of 1853, which cost the United States $10 million, was made to acquire land offering a likely route for a Pacific railroad. The idea of building a railroad linking together the new continental domain of the United States, though a great national goal, spawned sectional rivalries in still another quarter and reopened the slavery issue. Among the many transcontinental routes projected, the four most important were the northern route from Milwaukee to the Columbia River, a central route from St. Louis to San Francisco, another from Memphis to Los Angeles, and a more southerly route from New Orleans to San Diego via the Gadsden Purchase.

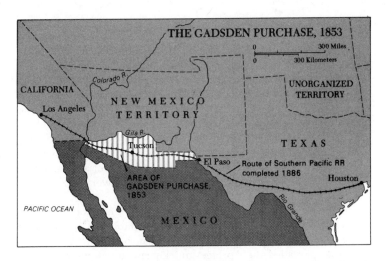

THE GADSDEN PURCHASE, 1853

CALIFORNIA

Los Angeles

Colorado R.

NEW MEXICO
TERRITORY

Gila R.

Tucson

AREA OF
GADSDEN PURCHASE,
1853

PACIFIC OCEAN

El Paso

MEXICO

UNORGANIZED
TERRITORY

TEXAS

Route of Southern Pacific RR
completed 1886

Houston

Rio Grande

0   300 Miles
0   300 Kilometers

DOUGLAS'S PROPOSAL   In 1852 and 1853 Congress debated and dropped several likely proposals. For various reasons, including terrain, climate, and sectional interest, Secretary of War Jefferson Davis favored the southern route and encouraged the Gadsden Purchase. Any other route, moreover, would go through the Indian country which stretched from Texas to the Canadian border.

Stephen A. Douglas of Illinois had an even better idea: Chicago ought to be the eastern terminus. Since 1845, therefore, Douglas and others had offered bills for a new territory in the lands west of Missouri and Iowa, bearing the Indian name Nebraska. In January 1854, as chairman of the committee on territories, Senator Douglas reported yet another Nebraska bill which became the Kansas-Nebraska Act. Unlike the others this one included the entire unorganized portion of the Louisiana Purchase to the Canadian border. At this point fateful connections began to transform his proposal from a railroad bill to a proslavery bill. To carry his point Douglas needed the support of southerners, and to win that support he needed to make some concession on slavery. This he did by writing popular sovereignty into the bill in language that specified that "all questions pertaining to slavery in the Territories, and in the new states to be formed therefrom are to be left to the people residing therein, through their appropriate representatives."

It was a clever dodge, since the Missouri Compromise would still exclude slaves until the territorial government had made a decision. Southerners quickly spotted the barrier and Douglas as quickly made two more concessions. He supported an amendment for repeal of the Missouri Compromise insofar as it excluded slavery north of 36°30′, and then agreed to organize two territories, Kansas, west of Missouri; and Nebraska, west of Iowa and Minnesota.

Douglas's motives are unclear. Railroads were surely foremost in his mind, but he was influenced also by the desire to win support for his bill in the South, by the hope that popular sovereignty would quiet the slavery issue and open the Northwest, or by a chance to split the Whigs. But he had blundered, had damaged his presidential chances, and had set his country on the road to civil war. The tragic flaw in his plan was his failure to appreciate the depth of antislavery feelings. Douglas himself preferred that the territories become free. Their climate and geography excluded plantation agriculture, he reasoned, and he could not comprehend how people could get so wrought up over abstract rights. Yet he had in fact opened the possibility that slavery might gain a foothold in Kansas.

The agreement to repeal the Missouri Compromise was less than a week old before six antislavery congressmen published a protest, the "Appeal of the Independent Democrats." The tone of moral indignation that pervaded their protest quickly spread among those who opposed Douglas. The document arraigned his bill "as a gross violation of a sacred pledge," and as "part and parcel of an atrocious plot" to create "a dreary region of despotism, inhabited by masters and slaves." They called upon their fellow citizens to protest against this "atrocious crime."

Across the North editorials, sermons, speeches, and petitions echoed this indignation. What had been radical opinion was fast becoming the common view of people in the North. But Douglas had the votes and,

Stephen Douglas.

once committed, forced the issue with tireless energy. President Pierce impulsively added his support. Southerners lined up behind Douglas, with notable exceptions such as Texas senator Sam Houston, who denounced the violation of two solemn compacts: the Missouri Compromise and the confirmation of the territory to the Indians "as long as grass shall grow and water run." He was not the only one to think of the Indians, however. Federal agents were already busy hoodwinking or bullying Indians into relinquishing their land claims. The Delaware were convinced to relocate to a small reservation and to rest content with an annual payment. Other tribes, such as the Shawnee and Miami, were relocated to the Indian Territory, out of the path of the proposed railroad routes. But Douglas and Pierce whipped reluctant Democrats into line (though about half the northern Democrats refused to yield), pushing the bill to final passage in May by 37 to 14 in the Senate and 113 to 100 in the House.

Very well, many in the North reasoned, if the Missouri Compromise was not a sacred pledge, then neither was the Fugitive Slave Act. On June 2 Boston witnessed the most dramatic demonstration against the act. After several attempts had failed to rescue a fugitive named Anthony Burns, a force of soldiers and marines marched him to a waiting ship through streets lined with people shouting "Kidnappers!" past buildings draped in black, while church bells tolled across the city. The event cost the federal government $14,000. Burns was the last to be returned from Boston, and was himself soon freed through purchase by the black community of Boston.

THE EMERGENCE OF THE REPUBLICAN PARTY   What John Calhoun had called the cords holding the Union together had already begun to part. The national church organizations of Baptists and Methodists, for instance, had split over slavery by 1845. The national parties, which had created mutual interests transcending sectional issues, were beginning to buckle under the strain. The Democrats managed to postpone disruption for yet a while, but their congressional delegation lost heavily in the North, enhancing the influence of the southern wing.

The strain of the Kansas-Nebraska Act, however, soon destroyed the Whig party. Southern Whigs now tended to abstain from voting, while Northern Whigs moved toward two new parties. One was the new American (Know-Nothing) party, which had raised the banner of native Americanism and the hope of serving the patriotic cause of Union. More Northern Whigs joined with independent Democrats and Free Soilers in spontaneous antislavery coalitions with a confusing array of names, including "Anti-Nebraska," "Fusion," and "People's party." These coalitions finally united in 1854 under the name "Republican," evoking the memory of Jefferson. The Know-Nothings and the Republicans, paradoxically, appealed to overlapping constituencies. As the historian David Potter aptly pointed out, "much of the rural, Protestant, puritan-oriented population of the North was sympathetic to antislavery and temperance and nativism and unsympathetic to the hard-drinking Irish Catholics."

"BLEEDING" KANSAS After passage of the Kansas-Nebraska Act, attention swung to the plains of Kansas, where opposing elements gathered to stage a rehearsal for civil war. All agreed that Nebraska would be free, but Kansas soon exposed the potential for mischief in popular sovereignty. The ambiguity of the law, useful to Douglas in getting it passed, only added to the chaos. The people of Kansas were "perfectly free to form and regulate their domestic institutions in their own way, subject only to the Constitution." That in itself invited conflicting interpretations, but the law was completely silent as to the time of decision, adding to each side's sense of urgency about getting control of the territory.

The settlement of Kansas therefore differed from the usual pioneering efforts. Groups sprang up North and South to hurry right-minded settlers westward. The first and best known was the New England Emigrant Aid Society. During 1855 and 1856 it sent fewer than 1,250 colonists, but its example encouraged other groups and individuals to follow suit. Southern efforts of the same kind centered in Missouri, which was separated from Kansas only by a surveyor's line. When Kansas's first governor arrived in October 1854, he found several thousand settlers already on the ground. He ordered a census and scheduled an election for a territorial legislature in March 1855. When the election took place, several thousand "Border Ruffians" crossed over from Missouri, illegally swept the polls for proslavery forces, and vowed to kill every "God-damned abolitionist in the Territory." The governor denounced the vote as a fraud, but did nothing to alter the results. The legislature so elected expelled the few antislavery members, adopted a drastic slave code, and made it a capital offense to aid a fugitive slave and a felony even to question the legality of slavery in the territory.

Free-state advocates rejected this "bogus" government and moved directly toward application for statehood. In October 1855 a constitutional convention, the product of an extralegal election, met in Topeka, drafted a state constitution excluding both slavery and free blacks from Kansas, and applied for admission to the Union. By March 1856 a free-state "governor" and "legislature" were functioning in Topeka. But the prospect of getting any government to command general authority in Kansas seemed dim, and both sides began to arm. The Emigrant Aid Society was soon in the business of gunrunning as well as helping settlers. The Reverend Henry Ward Beecher's name became especially

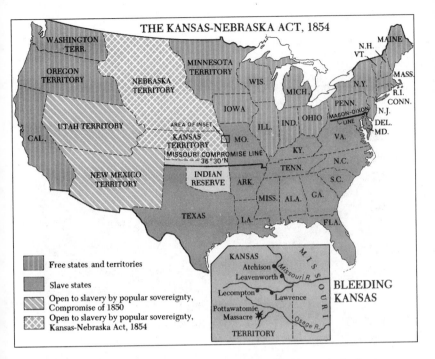

THE KANSAS-NEBRASKA ACT, 1854

WASHINGTON TERR.
OREGON TERRITORY
UTAH TERRITORY
CAL.
NEW MEXICO TERRITORY
NEBRASKA TERRITORY
MINNESOTA TERRITORY
AREA OF INSET
KANSAS TERRITORY
MISSOURI COMPROMISE LINE 36°30'N
INDIAN RESERVE
TEXAS
WIS.
IOWA
MO.
ARK.
LA.
MICH.
ILL.
IND.
OHIO
KY.
TENN.
MISS.
ALA.
GA.
N.H.
VT.
MAINE
N.Y.
MASS.
R.I.
CONN.
PENN.
N.J.
MASON-DIXON LINE
DEL.
MD.
VA.
N.C.
S.C.
FLA.

Free states and territories

Slave states

Open to slavery by popular sovereignty, Compromise of 1850

Open to slavery by popular sovereignty, Kansas-Nebraska Act, 1854

BLEEDING KANSAS

KANSAS
Atchison
Leavenworth
Lecompton
Lawrence
Pottawatomie Massacre
TERRITORY
MISSOURI
Missouri R.
Osage R.

identified with gunrunning because of "Beecher's Bibles," which were rifles supplied by his congregation.

Finally, confrontation began to slip into conflict. In May 1856 a proslavery mob entered the free-state town of Lawrence and destroyed newspaper presses, set fire to the free-state governor's private home, stole property that was not nailed down, and trained five cannon on the Free State Hotel, demolishing it.

The "sack of Lawrence" resulted in just one casualty, but the excitement aroused a fanatical free-soiler named John Brown, who had a history of instability. A companion described him later as one "impressed with the idea that God had raised him up on purpose to break the jaws of the wicked." Two days after the sack of Lawrence, Brown set out with four sons and three other men toward Pottawatomie Creek, site of a proslavery settlement, where they dragged five men from their houses and hacked them to death in front of their screaming families, ostensibly as revenge for the deaths of free-state men.

The Pottawatomie Massacre (May 24–25, 1856) set off a running guerrilla war in the territory that lasted through the fall. On August 30, Missouri ruffians raided the free-state settlement at Ossawatomie. They looted the houses, burned them to the ground, and shot John Brown's son Frederick through the heart. The elder Brown, who barely escaped, looked back at the site being devastated by "Satan's legions," and mut-

Ruins of the Free State Hotel *(Emigrant Aid Company headquarters)*, *Lawrence, Kansas, 1856.*

tered, "God sees it." He then swore to his surviving sons and followers: "I have only a short time to live —only one death to die, and I will die fighting for this cause." Altogether, by the end of 1856 Kansas lost about 200 killed and $2 million in property destroyed during the territorial civil war.

VIOLENCE IN THE SENATE   Violence in Kansas spilled over into Congress, where angry legislators began to trade recriminations, coming to the verge of blows. On May 22, 1856, the day after the sack of Lawrence, two days before the Pottawatomie Massacre, a sudden flash of violence on the Senate floor electrified the whole country. Just two days earlier Senator Charles Sumner of Massachusetts had finished an inflammatory speech on "The Crime against Kansas." Sumner, elected five years earlier by a coalition of Free Soilers and Democrats, displayed a complex mixture of traits: capable at once of eloquence and excess, a man of principle with limited tolerance for opinions different from his own. He had intended his speech to be "the most thorough philippic" ever heard.

What he produced was an exercise in studied insult. The proslavery Missourians who crossed into Kansas, Sumner charged, were "hirelings picked from the drunken spew and vomit of an uneasy civilization." Their treatment of Kansas was "the rape of a virgin territory," he said, "and it may be clearly traced to a depraved longing for a new slave State, the hideous offspring of such a crime. . . ." Senator A. P. Butler of South Carolina became a special target of his censure. Like Don Quixote in choosing Dulcinea, Butler had "chosen a mistress . . . who . . . though polluted in the sight of the world, is chaste in his sight—I mean the harlot, Slavery." Sumner said that Butler betrayed "an incapacity of accuracy," a constant "deviation of truth."

Sumner's rudeness might well have backfired had it not been for Butler's nephew Preston S. Brooks, a fiery-tempered congressman from Edgefield, South Carolina. For two days Brooks brooded over the insult to his uncle, Senator Butler. Knowing that Sumner would refuse a challenge to a duel, he considered but rejected the idea of taking a horsewhip to him. Finally, on May 22 he found Sumner writing at his Senate desk after an adjournment, accused him of libel against South Carolina and Butler, and commenced beating him about the head with a cane while stunned colleagues looked on. Sumner, struggling to rise, wrenched the desk from the floor and collapsed.

Brooks had satisfied his rage, but in doing so had created a martyr for the antislavery cause. Like so many other men in those years, he betrayed the zealot's gift for snatching defeat from the jaws of victory. For two and a half years Sumner's empty seat was a solemn reminder of the violence done to him. Some thought the senator was feigning injury, others that he really was physically disabled. In fact, although his injuries were bad enough, including two gashes to the skull, he seems to have suffered a psychosomatic shock that left him incapable of functioning adequately. When the House censured Brooks, he resigned, went home to Edgefield, and returned after being triumphantly reelected. His admirers presented him with new canes. Southerners

"Bully" Brooks's attack on Charles Sumner.
The incident worsened the strains on the
Union.

who never would have done what Brooks did now hastened to make excuses for him. Northerners who never would have said what Sumner said now hastened to his defense. The news of Sumner's beating drove John Brown "crazy," his eldest son remembered, *"crazy."* Men on each side, appalled at the behavior of the other, decided that North and South had developed into different civilizations with incompatible standards of honor. "I do not see," Emerson confessed, "how a barbarous community and a civilized community can constitute one state. We must either get rid of slavery, or get rid of freedom."

SECTIONAL POLITICS   Within the span of five days in May "Bleeding Kansas," "Bleeding Sumner," and "Bully Brooks" had set the tone for another presidential year. The major parties could no longer evade the slavery issue. Already in February it had split the hopeful American party wide open. Southern delegates, with help from New York, killed a resolution to restore the Missouri Compromise, and nominated Millard Fillmore for president. Later, what was left of the Whig party endorsed the same candidate.

At its first national convention the new Republican party passed over its leading figure, William H. Seward, who was awaiting a better chance in 1860. Following the Whig tradition, they sought out a military hero, John C. Frémont, the "Pathfinder" and leader in the conquest of California. The Republican platform owed much to the Whigs too. It favored a transcontinental railroad and, in general, more internal improvements. It condemned the repeal of the Missouri Compromise, the Democratic policy of expansion, and "those twin relics of barbarism—Polygamy and Slavery." The campaign slogan echoed that of the Free Soilers: "Free soil, free speech, and Frémont." It was the first time a major party platform had taken a stand against slavery.

The Republican position on slavery, the historian Eric Foner has argued, developed from an ideology of free labor. "Political antislavery was not merely a negative doctrine, an attack on southern slavery and the society built on it," Foner wrote; "it was an affirmation of the superiority of the social system of the North—a dynamic expanding capitalist society, whose achievements and destiny were almost wholly the result of the dignity and opportunities which it offered the average laboring man." Such a creed, he argued, could accommodate a variety of opinions on race, economics, or other issues, but it was "an ideology which blended personal and sectional interest with morality so perfectly that it became the most potent political force in the nation."

The Democrats, meeting two weeks earlier in June, had rejected Pierce, the hapless victim of so much turmoil. Douglas too was left out because of the damage done by his Kansas-Nebraska Act. The party therefore turned to James Buchanan of Pennsylvania, who had long

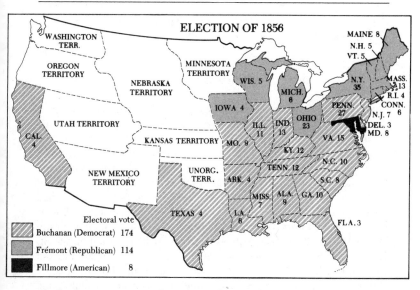

ELECTION OF 1856

Electoral vote

- Buchanan (Democrat) 174
- Frémont (Republican) 114
- Fillmore (American) 8

sought the nomination. The party and its candidate nevertheless hewed to Pierce's policies. The platform endorsed the Kansas-Nebraska Act and nonintervention. Congress, it said, should not interfere with slavery in either states or territories. The party reached out to its newly acquired ethnic voters by condemning nativism and endorsing religious liberty.

The campaign of 1856 resolved itself into two sectional campaigns. The "Black Republicans" had few southern supporters, and only a handful in the border states, where fears of disunion held many Whigs in line. Buchanan thus went into the campaign as the candidate of the only remaining national party. Although Fillmore won a larger vote in the South than Scott had, the slave states were safe for Buchanan. Frémont swept the northernmost states with 114 electoral votes, but Buchanan added five free states to his southern majority for a total of 174: Pennsylvania, New Jersey, Illinois, Indiana, and California, all but the last of which bordered on slave states.

Few presidents before Buchanan had a broader experience in politics and diplomacy. His career went back to 1815, when he started as a Federalist legislator in Pennsylvania before switching to Jackson in the 1820s. He had been over twenty years in Congress, minister to Russia and Britain, and Polk's secretary of state in between. His long quest for the presidency had been built on a southern alliance, and his political debts reinforced his belief that saving the Union depended on concessions to the South. Republicans charged that he lacked the backbone to stand up to the southerners who dominated the Democratic majorities in Congress. His choice of four slave-state and only three free-state men for his cabinet seemed another bad omen.

THE DEEPENING SECTIONAL CRISIS

THE DRED SCOTT CASE An old saying has it that troubles cluster in threes. In 1856 Lawrence, the Brooks-Sumner affair, and Pottawotamie came in quick succession. During Buchanan's first six months in 1857 he encountered the Dred Scott decision, new troubles in Kansas, and a business panic. On March 6, 1857, two days after the inauguration, the Supreme Court rendered a decision in the long-pending case of *Dred Scott v. Sandford*. Dred Scott, born a slave in Virginia about 1800, had been taken to St. Louis and sold to an army surgeon, who took him as body servant to Fort Armstrong, Illinois, then to Fort Snelling in the Wisconsin Territory (later Minnesota), and finally returned him to St. Louis in 1838. After his master's death in 1843 Scott apparently had tried to buy his freedom. In 1846, with help from white friends, he brought suit in Missouri courts claiming that residence in Illinois and the Wisconsin Territory had made him free. A jury decided in his favor, but the state supreme court ruled against him. When the case rose on appeal to the Supreme Court, the country anxiously awaited its opinion on the issue of slavery in the territories.

Each of the nine justices filed a separate opinion, except one who concurred with Chief Justice Roger B. Taney of Maryland. By different lines of reasoning seven justices ruled that Scott remained a slave. The aging Taney, whose opinion stood as the opinion of the Court, ruled that Scott lacked standing in court because he lacked citizenship. Taney argued that one became a federal citizen either by birth or by naturalization, which ruled out any former slave. He further argued that no state had ever accorded citizenship to blacks—a statement demonstrably in error. At the time the Constitution was adopted, Taney further said, blacks "had for more than a century been regarded as . . . so far inferior, that they had no rights which the white man was bound to respect."

To nail down further the definition of Scott's status, Taney moved to a second major question. Residency in a free state had not freed Scott since, in line with precedent, the decision of the state court governed. This left the question of residency in a free territory. On this point Taney argued that the Missouri Compromise had deprived citizens of property in slaves, an action "not warranted by the constitution." He strongly implied, but never said explicitly, that the compromise had violated the due-process clause of the Fifth Amendment, as Calhoun had earlier argued. The upshot was that the Supreme Court had declared

Dred Scott (left) and Chief Justice Roger B. Taney (right). The Supreme Court's decision on Dred Scott's suit for freedom fanned the flames of discord.

an act of Congress unconstitutional for the first time since *Marbury v. Madison* (1803), and a major act for the first time ever. Congress had repealed the Missouri Compromise in the Kansas-Nebraska Act three years earlier, but the decision now challenged popular sovereignty. If Congress itself could not exclude slavery from a territory, then presumably neither could a territorial government created by act of Congress.

By this decision the Supreme Court had thought to settle a question that Congress had dodged ever since the Wilmot Proviso surfaced. But far from settling it, they had only fanned the flames of dissension. Little wonder that Republicans protested: the Court had declared their program unconstitutional. It had also reinforced the suspicion that the slavocracy was hatching a conspiracy. Were not all but one of the justices who joined Taney southerners? And had not Buchanan chatted with the chief justice at the inauguration and then urged the people to accept the early decision as a final settlement, "Whatever this may be"? (Actually, Buchanan already knew the outcome because two other justices had spilled the beans in private letters.) Besides, if Dred Scott were not a citizen and had no standing in court, there was no case before it. The majority ruling was an *obiter dictum*—a statement not essential to deciding the case and therefore not binding, "entitled to just so much moral weight as would be the judgment of a majority of those congregated in any Washington bar-room."

Proslavery elements, of course, greeted the Court's opinion as binding. Now the fire-eaters among them were emboldened to yet another demand. It was not enough to deny Congress the right to interfere with slavery in the territories; Congress had an obligation to protect the property of slaveholders, making a federal slave code the next step. The idea, first broached by Alabama Democrats in the "Alabama Platform" of 1848, soon became orthodox southern doctrine.

THE LECOMPTON CONSTITUTION   Out in Kansas, meanwhile, the struggle continued. Just before Buchanan's inauguration the proslavery legislature called an election of delegates to a constitutional convention. Since no provision was made for a referendum on the constitution, the governor vetoed the measure and the legislature overrode his veto. The Kansas governor resigned on the day Buchanan took office, and the new president replaced him with Robert J. Walker. A native Pennsylvanian who had made a political career in Mississippi and a former member of Polk's cabinet, Walker had greater prestige than his predecessors, and like contemporaries such as Houston of Texas, Foote of Mississippi, and Benton of Missouri, put the Union above slavery in his scale of values. In Kansas he scented a chance to advance the cause of both the Union and his party. Under popular sovereignty, fair elections would produce a state that was both free and Democratic.

Walker arrived in May 1857, and, with Buchanan's approval, pledged to the free-state elements that the new constitution would be submitted to a fair vote. But in spite of his pleas, he arrived too late to persuade free-state men to vote for convention delegates in elections they were sure had been rigged against them. Later, however, Walker did persuade the free-state leaders to vote in the October election of a new territorial legislature.

As a result a polarity arose between an antislavery legislature and a proslavery constitutional convention. The convention, meeting at Lecompton, drew up a constitution under which Kansas would become a slave state. A referendum on the document was cunningly contrived so that voters could not vote against the proposed constitution. They could only accept it "with slavery" or "with no slavery," and even the latter meant that property in slaves already in Kansas would "in no measure be interfered with." The vote was set for December 21, 1857, with rules and officials chosen by the convention.

Although Kansas had only about 200 slaves at the time, free-state men boycotted the election on the claim that it too was rigged. At this point President Buchanan took a fateful step. Influenced by southern advisers and politically dependent upon southern congressmen, he decided to renege on his pledge to Walker and support the action of the Lecompton Convention. Walker resigned and the election went according to form: 6,226 for the constitution with slavery, 569 for the constitution without slavery. Meanwhile, the acting governor had convened the antislavery legislature, which called for another election to

President James Buchanan, whose support of the Lecompton constitution drove another wedge into the Democratic party.

vote the Lecompton constitution up or down. The result on January 4, 1858, was overwhelming: 10,226 against the constitution, 138 for the constitution with slavery, 24 for the constitution without slavery.

The combined results suggested a clear majority against slavery, but Buchanan stuck to his support of the Lecompton constitution, driving another wedge into the Democratic party. Senator Douglas, up for reelection, could not afford to run as a champion of Lecompton. He broke dramatically with the president in a tense confrontation, but Buchanan persisted in trying to drive Lecompton "naked" through the Congress. In the Senate, administration forces held firm, and in March 1858 Lecompton was passed. In the House, enough anti-Lecompton Democrats combined to put through an amendment for a new and carefully supervised popular vote in Kansas. Enough senators went along to permit passage of the House bill. Southerners were confident the vote would favor slavery, because to reject slavery the voters would have to reject the constitution, which would postpone statehood until the population reached 90,000. On August 2, 1858, Kansas voters nevertheless rejected Lecompton by 11,300 to 1,788. With that vote Kansas, now firmly in the hands of its antislavery legislature, largely ended its role in the sectional controversy.

THE PANIC OF 1857   The third crisis of Buchanan's first half year in office, a financial crisis, broke in August 1857. It was brought on by a reduction in demand for American grain caused by the end of the Crimean War (1854–1856), a surge in manufacturing that outran the growth of markets, and the continued weakness and confusion of the state banknote system. Failure of the Ohio Life Insurance and Trust

Company on August 24, 1857, precipitated the panic, which was followed by a depression from which the country did not emerge until 1859.

Everything in those years seemed to get drawn into the vortex of sectional conflict, and business troubles were no exception. Northern businessmen tended to blame the depression on the Democratic Tariff of 1857, which had set rates on imports at their lowest level since 1816. The agricultural South weathered the crisis better than the North. Cotton prices fell, but slowly, and world markets for cotton quickly recovered. The result was an exalted notion of King Cotton's importance to the world, and apparent confirmation of the growing argument that the southern system was superior to the free-labor system of the North.

DOUGLAS VS. LINCOLN   Amid the recriminations over Dred Scott, Kansas, and the depression, the center could not hold. The Lecompton battle put severe strains on the most substantial cord of Union that was left, the Democratic party. To many, Douglas seemed the best hope, one of the few remaining Democratic leaders with support in both sections. But now Douglas was being whipsawed between the extremes. Kansas-Nebraska had cast him in the role of "doughface," a southern sympathizer. His opposition to Lecompton, the fraudulent fruit of popular sovereignty, however, had alienated him from Buchanan's southern junta. But for all his flexibility and opportunism, Douglas had convinced himself that popular sovereignty was a point of principle, a bulwark of democracy and local self-government. In 1858 he faced reelection to the Senate against the opposition of Buchanan Democrats and Republicans. The year 1860 would give him a chance for the presidency, but first he had to secure his home base in Illinois.

To oppose him Illinois Republicans named Abraham Lincoln of Springfield, the lanky, rawboned former Whig state legislator and one-term congressman, a moderately prosperous small-town lawyer. Lincoln's early life had been the hardscrabble existence of the frontier farm. Born in a Kentucky log cabin in 1809, raised on frontier farms in Indiana and Illinois, the young Lincoln had the wit and will to rise above his coarse beginnings. With less than twelve months of sporadic schooling he learned to read, studied such books as came to hand, and eventually developed a prose style as muscular as the man himself. He worked at various farm tasks, operated a ferry, and made two trips down to New Orleans as a flatboatman. Striking out on his own, he managed a general store in New Salem, Illinois, learned surveying, served in the Black Hawk War (1832), won election to the legislature in 1834 at the age of twenty-five, read law, and was admitted to the bar in 1836.

As a Whig regular, Lincoln adhered to the economic philosophy of Henry Clay. He abhorred slavery but was no abolitionist. He did not believe the two races could coexist as equals. But he did oppose any further extension of slavery into new territories, assuming that over time it would die a "natural death." Slavery, he said in the 1840s, was a vexing but "minor question on its way to extinction." Lincoln stayed in the legislature until 1842, and in 1846 won a term in Congress. After a single term he retired from active politics to cultivate his law practice.

In 1854 the Kansas-Nebraska debate drew Lincoln back into the political arena. When Douglas appeared in Springfield to defend popular sovereignty, Lincoln spoke in refutation from the same platform. In Peoria he repeated the performance of what was known thereafter as the "Peoria speech." This speech began the journey toward his appointment with destiny, preaching an old but oft-neglected doctrine: hate the sin but not the sinner.

> When Southern people tell us they are no more responsible for the origin of slavery, than we; I acknowledge the fact. When it is said that the institution exists; and that it is very difficult to get rid of it, in any satisfactory way, I can understand and appreciate the saying. . . .
>
> But all this, to my judgment, furnishes no more excuses for permitting slavery to go into our own free territory, than it would for reviving the African slave trade by law.

At first Lincoln held back from the rapidly growing Republican party, but in 1856 he joined them, getting over 100 votes for their vice-presidential nomination, and gave some fifty speeches for the Frémont ticket in Illinois and nearby states. By 1858 he was the obvious choice to oppose Douglas for the Senate seat, and Douglas knew he was up against a formidable foe. Lincoln resorted to the classic ploy of the underdog: he challenged the favorite to debate with him. Douglas had little relish for drawing attention to his opponent, but agreed to meet him in seven places around the state.

Thus the legendary Lincoln-Douglas debates took place, August 21 to October 15, 1858. As they mounted the platform, the two men could not have presented a more striking contrast in appearance. Lincoln was well over six feet tall, sinewy, and craggy-featured, with a singularly long neck and deep-set, brooding, even melancholy eyes. Unassuming in manner, dressed in homely, well-worn clothes, and walking with a shambling gait, he lightened his essentially serious demeanor with a refreshing sense of humor. To sympathetic observers he conveyed an air of simplicity, sincerity, and common sense. Douglas, on the other hand, was short, rotund, bulb-nosed, stern, and cocky, attired in the finest custom-tailored suits, and possessed of supreme self-confidence. A man of considerable abilities and even greater ambition, he strutted to the platform with the pugnacious air of a predestined champion.

At the time and since, much attention focused on the second debate, at Freeport, where Lincoln asked Douglas how he could reconcile popular sovereignty with the Dred Scott ruling that citizens had the right to carry slaves into any territory. Douglas's answer, thenceforth known as the Freeport Doctrine, was to state the obvious. Whatever the Supreme Court might say about slavery, it could not exist anywhere unless supported by local police regulations.

Douglas tried to set some traps of his own. It is standard practice, of course, to put extreme constructions upon an adversary's stand. Douglas intimated that Lincoln belonged to the fanatical sect of abolitionists who planned to carry the battle to the slave states, just as Lincoln intimated the opposite about Douglas. Douglas accepted, without any apparent qualms, the conviction of black inferiority that most whites, North and South, shared at the time, and sought to pin on Lincoln the stigma of advocating racial equality. The question was a hot potato, which Lincoln handled with caution. There was "A physical difference between the white and black races," and it would "forever forbid the two races living together on terms of social and political equality," he said. He simply favored the containment of slavery where it existed so that "the public mind shall rest in the belief that it is in the course of ultimate extinction." But the basic difference between the two men, Lincoln insisted, lay in Douglas's professed indifference to the moral question of slavery: "He says he 'don't care whether it is voted up or voted down' in the territories. . . . Any man can say that who does not see anything wrong in slavery, but no man can logically say it who does see a wrong in it; because no man can logically say he don't care whether a wrong is voted up or down. . . ."

If Lincoln had the better of the argument, at least in the long view, Douglas had the better of the election. Still according to the Constitution, the voters actually had to choose a legislature, which would then elect the senator. Lincoln men won the larger total vote, but its distribution gave Douglas the legislature, 54 to 41. As the returns trickled in from the fall elections in 1858 —there was still no common election date —they recorded one loss after another for Buchanan men. When they were over, the administration had lost control of the House. But the new Congress would not meet in regular session until December 1859.

STORM WARNINGS   After the Lecompton fiasco the slavery issue was no longer before Congress in any direct way. The gradual return of prosperity in 1859 offered hope that the storms of the 1850s might yet pass. But the sectional issue still haunted the public mind, and like lightning on the horizon, warned that a storm was still pending. In the spring of 1859 there was a warning flash. The Supreme Court finally ruled in the case of *Ableman v. Booth,* which had arisen in 1854 when an abolitionist editor in Milwaukee, Sherman M. Booth, roused a mob to rescue a fugitive slave. Convicted in federal court of violating the Fugitive Slave Act, he got the Wisconsin supreme court to order him freed on the ground that the act was unconstitutional. A unanimous Supreme Court made short work of Wisconsin's interposition. Chief Justice Taney's opinion denied the right of state courts to interfere and reaffirmed the constitutionality of the Fugitive Slave Act. The Wisconsin legislature in turn responded with states'-rights resolutions that faintly echoed the Virginia and Kentucky Resolutions of 1798–1799.

The episode, like others at the time, illustrated the significant fact that both North and South seized on nationalism or states' rights for their own purposes—neither was a point on which many people could claim consistency. Since the early 1840s the Garrisonian abolitionists had openly championed disunion, but they were a small, if vocal, minority in the North. In the South few denied a state's right to dissolve the bond of Union in the same way that the original states had ratified it. And as the South became increasingly a conscious minority, beset by antislavery forces and aware of its growing isolation in the Western world, more and more were willing to consider secession a possibility. By 1855, when Peru acted to abolish slavery, the peculiar institution was left only in Brazil, in the Spanish colonies of Cuba and Puerto Rico, in the Dutch colonies of Guiana and the West Indies, and in the American South.

JOHN BROWN'S RAID   For a season sectional agitations were held in check. But in October 1859 John Brown once again surfaced. Since the Pottawatomie Massacre in 1856, he had led a furtive existence, engaging in fund-raising and occasional bushwhacking. His commitment to abol-

John Brown.

ish the "wicked curse of slavery," meanwhile, had intensified to a fever pitch. Self-righteous and demanding, he was a man driven by a fanatical sense of crusading zeal. His penetrating gray eyes, flowing beard, and religious certainty evoked images of a vengeful Abraham and struck fear into supporters and opponents alike.

Finally, on October 16, 1859, Brown was ready for his supreme gesture. From a Maryland farm he crossed the Potomac with nineteen men, including five blacks, and under cover of darkness occupied the federal arsenal in Harper's Ferry, Virginia (now West Virginia). His notion seems to have been that he would arm the many slaves who would flock to his cause, set up a black stronghold in the mountains of western Virginia, and provide a nucleus of support for slave insurrections across the South.

What he actually did was to take the arsenal by surprise, seize a few hostages, and hole up in the engine house until he was surrounded by militiamen and townspeople. The next morning Brown sent his son Watson and another supporter out under a white flag, but the enraged crowd shot them both. Intermittent shooting continued, and another Brown son was wounded. He begged his father to kill him so as to end his suffering, but the righteous Brown, befuddled and distraught by the unexpected collapse of his glorious insurrection, lashed out: "If you must die, die like a man." A few minutes later the son was dead.

That night Lieutenant-Colonel Robert E. Lee, U.S. Cavalry, arrived with his aide, Lieutenant J. E. B. Stuart, and a force of marines. The following morning, on October 18, Stuart and his troops broke down the barricaded doors and rushed into the engine room. A young lieutenant found Brown kneeling with his rifle cocked. Before the pious patriarch could fire, the marine plunged his dress sword into him with such force that the blade bent back double. He then used the hilt to beat Brown unconscious. By then the siege was over. Altogether Brown's men killed four people (including one marine) and wounded nine. Of their own force, ten died (including two of Brown's sons), seven were captured, and five escaped.

Brown was turned over to Virginia authorities, quickly tried for treason against the state and conspiracy to incite insurrection, convicted on October 31, and hanged on December 2 at Charlestown. Six others died on the gallows later. If Brown had failed in his purpose—whatever it was—he had achieved two things. He had become a martyr for the antislavery cause, and he had set off panic throughout the slaveholding South. At his sentencing he delivered one of the classic American speeches: "Now, if it is deemed necessary that I should forfeit my life for the furtherance of the ends of justice, and mingle my blood further with the blood of my children and with the blood of millions in this slave country whose rights are disregarded by wicked, cruel, and unjust enactments, I say, let it be done."

When Brown, still unflinching, met his end, there were solemn observances in the North. Prominent Republicans, including Lincoln and Seward, repudiated Brown's coup, but the discovery of Brown's correspondence revealed that he had enjoyed support among prominent antislavery leaders who, whether or not they knew at the time what they were getting into, later defended his deeds. "That new saint," Ralph Waldo Emerson said, "will make the gallows as glorious as the cross." William Lloyd Garrison, the lifelong pacifist, now wished "success to every slave insurrection at the South and in every slave country."

By far the gravest aftereffect of Brown's raid was to leave southerners in no mood to distinguish between John Brown and the Republican party. The southern mind now merged those who would contain slavery with those who would drown it in blood. All through the fall and winter of 1859–1860 rumors of conspiracy and insurrection swept the region. Every northern visitor, commercial traveler, or schoolteacher came under suspicion, and many were driven out. "We regard every man in our midst an enemy to the institutions of the South," said the Atlanta *Confederacy*, "who does not boldly declare that he believes African slavery to be a social, moral, and political blessing."

The Center Comes Apart

When the first session of the new Congress convened three days after the death of John Brown, the Democrats still controlled the Senate, but the House once again was thrown into deadlock over the choice of a Speaker. John Sherman of Ohio, the Republican candidate for Speaker, had committed the unforgivable sin in southern eyes of supporting the distribution of Hinton R. Helper's *The Impending Crisis of the South* (1857). Helper was a former North Carolinian who sought to demonstrate that slavery had impoverished non-slaveholding white southerners. The issue of "Helperism" kept enough votes from Sherman to prevent his selection. The House finally turned to William Pennington of New Jersey, an old Whig who supported the Fugitive Slave Act but also favored exclusion of slavery from the territories. He soon lined up with the Republicans. On the day after Pennington's election as Speaker, Jefferson Davis stood up in the Senate to introduce a set of resolutions for the defense of slavery, the main burden of which was a demand that the federal government extend "all needful protection" to slavery in the territories. Davis in effect asked for a federal slave code.

PROGRESSIVE DEMOCRACY—PROSPECT OF A SMASH UP.

Prospect of a Smash Up. *This 1860 cartoon shows the Democratic party—the last remaining national party—about to be split by sectional differences and the onrushing Republicans led by Lincoln.*

THE DEMOCRATS DIVIDE   Thus amid emotional hysteria and impossible demands the nation ushered in the year of another presidential election, destined to be the most fateful in its history. Four years earlier, in a moment of euphoria, the Democrats had settled on Charleston, South Carolina, as the site for their 1860 convention. Charleston in April, with the azaleas ablaze, was perhaps the most enticing city in the United States, but the worst conceivable place for such a meeting, except perhaps Boston. It was a hotbed of extremist sentiment, and lacked adequate accommodations for the crowds thronging in. South Carolina itself had chosen a remarkably moderate delegation, but the extreme southern-rights men held the upper hand in the delegations from the Gulf states.

Douglas men reaffirmed the platform of 1856, which simply promised congressional noninterference with slavery. Southern firebrands, however, were now demanding federal protection for slavery in the territories. Buchanan supporters, hoping to stop Douglas, encouraged the strategy. The platform debate reached a heady climax when the Alabama fire-eater William Yancey informed the northern Democrats that their error had been the failure to defend slavery as a positive good. An Ohio senator offered a blunt reply: "Gentlemen of the South," he said, "you mistake us—you mistake us. We will not do it."

When the southern planks lost, Alabama's delegates walked out of the convention, followed by those representing the other Gulf states, Georgia, South Carolina (except for two stubborn upcountry Unionists), and parts of the delegations from Arkansas and Delaware. This pattern foreshadowed with some fidelity the pattern of secession, in which the Deep South left the Union first. The convention then decided to leave the overwrought atmosphere of Charleston and reassemble in Baltimore on June 18. The Baltimore convention finally nominated Douglas on the 1856 platform. The Charleston seceders met first in Richmond, then in Baltimore, where they adopted the slave-code platform defeated in Charleston, and named Vice-President John C. Breckinridge of Kentucky for president. Thus another cord of union had snapped: the last remaining national party had fragmented.

LINCOLN'S ELECTION   The Republicans meanwhile gathered in Chicago. There everything suddenly came together for "Honest Abe" Lincoln, "the Railsplitter," the uncommon common man. Lincoln had suddenly emerged in the national view during his senatorial campaign two years before, and had since taken a stance designed to make him available for the nomination. He was strong enough on the containment of slavery to satisfy the abolitionists, yet moderate enough to seem less threatening than they were. In February 1860 he had gone east to address an audience of influential Republicans at the Cooper Union in New York City, where he emphasized his view of slavery "as an evil, not to be extended, but to be tolerated and protected only because of and so far as its actual presence among us makes that toleration and protection a necessity."

Chicago provided surroundings that gave Lincoln's people many advantages. His managers, for instance, could pack the galleries with

Abraham Lincoln, Republican candidate for president, June, 1860.

noisy supporters. They started out with little more support than the Illinois delegation, but worked to make Lincoln everybody else's second choice. William H. Seward was the early leader, but he had been tagged, perhaps wrongly, as an extremist for his earlier statements about an "irrepressible conflict" and a "higher law." On the first ballot Lincoln finished in second place. On the next ballot he drew almost even with Seward, and when he came within one and a half votes of a majority on the third count, Ohio quickly switched four votes to put him over the top. Later the same day Senator Hannibal Hamlin of Maine, a former Democrat, became the vice-presidential nominee.

The platform foreshadowed future policy better than most. It denounced John Brown's raid as "among the gravest of crimes," and promised the "maintenance inviolate of the right of each state to order and control its own domestic institutions." The party reaffirmed its resistance to the extension of slavery, and in an effort to gain broader support, endorsed a protective tariff for manufacturers, free homesteads for farmers, a more liberal naturalization law, and internal improvements, including a Pacific railroad. With this platform Republicans made a strong appeal to eastern businessmen, western farmers, and the large immigrant population.

Both major conventions revealed that opinion tended to become more radical in the upper North and Deep South. Attitude followed latitude. In the border states a sense of moderation, perhaps due to the fear that they would bear the brunt of any calamity, aroused the diehard Whigs there to make one more try at reconciliation. Meeting in Baltimore a week before the Republicans met in Chicago, they reorganized into the Constitutional Union party and named John Bell of Tennessee for president. Their only platform was "the Constitution of the Country, the Union of the States, and the Enforcement of the Laws."

Of the four candidates, not one was able to command a national following, and the campaig evolved into a choice between Lincoln and Douglas in the North, Breckinridge and Bell in the South. One consequence of these separate campaigns was that each section gained a false impression of the other. The South never learned to distinguish Lincoln from the radicals; the North failed to gauge the force of southern intransigence—and in this Lincoln was among the worst. He stubbornly refused to offer the South assurances or to amplify his position, which he said was a matter of public record.

The one man who tried to break through the veil that was falling between the sections was Douglas, who tried to mount a national campaign. Only forty-seven, but already weakened by drink, ill health, and disappointments, he wore himself out in one final glorious campaign. Early in October 1860, at Cedar Rapids, Iowa, he learned of Republican state victories in Pennsylvania and Indiana. "Mr. Lincoln is the next

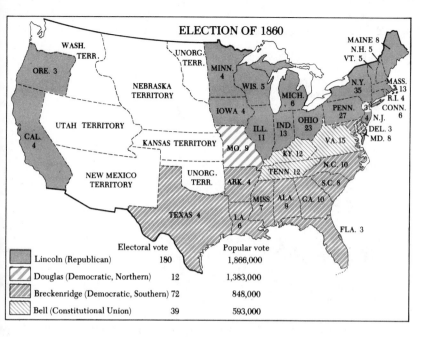

ELECTION OF 1860

	Electoral vote	Popular vote
Lincoln (Republican)	180	1,866,000
Douglas (Democratic, Northern)	12	1,383,000
Breckenridge (Democratic, Southern)	72	848,000
Bell (Constitutional Union)	39	593,000

President," he said. "We must try to save the Union. I will go South." Down through the hostile areas of Tennessee, Georgia, and Alabama Douglas carried appeals on behalf of the Union. "I do not believe that every Breckinridge man is a disunionist," he said, "but I do believe that every disunionist is a Breckinridge man." He was in Mobile when the election came.

By midnight of November 6 Lincoln's victory was clear. In the final count he had about 39 percent of the total popular vote, but a clear majority with 180 votes in the electoral college. He carried every one of the eighteen free states, and by a margin enough to elect him even if the votes for the other candidates had been combined. Among all the candidates, only Douglas had electoral votes from both slave and free states, but his total of 12 was but a pitiful remnant of Democratic Unionism. He ran last. Bell took Virginia, Kentucky, and Tennessee for 39 votes, and Breckinridge swept the other slave states to come in second with 72.

SECESSION OF THE DEEP SOUTH Soon after the election the South Carolina legislature, which had assembled to choose the state's electors, set a special election for December 6 to choose delegates to a convention. In Charleston on December 20, 1860, the convention unanimously voted an Ordinance of Secession, declaring the state's ratification of the Constitution repealed and the union with other states dissolved. A Declaration of the Causes of Secession reviewed the threats to slavery, and

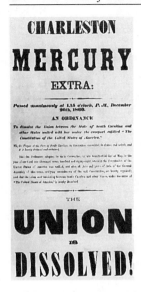

A handbill announcing South
Carolina's secession from the Union.

asserted that a sectional party had elected to the presidency a man
"whose opinions and purposes are hostile to slavery," who had declared
"Government cannot endure permanently half slave, half free," and
"that the public mind must rest in the belief that Slavery is in the course
of ultimate extinction."

By February 1, 1861, six more states had declared themselves out of
the Union. Texas was the last to act because its governor, staunch old
Jacksonian Sam Houston, had refused to assemble the legislature for a
convention call, but secessionist leaders called an irregular convention
that authorized secession. Only there was the decision submitted to a
referendum, which the secessionists carried handily. In some places the
vote for delegates revealed a close division, especially in Georgia and
Louisiana, but secession carried. On February 4 a convention of the
seven states met in Montgomery; on February 7 they adopted a provisional constitution for the Confederate States of America, and two days
later they elected Jefferson Davis its president. He was inaugurated
February 18, with Alexander Stephens of Georgia as vice-president.

In all seven states of the southernmost tier a solid majority had voted
for secessionist delegates, but their combined vote would not have been
a majority of the presidential vote in November. What happened, it
seemed, was what often happens in revolutionary situations: a determined and decisive group acted quickly in an emotionally charged climate and carried its program against a confused and indecisive opposition. Trying to decide whether or not a majority of the whites actually
favored secession probably is beside the point—a majority were vulnerable to the decisive action of the secessionists.

BUCHANAN'S WAITING GAME   History is full of might-have-beens. A bold stroke, even a bold statement, by the lame-duck president at this point might have changed things. "Oh, for one moment of Jackson!" many a Unionist lamented, but there was no Jacksonian will in Buchanan. Besides, a bold stroke might simply have hastened the conflict. No bold stroke came from Lincoln either, nor would he consult with the administration during the long months before his inauguration on March 4. He inclined all too strongly to the belief that secession was just another bluff and kept his public silence.

Buchanan followed his natural bent, the policy on which he had built a career: make concessions, seek a compromise to mollify the South. In his annual message on December 3 Buchanan made a forthright argument that secession was illegal, but that he lacked authority to coerce a state. "Seldom have we known so strong an argument come to so lame and impotent a conclusion," the Cincinnati *Enquirer* editorialized. There was, however, a hidden weapon in the president's reaffirmation of a duty to "take care that the laws be faithfully executed" insofar as he was able. If the president could enforce the law upon all citizens, he would have no need to "coerce" a state. Indeed his position became the policy of the Lincoln administration, which fought a war on the theory that individuals but not states as such were in rebellion.

Buchanan held firmly to his resolve, with some slight stiffening by the end of December 1860, when secession became a fact and the departure of two southerners removed the region's influence in his cabinet. He would retain positions already held, but would make no effort to assert federal authority provocatively. As the secessionists seized federal property, arsenals, and forts, this policy soon meant holding to isolated positions at Fort Pickens in Pensacola Harbor, some remote islands off southern Florida, and Fort Sumter in Charleston Harbor.

On the day after Christmas the small garrison at Fort Moultrie had been moved into the nearly completed Fort Sumter by Major Robert Anderson, a Kentucky Unionist. Anderson's move, designed to achieve both disengagement and greater security, struck South Carolina authorities as provocative, a violation of an earlier "gentleman's agreement" that the administration would make no changes in its arrangements, and commissioners of the newly "independent" state peremptorily demanded withdrawal of all federal forces.

They had overplayed their hand. Buchanan's cabinet, with only one southerner left, insisted it would be a gross violation of duty, perhaps grounds for impeachment, for the president to yield. His backbone thus stiffened, he sharply rejected the South Carolina ultimatum to withdraw: "This I cannot do: this I will not do." His nearest approach to coercion was to dispatch a steamer, *Star of the West,* to Fort Sumter with reinforcements and provisions. As the ship approached Charleston Harbor, Carolina batteries at Fort Moultrie and Morris Island opened fire and drove it away on January 9. It was in fact an act of war, but Buchanan chose to ignore the challenge. He decided instead to hunker down and ride out the remaining weeks of his term, hoping against hope that one of several compromise efforts would yet prove fruitful.

LAST EFFORTS AT COMPROMISE   Forlorn efforts at compromise continued in Congress until dawn of inauguration day. On December 18 Senator John J. Crittenden of Kentucky had proposed a series of amendments and resolutions the central features of which were the recognition of slavery in the territories south of 36°30′ and guarantees to maintain slavery where it already existed. A Senate Committee of Thirteen named to consider the proposal proved unable to agree. A House Committee of Thirty-three under Thomas Corwin of Ohio adopted two concessions to the South: an amendment guaranteeing slavery where it existed and granting statehood to New Mexico, presumably as a slave state. But the committee finished by submitting a set of proposals without endorsing any of them. The fight for a compromise was carried to the floor of each house by Crittenden and Corwin, and subjected to intensive debate during January and February.

Meanwhile a peace conference met in Willard's Hotel in February 1861, at the call of the Virginia legislature. Twenty-one states sent delegates and former president John Tyler presided, but the convention's proposal, substantially the same as the Crittenden Compromise, failed to win the support of either house of Congress. The only compromise proposal that met with any success was Corwin's amendment to guarantee slavery where it existed. Many Republicans, including Lincoln, were prepared to go that far to save the Union, but they were unwilling to repudiate their stand against slavery in the territories. As it happened, after passing the House the amendment passed the Senate without a vote to spare, by 24 to 12, on the dawn of inauguration day. It would have become the Thirteenth Amendment, with the first use of the word "slavery" in the Constitution, but the states never ratified it. When a Thirteenth Amendment was ratified in 1865, it did not guarantee slavery—it abolished slavery.

FURTHER READING

Surveys of the coming of the Civil War include Allan Nevins's *Ordeal of the Union* (2 vols., 1947), David M. Potter's *The Impending Crisis, 1848–1861* (1976),° James M. McPherson's *Battle Cry of Free-*

°These books are available in paperback editions.

dom: The Civil War Era (1988),° and Bruce Levine's *Half Slave and Half Free: The Roots of the Civil War* (1992). Interpretive essays can be studied in Eric Foner's *Politics and Ideology in the Age of the Civil War* (1980)° and Joel H. Silbey's *The Partisan Imperative* (1985).

Numerous works cover the crises of the 1850s. Holman Hamilton's *Prologue to Conflict: The Crisis and Compromise of 1850* (1964) probes that crucial dispute. Michael F. Holt's *The Political Crisis of the 1850s* (1978)° traces the demise of the Whigs. Eric Foner provides an interpretive introduction to how events and ideas combined in the formation of a new political party in *Free Soil, Free Labor, Free Men: The Ideology of the Republican Party before the Civil War* (1970).° Also good on the Republicans are William E. Gienapp's *The Origins of the Republican Party, 1852–1856* (1987), Hans L. Trefousse's *The Radical Republicans: Lincoln's Vanguard for Racial Justice* (1969), and David H. Donald's *Charles Sumner and the Coming of the Civil War* (1960). The economic, social, and political crises of 1857 are examined in Kenneth Stampp's *America in 1857: A Nation on the Brink* (1990).

Robert W. Johannsen's *Stephen A. Douglas* (1973) analyzes the issue of popular sovereignty. A more national perspective is provided in James A. Rawley's *Race and Politics: "Bleeding Kansas" and the Coming of the Civil War* (1969). On the role of John Brown in the sectional crisis, see Stephen B. Oates's *To Purge This Land with Blood: A Biography of John Brown* (2nd ed., 1984).° Two other issues that divided the nation can be studied in Stanley W. Campbell's *The Slave Catchers* (1970),° on attempts to enforce the Fugitive Slave Act, and Don E. Fehrenbacher's *Slavery, Law, and Politics* (1981),° on the Dred Scott case.

An excellent study of the South's journey to secession is William Freehling's *The Road to Disunion* (1990). Studies of southern states include J. Mills Thornton III's *Politics and Power in a Slave Society: Alabama, 1800–1860* (1978),° Michael P. Johnson's *Toward a Patriarchial Republic: The Secession of Georgia* (1977), and Steven A. Channing's *Crisis of Fear: Secession in South Carolina* (1970).° For developments in the border states, see Daniel W. Crofts's *Reluctant Confederates: Upper South Unionists in the Secession Crisis* (1989).

To gauge Lincoln's role in the coming crisis of war, see the biographies listed in Chapter 17; particularly good for Lincoln during the 1850s is Don E. Fehrenbacher's *Prelude to Greatness* (1962). Harry V. Jaffa's *Crisis of the House Divided* (1959) details the Lincoln-Douglas debates, and Richard N. Current's *Lincoln and the First Shot* (1963) treats the Fort Sumter controversy.

°These books are available in paperback editions.

17 ✒

THE WAR OF THE UNION

END OF THE WAITING GAME

During the four long months between his election and inauguration, Lincoln said little about future policies and less about past positions. "If I thought a *repetition* would do any good I would make it," he wrote to an editor in St. Louis. "But my judgment is it would do positive harm. The secessionists *per se,* believing they had alarmed me, would clamor all the louder." So he stayed in Springfield until mid-February 1861, biding his time. He then boarded a train for a long, roundabout trip, and began to drop some hints to audiences along the way. To the New Jersey legislature, which responded with prolonged cheering, he said: "The man does not live who is more devoted to peace than I am. . . . But it may be necessary to put the foot down." At the end of the journey, reluctantly yielding to rumors of plots against his life, he passed unnoticed on a night train through Baltimore and slipped into Washington before daybreak on February 23.

The furtive end to Lincoln's journey reinforced the fears of eastern sophisticates that the man lacked style. Lincoln, to be sure, lacked a formal education and training in the rules of etiquette. His tall frame shambled awkwardly, and he had an unseemly penchant for telling funny stories. But the qualities that had first called him to public attention would soon manifest themselves. His prose, at least, had style— and substance. So did his politics. What Nathaniel Hawthorne called his "Yankee shrewdness" guided him through the traps laid for the unwary in Washington. Whatever else people might think of him, they soon learned that he was not easily dominated.

LINCOLN'S INAUGURATION   Buchanan called for Lincoln at Willard's Hotel on a bright and blustery March 4, 1861. Together they rode in an open carriage to the Capitol. Along the way Buchanan confided to

Lincoln: "If you are as happy, my dear sir, on entering this house as I am in leaving it and returning home, you are the happiest man in the country." In his inaugural address Lincoln repeated his pledge not "to interfere with the institution of slavery in the States where it exists. I believe I have no lawful right to do so, and I have no inclination to do so."

But the immediate question had shifted from slavery to secession, and most of the speech emphasized Lincoln's view that "the Union of these States is perpetual." The Union, he asserted, preceded the Constitution itself, dating from the Articles of Association in 1774. It was "matured and continued" by the Declaration of Independence and the Articles of Confederation. Yet even if the United States were only a contractual association, "no State upon its own mere motion can lawfully get out of the Union." Lincoln promised to hold areas belonging to the government, collect taxes, and deliver the mails unless repelled, but beyond that "there will be no invasion, no using of force against or among the people anywhere." The final paragraph, based on a draft by Seward, offered an eloquent appeal for harmony:

> I am loath to close. We are not enemies, but friends. We must not be enemies. Though passion may have strained, it must not break our bonds of affection. The mystic chords of memory, stretching from every battlefield and patriot grave to every living heart and hearthstone all over this broad land, will yet swell the chorus of the Union, when again touched, as surely they will be, by the better angels of our nature.

Lincoln not only entered office amid the gravest crisis yet faced by a president, but he also faced unusual problems of transition. Republicans, in power for the first time, crowded Washington, hungry for office. Four of the seven new cabinet members had been rivals for the presidency: William H. Seward at State, Salmon P. Chase at the Treasury, Simon Cameron at the War Department, and Edward Bates as attorney-general. Four were former Democrats and three were former Whigs. They formed a group of better-than-average ability, though most were so strong-minded they thought themselves better qualified to lead than Lincoln. Only later did they acknowledge with Seward that "he is the best man among us."

THE FALL OF FORT SUMTER   For the time being Lincoln's combination of firmness and moderation differed little in effect from his predecessor's stance. Harsh judgments of Buchanan's waiting game overlook the fact that Lincoln kept it going. Indeed, his only other choices were to accept secession as an accomplished fact or to use force right away. On the day after he took office, however, word arrived from Charleston that time was running out. Major Anderson, in charge of Fort Sumter, had supplies for a month to six weeks, and Confederates were encircling the fort with a "ring of fire."

Events moved quickly to a climax in the next two weeks. On April 4, 1861, Lincoln decided to resupply the sixty-nine men at Fort Sumter. Two days later he notified the governor of South Carolina that "an attempt will be made to supply Fort Sumter with provisions only. . . ." On April 9 President Jefferson Davis and his cabinet in Montgomery decided against permitting Lincoln to maintain the status quo.

On April 11 Confederate general Pierre G. T. Beauregard, a dapper Creole from Louisiana who had studied artillery under Anderson at West Point, demanded a speedy surrender of Sumter. Major Anderson refused, but said his supplies would be used up in three more days. With the relief ships approaching, Anderson received an ultimatum to yield. He again refused, and at 4:30 A.M. on April 12 the shelling of Fort Sumter began. After more than thirty hours, his ammunition exhausted, Anderson agreed to give up, and on April 14 he lowered the flag. Although over 3,000 shells hit the fort, the only fatalities were two men killed in an explosion during a final salute to the colors, the first in a melancholy train of war dead.

The guns of Charleston signaled the end of the waiting game. "So Civil War is inaugurated at last," observed New York lawyer George Templeton Strong. "God defend the right." Equally committed was South Carolina's Mary Chesnut: "Woe to those who began this war if they were not in bitter earnest." On the day after Anderson's surrender, Lincoln called upon the loyal states to supply 75,000 militiamen to subdue a combination "too powerful to be suppressed by the ordinary course of judicial proceedings." Volunteers rallied around the flag at the recruiting stations. On April 19 Lincoln proclaimed a blockade of southern ports which, as the Supreme Court later ruled, confirmed the existence of war.

TAKING SIDES   In the free states and the Confederate states, Lincoln's proclamation reinforced the patriotic fervor of the day. In the upper South it brought dismay, and another wave of secession that swept four more states into the Confederacy. Many in those states abhorred both abolitionists and secessionists, but faced with a call for troops to suppress their sister states, decided to abandon the Union. Virginia acted first. Its convention passed an Ordinance of Secession on April 17. The Confederate Congress then chose Richmond as its new capital, and the government moved there in June.

Three other states followed Virginia in little over a month: Arkansas on May 6, Tennessee on May 7, and North Carolina on May 20. The Tar Heel State, next to last to ratify the Constitution, was last in secession. All four of the holdout states, especially Tennessee and Virginia,

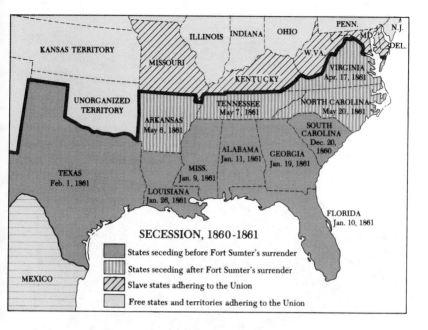

SECESSION, 1860-1861

- States seceding before Fort Sumter's surrender
- States seceding after Fort Sumter's surrender
- Slave states adhering to the Union
- Free states and territories adhering to the Union

had areas (mainly in the mountains) where both slaves and secessionists were scarce and where Union support ran strong. In Tennessee the mountain counties would supply more volunteers to the Union than to the Confederate cause. Unionists in western Virginia, bolstered by a Federal army from Ohio under General George B. McClellan, contrived a loyal government of Virginia that formed a new state. In 1863 Congress admitted West Virginia to the Union with a constitution that provided for gradual emancipation of the few slaves there.

Of the other slave states, Delaware, with but a token number of slaves, remained firmly in the Union, but Maryland, Kentucky, and Missouri went through bitter struggles for control. The secession of Maryland would have isolated Washington within the Confederacy. In fact Baltimore's mayor for a time did cut all connections to the capital. A mob attacked the Sixth Massachusetts Regiment on its way through Baltimore and killed four. To hold the state Lincoln took drastic measures of dubious legality: he suspended the writ of habeas corpus (under which judges could require arresting officers to produce their prisoners and justify their arrest) and rounded up pro-Confederate leaders and threw them in jail. The fall elections ended the threat of Maryland's secession by returning a solidly Unionist majority in the state.

Kentucky, native state of both Lincoln and Davis, harbored divided loyalties. But spring elections for a state convention returned a thumping Unionist majority, and the state legislature proclaimed Kentucky's "neutrality" in the conflict. Lincoln recognized the strategic value of his

U.S. Volunteers Attacked by the Mob, *St. Louis, Missouri, 1861.*

native state, situated on the south bank of the Ohio. "I think to lose Kentucky is nearly the same as to lose the whole game," he said. He promised to leave the state alone so long as the Confederates did likewise, and reassured its citizens that a war against secession was not a war against slavery. Kentucky's fragile neutrality lasted until September 3, when a Confederate force occupied several towns. General Ulysses S. Grant then moved Union soldiers into Paducah. Thereafter, Kentucky, though divided in allegiance, for the most part remained with the Union. It joined the Confederacy, some have said, only after the war.

Lincoln's effort to hold a middle course in Missouri ran afoul of the maneuvers of less patient men in the state. Unionists there had a numerical advantage, but there were many Confederate sympathizers. For a time the state, like Kentucky, kept an uneasy peace. But elections for a convention brought an overwhelming Union victory, while a pro-Confederate militia under the state governor began to gather near St. Louis. In the city Unionist forces rallied, and on May 10 they surprised and disarmed the militia at its camp. They pursued the pro-Confederate forces into the southwestern part of the state, and after a temporary setback on August 10, the Unionists pushed the Confederates back again, finally breaking their resistance at the Battle of Pea Ridge (March 6–8, 1862), just over the state line in Arkansas. Thereafter border warfare continued in Missouri, pitting against each other rival bands of gun-slingers who kept up their feuding and banditry for years after the war was over.

A "BROTHERS' WAR"   Robert E. Lee epitomized the agonizing choice facing many residents of the border states. Son of "Lighthorse Harry" Lee, a Revolutionary War hero, and married to a descendant of Martha Washington, Lee had served in the United States Army for thirty years. Now a colonel and master of Arlington, an estate that faced Washington across the Potomac, he was summoned by General Winfield Scott, another Virginian, and offered command of the Federal forces in the field. After a sleepless night pacing the floor, Lee told Scott that he could not go against his "country," meaning Virginia. Although Lee failed to "see the good of secession," he could not "raise my hand against my birthplace, my home, my children." Lee resigned his commission, retired to his estate, and soon answered a call to the Virginia—later the Confederate—service.

The conflict sometimes became literally a "brothers' war." At Hilton Head, South Carolina, Percival Drayton commanded a Federal gunboat while his brother led Confederate land forces. Franklin Buchanan, who

Soldier group. *Neither side in the Civil War was prepared for the magnitude of this first of "modern" wars.*

commanded the *Virginia* (formerly the *Merrimack*), sank the Union ship *Congress* with his brother on board. John J. Crittenden of Kentucky had a son in each army. J. E. B. Stuart of the Confederate cavalry was chased around the peninsula below Richmond by his Federal father-in-law. Lincoln's attorney-general had a son in the Confederate army, and Mrs. Lincoln herself had a brother, three half-brothers, and three brothers-in-law in the Confederate forces.

Many southerners made great sacrifices to remain loyal to the Union. Some left their native region once the fighting began. Others who remained in the South found ways to support the Union. In every Confederate state except South Carolina, whole regiments were organized to fight for the Union. Some 100,000 men from the southern states fought against the Confederacy. Of course, some of these southern "Tories" changed sides out of expediency rather than loyalty. Confederate soldiers who had been captured occasionally chose to switch sides and serve on the Indian frontier rather than remain in prison.

Others, however, never embraced the Confederate cause. Many of the loyalists were Irish or German immigrants who had no love for slavery or the planter elite. In the Fredericksburg–San Antonio region of Texas, German Americans opposed secession and the war once fighting erupted. The Confederate state government declared six counties in open rebellion in 1862 and sent in troops to suppress Union sentiment. Any German who criticized the Rebel cause was hanged, shot, or whipped. Confederate cavalry units caught one group of Germans trying to escape to Mexico and killed thirty-four of them. In south Texas almost a thousand Texas-Mexicans fought against Confederate troops. Whatever their motives, these and other southern loyalists played a significant role in helping the Union cause.

THE BALANCE OF FORCE

Shrouded in an ever-thickening mist of larger-than-life mythology, the Union triumph in the Civil War has acquired the mantle of inevitability. The Confederacy's fight for independence, on the other hand, has taken on the aura of a romantic lost cause, doomed from the start by the region's sparse industrial development, smaller pool of able-bodied men, paucity of capital resources and warships, and spotty transportation network. But in 1861 the military situation was by no means so clear-cut. For all of the South's obvious disadvantages, it did initially enjoy a captive labor force, superior officers, the prospects of foreign assistance, and the benefits of fighting a defensive campaign on familiar territory. Jefferson Davis and other Confederate leaders were genuinely confident that their cause would prevail on the battlefield. "If we husband our means and make a judicious use of our resources," Davis predicted in 1861, "it would be difficult to fix a limit to the period during which we could conduct a war against the adversary we now encounter." In short, the outcome of the Civil War was not inevitable: it was determined as much by human decisions and human willpower as by physical resources.

ECONOMIC ADVANTAGES   The South seceded in part out of a growing awareness of its minority status in the nation; a balance sheet of the sections in 1860 shows the accuracy of that perception. The Union held twenty-three states, including four border slave states, while the Confederacy had eleven, claiming also Missouri and Kentucky. Ignoring conflicts of allegiance within various states, which might roughly cancel each other out, the population count was about 22 million in the Union to 9 million in the Confederacy, and about 3½ million of the latter were slaves. The Union therefore had an edge of about four to one in potential human resources.

An even greater advantage for the North was its industry. In gross value of manufactures, the Union states had a margin of better than ten to one in 1860. The states that joined the Confederacy produced just 7.4 percent of the nation's manufactures on the eve of the war. What made the disparity even greater was that little of this was in heavy industry. The only iron industry of any size in the Confederacy was the Tredegar Iron Works in Richmond, which had long supplied the United States Army. Tredegar's existence strengthened the Confederacy's will to defend its capital. The Union states, in addition to making most of the country's shoes, textiles, and iron products, turned out 97 percent of the firearms and 96 percent of the railroad equipment. They had most of the trained mechanics, most of the shipping and mercantile firms, and the bulk of the banking and financial resources.

Even in farm production the northern states overshadowed the rural South, for most of the North's population was still rooted in the soil. As the progress of the war upset southern agricultural output, northern farms managed to increase theirs, despite the loss of workers to the army. The Confederacy produced enough to meet minimal needs, but the disruption of transport caused shortages in many places. One consequence was that the North produced a surplus of wheat for export at a time when drought and crop failures in Europe created a critical demand. King Wheat supplanted King Cotton as the nation's main export, becoming the chief means of acquiring foreign money and bills of exchange to pay for imports from abroad.

The North's advantage in transport weighed heavily as the war went on. The Union had more wagons, horses, and ships than the Confederacy, and an impressive edge in railroads: about 20,000 miles to the

South's 10,000. The actual discrepancy was even greater, for southern railroads were mainly short lines built to different gauges (widths), and had few replacements for rolling stock that broke down or wore out. The Confederacy had only one east-west connection, between Memphis and Chattanooga. The latter was an important rail hub with connections via Knoxville into Virginia and down through Atlanta to Charleston and Savannah. But the North already had an extensive railroad network. Three major lines gave western farmers an outlet to the eastern seaboard and greatly lessened their former dependence on the Mississippi River.

MILITARY ADVANTAGES   Against the weight of such odds the wonder is that the Confederacy managed to survive four years. Yet at the start certain factors evened the odds. The most important of these was geography: the Confederates could fight a defensive war on their own territory. In addition, the South initially had more experienced military leaders. A number of circumstances had given rise to a strong military tradition in the South: the long-standing Indian danger, the fear of slave insurrection, and a history of expansionism. Military careers had prestige, and military schools multiplied in the antebellum years, the most notable West Points of the South being The Citadel and Virginia Military Institute. West Point itself drew many southerners, producing an army corps dominated by men from the region, chief among them Winfield Scott. Many northern West Pointers, such as George B. McClellan and Ulysses S. Grant, dropped out of the service for civilian careers. A large proportion of the army's southern officers resigned their commissions to follow their states into the Confederacy. The head of the Louisiana Seminary of Learning and Military Academy (precursor of Louisiana State University), William Tecumseh Sherman, went the other way, rejoining the United States Army.

At the start of the war, Union seapower relied on about 90 ships, though only 42 were in active service and most were at distant stations. But under the able guidance of Secretary Gideon Welles, the Union navy eventually grew to 650 vessels of all types. It never completely sealed off the South, but it raised to desperate levels the hazards of blockade running. On the inland waters navy gunboats and transports played an even more direct role in ultimately securing the Union's control of the Mississippi and its larger tributaries, which provided easy routes into the center of the Confederacy.

EARLY STRATEGIES   Amid the furies of passion after the fall of Fort Sumter, hearts lifted on both sides with the hope that the war might end with one sudden bold stroke, the capture of Washington or the fall of Richmond. Strategic thought at the time remained under the spell of Napoleon, holding that everything would turn on one climactic battle in which a huge force, massed against an enemy's point of weakness, would demoralize its armies and break its will to resist. Such ideas had been instilled in a generation of West Point cadets, but these lessons neglected the massive losses Napoleon had suffered, losses that finally turned his victories into defeat.

General Scott, the seventy-five-year-old commander of the Union army, saw a long road ahead. Being older—his career dated from the War of 1812—he fell under the Napoleonic spell less than others. He proposed to use the navy to blockade the long Atlantic and Gulf coast-lines, and then to divide and subdivide the Confederacy by pushing southward along the main water routes: the Mississippi, Tennessee, and Cumberland Rivers. As word leaked out of Scott's plans, the newspapers impatiently derided his "Anaconda" strategy, which they judged far too slow, indicative of the commander's old age and caution. To the end, however, the Anaconda strategy of attrition remained Union policy: there was no Napoleonic climax.

BULL RUN   The outbreak of war gave Americans on both sides a sudden urgency of purpose that was absent from their daily routines. Caught up in the excitement of military preparation, neither side recognized how deadly earnest the other was; both predicted a quick and easy victory.

Nowhere was this naive optimism more clearly displayed than at the first battle at Bull Run. An eager public pressured both Lincoln and Davis to strike quickly and decisively. Davis allowed the battle-hungry General Beauregard to hurry his main forces in Virginia to the railroad center at Manassas Junction, about twenty-five miles west of Washington. Lincoln decided that General Irvin McDowell's hastily assembled army of some 37,000 might overrun the outnumbered Confederates and quickly march on to Richmond, the Confederate capital. There was a festive mood as hundreds of civilians rode out from Washington to picnic and watch the entertaining spectacle of a one-battle war. Instead they witnessed an entangling web of horror.

It was a hot, dry day on July 21, 1861, when McDowell's forces encountered Beauregard's army dug in behind a meandering little stream called Bull Run. The two generals, who had been classmates at West Point, adopted markedly similar plans—each would try to turn the other's left flank. The Federals almost achieved their purpose early in the afternoon, but reinforcements from canny General Joseph E. Johnston poured in to meet the Union offensive. Amid the fury, a South Carolina officer rallied his men by pointing to Thomas Jackson's brigade of Virginians: "Look, there is Jackson with his Virgini-

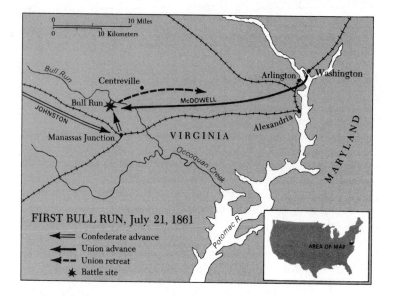

FIRST BULL RUN, July 21, 1861

← Confederate advance
← Union advance
←-- Union retreat
✱ Battle site

ans, standing like a stone wall." The reference thereafter served as his nickname.

After McDowell's last assault had faltered, he decided that discretion was the better part of valor. An orderly retreat in battle is one of the most difficult of maneuvers, and it proved too much for the raw Federal recruits. Their confused, frantic retreat turned into a panic as fleeing soldiers and terrified civilians clogged the Washington road. An Ohio congressman and several colleagues tried to rally the frenzied soldiers. "We called them cowards, denounced them in the most offensive terms, pulled out our heavy revolvers and threatened to shoot them, but in vain; a cruel, crazy, mad, hopeless panic possessed them." Lincoln read a gloomy dispatch from the front: "The day is lost. Save Washington and the remnants of this army. The routed troops will not re-form." Union army veterans remembered their retreat as "the great skedaddle."

Fortunately for the Federals, the Confederates were about as disorganized and exhausted by the battle as the Yankees were, and they failed to give chase. It would have been futile anyway, for the next day a summer downpour turned roads into quagmires. But the rain could not dampen the aroused spirits in the South. A Georgia secessionist proclaimed that the battle at Manassas had been *one of the decisive battles of the world. It has secured our independence.*" He exaggerated. Although some 4,500 men had been killed, wounded, or captured on both sides, the first major battle of the war was hardly decisive.

A MODERN WAR

Bull Run was a sobering experience for both sides. Much of the romance—the splendid uniforms, bright flags, rousing songs—gave way to the agonizing realization that this would be a long, mean, and costly struggle in which many—far too many—would die. *Harper's Weekly* bluntly warned: "From the fearful day at Bull Run dates war. Not polite war, not incredulous war, but war that breaks hearts and blights homes." The sobering Union defeat "will teach us in the first place . . . that this war must be prosecuted on scientific principles."

The Civil War was in many respects the first modern war. Its scope was unprecedented. One out of every twelve adult American males served in the war, and few families were unaffected by the event. Over 620,000 Americans died in the conflict, 50 percent more than in World War II. Because battlefield surgeons were constantly overworked and frequently lacked equipment, supplies, and knowledge, almost any stomach or head wound proved fatal, and gangrene was rampant. Fifty thousand of the survivors returned home with one or more limbs amputated. Disease, however, was the greatest threat to soldiers, killing twice as many as were lost in battle.

The Civil War was not neatly self-contained; it was a total war, fought not solely by professional armies but by and against whole soci-

Thirteen-inch mortars mounted at Battery No. 4 near Yorktown.

eties. Farms became battlefields, cities were transformed into armed encampments, and homes were commandeered for field hospitals. After the battle of Gettysburg, a woman recalled that "wounded men were brought into our house and laid side by side in our halls and first-story rooms . . . carpets were so saturated with blood as to be unfit for further use."

The Civil War was also modern in that much of the killing was distant, impersonal, and mechanical. The opposing forces used an array of new weapons and instruments of war made available by industrial advances: artillery with "rifled" or grooved barrels for greater accuracy, repeating rifles, ironclad ships, the telegraph, observation balloons, trenches, and wire entanglements. Cannons and rifles with grooved barrels soon replaced the conventional smooth-bore weapons, and the new guns were markedly more accurate. Firing the new .58-caliber minié ball, an inch-long bullet invented by a Frenchman, rifles were accurate at 250 yards—five times as far as the old muskets. Either attacking infantrymen were decimated by minié balls or grapeshot, or the defenders simply broke and ran. One general remarked that his soldiers' glittering bayonets were "rarely reddened with blood. The day of the bayonet is passed." Such long-range firepower gave defenders an overwhelming advantage: nine out of ten infantry assaults failed during the conflict.

MILITARY DEADLOCK

MOBILIZING VOLUNTEERS   When secession came, the United States Army numbered only 16,400 men and officers, most of whom were out west. The army remained a separate and very small part of the Union forces. Both sides, in the time-honored American way of war, looked to local militia and volunteers to beef up their armies, and in the beginning were swamped with light-hearted recruits.

Meeting in special session on July 4, 1861, Congress authorized a call for 500,000 more men, and after the Battle of Bull Run (or Manassas)° added another 500,000. By the end of the year the first half million had enlisted as a result mainly of state initiative and in many cases the efforts of groups, towns, and even individuals who raised and equipped regiments. This pell-mell mobilization left the army with a large number of "political" officers, commissioned by state governors or elected by the recruits.

°The Federals most often named battles for natural features, the Confederates for nearby towns, thus Bull Run (Manassas), Antietam (Sharpsburg), Stone's River (Murfreesboro), and the like.

Enlisting Union soldiers among Irish and German immigrants in New York, 1864.

Unlike today's army, the nineteenth-century army often organized its units along community and ethnic lines. The Union army, for example, included a Scandinavian regiment (the 15th Wisconsin Infantry), a Scottish Highlander unit (the 79th New York Infantry), a French regiment (the 55th New York Infantry), and a mixed unit of Poles, Hungarians, Germans, Spanish, and Italians (the 39th New York Infantry). There were also many German and Irish units. In the Confederate armies, large numbers of Germans served in Texas units. Some 2,500 Texas-Mexicans ("Tejanos") fought for the Rebel cause.

In the Confederacy, the first mass enlistment put a great strain on limited means. In March Davis was empowered to call 100,000 twelve-month volunteers and to employ state militia up to six months. In May, once the fighting had started, he was authorized to raise up to 400,000 three-year volunteers "without the delay of a formal call upon the respective states." Thus by early 1862, most of the veteran Confederate soldiers were nearing the end of their terms without having encountered much significant action. They were also resisting the incentives of bonuses and furloughs for reenlistment.

THE DRAFT   The Confederates adopted conscription first. By act of April 16, 1862, all white male citizens, eighteen to thirty-five, were declared members of the army for three years, and those already in service were required to serve out three years. In September 1862 the upper age was raised to forty-five, and in February 1864 the age limits were further extended to cover all from seventeen to fifty, with those under eighteen and over forty-five reserved for state defense.

Comprehensive as the law appeared on its face, it included two loopholes. First, a draftee might escape service either by providing an able-bodied substitute not of draft age or by paying $500 in commutation. Second, exemptions, designed to protect key civilian work, were all too subject to abuse by men seeking "bombproof" jobs. Exemption of state officials, for example, was flagrantly abused by the governors of Georgia and North Carolina, who were in charge of defining the vital jobs. The exclusion of teachers with twenty pupils inspired a sudden educational renaissance, and the exemption of one white man for each plantation with twenty or more slaves led to bitter complaints about "a rich man's war and a poor man's fight."

The Union took nearly another year to decide that volunteers would be too few after the first excitement. After flirting with conscription legislation in 1862, Congress finally acted in March 1863 to draft men aged twenty to forty-five. Exemptions were granted to specified federal and state officeholders and to others on medical or compassionate grounds, but one could still buy a substitute or, for $300, have one's service commuted. In both the North and the South conscription spurred men to volunteer, either to collect bounties or to avoid the disgrace of being drafted. Eventually the draft in the North produced about 46,000 conscripts and 118,000 substitutes, or only 6 percent of the Union armies.

The draft flouted an American tradition of voluntary service and was widely held to be arbitrary and unconstitutional. In the South the draft also sullied the cause of states' rights by requiring the exercise of a central power. It might have worked better had it operated through the states, some of which had set up their own drafts to meet the calls of President Davis. The governor of Georgia, who had one of the best records for raising troops at first, turned into a bitter critic of the draft, pronouncing it unconstitutional and trying to obstruct its enforcement. Few of the other governors gave it unqualified support, and Vice-President Stephens remained unreconciled to it throughout the war.

Widespread opposition limited enforcement of the draft acts both North and South. In New York City, which had long enjoyed commercial ties with the South, the announcement of a draft lottery on July 11, 1863, led to a week of rioting in which roving bands of immigrant working-class toughs took control of the streets. Although provoked by opposition to the draft, the riots exposed and crystallized emerging racial and ethnic tensions. The mobs assaulted conscription offices, factories, docks, and the homes of prominent Republicans. But they directed their wrath most furiously at blacks. In their tortured reasoning, they blamed blacks for causing the war and for threatening their own unskilled jobs. A white abolitionist watched in horror from her window as the "strange, wretched, abandoned creatures that flocked out from their dens and lairs" fell upon the city's black neighborhoods:

> A child of 3 years of age was thrown from a 4th story window and instantly killed. A woman one hour after her confinement was set upon and beaten with her tender babe in her arms. . . . Children were torn from their mother's embrace and their brains blown out in the very face of the afflicted mother. Men were burnt by slow fires.

The violence and pillaging ran completely out of control; 120 people died, and an estimated $2 million in property was destroyed before soldiers brought from Gettysburg restored order.

As important as the problem of manpower were problems of supply and logistics. If wars bring forth loyalty, they also bring forth greed, and the Civil War's frantic mobilization offered much room for profiteering. Simon E. Cameron, the politician whom Lincoln appointed secretary of war to round out his political coalition, tolerated wholesale fraud. Lincoln eased him out in January 1862, and his successor, Edwin M. Stanton, brought order and efficiency into the department. But he was never able entirely to eliminate the plague of overcharging for shoddy goods.

The War's Early Course

The battle of Bull Run demonstrated that the war would not be decided with one sudden stroke. Lincoln now fell back upon General Winfield Scott's three-pronged "Anaconda" strategy. It called first for the Army of the Potomac to defend Washington and exert constant pressure on the Confederate capital at Richmond. At the same time, the navy would blockade the southern coast and thereby dry up the Confederacy's access to foreign goods and weapons. In the final component of the plan, Union forces would divide the Confederacy by invading the South along the main water routes: the Mississippi, Tennessee, and Cumberland Rivers. This strategy would slowly entwine and crush the southern resistance.

The Confederate strategy was simpler. If the Union forces could be stalemated, Davis and others hoped, then the British or French might be convinced to join their cause, or perhaps public sentiment in the North would force Lincoln to seek a negotiated settlement. So at the same time that armies were forming in the South, Confederate diplomats were seeking assistance in London and Paris, and Confederate sympathizers in the North were urging an end to the North's war effort.

NAVAL ACTIONS After Bull Run, and for the rest of 1861 into early 1862, the most important actions involved naval war and blockade. The one great threat to the Union navy proved to be short-lived. The Confederates in Norfolk fashioned an ironclad ship from an abandoned Union steam frigate, the *Merrimack*. Rechristened the *Virginia*, it ventured out on March 8, 1862, and wrought havoc among Union ships at the Chesapeake entrance. But as luck would have it, a new Union ironclad, the *Monitor*, arrived from New York in time to engage the *Virginia* on the next day. They fought to a draw and the *Virginia* returned to port, where the Confederates destroyed it when they had to give up Norfolk soon afterward.

Gradually the "Anaconda" tightened its grip on the South. In November 1861 a Federal flotilla appeared at Port Royal, South Carolina, pounded the fortifications into submission, and seized the port and nearby sea islands. At Fortress Monroe, Virginia, Union forces held the tip of the peninsula between the James and York Rivers, the scene of much colonial and revolutionary history. The navy extended its bases

The Merrimack (center, top) *and the* Monitor (center, bottom) *exchange fire at Hampton Roads on March 9, 1862. This print is based on a sketch done at the scene.*

farther down the coast in the late summer and fall of 1862. Union troops then captured Hatteras Inlet on the Outer Banks of North Carolina in August, a foothold soon extended to Roanoke Island and New Bern on the mainland.

From there the navy's progress extended southward along the Georgia-Florida coast. To the north the Federals laid siege to Charleston; by 1863 Fort Sumter and the city itself had come under bombardment. In the spring of 1862 Flag Officer David Farragut forced open the lower Mississippi near its mouth and surprised the defenders New Orleans, who had expected any attack to come downstream. Farragut won a surrender on May 1, then moved quickly to take Baton Rouge in the same way.

THE WEST AND THE CIVIL WAR   During the Civil War, western settlement continued unabated. New discoveries of gold and silver along the eastern slopes of the Sierra Nevada and in Montana and Colorado lured thousands of prospectors and their suppliers. As the population grew and dispersed, new transportation and communication networks emerged. Telegraph lines sprouted above the plains, and stagecoach lines fanned out to serve the new communities. Dakota, Colorado, and Nevada gained territorial status in 1861, Idaho and Arizona in 1863, and Montana in 1864. Silver-rich Nevada gained statehood in 1864.

With the firing on Fort Sumter, many of the regular army units assigned to frontier outposts in the West began to head east to meet the Confederate threat. In Texas, the Indian Territory (Oklahoma), and southern New Mexico, Union soldiers left altogether. Elsewhere they left behind skeleton units to man the forts. Texas was the only western state to join the Confederacy. For the most part, the federal government maintained its control of the other western territories during the war.

But it was not easy. Fighting in Kansas and the Indian Territory was widespread and furious. By 1862 Lincoln was forced to dispatch new volunteer units to the West. He had two primary concerns: to protect the shipments of gold and silver and to win over western political support for the war and his presidency. The most intense fighting in the West during the Civil War occurred along the Kansas-Missouri border. There the disputes between proslavery and antislavery settlers of the 1850s turned into brutal guerrilla warfare. The most prominent pro-Confederate leader in the area was William C. Quantrill. He and his proslavery followers, mostly teenagers, fought under a black flag, meaning that they gave no quarter. In destroying Lawrence, Kansas, in 1863, Quantrill ordered his forces to "kill every male and burn every house." They did. By the end of the day 182 boys and men had been systematically killed. Their opponents—the Jayhawkers—responded in kind. They tortured and hanged prisoners, burned houses, and destroyed livestock.

Many Indian tribes found themselves caught up in the Civil War. Indian regiments fought on both sides of the war, and in the Indian country they fought against each other. Many Indians among the Five Civilized Tribes living in Indian Territory owned black slaves and felt a natural bond with southern whites. Oklahoma's proximity to Texas also influenced the Choctaws and Chickasaws to support the Confederacy.

The Cherokees, Creeks, and Seminoles were more divided in their loyalties. For these tribes, the Civil War served as a wedge that fractured their own unity. The Cherokees, for example, split in two, some supporting the Union and others supporting the South. John Ross, the Principal Chief of the Cherokee Nation, poignantly expressed his dilemma when he responded to a Confederate delegation soliciting an alliance: "I am—the Cherokees are—your friends, but we do not wish to be brought into the feuds between yourselves and your Northern Brethren. Our wish is for peace. Peace at home and peace among you."

Yet eventually Ross acceded to the demands of his followers to align themselves with the Confederacy. A regiment of Cherokee warriors fought with the Confederates during their victory at Wilson's Creek, Missouri, in August 1861. By the end of the year, Confederate and Union Cherokee factions were also at war with one another. During 1862, three Choctaw-Chickasaw regiments, a Creek regiment, a Creek-Seminole regiment, and two Cherokee regiments fought alongside white Confederates in Arkansas. One Cherokee leader attained the rank of brigadier general, and in 1865 he would be the last Confederate officer to surrender his troops, two months after Lee surrendered to Grant at Appomattox.

ACTIONS IN THE WESTERN THEATER   Except for the amphibious thrusts along the southern coast, little happened in the Eastern Theater (east of the Appalachians) before May 1862. The Western Theater (from the mountains to the Mississippi), on the other hand, flared up with several encounters and an important penetration of the Confederate states. In western Kentucky Confederate general Albert Sidney Johnston had perhaps 40,000 men stretched over some 150 miles. At the center, however, only about 5,500 men held Fort Henry on the Tennessee and Fort Donelson on the Cumberland.

Early in 1862 General Ulysses S. Grant made the first thrust against the weak center of Johnston's overextended lines. Moving out of Cairo and Paducah with a gunboat flotilla, he swung southward up the Tennessee River toward Fort Henry. After a pounding from the Union gunboats, Fort Henry fell on February 6. Grant then moved quickly overland to attack Fort Donelson. Donelson proved a harder nut to crack, but on February 16 it gave up with some 12,000 men. Grant's terms, "unconditional surrender," and his quick success sent a thrill

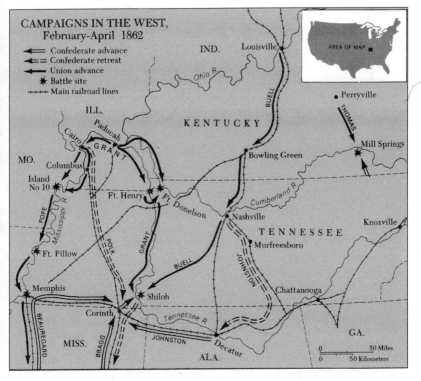

IND. Louisville

Ohio R.

• Perryville

ILL.

Paducah

Cairo

GRANT

KENTUCKY

Columbus

MO.

Island No 10

Ft. Henry

Ft. Donelson

Bowling Green

Cumberland R.

Mill Springs

THOMAS

Nashville

Knoxville

POPE

Mississippi R.

Ft. Pillow

POLK

GRANT

BUELL

Murfreesboro

TENNESSEE

JOHNSTON

Memphis

BEAUREGARD

Corinth

Shiloh

Tennessee R.

Chattanooga

JOHNSTON

Decatur

GA.

MISS.

BRAGG

ALA.

0   50 Miles
0   50 Kilometers

through the Union. U.S. "Unconditional Surrender" Grant had not only
opened a water route to Nashville, but had thrust his forces between
the two strongholds of the western Confederates. Johnston therefore
had to give up his foothold in Kentucky and abandon Nashville to Don
Carlos Buell's Army of the Ohio (February 25) in order to reunite his
forces at Corinth, Mississippi, along the Memphis and Chattanooga
Railroad.

SHILOH   Thus, the Union quickly regained most of Kentucky and western Tennessee, and stood poised in 1862 to strike at the Deep South.
But as Grant moved his forces southward along the Tennessee River
during the early spring of 1862, he made a costly mistake. While planning his attack on Corinth, Mississippi, he exposed his 42,000 troops on
a rolling plateau between two creeks flowing into the Tennessee and
failed to dig defensive trenches. General Johnston shrewdly recognized
Grant's oversight, and on the morning of April 6, the Kentuckian
ordered an attack on the vulnerable Federals, urging his men to be
"worthy of your race and lineage; worthy of the women of the South."

The Confederates struck suddenly at Shiloh, a log church in the center of the Union camp. There amid flowering dogwoods, peach trees,

and honeysuckle, they found most of Grant's troops still sleeping or groggily eating breakfast. Many died in their bedrolls. After a day of carnage and confusion, Grant's men were pinned against the river. But there they fended off a dozen assaults. Under the cover of gunboats and artillery at Pittsburg Landing, Grant and General William Tecumseh Sherman (who had two horses shot from under him and was himself wounded once) superbly rallied their troops. "We've had the devil's own day," Sherman told Grant that night. "Yes," Grant noted, "but we'll lick them tomorrow." Bolstered by reinforcements, Grant took the offensive the next day, and the Confederates withdrew to Corinth, leaving the Union army too battered to pursue.

Shiloh, a Hebrew word meaning "place of peace," was the costliest battle in which Americans had ever engaged, although worse was yet to come. Grant observed that the ground was "so covered with dead one could walk across the field without touching the ground." Combined casualties of nearly 25,000 exceeded the total dead and wounded of the Revolution, the War of 1812, and the Mexican War combined. Among the dead was the senior Confederate general, Albert Sidney Johnston, an artery in his leg severed by a gunshot. The Union, too, lost for a while the full services of its finest general. Grant had been caught napping and many northerners were shocked by the colossal loss of life. His superior, General Henry Halleck, already jealous of Grant's success, spread the false rumor that Grant had been drinking at Shiloh. Some called on Lincoln to fire Grant, but the president refused: "I can't spare this man; he fights." Halleck, however, took Grant's place as field commander, and as a result the Union thrust southward ground to a halt.

Nicknamed "Old Brains," the textbook strategist of offensive war, Halleck proved in the field to be unaccountably timid. Determined not to repeat Grant's mistake, he moved with profound caution on Corinth, taking at face value every inflated report of Rebel strength. But outnumbered better than two to one, P. G. T. Beauregard (Johnston's successor) abandoned Corinth to the Federals on May 30, falling back on Tupelo.

Halleck let slip the chance to overwhelm Beauregard, and for the remainder of 1862 the chief action in the Western Theater was a series of inconclusive maneuvers and two sharp engagements. Confederate general Braxton Bragg took his army to Kentucky, threatened Louisville, and was stopped by Buell's Army of the Ohio at Perryville on October 8. Kentuckians failed to rally to the Confederate flag, and Bragg pulled back into Tennessee. Buell, meanwhile, under pressure to sever the rail line at Chattanooga, proved to be one of the many Union generals who Lincoln said had "the slows." The administration replaced him with William S. Rosecrans, who moved out of Nashville and met Bragg in the costly engagement at Murfreesboro (or Stone's River), December 31 to January 3, after which Bragg cleared out of central Tennessee and fell

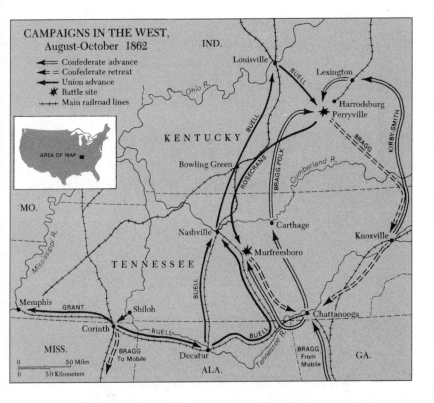

back on Chattanooga. But Lincoln still coveted eastern Tennessee, both for its many Unionists and for its railroads, which he wanted to cut to get between the Rebels and their "hog and hominy."

MCCLELLAN'S PENINSULAR CAMPAIGN   The Eastern Theater, aside from the coastal operations, remained fairly quiet for nine months after Bull Run. In the wake of the Union defeat, Lincoln had replaced McDowell with General George B. McClellan. Stonewall Jackson's classmate at West Point, McClellan had served as an army captain before resigning and becoming president of a railroad. After the firing on Fort Sumter, he was named a major-general overseeing Union forces in Ohio, Indiana, and Illinois. Now, as head of the Army of the Potomac, he set about building a powerful, well-trained army that would be ready for its next battle. The wide-shouldered, broad-chested McClellan exuded confidence and poise, as well as a certain flair for parade-ground showmanship. His troops adored him. Yet for all of McClellan's organizational ability and dramatic flair, his innate caution would prove crippling. His foremost concern was to avoid defeat rather than inflict it on the enemy.

Time passed, the army grew, and McClellan kept building his forces to meet the superior numbers that always seemed to be facing him. His intelligence service, headed by the private detective Allan Pinkerton, tended to overestimate enemy forces. Before moving, there was always the need to do this or that, to get 10,000 or 20,000 more men, always something. McClellan's Army of the Potomac was nine months in gestation after Bull Run, and then moved mainly because Lincoln insisted. In General Order No. 1, the president directed McClellan to begin forward movement by Washington's Birthday, February 22, 1862. The president wanted the army to move directly toward Richmond, keeping itself between the Confederate army and Washington. But McClellan, who dismissed Lincoln as a "well-meaning baboon," had another idea, and despite his reluctance to move, very nearly pulled it off. He sought to enter Richmond by the side door, so to speak, up the neck of land between the York and James Rivers, site of Jamestown, Williamsburg, and Yorktown, at the tip of which Federal forces already held Fortress Monroe, about seventy-five miles from Richmond.

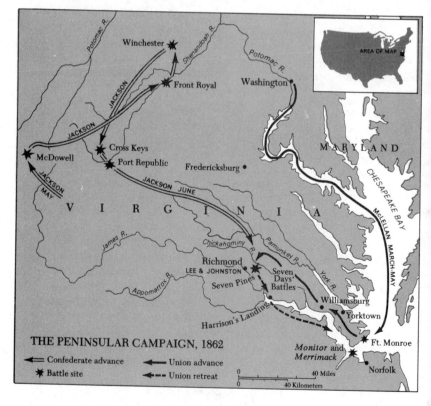

THE PENINSULAR CAMPAIGN, 1862

← Confederate advance   ← Union advance
✳ Battle site   ←--- Union retreat

Lincoln consented but specified, to McClellan's chagrin, that a force be left under McDowell to guard Washington. In mid-March 1862 McClellan's army finally embarked. In a brilliant maneuver, the Union forces went down the Potomac River and the Chesapeake Bay to the Virginia peninsula southeast of Richmond. This bold move put the Union forces within sixty miles of the Confederate capital. Advancing slowly up the thinly defended peninsula, taking no chances, McClellan brought Yorktown under siege from April 5 until May 4, when the Confederates slipped away, having accomplished their purpose of allowing General Joseph E. Johnston to get his outnumbered army in front of Richmond. Before the end of May McClellan's advance units sighted the church spires of Richmond. Thousands of Richmond residents fled the city in panic. President Davis sent his own family to a safe haven west of the city. But McClellan failed to capitalize on his situation. The Chickahominy River, which splits the peninsula north and east of Richmond, divided his army. Although Richmond lay south of the Chickahominy, part of the Confederate army was on the north bank to counter any southward move from Washington by McDowell.

McDowell, however, faced more urgent matters, or what seemed so. President Davis, at the urging of military adviser Robert E. Lee, sent Stonewall Jackson into the Shenandoah Valley on what proved to be a brilliant diversionary action. From March 23 to June 9, Jackson and some 18,000 men pinned down two separate armies with more than twice their numbers in the western Virginia mountains and at the northern end of the valley. While McDowell braced to defend Washington, Jackson hastened back to defend Richmond.

On May 31 Johnston struck at Union forces isolated on the south bank by the flooded river. In the Battle of Seven Pines (Fair Oaks), only the arrival of reinforcements, who somehow crossed the swollen river, prevented a disastrous Union defeat. Both sides took heavy casualties, and General Johnston was severely wounded.

At this point Robert E. Lee assumed command of the Army of Northern Virginia, a development that changed the course of the war. When McClellan heard the news, however, he declared that he preferred "Lee to Johnston. Lee is too cautious and weak under grave responsibility." He would soon change his opinion. Tall, erect, and wide-shouldered, Lee, who believed duty to be the "sublimest word in our language," projected a commanding presence. Unlike Johnston, he enjoyed Jefferson Davis's trust. More important, he knew how to use the talents of his superb field commanders: Stonewall Jackson, the pious, fearless, stern mathematics professor from Virginia Military Institute; James Longstreet, Lee's deliberate but tireless "war horse"; sharp-tongued D. H. Hill, the former engineering professor at Davidson College; Ambrose P. Hill, the consummate fighter who challenged one commander to a duel and feuded with Jackson; and J. E. B. Stuart, the courageous, colorful young cavalryman who once said: "All I ask of fate is that I may be killed leading a cavalry charge." He would get his wish.

Once in command, Lee quickly sized up the situation on the peninsula. He would hit the Union forces north of the Chickahominy with everything he had, leaving a token force in front of Richmond. But heavy losses frustrated Lee's plan. He launched a final desperate attack at Malvern Hill (July 1), where the Confederates suffered heavy casualties from Union artillery and gunboats in the James. This week of intense fighting, labeled the Seven Days' Battles (June 25 to July 1), had failed to dislodge the Union forces. McClellan was still near Richmond.

On July 9, when Lincoln visited McClellan's headquarters on the James, the general complained that the administration had failed to support him adequately and handed the president a strange document, the "Harrison's Landing Letter," in which, despite his critical plight, he instructed the president at length on war policies. It was ample reason to remove the general. Instead Lincoln returned to Washington and on July 11 called Halleck from the west to take charge as general-in-chief, a post that McClellan had temporarily vacated. Miffed at his demotion, McClellan angrily dismissed Halleck as an officer "whom I know to be my inferior."

SECOND BATTLE OF MANASSAS The new high command decided to evacuate the peninsula, which had become the graveyard of the last hope for a short war. McClellan was ordered to leave the peninsula and join the Washington defense force, now under John Pope, for a new overland assault on Richmond. In a letter to his wife, McClellan predicted that "Pope will be thrashed and disposed of" by Lee. As McClellan's Army of the Potomac began to pull out, Lee moved northward to strike Pope before McClellan arrived. Once again he adopted an audacious strategy. Dividing his forces, Lee sent Jackson's "foot cavalry" around Pope's right flank to attack his supply lines. At Second Bull Run (or Second Manassas), fought on almost the same site as the earlier battle, Pope assumed that he faced only Jackson, but Lee's main army by that time had joined in. On August 30 a crushing attack on Pope's flank drove the Federals from the field. In the next few days the Union forces pulled back into the fortifications around Washington, where McClellan once again took command and reorganized. He displayed his unflagging egotism in a letter to his wife: "Again I have been called upon to save the country." The disgraced Pope was dispatched to Minnesota to fight in the Indian wars.

ANTIETAM But Lee gave his adversary little time to prepare. Still on the offensive, determined to move the battlefield out of the South and

Lincoln and McClellan in the field, October 1862.

perhaps thereby gain foreign recognition for the Confederacy, he and his battle-tested troops invaded western Maryland in September 1862, headed for Pennsylvania. But Lee's bold strategy was uncovered when a Union soldier picked up a bundle of cigars and discovered a secret order from Lee wrapped around them. The paper revealed that Lee had again divided his army, sending Jackson off to take Harper's Ferry. McClellan boasted upon seeing the captured document: "Here is a paper with which, if I cannot whip Bobby Lee, I will be willing to go home." Instead of seizing his unexpected opportunity, however, he again delayed for sixteen crucial hours, still worried—as always—about enemy strength, and Lee was thereby able to reassemble most of his tired army behind Antietam Creek. Still, McClellan was optimistic, and Lincoln, too, relished the chance for a truly decisive blow: "God bless you and all with you," he wired McClellan. "Destroy the rebel army if possible."

On September 17, McClellan's forces attacked, commencing the furious Battle of Antietam (Sharpsburg). With the Confederate lines ready to break, A. P. Hill's division arrived from Harper's Ferry, having marched sixteen hot, dusty miles to the battlefield. Bone-weary and foot sore, they nevertheless plunged immediately into the fray, battering the Union army's left flank. It was a ghastly scene. "No tongue can tell, no mind conceive, no pen portray the horrible sights I witnessed this morning," a Pennsylvania soldier reported. Still outnumbered more than two to one, the Confederates were able to force a standoff in the bloodiest single day of the Civil War, a day participants thought would never end. The Union lost 2,108 dead and counted more than 10,000 wounded or missing. Lee's total losses were fewer, about 10,000, but they represented fully a fourth of his entire army. "God has been very kind to us this day," Stonewall Jackson declared with unintentional irony. The next day the battered Confederates slipped across the Potomac to the safety of Virginia.

Disgusted by McClellan's failure to follow up his success at Antietam and gain a truly decisive victory, Lincoln sent a curt message to the general: "I have just read your dispatch about sore-tongued and fatigued horses. Will you pardon me for asking what the horses of your army have done . . . that fatigues anything?" Later the president sent his commander a one-sentence letter: "If you don't want to use the army, I should like to borrow it for a while." Failing to receive a satisfactory answer, Lincoln removed McClellan and assigned him to recruiting duty in New Jersey. Never again would he command troops.

FREDERICKSBURG   Lee's invasion had failed and with it hopes of foreign recognition for the Confederacy. Yet the war was far from over. In his search for a fighting general Lincoln now made the worst choice of all. He turned to Ambrose E. Burnside, whose main achievements to that time had been to capture Roanoke Island and grow his famous side-whiskers. Burnside had twice before turned down the job on the grounds that he felt unfit for so large a command. But if the White House wanted him to fight, he would fight even in the face of oncoming winter. On December 13, 1862, Burnside sent his men across the icy Rappahannock River to assault Lee's forces, well entrenched west of Fredericksburg on Marye's Heights. Confederate artillery and muskets chewed up the blue columns as they crossed a mile of bottomland outside the town. Fourteen times the Union's suicidal assaults melted under the murderous fire issuing from protected positions above and below them. It was, a Federal general sighed, "a great slaughter-pen." The scene was both awful and awesome, prompting Lee to remark: "It is well that war is so terrible—we should grow too fond of it." After taking more than 12,000 casualties compared to fewer than 6,000 for the Confederates, Burnside wept as he gave the order to withdraw, and his battered forces limped back across the river.

The year 1862 ended with forces in the East deadlocked and the

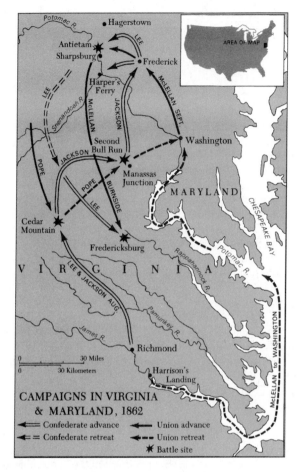

CAMPAIGNS IN VIRGINIA & MARYLAND, 1862

- ← Confederate advance
- ← = Confederate retreat
- ← Union advance
- ←--- Union retreat
- ✳ Battle site

Union advance in the West stalled since midyear. Union morale reached a low ebb. Northern Democrats were calling for a negotiated peace. At the same time Lincoln was under pressure from the Radicals of his own party, who were pushing for more stringent war measures, questioning the competence of the president, and demanding the removal of Secretary of State Seward. At the same time, Burnside was under fire from his own officers, some of whom were ready to testify publicly to his shortcomings.

But the deeper currents of the war were turning in favor of the Union: in a lengthening war its superior resources began to tell. In both the Eastern and Western Theaters the Confederate counterattack had been repulsed. And while the armies clashed, Lincoln by the stroke of a pen had changed the conflict from a war for the Union into a revolutionary struggle for abolition. On January 1, 1863, he signed the Emancipation Proclamation.

EMANCIPATION

It was the product of long and painful deliberation. In Lincoln's annual message of December 3, 1861, he had warned Congress to be "anxious and careful" that the war did not "degenerate into a violent and remorseless revolutionary struggle." At the outset he had upheld the promise of his party's platform to restore the Union but accept slavery where it existed. Congress too endorsed that position in the Crittendon-Johnson Resolutions, which passed both houses soon after the Battle of Bull Run with few dissenting votes. Once fighting began, the need to hold the border states dictated caution on the issue of emancipation. Beyond that, several other considerations deterred action. For one, Lincoln had to cope with a deep-seated racial prejudice in the North. Where most abolitionists promoted both complete emancipation and the social integration of the races, many antislavery activists only wanted slavery prohibited from the new territories and states. They were willing to allow slavery to continue in the South and were uneasy about racial integration. Lincoln himself harbored doubts about his authority to emancipate slaves so long as he clung to the view that the states remained legally in the Union. The only way around the problem would be to justify emancipation on the bases of military necessity and the president's war powers.

A MEASURE OF WAR   The war forced the issue. As Frederick Douglass predicted in 1861, the "American people and the Government at Washington may refuse to recognize it for a time, but the 'inexorable logic of events' will force it upon them in the end; that the war now being waged in this land is a war for and against slavery." He urged the northern armies to "teach the rebels and traitors that the price they are to pay for the attempt to abolish this government must be the abolition of slavery." As Federal forces pushed into the Confederacy, fugitive slaves began to turn up in Union army camps. In 1861 at Fortress Monroe, Virginia, Benjamin F. Butler declared vagabond or captured slaves to be "contraband of war" and put them to work on his fortifications. "Contrabands" soon became a common name for runaways in Union lines. But John C. Frémont pressed the issue one step too far. As commander of the Department of the West, in 1861 he simply liberated the slaves of all who actively helped the Rebel cause, an action that risked unsettling the yet-doubtful border states. Lincoln demanded that Frémont conform to the Confiscation Act of 1861, which freed only those slaves used

Former slaves, or "contrabands," on a farm in Cumberland Landing, Virginia, 1862.

by Rebel military services, as Butler's first "contrabands" had been. Then in 1862 General David Hunter declared free all slaves in South Carolina, Georgia, and Florida. He had no runaway slaves in his lines, he said, although some runaway masters had fled the scene. Lincoln quickly revoked the order, and took the brunt of the rising outrage among congressional Radicals who saw the war being fought to eliminate slavery everywhere.

Lincoln himself meanwhile edged toward emancipation. In March 1862 he proposed that federal compensation be offered any state that began gradual emancipation. The plan failed in Congress because of border-state opposition, but on April 16, 1862, Lincoln signed an act that abolished slavery in the District of Columbia, with compensation to owners; on June 19 another act excluded slavery from the territories, without offering owners compensation. A Second Confiscation Act, passed on July 17, liberated the slaves of all persons aiding the rebellion. Still another act forbade the army to help return runaways to their border-state owners.

To save the Union, Lincoln finally decided, complete emancipation would be required for several reasons: slave labor bolstered the Rebel cause, sagging morale in the North needed the lift of a moral cause, and public opinion was swinging that way as the war dragged on. Proclaiming a war on slavery, moreover, would end forever any chance that France or Britain would support the Confederacy. In July 1862 Lincoln first confided to his cabinet that he had in mind a proclamation that under his war powers would free the slaves of the enemy. At the time Seward advised him to wait for a Union victory in order to avoid any semblance of desperation.

The delay lasted through the long weeks during which Lee invaded Maryland and Bragg moved into Kentucky. As late as August 22, 1862, Lincoln responded to Horace Greeley's plea for emancipation: "My paramount object in this struggle is to save the Union and is not either to save or destroy slavery." The time to act finally came a month later, after Antietam. It was a dubious victory, but it did result in Lee's withdrawal. On September 22 Lincoln issued a preliminary Emancipation Proclamation, in which he repeated all his earlier stands: that his object was mainly to restore the Union and that he favored proposals for compensated emancipation and colonization. But the main burden of the document was his warning that on January 1, 1863, "all persons held as slaves within any state, or designated part of a state, the people whereof shall be in rebellion against the United States, shall be then, thenceforward and forever free."

In his annual message of December 1862 Lincoln once again raised the question of border-state compensation and ended with one of his most eloquent passages:

> We, even we here, hold the power and bear the responsibility. In giving freedom to the slave we assure freedom to the free—honorable alike in what we give and what we preserve. We shall nobly save or meanly lose the last, best hope of earth. Other means may succeed; this could not fail. The way is plain, peaceful, generous, just—a way which if followed the world will forever applaud and God must forever bless.

But this peroration was delivered with one eye to justifying the emancipation he had already promised. On January 1, 1863, Lincoln signed the second Emancipation Proclamation, giving effect to his promise of September, again emphasizing that this was a war measure based on his war powers. He also urged blacks to abstain from violence except in self-defense, and added that free blacks would now be received into the armed service of the United States.

For all its eloquence, the document set forth its points in commonplace terms. A newspaper in faraway Austria got the point better than many closer to home: "Lincoln is a figure *sui generis* in history. No pathos, no idealistic flights of eloquence, no posing, no wrapping himself in the toga of history. The most formidable decrees which he hurls against the enemy and which will never lose their historic significance, resemble—as the author intends them to—ordinary summonses sent by one lawyer to another on the opposing side." But as Henry Adams wrote from the London embassy, the Proclamation had created "an almost convulsive reaction in our favour."

REACTIONS TO EMANCIPATION   Among the Confederate states, Tennessee and the occupied parts of Virginia and Louisiana were exempted

Two views of the Emancipation Proclamation. *The Union view (top) shows a thoughtful Lincoln composing the Proclamation with the Constitution and the Holy Bible in his lap. The Confederate view (bottom) shows a demented Lincoln with his foot on the Constitution using an inkwell held by the devil.*

from its effect. The document, with few exceptions, freed no slaves who were within Union lines at the time, as cynics noted. Moreover, it went little further than the Second Confiscation Act. But these objections missed a point that black slaves readily grasped. "In a document proclaiming liberty," wrote the historian Benjamin Quarles, "the unfree never bother to read the fine print." Word spread quickly in the quarters, and in some cases masters learned of it first from their slaves. Though most slaves deemed it safer just to wait for the "day of jubilee" when Union forces arrived, some actively claimed their freedom. One spectacular instance was that of the black harbor pilot Robert Smalls, who one night took over a small Confederate gunboat, the *Planter,* and sailed his family through Charleston Harbor out to the blockading Union fleet. Later he served the Union navy as a pilot and still later became a congressman.

BLACKS IN THE MILITARY   From very early in the war Union commanders found "contrabands" like Smalls useful as guides to unfamiliar terrain and waterways, informants on the enemy, and at the very least common laborers. While menial labor by blacks was familiar enough to whites, military service was something else again. Though not unprecedented, it aroused in whites embedded fears. For more than a year the Lincoln administration warily evaded the issue.

Even after Congress authorized the enlistment of blacks in the Second Confiscation Act of July 1862, the administration ordered no general mobilization of black troops. Then, on January 1, 1863, Lincoln's Emancipation Proclamation reaffirmed the policy that blacks could enroll in the armed services and sparked new efforts to organize all-black units, to be led by white officers. Massachusetts organized the first northern all-black unit, the Massachusetts Fifty-fourth Regiment under Colonel Robert Gould Shaw. Rhode Island and other states soon followed suit. In May the War Department authorized general recruitment of blacks all over the country. This was a momentous decision, for it transformed a war to preserve the Union into a revolution to overthrow the social, economic, and racial status quo in the South. When one black soldier encountered his former master, now a prisoner of war, the former slave said, "Hello, Massa, bottom rail on top now."

By mid-1863 black units were involved in significant action in both the Eastern and Western Theaters. On July 18, 1863, Colonel Shaw, a Harvard graduate who was the son of a prominent abolitionist, led his black troops in a courageous assault against Fort Wagner, a massive earthwork barrier guarding Charleston, South Carolina. During the battle almost half of the Fifty-fourth Regiment were killed, including Colonel Shaw, who was slain while leading his men over the parapet. Enraged Confederates stripped Shaw's body and threw it into a ditch

Come and Join Us Brothers. *A poster recruiting freed slaves to join the "colored regiments" of the Union forces.*

serving as an unmarked mass grave for his men. When Shaw's father learned of the incident, he told a reporter: "The poor, benighted wretches thought they were heaping indignities upon his dead body, but the act recoils upon them. . . . They buried him with his brave, devoted followers who fell dead over him and around him. . . . We can imagine no holier place than that in which he is . . . nor wish him better company—what a bodyguard he has!"

The Fifty-fourth Regiment's unflinching attack in the face of murderous rifle and cannon fire resolved any doubts about the courage of the black soldier. "Through the cannon smoke of the dark night," went the description in the *Atlantic Monthly,* "the manhood of the colored race shines before many eyes that would not see." When the regiment's flag-bearer was slain, Sergeant William Carney retrieved the colors and carried them safely to the rear despite being shot in the head, chest, arm, and leg. He was the first of twenty-three African Americans to win the Congressional Medal of Honor.

The performance of the Fifty-fourth Regiment, and the use of African American units in the Vicksburg campaign, did much to win acceptance both for black soldiers and for emancipation, at least as a proper stratagem of war. Commenting on Union victories at Port Hud-

Sergeant J.L. Baldwin, 56th U.S. Colored Infantry, one of the few black officers in the Civil War. Born in Mississippi, Baldwin escaped slavery and went north to St. Louis, Missouri, where he enlisted in 1863. He was wounded in action in Arkansas, but returned to active duty.

son and Milliken's Bend, Mississippi, Lincoln reported that "some of our commanders . . . believe that . . . the use of colored troops constitutes the heaviest blow yet dealt to the rebels, and that at least one of these important successes could not have been achieved . . . but for the aid of black soldiers."

Some 178,000 African Americans served in the regiments of the United States Colored Troops, providing around 10 percent of the Union army total. Some 80 percent of the "colored troops" were former slaves or free blacks from the South. "This is the biggest thing that ever happened in my life," one enlistee declared. Of course, the African American soldiers encountered prejudice and skepticism within the Union ranks. But they persevered. Some 38,000 gave their lives. In the navy the 29,500 blacks accounted for about a fourth of all enlistments; of these more than 2,800 died. Not only black men but black women as well served in the war; Harriet Tubman and Susie King Taylor, for instance, were nurses with Clara Barton in the Sea Islands.

As the war entered its final months, freedom emerged more fully as a legal reality. Three major steps occurred in January 1865, when both Missouri and Tennessee abolished slavery by state action and the House of Representatives passed an abolition amendment introduced by Senator Lyman Trumbull of Illinois the year before. Upon ratification by three-fourths of the reunited states, the Thirteenth Amendment became part of the Constitution on December 18, 1865, and removed any lingering doubts about the legality of emancipation. By then, in fact, slavery remained only in the border states of Kentucky and Delaware.

WOMEN AND THE WAR

While breaking the bonds of slavery, the Civil War also loosened traditional restraints on female activity. "No conflict in history," a journalist wrote at the time, "was such a woman's war as the Civil War." Women played prominent roles in the conflict, and in the process many saw their outlook and status transformed. Initially the call to arms revived heroic images of female self-sacrifice and domestic skills. Women north and south sewed uniforms, composed uplifting poetry and songs, and raised money and supplies. Thousands of northern women worked with the United States Sanitary Commission, which organized medical relief and other services for soldiers. Others supported the freedmen's-aid movement to help impoverished blacks freed from bondage.

Mary Livermore of the Western Sanitary Commission recalled that patriotic women "planned money-making enterprises" that "yielded millions of dollars to be expended in the interest of sick and wounded soldiers." In the North alone, some 20,000 women served as nurses or other health-related volunteers. When war broke out, Mary Newcomb of Illinois was "so full of patriotism that if I had a dozen boys I have no doubt I should have said, 'Go! the country needs you.' " She thereafter became a nurse for the 11th Illinois Regiment. Nursing was as arduous and draining an enterprise as soldiering. A nurse working at a Maryland hospital recorded that she and her peers "endured the cold without sufficient bedding for our hard beds, and with no provision made for our fires. On bitter mornings we rose shivering, broke the ice in our pails, and washed our numb hands and faces, then went out into the raw air, up to our mess room, also without fire, thence to the wards."

Perhaps the two most famous nurses were Dorothea Dix and Clara Barton, both untiring volunteers in service to the wounded and dying. Dix, the veteran reformer of the nation's insane asylums, became the Union army's first Superintendent of Women Nurses. She soon found herself flooded with applications from around the country. Dix explained that nurses should be "sober, earnest, self-sacrificing, and self-sustained" women between the ages of thirty-five and fifty who could "bear the presence of suffering and exercise entire self control" and be "calm, gentle, quiet, active, and steadfast in duty."

Clara Barton (1821–1912), oversaw the distribution of vital medicines to Union troops, and later founded the American Red Cross.

Such a description fit Clara Barton well. Born in 1821, the fifth child of a Massachusetts family of modest means, she became an itinerant schoolteacher impatient with the gender discrimination of the day. Barton fought for equal pay and eventually became one of the first female clerks in the United States Patent Office in Washington, D.C. But she remained frustrated by her desire to find "something to do that *was* something." She discovered such fulfilling work as a nurse in the Civil War. Unlike Dix, Barton resisted the bureaucratic imperatives of the war effort. Instead of accepting an assignment to a general hospital, she followed the troops on her own, working in makeshift field hospitals. At Antietam she came so close to the fighting that as she worked on a wounded soldier a Confederate bullet ripped through the sleeve of her dress and killed the man.

Confederate Sally Tompkins of Richmond was equally unstinting. She and six others attended to 1,333 wounded men in her private hospital and kept all but 73 of them alive, a performance unmatched by any other hospital, North or South. Barton and other nurses challenged both male doctors' control of battlefield medicine and male bureaucrats' efforts to restrict the nurses' sphere of operations. In this way the war experience of women helped generate greater confidence in their own abilities. The war experience produced a generation of postwar female activists such as Annie Wittenmeyer of Iowa, who would become the first president of the Women's Christian Temperance Union, and Josephine Shaw Lowell, who would direct a variety of charitable organizations.

The departure of hundreds of thousands of men for the battlefields forced women to assume the public and private roles they left behind. Women suddenly found themselves in charge of households, farms, and businesses. They became farmers or plantation managers, clerks, munitions plant workers, and schoolteachers. Said one Georgia woman whose husband was killed in 1863, leaving her to manage three plantations and over a hundred slaves alone, "this cruel war imposes strange duties on us all." She added, however, that "I am willing to stand my lot." Some 400 women disguised themselves as men and fought in the war; dozens worked as spies; others traveled with the armies, cooking meals, writing letters, and assisting with amputations.

However, the conflict's unrelenting toll eventually eroded the martial enthusiasm of some home-front stalwarts. In mid-1862 a Virginia girl wrote her cousin that "this plagued, horrid, awful War/Has *proved to me romance too long.*" For many young women forced to shoulder new household burdens, the war's hardships accelerated their maturity and denied them an adolescence. In 1865 a southern woman confided that the war "commenced when I was thirteen, and I am now seventeen and no prospect yet of its ending. No pleasure, no enjoyment—nothing but rigid economy and hard work—nothing but the stern realities of life."

Others also saw the war's mounting death toll leach away its romance and nobility. A North Carolina mother lost seven sons in the fighting; another lost four, all at Gettysburg. Women who bore such loss or who witnessed daily suffering while serving as nurses were permanently altered by the experience. One New Hampshire–born writer who nursed convalescing soldiers later described the scene in one of her novels: "The wounded heroes were not poetical in appearance; they were simply a row of ordinary sick men, bandaged in various ways, often irritable, sometimes profane; their grammar was defective, and they cared more for tobacco than for texts, or even poetical quotations."

Still other women experienced what a West Virginia writer described as the "long, nervous strain" of waiting for news from the front. "No matter how gentle or womanly we might be, we read, we talked, we

Women workers filling cartridges with gunpowder at the federal arsenal in Watertown, Massachusetts.

thought perforce of nothing but slaughter." And the war's effects were enduring. The number of widows, spinsters, and orphans mushroomed. Many bereaved women on both sides came to look on the war with what the poet Emily Dickinson called a "chastened stare." South Carolina's Mary Boykin Chesnut wrote in her diary during the spring of 1862 that every "morning's paper [was] enough to kill a well woman [or] age a strong and hearty one. . . . The reality is hideous." Northerner Julia Ward Howe recalled that after the war ended many battle-scarred women in one way or another refused to revert to their "chimney corner life of the fifties." They struggled to find causes to serve or work to do outside the home.

Government During the War

Striking the shackles from 3.5 million slaves was a momentous social and economic revolution. But an even broader revolution began as power in Congress shifted from South to North with secession. Before the war southern congressmen had been able at least to frustrate the designs of both Free Soil and Whiggery. But once the secessionists abandoned Congress to the Republicans, a dramatic change occurred. The protective tariff, a transcontinental railroad, and a homestead act—all of which had been stalled by sectional controversy—were adopted before the end of 1862. The National Banking Act followed in 1863. Two other key pieces of legislation included the Morrill Land Grant Act (1862), which provided federal aid to state colleges of "agriculture and mechanic arts," and the Contract Labor Act (1864), which aided the importation of immigrant labor. All of these had great long-term significance.

UNION FINANCES   The more immediate problem for Congress was how to finance the costly war. Three options were available: higher taxes, printing paper money, and borrowing. The higher taxes came chiefly in the form of the Morrill Tariff and excise duties that one historian said "might be described with a near approach to accuracy as a tax on everything." Excise taxes were placed on manufactures and the practice of nearly every profession. A butcher, for example, had to pay 30¢ for every head of beef he slaughtered, 10¢ for every hog, 5¢ for every sheep. On top of the excises came an income tax that started in 1861 at 3 percent of income over $800 and increased in 1864 to a graduated rate rising from 5 percent of incomes over $600 to 10 percent of incomes over $10,000. To collect these the Revenue Act of 1862 created a Bureau of Internal Revenue.

But tax revenues trickled in so slowly—in the end they would meet only 21 percent of wartime expenditures—that Congress in 1862 forced upon a reluctant Treasury Secretary Chase the expedient of printing paper money, backed only by the proviso that it was legal tender for all debts. Beginning with the Legal Tender Act of 1862, Congress ultimately authorized $450 million of the notes, which soon became known as "greenbacks" because of their color. The number of greenbacks issued helped ease the financial crisis without causing the ruinous inflation that the unlimited issue of paper money caused in the Confederacy.

The net wartime issue of $431 million in greenbacks was only about a sixth of the total wartime indebtedness. From the beginning Chase had intended to rely for funds chiefly on the sale of bonds. Sales went slowly at first, although the issue of greenbacks, which depreciated in value against gold, encouraged the purchase of 6 percent bonds with the cheaper currency. But after October 1862 a Philadelphia banker named Jay Cooke (sometimes tagged "the Financier of the Civil War") mobilized a nationwide machinery of agents and propaganda for the sale of bonds. Eventually bonds amounting to more than $2 billion were sold, but not all by the patriotic ballyhoo of Jay Cooke and Company. New banks formed under the National Banking Act were required to invest part of their capital in the bonds, and encouraged to invest even more as security for the national bank notes they could issue.

For many businessmen, wartime ventures brought quick riches, which were made visible all too often in vulgar display and extravagance. "The world has seen its iron age, its silver age, its golden age and its brazen age," the New York *Herald* commented. "This is the age of shoddy . . . shoddy brokers in Wall Street, or shoddy manufacturers of shoddy goods, or shoddy contractors for shoddy articles for shoddy government. Six days a week they are shoddy businessmen. On the seventh day they are shoddy Christians." Not all the wartime fortunes, however, were made dishonestly. And they helped promote the capital accumulation with which American businessmen fueled later expansion. Wartime business thus laid the groundwork for the fortunes of such tycoons as J. P. Morgan, John D. Rockefeller, Andrew Mellon, and Andrew Carnegie.

CONFEDERATE FINANCES   Confederate finances were a disaster from the start. In the first year of its existence, the Confederacy levied export and import duties, but exports and imports were low. It enacted a tax of one-half of 1 percent on most forms of property, which should have yielded a hefty income, but the Confederacy farmed out its collection to the states, promising a 10 percent rebate on the take. The result was chaos. All but three states raised their quota by floating loans, which only worsened inflation.

In April 1863 the Confederate Congress passed a measure that, like Union excises, taxed nearly everything. A 10 percent tax in kind on all agricultural products did more to outrage farmers and planters than to supply the army, however. Enforcement was so poor and evasion so easy that the taxes produced only negligible amounts of depreciated currency.

Altogether, taxes covered no more than 5 percent of Confederate costs, perhaps less; bond issues accounted for less than 33 percent; and treasury notes for more than 66 percent. The last resort, the printing press, was in fact one of the early resorts. The first issue of $1 million in treasury notes in February 1861 was only the beginning: $20 million was authorized in May and $100 million in August, launching the Confederacy on an extended binge for which the only recourse was more of the same. Altogether the Confederacy turned out more than $1 billion in paper money. By March 1864 a wild turkey was offered in the Richmond market for $100, flour at $425 a barrel, home calls by doctors at $30, meal at $72 a bushel, and bacon at $10 a pound. Country folk were likely to have enough for subsistence, perhaps a little surplus to barter, but townspeople on fixed incomes were caught in a merciless squeeze.

CONFEDERATE DIPLOMACY   Civil wars often become international conflicts. Confederate diplomacy focused on gaining foreign help in the form of supplies, diplomatic recognition, or perhaps even intervention. The Confederates indulged the pathetic hope that diplomatic recognition would prove decisive, when in fact it more likely would have followed decisive victory in the field, which never came. An equally fragile illusion was the conviction that King Cotton would lure military aid and political sympathy from countries around the world dependent upon the fiber.

Indeed, to help foreign leaders make up their minds, the Confederates imposed a voluntary embargo on shipments of cotton, until the Union blockade began to strangle their foreign trade. European textile manufacturers meanwhile subsisted on the carryover from their purchase of the record crops of 1859 and 1860. By the time they needed cotton, it was available from new sources in Egypt, India, and elsewhere. Cotton textiles aside, the British economy was undergoing a boom from wartime trade with the Union and blockade-running into the Confederacy.

The first Confederate emissaries to England and France took hope when the British foreign minister received them informally after their arrival in London in 1861; they even won a promise from Napoleon III to recognize the Confederacy if Britain would lead the way. The key was therefore in London, but the British foreign minister refused to receive the Confederates again, partly because of Union pressures and partly out of British self-interest.

One incident early in the war threatened to upset British equanimity. In November 1861 a Union warship stopped a British mail packet, the *Trent,* and took into custody two Confederate commissioners, James M. Mason and John Slidell, en route from Havana to Europe. Celebrated as a heroic deed by a northern public still starved for victories, the *Trent* affair roused a storm of protest in Britain. An ultimatum for the captives' release was delivered to Washington, confronting Lincoln and Seward with an explosive crisis. To interfere with a neutral ship on the high seas violated long-settled American principle, and Seward finally decided to face down popular clamor and release Mason and Slidell, much to their own chagrin. As martyrs in Boston, they were more useful to their own cause than they could ever be in London and Paris.

In contrast to the futility of Confederate attempts at King Cotton diplomacy, Confederate commissioners scored some successes in getting supplies. The most spectacular feat was the procurement of Confederate raiding ships. Although British law forbade the sale of warships to belligerents, a Confederate commissioner contrived to have the ships built and then, on trial runs, to escape to the Azores or elsewhere for outfitting with guns. In all, eighteen such ships were activated and saw action in the Atlantic, Pacific, and Indian Oceans, where they sank hundreds of Yankee ships and threw terror into the rest. The most spectacular of the Confederate raiders were the first two, the *Florida* and the *Alabama,* which took thirty-eight and sixty-four prizes, respectively.

UNION POLITICS AND CIVIL LIBERTIES   On the home fronts there was no moratorium on partisan politics, north or south. Within his own party Lincoln faced a Radical wing composed mainly of prewar abolitionists. By the end of 1861 they were getting restless with the policy of fighting solely to protect the Union. The congressional Joint Committee on the Conduct of the War became an instrument of their cause. Led by men such as Thaddeus Stevens and George W. Julian in the House, and Charles Sumner, Benjamin F. Wade (the chairman), and Zachariah Chandler in the Senate, they pushed for confiscation of plantations, emancipation of slaves, and a more vigorous prosecution of the war. The greater body of Republicans, however, continued to back Lincoln's more cautious approach. And the party was generally united on economic policy.

The Democratic party suffered the loss of its southern wing and the death of its leader, Stephen A. Douglas, in June 1861. By and large, northern Democrats supported a war for the "Union as it was" before 1860, giving reluctant support to war policies but opposing restraints on civil liberties and the new economic legislation. "War Democrats" such as Senator Andrew Johnson and Secretary of War Edwin M. Stanton fully supported Lincoln's policies, however, while a Peace Wing of the party preferred an end to the fighting, even at risk to the Union. An extreme fringe of the Peace Wing even flirted with outright disloyalty. The "Copperheads," as they were called, organized secret societies for purposes that were none too clear and often suspect. They were strongest in states such as Ohio, Indiana, and Illinois, all leavened with native southerners, some of whom were pro-Confederate.

Coercive measures against disloyalty were perhaps as much a boost as a hindrance to Democrats, who took up the cause of civil liberty. Early in the war Lincoln assumed the power to suspend the writ of habeas corpus, which entitles people who have been jailed to a speedy hearing. Lincoln also subjected "disloyal" persons to martial law—often on vague suspicion. The Constitution said only that habeas corpus should be suspended in cases of rebellion or invasion, but congressional leaders argued that Congress alone had authority to act, since the provision fell in Article I, which deals with the powers of Congress. When Congress, by the Habeas Corpus Act of 1863, finally authorized the president to suspend the writ, it required officers to report the names of all arrested

A cartoon lampooning Copperhead Democrats for their subservience to the Confederacy, 1864.

persons to the nearest district court, and provided that if the grand jury found no indictment, those arrested could be released upon taking an oath of allegiance.

There were probably more than 14,000 arrests made without recourse to a writ of habeas corpus. Most of those arrested were Confederate citizens accused of blockade running, or foreign nationals. But Union citizens were also detained. One celebrated case arose in 1863 when Federal soldiers hustled the Democrat Clement L. Vallandigham out of his home in Dayton, Ohio. A military commission condemned Ohio's most prominent Copperhead to confinement for the duration of the war because he had questioned arbitrary arrests. The muzzling of a political opponent proved such an embarrassment to Lincoln that he commuted the sentence, but only by another irregular device, banishment behind the Confederate lines. Vallandigham eventually found his way to Canada. In 1863 he ran as the Democratic candidate for Ohio governor *in absentia*, and in 1864 slipped back into the country. He was left alone at Lincoln's order, took part in the Democratic national convention, and ultimately his pro-southern proved more of an embarrassment to the Democrats than to the president.

At their 1864 national convention in Chicago, the Democrats called for an armistice to be followed by a national convention that would restore the Union. They named General George B. McClellan as their candidate, but McClellan distanced himself from the peace platform by declaring that agreement on Union would have to precede peace.

Radical Republicans, who still regarded Lincoln as soft on treason, tried to thwart his nomination, but he outmaneuvered them at every turn. Lincoln brought about the vice-presidential nomination of Andrew Johnson, a War Democrat from Tennessee, on the "National Union" ticket, so named to minimize partisanship. As the war dragged on through 1864, however, with Grant taking heavy losses in Virginia, Lincoln fully expected to lose. Then Admiral Farragut's capture of Mobile in August and Sherman's capture of Atlanta on September 2 turned the tide. McClellan carried only New Jersey, Delaware, and Kentucky, with 21 electoral votes to Lincoln's 212, and 1.8 million popular votes (45 percent) to Lincoln's 2.2 million (55 percent).

CONFEDERATE POLITICS   Unlike Lincoln, Jefferson Davis never had to contest a presidential election. He and his vice-president, Alexander Stephens, were elected without opposition in 1861 for a six-year term. But discontent flourished as events went from bad to worse, and came very close to home in the Richmond bread riot of April 2, 1863, which ended only when Davis himself persuaded the mob (mostly women) to

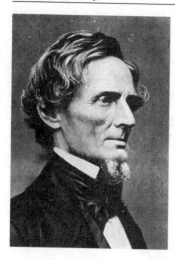

Jefferson Davis, president of the Confederacy.

disperse. After the congressional elections of 1863, the second and last in the Confederacy, about a third of the legislators were anti-administration. Although parties as such did not figure in the elections, it was noteworthy that many ex-Whigs and other opponents of secession were chosen.

Davis, like Lincoln, had to contend with dissenters. Large pockets of Union loyalists appeared in the German counties of Texas, the hill country of Arkansas, the North Carolina Piedmont, and most of all along the Appalachian spine that reached as far south as Alabama and Georgia. Many Unionists followed their states into the Confederacy reluctantly, and were receptive to talk of peace. They were less troublesome to Davis, however, than the states'-rights men who had embraced secession and then guarded states'-rights against the Confederacy as zealously as they had against the Union. Georgia, and to a lesser degree North Carolina, were strongholds of such sentiment, which prevailed widely elsewhere as well. The states' rights advocates challenged, among other things, the legality of conscription, taxes on farm produce, and above all the suspension of habeas corpus. Vice-President Stephens carried on a running battle against Davis's effort to establish "military despotism," left Richmond to sulk at his Georgia home for eighteen months, and warned the Georgia legislature in 1864, on the eve of Sherman's march, against the "siren song, 'Independence first and liberty afterwards.' "

The ultimate failure of the Confederacy has been attributed to many things. Among other things, the Confederacy died of dogma. Where Lincoln was the consummate pragmatist, Davis was a brittle dogmatist with a waspish temper. His fundamental insecurity made him indecisive. But once he made a decision, nothing could change his mind. One southern politician said that he was "as stubborn as a mule." Davis could never find it in himself to admit that he had made a mistake. Such a personality was ill-suited to the chief executive of an infant nation.

THE FALTERING CONFEDERACY

In 1863 the hinge of fate began to close the door on the brief career of the Confederacy. After the Union disaster at Fredericksburg, Lincoln's search for a capable general turned to one of Burnside's disgruntled lieutenants, Joseph E. Hooker, whose pugnacity had given him the name of "Fighting Joe." After the appointment, Lincoln wrote his new commander, "there are some things in regard to which, I am not quite satisfied with you." Hooker had been saying the country needed a dictator, and word had reached Lincoln. "Only those generals who gain successes can set up dictators," the president wrote. "What I now ask of you is military success, and I will risk the dictatorship." But the risk was not great. Hooker was no more able than Burnside to deliver the goods. He failed his test at Chancellorsville, Virginia, May 1–5, 1863.

CHANCELLORSVILLE   With a force of perhaps 130,000, the largest Union army yet gathered, and a brilliant plan, Hooker suffered a loss of control, perhaps a failure of nerve, at the critical juncture. Lee, with perhaps half that number, staged what became a textbook example of daring and maneuver. Hooker's plan was to leave his base, opposite Fredericksburg, on a sweeping movement upstream across the Rappahannock and Rapidan rivers to flank Lee's position. A diversionary force was to cross below the town. Lee, however, sniffed out the ruse and pulled his main forces back to meet Hooker. At Chancellorsville, after a preliminary skirmish, Lee divided his army again, sending Jackson with more than half the men on a long march to hit the enemy's exposed right flank.

On May 2, toward evening, Jackson surprised the Federals at the edge of a wooded area called the Wilderness, throwing things into chaos, but the fighting died out in confusion as darkness fell. The next day, Lee forced Hooker's army back across the Rappahannock. It was the peak of Lee's career, but Chancellorsville was his last significant victory. And his costliest: the South suffered some 12,000 casualties and more than 1,600 killed, among them Stonewall Jackson, mistakenly felled by his own men. "I have lost my right arm," Lee lamented.

VICKSBURG   While Lee held the Federals at bay in the East, a reinstated Ulysses Grant had been groping his way down the Mississippi River toward Vicksburg. Located on a bluff 200 feet above the river, Vicksburg had withstood naval attacks and a downriver expedition led by William T. Sherman. Grant positioned his army about fifteen miles north of the city, but the surrounding bayous baffled efforts to reach the goal. Grant finally gave up the idea of a northern approach. He crossed over to Louisiana, and while the navy ran gunboats and transports past the Confederate batteries at Vicksburg, he moved south to meet them, crossed back, and reached dry ground south of Vicksburg at the end of April. From there Grant adopted a new expedient. He would forget supply lines and live off the country. Grant then swept eastward on a campaign that Lincoln later called "one of the most brilliant in the world," took Jackson, Mississippi, where he seized or destroyed supplies, then turned westward and on May 18 pinned the 30,000 Confederates inside Vicksburg. He resolved to wear them down and starve them out.

GETTYSBURG   The plight of Vicksburg put the Confederate high command in a quandary. Joseph E. Johnston, now in charge of the western forces but with few men under his personal command, would have preferred to focus on the Tennessee front and thereby perhaps force Grant to relax his grip. Lee had another idea for a diversion. If he could win a victory on northern soil, he might do more than just relieve the pres-

Wilderness
Battlefield
Scene, 1863,
*photograph
by Alexander
Gardner.*

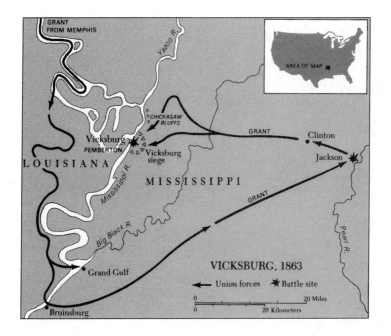

GRANT
FROM MEMPHIS

Yazoo R.

AREA OF MAP

CHICKASAW
BLUFFS

GRANT

Clinton

Vicksburg
PEMBERTON

Vicksburg
siege

Jackson

LOUISIANA

Mississippi R.

MISSISSIPPI

GRANT

Pearl R.

Big Black R.

Grand Gulf

VICKSBURG, 1863

Union forces   Battle site

0   20 Miles

0   20 Kilometers

Bruinsburg

sure at Vicksburg. In June he moved his army into the Shenandoah Valley and northward again across Maryland.

Hooker followed, keeping his forces between Lee's army and Washington, but, demoralized by defeat at Chancellorsville and quarrels with Halleck, he turned in his resignation. On June 28 Major-General George G. Meade took command. Neither side chose Gettysburg, Pennsylvania, as the site for the climactic battle, but a Confederate scavenging party entered the town in search of shoes and encountered units of Union cavalry on June 30. The main forces quickly converged on that point. On July 1 the Confederates pushed the Federals out of the town, but into stronger positions on high ground to the south. Meade hastened reinforcements to his new lines along the heights. On July 2 Lee—with uncharacteristic tardiness—mounted furious assaults at both the extreme left and right flanks of Meade's army, but in vain. General Longstreet said that it was the "best three hours' fighting I had seen done by any troops on any battle-field." As darkness settled over the battlefield, a grievously wounded Lieutenant Barzilia J. Inman of the 148th Pennsylvania struggled all night to stay awake so as to fend off the hog that was eating the flesh of the dead around him.

On July 3 Lee staked everything on one final assault on the Union center at Cemetery Ridge. About 2 P.M. General George E. Pickett's 15,000 troops emerged from the woods into the brilliant sunlight,

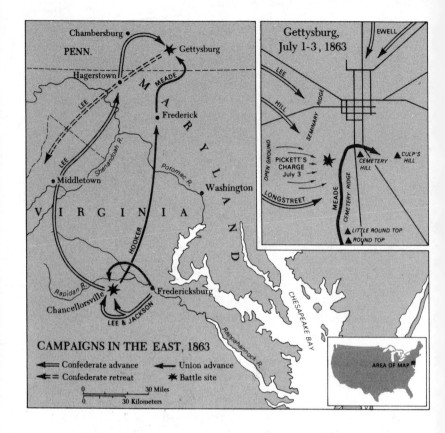

CAMPAIGNS IN THE EAST, 1863

←← Confederate advance   ← Union advance
←= Confederate retreat   ✳ Battle site

0 ————————— 30 Miles
0 ————————— 30 Kilometers

Gettysburg, July 1-3, 1863

PICKETT'S CHARGE July 3

AREA OF MAP

formed neat ranks, and began their suicidal advance across open ground commanded by Union artillery. It was as hopeless as Burnside's assault at Fredericksburg. Only 5,000 of Pickett's men reached the ridge, and the few who got within range of hand-to-hand combat were quickly overwhelmed. As he watched the few survivors returning from the bloody field, Lee muttered: "All this has been my fault." He then told Pickett to regroup his division to repulse a possible counterattack, only to have Pickett tartly reply, "General Lee, I have no division now." Pickett never forgave Lee. Years later he charged: "That old man had my division slaughtered."

With nothing left to do but retreat, on July 4 Lee's dejected and mangled army, with about a third of its number gone, began to slog south through a driving rain. "I started from Texas to find a fight," one Confederate wrote home, "and I have made a success of it." They had failed in all their purposes, not the least being to relieve the pressure on Vicksburg. On that same July 4, the Confederate commander at Vicksburg reached the end of his tether and surrendered his entire garrison. Four days later the last remaining Confederate stronghold on the Mississippi, Port Hudson, under siege since May by Union forces, gave up. "The father of waters," Lincoln said, "flows unvexed to the sea." The Confederacy was irrevocably split. Had Meade pursued Lee, he might have delivered the *coup de grace* before the Rebels could get back across the flooded Potomac.

CHATTANOOGA   The third great Union victory of 1863 occurred in fighting around Chattanooga, the railhead of eastern Tennessee and gateway to northern Georgia. In the late summer a Union army led by General William Rosecrans took Chattanooga and then rashly pursued General Braxton Bragg's forces into Georgia, where they met at Chickamauga. The battle (September 19 –20) had the makings of a Union disaster, since it was one of the few times when the Confederates had a numerical advantage (about 70,000 to 56,000). On the second day Bragg smashed the Federals' right, and only the stubborn stand of troops under George H. Thomas (thenceforth "the Rock of Chickamauga") prevented a general rout. The battered Union forces fell back into Chattanooga, while Bragg cut the railroad from the west and held the city virtually under siege from the heights to the south and east.

Rosecrans seemed stunned and apathetic, but Lincoln urged him to hang on: "If we can hold Chattanooga, and East Tennessee, I think rebellion must dwindle and die." The Union command sent reinforcements from Virginia, while Grant and Sherman arrived with more from the west. Grant, given overall command of the Western theater of operations on October 16, pushed his way into Chattanooga a few days later,

Harvest of Death. *T. H. O'Sullivan's grim photograph of the dead at Gettysburg.*

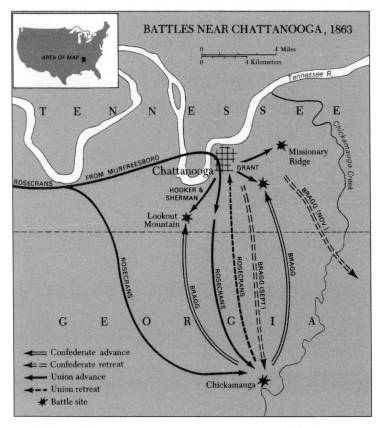

BATTLES NEAR CHATTANOOGA, 1863

AREA OF MAP

0   4 Miles
0   4 Kilometers

Tennessee R.

T E N N E S S E E

FROM MURFREESBORO

ROSECRANS

Chattanooga

GRANT

Missionary Ridge

HOOKER & SHERMAN

Lookout Mountain

Chickamauga Creek

BRAGG (NOV.)

ROSECRANS

BRAGG

ROSECRANS

ROSECRANS

BRAGG (SEPT.)

BRAGG

G E O R G I A

←━ Confederate advance
←= Confederate retreat
←━ Union advance
◄-- Union retreat
✶ Battle site

Chickamauga

forcing open a supply route as he came. He replaced Rosecrans with Thomas. On November 24 the Federals began to move, hitting the Confederate flanks at Lookout Mountain and Signal Hill while Thomas created a diversion at the center. The Union troops took Lookout Mountain in what was mainly a feat of mountaineering, but Sherman's forces stalled at Signal Hill. On the second day of the battle Grant ordered Thomas forward to positions at the foot of Missionary Ridge. Successful there, but still exposed, the men spontaneously began to move on up toward the crest 400 to 500 feet above. They might well have been cut up badly, but the Rebels were unable to lower their big guns enough. In the face of thousands of Union troops swarming up the hill, the Confederate defenders panicked and fled.

Bragg was unable to regroup his forces until they were many miles to the south, and the Battle of Chattanooga was the end of his active career. Jefferson Davis, who had backed Bragg against all censure, reluctantly replaced him with Johnston and called Bragg back to Richmond as an adviser. Soon after the battle the Federals linked up with Burnside, who had taken Knoxville, and proceeded to secure their control of eastern Tennessee, where the hills were full of native Unionists.

Chattanooga had another consequence. Though the Federals won the battle by rushing up Missionary Ridge, against orders, the victory nonetheless confirmed the impression of Grant's genius. Lincoln had at last found his general. In March 1864 Grant arrived in Washington to assume the rank of lieutenant-general and a new position as general-in-chief. Halleck became chief of staff and continued in his role as channel of communication between the president and commanders in the field. Within the Union armies at least, a modern command system was emerging; the Confederacy never had a unified command.

THE CONFEDERACY'S DEFEAT

Lincoln's main targets now were Lee's army in Virginia and General Joseph Johnston's in Georgia. Grant personally would accompany Meade, who retained direct command over the Army of the Potomac; operations in the West were entrusted to Grant's long-time lieutenant, William T. Sherman. As Sherman put it later, Grant "was to go for Lee,

General Ulysses S. Grant.

and I was to go for Joe Johnston. That was his plan." Grant brought with him a new strategy against Lee. Where his predecessors had all hoped for the climactic single battle, he adopted a policy of attrition. He would attack, attack, attack, keeping the pressure on the Confederates, grinding down their numbers and taking away their initiative and will to fight. As he ordered Meade, "Wherever Lee goes, there you will go also." Grant would also wage total war, confiscating or destroying any and all civilian property of military use. It was a brutal, costly, but ultimately effective plan.

GRANT'S PURSUIT OF LEE   In May 1864, the Army of the Potomac, numbering about 115,000 to Lee's 65,000, moved south across the Rappahannock and the Rapidan into the Wilderness, where Hooker had come to grief in the Battle of Chancellorsville. In the Battle of the Wilderness (May 5–6), the armies fought blindly through the woods, the horror and suffering of the scene heightened by crackling brushfires. Grant's men suffered heavier casualties than the Confederates, but the Rebels were running out of replacements.

Many of the Union officers in the Army of the Potomac whom Grant inherited were still in awe of Lee. They feared another decisive counterattack on their flanks. When one of his officers expressed concern about what Lee might do, Grant exploded: "Oh, I am heartily tired of hearing about what Lee is going to do. Some of you always seem to

The tattered colors of the 56th and 36th Massachusetts regiments, marching through Virginia, 1864.

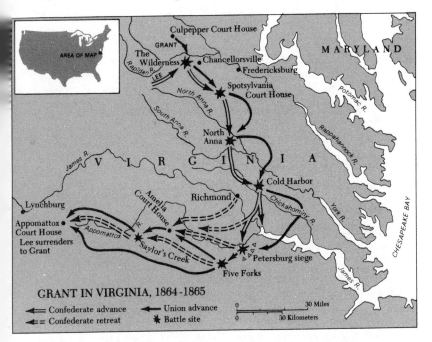

GRANT IN VIRGINIA, 1864-1865

⟸= Confederate advance   ⟵ Union advance
⟸= Confederate retreat   ✹ Battle site

think he is suddenly going to turn a double somersault, and land in our rear and on both flanks at the same time. Go back to your command, and try to think what we are going to do ourselves, instead of what Lee is going to do." Always before when bloodied by Lee's troops, Union forces had pulled back to nurse their wounds, but Grant slid off to his left and continued his relentless advance southward, now toward Spotsylvania Court House.

There Lee's advance guard barely arrived in time to stall the movement, and the armies settled down for five days of bloody warfare, May 8–12. Grant sent word back to Halleck: "I propose to fight it out along this line if it takes all summer." But again Grant slid off to his left, and kept moving. Along the banks of the Chickahominy, the two sides clashed at Cold Harbor (June 1–3). In twenty minutes, 7,000 attacking Federals were killed or wounded. Many of them predicted as much. After the failed assault, Confederates retrieved a diary from a dead Massachusetts soldier. The final entry read: "June 3, 1864, Cold Harbor, Virginia. I was killed." Battered and again repulsed, Grant cut away yet again. For several days Lee lost sight of the Federals while they crossed the James on a pontoon bridge and headed for Petersburg, at the junction of railroads into Richmond from the south.

Grant dug in for a siege along lines that extended for twenty-five miles above and below Petersburg. On July 30 a huge mine exploded in a tunnel under the Confederate line. In the ensuing Battle of the Crater, the Union soldiers who were supposed to exploit the opening milled around aimlessly in the pit while Rebels shot them like fish in a pond. For nine months the two armies faced each other down while Grant kept pushing toward his left flank to break the railroad arteries that were Lee's lifeline. He would fight it out along *this* line all summer, all autumn, and all winter, generously supplied by Union vessels moving up the James, while Lee's forces, beset by hunger, cold, and desertion, wasted away. Petersburg had become Lee's prison while disasters piled up for the Confederacy elsewhere.

SHERMAN'S MARCH   When Grant headed south, so did Sherman—toward the railroad hub of Atlanta, with 90,000 men against Joe Johnston's 60,000. Sherman's campaign, like Grant's, developed into a war of maneuver, but without the pitched battles. Sherman kept moving to his right, but the wily Johnston was always one step ahead of him—turning up in secure positions along the north Georgia ridges, drawing Sherman farther from his Chattanooga base, harassing the Union supply lines with Joe Wheeler's cavalry, and keeping his own main force intact. But Johnston's skillful defensive tactics caused an impatient President Davis finally to replace him with the combative but reckless John B. Hood. A towering, blond-bearded Texan, Hood did not know the meaning of retreat. Lee described him as being "all lion." He had "none of the fox" in him. Having had an arm crippled by a bullet at Gettysburg

William Tecumseh Sherman.

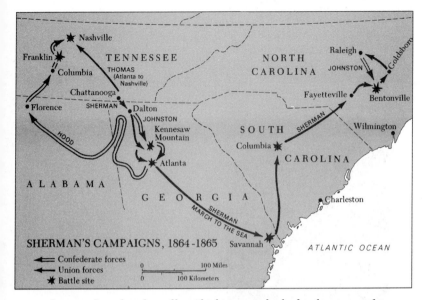

SHERMAN'S CAMPAIGNS, 1864-1865

and most of one leg shot off at Chickamauga, he had to be strapped to his horse. Three times in eight days Hood lashed out at the Union lines, each time meeting a bloody rebuff. Sherman at first resorted to a siege of Atlanta, then slid off to the right again, cutting the rail lines below Atlanta. Hood evacuated on September 1, but kept his army intact.

Sherman now laid plans for a march through central Georgia, where no organized armies remained. Hood meanwhile had hatched an equally audacious plan. He would cut away to northern Alabama and push on into Tennessee, forcing Sherman into pursuit. Sherman refused to take the bait, although he did send a Union force back to Tennessee to keep watch. So the curious spectacle unfolded of the main armies moving off in opposite directions. But it was a measure of the Confederates' plight that Sherman could cut a swath across Georgia with impunity, while Hood was soon outnumbered again. In the Battle of Franklin (November 30), Hood sent his army across two miles of open ground. Six waves broke against the Union lines, leaving the ground strewn with Confederates. Total Rebel casualties numbered 6,000. With what he had left, Hood dared not attack Nashville, nor did he dare withdraw for fear of final disintegration. Finally, in the Battle of Nashville (December 15–16), the Federals broke and scattered what was left of the Confederate Army of Tennessee. The Confederate front west of the Appalachians had collapsed, leaving only a few units scattered in the field.

During all this, Sherman's army was marching through Georgia, pioneering the modern practice of total war against a people's resources and against their will to resist. He was determined to "make Georgia

Ruins of Georgia Railround Roundhouse at Atlanta, 1864. *In the wake of Sherman's march, abandoned locomotives and twisted rails marked the destruction in Atlanta.*

howl." And he did. On November 15, 1864, he destroyed Atlanta's warehouses and railroad facilities while spreading fires that consumed about a third of the city. The Union army moved out in four columns over a front twenty to sixty miles wide, living off the land and destroying any provisions that might serve Confederate forces. Bands of stragglers and deserters from both armies joined in looting along the flanks, while Union cavalry destroyed Rebel supplies to keep them out of enemy hands. When, after a month, Sherman arrived in Savannah, he had cut a swath of desolation 250 miles long. On December 21 Sherman marched into Savannah, and three days later he wired Lincoln that the captured city was his Christmas gift to the Union.

Pushing across the Savannah river into that "hell-hole of secession," South Carolina, Sherman's men wrought even greater destruction. More than a dozen towns were burned in whole or part, including the state capital of Columbia, captured on February 17, 1865. Meanwhile, Charleston's defenders abandoned the city and pulled north to join an army that Joseph E. Johnston was desperately pulling together. Johnston mounted one final attack on Sherman's left wing at Bentonville (March 19–20), but that was his last major battle.

APPOMATTOX   During this final season of the Confederacy, Grant kept pushing, probing, and battering the Petersburg defenses. Raids by

Philip H. Sheridan's cavalry had desolated Lee's breadbasket in the Shenandoah Valley, and winter left his men on short rations. News of Sherman's progress through Georgia and South Carolina added to the gloom and the impulse to desert. By March 1865, the Confederate lines had thinned out to about 1,000 men per mile. Lee began to lay plans for his beseiged forces to escape and join Johnston's army in North Carolina. On April 2 he abandoned Richmond and Petersburg in a desperate flight toward Lynchburg and rails south. President Davis, exhausted but still defiant, gathered what archives and treasure he could and made it out by train ahead of the advancing Federals, only to be captured in Georgia by Union cavalry on May 10.

By then the Confederacy was already dead. Lee moved out with Grant in hot pursuit, and soon found his escape route cut by Sheridan's calvary forces. On April 9 (Palm Sunday) he donned a crisp dress uniform and met the mud-spattered Grant in the parlor of the McLean home at Appomattox to tender his surrender, four years to the day after Davis and his cabinet decided to attack Fort Sumter. Grant, at Lee's request, let the Rebel officers keep their sidearms and permitted soldiers to keep personal horses and mules. On April 18, Johnston surrendered to Sherman at the Bennett house near what would soon become the thriving tobacco town of Durham. During May the remaining Confederate forces surrendered as well.

The debate over why the North won and the South lost the Civil War will probably never end, but Lee's own explanation of the Confederate defeat retains an enduring legitimacy: "After four years of arduous service marked by unsurpassed courage and fortitude, the Army of North-

Robert E. Lee. *Mathew Brady took this photograph in Richmond eleven days after Lee's surrender at Appomattox.*

ern Virginia has been compelled to yield to overwhelming numbers and resources."

BITTERSWEET VICTORY   In Charleston, the Confederate "holy of holies," the first occupation troops to arrive in February 1865 were black units, including the Third and Fourth South Carolina Regiments, some of whom had been among the city's slaves in 1860. It was little more than four years since the secession convention had met, not quite five years since the disruption of the Democratic party in the same city. Soon after the occupation, the War Department staged a massive celebration at Fort Sumter on the fourth anniversary of its fall. On April 14, 1865, the fort was filled with dignitaries, and a few hundred black soldiers brought out by the *Planter,* the boat on which Captain Robert Smalls had fled slavery three years before. At noon Major Anderson ran up the flag he had lowered just four years previously, while gaily decorated ships and all the forts in the harbor sounded a salute.

The same day President Lincoln spent the afternoon discussing post-war policy with his cabinet. That night Mr. and Mrs. Lincoln went to the theater.

FURTHER READING

The best one-volume overview of the Civil War period is James M. McPherson's *Battle Cry of Freedom: The Civil War Era* (1988).° The most comprehensive treatment is Allan Nevins's *The War for the Union* (4 vols., 1959–1971). Other good surveys are William C. Davis's *The Imperiled Union* (3 vols., 1982–1989) and James M. McPherson's *Ordeal by Fire: The Civil War and Reconstruction* (1982).° The many military histories by Bruce Catton are extremely readable; begin with *This Hallowed Ground* (1956).° *The Image of War, 1861–1865* (6 vols., 1981–1989), edited by William C. Davis, is a useful collection of photographs.

The Civil War period features a number of firsthand accounts. Among the better are *Mary Chesnut's Civil War* (1981),° edited by C. Vann Woodward, and *The Children of Pride* (1972; abridged ed., 1984),° edited by Robert M. Myers. The life of the common soldier is well treated by Bell I. Wiley in *The Life of Johnny Reb* (1943) and *The Life of Billy Yank* (1943). For the black soldier's perspective, see *On The Altar of Freedom: A Black Soldier's Civil War Letters From The Front* (1991), edited by Virginia M. Adams.

For emphasis on the South, turn first to Emory M. Thomas's *The*

°These books are available in paperback editions.

Confederate Nation, 1861–1865 (1979). Older, but still reliable, is Clement Eaton's *A History of the Southern Confederacy* (1954). For a sparkling account of the birth of the Rebel nation, see William C. Davis's *"A Government of Our Own": The Making of the Confederacy* (1994). The same author provides a fine biography of Jefferson Davis in *Jefferson Davis: The Man and His Hour* (1992).

Shelby Foote's *The Civil War* (3 vols., 1958–1974)° gives the most thorough treatment of the military conflict from the southern perspective. The war in the Eastern Theater is handled in the several biographies of Robert E. Lee, among them Douglas S. Freeman's *R. E. Lee: A Biography* (4 vols., 1934–1936) and Thomas L. Connelly's *Marble Man* (1977).° For a revisionist's view of Lee, see Alan T. Nolan's *Lee Considered: General Robert E. Lee and Civil War History* (1991).

More recent scholarship on the military conflict includes Steven E. Wordsworth's *Jefferson Davis and His Generals: The Failure of Confederate Command in the West* (1991) and Paul D. Casdorph's *Lee and Jackson: Confederate Chieftains* (1992). Those interested in learning more about one of Lee's greatest lieutenants should consult Jeffrey D. West's *General James Longstreet: The Confederacy's Most Controversial Soldier* (1992). A cultural interpretation of Confederate military behavior is Grady McWhiney and Perry D. Jamieson's *Attack and Die* (1982). MacKinlay Kantor's *Andersonville* (1955)° covers that tragedy.

The history of the North is surveyed in Philip S. Paludan's *"A People's Contest": The Union at War, 1861–1865* (1988). Treatments of northern politics during the war include David H. Donald's *Charles Sumner and the Rights of Man* (1970), Harold M. Hyman's *A More Perfect Union* (1973), and Allan G. Bogue's *The Earnest Men: Republicans of the Civil War Senate* (1981). Diplomatic relations with Europe are covered in Glyndon Van Deusen's *William Henry Seward* (1967).

The central political figure, Abraham Lincoln, is the subject of many books. Good single-volume biographies are Stephen B. Oates's *With Malice toward None* (1977)° and Benjamin P. Thomas's *Abraham Lincoln* (1952). Carl Sandburg's *Lincoln: The War Years* (4 vols., 1939) gives the fullest treatment of his presidential career. Varying interpretations of Lincoln can be found in David H. Donald's *Lincoln Reconsidered* (1956), Garry Wills's *Lincoln at Gettysburg* (1992), and Richard N. Current's *The Lincoln Nobody Knows* (1958). On Lincoln's assassination, see William Hanchett's *The Lincoln Murder Conspiracies* (1983). For his wife see Jean H. Baker's *Mary Todd Lincoln: A Biography* (1987).

The emphasis is also on Lincoln in a number of works dealing with northern military strategy. A fine interpretive work is T. Harry

°These books are available in paperback editions.

Williams's *Lincoln and His Generals* (1952).° Concerning specific military campaigns, see Stephen W. Sears's *Landscape Turned Red: The Battle of Antietam* (1983) and *To the Gates of Richmond* (1993), James Lee McDonough and James Pickett Jones's *War So Terrible: Sherman and Atlanta* (1992), Robert Garth Scott's *Into The Wilderness with the Army of The Potomac* (1985), and Albert Castel's *Decision in The West: The Atlanta Campaign of 1864* (1992). Biographical studies of the northern military leaders include T. Harry Williams's *McClellan, Sherman and Grant* (1962), Brooks D. Simpson's *Let Us Have Peace: U. S. Grant and The Politics of War and Reconstruction, 1861–1868* (1991), John F. Marszalek's *Sherman, A Soldier's Passion for Order* (1993), and Charles Royster's *The Destructive War: William Tecumseh Sherman, Stonewall Jackson, and the Americans* (1991), and William S. McFeely's *Grant: A Biography* (1981).° The views of northern intellectuals on the war is the subject of George M. Fredrickson's fine work, *The Inner Civil War* (1965).

How the emancipated slave fared during the war has drawn some scholarly attention. The standard overview is Benjamin Quarles's *The Negro in the Civil War* (1953).° The career of the black soldier is found in Joseph T. Glatthaar's *Forged in Battle: The Civil War Alliance of Black Soldiers and White Officers* (1989), Dudley T. Cornish's *The Sable Arm* (1956), and *Freedom: A Documentary History of Emancipation, 1861–1867,* edited by Ira Berlin, Joseph P. Reidy, and Leslie S. Rowland (1982). Willie Lee Rose's *Rehearsal for Reconstruction: The Port Royal Experiment* (1964) and Louis S. Gerteis's *From Contraband to Freedman: Federal Policy toward Southern Blacks, 1861–1865* (1973) both trace the federal government's policies dealing with freed slaves during the war. For Lincoln's viewpoint, see LaWanda Cox's *Lincoln and Black Freedom: A Study in Presidential Leadership* (1981).° The Confederate viewpoint is handled in Robert F. Durden's *The Gray and the Black* (1972). For the black woman's experience, see Susie King Taylor's *Reminiscences of My Life: A Black Woman's Civil War Memoirs* (1988) and Jacqueline Jones's *Labor of Love, Labor of Sorrow: Black Women, Work and the Family from Slavery to Present* (1985).

Recent gender and ethnic studies include *Divided Houses: Gender and The Civil War,* edited by Catherine Clinton and Nina Silber (1992), Shirley Samuels's *The Culture of Sentiment: Race, Gender, and Sentimentality in 19th-Century America* (1992), George C. Rable's *Civil Wars: Women and the Crises of Southern Nationalism* (1989), and William L. Burton's *Melting Pot Soldiers: The Union's Ethnic Regiments* (1988). For a fine biography of the North's most famous nurse, see Stephen B. Oates's *A Woman of Valor: Clara Barton and the Civil War* (1994).

°These books are available in paperback editions.

18 ✐

RECONSTRUCTION:
NORTH AND SOUTH

The War's Aftermath

In the spring of 1865 the cruel war was over. At the frightful cost of 620,000 lives and the destruction of the southern economy and much of its landscape, American nationalism emerged triumphant, and some 4 million slaves emerged free. Ratification of the Thirteenth Amendment in December 1865 abolished slavery throughout the Union.

But peace had come only on the battlefields. "Cannon conquer," recognized a northern editor, "but they do not necessarily convert." Now the North faced the task of "reconstructing" a ravaged and resentful South. A few northerners thought the task was relatively simple. The Boston poet and professor James Russell Lowell wrote a friend in April 1865: "I worry a little about reconstruction, but am inclined to think that matters will very much settle themselves." He was wrong. An array of difficult issues confronted northern politicians. Should the Confederate leaders be tried for treason? How should new governments be formed? How and at whose expense was the South's economy to be rebuilt? What was to be done with the freed slaves? Were they to be given land? social equality? education? voting rights? Such complex questions required sober reflection and careful planning, but policy makers did not have the luxury of time or the benefits of consensus.

DEVELOPMENT IN THE NORTH   To some Americans the Civil War had been more truly a social revolution than the War of Independence, for it reduced the once-dominant power of planter agrarians in the national councils and elevated that of the "captains of industry." It is easy to

The Grand Review of Union Troops in Victory, *Washington, D.C., May 1865.*

exaggerate the profundity of this change, but government did become subtly more friendly to businessmen and unfriendly to those who would probe into their activities. The wartime Republican Congress had delivered on the major platform promises of 1860, which had cemented the allegiance of northeastern businessmen and western farmers to the party of free labor.

In the absence of southern members, Congress during the war had passed the Morrill Tariff, which brought the average level of duties up to about double what it had been on the eve of conflict. The National Banking Act created a uniform system of banking and bank-note currency, and helped to finance the war. Congress also passed legislation guaranteeing that the first transcontinental railroad would run along a north-central route from Omaha to Sacramento, and donated public lands and public bonds to ensure its financing. In the Homestead Act of 1862, moreover, Congress voted free homesteads of 160 acres to settlers. They had to occupy the land for five years. The Morrill Land Grant Act of the same year conveyed to each state 30,000 acres of public land per member of Congress from the state, the proceeds from the sale of which went to create colleges of "agriculture and mechanic arts." Such measures helped stimulate the North's economy in the years after the Civil War.

DEVASTATION IN THE SOUTH   The postwar South, where most of the fighting had occurred, offered a sharp contrast to the victorious North. Along the path of General Sherman's army, one observer reported in 1866, the countryside still "looked for many miles like a broad black streak of ruin and desolation." Columbia, South Carolina, said another witness, was "a wilderness of ruins," Charleston a place of "vacant houses, of widowed women, of rotting wharves, of deserted warehouses, of weed-wild gardens, of miles of grass-grown streets, of acres of pitiful and voiceless barrenness." In the Tennessee River valley, a British visitor reported: "The trail of war is visible . . . in burnt-up gin houses, ruined bridges, mills, and factories." The border states of Missouri and Kentucky had experienced a guerrilla war that lapsed into postwar anarchy perpetrated by marauding bands of bushwhackers turned outlaws, such as the notorious James boys, Frank and Jesse.

Throughout the South, property values had collapsed. Confederate bonds and money became worthless; railroads were damaged or destroyed. Cotton that had escaped destruction was seized as Confederate property or in forfeit of federal taxes. Emancipation of the slaves wiped out perhaps $4 billion invested in human flesh and left the labor

The "burned district" of Richmond, Virginia, April, 1865.

system in disarray. The great age of expansion in the cotton market was over. Not until 1879 would the cotton crop again equal the record harvest of 1860; tobacco production did not regain its prewar level until 1880; the sugar crop of Louisiana not until 1893; and the old rice industry of the Tidewater and the hemp industry of the Kentucky Bluegrass never regained their prewar status.

FORCED DOMESTICITY   The defeat of the Confederacy transformed much of southern society. The freeing of slaves, the destruction of property, and the free fall in land values left many among the former planter elite destitute and homeless. Amanda Worthington, a plantation mistress from Mississippi, saw her whole world destroyed. In the fall of 1865, she assessed the damage: "None of us can realize that we are no longer wealthy—yet thanks to the yankees, the cause of all unhappiness, such is the case. As long as I thought we would conquer in our just cause, I cared nothing for the loss of property for I felt as if we would be rich if we had *Our Rights & Our Country* left us—but now they are lost too, & *we have suffered in vain. In vain!* There is where the bitterness lies!"

Genteel southerners now found themselves forced to rebuild lives and families without the help of slaves. Women accustomed to relying on slaves for their every need were unprepared for the tasks at hand. One girl could not even comb her own hair; a matron cried at night because she had no one to wash her feet. "I did the washing for six weeks," one tired woman wrote, "[and] came near ruining myself for life as I was too delicately raised for such hard work." Those who still had some money after the war often recruited former slaves to work as domestic servants. Now, however, they had to pay for their services.

BITTER IN DEFEAT   After the Civil War many former Confederates were so embittered by defeat and so resistant to the idea of living under northern rule that they abandoned their native region rather than submit to "Yankee rule." Some migrated to Canada, Europe, Mexico, South America, and Asia. Others preferred the western territories and states. Still others moved north, settling in northern and midwestern cities on the assumption that educational and economic opportunities would be better among the victors.

Most of those who remained in the South returned to find their farms and homes and communities transformed. One Confederate army captain reported that on his father's plantation "Our negroes are living in great comfort. They were delighted to see me with overflowing affection. They waited on me as before, gave me breakfast, splendid dinners, etc. But they firmly and respectfully informed me: 'We own this land now. Put it out of your head that it will ever be yours again.'"

As Union troops fanned out across the defeated South, it was readily apparent that many former Confederates resented and resisted their presence. People cursed and spat upon the troops as they marched into town. Acts of sabotage kept the federal forces on the alert. A Virginia woman expressed a spirited defiance common among her circle of friends: "Every day, every hour, that I live increases my hatred and detestation, and loathing of that race. They [Yankees] disgrace our common humanity. As a people I consider them vastly inferior to the better classes of our slaves." Fervent southern nationalists, both men and women, planted in their children a similar hatred of Yankees and a defiance of northern rule. One mother said that she trained her children to "fear God, love the South, and live to avenge her."

LEGALLY FREE, SOCIALLY BOUND   In the former Confederate states, the newly freed slaves suffered most of all. According to Frederick Douglass, the black abolitionist, the former slave remained dependent: "He had neither money, property, nor friends. He was free from the old plantation, but he had nothing but the dusty road under his feet. He was free from the old quarter that once gave him shelter, but a slave to the rains of summer and the frosts of winter. He was turned loose, naked, hungry, and destitute to the open sky."

A few northerners argued that what the ex-slaves needed most was their own land. But even dedicated abolitionists shrank from endorsing measures of land reform that might have given the freed slaves more self-support and independence. Citizenship and legal rights were one

According to a former Confederate general, recently freed blacks had "nothing but freedom."

thing, wholesale confiscation and land distribution quite another. Instead of land or material help, the freed slaves more often got advice and moral platitudes.

In 1865 Representative George Julian of Indiana and Senator Charles Sumner of Massachusetts proposed to give freed slaves forty-acre homesteads carved out of Rebel lands taken under the Confiscation Act of 1862. But their plan for outright grants was replaced by a program of rentals since, under the law, confiscation was effective only for the lifetime of the offender. Discussions of land distribution, however, fueled rumors that freed slaves would get "forty acres and a mule," a slogan that swept the South at the end of the war. Its source remains unknown, but the aspirations that gave rise to it are clear enough. As one black man in Mississippi put it: "Gib us our own land and we take care ourselves; but widout land, de ole massas can hire us or starve us, as dey please." More lands were seized as "abandoned lands" under an act of 1864, and for default on the direct taxes that Congress had levied early in the war, than under the Confiscation Act. The most conspicuous example of confiscation was the estate of Robert E. Lee and the Custis family, which became Arlington National Cemetery, but larger amounts were taken in the South Carolina Sea Islands and elsewhere. Some of these lands were sold to freed blacks, some to Yankee speculators.

THE FREEDMEN'S BUREAU   On March 3, 1865, Congress set up within the War Department the Bureau of Refugees, Freedmen, and Abandoned Lands, to provide "such issues of provisions, clothing, and fuel"

The Freedmen's Bureau set up schools such as this throughout the former Confederate states.

as might be needed to relieve "destitute and suffering refugees and freedmen and their wives and children." The Freedmen's Bureau would also take over abandoned and confiscated land for rental in forty-acre tracts to "loyal refugees and freedmen," who might buy the land at a fair price within three years. But the amount of such land was limited. Under General Oliver O. Howard as commissioner, and assistant commissioners in each state of the former Confederacy, agents were entrusted with negotiating labor contracts (something new for both blacks and planters), providing medical care, and setting up schools, often in cooperation with northern agencies such as the American Missionary Association and the Freedmen's Aid Society. The bureau had its own courts to deal with labor disputes and land titles, and its agents were further authorized to supervise trials involving blacks in other courts. White intransigence and the failure to grasp the intensity of racial prejudice increasingly thwarted the efforts of Freedmen's Bureau agents to protect and assist the former slaves.

And Congress was not willing to strengthen the powers of the Freedmen's Bureau to reflect such problems. Beyond temporary relief measures, no program of reconstruction ever incorporated much more than constitutional and legal rights for freedmen. These were important in themselves, of course, but the extent to which even these should go was very uncertain, to be settled more by the course of events than by any clear-cut commitment to equality.

THE BATTLE OVER RECONSTRUCTION

The problem of reconstructing the South arose first at the very beginning of the Civil War, when the western counties of Virginia refused to go along with secession. In 1861 a loyal state government of Virginia was proclaimed at Wheeling, and this government in turn consented to the formation of a new state called West Virginia, duly if irregularly admitted to the Union in 1863. The loyal government of Virginia then carried on from Alexandria, its reach limited to that part of the state that the Union controlled. As Union forces advanced into the South, Lincoln in 1862 named military governors for Tennessee, Arkansas, and Louisiana. By the end of the following year he had formulated a plan for regular governments in those states and any others that might qualify.

LINCOLN'S PLAN AND CONGRESS'S RESPONSE   Acting under his pardon power, President Lincoln issued in December 1863 a Proclamation of Amnesty and Reconstruction, under which any rebel state could form a Union government whenever a number equal to 10 percent of those who had voted in 1860 took an oath of allegiance to the Constitution and the Union, and had received a presidential pardon. Participants also had to swear support for laws and proclamations dealing with emancipation. Certain groups, however, were excluded from the pardon: civil and diplomatic officers of the Confederacy; senior officers of the Confederate army and navy; judges, congressmen, and military officers of the United States who had left their posts to aid the rebellion; and those accused of failure to treat captured black soldiers and their officers as prisoners of war. Under this plan loyal governments appeared in Tennessee, Arkansas, and Louisiana, but Congress recognized them neither by representation nor in counting the electoral votes of 1864.

In the absence of any specific provisions for reconstruction in the Constitution, politicians disagreed as to where authority properly rested. Lincoln claimed the right to direct reconstruction under the clause that set forth the presidential pardon power, and also under the constitutional obligation of the United States to guarantee each state a republican form of government. Republican congressmen, however, argued that this obligation implied a power of Congress to act.

A few conservative and most moderate Republicans supported Lincoln's program of immediate restoration. A small but influential group known as Radical Republicans, however, favored a sweeping transformation of southern society based on granting freedmen full-fledged citizenship. The Radicals hoped to reconstruct southern society so as to mirror the North's emphasis on small-scale competitive capitalism. This meant thwarting the efforts of the old planter class to reestablish a caste system and keep the freed blacks in a state of peonage.

The Radicals also maintained that Congress, not the president, should supervise the reconstruction program. To this end they helped pass in 1864 the Wade-Davis Bill, sponsored by Senator Benjamin Wade of Ohio and Representative Henry Winter Davis of Maryland. It proposed much more stringent requirements than Lincoln had. In contrast to Lincoln's 10 percent plan, the Wade-Davis Bill required that a majority of white male citizens declare their allegiance and that only those who could take an "ironclad" oath (required of federal officials since 1862) attesting to their *past* loyalty could vote or serve in the state constitutional conventions. The conventions, moreover, would have to abolish slavery, exclude from political rights high-ranking civil and military officers of the Confederacy, and repudiate debts incurred "under the sanction of the usurping power."

Passed during the closing day of the session, the Wade-Davis Bill never became law. Lincoln exercised a pocket veto. That is, he simply refused to sign it, but he issued an artful statement that he would accept any state that preferred to present itself under the congressional plan. The sponsors responded with the Wade-Davis Manifesto, which accused the president, among other sins, of usurping power and attempting to use readmitted states to ensure his reelection.

Lincoln offered his last public words on reconstruction in his final public address, on April 11, 1865. Speaking from the White House balcony, he pronounced that the Confederate states had never left the Union. These states were simply "out of their proper practical relation with the Union," and the object was to get them "into their proper practical relation." It would be easier to do this by merely ignoring the abstract issue: "Finding themselves safely at home, it would be utterly immaterial whether they had been abroad." At a cabinet meeting, Lincoln proposed to get state governments in operation before Congress met in December. He said that there were men in Congress who, if their motives were good, were nevertheless impracticable, and who possessed feelings of hate and vindictiveness with which he did not sympathize and could not participate. He wanted "no persecution, no bloody work," no radical restructuring of southern social and economic life.

THE ASSASSINATION OF LINCOLN   That evening Lincoln went to Ford's Theater and his rendezvous with death. Shot by John Wilkes Booth, a

City Hall in New York City, on April 24, is thronged with people anxious for a last look at Lincoln.

crazed actor and Confederate zealot who thought he was helping the South, the president died the next morning. Accomplices had also targeted Vice-President Andrew Johnson and Secretary of State William Seward. Seward and four others, including his son, were victims of severe but not fatal stab wounds. Johnson escaped injury, however, because his would-be assassin got cold feet and wound up tipsy in the barroom of Johnson's hotel.

Martyred in the hour of victory, Lincoln entered into the national mythology even while the funeral train took its mournful burden north to New York and westward home to Springfield. The nation extracted a full measure of vengeance from the conspirators. Pursued into Virginia, Booth was trapped and shot in a burning barn. His last words were: "Tell Mother I die for my country. I thought I did for the best." Three of Booth's collaborators were brought to trial by a military commission and hanged, along with the woman at whose boardinghouse they had plotted. Three others got life sentences, including a Maryland doctor who set the leg Booth had broken when he jumped to the stage. President Johnson eventually pardoned them all, except one who died in prison. The doctor achieved lasting fame by making common a once obscure expression. His name was Mudd. Apart from those cases, however, there was only one other execution in the aftermath of war: Henry Wirz, who commanded the infamous prison at Andersonville, Georgia, where Union prisoners were probably more the victims of war conditions than of deliberate cruelty.

JOHNSON'S PLAN Lincoln's death suddenly elevated to the White House Andrew Johnson of Tennessee, a man whose state was still in legal limbo and whose party affiliation was unclear. He was a War Democrat who had been put on the Union ticket in 1864 as a gesture of unity. Of humble origins like Lincoln, Johnson had moved as a youth from his birthplace in Raleigh, North Carolina, to Greeneville, Tennessee, where he became proprietor of a tailor shop. Self-educated with the help of his wife, he had made himself into an effective orator of the rough-and-tumble school, served as mayor, congressman, governor, and senator, then as military governor of Tennessee before he became vice-president. In the process he had become an advocate of the small farmers against the privileges of the large planters. He also shared the racial attitudes of most white yeomen. "Damn the negroes," he exclaimed to a friend during the war, "I am fighting those traitorous aristocrats, their masters."

Some of the Radicals at first thought Johnson, unlike Lincoln, to be one of them. Johnson had, for example, once asserted that treason "must be made infamous and traitors must be impoverished." Senator Benjamin Wade loved such language. "Johnson, we have faith in you," he promised. "By the gods, there will be no trouble now in running this government." But Wade would soon find him as unsympathetic as Lincoln, if for different reasons.

Johnson's very loyalty to the Union sprang from a strict adherence to the Constitution. Given to dogmatic abstractions that were alien to Lincoln's temperament, he nevertheless arrived by a different route at similar objectives. The states should be brought back into their proper relation to the Union not by ignoring as a pernicious abstraction the theoretical question of their status, but because the states and the Union were indestructible. And like many other whites, he found it hard to accept the growing Radical movement toward suffrage for blacks. By May 1865 he was saying "there is no such thing as reconstruction. Those States have not gone out of the Union. Therefore reconstruction is unnecessary."

Johnson's plan to restore the Union thus closely resembled Lincoln's. A new Proclamation of Amnesty (May 1865) added to those Lincoln had excluded from pardon everybody with taxable property worth more than $20,000. These wealthy planters, bankers, and merchants were the people Johnson believed had led the South into secession. But those in the excluded groups might make special applications for pardon, and before the year was out Johnson had issued some 13,000 such pardons.

Andrew Johnson.

In every case Johnson ruled that pardon, whether by general amnesty or special clemency, restored one's property rights in land. He defined as "confiscated" only lands already sold under court decree. This applied to lands set aside by order of General Sherman, who had allocated for the exclusive use of freed slaves a coastal strip thirty miles wide from Charleston south to the St. John's River in Florida.

Johnson's rulings nipped in the bud an experiment in land distribution that had barely begun. More than seventy years later, one freed slave, born in Orange County, North Carolina, spoke bluntly of his dashed hopes: "Lincoln got the praise for freeing us, but did he do it? He give us freedom without giving us any chance to live to ourselves and we still had to depend on the southern white man for work, food and clothing, and he held us through our necessity and want in a state of servitude but little better than slavery." A South Carolina Land Commission, established by the Radical state government in 1869, distributed lands to more than 5,000 black families. One black community in the upcountry, Promised Land, still retains its identity more than a century later, an obscure reminder of what might have been.

On the same day that Johnson announced his amnesty program, he issued another proclamation to his native state of North Carolina. Within six more weeks, he issued similar edicts for the other rebel states not already organized. In each a native Unionist became provisional governor with authority to call a convention elected by loyal voters. Lincoln's 10 percent requirement was omitted. Johnson called upon the conventions to invalidate the secession ordinances, abolish slavery, and repudiate all debts incurred to aid the Confederacy. Each state, moreover, was to ratify the Thirteenth Amendment. Lincoln had privately advised the governor of Louisiana to consider a grant of suffrage to some blacks, "the very intelligent and those who have fought gallantly in our ranks." In his final public address he had also endorsed a limited black suffrage. Johnson repeated Lincoln's advice. He reminded the provisional governor of Mississippi, for example, that the state conventions might "with perfect safety" extend suffrage to blacks with education or with military service so as to "disarm the adversary"—the adversary being "radicals who are wild upon Negro franchise."

The state conventions for the most part met Johnson's requirements, although South Carolina and Mississippi did not repudiate their debt and the new Mississippi legislature refused to ratify the Thirteenth Amendment. Presidential agents sent to the South reported "that the mass of thinking men of the south accept the present situation of affairs in good faith." But Carl Schurz of Missouri found "an *utter absence of national feeling* . . . and a desire to preserve slavery . . . as much and as long as possible." The discrepancy between the two reports is perhaps only apparent: southern whites accepted the situation because they thought so little had changed after all. Emboldened by Johnson's indulgence, they ignored his counsels of expediency. Suggestions of black suffrage were scarcely raised in the conventions and promptly squelched when they were.

SOUTHERN INTRANSIGENCE   When Congress met in December 1865, for the first time since the end of the war, it had only to accept the accomplished fact that state governments were functioning in the South. But there was the rub. The new governments were remarkably like the old. Southern voters had acted with extreme disregard of northern feelings. Among the new legislative members presenting themselves were Georgia's Alexander H. Stephens, ex-vice-president of the Confederacy, now claiming a seat in the Senate, four Confederate generals, eight colonels, six cabinet members, and a host of lesser Rebels. The Congress forthwith denied seats to all members from the eleven former Confederate states. It was too much to expect, after four bloody years, that Unionists would welcome ex-Confederates like prodigal sons.

Furthermore, the new southern legislatures, in passing repressive Black Codes regulating the freedom of blacks, demonstrated that they intended to preserve slavery as nearly as possible. As one white southerner stressed, "the ex-slave was not a free man; he was a free Negro," and the Black Codes were intended to highlight the distinction. The codes extended to blacks certain rights they had not hitherto enjoyed, but universally set them aside as a separate caste subject to special restraints. Details varied from state to state, but some provisions were common. Existing marriages, including common-law marriages, were recognized, and testimony of blacks was accepted in legal cases involving blacks—and in six states, in all cases. Blacks could hold property. They could sue and be sued in the courts. On the other hand, blacks could not own farm lands in Mississippi or city lots in South Carolina. In some states they could not carry firearms without a license to do so.

The codes' labor provisions confirmed suspicions that whites were seeking to preserve the slave labor system. Blacks were required to enter into annual labor contracts, with provision for punishment in case of violation. Dependent children were subject to compulsory apprenticeship and corporal punishment by masters. Vagrants were punished with severe fines and could be sold into private service if unable to pay. To many people it indeed seemed that slavery was on the way back in another guise. The new Mississippi penal code virtually said so: "All penal and criminal laws now in force describing the mode of punishment of crimes and misdemeanors committed by slaves, free negroes, or mulattoes are hereby reenacted, and decreed to be in full force against all freedmen, free negroes and mulattoes."

Faced with such evidence of southern intransigence, moderate

Slavery Is Dead (?) *Thomas Nast's cartoon suggests that, in 1866, slavery was only legally dead.*

Republicans drifted more and more toward Radical views. Having excluded southern members, the new Congress set up a Joint Committee on Reconstruction, with nine members from the House and six from the Senate, to gather evidence and submit proposals. Headed by the moderate Senator William Pitt Fessenden, the committee fell under greater Radical influence as a parade of witnesses testified to the Rebels' impenitence. Initiative on the committee fell to determined Radicals who knew what they wanted: Ben Wade of Ohio, George W. Julian of Indiana—and most conspicuously of all, Thaddeus Stevens of Pennsylvania and Charles Sumner of Massachusetts.

THE RADICALS   The motivations of the Radical Republicans were mixed, and perhaps little purpose is served in attempting to sort them out. Purity of motive is rare in an imperfect world. Most Radicals had been connected with the antislavery cause. While one could be hostile to both slavery and blacks, many whites approached the question of black rights with a humanitarian impulse. Few could escape the bitterness bred by the long and bloody war, however, or remain unaware of the partisan advantage that would come to the Republican party from black suffrage. But the party of Union and freedom, after all, could best guarantee the fruits of victory, they reasoned, and black suffrage could best guarantee black rights.

The growing conflict of opinion over reconstruction policy brought about an inversion in constitutional reasoning. Secessionists—and Johnson—were now arguing that their states had in fact remained in the Union, and some Radicals were contriving arguments that they had left the Union after all. Thaddeus Stevens argued that the Confederate states were now conquered provinces, subject to the absolute will of the victors. Charles Sumner maintained that the southern states, by their pretended acts of secession, had in effect committed suicide and reverted to the status of unorganized territories subject to the will of Congress. But few ever took such ideas seriously. Republicans converged instead on the "forfeited-rights theory," later embodied in the report of the Joint Committee on Reconstruction. This held that the states as entities continued to exist, but by the acts of secession and war had forfeited "all civil and political rights under the constitution." And Congress was the proper authority to determine conditions under which such rights might be restored.

JOHNSON'S BATTLE WITH CONGRESS   A long year of political battling remained, however, before this idea triumphed. By the end of 1865, Radical views had gained a majority in Congress, if one not yet large enough to override presidential vetoes. But the critical year 1866 saw the gradual waning of Johnson's power and influence; much of this was self-induced. Johnson first challenged Congress in February 1866, when he vetoed a bill to extend the life of the Freedmen's Bureau. The measure, he said, assumed that wartime conditions still existed, whereas the country had returned "to a state of peace and industry." No longer valid as a war measure, the bill violated the Constitution in several ways he declared. It made the federal government responsible for the care of indigents. It was passed by a Congress in which eleven states were denied seats. And it used vague language in defining the "civil rights

Two leading Radicals: Senator Charles Sumner (left) *and Representative Thaddeus Stevens.*

and immunities" of blacks. The Congress soon moved to correct that particular defect, but for the time being Johnson's prestige remained sufficiently intact that the Senate upheld his veto.

Three days after the veto, however, Johnson undermined his already weakening prestige with a gross assault on Radical leaders during an impromptu speech. The Joint Committee on Reconstruction, he charged, was "an irresponsible central directory" that had repudiated the principle of an indestructible Union and accepted the legality of secession by entertaining conquered-province and state-suicide theories. From that point forward moderate Republicans backed away from a president who had opened himself to counterattack. He was "an alien enemy of a foreign state," Stevens declared. Sumner called him "an insolent drunken brute"—and Johnson was open to the charge because of an incident at his vice-presidential inauguration. Weakened by illness at the time, he had taken a belt of brandy to get him through the ceremony and, under the influence of fever and alcohol, had become incoherent.

In mid-March 1866 Congress passed the Civil Rights Act. A response to the Black Codes, this bill declared that "all persons born in the United States and not subject to any foreign power, excluding Indians not taxed," were citizens entitled to "full and equal benefit of all laws." The grant of citizenship to native-born blacks, Johnson fumed, went beyond anything formerly held to be within the scope of federal power. It would, moreover, "foment discord among the races." This time, on April 9, 1866, Congress overrode the presidential veto. On July 16 it enacted a revised Bureau Bill, again overriding a veto. From that point on Johnson steadily lost both public and political support.

THE FOURTEENTH AMENDMENT   To remove all doubt about the constitutionality of the new Civil Rights Act, which was justified as implementing freedom under the Thirteenth Amendment, the Joint Committee recommended a new amendment, which passed Congress on June 16, 1866, and was ratified by July 28, 1868. The Fourteenth Amendment, however, went far beyond the Civil Rights Act. It merits close scrutiny because of its broad impact on subsequent laws and litigation.

The first section asserted four principles: it reaffirmed state and federal citizenship for persons born or naturalized in the United States, and it forbade any *state* (the word "state" was important in later litigation) to abridge the "privileges and immunities" of citizens, to deprive any *person* (again an important term) of life, liberty, or property without "due process of law," or to deny any person "the equal protection of the laws."

Extract Const. Amend. *Referring to the recently ratified Fourteenth Amendment, Uncle Sam advises the president in this cartoon, "Now, ANDY, take it right down. More you Look at it, worse you'll Like it."*

The last three of these clauses have been the subject of long and involved lawsuits resulting in applications not widely, if at all, foreseen at the time. The "due-process clause" has come to mean that state as well as federal power is subject to the Bill of Rights, and it has been used to protect corporations, as legal "persons," from "unreasonable" regulation by the states. Other provisions of the amendment had less far-reaching effects. One section specified that the debt of the United States "shall not be questioned," but declared "illegal and void" all debts contracted in aid of the rebellion. Another section specified the power of Congress to pass laws enforcing the amendment.

Johnson's home state was among the first to ratify the Fourteenth Amendment. In Tennessee, which had harbored probably more Unionists than any other Confederate state, the government had fallen under Radical control. The state's governor, in reporting the results to the secretary of the Senate, added: "Give my respects to the dead dog of the White House." His words afford a fair sample of the growing acrimony on both sides of the reconstruction debates. In May and July bloody race riots in Memphis and New Orleans added fuel to the flames. Both incidents involved indiscriminate massacres of blacks by local police and white mobs. The carnage, Radicals argued, was the natural fruit of Johnson's policy. "Witness Memphis, witness New Orleans," Sumner cried. "Who can doubt that the President is the author of these tragedies?"

RECONSTRUCTING THE SOUTH

THE TRIUMPH OF CONGRESSIONAL RECONSTRUCTION   As 1866 drew to an end, the congressional elections promised to be a referendum on the growing split between Johnson and the Radicals. In August Johnson's friends staged a National Union Convention in Philadelphia. Men from Massachusetts and South Carolina marched down the aisle arm in arm to symbolize national reconciliation. The Radicals countered with a convention of their own and organized a congressional campaign committee to coordinate their propaganda.

Johnson responded with a speaking tour of the Midwest, a "swing around the circle," which turned into an undignified shouting contest between Johnson and his critics. Subjected to attacks on his integrity, Johnson responded in kind. In Cleveland he described the Radicals as "factious, domineering, tyrannical" men, and he foolishly exchanged hot-tempered insults with a heckler. At another stop, while Johnson was speaking from an observation car, the engineer mistakenly pulled the train out of the station, making the president appear quite the fool. Johnson may have been, as Secretary Seward claimed, the best stump speaker in the country. The trouble was, as another cabinet officer responded, the president ought not to be a stump speaker. It tended to confirm his image as a "ludicrous boor" and "drunken imbecile," which Radical papers projected. When the returns of the congressional elections came in, the Republicans had well over a two-thirds majority in each house, a comfortable margin with which to override any presidential vetoes.

The Congress in fact enacted a new program even before new members took office. Two acts passed in 1867 extended the suffrage to African Americans in the District of Columbia and the territories. Another law provided that the new Congress would convene on March 4 instead of the following December, depriving Johnson of a breathing spell. On March 2, 1867, two days before the old Congress expired, it passed three basic laws of congressional reconstruction over Johnson's vetoes: the Military Reconstruction Act, the Command of the Army Act (an amendment to an army appropriation), and the Tenure of Office Act.

The first of the three acts prescribed new conditions under which the formation of southern state governments should begin all over again. The other two sought to block obstruction by the president. The Command of the Army Act required that all orders from the commander-in-chief go through the headquarters of the general of the army, then Ulysses S. Grant, who could not be reassigned outside Washington without the consent of the Senate. The Radicals had faith in Grant, who was already leaning their way. The Tenure of Office Act required the

*This cartoon appeared at the time of the 1866
congressional elections. It shows "King Andy I"
approving the execution of Radical leaders in Congress.*

consent of the Senate for the president to remove any officeholder
whose appointment the Senate had to confirm in the first place. The
purpose of at least some congressmen was to retain Secretary of War
Edwin M. Stanton, the one Radical sympathizer in Johnson's cabinet.
But an ambiguity crept into the wording of the act. Cabinet officers, it
said, should serve during the term of the president who appointed
them—and Lincoln had appointed Stanton, although, to be sure, Johnson was serving out Lincoln's term.

The Military Reconstruction Act, often hailed or denounced as the
triumphant victory of "Radical" Reconstruction, actually represented a
compromise that fell short of a thoroughgoing radicalism. As first
reported from the Reconstruction Committee by Thaddeus Stevens, it
would have given military commanders in the South ultimate control
over law enforcement and would have left open indefinitely the terms of
future restoration. More moderate elements, however, pushed through
the "Blaine Amendment." Along with programs of land confiscation and
education, it scrapped the prolonged national control under which Radicals hoped to put through the far more revolutionary program of reducing the rebel states to territories. With the Blaine Amendment in place
the Reconstruction program boiled down to little more than a require-

ment that southern states accept black suffrage and ratify the Fourteenth Amendment. Years later Albion W. Tourgée, after a career as a "carpetbagger" in North Carolina, wrote: "Republicans gave the ballot to men without homes, money, education, or security, and then told them to use it to protect themselves. . . . It was cheap patriotism, cheap philanthropy, cheap success!"

The act began with a pronouncement that "no legal state governments or adequate protection for life and property now exists in the rebel States. . . ." One state, Tennessee, which had ratified the Fourteenth Amendment, was exempted from the application of the act. The other ten were divided into five military districts, and the commanding officer of each was authorized to keep order and protect the "rights of persons and property." To that end he might use military tribunals in place of civil courts when he judged it necessary. The Johnson governments remained intact for the time being, but new constitutions were to be framed "in conformity with the Constitution of the United States," in conventions elected by male citizens twenty-one and older "of whatever race, color, or previous condition." Each state constitution had to provide the same universal male suffrage. Then, once the constitution was ratified by a majority of voters and accepted by Congress, other criteria had to be met. The state legislature had to ratify the Fourteenth Amendment, and once the amendment became part of the Constitution, any given state would be entitled to representation in Congress. Persons excluded from officeholding by the proposed amendment were also excluded from participation in the process.

Johnson reluctantly appointed military commanders under the act, but the situation remained uncertain for a time. Some people expected the Supreme Court to strike down the act, and for the time being no machinery existed for the new elections. Congress quickly remedied that on March 23, 1867, with the Second Reconstruction Act, which directed the commanders to register for voting all adult males who swore they were qualified. A Third Reconstruction Act, passed on July 19, directed registrars to go beyond the loyalty oath and determine each person's eligibility to take it, and also authorized district commanders to remove and replace officeholders of any existing "so-called state" or division thereof. Before the end of 1867 new elections had been held in all the states but Texas.

Having clipped the president's wings, the Republican Congress moved a year later to safeguard its program from possible interference by the Supreme Court, which in a series of decisions had shown a readiness to question certain actions related to Reconstruction. With the Court considering *Ex parte McCardle*, the case of a Vicksburg editor arrested for criticizing the administration of the Fourth Military District who now sought release under the Habeas Corpus Act of 1867,

Congress acted. On March 27, 1868, it simply removed the power of the Supreme Court to review cases arising under the law, which Congress clearly had the right to do under its power to define the Court's appellate jurisdiction. The Court accepted this curtailment on the same day it affirmed the principle of an "indestructible union" in *Texas v. White* (1868). In that case it also asserted the right of Congress to reframe state governments.

THE IMPEACHMENT AND TRIAL OF JOHNSON   Congress's move to restrain the Supreme Court preceded by just a few days the opening arguments in the trial of the president in the Senate on an impeachment brought in by the House. Johnson, though hostile to the congressional program, had gone through the motions required of him. He continued, however, to pardon former Confederates in wholesale lots and replaced several district commanders whose Radical sympathies offended him. He and his cabinet members, moreover, largely ignored the Test Oath Act of 1862 by naming former Confederates to head post offices and other federal positions. Nevertheless a lengthy investigation by the House Judiciary Committee, extending through most of 1867, had failed to convince the House that grounds for impeachment existed.

Johnson himself provided the occasion for impeachment when he deliberately violated the Tenure of Office Act in order to test its constitutionality in the courts. Secretary of War Edwin M. Stanton had become a thorn in the president's side, refusing to resign despite his disagreements with the president's reconstruction policy. On August 12, 1867, during a congressional recess, Johnson suspended Stanton and named General Grant in his place. Grant's political stance was ambiguous at the time, but his acceptance implied cooperation with Johnson. When the Senate refused to confirm Johnson's action, however, Grant returned the office to Stanton. The president thereupon named General Lorenzo Thomas as secretary of war after a futile effort to interest General William T. Sherman. Three days later, on February 24, 1868, the House voted impeachment, to be followed by specific charges. In due course a special committee of seven brought in its report.

Of the eleven articles of impeachment, eight focused on the charge that he had unlawfully removed Stanton and had failed to give the Senate the name of a successor. Article 9 accused the president of issuing orders in violation of the Command of the Army Act. The last two in effect charged him with criticizing Congress by "inflammatory and scandalous harangues" and by claiming that the Congress was not legally valid without southern representatives. But Article 11 accused Johnson of "unlawfully devising and contriving" to violate the Reconstruction Acts, contrary to his obligation to execute the laws. At the least, it stated,

House of Representatives managers of the impeachment proceedings and trial of Andrew Johnson. Among them were Benjamin Butler (R-Mass., seated left) and Thaddeus Stevens (R-Pa., seated with cane).

Johnson had tried to obstruct Congress's will while observing the letter of the law.

The Senate trial opened on March 5 and continued until May 26, with Chief Justice Salmon P. Chase presiding. Seven managers from the House, including Thaddeus Stevens and Benjamin F. Butler, directed the prosecution. The president was spared the humiliation of a personal appearance. His defense counsel shrewdly insisted on narrowing the trial to questions that would be indictable offenses under the law, and steered the questions away from Johnson's manifest wish to frustrate the will of Congress. Such questions, they contended, were purely political in nature. In the end, enough Republican senators joined their pro-Johnson colleagues to prevent conviction. On May 16 the crucial vote came on Article 9: 35 votes guilty and 19 not guilty, one vote short of the two-thirds needed to convict. The trial then adjourned for a week. Reconvening on May 26, the Senate voted on Articles 2 and 3 by the same division, 35 to 19. Thereupon the Senate dissolved the tribunal.

In a parliamentary system Johnson probably would have been removed as leader of the government long before then. But by deciding the case on the narrowest grounds, the Senate made it unlikely that any future president could ever be removed except for the gravest offenses, and almost surely not for flouting the will of Congress in executing the laws. Impeachment of Johnson was in the end a great political mistake, for the failure to remove the president damaged Radical morale and support. Nevertheless, the Radical cause did gain something. To blunt the opposition, Johnson agreed not to obstruct the process of Reconstruction, named a secretary of war who was committed to enforcing the new laws, and sent to Congress the new Radical constitutions of Arkansas and South Carolina. Thereafter his obstruction ceased and Radical Reconstruction began in earnest.

REPUBLICAN RULE IN THE SOUTH   In June 1868 Congress agreed that seven states had met the conditions for readmission, all but Virginia, Mississippi, and Texas. Congress rescinded Georgia's admission, however, when the state legislature expelled twenty-eight black members on the pretext that the state constitution had failed to specify their eligibility, and seated some former Confederate leaders. The military commander of Georgia then forced the legislature to reseat the black members and remove the Confederates, and the state was compelled to ratify the Fifteenth Amendment before being admitted in July 1870. Mississippi, Texas, and Virginia had returned earlier in 1870, under the added requirement that they too ratify the Fifteenth Amendment. This amendment, submitted to the states in 1869, ratified in 1870, forbade the states to deny any person the vote on grounds of race, color, or previous condition of servitude.

Long before the new governments were established, Republican groups began to spring up in the South, chiefly sponsored by the Union League, founded at Philadelphia in 1862 to promote support for the Union. Emissaries of the league enrolled African Americans and loyal whites, initiated them into the secrets and rituals of the order, and instructed them "in their rights and duties." The league emphasized the display of such symbols as the Bible, the flag, the Constitution, and the Declaration of Independence. Agents of the Freedmen's Bureau, northern missionaries, teachers, and soldiers aided the cause and spread its influence. When the time came for political action, they were ready. In October 1867, for instance, on the eve of South Carolina's choice of convention delegates, the league reported eighty-eight chapters, which claimed to have enrolled almost every adult black male in the state.

BLACKS IN THE RECONSTRUCTED SOUTH

To focus solely on what white Republicans did to reconstruct the defeated South creates the false impression that the freed slaves were

A celebration by African Americans of the adoption of the Fifteenth Amendment, New York City, April 1870.

simply pawns in the hands of others. Such a stereotype appeared early. "The Negroes are to be pitied," wrote South Carolinian Julius J. Fleming, a white teacher, minister, and public official. "They do not understand the liberty which has been conferred upon them."

In fact, however, southern blacks were active agents in affecting the course of Reconstruction. Although many of them found themselves liberated but destitute after the fighting ended, the mere promise of freedom raised their hopes about achieving a biracial democracy, equal justice, and economic opportunity. "Most anyone ought to know that a man is better off free than as a slave, even if he did not have anything," said the Reverend E. P. Holmes, a black Georgia preacher and former domestic servant. "I would rather be free and have my liberty."

Participation in the Union army or navy gave many freedmen a training ground in leadership. Black military veterans would form the core of the first generation of African American political leaders in the postwar South. Military service provided many former slaves the first opportunities to learn to read and write. "A large portion of the regiment have been going to school during the winter months," wrote a black sergeant from Virginia in 1865. Army life also alerted them to alternative social choices and to new opportunities for advancement and respectability. "No negro who has ever been a soldier," reported a northern official after visiting a black unit, "can again be imposed upon; they have learnt what it is to be free and they will infuse their feelings into others."

Fighting for the Union cause also instilled a fervent sense of nationalism. "We are Americans," announced a gathering of Virginia blacks, "we know no other country, we love the land of our birth." Another Virginia freedman explained that the United States was "now *our* country—made emphatically so by the blood of our brethren."

The pent-up desire among former slaves for freedom from white control led them to establish independent black churches after the war, churches that would serve as the foundation of African American community life. In war-ravaged Charleston, South Carolina, the first new building to appear after the war was a black church on Calhoun Street; by 1866 ten more had been built. Blacks preferred Baptist churches over other denominations, in part because of their decentralized structure that allowed each congregation to worship in its own way. By 1890 there were over 1.3 million black Baptists in the South, nearly three times as many as any other black denomination. For many former slaves, churches were the first institutions they owned and controlled. In addition to forming viable new congregations, freed blacks organized thousands of fraternal, benevolent, and mutual-aid societies, clubs, lodges, and associations. Memphis, for example, had over two hundred such organizations; Richmond boasted twice that number.

The freed slaves, both women and men, also hastened to reestablish

First African Church, Richmond, Virginia, 1865.

and reaffirm families. Marriages that had been prohibited were now legitimized through the assistance of the Freedmen's Bureau. By 1870 a preponderant majority of former slaves lived in two-parent households. One white editor in Georgia, lamenting the difficulty of finding black women to serve as house servants, reported that "every negro woman wants to set up house keeping" for herself and her family. To do so they often chose to be sharecropping farmers. With little money or technical training, freed slaves faced the prospect of becoming wage laborers. Yet in order to retain as much autonomy over their productive energies and those of their children on both a daily and seasonal basis, many husbands and wives chose sharecropping. This enabled mothers and wives to devote more of their time to domestic needs while still contributing to family income.

Black communities in the postwar South also quickly sought to establish schools. The antebellum planter elite had denied education to blacks because they feared that literate slaves would organize uprisings. After the war the white elite feared that education programs would encourage both poor whites and blacks to leave the South in search of better social and economic opportunities. Economic leaders wanted to protect the competitive advantage afforded by the region's low-wage labor market.

The general resistance among the former slaveholding class to new education initiatives forced the freed slaves to rely on northern assistance or take their own initiative. A Mississippi Freedmen's Bureau agent noted in 1865 that when he told a gathering of some 3,000 former slaves that they "were to have the advantages of schools and education, their joy knew no bounds. They fairly jumped and shouted in gladness." Black churches and individuals helped raise the money and often built the schools and paid the teachers. Soldiers who had acquired some reading and writing skills often served as the first teachers, and the students included adults as well as children. A Florida teacher reported that a sixty-year-old former slave woman in her class was so excited by literacy that she "spells her lesson all the evening, then she dreams about it, and wakes up thinking about it."

BLACKS IN SOUTHERN POLITICS   The new role of African Americans in politics caused the most controversy, then and afterward. If largely illiterate and inexperienced in the rudiments of politics, they were little different from millions of whites enfranchised in the age of Jackson or immigrants herded to the polls by political bosses in New York and other cities after the war. Some freedmen frankly confessed their disadvantages. Beverly Nash, a black delegate in the South Carolina convention of 1868, told his colleagues: "I believe, my friends and fellow-citizens, we are not prepared for this suffrage. But we can learn.

A lithograph depicting five of the major black political figures of the Reconstruction period: Hiram Revels (top left) and Blanche K. Bruce (center) served in the U.S. Senate, Joseph H. Rainey (bottom left), John R. Lynch (bottom right), and James T. Rapier (top right) in the House of Representatives.

Give a man tools and let him commence to use them, and in time he will learn a trade. So it is with voting."

Several hundred black delegates participated in the statewide political conventions. Most had been selected by local political meetings or by churches, fraternal societies, Union Leagues, and black army units, although a few simply appointed themselves. "Some bring credentials," explained a North Carolina black leader, "others had as much as they could to bring themselves, having to escape from their homes stealthily at night" to avoid white assaults. The African American delegates "ranged all colors and apparently all conditions," but free mulattoes from the cities played the most prominent roles. At Louisiana's Republican state convention, for instance, nineteen of the twenty black delegates had been born free.

By 1867, however, former slaves began to gain political influence, and this led to debates that revealed emerging tensions within the black community. Some southern blacks resented the presence of northern brethren, while others complained that few ex-slaves were represented in leadership positions. Northern blacks and the southern free black elite, most of whom were urban dwellers, tended to oppose efforts to confiscate and redistribute land to the rural freedmen, and many insisted that political equality did not mean social equality. As an Alabama black leader stressed, "We do not ask that the ignorant and degraded shall be put on a social equality with the refined and intelligent." In general, however, unity rather than dissension prevailed, and blacks focused on common concerns such as full equality under the law.

Brought suddenly into politics in times that tried the most skilled of statesmen, many African Americans nevertheless served with distinction. Yet the derisive label "black Reconstruction" used by later critics exaggerates black political influence, which was limited mainly to voting, and overlooks the large numbers of white Republicans, especially in the mountain areas of the upper South. Only one of the new conventions, South Carolina's, had a black majority, 76 to 41. Louisiana's was evenly divided racially, and in only two other conventions were more than 20 percent of the members black: Florida's, with 40 percent, and Virginia's, with 24 percent. The Texas convention was only 10 percent black, and North Carolina's 11 percent—but that did not stop a white newspaper from calling it a body consisting of "baboons, monkeys, mules . . . and other jackasses."

In the new state governments, any African American participation was a novelty. Although some 600 blacks—most of them former slaves—served as state legislators, no black man was ever elected governor. Only a few served as judges, although in Louisiana Pinckney B. S. Pinchback, a northern black and former Union soldier, won the office of lieutenant-governor and served as acting governor when the white governor was indicted for corruption. Several blacks were elected lieutenant-governors, state treasurers, or secretaries of state. There were two black senators in Congress, Hiram Revels and Blanche K. Bruce, both Mississippi natives who had been educated in the North, and fourteen black members of the House during Reconstruction. Among these were some of the ablest congressmen of the time. African Americans served in every state legislature, and in South Carolina they made up a majority in both houses for two years.

CARPETBAGGERS AND SCALAWAGS   The top positions in southern state governments went for the most part to white Republicans, whom the opposition whites soon labeled "carpetbaggers" and "scalawags," depending on their place of birth. The northern opportunists who allegedly rushed south with all their belongings in carpetbags to grab the political spoils were more often than not Union veterans who had arrived as early as 1865 or 1866, drawn south by the hope of economic opportunity and by other attractions that many of them had seen in Union service. Many other so-called carpetbaggers were teachers, social workers, or preachers animated by a missionary impulse. Albion W. Tourgée, for instance, a badly wounded Union veteran, moved to North Carolina in 1865, seeking a milder climate for reasons of health. He invested $5,000 in a nursery and promptly lost it. He would have needed a fine crystal ball indeed to see two years in advance the chance for political office under the Radical program. As it turned out, he served in the state constitutional convention of 1868 and later as a state judge.

The "scalawags," or native white Republicans, were even more reviled and misrepresented. A jaundiced editor of a Nashville paper called them the "merest trash that could be collected in a civilized community, of no personal credit or social responsibility." Most "scalawags" had opposed secession, forming a Unionist majority in many mountain counties as far south as Georgia and Alabama, and especially in the hills of eastern Tennessee. Among the "scalawags" were several distinguished figures, including former Confederate general James A. Longstreet, who decided after Appomattox that the Old South must change its ways. He became a successful cotton broker in New Orleans, joined the Republican party, and supported the Radical Reconstruction program. Other "scalawags" were former Whigs who found the Republican party's economic program of industrial and commercial expansion in keeping with Henry Clay's earlier "American System." Unionists, whether Whig or Democratic before the war, and even some secessionists, agreed with Georgia's Confederate governor and later Democratic senator: "The statesman, like the businessman, should take a practical view of questions as they arise." For the time a practical view dictated joining the Republicans. Mississippi's James L. Alcorn, wealthy planter and former Whig, was among the prominent whites who joined the Republicans in the hope of moderating Radical policies. Such men were ready to concede black suffrage in the hope of influencing African American voters. Alcorn became the first Republican governor of Mississippi.

THE REPUBLICAN RECORD   The new state constitutions were objectionable to adherents of the old order more because of their origins than because of their contents, excepting their provisions for black suffrage and civil rights. Otherwise the documents were in keeping with other state constitutions of the day, their provisions often drawn from the basic laws of northern states. Most remained in effect for some years after the end of Radical control, and later constitutions incorporated many of their features. Conspicuous among Radical innovations were such steps toward greater democracy as requiring universal manhood suffrage, reapportioning legislatures more nearly according to population, and making more state offices elective.

Given the hostile circumstances under which the Radical governments operated, their achievements are remarkable. For the first time in most of the South they established state school systems, however inadequate and ill-supported at first. The testimony is almost universal that African Americans eagerly sought education for themselves and their children. Some 600,000 black pupils were in southern schools by 1877. State governments under the Radicals also gave more attention than ever before to poor relief and to public institutions for the disadvantaged and handicapped: orphanages, asylums, and institutions for the deaf, dumb, and blind of both races. Public roads, bridges, and buildings were repaired or rebuilt. Blacks achieved new rights and opportunities that would never again be taken away, at least in principle: equality before the law and the rights to own property, carry on business, enter professions, attend schools, and learn to read and write.

Yet several of these Republican regimes also engaged in corrupt practices. Contracts were let at absurd prices, and public officials took their cut. Public money and public credit were often voted to privately owned corporations, notably railroads, under conditions that invited influence peddling. But governmental subsidies—especially for transportation— were common before and after Reconstruction (and still are), and the extension of public aid had general support among all elements, including the Radicals and their enemies. Taxes and public debt rose in every state. Yet the figures of taxation and debt hardly constitute an unqualified indictment of Radical governments, since they then faced unusual and inflated costs for the physical reconstruction of public works in the South. Most states, moreover, had to float loans at outrageous discounts, sometimes at 50–75 percent of face value, because of uncertain conditions.

Nor, for that matter, were the breaches of public morality limited to the South or to Republicans. The Democratic Tweed Ring at the time was robbing New York City of more than $75 million, while the Republican "Gas Ring" in Philadelphia was also lining its pockets. In national politics a number of scandals plagued the Grant administration (1869–1877). Corruption was not invented by the Radical regimes, nor did it die with them. Louisiana's "carpetbag" governor recognized as much: "Why," he said, "down here everybody is demoralized. Corruption is the fashion." In three years Louisiana's printing bill ran to $1.5 million, about half of which went to a newspaper belonging to the young governor, who left office with a tidy nest egg and settled down to a long life as a planter. About the same time Mississippi's Democratic state treasurer embezzled over $315,000. During Republican rule in Mississippi, on the other hand, there was no evidence of major corruption.

WHITE TERROR   The case of Mississippi strongly suggests that whites were hostile to Republican regimes less because of their corruption than their inclusion of blacks. Most white southerners remained unreconstructed, so conditioned by slavery that they were unable to conceive of blacks as citizens or even free agents. White women in the postwar South were as violently opposed as men to northern rule. "I have always been down on Reconstruction," declared Ella Cooper, "and never should one Southern man accept it with my consent. I opposed it to the last. They can force it on us, but I say 'never accept it.' " In some places hostility to the new biracial regimes took on the form of white terror. In Grayson County, Texas, three whites murdered three freed slaves because they felt the need to "thin the niggers out and drive them to their holes." Efforts to oust Republican rule focused largely on violence. Said one unreconstructed Mississippian, "Carry the election peaceably if we can, forcibly if we must."

The prototype of terrorist groups was the Ku Klux Klan, first organized in 1866 by some young men of Pulaski, Tennessee, as a social club with the costumes, secret ritual, and mumbo-jumbo common to fraternal groups. At first a group devoted to practical jokes, the founders soon turned to intimidation of blacks and white Republicans, and the KKK

This Thomas Nast cartoon chides the Ku Klux Klan and the White League for promoting conditions "worse than slavery" for southern blacks after the Civil War.

and imitators like Louisiana's Knights of the White Camellia spread rapidly across the South in answer to the Union League. Klansmen rode about the countryside hiding under masks and robes, spreading horrendous rumors, issuing threats, harassing African Americans, and occasionally running amok wreaking violence and destruction.

Klansmen focused their terror on prominent Republicans, black and white. In Mississippi they killed a black Republican leader in front of his family. Three white "scalawag" Republicans were murdered in Georgia in 1870. That same year an armed mob of whites assaulted a Republican political rally in Alabama, killing four blacks and wounding fifty-four. In South Carolina the Klan was especially active. Virtually the entire white male population of York County joined the Klan, and they were responsible for eleven murders and hundreds of whippings. In 1871 some 500 masked men laid siege to the Union County jail and eventually lynched eight black prisoners. Although most Klansmen were poor farmers and tradesmen, middle-class whites—planters, merchants, bankers, lawyers, doctors, even ministers—also joined the group and participated in its brutalities.

Congress struck back with three Enforcement Acts (1870–1871) to protect black voters. The first of these measures levied penalties on persons who interfered with any citizen's right to vote. A second placed the election of congressmen under surveillance by federal election supervisors and marshals. The third (the Ku Klux Klan Act) outlawed the characteristic activities of the Klan—forming conspiracies, wearing disguises, resisting officers, and intimidating officials—and authorized the president to suspend habeas corpus where necessary to suppress "armed combinations." President Grant, in October 1871, singled out nine counties in upcountry South Carolina as an example, suspended habeas corpus, and pursued mass prosecutions that brought an abrupt halt to the Klan outrages. The program of federal enforcement broke the back of the Klan, whose outrages declined steadily as conservative southerners resorted to more subtle methods.

CONSERVATIVE RESURGENCE   The Klan's impact on politics varied from state to state. In the upper South it played only a modest role in facilitating a Democratic resurgence. But in the Deep South, Klan violence and intimidation had some effect. In Georgia, for instance, Republicans virtually quit campaigning and voting. In overwhelmingly black Yazoo County, Mississippi, vengeful whites used violence to reverse the political balance of power. In the 1873 elections the Republicans cast 2,449 votes and the Democrats 638; two years later the Democrats polled 4,049 votes, the Republicans 7. Throughout the South the activities of the Klan weakened black and Republican morale, and in the North they encouraged a growing weariness with the whole southern question.

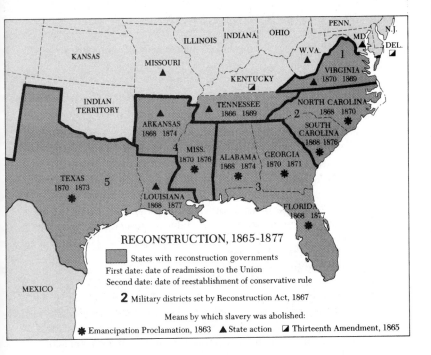

RECONSTRUCTION, 1865-1877

States with reconstruction governments
First date: date of readmission to the Union
Second date: date of reestablishment of conservative rule

2 Military districts set by Reconstruction Act, 1867

Means by which slavery was abolished:
✳ Emancipation Proclamation, 1863 ▲ State action ◪ Thirteenth Amendment, 1865

"The plain truth is," noted the New York *Herald,* "the North has got tired of the Negro."

Americans had other fish to fry anyway. Western expansion, Indian wars, economic growth, and political controversy over the tariff and the currency distracted attention from southern outrages. Republican control in the South gradually loosened as "Conservative" parties—Democrats used that name to mollify former Whigs—mobilized the white vote. Scalawags, and many carpetbaggers, drifted away from the Radical ranks under pressure from their white neighbors. Few of them had joined the Republicans out of concern for black rights in the first place. And where persuasion failed to work, Democrats were willing to use chicanery. As one enthusiastic Democrat boasted, "the white and black Republicans may outvote us, but we can outcount them."

Republican control collapsed in Virginia and Tennessee as early as 1869, in Georgia and North Carolina in 1870, although North Carolina had a Republican governor until 1876. Reconstruction lasted longest in the Deep South states with the largest black population, where whites abandoned Klan masks for barefaced intimidation in paramilitary groups such as the Mississippi Rifle Club and the South Carolina Red Shirts. By 1876 Radical regimes survived only in Louisiana, South Carolina, and Florida, and these all collapsed after the elections of that year. Later the last carpetbag governor of South Carolina explained that "the uneducated negro was too weak, no matter what his numbers, to cope with the whites."

THE GRANT YEARS

GRANT'S ELECTION   Ulysses S. Grant, who presided over the collapse of Republican rule in the South, brought to the presidency less political experience than any man who ever occupied the office, except perhaps Zachary Taylor, and perhaps less political judgment than any other. But in 1868 the rank-and-file voter could be expected to support "the Lion of Vicksburg" because of his record as a war leader. Both parties wooed him, but his falling-out with President Johnson pushed him toward the Republicans and built trust in him among the Radicals. They were, as Thad Stevens said, ready to "let him into the church." When the Republicans gathered in Chicago to name their candidate, Grant was the unanimous choice. The platform endorsed the Reconstruction policy of Congress, congratulating the country on the "assured success" of the program. One plank cautiously defended black suffrage as a necessity in the South, but a matter each northern state should settle for itself. Another urged payment of the national debt "in the utmost good faith to all creditors," which meant in gold. More important than the platform were the great expectations of a soldier-president and his slogan: "Let us have peace."

The Democrats took opposite positions on both Reconstruction and the debt. The Republican Congress, the platform charged, instead of restoring the Union had "so far as in its power, dissolved it, and subjected ten states, in the time of profound peace, to military despotism and Negro supremacy." As to the public debt, the party endorsed Representative George H. Pendleton's "Ohio idea" that, since most bonds had been bought with depreciated greenbacks, they should be paid off in greenbacks unless they specified payment in gold. With no conspicuously available candidate in sight, the convention turned to Horatio Seymour, war governor of New York and chairman of the convention. His friends had to hustle him out of the hall to prevent his withdrawal. The Democrats made a closer race of it than showed up in the electoral vote. Eight states, including New York and New Jersey, went for Seymour. While Grant swept the electoral college by 214 to 80, his popular majority was only 307,000 out of a total of over 5.7 million votes. More than 500,000 black voters accounted for Grant's margin of victory.

EARLY APPOINTMENTS   Grant had proven himself a great leader in the war, but in the White House he seemed blind to the political forces and influence peddlers around him. He was awestruck by men of wealth

President Grant, seated at left, with Mrs. Grant next to him, in a family portrait, 1870.

and unaccountably loyal to some who betrayed his trust. The historian Henry Adams, who lived in Washington at the time, noted that to his friends "Grant appeared as intermittent energy, immensely powerful when awake, but passive and plastic in repose. . . . They could never measure his character or be sure when he would act. They could never follow a mental process in his thought. They were not sure that he did think." His conception of the presidency was "Whiggish." The chief executive carried out the laws; in the formulation of policy he passively followed the lead of Congress. This approach endeared him at first to party leaders, but it left him at last ineffective and left others disillusioned with his leadership.

At the outset Grant consulted nobody on his cabinet appointments. Some of his choices indulged personal whims; others simply displayed bad judgment. In some cases appointees learned of their nomination from the newspapers. As time went by Grant betrayed a fatal gift for losing men of talent and integrity from his cabinet. Secretary of State Hamilton Fish of New York turned out to be a happy exception; he guided foreign policy throughout the Grant presidency.

At first it looked as if Grant's freewheeling style of choosing a cabinet signaled a sharp departure from the spoils system. But once Grant had taken care of his friends and relatives, he began to take care of party leaders. Cabinet members who balked at the procedure were soon eased out. This strengthened a nascent movement for a merit system in the civil service, modeled on systems recently adopted in Great Britain, Germany, and France. Grant finally approved a measure to set up a commission to look into the matter in 1872, a good gesture in a political year. The group duly brought in recommendations which in turn were duly shelved and forgotten once the election was over.

THE GOVERNMENT DEBT   Financial issues dominated the political agenda during Grant's presidency. After the war the Treasury had assumed that the $400 million worth of greenbacks issued during the conflict would be retired from circulation and that the nation would revert to a "hard-money" currency—gold coins. Many agrarian and debtor groups resisted this contraction of the money supply, believing that it would mean lower prices for their crops and would make it harder for them to pay long-term debts. They were joined by a large number of Radicals who thought a combination of high tariffs and inflation would generate more rapid economic growth. In 1868 congressional supporters of such a "soft-money" policy halted the retirement of greenbacks, leaving $356 million outstanding. There matters stood when Grant took office.

The "sound" or hard-money advocates, mostly bankers and merchants, claimed that Grant's election was a mandate to save the country from the Democrats' "Ohio idea." (the idea put forward by former Ohio Congressman George H. Pendleton that the government bonds should be repaid in greenbacks). Quite influential in Republican circles, the "sound-money" advocates also had the benefit of a deeply ingrained popular assumption that hard money was morally preferable to paper currency. Grant agreed, and in his inaugural address he endorsed payment of the national debt in gold as a point of national honor. On March 18, 1869, the Public Credit Act endorsing that principle became the first act of Congress that he signed. Under the Refunding Act of 1870, the Treasury was able to replace 6 percent Civil War bonds with a new issue promising 4–5 percent in gold.

SCANDAL AND REFORM   The complexities of the "money question" exasperated Grant, but that was the least of his worries, for his administration soon fell into a cesspool of scandal. The first hint of scandal touched Grant in the summer of 1869, when the crafty Jay Gould and the flamboyant Jim Fisk connived with the president's brother-in-law to corner the gold market. Gould concocted an argument that the government should refrain from selling gold on the market because the resulting rise in gold prices would raise temporarily depressed farm prices. Grant apparently smelled a rat from the start, but was seen in public with the

The People's Handwriting on the Wall. *An 1872 engraving comments on the corruption engulfing Grant.*

speculators. As the rumor spread on Wall Street that the president had bought the argument, gold rose from $132 to $163 an ounce. When Grant finally persuaded his brother-in-law to pull out of the deal, Gould began quietly selling out. Finally, on "Black Friday," September 24, 1869, Grant ordered the Treasury to sell a large quantity of gold, and the bubble burst. Fisk got out by repudiating his agreements and hiring thugs to intimidate his creditors. "Nothing is lost save honor," he said.

The plot to corner the gold market was only the first of several scandals that rocked the Grant administration. During the campaign of 1872 the public first learned about the financial buccaneering of the Crédit Mobilier, a construction company that had milked the Union Pacific Railroad for exorbitant fees in order to line the pockets of insiders who controlled both firms. Rank-and-file Union Pacific shareholders were left holding the bag. One congressman had distributed Crédit Mobilier shares at bargain rates where, he said, "it will produce much good to us." This chicanery had transpired before Grant's election in 1868, but it now touched a number of prominent Republicans. The beneficiaries had included Speaker Schuyler Colfax, later vice-president, and Representative James A. Garfield, later president. Of thirteen members of Congress involved, only two were censured by a Congress which, before it adjourned in March 1873, voted itself a pay raise from $5,000 to $7,500—retroactive, it decided, for two years. A public uproar forced repeal, leaving only the raises voted the president ($25,000 to $50,000) and Supreme Court justices.

Even more odious disclosures soon followed, and some involved the president's cabinet. The secretary of war, it turned out, had accepted bribes from merchants at army posts in the West who traded with Indians. He was impeached, but resigned in time to elude a Senate trial. Post-office contracts, it was revealed, went to carriers who offered the highest kickbacks. The secretary of the treasury had awarded a political friend a commission of 50 percent for the collection of overdue taxes. In St. Louis a "Whiskey Ring" bribed tax collectors to bilk the government of millions in revenue. Grant's private secretary was enmeshed in that scheme, taking large sums of money and other valuables in return for inside information. There is no evidence that Grant himself was ever involved in, or that he personally profited from, any of the fraud, but his poor choice of associates earned him the public censure that was heaped upon his head.

Long before Grant's first term ended, a reaction against the Reconstruction measures and against incompetence and corruption in the administration had incited mutiny within the Republican ranks. Open revolt broke out first in Missouri where Carl Schurz, a German immigrant and war hero, led a group that elected a governor with Democratic help in 1870 and sent Schurz to the Senate. In 1872 the Liberal Republicans (as they called themselves) held a national convention at Cincinnati that produced a compromise platform condemning the party's southern policy and favoring civil service reform, but remained silent on the protective tariff. The delegates embraced an anomalous presidential candidate: Horace Greeley, editor of the New York *Tribune*, a longtime champion of just about every reform of his times. His image as a visionary eccentric was complemented by his record of hostility to Democrats, whose support the Liberals needed. The Democrats nevertheless swallowed the pill and gave their nomination to Greeley as the only hope of beating Grant.

The result was a foregone conclusion. Republican regulars duly endorsed Radical Reconstruction and the protective tariff. Grant still had seven carpetbag states in his pocket, generous contributions from business and banking interests, and the stalwart support of the Radicals. Above all, he still evoked the imperishable glory of Appomattox. Greeley, despite an exhausting tour of the country—still unusual for a presidential candidate—carried only six southern and border states and none in the North. Greeley's wife had died during the campaign, and worn out with grief and fatigue, he too was gone three weeks after the election.

PANIC AND REDEMPTION   Economic distress followed close upon the public scandals besetting the Grant administration. Contraction of the

Horace Greeley, editor of the New York Tribune and reform candidate for president in 1872.

money supply brought about by the withdrawal of greenbacks and expansion of the railroads into sparsely settled areas had made investors cautious and helped precipitate a crisis. During 1873 the market for railroad bonds turned sour as some twenty-five railroads defaulted on their interest payments before the end of August. The investment-banking firm of Jay Cooke and Company, unable to sell the bonds of the Northern Pacific Railroad, financed them with short-term deposits in hope that a European market would develop. But in 1873 the opposite happened when a financial panic in Vienna forced many financiers to unload American stocks and bonds. Caught short, Cooke and Company went bankrupt on September 18, 1873. The ensuing stampede of investors to exchange securities for cash forced the stock market to close for ten days. The Panic of 1873 set off a depression that lasted for six years, the longest and most severe that Americans had yet suffered, marked by widespread bankruptcies, unemployment, and a drastic slow-down in railroad building.

Hard times and scandals hurt Republicans in the midterm elections of 1874. The Democrats won control of the House of Representatives and gained in the Senate. The new Democratic House immediately launched inquiries into the scandals and unearthed further evidence of corruption in high places. The panic meanwhile focused attention once more on greenback currency.

Since greenbacks were valued less than gold, they had become the chief circulating medium. Most people spent greenbacks first and held their gold or used it to settle foreign accounts, which drained much gold out of the country. The postwar reduction of greenbacks in circulation from $432 million to $356 million had made for tight money. To relieve deflation and stimulate business, therefore, the Treasury reissued $26 million in greenbacks that had been previously withdrawn.

For a time the advocates of paper money were riding high. But in 1874 Grant vetoed a bill to issue more greenbacks. Then, in his annual message that December he called for the gradual resumption of specie payments—that is, the redemption of greenbacks in gold. This would make greenbacks "good as gold" and raise their value to a par with the gold dollar. In January, before the Republicans gave up control of the House, Congress obliged by passing the Resumption Act of 1875. The payment in gold to people who turned in their paper money began on January 1, 1879, after the Treasury had built a gold reserve for that purpose and reduced the value of greenbacks in circulation. This act infuriated those promoting an inflationary monetary policy and provoked the formation of the National Greenback party, which elected fourteen congressmen in 1878. The much-debated "money question" was destined to remain one of the most divisive issues in American politics.

THE COMPROMISE OF 1877   Grant, despite the controversies swirling around him, was eager to run again in 1876, but the recent scandals discouraged any challenge to the two-term tradition. James G. Blaine of Maine, former Speaker of the House, emerged as the Republican front-runner, but he too bore the taint of scandal. Letters in the possession of James Mulligan of Boston linked Blaine to some dubious railroad dealings, and these "Mulligan letters" found their way into print.

The Republican convention in Cincinnati therefore eliminated Blaine and several other hopefuls in favor of Ohio's favorite son, Rutherford B. Hayes. Three times elected governor of Ohio, most recently as an advocate of hard money, Hayes had also made a name as a civil service reformer. But his chief virtue was that he offended neither Radicals nor reformers. As Henry Adams put it, he was "a third rate nonentity, whose only recommendation is that he is obnoxious to no one."

The Democratic convention in St. Louis was abnormally harmonious from the start. The nomination went on the second ballot to Samuel J. Tilden, millionaire corporation lawyer and reform governor of New York who had directed a campaign to overthrow first the notorious

*A Republican campaign piece from the 1876 election: "Yankee Doodle,
that's the talk—/ We've found an honest dealer;/ And o'er the course we
ride or walk,/ We'll go for Hayes and Wheeler."*

Tweed Ring controlling New York City politics and then another ring in
Albany that had bilked the state of millions.

The campaign generated no burning issues. Both candidates favored
the trend toward conservative rule in the South. During one of the most
corrupt elections ever, both candidates also favored civil service reform.
In the absence of strong differences, Democrats waved the Republicans' dirty linen. In response, Republicans waved the bloody shirt,
which is to say that they engaged in verbal assaults on former Confederates and the spirit of rebellion, linking the Democratic party with
secession and with the outrages committed against the black and white
Republicans in the South. As one Republican speaker insisted, "Every
man that tried to destroy this nation was a Democrat. . . . The man that
assassinated Abraham Lincoln was a Democrat. . . . Soldiers, every scar
you have on your heroic bodies was given you by a Democrat!" The
phrase "waving the bloody shirt" originated at the impeachment trial of
President Johnson when Benjamin F. Butler, speaking for the prosecution, displayed the bloody shirt a Mississippi carpetbagger had been
wearing when hauled out of bed and beaten by Klansmen.

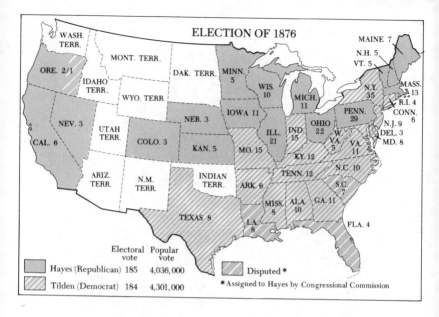

ELECTION OF 1876

	Electoral vote	Popular vote
Hayes (Republican)	185	4,036,000
Tilden (Democrat)	184	4,301,000
Disputed *		

*Assigned to Hayes by Congressional Commission

Early election returns pointed to a Tilden victory. Tilden enjoyed a 300,000 edge in the popular vote and had 184 electoral votes, just one short of a majority, but Republicans claimed nineteen doubtful votes from Florida, Louisiana, and South Carolina, while Democrats laid a counterclaim to Oregon. But the Republicans had clearly carried Oregon. In the South the outcome was less certain, and given the fraud and intimidation perpetrated on both sides, nobody will ever know what might have happened if, to use a slogan of the day, "a free ballot and a fair count" had prevailed. As good a guess as any may be, as one writer suggested, that the Democrats stole the election first and the Republicans stole it back.

In all three of the disputed southern states rival canvassing boards sent in different returns. In Florida, Republicans conceded the state election, but in Louisiana and South Carolina rival state governments also appeared. The Constitution offered no guidance in this unprecedented situation. Even if Congress were empowered to sort things out, the Democratic House and the Republican Senate proved unable to reach an agreement.

Finally, on January 29, 1877, the two houses decided to set up a special Electoral Commission to investigate and report its findings. It had fifteen members, five each from the House, the Senate, and the Supreme Court. The decision on each state went by a vote of 8 to 7, along party lines, in favor of Hayes. After much bluster and threat of filibuster by Democrats, the House voted on March 2 to accept the report and declare Hayes the victor by an electoral vote of 185 to 184.

Critical to this outcome was the defection of southern Democrats who had made several informal agreements with the Republicans. On February 26, 1877, prominent Ohio Republicans and powerful southern Democrats struck a bargain at the Wormley House, a Washington hotel. The Republicans promised that, if elected, Hayes would withdraw the last federal troops from Louisiana and South Carolina, letting the Republican governments there collapse. In return the Democrats promised to withdraw their opposition to Hayes, to accept in good faith the Reconstruction amendments, and to refrain from partisan reprisals against Republicans in the South.

With this agreement in hand, southern Democrats could justify deserting Tilden because this so-called Compromise of 1877 brought a final "redemption" from the "Radicals" and a return to "home rule," which actually meant rule by white Democrats. Other, more informal promises, less noticed by the public, bolstered the Wormley House agreement. Hayes's friends pledged more support for Mississippi levees and other internal improvements, including federal subsidy for a transcontinental railroad along a southern route. Southerners extracted a further promise that Hayes would name a white southerner as postmaster-general, the cabinet position with the most patronage jobs at hand. In return, southerners would let Republicans make James A. Garfield Speaker of the new House.

THE END OF RECONSTRUCTION   After Hayes took office, most of these promises were either renounced or forgotten. They had served their purpose of ending the crisis. In April 1877 Hayes withdrew federal troops from the state houses in Louisiana and South Carolina, and the Republican governments there collapsed—along with much of Hayes's claim to legitimacy. Hayes chose a Tennessean and former Confederate as postmaster-general. But after southern Democrats failed to permit the choice of Garfield as Speaker, Hayes expressed doubt about any further subsidy for railroad building, and none was voted.

As to southern promises regarding the civil rights of blacks, only a few Democratic leaders, such as the new governors of South Carolina and Louisiana, remembered them for long. Over the next three decades those rights crumbled under the pressure of white rule in the South and the force of Supreme Court decisions narrowing the application of the Reconstruction amendments. Radical Reconstruction never offered more than an uncertain commitment to equality before the law. Yet it left an enduring legacy, the Thirteenth, Fourteenth, and Fifteenth Amendments—not dead but dormant, waiting to be awakened.

FURTHER READING

Reconstruction has long been "a dark and bloody ground" of conflicting interpretations. The most recent reinterpretation is Eric Foner's *Reconstruction: America's Unfinished Revolution, 1863–1877* (1988)°. Other recent surveys are Michael Perman's *Emancipation and Reconstruction, 1862–1879* (1987) and James M. McPherson's *Ordeal by Fire: The Civil War and Reconstruction* (1982). John Hope Franklin's *Reconstruction after the Civil War* (1961)° and Kenneth M. Stampp's *The Era of Reconstruction, 1865–1877* (1965)° are also valuable.

More specialized works give closer scrutiny to the aims of the principal political figures. Peyton McCrary's *Abraham Lincoln and Reconstruction* (1978) deals with the Lincoln policies as they were carried out in Louisiana. For a study of Andrew Johnson, see Hans L. Trefousse's *Andrew Johnson: A Biography* (1989). Eric L. McKitrick's *Andrew Johnson and Reconstruction* (1960), LaWanda Cox and John H. Cox's *Politics, Principle, and Prejudice, 1865–1866* (1963), and William R. Brock's *An American Crisis* (1963)° criticize Johnson's policies. Why Johnson was impeached is detailed in Michael Les Benedict's *The Impeachment and Trial of Andrew Johnson* (1973)° and Hans L. Trefousse's *Impeachment of a President* (1975).

Scholars have been fairly sympathetic to the aims and motives of the Radical Republicans. See, for instance, Herman Belz's *Reconstructing the Union* (1969) and Richard Nelson Current's *Those Terrible Carpetbaggers: A Reinterpretation* (1988).° The ideology of these Radicals is explored in Michael Les Benedict's *A Compromise of Principle: Congressional Republicans and Reconstruction* (1974).

The intransigence of southern white attitudes is examined in Michael Perman's *Reunion without Compromise* (1973).° Allen W. Trelease's *White Terror* (1971)° covers the various organizations that practiced vigilante tactics, chiefly the Ku Klux Klan. The difficulties former planters had in adjusting to the new labor system are documented in James L. Roark's *Masters without Slaves* (1977).° Books on southern politics during Reconstruction include Michael Perman's *The Road to Redemption* (1984), Terry L. Seip's *The South Returns to Congress* (1983), Mark W. Summers's *Railroads, Reconstruction, and the Gospel of Prosperity* (1984), Dan T. Carter's *When the War Was Over* (1985), and George C. Rable's *But There Was No Peace* (1984).

Numerous works have appeared on the freed blacks' experience in the South. Start with Leon F. Litwack's *Been in the Storm So Long* (1979),° which covers wonderfully the transition from slavery to free-

°These books are available in paperback editions.

dom. Willie Lee Rose's *Rehearsal for Reconstruction* (1964)° examines Union efforts to define the social role of former slaves during wartime emancipation. Joel Williamson's *After Slavery* (1965)° argues that South Carolina blacks took an active role in pursuing their political and economic rights. For works concerning the political activity of freed slaves in other areas of the South, see Howard N. Rabinowitz's *Southern Black Leaders of the Reconstruction* (1982) and Edmund L. Drago's *Black Politicians and Reconstruction in Georgia: A Splendid Failure* (1982). Peter Kolchin's *First Freedom* (1972), a study of freed slaves in Alabama, is also useful. The role of the Freedman's Bureau is explored in William S. McFeely's *Yankee Stepfather: General O. O. Howard and the Freedmen* (1968).° The situation of freed slave women, which was often quite different from that of freed slave men, is discussed in Jacqueline Jones's *Labor of Love, Labor of Sorrow: Black Women, Work and the Family from Slavery to Present* (1985) and Dorothy Sterling's *We Are Your Sisters* (1984).

The land confiscation issue is discussed in Eric Foner's *Politics and Ideology in the Age of the Civil War* (1980)°; Beth Bethel's *Promiseland* (1981), on a South Carolina black community; and Janet S. Hermann's *The Pursuit of a Dream* (1981),° on the Davis Bend experiment in Mississippi.

The politics of corruption outside the South is depicted in Allan Nevin's *Hamilton Fish: The Inner History of the Grant Administration* (1936) and William S. McFeely's *Grant: A Biography* (1981).° The political maneuvers of the election of 1876 and the resultant crisis and compromise are explained in C. Vann Woodward's *Reunion and Reaction* (1951)° and William Gillette's *Retreat from Reconstruction, 1869–1879* (1979).°

For an examination of the lives of southern men and women who moved north between 1865 and 1880, see Daniel E. Sutherland's *The Confederate Carpetbaggers* (1992).

°These books are available in paperback editions.

APPENDIX

THE DECLARATION OF INDEPENDENCE

WHEN IN THE COURSE OF HUMAN EVENTS, it becomes necessary for one people to dissolve the political bands which have connected them with another, and to assume the Powers of the earth, the separate and equal station to which the Laws of Nature and of Nature's God entitle them, a decent respect to the opinions of mankind requires that they should declare the causes which impel them to the separation.

We hold these truths to be self-evident, that all men are created equal, that they are endowed by their Creator with certain unalienable rights, that among these are Life, Liberty, and the pursuit of Happiness. That to secure these rights, Governments are instituted among Men, deriving their just powers from the consent of the governed. That whenever any Form of Government becomes destructive of these ends, it is the Right of the People to alter or to abolish it, and to institute new Government, laying its foundation on such principles and organizing its powers in such form, as to them shall seem most likely to effect their Safety and Happiness. Prudence, indeed, will dictate that Governments long established should not be changed for light and transient causes; and accordingly all experience hath shown, that mankind are more disposed to suffer, while evils are sufferable, than to right themselves by abolishing the forms to which they are accustomed. But when a long train of abuses and usurpations, pursuing invariably the same Object evinces a design to reduce them under absolute Despotism, it is their right, it is their duty, to throw off such Government, and to provide new Guards for their future security.—Such has been the patient sufferance of these Colonies; and such is now the necessity which constrains them to alter their former Systems of Government. The history of the present King of Great Britain is a history of repeated injuries and usurpations, all having in direct object the establishment of an absolute Tyranny over these States. To prove this, let Facts be submitted to a candid world.

He has refused his Assent to Laws, the most wholesome and necessary for the public good.

He has forbidden his Governors to pass Laws of immediate and pressing importance, unless suspended in their operation till his Assent should be obtained; and when so suspended, he has utterly neglected to attend to them.

He has refused to pass other Laws for the accommodation of large districts of people, unless those people would relinquish the right of Representation in the Legislature, a right inestimable to them and for midable to tyrants only.

He has called together legislative bodies at places unusual, uncomfortable, and distant from the depository of their public Records, for the sole purpose of fatiguing them into compliance with his measures.

He has dissolved Representative Houses repeatedly, for opposing with manly firmness his invasions on the rights of the people.

He has refused for a long time, after such dissolutions, to cause others to be elected; whereby the Legislative powers, incapable of Annihilation, have returned to the People at large for their exercise; the State remaining in the mean time exposed to all dangers of invasion from without, and convulsions within.

He has endeavoured to prevent the population of these States; for that purpose obstructing the Laws of Naturalization of Foreigners; refusing to pass others to encourage their migrations hither, and raising the conditions of new Appropriations of Lands.

He has obstructed the Administration of Justice, by refusing his Assent to Laws for establishing Judiciary powers.

He has made Judges dependent on his Will alone, for the tenure of their offices, and the amount and payment of their salaries.

He has erected a multitude of New Offices, and sent hither swarms of Officers to harass our People, and eat out their substance.

He has kept among us, in times of peace, Standing Armies without the Consent of our legislature.

He has affected to render the Military independent of and superior to the Civil Power.

He has combined with others to subject us to a jurisdiction foreign to our constitution, and unacknowledged by our laws; giving his Assent to their Acts of pretended Legislation:

For quartering large bodies of armed troops among us:

For protecting them, by a mock Trial, from Punishment for any Murders which they should commit on the Inhabitants of these States:

For cutting off our Trade with all parts of the world:

For imposing taxes on us without our Consent:

For depriving us of many cases, of the benefits of Trial by jury:

For transporting us beyond Seas to be tried for pretended offences:

For abolishing the free System of English Laws in a neighbouring Province, establishing therein an Arbitrary government, and enlarging its Boundaries so as to render it at once an example and fit instrument for introducing the same absolute rule into these Colonies:

For taking away our Charters, abolishing our most valuable Laws, and altering fundamentally the Forms of our Governments:

For suspending our own Legislatures, and declaring themselves in vested with Power to legislate for us in all cases whatsoever.

He has abdicated Government here, by declaring us out of his Protection and waging War against us.

He has plundered our seas, ravaged our Coasts, burnt our towns, and destroyed the lives of our people.

He is at this time transporting large armies of foreign mercenaries to compleat the works of death, desolation, and tyranny, already begun with circumstances of Cruelty & perfidy scarcely paralleled in the most barbarous ages, and totally unworthy the Head of a civilized nation.

He has constrained our fellow Citizens taken Captive on the high Seas to bear Arms against their Country, to become the executioners of their friends and Brethren, or to fall themselves by their Hands.

He has excited domestic insurrections amongst us, and has endeavoured to bring on the inhabitants of our frontiers, the merciless Indian Savages, whose known rule of warfare, is an undistinguished destruction of all ages, sexes, and conditions.

In every stage of these Oppressions We have Petitioned for Redress in the most humble terms: Our repeated Petitions have been answered only by repeated injury. A Prince, whose character is thus marked by every act which may define a Tyrant, is unfit to be the ruler of a free people.

Nor have We been wanting in attention to our British brethren. We have warned them from time to time of attempts by their legislature to extend an unwarrantable jurisdiction over us. We have reminded them of the circumstances of our emigration and settlement here. We have appealed to their native justice and magnanimity, and we have conjured them by the ties of our common kindred to disavow these usurpations, which, would inevitably interrupt our connections and correspondence. They too must have been deaf to the voice of justice and of consanguinity. We must, therefore, acquiesce in the necessity, which denounces our Separation, and hold them, as we hold the rest of mankind, Enemies in War, in Peace Friends.

WE, THEREFORE, the Representatives of the UNITED STATES OF AMERICA, in General Congress, Assembled, appealing to the Supreme Judge of the world for the rectitude of our intentions, do, in the Name, and by Authority of the good People of these Colonies, solemnly publish and declare, That these United Colonies are, and of Right ought to be FREE AND INDEPENDENT STATES; that they are Absolved from all Allegiance to the British Crown, and that all political connection between them and the State of Great Britain, is and ought to be totally dissolved; and that as Free and Independent States, they have full Power to levy War, conclude Peace, contract Alliances, establish Commerce, and to do all other Acts and Things which Independent States may of right do. And for the support of this Declaration, with a firm reliance on the Protection of Divine Providence, we mutually pledge to each other our Lives, our Fortunes, and our sacred Honor.

The foregoing Declaration was, by order of Congress, engrossed, and signed by the following members:

John Hancock

NEW HAMPSHIRE
Josiah Bartlett
William Whipple
Matthew Thornton

MASSACHUSETTS BAY
Samuel Adams
John Adams
Robert Treat Paine
Elbridge Gerry

RHODE ISLAND
Stephen Hopkins
William Ellery

CONNECTICUT
Roger Sherman
Samuel Huntington
William Williams
Oliver Wolcott

NEW YORK
William Floyd
Philip Livingston
Francis Lewis
Lewis Morris

NEW JERSEY
Richard Stockton
John Witherspoon
Francis Hopkinson
John Hart
Abraham Clark

PENNSYLVANIA
Robert Morris
Benjamin Rush
Benjamin Franklin
John Morton
George Clymer
James Smith
George Taylor
James Wilson
George Ross

DELAWARE
Caesar Rodney
George Read
Thomas M'Kean

MARYLAND
Samuel Chase
William Paca
Thomas Stone
*Charles Carroll, of
    Carrollton*

VIRGINIA
George Wythe
Richard Henry Lee
Thomas Jefferson
Benjamin Harrison
Thomas Nelson, Jr.
Francis Lightfoot Lee
Carter Braxton

NORTH CAROLINA
William Hooper
Joseph Hewes
John Penn

SOUTH CAROLINA
Edward Rutledge
Thomas Heyward, Jr.
Thomas Lynch, Jr.
Arthur Middleton

GEORGIA
Button Gwinnett
Lyman Hall
George Walton

Resolved, That copies of the Declaration be sent to the several assemblies, conventions, and committees, or councils of safety, and to the several commanding officers of the continental troops; that it be proclaimed in each of the United States, at the head of the army.

ARTICLES OF CONFEDERATION

To all to whom these Presents shall come, we the undersigned Delegates of the States affixed to our Names send greeting.

Whereas the Delegates of the United States of America in Congress assembled did on the fifteenth day of November in the Year of our Lord One Thousand Seven Hundred and Seventy-seven, and in the Second Year of the Independence of America agree to certain articles of Confederation and perpetual Union between the States of Newhampshire, Massachusetts-bay, Rhodeisland and Providence Plantations, Connecticut, New York, New Jersey, Pennsylvania, Delaware, Maryland, Virginia, North-Carolina, South-Carolina and Georgia in the Words following, viz.

Articles of Confederation and perpetual Union between the States of Newhampshire, Massachusetts-bay, Rhodeisland and Providence Plantations, Connecticut, New-York, New-Jersey, Pennsylvania, Delaware, Maryland, Virginia, North-Carolina, South-Carolina and Georgia.

ARTICLE I. The stile of this confederacy shall be "The United States of America."

ARTICLE II. Each State retains its sovereignty, freedom and independence, and every power, jurisdiction and right, which is not by this confederation expressly delegated to the United States, in Congress assembled.

ARTICLE III. The said States hereby severally enter into a firm league of friendship with each other, for their common defence, the security of their liberties, and their mutual and general welfare, binding themselves to assist each other, against all force offered to, or attacks made upon them, or any of them, on account of religion, sovereignty, trade or any other pretence whatever.

ARTICLE IV. The better to secure and perpetuate mutual friendship and intercourse among the people of the different States in this Union, the free inhabitants of each of these States, paupers, vagabonds and fugitives from justice excepted, shall be entitled to all privileges and immunities of free citizens in the several States; and the people of each State shall have free ingress and regress to and from any other State, and shall enjoy therein all the privileges of trade and commerce, subject to the same duties, impositions and restrictions as the inhabitants thereof respectively, provided that such restrictions shall not extend so far as to prevent the removal of property imported into any State, to any other State of which the owner is an inhabitant; provided also that no imposition, duties or restriction shall be laid by any State, on the property of the United States, or either of them.

If any person guilty of, or charged with treason, felony, or other high misdemeanor in any State, shall flee from justice, and be found in any of the United States, he shall upon demand of the Governor or Executive power, of the State from which he fled, be delivered up and removed to the State having jurisdiction of his offence.

Full faith and credit shall be given in each of these States to the records, acts and judicial proceedings of the courts and magistrates of every other State.

ARTICLE V. For the more convenient management of the general interests of the United States, delegates shall be annually appointed in such manner as the legislature of each State shall direct, to meet in Congress on the first Monday in November, in every year, with a power reserved to each State, to recall its delegates, or any of them, at any time within the year, and to send others in their stead, for the remainder of the year.

No State shall be represented in Congress by less than two, nor by more than seven members; and no person shall be capable of being a delegate for more than three years in any term of six years; nor shall any person, being a delegate, be capable of holding any office under the United States, for which he, or another for his benefit receives any salary, fees or emolument of any kind.

Each State shall maintain its own delegates in a meeting of the States, and while they act as members of the committee of the States.

In determining questions in the United States, in Congress assembled, each State shall have one vote.

Freedom of speech and debate in Congress shall not be impeached or questioned in any court, or place out of Congress, and the members of Congress shall be protected in their persons from arrests and imprisonments, during the time of their going to and from, and attendance on Congress, except for treason, felony, or breach of the peace.

ARTICLE VI. No State without the consent of the United States in Congress assembled, shall send any embassy to, or receive any embassy from, or enter into any conference, agreement, alliance or treaty with any king, prince or state; nor shall any person holding any office of profit or trust under the United States, or any of them, accept of any present, emolument, office or title of any kind whatever from any king, prince or foreign state; nor shall the United States in Congress assembled, or any of them, grant any title of nobility.

No two or more States shall enter into any treaty, confederation or alliance whatever between them, without the consent of the United States in Congress assembled, specifying accurately the purposes for which the same is to be entered into, and how long it shall continue.

No State shall lay any imposts or duties, which may interfere with any stipulations in treaties, entered into by the United States in Congress assembled, with any king, prince or state, in pursuance of any treaties already proposed by Congress, to the courts of France and Spain.

No vessels of war shall be kept up in time of peace by any State, except such number only, as shall be deemed necessary by the United States in Congress assembled, for the defence of such State, or its trade; nor shall any body of forces be kept up by any State, in time of peace, except such number only, as in the judgment of the United States, in Congress assembled, shall be deemed requisite to garrison the forts necessary for the defence of such State; but every State shall always keep up a well regulated and disciplined militia, sufficiently armed and accoutred, and shall provide and constantly have ready for use, in public stores, a due number of field pieces and tents, and a proper quantity of arms, ammunition and camp equipage.

No State shall engage in any war without the consent of the United States in Congress assembled, unless such State be actually invaded by enemies, or shall have received certain advice of a resolution being formed by some nation of Indians to invade such State, and the danger is so imminent as not to admit of a delay, till the United States in Congress assembled can be consulted: nor shall any State grant commissions to any ships or vessels of war, nor letters of marque or reprisal, except it be after a declaration of war by the United States in Congress assembled, and then only against the kingdom or state and the subjects thereof, against which war has been so declared, and under such regulations as shall be established by the United States in Congress assembled, unless such State be infested by pirates, in which case vessels of war may be fitted out for that occasion, and kept so long as the danger shall continue, or until the United States in Congress assembled shall determine otherwise.

Article VII. When land-forces are raised by any State of the common defence, all officers of or under the rank of colonel, shall be appointed by the Legislature of each State respectively by whom such forces shall be raised, or in such manner as such State shall direct, and all vacancies shall be filled up by the State which first made the appointment.

Article VIII. All charges of war, and all other expenses that shall be incurred for the common defence or general welfare, and allowed by the United States in Congress assembled, shall be defrayed out of a common treasury, which shall be supplied by the several States, in proportion to the value of all land within each State, granted to or surveyed for any person, as such land and the buildings and improvements thereon shall be estimated according to such mode as the United States in Congress assembled, shall from time to time direct and appoint.

The taxes for paying that proportion shall be laid and levied by the authority and direction of the Legislatures of the several States within the time agreed upon by the United States in Congress assembled.

Article IX. The United States in Congress assembled, shall have the sole and exclusive right and power of determining on peace and war, except in the cases mentioned in the sixth article—of sending and receiving ambassadors—entering into treaties and alliances, provided that no treaty of commerce shall be made whereby the legislative power of the respective States shall be restrained from imposing such imposts and duties on foreigners, as their own people are subjected to, or from prohibiting the exportation or importation of and species of goods or commodities whatsoever—of establishing rules for deciding in all cases, what captures on land or water shall be legal, and in what manner prizes taken by land or naval forces in the service of the United States shall be divided or appropriated—of granting letters of marque and reprisal in times of peace—appointing courts for the trial of piracies and felonies committed on the high seas and establishing courts for receiving and determining finally appeals in all cases of captures, provided that no member of Congress shall be appointed a judge of any of the said courts.

The United States in Congress assembled shall also be the last resort on appeal in all disputes and differences now subsisting or that hereafter may arise between two or more States concerning boundary, jurisdiction or any other cause whatever; which authority shall always be exercised in the manner following. Whenever the legislative or executive authority or lawful agent of any State in controversy with another shall present a petition to Congress, stating the matter in question and praying for a hearing, notice thereof shall be given by order of Congress to the legislative or executive authority of the other State in controversy, and a day assigned for the appearance of the parties by their lawful agents, who shall then be directed to appoint by joint consent, commissioners or judges to constitute a court for hearing and determining the matter in question: but if they cannot agree, Congress shall name three persons out of each of the United States, and from the list of such persons each party shall alternately strike out one, the petitioners beginning, until the number shall be reduced to thirteen; and from that number not less than seven, nor more than nine names as Congress shall direct, shall in the presence of Congress be drawn out by lot, and the persons whose names shall be so drawn or any five of them, shall be commissioners or judges, to hear and finally determine the controversy, so always as a major part of the judges who shall hear the cause shall agree in the determination: and if either party shall neglect to attend at the day appointed, without reasons, which Congress shall judge sufficient, or being present shall refuse to strike, the Congress shall proceed to nominate three persons out of each State, and the Secretary of Congress shall strike in behalf of such party absent or refusing; and the judgment and sentence of the court to be appointed, in the manner before prescribed, shall be final and conclusive; and if any of the parties shall refuse to submit to the authority of such court, or to appear or defend their claim or cause, the court shall nevertheless proceed to pronounce sentence, or judgment, which shall in like manner be final and decisive, the judgment or sentence and other proceedings being in either case transmitted to Congress, and lodged among the acts of Congress for the security of the parties concerned: provided that every commissioner, before he sits in judgment, shall take an oath to be administered by one of the judges of the supreme or superior court of the State where the case shall be tried, "well and truly to hear and determine the matter in question, according to the best of his judgment, without favour, affection or hope of reward:" provided also that no State shall be deprived of territory for the benefit of the United States.

All controversies concerning the private right of soil claimed under different grants of two or more States, whose jurisdiction as they may respect such lands, and the states which passed such grants are adjusted, the said grants or either of them being at the same time claimed to have originated antecedent to such settlement of jurisdiction, shall on the petition of either party to the Congress of the United States, be finally determined as near as may be in the same manner as is before prescribed for deciding disputes respecting territorial jurisdiction between different States.

The United States in Congress assembled shall also have the sole and exclusive right and power of regulating the alloy and value of coin struck by their own authority, or by that of the respective States—fixing the standard of weights and measures throughout the United States—regulating the trade and managing all affairs with the Indians, not members of any of the States, provided that the legislative right of any State within its own limits be not infringed or violated—establishing and regulating post-offices from one State to another, throughout all of the United States, and exacting such postage on the papers passing thro' the same as may be requisite to defray the expenses of the said office—appointing all officers of the land forces, in the service of the United States, excepting regimental officers—appointing all the officers of the naval forces, and commissioning all officers whatever in the service of the United States—making rules for the government and regulation of the said land and naval forces, and directing their operations.

The United States in Congress assembled shall have authority to appoint a committee, to sit in the recess of Congress, to be denominated "a Committee of the States," and to consist of one delegate from each State; and to appoint such other committees and civil officers as may be necessary for managing the general affairs of the United States under their direction—to appoint one of their number to preside, provided that no person be allowed to serve in the office of president more than one year in any term of three years; to ascertain the necessary sums of money to be raised for the service of the United States, and to appropriate and apply the same for defraying the public expenses—to borrow money, or emit bills on the credit of the United States, transmitting every half year to the respective States an account of the sums of money so borrowed or emitted,—to build and equip a navy—to agree upon the number of land forces, and to make requisitions from each State for its quota, in proportion to the number of white inhabitants in such State; which requisition shall be binding, and thereupon the Legislature of each State shall appoint the regimental officers, raise the men and cloath, arm and equip them in a soldier like manner, at the expense of the United States; and the officers and men so cloathed, armed and equipped shall march to the place appointed, and within the time agreed on by the United States in Congress assembled: but if the United States in Congress assembled shall, on consideration of circumstances judge proper that any State should not raise men, or should raise a smaller number of men than the quota thereof, such extra number shall be raised, officered, cloathed, armed and equipped in the same manner as the quota of such State, unless the legislature of such State shall judge that such extra number cannot be safely spared out of the same, in which case they shall raise officer, cloath, arm and equip as many of such extra number as they judge can be safely spared. And the officers and men so cloathed, armed and equipped, shall march to the place appointed, and within the time agreed on by the United States in Congress assembled.

The United States in Congress assembled shall never engage in a war, nor grant letters of marque and reprisal in time of peace, nor enter into any treaties or alliances, nor coin money, nor regulate the value thereof, nor ascertain the sums and expenses necessary for the defence and welfare of the United States, or any of them, nor emit bills, nor borrow money on the credit of the United States, nor appropriate money, nor agree upon the number of vessels to be built or purchased, or the number of land or sea forces to be raised, nor appoint a commander in chief of the army or navy, unless nine States assent to the same: nor shall a question on any other point, except for adjourning from day to day be determined, unless by the votes of a majority of the United States in Congress assembled.

The Congress of the United States shall have power to adjourn to any time within the year, and to any place within the United States, so that no period of adjournment be for a longer duration than the space of six months, and shall publish the journal of their proceedings monthly, except such parts thereof relating to treaties, alliances or military operations, as in their judgment require secresy; and the yeas and nays of the delegates of each State on any question shall be entered on the Journal, when it is desired by any delegate; and the delegates of a State, or any of them, at his or their request shall be furnished with a transcript of the said journal, except such parts as are above excepted, to lay before the Legislatures of the several States.

ARTICLE X. The committee of the States, or any nine of them, shall be authorized to execute, in the recess of Congress, such of the powers of Congress as the United States in Congress assembled, by the consent of nine States, shall from time to time think expedient to vest them with; provided that no power be delegated to the said committee, for the exercise of which, by the articles of confederation, the voice of nine States in the Congress of the United States assembled is requisite.

ARTICLE XI. Canada acceding to this confederation, and joining in the measures of the United States, shall be admitted into, and entitled to all the advantages of this Union: but no other colony shall be admitted into the same, unless such admission be agreed to by nine States.

ARTICLE XII. All bills of credit emitted, monies borrowed and debts contracted by, or under the authority of Congress, before the assembling of the United States, in pursuance of the present confederation, shall be deemed and considered as a charge against the United States, for payment and satisfaction whereof the said United States, and the public faith are hereby solemnly pledged.

ARTICLE XIII. Every State shall abide by the determinations of the United States in Congress assembled, on all questions which by this confederation are submitted to them. And the articles of this confederation shall be inviolably observed by every State, and the Union shall be perpetual; nor shall any alteration at any time hereafter be made in any of them; unless such alteration be agreed to in a Congress of the United States, and be afterwards confirmed by the Legislatures of every State.

And whereas it has pleased the Great Governor of the world to incline the hearts of the Legislatures we respectively represent in Congress, to approve of, and to authorize us to ratify the said articles of confederation and perpetual union. Know ye that we the undersigned delegates, by virtue of the power and authority to us given for that purpose, do by these presents, in the name and in behalf of our respective constituents, fully and entirely ratify and confirm each and every of the said articles of confederation and perpetual union, and all and singular the matters and things therein contained: and we do further solemnly plight and engage the faith of our respective constituents, that they shall abide by the determinations of the United States in Congress assembled, on all questions, which by the said confederation are submitted to them. And that the articles thereof shall be inviolably observed by the States we respectively represent, and that the Union shall be perpetual.

In witness thereof we have hereunto set our hands in Congress. Done at Philadelphia in the State of Pennsylvania the ninth day of July in the year of our Lord one thousand seven hundred and seventy-eight, and in the third year of the independence of America.

THE CONSTITUTION OF
THE UNITED STATES

WE THE PEOPLE OF THE UNITED STATES, in order to form a more perfect Union, establish Justice, insure domestic Tranquility, provide for the common defence, promote the general Welfare, and secure the Blessings of Liberty to ourselves and our Posterity, do ordain and establish this Constitution for the United States of America.

ARTICLE. I.

Section. 1. All legislative Powers herein granted shall be vested in a Congress of the United States, which shall consist of a Senate and House of Representatives.

Section. 2. The House of Representatives shall be composed of Members chosen every second Year by the People of the several States, and the Electors in each State shall have the Qualifications requisite for Electors of the most numerous Branch of the State Legislature.

No Person shall be a Representative who shall not have attained to the Age of twenty five Years, and been seven Years a Citizen of the United States, and who shall not, when elected, be an Inhabitant of that State in which he shall be chosen.

Representatives and direct Taxes shall be apportioned among the several States which may be included within this Union, according to their respective Numbers, which shall be determined by adding to the whole Number of free Persons, including those bound to Service for a Term of Years, and excluding Indians not taxed, three fifths of all other Persons. The actual Enumeration shall be made within three Years after the first Meeting of the Congress of the United States, and within every subsequent Term of ten Years, in such Manner as they shall by Law direct. The Number of Representatives shall not exceed one for every thirty Thousand, but each State shall have at Least one Representative; and until such enumeration shall be made, the State of New Hampshire shall be entitled to chuse three, Massachusetts eight, Rhode-Island and Providence

Plantations one, Connecticut five, New-York six, New Jersey four, Pennsylvania eight, Delaware one, Maryland six, Virginia ten, North Carolina five, South Carolina five, and Georgia three.

When vacancies happen in the Representation from any state, the Executive Authority thereof shall issue Writs of Election to fill such Vacancies.

The House of Representatives shall chuse their Speaker and other Officers; and shall have the sole Power of Impeachment.

Section. 3. The Senate of the United States shall be composed of two Senators from each State, chosen by the legislature thereof, for six Years; and each Senator shall have one Vote.

Immediately after they shall be assembled in Consequence of the first Election, they shall be divided as equally as may be into three Classes. The Seats of the Senators of the first Class shall be vacated at the Expiration of the second Year, of the second Class at the Expiration of the fourth Year, and of the third Class at the Expiration of the sixth Year, so that one third maybe chosen every second Year; and if Vacancies happen by Resignation, or otherwise, during the Recess of the Legislature of any State, the Executive thereof may make temporary Appointments until the next Meeting of the Legislature, which shall then fill such Vacancies.

No Person shall be a Senator who shall not have attained to the Age of thirty Years, and been nine Years a Citizen of the United States, and who shall not, when elected, be an Inhabitant of that State for which he shall be chosen.

The Vice President of the United States shall be President of the Senate, but shall have no Vote, unless they be equally divided.

The Senate shall chuse their other Officers, and also a President pro tempore, in the Absence of the Vice President, or when he shall exercise the Office of President of the United States.

The Senate shall have the sole Power to try all Impeachments. When sitting for that Purpose, they shall be on Oath or Affirmation. When the President of the United States is tried, the Chief Justice shall preside: And no Person shall be convicted without the Concurrence of two thirds of the Members present.

Judgment in Cases of Impeachment shall not extend further than to removal from Office, and disqualification to hold and enjoy any Office of honor, Trust or Profit under the United States: but the Party convicted shall nevertheless be liable and subject to Indictment, Trial, Judgment and Punishment, according to Law.

Section. 4. The Times, Places and Manner of holding Elections for Senators and Representatives, shall be prescribed in each State by the Legislature thereof; but the Congress may at any time by Law make or alter such Regulations, except as to the Places of chusing Senators.

The Congress shall assemble at least once in every Year, and such Meeting shall be on the first Monday in December, unless they shall by Law appoint a different Day.

Section. 5. Each House shall be the Judge of the Elections, Returns and Qualifications of its own Members, and a Majority of each shall constitute a Quorum to do Business; but a smaller Number may adjourn from day to day, and may be authorized to compel the Attendance of absent Members, in such Manner, and under such Penalties as each House may provide.

Each House may determine the Rules of its Proceedings, punish its Members for disorderly Behaviour, and, with the Concurrence of two thirds, expel a Member.

Each House shall keep a Journal of its Proceedings, and from time to time publish the same, excepting such Parts as may in their Judgment require Secrecy; and the Yeas and Nays of the Members of either House on any question shall, at the Desire of one fifth of those Present, be entered on the Journal.

Neither House, during the Session of Congress, shall, without the Consent of the other, adjourn for more than three days, not to any other Place than that in which the two Houses shall be sitting.

Section. 6. The Senators and Representatives shall receive a Compensation for their Services, to be ascertained by Law, and paid out of the Treasury of the United States. They shall in all Cases, except Treason, Felony and Breach of the Peace, be privileged from Arrest during their Attendance at the Session of their respective Houses, and in going to and returning from the same; and for any Speech or Debate in either House, they shall not be questioned in any other Place.

No Senator or Representative shall, during the Time for which he was elected, be appointed to any civil Office under the Authority of the United States, which shall have been created, or the Emoluments whereof shall have been encreased during such time; and no Person holding any Office under the United States, shall be a Member of either House during his Continuance in Office.

Section. 7. All Bills for raising Revenue shall originate in the House of Representatives; but the Senate may propose or concur with Amendments as on other Bills.

Every Bill which shall have passed the House of Representatives and the Senate shall, before it become a Law, be presented to the President of the United States; If he approve he shall sign it, but if not he shall return it, with his Objections to that House in which it shall have originated, who shall enter the Objections at large on their Journal, and proceed to reconsider it. If after such Reconsideration two thirds of that House shall agree to pass the Bill, it shall be sent, together with the Objections, to the other House, by which it shall likewise be reconsidered, and if approved by two thirds of that House, it shall become a Law. But in all such Cases the Votes of both Houses shall be determined by yeas and Nays, and the Names of the Persons voting for and against the Bill shall be entered on the Journal of each House respectively. If any Bill shall not be returned by the President within ten Days (Sundays excepted) after it shall have been presented to him, the Same shall be a Law, in like Manner as if he had signed it, unless the Congress by their Adjournment prevent its Return, in which Case it shall not be a Law.

Every Order, Resolution, or Vote to which the Concurrence of the Senate and House of Representatives may be necessary (except on a question of Adjournment) shall be presented to the President of the United States; and before the Same shall take Effect, shall be approved by him, or being disapproved by him, shall be repassed by two thirds of the Senate and House of Representatives, according to the Rules and Limitations prescribed in the Case of a Bill.

Section. 8. The Congress shall have Power To lay and collect Taxes, Duties, Imposts and Excises, to pay the Debts and provide for the common Defence and general Welfare of the United States; but all Duties, Imposts and Excises shall be uniform throughout the United States;

To borrow Money on the credit of the United States;

To regulate Commerce with foreign Nations, and among the several States, and with the Indian Tribes;

To establish an uniform Rule of Naturalization, and uniform Laws on the subject of Bankruptcies throughout the United States;

To coin Money, regulate the Value thereof, and of foreign Coin, and fix the Standard of Weights and Measures;

To provide for the Punishment of counterfeiting the Securities and current Coin of the United States;

To establish Post Offices and Post Roads;

To promote the Progress of Science and useful Arts, by securing for limited Times to Authors and Inventors the exclusive Right to their respective Writings and Discoveries;

To constitute Tribunals inferior to the supreme Court;

To define and punish Piracies and Felonies committed on the high Seas, and Offences against the Law of Nations;

To declare War, grant Letters of Marque and Reprisal, and make Rules concerning Captures on land and Water;

To raise and support Armies, but no Appropriation of Money to that Use shall be for a longer Term than two Years;

To provide and maintain a Navy;

To make Rules for the Government and Regulation of the land and naval Forces;

To provide for calling forth the Militia to execute the Laws of the Union, suppress Insurrections and repel Invasions;

To provide for organizing, arming, and disciplining, the Militia, and for governing such Part of them as may be employed in the Service of the United States, reserving to the States respectively, the Appointment of the Officers, and the Authority of training the Militia according to the discipline prescribed by Congress.

To exercise exclusive Legislation in all Cases whatsoever, over such District (not exceeding ten Miles square) as may, by Cession of Particular States, and the Acceptance of Congress, become the Seat of the Government of the United States, and to exercise like Authority over all Places purchased by the Consent of the Legislature of the State in which the Same shall be, for the Erection of Forts, Magazines, Arsenals, dock-Yards, and other needful Buildings;—And

To make all Laws which shall be necessary and proper for carrying into Execution the foregoing Powers, and all other Powers vested by this Constitution in the Government of the United States, or in any Department or Officer thereof.

Section. 9. The Migration or Importation of such Persons as any of the States now existing shall think proper to admit, shall not be prohibited by the Congress prior to the Year one thousand eight hundred and eight, but a Tax or duty may be imposed on such Importation, not exceeding ten dollars for each Person.

The Privilege of the Writ of Habeas Corpus shall not be suspended, unless when in Cases of Rebellion or Invasion the public Safety may require it.

No Bill of Attainder or ex post facto Law shall be passed.

No Capitation, or other direct, Tax shall be laid, unless in Proportion to the Census or Enumeration herein before directed to be taken.

No Tax or Duty shall be laid on Articles exported from any State.

No Preference shall be given by any Regulation of Commerce or Revenue to the Ports of one State over those of another: nor shall Vessels bound to, or from, one State, be obliged to enter, clear, or pay Duties in another.

No Money shall be drawn from the Treasury, but in Consequence of Appropriations made by Law; and a regular Statement and Account of the Receipts and Expenditures of all public Money shall be published from time to time.

No Title of Nobility shall be granted by the United States: And no Person holding any Office of Profit or trust under them, shall, without the Consent of the Congress, accept of any present, Emolument, Office, or Title, of any kind whatever, from any King, prince, or foreign State.

Section 10.

No State shall enter into any Treaty, Alliance, or Confederation; grant Letters of Marque and Reprisal; coin Money; emit Bills of Credit; make any Thing but gold and silver Coin a Tender in Payment of Debts; pass any Bill of Attainder, ex post facto Law, or Law impairing the Obligation of Contracts, or grant any Title of Nobility.

No State shall, without the Consent of the Congress, lay any Imposts or Duties on Imports or Exports, except what may be absolutely necessary for executing it's inspection Laws: and the net Produce of all Duties and Imposts, laid by any State on Imports or Exports, shall be for the Use of the Treasury of the United States; and all such Laws shall be subject to the Revision and Controul of the Congress.

No State shall, without the Consent of Congress, lay any Duty of Tonnage, keep Troops, or Ships of War in time of Peace, enter into any Agreement or Compact with another State, or with a foreign Power, or engage in War, unless actually invaded, or in such imminent Danger as will not admit of delay.

Article. II.

Section. 1. The executive Power shall be vested in a President of the United States of America. He shall hold his Office during the term of four Years, and, together with the Vice President, chosen for the same Term, be elected, as follows

Each State shall appoint, in such Manner as the Legislature thereof may direct, a Number of Electors, equal to the whole Number of Senators and Representatives to which the State may be entitled in the Congress: but no Senator or Representative, or Person holding an Office of Trust or Profit under the United States, shall be appointed an Elector.

The Electors shall meet in their respective States, and vote by Ballot for two Persons, of whom one at least shall not be an Inhabitant of the same State with themselves. And they shall make a List of all the Persons voted for, and of the Number of Votes for each; which List they shall sign and certify, and transmit sealed to the Seat of the Government of the United States, directed to the President of the Senate. The President of the Senate shall, in the Presence of the Senate and House of Representatives, open all the Certificates, and the Votes shall then be counted. The Person having the greatest Number of Votes shall be the President, if such Number be a Majority of the whole Number of Electors appointed; and if there be more than one who have such Majority, and have an equal Number of Votes, then the House of Representatives shall immediately chuse by Ballot one of them for President; and if no Person have a Majority, then from the five highest on the List the said House shall in like Manner chuse the President. But in chusing the President, the Votes shall be taken by States, the Representation from each State having one Vote; A quorum for this Purpose shall consist of a Member or Members from two thirds of the States, and a Majority of all the States shall be necessary to a Choice. In every Case, after the Choice of the President, the Person having the greatest Number of Votes of the Electors shall be the Vice President. But if there should remain two or more who have equal Votes, the Senate shall chuse from them by Ballot the Vice President.

The Congress may determine the Time of chusing the Electors, and the Day on which they shall give their Votes; which Day shall be the same throughout the United States.

No Person except a natural born Citizen, or a Citizen of the United States, at the time of the Adoption of this Constitution, shall be eligible to the Office of President; neither shall any Person be eligible to that Office who shall not have attained to the Age of thirty five Years, and been fourteen Years a Resident within the United States.

In Case of the Removal of the President from Office, or of his Death, Resignation, or Inability to discharge the Powers and Duties of the said Office, the Same shall devolve on the Vice President, and the Congress may by Law provide for the Case of Removal, Death, Resignation or Inability, both of the President and Vice President, declaring what Officer shall then act as President, and such Officer shall act accordingly, until the Disability be removed, or a President shall be elected.

The President shall, at stated Times, receive for his Services, a Compensation, which shall neither be encreased or diminished during the Period for which he shall have been elected, and he shall not receive within that Period any other Emolument from the United States, or any of them.

Before he enters on the Execution of his Office, he shall take the following Oath or Affirmation:—"I do solemnly swear (or affirm) that I will faithfully execute the Office of President of the United States, and will to the best of my Ability, preserve, protect and defend the Constitution of the United States."

Section. 2. The President shall be Commander in Chief of the Army and Navy of the United States, and of the Militia of the several States, when called into the actual Service of the United States; he may require the Opinion, in writing, of the principal Officer in each of the executive Departments, upon any Subject relating to the Duties of their respective Offices, and he shall have Power to grant Reprieves and Pardons for Offences against the United States, except in Cases of Impeachment.

He shall have Power, by and with the Advice and Consent of the Senate, to make Treaties, provided two thirds of the Senators present concur; and he shall nominate, and by and with the Advice and Consent of the Senate, shall appoint Ambassadors, other public Ministers and Consuls, Judges of the supreme Court, and all other Officers of the United States, whose Appointments are not herein otherwise provided for, and which shall be established by Law; but the Congress may by Law vest the Appointment of such inferior Officers, as they think proper, in the President alone, in the Courts of Law, or in the Heads of Departments.

The President shall have Power to fill up all Vacancies that may happen during the Recess of the Senate, by granting Commissions which shall expire at the End of their next Session.

Section. 3. He shall from time to time give to the Congress Information of the State of the Union, and recommend to their Consideration such Measures as he shall judge necessary and expedient; he may, on extraordinary Occasions, convene both Houses, or either of them, and in Case of Disagreement between them, with Respect to the Time of Adjournment, he may adjourn them to such Time as he shall think proper; he shall receive Ambassadors and other public Ministers; he shall take Care that the Laws be faithfully executed, and shall Commission all the Officers of the United States.

Section. 4. The President, Vice President and all civil Officers of the United States, shall be removed from Office on Impeachment for, and Conviction of, Treason, Bribery, or other high Crimes and Misdemeanors.

ARTICLE. III.

Section. 1. The judicial Power of the United States, shall be vested in one supreme Court, and in such inferior Courts as the Congress may from time to time ordain and establish. The Judges, both of the supreme and inferior Courts, shall hold their Offices during good Behavior, and shall, at stated Times, receive for their Services, a Compensation, which shall not be diminished during their Continuance in Office.

Section. 2. The judicial Power shall extend to all Cases, in Law and Equity, arising under this Constitution, the Laws of the United States, and Treaties made, or which shall be made, under their Authority;—to all Cases affecting Ambassadors, other public Ministers and Consuls;—to all Cases of admiralty and maritime Jurisdiction;—the Controversies to which the United States shall be a Party;—to Controversies between two or more States;—between a State and Citizens of another State;—between Citizens of different States;—between Citizens of the same State claiming Lands under Grants of different States, and between a State, or the Citizens thereof, and foreign States, Citizens or Subjects.

In all cases affecting Ambassadors, other public Ministers and Consuls, and those in which a State shall be Party, the supreme Court shall have original Jurisdiction. In all the other Cases before mentioned, the supreme Court shall have appellate Jurisdiction, both as to Law and Fact, with such Exceptions, and under such Regulations as the Congress shall make.

The Trial of all Crimes, except in Cases of Impeachment, shall be by Jury; and such Trial shall be held in the State where the said Crimes shall have been committed; but when not committed within any State, the Trial shall be at such Place or Places as the Congress may by Law have directed.

Section. 3. Treason against the United States, shall consist only in levying War against them, or in adhering to their Enemies, giving them Aid and Comfort. No Person shall be convicted of Treason unless on the Testimony of two Witnesses to the same overt Act, or on Confession in open Court.

The Congress shall have Power to declare the Punishment of Treason, but no Attainder of Treason shall work Corruption of Blood, or Forfeiture except during the Life of the Person attainted.

ARTICLE. IV.

Section. 1 Full Faith and Credit shall be given in each State to the public Acts, Records, and judicial Proceedings of every other State. And the Congress may by general Laws prescribe the Manner in which such Acts, Records and Proceedings shall be proved, and the Effect thereof.

Section. 2. The Citizens of each State shall be entitled to all Privileges and Immunities of Citizens in the several States.

A Person charged in any State with Treason, Felony, or other Crime, who shall flee from Justice, and be found in another State, shall on Demand of the executive Authority of the State from which he fled, be delivered up, to be removed to the State having Jurisdiction of the Crime.

No Person held to Service or Labour in one State, under the Laws thereof, escaping into another, shall, in Consequence of any Law or Regulation therein, be discharged from such Service or Labour, but shall be delivered up on Claim of the Party to whom such Service or Labour may be due.

Section. 3. New States may be admitted by the Congress into this Union; but no new State shall be formed or erected within the Jurisdiction of any other State; nor any State be formed by the Junction of two or more States, or Parts of States, without the consent of the Legislatures of the States concerned as well as of the Congress.

The Congress shall have Power to dispose of and make all needful Rules and Regulations respecting the Territory or other Property belonging to the United States; and nothing in this Constitution shall be so construed as to Prejudice any Claims of the United States, or of any particular States.

Section. 4. The United States shall guarantee to every State in this Union a Republican Form of Government, and shall protect each of them against Invasion; and on Application of the Legislature, or of the Executive (when the Legislature cannot be convened) against domestic Violence.

ARTICLE. V.

The Congress, whenever two thirds of both Houses shall deem it necessary, shall propose Amendments to this Constitution, or, on the Application of the Legislatures of two thirds of the several States, shall call a Convention for proposing Amendments, which, in either Case, shall be valid to all Intents and Purposes, as Part of this Constitution, when ratified by the Legislatures of three fourths of the several States, or by Conventions in three fourths thereof, as the one or the other Mode of Ratification may be proposed by the Congress; Provided that no Amendment which may be made prior to the Year One thousand eight hundred and eight shall in any Manner affect the first and fourth Clauses in the Ninth Section of the first Article; and that no State, without its Consent, shall be deprived of its equal Suffrage in the Senate.

ARTICLE. VI.

All Debts contracted and Engagements entered into, before the Adoption of this Constitution, shall be as valid against the United States under this Constitution, as under the Confederation.

This Constitution, and the Laws of the United States which shall be made in Pursuance thereof; and all Treaties made, or which shall be made, under the Authority of the United States, shall be the supreme Law of the Land; and the Judges in every State shall be bound thereby, any Thing in the Constitution or Laws of any State to the Contrary notwithstanding.

The Senators and Representatives before mentioned, and the Members of the several State Legislatures, and all executive and judicial Officers, both of the United States and of the several States, shall be bound by Oath or Affirmation, to support this Constitution; but no religious Test shall ever be required as a Qualification to any Office or public Trust under the United States.

ARTICLE. VII.

The Ratification of the Conventions of nine States, shall be sufficient for the Establishment of this Constitution between the States so ratifying the Same.

Done in Convention by the Unanimous Consent of the States present the Seventeenth Day of September in the Year of our Lord one thousand seven hundred and Eighty seven and of the Independence of the United States of

America the Twelfth. In witness thereof We have hereunto subscribed our Names,

G°. WASHINGTON—Presd'.
and deputy from Virginia.

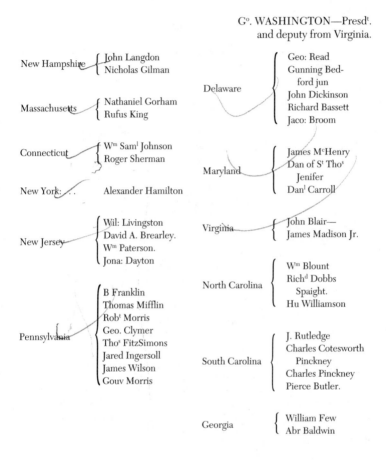

New Hampshire { John Langdon
Nicholas Gilman

Massachusetts { Nathaniel Gorham
Rufus King

Connecticut { Wᵐ Samˡ Johnson
Roger Sherman

New York: Alexander Hamilton

New Jersey { Wil: Livingston
David A. Brearley.
Wᵐ Paterson.
Jona: Dayton

Pennsylvania { B Franklin
Thomas Mifflin
Robᵗ Morris
Geo. Clymer
Thoˢ FitzSimons
Jared Ingersoll
James Wilson
Gouv Morris

Delaware { Geo: Read
Gunning Bedford jun
John Dickinson
Richard Bassett
Jaco: Broom

Maryland { James MᶜHenry
Dan of Sᵗ Thoˢ Jenifer
Danˡ Carroll

Virginia { John Blair—
James Madison Jr.

North Carolina { Wᵐ Blount
Richᵈ Dobbs Spaight.
Hu Williamson

South Carolina { J. Rutledge
Charles Cotesworth Pinckney
Charles Pinckney
Pierce Butler.

Georgia { William Few
Abr Baldwin

AMENDMENTS TO THE CONSTITUTION

ARTICLES IN ADDITION TO, and Amendment of the Constitution of the United States of America, proposed by Congress, and ratified by the Legislatures of the several States, pursuant to the fifth Article of the original Constitution.

AMENDMENT I.

Congress shall make no law respecting an establishment of religion, or prohibiting the free exercise thereof; or abridging the freedom of speech, or of the press;

or the right of the people peaceably to assemble, and to petition the Government for a redress of grievances.

AMENDMENT II.

A well regulated Militia, being necessary to the security of a free State, the right of the people to keep and bear Arms, shall not be infringed.

AMENDMENT III.

No Soldier shall, in time of peace be quartered in any house, without the consent of the Owner, nor in time of war, but in a manner to be prescribed by law.

AMENDMENT IV.

The right of the people to be secure in their persons, houses, papers, and effects, against unreasonable searches and seizures, shall not be violated, and no Warrants shall issue, but upon probable cause, supported by Oath or affirmation, and particularly describing the place to be searched, and the persons or things to be seized.

AMENDMENT V.

No person shall be held to answer for a capital, or otherwise infamous crime, unless on a presentment or indictment of a Grand Jury, except in cases arising in the land or naval forces, or in the Militia, when in actual service in time of War or public danger; nor shall any person be subject for the same offence to be twice put in jeopardy of life or limb; nor shall be compelled in any criminal case to be a witness against himself, nor be deprived of life, liberty, or property, without due process of law; nor shall private property be taken for public use, without just compensation.

AMENDMENT VI.

In all criminal prosecutions, the accused shall enjoy the right to a speedy and public trial, by an impartial jury of the State and district wherein the crime shall have been committed, which district shall have been previously ascertained by law, and to be informed of the nature and cause of the accusation; to be confronted with the witnesses against him; to have compulsory process for obtaining witnesses in his favor, and to have the Assistance of Counsel for his defence.

AMENDMENT VII.

In Suits at common law, where the value in controversy shall exceed twenty dollars, the right of trial by jury shall be preserved, and no fact tried by a jury, shall be otherwise re-examined in any Court of the United States, than according to the rules of the common law.

AMENDMENT VIII.

Excessive bail shall not be required, nor excessive fines imposed, nor cruel and unusual punishments inflicted.

AMENDMENT IX.

The enumeration in the Constitution, of certain rights, shall not be construed to deny or disparage others retained by the people.

AMENDMENT X.

The powers not delegated to the United States by the Constitution, nor prohibited by it to the States, are reserved to the States respectively, or to the people. [The first ten amendments went into effect December 15, 1791.]

AMENDMENT XI.

The Judicial power of the United States shall not be construed to extend to any suit in law or equity, commenced or prosecuted against one of the United States by Citizens of another State, or by Citizens or Subjects of any Foreign State. [January 8, 1798.]

AMENDMENT XII.

The Electors shall meet in their respective states, and vote by ballot for President and Vice-President, one of whom, at least, shall not be an inhabitant of the same state with themselves; they shall name in their ballots the person voted for as President, and in distinct ballots the person voted for as Vice-President, and they shall make distinct lists of all persons voted for as President, and of all persons voted for as Vice President, and of the number of votes for each, which lists they shall sign and certify, and transmit sealed to the seat of the government of the United States, directed to the President of the Senate;—The President of the Senate shall, in the presence of the Senate and House of Representatives, open all the certificates and the votes shall then be counted;—The person having the greatest number of votes for President, shall be the President, if such number be a majority of the whole number of Electors appointed; and if no person have such majority, then from the persons having the highest numbers not exceeding three on the list of those voted for as President, the House of Representatives shall choose immediately, by ballot, the President. But in choosing the President, the votes shall be taken by states, the representation from each state having one vote; a quorum for this purpose shall consist of a member or members from two-thirds of the states, and a majority of all the states shall be necessary to a choice. And if the House of Representatives shall not choose a President whenever the right of choice shall devolve upon them, before the fourth day of March next following, then the Vice-President shall act as President, as in the case of the death or other constitutional disability of the President.—The person having the greatest number of votes as Vice-President, shall be the Vice-President, if such number be a majority of the whole number of Electors appointed, and if no person have a majority, then from the two highest numbers on the list, the Senate shall choose the Vice-President; a quorum for the purpose shall consist of two-thirds of the whole number of Senators, and a majority of the whole number shall be necessary to a choice. But no person constitutionally ineligible to the office of President shall be eligible to that of Vice-President of the United States. [September 25, 1804.]

AMENDMENT XIII.

Section 1. Neither slavery nor involuntary servitude, except as a punishment for crime whereof the party shall have been duly convicted, shall exist within the United States, or any place subject to their jurisdiction.

Section 2. Congress shall have power to enforce this article by appropriate legislation. [December 18, 1865.]

AMENDMENT XIV.

Section 1. All persons born or naturalized in the United States, and subject to the jurisdiction thereof, are citizens of the United States and of the State wherein they reside. No State shall make or enforce any law which shall abridge the privileges or immunities of citizens of the United States; nor shall any State deprive any person of life, liberty, or property, without due process of law; nor deny to any person within its jurisdiction the equal protection of the laws.

Section 2. Representatives shall be apportioned among the several States according to their respective numbers, counting the whole number of persons in each State, excluding Indians not taxed. But when the right to vote at any election for the choice of electors for President and Vice President of the United States, Representatives in Congress, the Executive and Judicial officers of a State, or the members of the Legislature thereof, is denied to any of the male inhabitants of such State, being twenty-one years of age, and citizens of the United States, or in any way abridged, except for participation in rebellion, or other crime, the basis of representation therein shall be reduced in the proportion which the number of such male citizens shall bear to the whole number of male citizens twenty-one years of age in such State.

Section 3. No person shall be a Senator or Representative in Congress, or elector of President and Vice President, or hold any office, civil or military, under the United States, or under any State, who, having previously taken an oath, as a member of Congress, or as an officer of the United States, or as a member of any State legislature, or as an executive or judicial officer of any State, to support the Constitution of the United States, shall have engaged in insurrection or rebellion against the same, or given aid or comfort to the enemeis thereof. But Congress may by a vote of two-thirds of each House, remove such disability.

Section 4. The validity of the public debt of the United States, authorized by law, including debts incurred for payment of pensions and bounties for services in suppressing insurrection or rebellion, shall not be questioned. But neither the United States nor any State shall assume or pay any debt or obligation incurred in aid of insurrection or rebellion against the United States, or any claim for the loss or emancipation of any slave; but all such debts, obligations and claims shall be held illegal and void.

Section 5. The Congress shall have power to enforce, by appropriate legislation, the provisions of this article. [July 28, 1868.]

AMENDMENT XV.

Section 1. The right of citizens of the United States to vote shall not be denied or abridged by the United States or by any State on account of race, color, or previous condition of servitude—

Section 2. The Congress shall have power to enforce this article by appropriate legislation.—[March 30, 1870.]

AMENDMENT XVI.

The Congress shall have power to lay and collect taxes on incomes, from whatever source derived, without apportionment among the several States, and without regard to any census or enumeration. [February 25, 1913.]

AMENDMENT XVII.

The Senate of the United States shall be composed of two senators from each State, elected by the people thereof, for six years; and each Senator shall have one vote. The electors in each State shall have the qualifications requisite for electors of the most numerous branch of the State legislature.

When vacancies happen in the representation of any State in the Senate, the executive authority of such State shall issue writs of election to fill such vacancies: *Provided,* That the legislature of any State may empower the executive thereof to make temporary appointments until the people fill the vacancies by election as the legislature may direct.

This amendment shall not be so construed as to affect the election or term of any senator chosen before it becomes valid as part of the Constitution. [May 31, 1913.]

AMENDMENT XVIII.

After one year from the ratification of this article, the manufacture, sale, or transportation of intoxicating liquors within, the importation thereof into, or the exportation thereof from the United States and all territory subject to the jurisdiction thereof for beverage purposes is hereby prohibited.

The Congress and the several States shall have concurrent power to enforce this article by appropriate legislation.

This article shall be inoperative unless it shall have been ratified as an amendment to the Constitution by the legislatures of the several States, as provided in the Constitution, within seven years from the date of the submission thereof to the States by Congress. [January 29, 1919.]

AMENDMENT XIX.

The right of citizens of the United States to vote shall not be denied or abridged by the United States or by any State on account of sex.

The Congress shall have power by appropriate legislation to enforce the provisions of this article. [August 26, 1920.]

AMENDMENT XX.

Section 1. The terms of the President and Vice-President shall end at noon on the twentieth day of January, and the terms of Senators and Representatives at noon on the third day of January, of the years in which such terms would have ended if this article had not been ratified; and the terms of their successors shall then begin.

Section 2. The Congress shall assemble at least once in every year, and such meeting shall begin at noon on the third day of January, unless they shall by law appoint a different day.

Section 3. If, at the time fixed for the beginning of the term of the President, the President-elect shall have died, the Vice-President-elect shall become President. If a President shall not have been chosen before the time fixed for the beginning of his term, or if the President-elect shall have failed to qualify, then the Vice-President-elect shall act as President until a President shall have qualified; and the Congress may by law provide for the case wherein neither a President-elect nor a Vice-President-elect shall have qualified, declaring who shall then act as President, or the manner in which one who is to act shall be selected, and such person shall act accordingly until a President or Vice-President shall have qualified.

Section 4. The Congress may by law provide for the case of the death of any of the persons from whom the House of Representatives may choose a President whenever the right of choice shall have devolved upon them, and for the case of the death of any of the persons from whom the Senate may choose a Vice-President whenever the right of choice shall have devolved upon them.

Section 5. Sections 1 and 2 shall take effect on the 15th day of October following the ratification of this article.

Section 6. This article shall be inoperative unless it shall have been ratified as an amendment to the Constitution by the legislatures of three-fourths of the several States within seven years from the date of its submission. [February 6, 1933.]

AMENDMENT XXI.

Section 1. The eighteenth article of amendment to the Constitution of the United States is hereby repealed.

Section 2. The transportation or importation into any State, Territory or possession of the United States for delivery or use therein of intoxicating liquors, in violation of the laws thereof, is hereby prohibited.

Section 3.
This article shall be inoperative unless it shall have been ratified as an amendment to the Constitution by convention in the several States, as provided in the Constitution, within seven years from the date of the submission thereof to the States by the Congress. [December 5, 1933.]

AMENDMENT XXII.

Section 1. No person shall be elected to the office of the President more than twice, and no person who has held the office of President, or acted as President, for more than two years of a term to which some other person was elected President shall be elected to the office of the President more than once. But this Article shall not apply to any person holding the office of President when this Article was proposed by the Congress, and shall not prevent any person who may be holding the office of President, or acting as President, during the term within which this Article becomes operative from holding the office of President or acting as President during the remainder of such term.

Section 2. This article shall be inoperative unless it shall have been ratified as an amendment to the Constitution by the legislatures of three-fourths of the several states within seven years from the date of its submission to the States by the Congress. [February 27, 1951.]

AMENDMENT XXIII.

Section 1. The District constituting the seat of government of the United States shall appoint in such manner as the Congress may direct:

A number of electors of President and Vice-President equal to the whole number of Senators and Representatives in Congress to which the District would be entitled if it were a State, but in no event more than the least populous State; they shall be in addition to those appointed by the States, but they shall be considered, for the purposes of the election of President and Vice-President, to be electors appointed by a State; and they shall meet in the District and perform such duties as provided by the twelfth article of amendment.

Section 2. The Congress shall have the power to enforce this article by appropriate legislation. [March 29, 1961.]

AMENDMENT XXIV.

Section 1. The right of citizens of the United States to vote in any primary or other election for President or Vice President, for electors for President or Vice President, or for Senator or Representative in Congress, shall not be denied or abridged by the United States or any State by reason of failure to pay any poll tax or other tax.

Section 2. The Congress shall have power to enforce this article by appropriate legislation. [January 23, 1964.]

AMENDMENT XXV.

Section 1. In case of the removal of the President from office or of his death or resignation, the Vice President shall become President.

Section 2. Whenever there is a vacancy in the office of Vice President, the President shall nominate a Vice President who shall take office upon confirmation by a majority vote of both Houses of Congress.

Section 3. Whenever the President transmits to the President pro tempore of the Senate and the Speaker of the House of Representatives his written declaration that he is unable to discharge the powers and duties of his office, and until he transmits to them a written declaration to the contrary, such powers and duties shall be discharged by the Vice President as Acting President.

Section 4. Whenever the Vice President and a majority of either the principal officers of the executive departments or of such other body as Congress may by law provide, transmit to the President pro tempore of the Senate and the Speaker of the House of Representatives their written declaration that the President is unable to discharge the powers and duties of his office, the Vice President shall immediately assume the powers and duties of the office as Acting President.

Thereafter, when the President transmits to the President pro tempore of the Senate and the Speaker of the House of Representatives his written declaration that no inability exists, he shall resume the powers and duties of his office unless the Vice President and a majority of either the principal officers of the executive departments or of such other body as Congress may by law provide, transmit within four days to the President pro tempore of the Senate and the Speaker of the House of Representatives their written declaration that the President is unable to discharge the powers and duties of his office. Thereupon Congress shall decide the issue, assembling within forty-eight hours for that purpose if not in session. If the Congress, within twenty-one days after receipt of the latter written declaration, or, if Congress is not in session, within twenty-one days after Congress is required to assemble, determines by two-thirds vote of both Houses that the President is unable to discharge the powers and duties of his office, the Vice President shall continue to discharge the same as Acting President; otherwise, the President shall resume the powers and duties of his office. [February 10, 1967.]

AMENDMENT XXVI.

Section 1. The right of citizens of the United States, who are eighteen years of age or older, to vote shall not be denied or abridged by the United States or by any State on account of age.

Section 2. The Congress shall have power to enforce this article by appropriate legislation [June 30, 1971.]

AMENDMENT XXVII.

No law, varying the compensation for the services of the Senators and Representatives shall take effect, until an election of Representatives shall have intervened. [May 8, 1992.]

PRESIDENTIAL ELECTIONS

Year	Number of States	Candidates	Parties	Popular Vote	% of Popular Vote	Electoral Vote	% Voter Participation
1789	11	**GEORGE WASHINGTON**	No party designations			69	
		John Adams				34	
		Other candidates				35	
1792	15	**GEORGE WASHINGTON**	No party designations			132	
		John Adams				77	
		George Clinton				50	
		Other candidates				5	
1796	16	**JOHN ADAMS**	Federalist			71	
		Thomas Jefferson	Democratic-Republican			68	
		Thomas Pinckney	Federalist			59	
		Aaron Burr	Democratic-Republican			30	
		Other candidates				48	
1800	16	**THOMAS JEFFERSON**	Democratic-Republican			73	
		Aaron Burr	Democratic-Republican			73	
		John Adams	Federalist			65	
		Charles C. Pinckney	Federalist			64	
		John Jay	Federalist			1	

Year	Number of States	Candidates	Parties	Popular Vote	% of Popular Vote	Electoral Vote	% Voter Participation
1804	17	THOMAS JEFFERSON	Democratic-Republican			162	
		Charles C. Pinckney	Federalist			14	
1808	17	JAMES MADISON	Democratic-Republican			122	
		Charles C. Pinckney	Federalist			47	
		George Clinton	Democratic-Republican			6	
1812	18	JAMES MADISON	Democratic-Republican			128	
		DeWitt Clinton	Federalist			89	
1816	19	JAMES MONROE	Democratic-Republican			183	
		Rufus King	Federalist			34	
1820	24	JAMES MONROE	Democratic-Republican			231	
		John Quincy Adams	Independent			1	
1824	24	JOHN QUINCY ADAMS	Democratic-Republican	108,740	30.5	84	26.9
		Andrew Jackson	Democratic-Republican	153,544	43.1	99	
		Henry Clay	Democratic-Republican	47,136	13.2	37	
		William H. Crawford	Democratic-Republican	46,618	13.1	41	
1828	24	ANDREW JACKSON	Democratic	647,286	56.0	178	57.6
		John Quincy Adams	National-Republican	508,064	44.0	83	

Year	Number of States	Candidates	Parties	Popular Vote	% of Popular Vote	Electoral Vote	% Voter Participation
1832	24	**ANDREW JACKSON**	Democratic	688,242	54.5	219	55.4
		Henry Clay	National-Republican	473,462	37.5	49	
		William Wirt	Anti-Masonic	101,051	8.0	7	
		John Floyd	Democratic			11	
1836	26	**MARTIN VAN BUREN**	Democratic	765,483	50.9	170	57.8
		William H. Harrison	Whig			73	
		Hugh L. White	Whig	739,795	49.1	26	
		Daniel Webster	Whig			14	
		W. P. Mangum	Whig			11	
1840	26	**WILLIAM H. HARRISON**	Whig	1,274,624	53.1	234	80.2
		Martin Van Buren	Democratic	1,127,781	46.9	60	
1844	26	**JAMES K. POLK**	Democratic	1,338,464	49.6	170	78.9
		Henry Clay	Whig	1,300,097	48.1	105	
		James G. Birney	Liberty	62,300	2.3		
1848	30	**ZACHARY TAYLOR**	Whig	1,360,967	47.4	163	72.7
		Lewis Cass	Democratic	1,222,342	42.5	127	
		Martin Van Buren	Free Soil	291,263	10.1		
1852	31	**FRANKLIN PIERCE**	Democratic	1,601,117	50.9	254	69.6
		Winfield Scott	Whig	1,385,453	44.1	42	
		John P. Hale	Free Soil	155,825	5.0		
1856	31	**JAMES BUCHANAN**	Democratic	1,832,955	45.3	174	78.9
		John C. Frémont	Republican	1,339,932	33.1	114	
		Millard Fillmore	American	871,731	21.6	8	

Year	No.	Candidates	Parties	Popular Vote	% Popular	Electoral Vote	% Participation
1860	33	**ABRAHAM LINCOLN**	Republican	1,865,593	39.8	180	81.2
		Stephen A. Douglas	Democratic	1,382,713	29.5	12	
		John C. Breckinridge	Democratic	848,356	18.1	72	
		John Bell	Constitutional Union	592,906	12.6	39	
1864	36	**ABRAHAM LINCOLN**	Republican	2,206,938	55.0	212	73.8
		George B. McClellan	Democratic	1,803,787	45.0	21	
1868	37	**ULYSSES S. GRANT**	Republican	3,013,421	52.7	214	78.1
		Horatio Seymour	Democratic	2,706,829	47.3	80	

Candidates receiving less than 1 percent of the popular vote have been omitted. Thus the percentage of popular vote given for any election year may not total 100 percent.

Before the passage of the Twelfth Amendment in 1804, the Electoral College voted for two presidential candidates; the runner-up became vice-president.

ADMISSION OF STATES

Order of Admission	State	Date of Admission	Order of Admission	State	Date of Admission
1	Delaware	December 7, 1787	26	Michigan	January 26, 1837
2	Pennsylvania	December 12, 1787	27	Florida	March 3, 1845
3	New Jersey	December 18, 1787	28	Texas	December 29, 1845
4	Georgia	January 2, 1788	29	Iowa	December 28, 1846
5	Connecticut	January 9, 1788	30	Wisconsin	May 29, 1848
6	Massachusetts	February 7, 1788	31	California	September 9, 1850
7	Maryland	April 28, 1788	32	Minnesota	May 11, 1858
8	South Carolina	May 23, 1788	33	Oregon	February 14, 1859
9	New Hampshire	June 21, 1788	34	Kansas	January 29, 1861
10	Virginia	June 25, 1788	35	West Virginia	June 30, 1863
11	New York	July 26, 1788	36	Nevada	October 31, 1864
12	North Carolina	November 21, 1789	37	Nebraska	March 1, 1867
13	Rhode Island	May 29, 1790	38	Colorado	August 1, 1876
14	Vermont	March 4, 1791	39	North Dakota	November 2, 1889
15	Kentucky	June 1, 1792	40	South Dakota	November 2, 1889
16	Tennessee	June 1, 1796	41	Montana	November 8, 1889
17	Ohio	March 1, 1803	42	Washington	November 11, 1889
18	Louisiana	April 30, 1812	43	Idaho	July 3, 1890
19	Indiana	December 11, 1816	44	Wyoming	July 10, 1890
20	Mississippi	December 10, 1817	45	Utah	January 4, 1896
21	Illinois	December 3, 1818	46	Oklahoma	November 16, 1907
22	Alabama	December 14, 1819	47	New Mexico	January 6, 1912
23	Maine	March 15, 1820	48	Arizona	February 14, 1912
24	Missouri	August 10, 1821	49	Alaska	January 3, 1959
25	Arkansas	June 15, 1836	50	Hawaii	August 21, 1959

POPULATION OF THE UNITED STATES

Year	Number of States	Population	% Increase	Population per Square Mile
1790	13	3,929,214		4.5
1800	16	5,308,483	35.1	6.1
1810	17	7,239,881	36.4	4.3
1820	23	9,638,453	33.1	5.5
1830	24	12,866,020	33.5	7.4
1840	26	17,069,453	32.7	9.8
1850	31	23,191,876	35.9	7.9
1860	33	31,443,321	35.6	10.6
1870	37	39,818,449	26.6	13.4
1880	38	50,155,783	26.0	16.9
1890	44	62,947,714	25.5	21.1
1900	45	75,994,575	20.7	25.6
1910	46	91,972,266	21.0	31.0
1920	48	105,710,620	14.9	35.6
1930	48	122,775,046	16.1	41.2
1940	48	131,669,275	7.2	44.2
1950	48	150,697,361	14.5	50.7
1960	50	179,323,175	19.0	50.6
1970	50	203,235,298	13.3	57.5
1980	50	226,504,825	11.4	64.0
1985	50	237,839,000	5.0	67.2
1990	50	250,122,000	5.2	70.6
1995	50	263,411,707	5.3	74.4

IMMIGRATION TO THE UNITED STATES, FISCAL YEARS 1820–1990

Year	Number	Year	Number	Year	Number	Year	Number
1820–1989	55,457,531	1871–80	2,812,191	1921–30	4,107,209	1971–80	4,493,314
1820	8,385	1871	321,350	1921	805,228	1971	370,478
1821–30	143,439	1872	404,806	1922	309,556	1972	384,685
1821	9,127	1873	459,803	1923	522,919	1973	400,063
1822	6,911	1874	313,339	1924	706,896	1974	394,861
1823	6,354	1875	227,498	1925	294,314	1975	386,914
1824	7,912	1876	169,986	1926	304,488	1976	398,613
1825	10,199	1877	141,857	1927	335,175	1976, TQ	103,676
1826	10,837	1878	138,469	1928	307,255	1977	462,315
1827	18,875	1879	177,826	1929	279,678	1978	601,442
1828	27,382	1880	457,257	1930	241,700	1979	460,348
1829	22,520	1881–90	5,246,613	1931–40	528,431	1980	530,639
1830	23,322	1881	669,431	1931	97,139	1981–90	7,338,062
1831–40	599,125	1882	788,992	1932	35,576	1981	596,600
1831	22,633	1883	603,322	1933	23,068	1982	594,131
1832	60,482	1884	518,592	1934	29,470	1983	559,763
1833	58,640	1885	395,346	1935	34,956	1984	543,903
1834	65,365	1886	334,203	1936	36,329	1985	570,009
1835	45,374	1887	490,109	1937	50,244	1986	601,708
1836	76,242	1888	546,889	1938	67,895	1987	601,516
1837	79,340	1889	444,427	1939	82,998	1988	643,025
1838	38,914	1890	455,302	1940	70,756	1989	1,090,924
1839	68,069	1891–1900	3,687,564	1941–50	1,035,039	1990	1,536,483
1840	84,066	1891	560,319	1941	51,776		
1841–50	1,713,251	1892	579,663	1942	28,781		
1841	80,289	1893	439,730	1943	23,725		
1842	104,565	1894	285,631	1944	28,551		
		1895	258,536	1945	38,119		
		1896	343,267	1946	108,721		

Year	Number
1843	52,496
1844	78,615
1845	114,371
1846	154,416
1847	234,968
1848	226,527
1849	297,024
1850	369,980
1851–60	**2,598,214**
1851	379,466
1852	371,603
1853	368,645
1854	427,833
1855	200,877
1856	200,436
1857	251,306
1858	123,126
1859	121,282
1860	153,640
1861–70	**2,314,824**
1861	91,918
1862	91,985
1863	176,282
1864	193,418
1865	248,120
1866	318,568
1867	315,722
1868	138,840
1869	352,768
1870	387,203

Year	Number
1897	230,832
1898	229,299
1899	311,715
1900	448,572
1901–10	**8,795,386**
1901	487,918
1902	648,743
1903	857,046
1904	812,870
1905	1,026,499
1906	1,100,735
1907	1,285,349
1908	782,870
1909	751,786
1910	1,041,570
1911–20	**5,735,811**
1911	878,587
1912	838,172
1913	1,197,892
1914	1,218,480
1915	326,700
1916	298,826
1917	295,403
1918	110,618
1919	141,132
1920	430,001

Year	Number
1947	147,292
1948	170,570
1949	188,317
1950	249,187
1951–60	**2,515,479**
1951	205,717
1952	265,520
1953	170,434
1954	208,177
1955	237,790
1956	321,625
1957	326,867
1958	253,265
1959	260,686
1960	265,398
1961–70	**3,321,677**
1961	271,344
1962	283,763
1963	306,260
1964	292,248
1965	296,697
1966	323,040
1967	361,972
1968	454,448
1969	358,579
1970	373,326

Source: U.S. Immigration and Naturalization Service, 1991.

IMMIGRATION BY REGION AND SELECTED COUNTRY OF LAST RESIDENCE, FISCAL YEARS 1820–1989

Region and Country of Last Residence[1]	1820	1821–30	1831–40	1841–50	1851–60	1861–70	1871–80	1881–90
All countries	8,385	143,439	599,125	1,713,251	2,598,214	2,314,824	2,812,191	5,246,613
Europe	7,690	98,797	495,681	1,597,442	2,452,577	2,065,141	2,271,925	4,735,484
Austria-Hungary	—[2]	—[2]	—[2]	—[2]	—[2]	7,800	72,969	353,719
Austria	—[2]	—[2]	—[2]	—[2]	—[2]	[3]7,124	63,009	226,038
Hungary						[3]484	9,960	127,681
Belgium	1	27	22	5,074	4,738	6,734	7,221	20,177
Czechoslovakia	—[4]	—[4]	—[4]	—[4]	—[4]	—[4]	—[4]	
Denmark	20	169	1,063	539	3,749	17,094	31,771	88,132
France	371	8,497	45,575	77,262	76,358	35,986	72,206	50,464
Germany	968	6,761	152,454	434,626	951,667	787,468	718,182	1,452,970
Greece		20	49	16	31	72	210	2,308
Ireland[5]	3,614	50,724	207,381	780,719	914,119	435,778	436,871	655,482
Italy	30	409	2,253	1,870	9,231	11,725	55,759	307,309
Netherlands	49	1,078	1,412	8,251	10,789	9,102	16,541	53,701
Norway-Sweden	3	91	1,201	13,903	20,931	109,298	211,245	568,362
Norway	—[6]	—[6]	—[6]	—[6]	—[6]	—[6]	95,323	176,586
Sweden	—[6]	—[6]	—[6]	—[6]	—[6]	—[6]	115,922	391,776
Poland	5	16	369	105	1,164	2,027	12,970	51,806
Portugal	35	145	829	550	1,055	2,658	14,082	16,978
Romania	—[7]	—[7]	—[7]	—[7]	—[7]	—[7]	11	6,348
Soviet Union	14	75	277	551	457	2,512	39,284	213,282
Spain	139	2,477	2,125	2,209	9,298	6,697	5,266	4,419
Switzerland	31	3,226	4,821	4,644	25,011	23,286	28,293	81,988
United Kingdom[5,8]	2,410	25,079	75,810	267,044	423,974	606,896	548,043	807,357
Yugoslavia	—[9]	—[9]	—[9]	—[9]	—[9]	—[9]	—[9]	—[9]
Other Europe		3	40	79	5	8	1,001	682

Region / Country								
Asia	6	30	55	141	41,538	64,759	124,160	69,942
China[10]	1	2	8	35	41,397	64,301	123,201	61,711
Hong Kong	—[11]	—[11]	—[11]	—[11]	—[11]	—[11]	—[11]	—[11]
India	1	8	39	36	43	69	163	269
Iran	—[12]	—[12]	—[12]	—[12]	—[12]	—[12]	—[12]	—[12]
Israel	—[13]	—[13]	—[13]	—[13]	—[13]	—[13]	—[13]	—[13]
Japan	—[14]	—[14]	—[14]	—[14]	83	186	149	2,270
Korea	—[15]	—[15]	—[15]	—[15]	—[15]	—[15]	—[15]	—[15]
Philippines	—[16]	—[16]	—[16]	—[16]	—[16]	—[16]	—[16]	—[16]
Turkey	1	20	7	59		131	404	3,782
Vietnam	—[11]	—[11]	—[11]	—[11]	—[11]	—[11]	—[11]	—[11]
Other Asia	3		1	11	15	72	243	1,910
America	387	11,564	33,424	62,469	74,720	166,607	404,044	426,967
Canada & Newfoundland[17,18]	209	2,277	13,624	41,723	59,309	153,878	383,640	393,304
Mexico[8]	1	4,817	6,599	3,271	3,078	2,191	5,162	1,913[19]
Caribbean	164	3,834	12,301	13,528	10,660	9,046	13,957	29,042
Cuba	—[12]	—[12]	—[12]	—[12]	—[12]	—[12]	—[12]	—[12]
Dominican Republic	—[20]	—[20]	—[20]	—[20]	—[20]	—[20]	—[20]	—[20]
Haiti	—[20]	—[20]	—[20]	—[20]	—[20]	—[20]	—[20]	—[20]
Jamaica	—[21]	—[21]	—[21]	—[21]	—[21]	—[21]	—[21]	—[21]
Other Caribbean	164	3,834	12,301	13,528	10,660	9,046	13,957	29,042
Central America	2	105	44	368	449	95	157	404
El Salvador	—[20]	—[20]	—[20]	—[20]	—[20]	—[20]	—[20]	—[20]
Other Central America	2	105	44	368	449	95	157	404
South America	11	531	856	3,579	1,224	1,397	1,128	2,304
Argentina	—[20]	—[20]	—[20]	—[20]	—[20]	—[20]	—[20]	—[20]
Colombia	—[20]	—[20]	—[20]	—[20]	—[20]	—[20]	—[20]	—[20]
Ecuador	—[20]	—[20]	—[20]	—[20]	—[20]	—[20]	—[20]	—[20]
Other South America	11	531	856	3,579	1,224	1,397	1,128	2,304
Other America	—[22]	—[22]	—[22]	—[22]	—[22]	—[22]	—[22]	—[22]
Africa	1	16	54	55	210	312	358	857
Oceania	1	2	9	29	158	214	10,914	12,574
Not specified[22]	300	33,030	69,902	53,115	29,011	17,791	790	789

Source: U.S. Immigration and Naturalization Service, 1991.

Region and Country of Last Residence[1]	1891–1900	1901–10	1911–20	1921–30	1931–40	1941–50	1951–60	1961–70
All countries	3,687,564	8,795,386	5,735,811	4,107,209	528,431	1,035,039	2,515,479	3,321,677
Europe	3,555,352	8,056,040	4,321,887	2,463,194	347,566	621,147	1,325,727	1,123,492
Austria-Hungary	592,707[23]	2,145,266[23]	896,342[23]	63,548	11,424	28,329	103,743	26,022
Austria	234,081[3]	668,209[3]	453,649	32,868	3,563[34]	24,860[34]	67,106	20,621
Hungary	181,288[3]	808,511[3]	442,693	30,680	7,861	3,469	36,637	5,401
Belgium	18,167	41,635	33,746	15,846	4,817	12,189	18,575	9,192
Czechoslovakia		—[4]	3,426[4]	102,194	14,393	8,347	918	3,273
Denmark	50,231	65,285	41,983	32,430	2,559	5,393	10,984	9,201
France	30,770	73,379	61,897	49,610	12,623	38,809	51,121	45,237
Germany	505,152[23]	341,498[23]	143,945[23]	412,202	114,058[34]	226,578[34]	477,765	190,796
Greece	15,979	167,519	184,201	51,084	9,119	8,973	47,608	85,969
Ireland[5]	388,416	339,065	146,181	211,234	10,973	19,789	48,362	32,966
Italy	651,893	2,045,877	1,109,524	455,315	68,028	57,661	185,491	214,111
Netherlands	26,758	48,262	43,718	26,948	7,150	14,860	52,277	30,606
Norway-Sweden	321,281	440,039	161,469	165,780	8,700	20,765	44,632	32,600
Norway	95,015	190,505	66,395	68,531	4,740	10,100	22,935	15,484
Sweden	226,266	249,534	95,074	97,249	3,960	10,665	21,697	17,116
Poland	96,720[23]	—[23]	4,813[33]	227,734	17,026	7,571	9,985	53,539
Portugal	27,508	69,149	89,732	29,994	3,329	7,423	19,588	76,065
Romania	12,750	53,008	13,311	67,646	3,871	1,076	1,039	2,531
Soviet Union	505,290[23]	1,597,306[23]	921,201[23]	61,742	1,370	571	671	2,465
Spain	8,731	27,935	68,611	28,958	3,258	2,898	7,894	44,659
Switzerland	31,179	34,922	23,091	29,676	5,512	10,547	17,675	18,453
United Kingdom[5,8]	271,538	525,950	341,408	339,570	31,572	139,306	202,824	213,822
Yugoslavia	—[9]	—[9]	1,888[9]	49,064	5,835	1,576	8,225	20,381
Other Europe	282	39,945	31,400	42,619	11,949	8,486	16,350	11,604

Asia	74,862	323,543	247,236	112,059	16,595	37,028	153,249	427,642
China[10]	14,799	20,605	21,278	29,907	4,928	16,709	9,657	34,764
Hong Kong	—[11]	—[11]	—[11]	—[11]	—[11]	—[11]	15,541[11]	75,007
India	68	4,713	2,082	1,886	496	1,761	1,973	27,189
Iran	—[12]	—[12]	—[12]	241[12]	195	1,380	3,388	10,339
Israel	—[13]	—[13]	—[13]	—[13]	—[13]	476[13]	25,476	29,602
Japan	25,942	129,797	83,837	33,462	1,948	1,555	46,250	39,988
Korea	—[15]	—[15]	—[15]	—[15]	—[15]	107[15]	6,231	34,526
Philippines	—[16]	—[16]	—[16]	—[16]	528[16]	4,691	19,307	98,376
Turkey	30,425	157,369	134,066	33,824	1,065	798	3,519	10,142
Vietnam	—[11]	—[11]	—[11]	—[11]	—[11]	—[11]	335[11]	4,340
Other Asia	3,628	11,059	5,973	12,739	7,435	9,551	21,572	63,369
America	38,972	361,888	1,143,671	1,516,716	160,037	354,804	996,944	1,716,374
Canada & Newfoundland[17,18]	3,311	179,226	742,185	924,515	108,527	171,718	377,952	413,310
Mexico[18]	971[19]	49,642	219,004	459,287	22,319	60,589	299,811	453,937
Caribbean	33,066	107,548	123,424	74,899	15,502	49,725	123,091	470,213
Cuba	—[12]	—[12]	—[12]	15,901[12]	9,571	26,313	78,948	208,536
Dominican Republic	—[20]	—[20]	—[20]	—[20]	1,150[20]	5,627	9,897	93,292
Haiti	—[20]	—[20]	—[20]	—[20]	191[20]	911	4,442	34,499
Jamaica	—[21]	—[21]	—[21]	—[21]	—[21]	—[21]	8,869[21]	74,906
Other Caribbean	33,066	107,548	123,424	58,998	4,590	16,574	20,935[21]	58,980
Central America	549	8,192	17,159	15,769	5,861	21,665	44,751	101,330
El Salvador	—[20]	—[20]	—[20]	—[20]	673[20]	5,132	5,895	14,992
Other Central America	549	8,192	17,159	15,769	5,188	16,533	38,856	86,338
South America	1,075	17,280	41,899	42,215	7,803	21,831	91,628	257,954
Argentina	—[20]	—[20]	—[20]	—[20]	1,349[20]	3,338	19,486	49,721
Colombia	—[20]	—[20]	—[20]	—[20]	1,223[20]	3,858	18,048	72,028
Ecuador	—[20]	—[20]	—[20]	—[20]	337[20]	2,417	9,841	36,780
Other South America	1,075	17,280	41,899	42,215	4,894	12,218	44,253	99,425
Other America	—[22]	—[22]	—[22]	31[22]	25	29,276	59,711	19,630
Africa	350	7,368	8,443	6,286	1,750	7,367	14,092	28,954
Oceania	3,965	13,024	13,427	8,726	2,483	14,551	12,976	25,122
Not specified[22]	14,063	33,523[25]	1,147	228	—	142	12,491	93

Region and Country of Last Residence[1]	1971–80	1981–89	1984	1985	1986	1987	1988	1989	Total 170 Years 1820–1989
All countries	4,493,314	5,801,579	543,903	570,009	601,708	601,516	643,025	1,090,924	55,457,531
Europe	800,368	637,524	69,879	69,526	69,224	67,967	71,854	94,338	36,977,034
Austria-Hungary	16,028	20,152	2,846	2,521	2,604	2,401	3,200	3,586	4,338,049
Austria	9,478	14,566	2,351	1,930	2,039	1,769	2,493	2,845	1,825,172[3]
Hungary	6,550	5,586	495	591	565	632	707	741	1,666,801[3]
Belgium	5,329	6,239	787	775	843	859	706	705	209,729
Czechoslovakia	6,023	6,649	693	684	588	715	744	526	145,223
Denmark	4,439	4,696	512	465	544	515	561	617	369,738
France	25,069	28,088	3,335	3,530	3,876	3,809	3,637	4,101	783,322
Germany	74,414	79,809	9,375	10,028	9,853	9,923	9,748	10,419	7,071,313
Greece	92,369	34,490	3,311	3,487	3,497	4,087	4,690	4,588	700,017
Ireland[5]	11,490	22,229	1,096	1,288	1,757	3,032	5,121	6,983	4,715,393
Italy	129,368	51,008	6,328	6,351	5,711	4,666	5,332	11,089	5,356,862
Netherlands	10,492	10,723	1,313	1,235	1,263	1,303	1,152	1,253	372,717
Norway-Sweden	10,472	13,252	1,455	1,557	1,564	1,540	1,669	1,809	2,144,024
Norway	3,941	3,612	403	386	367	372	446	556	800,672[6]
Sweden	6,531	9,640	1,052	1,171	1,197	1,168	1,223	1,253	1,283,097[6]
Poland	37,234	64,888	7,229	7,409	6,540	5,818	7,298	13,279	587,972[6]
Portugal	101,710	36,365	3,800	3,811	3,804	4,009	3,290	3,861	497,195
Romania	12,393	27,361	2,956	3,764	3,809	2,741	2,915	3,535	201,345
Soviet Union	38,961	42,898	3,349	1,532	1,001	1,139	1,408	4,570	3,428,927
Spain	39,141	17,689	2,168	2,278	2,232	2,056	1,972	2,179	282,404
Switzerland	8,235	7,561	795	980	923	964	920	1,072	358,151
United Kingdom[5,8]	137,374	140,119	16,516	15,591	16,129	15,889	14,667	16,961	5,100,096
Yugoslavia	30,540	15,984	1,404	1,521	1,915	1,793	2,039	2,464	133,493
Other Europe	9,287	7,324	611	719	771	708	785	741	181,064

Asia	1,588,178	2,416,278	247,775	255,164	258,546	248,293	254,745	296,420	5,697,301
China[10]	124,326	306,108	29,109	33,095	32,389	32,669	34,300	39,284	873,737
Hong Kong	113,467	83,848	12,290	10,795	9,930	8,785	11,817	15,257	287,863[11]
India	164,134	221,977	23,617	24,536	24,808	26,394	25,312	28,599	426,907
Iran	45,136	101,267	11,131	12,327	12,031	10,323	9,846	13,027	161,946[12]
Israel	37,713	38,367	4,136	4,279	5,124	4,753	4,444	5,494	131,634[13]
Japan	49,775	40,654	4,517	4,552	4,444	4,711	5,085	5,454	455,813[14]
Korea	267,638	302,782	32,537	34,791	35,164	35,397	34,151	33,016	611,284[15]
Philippines	354,987	477,485	46,985	53,137	61,492	58,315	61,017	66,119	955,374[16]
Turkey	13,399	20,028	1,652	1,690	1,975	2,080	2,200	2,538	409,122
Vietnam	172,820	266,027	25,803	20,367	15,010	13,073	12,856	13,174	443,522[21]
Other Asia	244,783	557,735	55,998	55,595	56,179	51,793	53,717	74,458	940,099
America	1,982,735	2,564,698	208,111	225,519	254,078	265,026	294,906	672,639	12,017,021
Canada & Newfoundland[17,18]	169,939	132,296	15,659	16,354	16,060	16,741	15,821	18,294	4,270,943
Mexico[18]	640,294	975,657	57,820	61,290	66,753	72,511	95,170	405,660	3,208,543
Caribbean	741,126	759,416	68,368	79,374	98,527	100,615	110,949	87,597	2,590,542
Cuba	264,863	135,142	5,699	17,115	30,787	27,363	16,610	9,523	739,274[12]
Dominican Republic	148,135	209,899	23,207	23,861	26,216	24,947	27,195	26,744	468,000[20]
Haiti	56,335	118,510	9,554	9,872	12,356	14,643	34,858	13,341	214,888[20]
Jamaica	137,577	184,481	18,997	18,277	18,916	22,430	20,474	23,572	405,833[21]
Other Caribbean	134,216	111,384	10,911	10,249	10,252	11,232	11,812	14,417	762,547
Central America	134,640	321,845	27,626	28,447	30,086	30,366	31,311	101,273	673,385
El Salvador	34,436	133,938	8,753	10,093	10,881	10,627	12,043	57,628	195,066[20]
Other Central America	100,204	187,907	18,873	18,354	19,205	19,739	19,268	43,645	478,319
South America	295,741	375,026	38,636	40,052	42,650	44,782	41,646	59,812	1,163,482
Argentina	29,897	21,374	2,287	1,925	2,318	2,192	2,556	3,766	125,165[20]
Colombia	77,347	99,066	10,897	11,802	11,213	11,482	10,153	14,918	271,570[20]
Ecuador	50,077	43,841	4,244	4,601	4,518	4,656	4,736	7,587	143,293[20]
Other South America	138,420	210,745	21,208	21,724	24,601	26,452	24,201	33,541	623,454
Other America	995	458	2	2	2	11	9	3	110,126
Africa	80,779	144,096	13,594	15,236	15,500	15,730	17,124	22,485	301,348
Oceania	41,242	38,401	4,249	4,552	4,352	4,437	4,324	4,956	197,818
Not specified[22]	12	582	295	12	8	63	72	86	267,009

[1]Data for years prior to 1906 relate to country whence alien came; data from 1906–79 and 1984–89 are for country of last permanent residence; and data for 1980–83 refer to country of birth. Because of changes in boundaries, changes in lists of countries, and lack of data for specified countries for various periods, data for certain countries, especially for the total period 1820–1989, are not comparable throughout. Data for specified countries are included with countries to which they belonged prior to World War I.

[2]Data for Austria and Hungary not reported until 1861.

[3]Data for Austria and Hungary not reported separately for all years during the period.

[4]No data available for Czechoslovakia until 1920.

[5]Prior to 1926, data for Northern Ireland included in Ireland.

[6]Data for Norway and Sweden not reported separately until 1871.

[7]No data available for Romania until 1880.

[8]Since 1925, data for United Kingdom refer to England, Scotland, Wales, and Northern Ireland.

[9]In 1920, a separate enumeration was made for the Kingdom of Serbs, Croats, and Slovenes. Since 1922, the Serb, Croat, and Slovene Kingdom recorded as Yugoslavia.

[10]Beginning in 1957, China includes Taiwan.

[11]Data not reported separately until 1952.

[12]Data not reported separately until 1925.

[13]Data not reported separately until 1949.

[14]No data available for Japan until 1861.

[15]Data not reported separately until 1948.

[16]Prior to 1934, Philippines recorded as insular travel.

[17]Prior to 1920, Canada and Newfoundland recorded as British North America. From 1820 to 1898, figures include all British North America possessions.

[18]Land arrivals not completely enumerated until 1908.

[19]No data available for Mexico from 1886 to 1893.

[20]Data not reported separately until 1932.

[21]Data for Jamaica not collected until 1953. In prior years, consolidated under British West Indies, which is included in "Other Caribbean."

[22]Included in countries "Not specified" until 1925.

[23]From 1899 to 1919, data for Poland included in Austria-Hungary, Germany, and the Soviet Union.

[24]From 1938 to 1945, data for Austria included in Germany.

[25]Includes 32,897 persons returning in 1906 to their homes in the United States.

—represents zero.

NOTE: From 1820 to 1867, figures represent alien passengers arrived at seaports; from 1868 to 1891 and 1895 to 1897, immigrant aliens arrived; from 1892 to 1894 and 1898 to 1989, immigrant aliens admitted for permanent residence. From 1892 to 1903, aliens entering by cabin class were not counted as immigrants. Land arrivals were not completely enumerated until 1908. For this table, fiscal year 1843 covers 9 months ending September 1843; fiscal years 1832 and 1850 cover 15 months ending December 31 of the respective years; and fiscal year 1868 covers 6 months ending June 30, 1868.

PRESIDENTS, VICE-PRESIDENTS, AND SECRETARIES OF STATE

President	Vice-President	Secretary of State
1. George Washington, Federalist 1789	John Adams, Federalist 1789	T. Jefferson 1789 E. Randolph 1794 T. Pickering 1795
2. John Adams, Federalist 1798	Thomas Jefferson, Dem.-Rep. 1797	T. Pickering 1797 John Marshall 1800
3. Thomas Jefferson, Dem.-Rep. 1801	Aaron Burr, Dem.-Rep. 1801 George Clinton, Dem.-Rep. 1805	James Madison 1801
4. James Madison, Dem.-Rep. 1809	George Clinton, Dem.-Rep. 1809 Elbridge Gerry, Dem.-Rep. 1813	Robert Smith 1809 James Monroe 1811
5. James Monroe, Dem.-Rep. 1817	D. D. Tompkins, Dem.-Rep. 1817	J. Q. Adams 1817
6. John Quincy Adams, Dem.-Rep. 1825	John C. Calhoun, Dem.-Rep. 1825	Henry Clay 1825
7. Andrew Jackson, Democratic 1829	John C. Calhoun, Democratic 1829 Martin Van Buren, Democratic 1833	M. Van Buren 1829 E. Livingston 1831 Louis McLane 1833 John Forsyth 1834
8. Martin Van Buren, Democratic 1837	Richard M. Johnson, Democratic 1837	John Forsyth 1837
9. William H. Harrison, Whig 1841	John Tyler, Whig 1841	Daniel Webster 1841

	President	Vice-President	Secretary of State
10.	John Tyler, Whig and Democratic 1841		Daniel Webster 1841 Hugh S. Legare 1843 Abel P. Upshur 1843 John C. Calhoun 1844
11.	James K. Polk, Democratic 1845	George M. Dallas, Democratic 1845	James Buchanan 1845
12.	Zachary Taylor, Whig 1849	Millard Fillmore, Whig 1848	John M. Clayton 1849
13.	Millard Fillmore, Whig 1850		Daniel Webster 1850 Edward Everett 1852
14.	Franklin Pierce, Democratic 1853	William R. D. King, Democratic 1853	W. L. Marcy 1853
15.	James Buchanan, Democratic 1857	John C. Breckinridge, Democratic 1857	Lewis Cass 1857 J. S. Black 1860
16.	Abraham Lincoln, Republican 1861	Hannibal Hamlin, Republican 1861 Andrew Johnson, Unionist 1865	W. H. Seward 1861
17.	Andrew Johnson, Unionist 1865		W. H. Seward 1865
18.	Ulysses S. Grant, Republican 1869	Schuyler Colfax, Republican 1869 Henry Wilson, Republican 1873	E. B. Washburne 1869 H. Fish 1869

CHRONOLOGY OF
SIGNIFICANT EVENTS

16,000–14,000 B.C.	Likely period for first crossing of land bridge from Old World to New World
5000 B.C.	Hunting and gathering established as a way of life in New World
2000–1500 B.C.	Permanent towns appear in Mexico
800 B.C.–A.D. 600	Adena-Hopewell culture (northeast United States)
400 B.C.-present	Pueblo-Hohokam culture (southwest United States)
A.D. 300–900	Mayan culture
600–1500	Mississippian culture (southeast United States)
1000	Leif Ericsson sights Newfoundland
1215	Magna Carta adopted in England
1300–1519	Aztec culture
1300–1598	Inca culture
1440	Gutenberg invents movable type
1477	Marco Polo's *Travels* published
1492–1504	Columbus's four voyages to New World
1493	Pope declares demarcation line
1517	Martin Luther launches Protestant Reformation
1519	Cortés conquers Aztec empire
1536	John Calvin publishes *The Institutes*
1558–1603	Reign of Queen Elizabeth I
1565	Town of St. Augustine founded by the Spanish
1587	Sir Walter Raleigh's "lost colony" at Roanoke
1588	Defeat of the Spanish Armada by the English

1603–1625	Reign of James I, first of England's Stuart kings
1606	Virginia Company chartered
1607	Jamestown founded
1614	Dutch trading post set up on Manhattan Island
1616	Tobacco becomes an export staple for Virginia
1619	Virginia's General Assembly first convenes
1619	First Africans brought to English America
1620	*Mayflower* lands at Plymouth
1625	Population of English colonies in America at 2,000
1625–1649	Reign of Charles I in England
1630	Gov. John Winthrop leads the Puritan migration to Massachusetts Bay
1634	First settlement in Maryland
1636	Harvard College founded
1638	Anne Hutchinson banished from Massachusetts in Antinomian controversy
1642–1649	English Civil War
1649–1660	The Commonwealth and Protectorate in England
1651	William Bradford completes *Of Plymouth Plantation*
1660	English monarchy restored under Charles II
1662	Half-Way Covenant adopted by New England Congregational churches
1664	Dutch New Netherland colony becomes English New York
1675	King Philip's War
1676	Bacon's Rebellion
1681	Pennsylvania founded
1685–1688	Reign of James II
1687	Newton's *Principia* published
1688	England's Glorious Revolution
1689	John Locke's *Two Treatises on Civil Government* published
1689–1697	King William's War (War of the League of Augsburg)
1692	Salem witch trials
1700	Population of English colonies in America at 250,000
1702–1713	Queen Anne's War (War of the Spanish Succession)
1704	First enduring newspaper published in America

1789	Bill of Rights submitted to the states
1790–1791	Hamilton's *Reports*
1790	Samuel Slater's cotton mill set up in Rhode Island
1793	Eli Whitney invents the cotton gin
1794	Whiskey Rebellion
1794	Jay Treaty
1795	Pinckney Treaty
1795	North Carolina opens first state university
1796	John Adams elected president
1797	XYZ Affair
1797–1810	Revivalism on the frontier
1798–1800	Undeclared war with France
1798	Alien and Sedition Acts
1798	Kentucky and Virginia Resolutions
1800	Thomas Jefferson elected president
1803	*Marbury v. Madison*
1803	Louisiana Purchase
1803–1806	Lewis and Clark expedition
1807	Embargo Act
1809	Non-Intercourse Act
1811	Battle of Tippecanoe
1811	National Road started
1812	Congress declares war on Great Britain
1814	Hartford Convention
1815	Battle of New Orleans
1815	Peace of Ghent
1817–1825	Construction of the Erie Canal
1819	*McCulloch v. Maryland*
1819	Adams-Onis Treaty
1820	Washington Irving's *The Sketch Book*
1820	Missouri Compromise
1820	Significant Irish immigration begins
1821	Boston opens first public secondary school
1821–1822	Santa Fe Trail opened
1822	Cotton mills opened in Lowell, Massachusetts
1823	Monroe Doctrine
1826	James Fenimore Cooper's *The Last of the Mohicans*
1828	Andrew Jackson elected president
1828	Calhoun's *South Carolina Exposition and Protest*
1829–1837	Battle over recharter of the Bank of the United States

1858	Lincoln-Douglas debates
1859	John Brown's Raid
1859	Charles Darwin's *Origin of Species*
1860	Abraham Lincoln elected president
1860–1861	Southern states secede from the Union
1861	The Civil War breaks out
1861	First Battle of Bull Run
1861–1890	Indian wars in the West
1862	Battle of Antietam
1862	Battle of Shiloh
1862	The Homestead Act
1863	Battle of Gettysburg
1863	New York City Draft Riots
1863	Lincoln issues the Emancipation Proclamation
1864	Sherman's March to the Sea
1865	Lee surrenders to Grant at Appomattox Courthouse
1865	Freedmen's Bureau established
1865	Assassination of President Lincoln
1866–1868	Fourteenth Amendment passed and ratified
1867	First Reconstruction Act
1867–1877	Congressional Reconstruction of the South
1867	United States purchases Alaska
1868	Impeachment of President Andrew Johnson
1869	Completion of first transcontinental railroad
1869	National Woman Suffrage Association founded
1870	Standard Oil Company of Ohio established by John D. Rockefeller
1873	Crédit-Mobilier Scandal

ILLUSTRATION CREDITS

Note: The sequence of the credits follows that of the illustrations.

CHAPTER 1 / Museum of the American Indian, Heye Foundation. / Peabody Museum, Harvard University. / Milwaukee Public Museum. / Denver Convention & Visitors Bureau. / Museo Naval, Madrid. / The New York Public Library. / The New York Public Library. / British Museum. / Courtesy of the John Carter Brown Library at Brown University. / Neg. No. 286821, courtesy Department of Library Services, American Museum of Natural History. / The British Library. / Newberry Library, Chicago. / Royal Library, Copenhagen. / Editorial Photocolor Archives. / Musée Historique de la Reformation. / The Warder Collection. / National Maritime Museum, London. / Library of Congress.

CHAPTER 2 / National Portrait Gallery, London. / National Portrait Gallery, London. / National Portrait Gallery, London. / Huntington Library. / Library of Congress. / Huntington Library. / Society of Antiquaries, London. / Stadelschen Kunstinstituts Frankfurt, photo © Ursula Edelmann. / Pilgrim Society, Boston. / American Antiquarian Society. / American Antiquarian Society. / The Warder Collection. / Library Company of Philadelphia. / Massachusetts Historical Society. / National Portrait Gallery, London. / Courtesy of the John Carter Brown Library at Brown University. / South Caroliniana Library. / The New York Public Library. / Canadian Museum of Civilization. / Cranbrook Institute of Science. / Historical Society of Pennsylvania. / Museum of Fine Arts, Boston. / The Mariners Museum, Newport News, Virginia.

CHAPTER 3 / Yale University Library. / The Worcester Art Museum. / National Gallery, Washington, DC / Connecticut Historical Society. / Colonial Williamsburg Foundation. / Metropolitan Museum of Art. / South Caroliniana Library. / British Museum. / American Antiquarian Society. / Statue of Liberty National Monument. / The Abby Aldridge Rockefeller Folk Art Center, Williamsburg, Virginia. / National Museum of American History, Smithsonian. / Courtesy, Henry Francis du Pont Winterthur Museum. / Historic Christ's Church, Virginia. / Massachusetts Historical Society. / Courtesy, Peabody Essex Museum, Salem, MA. / Essex Institute. / From Ralph Gardiner, *England's Grievance Discovered*, 1655. / From Sachse, *The German Sectarians of Pennsylvania*. / The New York Public Library. / Harvard University. / American Antiquarian Society. / Yale University Art Gallery.

CHAPTER 4 / Courtesy, Henry Francis du Pont Winterthur Museum. / National Maritime Museum, London. / The Colonial Williamsburg Foundation. / National Library of Canada, Rare Books and Manuscripts Division, Ottawa. / Public Archives of Canada. / Public Archives of Canada. / Public Archives of Canada. / Historical Society of Pennsylvania. / Library of Congress. / National Army Museum, London. / Public Archives of Canada.

CHAPTER 5 / Courtauld Institute of Art. / Collection, Washington University, St. Louis. / Christ Church, Oxford. / British Museum. / Historical Society of Pennsylvania. / Brown University Library. / Historical Society of Pennsylvania. / Museum of Fine Arts, Boston. / Library of Congress. / Boston Public Library. / Massachusetts Historical Society. / Library of Congress. / Cartoon History of the American Revolution. / The New York Public Library. / The Library Company of Philadelphia. / British Museum. / Courtesy of the John Carter Brown Library at Brown University. / National Gallery of Art, Washington. / American Antiquarian Society. / Library of Congress.

CHAPTER 6 / Brown University Library. / Courtesy Pennsylvania Academy of the Fine Arts. / Brown Brothers. / Historical Society of Pennsylvania. / Frick Collection. / Courtesy, Independence National Historical Park. / Library of Congress. / The New-York Historical Society. / The Historical Society of Pennsylvania. / Musée de Versailles, Photo courtesy Réunion des Musées Nationaux. / Courtesy, Henry Francis du Pont Winterthur Museum. / Cartoon History of the American Revolution. / Maryland Historical Society. / Massachusetts Historical Society. / Library Company of Philadelphia. / Museum of Art, Rhode Island School of Design. / Yale University Art Gallery. / Metropolitan Toronto Library Board.

CHAPTER 7 / Independence National Historical Park Collection. / American Philosophical Society. / Library Company of Philadelphia. / The British Library. / Boston Athenaeum. / Historical Society of Pennsylvania. / Historical Society of Pennsylvania. / Historical Society of Pennsylvania. / Library of Congress. / Library of Congress. / Independence National Historical Park Collection. / Library of Congress. / American Antiquarian Society.

CHAPTER 8 / Library of Congress. / Library of Congress. / Collection of the Albany Institute of History & Art. / The Metropolitan Museum of Art. / Library of Congress. / Library Company of Philadelphia. / Independence National Historical Park. / Detroit Public Library. / The Warder Collection. / The New York Public Library. / The Maryland Historical Society. / American Antiquarian Society. / The Warder Collection. / Henry E. Huntington Library and Art Gallery. / The New York Public Library.

CHAPTER 9 / The New York Public Library. / Library of Congress. / The Cincinnati Historical Society. / The Bettmann Archive. / Library of Congress. / National Portrait Gallery and Art Resource, NY / The New York Public Library. / The New York Public Library. / The New-York Historical Society. / American Museum of Natural History. / The New-York Historical Society. / Peale Museum, Baltimore. / The Massachusetts Historical Society. / The Warder Collection.

CHAPTER 10 / Maryland Historical Society. / Historical Society of Pennsylvania. / The Smithsonian Institution. / The Historical Society of Pennsylvania. / Historical Museum of Southern Florida. / The Warder Collection. / Henry Clay Memorial Foundation. / Library of Congress. / Metropolitan Museum of Art. / New-York Historical Society. / New York Office of Parks, Recreation and Historic Preservation, Philipse Manor Hall State Historic Site. / New-York Historical Society. / New-York Historical Society.

CHAPTER 11 / Library of Congress. / National Museum of American History. / Frick Art Reference Library. / Library of Congress. / Boston Art Commission. / American Antiquarian Society. / Western History Collections, University of Oklahoma Library. / The New-York Historical Society. / Boatmen's National Bank of St. Louis. / The New-York Historical Society. / The New-York Historical Society. / The New-York Historical Society. / Library of Congress. / Library of Congress. / The New-York Historical Society. / Library of Congress.

CHAPTER 12 / Merrimack Valley Textile Museum. / Amon Carter Museum. / Minnesota Historical Society Press. / State University of New York, Albany, Press. / Statue of Liberty National Monument. / Library of Congress. / New York State Historical Society. / The Science Museum, London. / Library of Congress. / US Air Force. / The New York Public Library. / Oklahoma University Press. / Library of Congress. / Historical Society of Pennsylvania.

CHAPTER 13 / Library of Congress. / Keith Hardiman. / The Church of Jesus Christ of Latter-Day Saints. / American Antiquarian Society. / Warner Collection of Gulf States Paper Corp. / New England Magazine. / Concord Free Public Library. / The Essex Institute. / American Antiquarian Society. / Old Dartmouth Historical Society—New Bedford Whaling Museum. / Amon Carter Museum. / Gilman Paper Company. / Erie Canal Museum. / University of Virginia Manuscript Department. / Lake County Historical Society. / Library of Congress. / The New York Public Library. / National Portrait Gallery, Smithsonian Institution and Art Resource, NY / Courtesy, Henry Francis du Pont Winterthur Museum. / The Warder Collection. / Metropolitan Museum of Art. / By Shaker Hands.

CHAPTER 14 / Museum of New Mexico. / Museum of New Mexico. / Metropolitan Museum of Art. / The Henry E. Huntington Library and Art Gallery. / California State Library. / The Bancroft Library. / Library of Congress. / Library of Congress. / The Corcoran Gallery of Art. / Library of Congress. / Library of Congress. / The Warder Collection.

CHAPTER 15 / Library of Congress. / The New York Public Library. / Library of Congress. / Library of Congress. / Historical Society of Pennsylvania. / Charleston Museum. / Library of Congress. / Peabody Museum, Harvard University. / Library of Congress. / The New-York Historical Society. / South Carolina Historical Society. / National Portrait Gallery, Smithsonian Institution and Art Resource, NY / The New-York Historical Society.

CHAPTER 16 / Library of Congress. / California State Library. / California State Library. / The Metropolitan Museum of Art. / Library of Congress. / Library of Congress. / The New-York Historical Society. / Library of Congress. / National Portrait Gallery, Smithsonian Institution and Art Resource, NY / Library of Congress. / The New York Public Library. / Missouri Historical Society. / National Archives, Washington. / Library of Congress. / Boston Athenaeum. / Library of Congress. / Chicago Historical Society. / The New York Public Library.

CHAPTER 17 / Library of Congress. / Library of Congress. / Library of Congress. / Library of Congress. / The New York Public Library. / Library of Congress. / Library of Congress. / Library of Congress. / Library of Congress. / Library of Congress. / National Archives, Washington. / Chicago Historical Society. / Library of Congress. / Library of Congress. / Library of Congress. / Gilman Paper Company. / Library of Congress. / Chicago Historical Society. / US Army Military History Institute. / US Army Military History Institute. / Library of Congress. / Library of Congress.

CHAPTER 18 / Library of Congress. / Library of Congress. / Library of Congress. / Library of Congress. / The George Eastman House. / Library of Congress. / *Harper's Weekly.* / Library of Congress. / National Archives, Washington. / The Warder Collection. / National Portrait Gallery, Smithsonian Institution and Art Resource, NY / National Archives, Washington. / Library of Congress. / Library of Congress. / National Archives, Washington. / Library of Congress. / National Portrait Gallery, Smithsonian Institution and Art Resource, NY / Library of Congress. / Library of Congress. / Library of Congress.

INDEX

THE WORLD

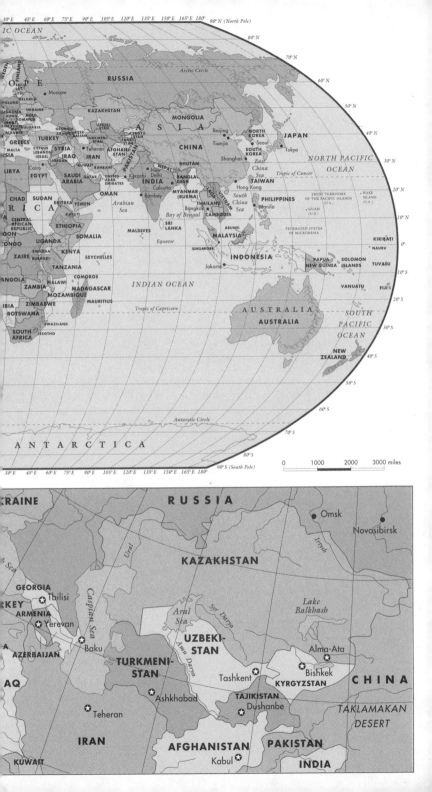